THE PAPERS

of

JOHN C. CALHOUN

John C. Calhoun

This oil-on-canvas portrait was painted by George P.A. Healy and is dated 1845. It was a gift from W. Thomas Smith to the Greenville County Museum of Art in 1986.

THE PAPERS

of

JOHN C. CALHOUN

Volume XVIII, 1844

Edited by

CLYDE N. WILSON

Shirley Bright Cook, *Associate Editor*

Alexander Moore, *Assistant Editor*

UNIVERSITY OF SOUTH CAROLINA PRESS, 1988

*Publication of this book was made possible
by a grant from the National Historical Publications
and Records Commission.*

International Standard Book Number: 0–87249–606–6
Library of Congress Catalog Card Number: 59–10351

Manufactured in the United States of America

CONTENTS

Ⅲ

CONTENTS

II

v

PREFACE

It has been decided to publish the papers relating to the one-year period of Calhoun's tenure as Secretary of State in three volumes, of which this is the first. Using a fairly broad but reasonable definition of what constitutes a Calhoun document, there are for this period about 7,000 extant documents, not counting several thousand multiple copies and enclosures—more than the total number of documents for all of the amply-documented last five years of Calhoun's life.

Despite what must seem an extensive publication, the three volumes are highly selective. Only a little over a third of the extant documents will be published, and many of those only in abbreviated summary. This is approximately the same proportion of documents in relation to the total corpus of material that was published for the period of Calhoun's administration as Secretary of War (vols. II through IX of this edition), a period when both the unofficial and official correspondence were less voluminous.

When opportunity came to make a selection for publication, almost all the material was already collected and edited. It was apparent that this was a very rich body of documentation for a critical, expansive period in the history of the Union and its diplomacy, which is not well-represented in published documents, at least below the highest level of official correspondence. Calhoun's tenure in the State Department was at the heart of climactic developments in regard to Texas and Oregon, the most important issues in American foreign relations between the War of 1812 and the Spanish-American War, possibly between the Louisiana Purchase and World War I. It was also an instructive period in the development of American engagement with the outside world that was to become increasingly significant. It is the period of the first major formal American missions in China and the Sandwich Islands (Hawaii); of significant events in the Caribbean and Central America; of unprecedentedly extensive American negotiations with various German states; of the development of an American presence, not always official, in nearly every corner of the globe, including, for instance, the appearance of missionaries in Persia. These matters are of permanent and wide interest.

In considering this material it was also apparent that it had more pertinence for Calhoun's later career than has generally been recognized. Most of his major speeches and political moves, from the time he returned to the Senate in December, 1845, until his death in March, 1850, related either to the conflict with Mexico in all its ramifications or to the question of slavery in the territories which grew directly out of it. The later years of Calhoun's career cannot be understood fully without awareness of the view of the South's position in the world presented to him as Secretary of State, a period that has not, for the most part, been given exhaustive treatment in Calhoun scholarship.

The principles of selection used in this volume (as well as other editorial considerations) are described in the Introduction. A more extensive and detailed accounting of the omitted material will be given in Volume XX. As has always been the practice, photocopies and transcripts or abstracts of the many omitted documents will be kept as a permanent archive. Possibly one day, should human and economic resources endure, the omitted material will become a microform publication in supplement of this edition.

This continuing publication is made possible by support from the University of South Carolina, the Program for Editions of the National Endowment for the Humanities, and the National Historical Publications and Records Commission.

CLYDE N. WILSON

Columbia, August, 1987

INTRODUCTION

〖〗

President John Tyler appointed John C. Calhoun to be Secretary of State on March 6, 1844. The appointment was confirmed by the United States Senate on the same day in simple and unanimous proceedings. Calhoun, at home at Fort Hill, learned of his appointment on March 15 and wrote his somewhat reluctant acceptance the next day. He arrived in Washington on March 29 and took up the duties of the office on Monday, April 1.

This volume covers approximately the first third of Calhoun's administration of the State Department, a brief but intense period ending on June 8, 1844, the date on which the Senate refused its consent to the treaty of annexation that Calhoun had concluded with the representatives of the independent Republic of Texas nearly two months before.

The questions raised by Texas annexation were galvanic for Texas, for American politics and public opinion, for Mexico, and perhaps for other powers. But there were other reasons, as well, why this proved to be an intense period for Calhoun. Only a few weeks before Calhoun's appointment a new British plenipotentiary, Richard Pakenham, arrived in Washington with powers to settle the largest outstanding question between the two great Anglo-Saxon powers, which was the future of the vast northwestern territory of Oregon. Calhoun's predecessor Secretary of State, Abel P. Upshur, had met with Pakenham on this question for the first time on February 27, the day before he died. Calhoun seems to have managed to put off further negotiations on Oregon until later in the year, after the Texas treaty had been concluded and Congress had adjourned.

There were other matters pending. A few days before Calhoun reached Washington, the American Minister in Prussia, Henry Wheaton, had concluded a major commercial treaty with the nineteen states of the German Customs Union, a treaty which would provide advantages for American agriculture and which could be considered as a step toward Calhoun's great desideratum of free trade. Other negotiations were pending, to settle claims in South America and to formalize American relations with the Hawaiian

Islands and the empire of China in the far Pacific, a region just beginning to emerge into lasting significance for Americans. Civil war, slave revolt, and repression gripped two near Caribbean islands where Americans were in considerable presence as residents and traders—independent Haiti and the Spanish colony of Cuba. The northeastern boundary with Canada had been put on track to be peacefully arranged by the Treaty of 1842, but the settlement remained to be fully implemented in detail.

In addition to facing Texas and Oregon, the largest issues that had concerned American foreign policy since the Treaty of Ghent, and all the other matters, Calhoun had to take over the day-to-day administration of a large department which had had only an interim direction for over a month since Upshur's sudden death. The normally heavy business of a department head was multiplied many times because Congress was in session and grappling with appointments, appropriations, and other controversial matters.

And, though Calhoun had seemingly hoped to avoid politics, the period was necessarily one of political intensity. He became a member of an administration that was the most beleaguered in the history of the Union and which was in its last year. President Tyler could count on support from neither Whigs nor Democrats, and his measures and appointments faced regular rejection in the Congress. Yet the President still hoped against hope that he might emerge from the ongoing Presidential maneuverings with a nomination to succeed himself.

Calhoun, of course, had been until quite recently a significant player in these maneuverings, and was still considered to be so by some, though not by himself. A convention of Tyler supporters and the Democratic National Convention both met in Baltimore in late May. The Democratic National Convention gathered amidst intense maneuverings among party leaders and volatile clashings of public opinion, resulting from the joint determination of Henry Clay, leader and presidential nominee of the Whig party, and Martin Van Buren, until recently leader of the Democrats, to oppose the annexation of Texas at this time, an opposition which became public on April 27.

Richard K. Crallé came up from Virginia to serve as Calhoun's Chief Clerk in the administration of the State Department. Excluding the Patent Office, for which the Secretary of State was responsible but which had its own Commissioner and operated somewhat independently, the State Department had about sixteen full-time Clerks to handle the diplomatic and consular business of the federal government and the many miscellaneous domestic matters that fell to the Secretary of State's jurisdiction in that day before the creation of an Interior Department.

The veteran Clerks were chiefly Marylanders and Virginians with political connections and social prominence, and Calhoun was probably already acquainted with most of them. One was Francis Markoe, a son-in-law of Calhoun's late intimate friend Virgil Maxcy. Another was Robert Greenhow, whose kinsman, Washington Greenhow, was the editor of the chief Calhoun newspaper in Virginia. The staff was divided into a diplomatic bureau, a consular bureau, and a home bureau. In addition, Greenhow served as Librarian and chief translator, and there was a financial officer known as the Disbursing Agent. There were also numerous part-time Clerks, as occasion demanded.

Exactly how much business Calhoun took a direct hand in is not clear. Crallé probably ran interference for the Secretary and handled many routine matters. Yet, though he had been out of executive office for nearly twenty years, Calhoun was one of the most experienced administrators in Washington, and the staff was not large enough that the head of the department could be immune from much day-to-day routine. Robert M.T. Hunter, who visited Calhoun on his way to the Baltimore convention, found that Calhoun "had taken rather a fancy to the work in his Department." Calhoun told Hunter that his predecessors had concentrated on a few large issues and had neglected "the small work" of the department, a situation which he intended to correct.[1]

Calhoun's private life in Washington, though he was lodged in a comfortable boarding establishment, could not be compared with that when he had been Secretary of War and had been with his family a fixture of Georgetown society. However, it seems to have been pleasant and active enough. Calhoun gave and received invitations.[2] The very young and charming second wife of the President, Julia Gardiner Tyler, reported that Calhoun sat next to her at dinner and made himself agreeable by reciting verses to her.[3] An unusual number of first-hand impressions of Calhoun have survived in writing for his first months in the State Department, and these agree that

[1] Hunter's ms. memoir of Calhoun, p. 286, Robert M.T. Hunter Papers, Virginia State Library.

[2] See the bill from [Mrs.] E. King, dated May 28, 1844, below in this volume. Also the diary of Charles J. Ingersoll, Chairman of the House Foreign Affairs Committee, as printed in William M. Meigs, *The Life of Charles Jared Ingersoll* (Philadelphia: J.B. Lippincott, 1900), p. 267.

[3] Robert Seager II, *And Tyler Too: A Biography of John and Julia Gardiner Tyler* (New York: McGraw-Hill, 1963), p. 246.

the sixty-two-year-old South Carolinian was relaxed, content, in good form, and in relatively good health.[4]

The Papers of the Secretary of State

During the nineteenth century the record-keeping of the executive branch of the federal government was comprehensive, leaving an embarrassment of riches for anyone who undertakes to edit the papers of the head of an executive department such as John C. Calhoun (Secretary of War: December 10, 1817, to March 3, 1825; Secretary of State: April 1, 1844, to March 10, 1845). Several decades of diligent search have uncovered a total corpus of upwards of 7,000 documents relating to Calhoun's year as head of the State Department. (This total includes his personal papers for the period but does not count many hundreds of variant versions and enclosures.) This collection, out of which a selection of a little more than one-third has been made for publication, is as comprehensive as it has been possible to assemble. Even so, there are probably a few documents in obscure files among the immense holdings of the National Archives that have been overlooked. There are conceivably also documents in European archives, which it has been possible to examine only summarily and indirectly, but it is unlikely that any significant documents will be found there that are not already known in other versions.

The State Department and other executive departments in the 1840's kept systematic files of letters sent and received, at least in regard to all but the most minor activities. Often multiple versions of one letter are to be found in the National Archives. If the Secretary of State wrote the Secretary of the Navy, a file copy of the letter sent may be found in the records of the State Department and a recipient's copy in the records of the Navy Department. Not infrequently, still further copies of the same letter may be found—for instance, a copy might be made later to be sent to a Congressional committee or to another official for information.[5]

---

[4] See Hunter's memoir and the Ingersoll diary cited above; the notes to letters below in this volume from Caleb Atwater, April 6, 1844, and George R. Gliddon, May 17, 1844. Also Frederick von Raumer, *America and the American People* (New York: J. & H.G. Langley, 1846), p. 417; Charles M. Wiltse, *John C. Calhoun* (3 vols. Indianapolis: The Bobbs-Merrill Co., Inc., c. 1944, 1949, 1951), 3:165; Richard Pakenham to Lord Aberdeen, April 14, 1844, British Museum, Aberdeen Papers, folios 68–70.

[5] As has always been the practice in this edition, all known ms. versions of a document have been compared and cited. It has been also customary in this

The greater part of the Secretary of State's official correspondence in Calhoun's time can be found in the National Archives in Record Group 59, General Records of the Department of State, which is cited herein as "DNA, RG 59 (State Department)." Most of the significant correspondence in this record group is found in ten files or series, five of them of letters sent and five of letters received. These ten series are described briefly below, beginning with the abbreviated titles used herein in citations for individual documents.

Diplomatic Instructions. (Diplomatic Instructions of the Department of State, 1801–1906.) Retained copies of correspondence sent to U.S. legations abroad; arranged by country.

Diplomatic Despatches. (Diplomatic Despatches, 1789–1906.) Correspondence received from U.S. legations abroad; arranged by country.

Notes to Foreign Legations. (Notes to Foreign Legations from the Department of State, 1834–1906.) Retained copies of correspondence sent to foreign representatives in the U.S.; arranged by country.

Notes from Foreign Legations. (Notes from Foreign Legations in the United States, 1789–1906.) Correspondence received from foreign representatives in Washington; arranged by country.

Consular Instructions. (Instructions to Consular Officers, 1800–1906.) Retained copies of correspondence sent to Consuls and other U.S. representatives abroad below the legation level, and also to other persons concerning consular business; arranged in one chronological series.

Consular Despatches. (Consular Despatches, 1789–1906.) Correspondence received at the State Department from U.S. representatives abroad at the consular level; arranged by post.

Domestic Letters. (Domestic Letters of the Department of State,

---

edition to provide a citation to all previous significant printings of the documents that are presented. Some of the major official documents written and received by Calhoun as Secretary of State have been reprinted so often in compilations of diplomatic documents that this has proved impractical. Some of the documents printed herein have been previously printed in the following six collections for which citations have not been provided for individual documents. Full citations to these collections are in the Bibliography: Kenneth Bourne, ed., *British Documents on Foreign Affairs*; *British and Foreign State Papers*, vols. 33 and 34; Jules Davids, ed., *American Diplomatic and Public Papers: The United States and China*; George P. Garrison, ed., *Diplomatic Correspondence of the Republic of Texas*; William R. Manning, ed., *Diplomatic Correspondence of the United States: Canadian Relations, 1784–1860* and *Inter-American Affairs, 1831–1860*. Except for these six collections, previous printings of documents included herein have been cited.

1784–1906.) Retained copies of letters sent to private persons and to officials who do not fall into the category of diplomatic or consular personnel; arranged in one chronological series.

Miscellaneous Letters. (Miscellaneous Letters of the Department of State, 1789–1906.) Correspondence received from private sources and official sources other than diplomatic and consular personnel; arranged in one chronological series.

Reports of the Secretary of State to the President and Congress. (Reports of the Secretary of State to the President and Congress, 1790–1906.) Retained copies of formal communications in response to resolutions of the houses of Congress; arranged chronologically.

Applications and Recommendations, 1837–1845. (Letters of Application and Recommendation During the Administrations of Martin Van Buren, William Henry Harrison, and John Tyler, 1837–1845.) Letters received from applicants for Presidential appointments and their endorsers; a file administered in the State Department and arranged alphabetically by the name of the applicant.

These series contain the greater part of the Secretary of State's more significant official correspondence. However, there are other files in Record Group 59. Passports, pardons, the settlement of accounts and certain other transactions with the Treasury Department, foreign Consuls in the United States, and a few other matters enjoyed separate files.

There are two other record groups arising out of State Department activities that need mention. These are Record Group 76, Records of Boundary and Claims Commissions and Arbitrations, which contains an occasional document of interest not found elsewhere, and Record Group 84, Records of Foreign Service Posts of the Department of State. The latter consists of records maintained at foreign posts and later brought to Washington. They are for the most part copies of documents already known in the files of the State Department, but occasionally contain a document not otherwise known.

In addition, copies of the Secretary of State's letters can be found in the record groups of other parts of the federal government, such as the Navy Department, the Treasury Department, the two houses of Congress, and others.

Despite massive and systematic record keeping, there are now and then small lacunae in the National Archives. It was always possible for the Secretary, for reasons that seemed good at the time, to communicate outside of official channels, and it also seems that a few documents have simply been lost or removed from the files in the nearly century and a half since they were created.

In making a comprehensive collection of Calhoun's official papers as Secretary of State it was necessary to consider questions of time and transportation. For instance, a despatch written to the State Department by the American representative in Mexico City had to be sent either by regular mail service or by private messenger from Mexico City to Vera Cruz, where the U.S. Consul had to find the best means to get it safely by sea to New Orleans. In New Orleans the Collector of Customs had then to arrange to get the message to Washington. The whole process consumed normally more than a month.

For more remote posts and less urgent business the time lag was even greater. Sometimes an outgoing message had to wait for the services of a Navy or private vessel bound for the far Pacific or some other distant or little-frequented spot. Despatch Agents were maintained by the State Department at New York City, Boston, and Panama to facilitate this process; and the U.S. Minister at London was a funnel and facilitator for most of the correspondence with Europe and other quarters farther east. Since the transmission of letters to and from places abroad was often a matter of months, there are anomalies in the identification of official correspondence at both the beginning and the end of Calhoun's service.

The U.S. Consul in Zanzibar sat down on July 1, 1843, to write a despatch to the Secretary of State. He addressed it to Daniel Webster, who had ceased being Secretary of State almost two months before, a fact he had no way of knowing. This despatch was received in Washington on May 4, 1844, over a month after Calhoun had become Secretary of State and almost a year after it had been written.[6] There had been two other Secretaries of State and two interim administrations in the meantime. In making our collection, such letters have been considered Calhoun documents, since Calhoun was the official recipient and was responsible for whatever response, if any, was to be made.

Another example: James C. Pickett, the U.S. Chargé d'Affaires in Peru, on the Pacific coast of South America, could communicate more readily with California or Tahiti than with Washington. On March 23, 1844, he wrote to Secretary of State Upshur, who had

---

[6] Richard P. Waters, Zanzibar, to Daniel Webster, July 1, 1843, in DNA, RG 59 (State Department), Consular Despatches, Zanzibar, vol. 1 (M-468:1, frames 193–194).

been dead for nearly a month, informing him that he had just received word of Upshur's appointment as Secretary of State the previous June. He did not receive notice of Upshur's death (in February 1844) until June 7, after Calhoun had been in office for three months. On September 3, 1844, nearly six months after the event, he received official notice of Calhoun's appointment as Secretary of State.[7] Thus, most of the letters actually received by Calhoun from Pickett while Calhoun was Secretary of State were not addressed to Calhoun by name, while most of Pickett's letters that were addressed to Calhoun by name were not received in Washington until after Calhoun had left the office and landed on the desk of Calhoun's successor, James Buchanan. There were also American representatives abroad who were sticklers for protocol, like Edward Everett. Everett persisted in addressing his despatches to Calhoun's interim predecessor for many weeks after he knew for a certainty that Calhoun was Secretary of State—because the official notification had not reached him.

To identify the letters written (or at least signed) by Calhoun as Secretary of State is a fairly easy matter. For the reasons mentioned, however, to identify the letters received, which are much more numerous, is a more complicated undertaking—made even more so by the fact that there was an interim period of more than a month between Abel P. Upshur's death and Calhoun's entrance into office.

In making a collection, Calhoun documents have been defined as comprehensively as possible. Thus we have considered as Calhoun documents 1) letters addressed to Calhoun by name or to the Secretary of State by title during the time Calhoun held the office; 2) letters addressed by name to Calhoun's predecessors in office after Calhoun had been appointed; 3) letters written to Calhoun's predecessors before his appointment but received in the State Department after his appointment; 4) and letters addressed to Calhoun by name after he had left the office. In selecting for publication, however, most of the many hundreds of documents in category 3 have been excluded and all of those in category 4.

Calhoun took over a department in which several major matters were in midstream. The first section of this volume contains a small selection from the many hundreds of documents written before he entered office on April 1, but which were received after he became Secretary of State on March 6. In the first section also are a few

---

[7] Pickett's letters to the Secretaries of State during 1844 in DNA, RG 59 (State Department), Diplomatic Despatches, Peru, vol. 6 (T-52:6, frames 477 ff.).

other documents of his predecessors which set the parameters of action on some major questions with which Calhoun had to deal or which, though received earlier, were still awaiting action or answer. In the first section (documents dated before April 1) the headings show to whom the letter was addressed, usually Abel P. Upshur. For documents dated after April 1, if a letter is addressed to a predecessor Secretary of State, it is stated in the note to that letter rather than the heading. If the letter is addressed to Calhoun by name or to the Secretary of State without name, no notice is taken.

Because of the importance of the time element, the citation herein to each official document from abroad contains the date of its receipt in Washington, where known. (This was usually noted on the document itself at the time.) Knowledge of the date of its receipt in Washington is essential to the understanding and usefulness of every foreign despatch. We have also included in such documents the despatch numbers used at the time. A representative abroad usually numbered his letters to the State Department consecutively from the time he accepted appointment until his return to the U.S. These numbers provide a rough guide to how long the official had been in his post and also indicate how many intervening despatches may have been omitted from publication.

It must be noted that occasionally correspondence of the Chief Clerk or other Clerks of the State Department acting on the Secretary's behalf and correspondence of the President referred to the Secretary of State for action have been treated as Calhoun documents.

There are several dozen documents—memoranda and correspondence—which can be considered of an official or at least a semi-official nature, which are not in the files in the National Archives, but which are found among Calhoun's personal papers at Clemson University or the personal papers of his Chief Clerk, Richard K. Crallé, at the University of Virginia. All such documents that fall within the period of Calhoun's service as Secretary of State have been included herein for publication. Perhaps a third of such documents, however, are dated before Calhoun's entry into the State Department. These are documents that belonged to Abel P. Upshur and which were evidently retained by Calhoun or Crallé as reference material in regard to matters that came up after their dates. All these early documents found among private papers are mentioned somewhere in the notes to our published documents, in connection with the later matters to which they appear to relate.

Principles of Selection

The main files of official correspondence of the Secretary of State are clearly and logically arranged and for the most part quite easy of use. Most have appeared in published microcopies of the National Archives (citations to which are included with our documents). However, the primary files that have been described are built around provenance rather than subject matter, so that to find all the relevant documents about a particular event one has often to look through several files.

A hypothetical case: a conflict between British and American trade regulations on the Maine-New Brunswick border. Such a question might involve the Secretary of State in correspondence with the British Minister in Washington and through him with British officials in London or Canada. Others might come into the picture: the American Minister in London; the Treasury Department in Washington or one of its Collectors at a port; a U.S. District Attorney in the region; the President; a Congressional committee; private citizens; State officials; American consuls in Canada. Thus, not all of the correspondence relating to this matter, or even all of one side of the correspondence, would be found in one file, but would be spread over many.

While the files are organized mainly by provenance, the omissions and inclusions of documents for publication in the three volumes of this edition which will cover Calhoun's term as Secretary of State have been decided on the basis of subject matter. There has been no summary exclusion of documents by provenance or type. Rather, there has been a thorough examination of all known files, even the most unpromising, before a selection for publication has been made. While there are routine and minor documents, there are no routine and minor files, for each file represents the written remnants of an extensive human activity in which something surprising or interesting can always appear. On the other hand, no documents have been selected for inclusion on the basis of provenance alone. Thus for even the most important correspondents, lesser or repetitive documents have been omitted. To make decisions on the basis of subject matter is perhaps more subjective than to make them on the basis of category. It is also a much more useful and more demanding approach to the necessary evil of selectivity.

There follows a general description of the subjects that have been preferred in selecting for publication.

All of Calhoun's normal personal and political correspondence found outside the official files of the National Archives.

Most correspondence relating to

—U.S. relations with the Republics of Texas and Mexico and with other powers in regard to Texas, whether from legation, consular, or private sources.

—the Oregon question.

—the seeking of offices or other patronage and the appointment or removal of government officers. (While not always involving Calhoun very directly, such correspondence provides a significant part of the history of the Tyler administration; indicates lines of political allegiance and influence, actual or anticipated; and identifies and reflects the activities of Calhoun's political "friends.")

—official relations with Congressional committees or with the houses of Congress formally (though not a great deal of correspondence with individual members of Congress on constituent or minor business).

—the implementation of the Treaty of Washington of 1842 with Great Britain. (Papers relating to the northeastern boundary settlement, relations along the boundary, the African slave trade, and other matters are included, but not those relating to the treaty's extradition provision except as it concerned fugitive American slaves in British colonies.)

—relations with foreign legations in the United States on significant and current matters (but not a great deal of correspondence relating to ceremony, private claims, issuing exequaturs for foreign Consuls in the U.S., extradition, and minor customs matters).

—the international slave trade and relations with Great Britain in regard to it (except for some correspondence relating to very old and previously-settled claims against Britain for ship seizures on the coast of Africa).

A selective but substantial representation of correspondence relating to

—the commercial treaty concluded by Henry Wheaton with the German Zollverein in March, 1844, and to the related American interest in and expansion of trade and other relations in northern and central Europe.

—significant events occurring in the Caribbean, particularly Cuba and Haiti, where Americans were in extensive presence as traders and residents.

—those South American states where active negotiations were under way for the settlement of claims.

—a variety of non-routine matters of large and lasting interest, such as the U.S. Commissioners in Hawaii and China and other expansive activities in the Pacific.

—tangible day-to-day activities and decisions of Calhoun as Secretary of State.

In general, the selection of documents for publication reflects a bias in favor of the New World over the Old and a bias in favor of areas of change and movement over those of routine and stable, even if significant, relationships.

Principles of Omission

There follows a general explanation of materials of Calhoun as Secretary of State that were not selected for publication in this edition.

All documents that were not correspondence and required only the signature of the Secretary of State ex officio, of which there are many types: the laws of the United States, certified copies of public documents, commissions of many officers of the government, passports, ships' papers, patents, and others.

Most correspondence relating to

—the Secretary of State's administration of the Territories under the President (except for one incident which involved Calhoun in a controversy with the Governor of Florida Territory).

—the Secretary's administration of the District of Columbia under the President.

—the Secretary's administration of the federal justice system (U.S. Marshals and District Attorneys) under the President.

—the Secretary's administration of the pardoning power for the President (except for one case, politically significant in Missouri, in which an effort was made to get Calhoun personally involved because he was acquainted with relatives of the condemned).

—the State Department's administration of passports.

—individual cases of extradition to and from the United States.

—the activities of the State Department as an official repository of documents. (The Department was the official archive and register of authenticity for laws, treaties, and other public documents of the United States, for the public and other departments of the government. It was responsible for the publication and dissemination of the laws and other public documents to Congressmen, judges, States, educational institutions, and others. It maintained collections of the laws of the States and Territories, a library, and a large collection of

Revolutionary War materials known as the "Washington Papers" which were in constant use for pension applications and historical research. All of this created an extensive correspondence.)

—individual claims of American citizens against foreign governments, especially older claims (which seem to have been resuscitated every time a new Secretary was appointed) and claims against European governments. (However, claims against Mexico and more recent and active claims against other Latin American states have been included.)

—financial transactions, such as the payment of salaries and the transfer of funds (both of which involved correspondence with the Treasury Department and private banking houses in the United States and abroad, and others).

—the settlement of accounts of Americans who had served abroad (though some papers relating to major and recent cases, which necessitated decisions by Calhoun, have been included).

—the business of foreign Consuls in the United States (of whom there were nearly 200) except in matters of unusual interest and for countries which had no representative in the U.S. above Consul.

—relations with the foreign legations in Washington, of which there were sixteen in 1844. (This correspondence is not voluminous, presumably because in-person discussion was possible. But most is omitted: that having to do with ceremony, securing exequaturs for Consuls in the U.S., extradition, individual claims and other private business of citizens of either country, and minor customs matters. Papers relating to significant and current matters are included, however.)

In addition to the omissions indicated above, pursuance of the principles of inclusion and selectivity that have been described in this Introduction results in the omission of the greater part of a large amount of correspondence to, from, and about U.S. representatives abroad at both the legation and the consular level.

In 1844 there were twenty-seven representatives of the United States abroad with the rank of Minister, Chargé d'Affaires, or Commissioner. The greater part of the papers relating to these officers has been omitted. Omissions include most papers relating to such matters as: reports on affairs in foreign countries with no direct and immediate relation to American interests; securing exequaturs for U.S. Consuls in foreign lands and their colonies; ceremonial exchanges; the transmission and receipt of documents; postal conventions; financial transactions; most cultural, scientific, and economic information and exchange; most claims of individual American citizens; most other affairs and interests of individual Americans abroad.

Most American representatives abroad at legation rank are, as a result, represented by a few documents each in this edition, selected out of a large correspondence. In a number of other cases, such as Henry Wheaton in Prussia, Edward Everett in Great Britain, Caleb Cushing in China, and the representatives in some South American states, a larger number of documents will be published; but, even so, the published materials represent only a fraction of a voluminous extant correspondence. The most comprehensively represented are the legations in Mexico and Texas. Even here the record is selective.

The exact number of U.S. representatives abroad at the consular level in 1844 cannot be stated because there were always vacancies, turnovers underway, and posts being opened and closed. Counting Commercial Agents, who performed functions similar to Consuls with a more modest establishment and accreditation, there were approximately 170. The Consuls and Commercial Agents were largely an arm of American commerce. They were located mostly, though not entirely, in ports, in all parts of the inhabited world's coasts, islands, and navigable rivers, wherever indefatigable New England traders and whalers might appear. In a major city where there was much American activity, or in a country where there was no diplomatic representative, a Consul might have a large establishment with Vice-Consuls located at other points in the region which was his responsibility. In lesser places the Consul might be merely a resident merchant or professional man who exercised consular responsibilities only occasionally, as needed—sometimes such persons were not even American citizens.

The greatest single variety of the extant official correspondence of the Secretary of State in 1844 and 1845 falls under the description of consular business, and most of this huge body of material has been omitted from publication. Omitted are papers related to such matters as: the equipping of consulates; the bonding of Consuls; appointments of Vice-Consuls; leaves of absence; financial transactions; reports of commercial and navigational information forwarded for publication in the United States for the benefit of the American merchant marine; required semi-annual reports from each post of fees, accounts, visits by U.S. ships, and activities in behalf of distressed American seamen; the often complicated navigational and legal distresses of American merchant vessels; the affairs of individual American citizens abroad—deaths, inheritances, disappearances, strandings, civil and criminal difficulties, and other problems and interests; re-

ports on affairs and events in foreign countries that were of no immediate interest to the United States.

As a result of these policies of selection many of the Consuls will
not appear at all in the published documents. Others will be represented by only one or two documents. For none is all the extant
correspondence published, but the most fully represented are the
Consuls in the Texas Republic; in some but not all regions of Mexican territory; in the hot spots of the Caribbean; and to a lesser extent
in northern and central Europe where diplomatic and trade initiatives
and an accompanying expansion of the consular establishment appear to have been under way.

As with Ministers, the bias in selection from the immense consular
correspondence has been in favor of the New World over the Old
and in favor of change over large but static activities. A great part
of regular consular business was carried on in the old ports of Europe,
and this routinized business, though generating a large correspondence, does not appear prominently in the published documents.
The consular correspondence is a tremendously interesting and under-
used source of information about events and conditions in many
parts of the world at the time, most of which has had to be omitted
from publication. The American Consuls in North Africa (at Tunis,
Tangier, and Tripoli), for instance, wrote frequent and informative
reports of conditions in that region and the imperial maneuverings
of the European powers there, that could not be fitted into our
publication.

All of the documents selected for omission, nearly two-thirds
of the total extant, are of an official character. That is to say, almost all of the omitted documents are from the National Archives,
except for a few found in unofficial repositories that are copies of or
of a type of official document. It should be noted that the census,
at least at this time, and the Patent Office, which had its own Commissioner and staff, did not generate much correspondence on the
part of the Secretary of State.

The principles of inclusion and exclusion which have been stated
constitute a general description and not an ironclad set of categories.
Many documents fit into two or more descriptive categories, and
others fit into none. It has been beyond the mission and the resources
of the Calhoun edition to provide a comprehensive documentary
history of American foreign relations while Calhoun was Secretary
of State, as tempting as it might be. What we have sought to provide is a rich rendering of the more active side of a vast body of

significant historical material that, though relatively accessible, has been relatively unknown and unused.

Calhoun and Texas

Calhoun was on the losing side of history, insofar as history, in the largest sense, can be said to have a losing side. He stood athwart the course of democratic consolidation and egalitarianism, as it has subsequently unfolded, which it would be silly and futile to deny. As a result he has paid the penalty of a negative and unfavorable image in that greater part of American historical writing which is devoted to celebrating the tendencies which he opposed.

Yet Calhoun has never ceased to have admirers and defenders. A surprisingly large minority of observers, of diverse times and viewpoints, have found his thought and his career of lasting interest and of lasting relevance to the problems of later generations, often more so than the careers and ideas of much more conventionally successful and popular figures.

At no point in his long and stormy role in the drama of American history does the company of his defenders shrink to smaller numbers than the critical year of his service as Secretary of State. Not even Nullification has drawn less sympathy than this part of his career. The story of Texas and sectional conflict over the Western territories began long before Calhoun was Secretary of State and continued long after. Yet the vast secondary literature on this subject, most of it quite superficial, has focused (quite reasonably) on this episode as a turning point in the hardening of sectional conflict and (less reasonably) on Calhoun as the villain of this development, as if it would not have occurred without him.

It is a volatile and complicated point in history. To understand the period 1844–1845 requires an immense effort in sorting out the varying perspectives, attitudes, and tactical judgments that characterized many different segments of sectional and factional opinion. There was a chaos of impulses, ideas, interests, and ambitions at loose in the expansive American society at that moment, and only a shallow or partisan historian would be too quick with summary judgments about what political leaders were good or bad, wise or misguided. In fact, no leader, no party, and no set of policies could achieve a satisfactory consensus or even a very satisfactory accommodation. We are, after all, on the threshold of thirty years of hot and cold civil war.

That segment of opinion and tendency that Calhoun represented in this situation was described perhaps better by one of his correspondents than by himself. A Tennessee politician wrote:

> It is time that the South should set up for herself. A large majority of our people are determined to have Texas cost what it may. We feel that the opposition to Texas is a concession to abolition & to the fears of Tariff monopolists. We have submitted to the open insults of the one & grinding oppressions of the other long enough. To yield the Texas question is to agree quietly to be tied hand & foot & oppressed in all time to come . . . . We look to you to hold the helm and pilot us through the difficulties which surround us.[8]

Anyone who wishes to understand Calhoun's position at this juncture will find it well laid out in the "Preliminary Remarks" with which Richard K. Crallé prefaced his publication of correspondence about the Texas question in his edition of Calhoun's works.[9] And the biographies by Charles M. Wiltse and Margaret L. Coit, by a thorough examination of the context and the chronology, add understanding of Calhoun at this controversial point.[10]

In the first weeks of his service as Secretary of State in the John Tyler administration, Calhoun concluded with the representatives of the Texas Republic a treaty annexing that Republic to the United States. Texas had been independent and waiting at the door of the Union to be admitted since 1836, something clearly desired by its people, but which had not been consummated, though favored to some degree by every administration and by much if not all American opinion. There were two reasons for holding back. One was fear of war with Mexico. Calhoun hoped to obviate this possibility by leaving open the question of border and otherwise maintaining a temperate stance towards the concerns of the Republic of Mexico. There was considerable evidence that this might have worked had it been carried out skilfully,[11] and nothing in later events, including

---

[8] From L[evoritt] H. Coe, May 11, 1844, herein.

[9] Richard K. Crallé, ed., *The Works of John C. Calhoun* (6 vols. Columbia, S.C.: printed by A.S. Johnston, 1851, and New York: D. Appleton & Co., 1853–1857), 5:311–320.

[10] Wiltse, *John C. Calhoun,* 3:150–182; Margaret L. Coit, *John C. Calhoun: American Portrait* (Boston: Houghton Mifflin Co., c. 1950), pp. 363–372.

[11] Ben E. Green, one of the best situated Americans to assess Mexican politics, thought so. See Green to Lyon G. Tyler, August 8, 1889, in the Duff Green Papers, Southern Historical Collection, University of North Carolina (published microfilm, roll 17, frames 803–812). The British Minister, Richard Pakenham, reported to his government that Calhoun "said he intended to endeavor to obtain the consent of Mexico to the proposed arrangement by the offer of a pecuniary compensation, and that the Mexican Minister at Washington [Juan N. Almonte]

the development of armed conflict over the border question, disproves it.

The second reason for opposition was sectional. It was not created by Calhoun, but had been implicit in the American body politic at least since the Missouri controversy. The adding of territory to the Union that would increase the strength of the South was, at least in the perception of many, incompatible with the economic and moral goals of the North that were steadily growing in focus and potency.

Calhoun had not made the decision to annex Texas. This had already been initiated as a primary policy of the administration before he was appointed. Nor did Calhoun invent the policy of placing much of the defense of annexation on the threat to slavery in the South from the potential machinations of British abolitionism in a vulnerable Texas. This was already administration policy and had already been widely discussed in the public press. He did make this reasoning quite explicit in his correspondence with the British minister at the time. And the leaking of this correspondence from the confidential papers of the Senate to the press by an Ohio Free Soiler did add heat to the public discussion and mobilize the opinion not only of many Northerners but also of cautious Southerners against the treaty.

It has often been charged that Calhoun's insistence on inserting a sectional defense of slavery into the case for Texas led to the defeat (on June 8 by a vote of 16 to 35) of the treaty. It was convenient for many to accept this interpretation. It provided an excuse for Thomas H. Benton and for certain Northern Democrats who were not free soilers and who had always been expansionists to oppose the treaty, thus deflecting free-soil resentment and at the same time saving the political dividends of pro-Texas sentiment to accrue to themselves at a later time. It was also, in retrospect, convenient for the few defenders of John Tyler to allow Calhoun to accept blame for the defeat, when in fact he merely had expressed what had been consistently the administration policy and when the defeat had as much to do with the general pattern of failure by the administration as it had to do with anything that Calhoun wrote.

An examination of the context and of the vote and of later developments indicates pretty clearly that the treaty was doomed whatever Calhoun did, and its doom resulted, just as Calhoun main-

---

had listened favorably to these suggestions and had undertaken to communicate them to his Govt." Pakenham to Lord Aberdeen, April 14, 1844, Aberdeen Papers, British Museum.

tained, from Presidential politics. The defection of Van Buren Democrats crippled it, and the all but unanimous defection of the Southern and Border State Whigs in the Senate, twelve in number, made defeat certain. The actions of these had to do not with free-soil but with the strategy of their party and its leader, Henry Clay. And Clay himself, throughout the ensuing presidential campaign, backed steadily away from his anti-Texas position and in Calhoun's direction, under the pressure of public opinion.

It remains a fact to be explained that Calhoun raised the sectional issue in a provocative fashion, though he did not know, of course, that his letters to Pakenham would be published while the treaty was pending in the Senate. And it is hard to see this as anything other than a tactical mistake since it would tend to render politically vulnerable if not alienate moderate Northerners. Thus the independent-minded and pro-annexation Charles J. Ingersoll of Pennsylvania could see Calhoun at this juncture as committing "a great blunder . . . . Calhoun, with superior talents, is extremely sectional and southern . . . . felo de se."[12]

The fear of British abolitionism *was*, in fact, the only *urgent* reason for annexation (which, after all had been in abeyance for eight years) and it had already been accepted as such. A more pragmatic politician than Calhoun would have stated this fact less forthrightly. But Calhoun believed in the importance of precedents and of meeting attacks at the threshold, and he desired to have on record a principled opposition by the federal government to the proposition that British power could presume to interfere with the interests or morals of American slaveholders. And he hoped to mobilize a lethargic South by getting a British admission of such intent on record. Possibly, also, he thought mistakenly that, rather than offending wavering Northerners, a clear stand might provide a countervailing pressure that would keep them in place. To wish to add new territory to the Union, to resent the opposition to new territory on anti-slavery grounds, and to resent the implications of British interference was all completely within the mainstream of Jeffersonian nationalism, and he did not see himself as an innovator.

In other words, as Calhoun saw it, he did not raise the sectional issue, he simply met it more forthrightly than most people in 1844 preferred. Calhoun was, like everyone else, caught up in the impending sectional maelstrom. The conflict at that moment was not between nationalists and sectionalists but between pragmatists and

[12] Meigs, *Life of Ingersoll*, p. 266.

idealists, each of which came in a Northern and a Southern variety. Calhoun represented Southern idealism, a minority, as the vote on the Texas treaty showed. Southern pragmatists like the Whigs were content to defeat annexation for the time being and leave it for some future date when the benefit would accrue to their party, or were ready, like the Democrat James K. Polk, to take short-term gains and ignore those long-term implications of sectional conflict that the provocative and impractical Calhoun insisted on bringing up. The North, of course, was carrying on its own dialectic between pragmatists and idealists, though these, perhaps, were not as far apart in their ultimate goals as the Southern variety. The two dialogues increasingly operated in separate universes of discourse, which was the most portentous fact in the whole situation and which Calhoun was one of the few far-sighted enough to discern and to face frankly.

Perhaps Calhoun's stand at this critical juncture is explained as well as can be by the observations made by Friedrich von Raumer, a historian and liberal monarchist from Prussia, who met him at just this time:

> My high esteem for Mr. C[alhoun] has been fully confirmed by personal acquaintance; and his Speeches which he has given me with his own marginal notes, will be a treasured token of remembrance. I had already made myself acquainted with them in Berlin. Every one speaks in the highest terms of C[alhoun]'s morality and excellent character; though some, half in reproach, call him a *metaphysician*. I am well aware that by this is understood nothing of what has been called so from Aristotle to Schelling. In a like manner the minister Struensee used the word *poetry*. If he said, "That is poetry," he meant, that is unpractical, impossible, empty dreaming. Assuredly C[alhoun] cherishes none of the whims of impractical philosophers . . . . His metaphysics consist essentially in this, that he will not attribute absolute truth and omnipotence to the opinions and crotchets of this or that day; nay, as the defender of the slave states, he has practically opposed a kind of metaphysics of the north. . . . men of the logical sagacity of Mr. C[alhoun] are a necessary counterpoise to mere rhetorical talent.[13]

[13] From a letter written on May 7, 1844, from Charleston, in Frederick von Raumer, *America and the American People*, translated from the German by William W. Turner (New York: J. & H.G. Langley, 1846), p. 417. Raumer (1781–1873) was a professor of history and jurisprudence, a member of the "right center" in the Frankfort Parliament in 1848, and an advocate of German unification under a Prussian prince but along the lines of American federalism.

THE PAPERS

of

JOHN C. CALHOUN

▯

Volume XVIII

JANUARY 1– MARCH 31
1844

▥

When John Tyler was elevated suddenly into the Presidency in April, 1841, by the death of William Henry Harrison, he inherited Daniel Webster as his Secretary of State. All of Harrison's Cabinet except Webster resigned in September, 1841, joining with the Whig leadership in Congress to read President Tyler out of their party for his refusal to acquiesce in the rechartering of a national bank. Webster remained behind, justifying himself to his fellow Whigs on the grounds that important negotiations were under way with Great Britain.

Webster resigned in May, 1843, having concluded the Treaty of Washington with Great Britain the previous year, having filled as many offices as possible with his political allies, and having launched several important initiatives, such as sending Commissioners for the first time to China and to the King of Hawaii. The independently-Whiggish South Carolinian Hugh S. Legaré was appointed to succeed Webster in the State Department, but died suddenly within weeks of his appointment. After Calhoun declined an overture for the office, Tyler promoted his fellow Virginian Abel P. Upshur from the Navy Department to the State Department.

Upshur consulted freely with Calhoun, and Calhoun was well informed about the administration's major diplomatic plans, especially the initiative which Upshur, with the President's concurrence, had launched to secure the consent of the independent Republic of Texas to a treaty annexing itself to the Union of the States. On February 28, 1844, as this plan was coming to a head, Upshur was killed, with others, by an accidental explosion on a U.S. warship during a social excursion. Only shortly before, a new British plenipotentiary, Richard Pakenham, had arrived in Washington with powers to settle the troublesome status of the vast Oregon Territory. Upshur and Pakenham had met formally for the first time the day before Upshur's death.

Without consulting Calhoun, President Tyler on March 6, 1844,

3

sent Calhoun's nomination to the Senate as Secretary of State, a nomination which the Senate confirmed immediately without dissent. Calhoun learned of this on March 15, and the next day wrote his reluctant acceptance. During the month between Upshur's death and Calhoun's arrival in Washington on March 29, Tyler's Attorney General, John Nelson, acted as interim Secretary of State, supervising the routine business and transacting the urgent business of the department.

Calhoun entered on official duties on April 1, a Monday. He had already met socially with Pakenham and with the leading members of the Senate Foreign Relations Committee. Also with the representatives of the Texas Republic—Isaac Van Zandt, the Chargé d'Affaires, and J. Pinckney Henderson, who had been sent direct from Texas to join in the negotiation and had arrived in Washington only shortly before Calhoun.

The papers of the following section, covering the first three months of 1844, overlap with the documents presented in the last section of Volume XVII of The Papers of John C. Calhoun. *The last section of Volume XVII contains Calhoun's personal correspondence for the period of January through March, 1844, but not his official correspondence, except for a few letters written to the newly-appointed Secretary of State before he took office from persons seeking appointments to office. The section which follows in this volume contains a highly selective presentation of Calhoun's most important official documents as Secretary of State for the same time period.*

More specifically, the section which follows contains 1) a few of the many hundreds of documents addressed to the Secretary of State before Calhoun took office, but which were received by him after he entered the office; 2) a few important items that had already been received but which had not yet been acted on; and 3) a few other papers of Calhoun's predecessors that had set policies and parameters within which the new Secretary would be obliged to operate.

Ⅲ

George Brown to A[bel] P. Upshur

Honolulu, Jan[uar]y 16, 1844

Dear Sir, Having now been resident here during three months, it may be supposed that I have in that time made myself somewhat acquainted with the state of civilization and of affairs generally, and although I am not aware that I shall be able to give much new information, so many works having been published on these islands, yet as it may be expected of me, I consider it my duty to give you my impressions, from the information I have acquired.

First in regard to Population. From a census taken in 1836 the population of the different islands was as follows, Kauai 9,927, Oahu 27,798, Maui 24,195, Molokai 6,000, Lanai 1,200, Hawaii 39,193, Kahoolawe 80. The Census however was taken by natives, and it is very doubtful if it more than approaches to correctness. In comparison to a former census taken a few years previous, this shews a considerable diminution in numbers, over twenty thousand, a number much too great to be correct. It is however a fact undenied that there has been heretofore a steady diminution in the population, at least untill within the last two or three years and the causes to which such a result is owing are divers; I will mention two or three.

In the first place the vices and diseases introduced by foreigners, Debauchery and drunken[n]ess. It is true that the natives long before the discovery of their islands by [Captain James] Cook were accustomed to use the "Awa" an intoxicating liquor, but that had neither the quick or injurious effects of those liquors afterwards introduced by foreigners, and neither were its effects connected with those of the disease introduced by the earliest discoverers of the islands, and which effects united, have no doubt had the greatest share in the diminution of the population. Next to these may be mentioned the manner of living which is not calculated to induce long life. A large proportion of the people live in grass houses, that is, houses formed by inserting long posts into the ground, interwoven with withes, and covered & thatched with dry grass. These houses answer very well for the dry seasons, but are damp and unwholesome in the times of the rains, or in low and wet situations. This evil however is diminishing to a considerable extent at least in the towns; "Adobe" houses or houses built of mud bricks baked in the sun, are substituted by all who have become connected with foreigners & who can bear the expense. I have been informed by a respectable physician here, that many of the fatal diseases of this country may be attributed to the occupancy of straw houses.

The food of the inhabitants consisting principally of fish and "Poi," a dish made from the Taro, is not conducive to longevity, puffing up & bloating the flesh, and producing flatulency & diarrhaes. The inhabitants however in the large towns are getting into the habit of using meat to a small extent, and most of the vegetables of America are now raised somewhat abundantly, and coming into more general use.

The Climate of these islands, is most delightful, the thermometer seldom ranging below seventy or above eighty six on the low lands, and by ascending, almost any temperature down to Zero may be obtained.

These Islands are well calculated to produce all the fruits & vegetables that are grown in the East or West Indies. The Coffee is of fine flavor and the trees very productive. Sugar is made of excellent quality, and some hundred tons are annually exported, principally from plantations owned by foreigners. The native woods are in many instances very beautiful, and splendid articles of furniture are made from them. I have been informed that there are over one hundred varieties of the different kinds of wood suitable for building & cabinet work. I hope to be able to send to the department samples of the latter kind.

I am sorry I cannot give so flattering an account of the morals of these people as I could wish. The American missionaries have done, under the blessings of God, wonders, but there is much more to be done. Licentiousness yet prevails to a considerable extent in the towns & villages inhabited by & the ports frequented by foreigners. Intemperance for the present at least, is checked. Severe penal laws are made against the use of spirits to excess by the natives, and as yet I have not seen one native intoxicated. If it was not for the compulsatory treaty made by the Captain of a French man of war, whereby brandy is to be admitted at a nominal duty, the Government here would undoubtedly prohibit the importation of all Kinds of spirits, and it is to be hoped that their Envoys have succeeded in getting that treaty annulled by the French Government. It is only about two years since, the King and the most of the chiefs were in the habit of using intoxicating liquors to an unlimited extent, and of course their example was followed by the common people, but a new order of things has resulted from the labors of the missionaries, which is alike creditable to them, and the people under their charge.

The people are naturally indolent, but if an adequate object to industry is placed before them, they will work and work well with good overseers. The wages of common laboring men are from four to six dollars p[e]r month, they finding themselves food & lodging.

Their mental faculties, as far as I have been able to judge, are respectable, and instances could be named of individuals, who would do credit to the most civilized communities. The Present Governor of this island is a well informed, energetic and fine looking man, respected by all the foreigners who are themselves respectable. A considerable proportion of the people, I understand can read, and many of them are well informed though not to the extent they ought to be. One great mistake I am afraid has been made by the missionaries; they have employed more of their time in *preaching* than *teaching*. Civilization and Christianity ought to go hand in hand. There is now however a flourishing academy at Lahainaluna, on Maui; one here for the children of the chiefs, and one for half castes, besides a number of common schools. The children receive instruction readily, when their parents can be induced to send them to school, but I am sorry to find too many idle children of both sexes in the streets.

The Government is of a mixed character. The present King [Kamehameha III] is not absolute by law, but has associated with him a high female chief without whose assent no laws are binding. Together, they may enact laws, though these are generally made by the Congress, consisting of the council of chiefs, which forms the upper house, and of the representatives of the different islands, as a lower house, chosen by the majority of the people. The Congress meets once a year. The Laws having been made at different times, as occasions demanded, and never having been revised, are faulty in many respects, and sometimes contradictory, and by no means sufficiently ample. At the next session of Congress however, if the Envoys return in the mean time, they are to be revised, and a new code, better adapted to the present condition of the nation, adopted.

The Revenue of the islands is about forty thousand dollars the past year, but this is not a criterion. It has some years been as high as one hundred thousand. It is produced by the duties on imports, and the capitation tax of one dollar on adult males, down to a rial on children below fourteen years of age. Besides the taxes in money or produce each inhabitant capable of labor, is obliged to give a certain number of days per annum, in work on the roads or to the chief from whom he holds his land. The people however on some of the islands are becoming more democratic, and will not work for the chiefs unless they are paid a rial per day. Ere long I think they will be able to obtain their lands in fee simple. They are now held by the King or chiefs. There are about four hundred American residents on these islands including Missionaries and children born here of Am[erican] Parants, and to a great extent, they are a well behaved and respectable class of people. Of this number about half are connected with the mission. Of the remainder between thirty & forty are merchants & Storekeepers, and the remainder of the males, mechanics, boarding house keepers, and professional men. There are some five or six highly respectable mercantile firms, holders of considerable landed property, and doing a good & safe business. Their property may be estimated from fifteen to one hundred thousand dollars each. Of other foreign residents there are not over one hundred. There is however a floating population of about one hundred more of all nations, principally sick & other seamen discharged from their vessels. Some sixty Americans are married to native females & have by them about one hundred & twenty half caste children.

The question now arises whether this people are capable of governing themselves. In my opinion *they are entirely so.* They are naturally courageous but very inoffensive, and if they are not imposed upon by a nation of greater power, and the laws made for their own government, and for that of those who choose to reside among them, are not interfered with, I see no reason why they may not go on prosperous & happy. They are willing and happy in being taught, and have every desire to live in peace with all nations. Their knowledge of international law is but small, but they are by no means ignorant of international rights, and have always shewn their good sense in asking advice of those foreigners whose conduct and character have given them confidence. I doubt whether in the history of the world a case can be quoted, to compare with that of the Hawaiian Nation. But little more than twenty years have elapsed since they emerged from a state of barbarism, and they would lose little in a comparison with some of the small South American states. I have visited a number of times, the seminary where the young male & female chiefs are educated, and have been struck with their talents & improvement. Most of them speak English well and are well versed in the common branches of English studies. Some play well on the piano, considering the little time spent in learning, and others draw with considerable taste. The heir apparent to the throne, the son of the Governor of Oahu, is a remarkable bright boy, with a very good disposition.

Owing to the want of a knowledge of foreign languages, among the older portion of the natives, they have been compelled to employ foreigners, in their intercourse with foreigners, and the Sec[re]t[ar]y of State for Foreign affairs, Collectors, & chiefs of Police are foreigners, I believe in nearly every instance native Americans. Our Countrymen, stand altogether higher in the estimation of the people & government, than those of any other nation, and I believe from their conduct deserve the preference.

In conclusion I would say, that this government feels its weakness. It is all the time or has been heretofore, in continual fear of the visits of some foreign man of war, with an ignorant or unprincipalled commander, who listening to the unfounded complaints of some of his own debauched or unprincipled countrymen, would make demands for redress where no injury had been sustained, and who would support the most unjust and iniquitous demands, made by men, whose residence would be a disgrace to any country. The way to make these islands of benefit to all commercial nations, is to make their Government a strong one, and to give it full power to banish from the territory, any foreigners who by their conduct and example are obnoxious. They are not yet able to erect prisons and bear the expense of keeping a parcel of convicts in confinement, and they heretofore have been cursed with but few from the native population. It is hard that they should be obliged to take care of those of other nations, or let them run riot in their course.

February 9th 1844

The "Hazard" H.B.M. Corvette, arrived from Mazatlan and St. Blas [Mexico] on the 3d inst. bringing the English Consul General William Miller Esq. I received no letters from the Department but files of newspapers from Sept[embe]r 26th to Oct[obe]r 28th were received. I presume my letters and dispatches from the Department if any are on the coast either at Paita or Calao.

Gen[era]l Miller the new Consul Gen[era]l appears to be a gentlemanly man, and I think will be popular, both with the Government & the residents here. He came prepared to restore the sov[e]reignty of the Islands to the King but had been forestalled by Admiral [Richard] Thomas. It appears by documents sent to the Govt. here by their agents [in Europe] Mess[rs. William] Richards & Haalilia, that the English Government had in every instance sustained this Government in the course they had taken, and confirmed the proceedings of the courts here in all their decisions except one, where interest was allowed on a claim from the date of the liability, and where the English lawyers think interest ought to be allowed only from the time of judgement. Every thing indeed appears to be satisfactorily arranged. Mr. Miller in an interview with me, said, that the policy of his Government was undoubtedly the same as mine, viz. to do every thing in their power to advance the interests of these islands, by protecting & benefitting the Government and people, and that he would with pleasure unite with me in any measures likely to tend to that end. Mr. M[iller] with the Admiral have gone to La-haina to visit the King. They left yesterday in the Hazard and will probably be absent a week.

Some time since I, in a conversation with Mr. [G.P.] Judd the Sec[re]t[ar]y of State of Foreign Affairs, told him that I should probably find it necessary to protest against the treaty made between this Govt. & Admiral Thomas, especially that part which provided, that in case of suits between Englishmen & Foreigners, the Jury were to be half English, as it was notorious that there were not six English-men here fit to sit upon a jury. He stated at that time, that his opinion coincided with mine, and that he should use his endeavors at the proper time to have that treaty abrogated. Since the arrival of Gen[era]l Miller, he has informed me that Gen. M[iller] has told him that he considers the treaty null & void, the Admiral having no powers to make one and that he looked upon it, at least in part, as a foolish & unjust one.

Dr. Judd also informed me that the only case of any importance, in which an Englishman and American were concerned, and where judgement had been rendered in favor of the latter, had been sub-mitted to the Eng[lish] Govt. and the doings here been confirmed; and the money, now in the hands of the Eng[lish] Consul, where it had been placed by Lord George Paulett[']s usurped power, would be paid over to the American Claimant. I have no doubt that here-after every thing will go along smoothly here, and that no further attempts will be made by the English or French men of war, to trouble this people.

On the 5th instant I received from Mr. [William] Hooper, Act-[in]g Com[mercia]l Agent [here at Honolulu], a note, of which I forward a copy informing me that he had appointed Milo Calkin Esq. U.S. Com[mercial] Agent at Lahaina Maui. My answer to that note is also forwarded, and I beg leave to say to you that the appointment is a very good & popular one. Mr. Calkin is much liked by the Americans here and his absence from this place, where he has resided some years, is much regretted. If the Com[mercia]l Agency here, is altered to that of Consulate as I have heretofore advised, that of Lahaina will of course be a Vice Consulate, & you will be good enough to send out a flag, seal, & the usual articles furnished to those offices, as they cannot be obtained here.

On the first instant I addressed a note to Mr. Judd, a copy of which marked A, accompanies this, to which he replied as per copy marked B. The notes speak for themselves & I will only farther say, that I have no doubt that this Government will do every thing in their power to further the interests of the United States in regard to the establishment of a Naval depot here. I was induced to address the note I did, from a conversation I had with you when Sec[re]t[ar]y of the Navy, before I left Washington the last time. In a few days I intend visiting the different ports in the islands, and will write you the result of my observations, though I have now, little doubt but that Honolulu is the best port by far, for the depot, if one is established.

Feb[ruar]y 16th 1844

The Hazard returned from Lahaina on the 13th. That morning I called upon the Sec[re]t[ar]y for foreign affairs, Dr. Judd, when he informed me among other things, that a treaty had been negotiated between the King and Consul Gen[era]l Miller on the part of H.B. Majesty. I expressed to him my surprise, that this should have been done without apprising me, and requested him to allow me to see it, which he did, when to my astonishment I found that it was in all material points the same that had been forced from this Government by Capt. La Place of the French navy, and which was derogatory to ["the" *interlined*] Character and injurious to the interests of this nation. I again expressed my surprise to Dr. Judd that such a treaty should have been signed at all, and at any rate with so much haste. I pointed out to him the injustice of some of the provisions, especially that in the second article, where the *same privileges* were allowed to *foreigners* which the King allowed to his *own people.* That, in the sixth article, where this Government was not allowed to charge more than five per cent duties on English goods or those brought in Eng[lish] vessels, while they were only permitted to ["import" *altered to* "export"] their own products to Great Britain, subject to whatever duties the Eng[lish] Government think proper to impose. But I told him that of these I had no right to complain, I only suggested them to him to prove, that this Government had been hasty in its movements, especially when they had no definitive information as to what the Envoys it had sent to Europe had done, and that it would have been as well to have delayed signing the treaty, at least untill the return of Mess. Richards & Haalilio.

I however stated that there was one article to which I had objections (the third), and that I should address him a note on the subject, which I did on the 14th inst., a copy of which you will find attached, marked "E."

On the 16th inst., Dr. Judd called on me and handed me the answer to my note of the 14th, and said that he regretted much that he had not Submitted to me the treaty previous to its being signed—that he was aware it was not what it ought to be, and that he was satisfied the King had been too hasty in signing it. He said also that Gen[era]l Miller told him, that he was not authorised by his Government to alter a single word in the treaty, and that his authority only extended to the signing it. He also informed me that since receiving my note he had submitted my objections to Gen[era]l Miller who had acknowledged their force, and had stated that he himself, thought that the treaty was not an equitable one & that he would write to Lord Aberdeen expressing his opinion to that effect, which as Dr. Judd has informed me has been done & that Gen[era]l Miller has shewn him a copy of his communication. Dr. J[udd] also said that he should write to Lord Aberdeen and that he would shew me a copy. His letter to me is furnished with this as per copy marked "F."

I am satisfied that the English Government, did intend to overreach the Hawaiian Govt. in this treaty as they had refused to negotiate with Richards & Haalilio in England, and sent out this, as is said, ready written, without having submitted it to them, being satisfied that they would not have signed such an one there, and hoping to work upon the feelings of the King here, by restoring his flag, which they were not aware had been done, when Gen[era]l Miller left. Dr. Judd has concluded ["to" *interlined*] publish the treaty with the correspondence between this Govt. & Gen[era]l Miller as also the Admiral, and requested me to consent that our notes should also be published, but I thought it would not be correct so to do, untill they had been submitted to you & therefore declined giving my consent, at the same time saying that he had the *right* to do as he pleased. He appeared to think that my note might be of service if published, but as he can give the substance of it to Lord Aberdeen, I do not think the publication could be of the least benefit. I trust my proceedings in this affair will meet your approbation and that of the President [John Tyler].

I am pretty well satisfied that *this Government* is still fearful that they are not yet safe from the encroachments of the English, and they do not feel strong enough to resist demands, even if unjust. I do not myself however think they have any, at least immediate, cause.

Feb[ruar]y 21.

Some days previous to this, I had a conversation with Dr. Judd, as to the propriety and feasibility of sending in to Mexico at least once in three months, a government vessel, to answer as a packet and I urged upon him the advantages, that by such an arrangement, would accrue to this Government, and the mercantile interests generally. Yesterday I received a note from him, inviting me to meet the representatives of France & Great Britain at his office, to consult on the subject. We accordingly met to day at eleven o[']clock. Dr. Judd stated that this Government would send in to [the Mexican Pacific ports of] either Mazatlan or St. Blas, one of the Govt. vessels, as often as once in three months, if sufficient money could be pledged to pay the expenses of victualling and manning her, which was estimated at about four hundred dollars p[e]r month. He said he was aware that it would be advantageous to the Govt. to have frequent communications with the U. States and Europe, but that it was poor, and if it gave the services of the vessel, and bore the expenses of her wear and tear, it was as much as it could do at present. I told him that I would write to my Government on the subject, and recommend that a sum should be appropriated to the purpose, but that I could guarantee nothing. I also said that I had little doubt but that the merchants of New Bedford, Nantucket, New London and other whaling towns, as well as the different Insurance Companies, would subscribe, something, towards the enterprise, and that I would write to my friends in those towns, to see what they would do.

The English Consul General wanted to have the things on a grander scale, and that Packets should sail once a month. Dr. Judd had no objection, were the money to carry the enterprise on, to be had. Both Consuls stated they would propose it to their Governments, and the French Consul also stated, that he would write to Mons[ieu]r Bruat Governor of Tahiti. Will you be good enough to write me whether the Govt. of the U. States will do any thing and to what amount?

Feb[ruar]y 23d

Yesterday H.B. Majesty's Ship Dublin arrived from Tahiti via Hilo, and the Corvette Modeste from Mazatlan & St. Blas. By the latter vessel I received a dispatch from your department dated 30th May 1843, referring to the Ship W[illia]m & Eliza of New Bedford, whose commander, the owners suspected intended to commit barratry. The W[illia]m & Eliza sailed for New York in December last, and the owners must have labored under a great mistake. The dispatch was sent from Valparaiso to Mazatlan, and has been some months reaching me, while by the same vessel that brought it here, I received the President's message, and New Orleans papers up to the 18th December, which proves that the best plan to send letters here is via Mexico, Mazatlan or St. Blas. The message reached Mazatlan in 27 days from

13

the U. States. By the Frigate Dublin I received a letter from Tahiti stating that the [French] Governor of that island had refused to acknowledge Mr. Pritchard as British Consul. Every thing was quiet there.

The Eng[lish] Frigate Dublin[,] Admiral Thomas, leaves this port for Valparaiso, and the Sloop Hazard for Sydney next week. The Sloop Modeste will remain on this Station for the present. I understand it is the intention of the Admiral that, one of his Squadron shall be here nearly all the time. His Hawaiian Majesty's Schooner "Hoikaika" (The Swift) will go into the coast in a few days. I have the honor to be with great respect, Y[ou]r Very Ob[edien]t S[e]r-[vant], George Brown, Commissioner to the King of Hawaii.

ALS (No. 11) with Ens in DNA, RG 59 (State Department), Diplomatic Despatches, Hawaii, vol. 1 (T-30:1, frames 62–79), received 5/11. NOTE: Brown, from Beverly, Mass., was appointed to Hawaii by John Tyler in 3/1843. He was lost at sea in 1845 on his return voyage to the U.S.

ISAAC VAN ZANDT to A[bel] P. Upshur

Legation of Texas
Washington, 17th Jan[uar]y 1844

Sir, It is known to you that an armistice has been proclaimed between Mexico and Texas; that, that armistice has been obtained through the intervention of several great Powers mutually friendly, and that negociations are now pending, having for their object a settlement of the difficulties heretofore existing between the two countries. A proposition likewise having been submitted by the President of the United States [John Tyler] through you for the annexation of Texas to this country, therefore (without indicating the nature of the reply which the President of Texas [Samuel Houston] may direct to be made to this proposition) I beg leave to suggest, that it may be apprehended should a treaty of annexation be concluded, Mexico may think proper to at once terminate the armistice, break off all negociations for peace and again threaten, or commence hostilities against Texas; and that some of the other Governments, who have been instrumental in obtaining their cessation if they do not not [sic] throw their influence into the Mexican scale, may altogether withdraw their good offices of mediation thus loosing to Texas their friendship and exposing her to the unrestrained menaces of Mexico. In view then of these things I desire to submit, through you, to His Excellency the

President of the United States this inquiry; Should the President of Texas accede to the proposition of annexation, would the President of the United States, after the signing of that treaty, and before it shall be ratified and receive the final action of the other branches of both Governments, in case Texas should desire it or with her consent, order such number of the military and naval forces of the United States to such necessary points, upon the territory or borders of Texas, or the Gulf of Mexico, as shall be sufficient to protect her against foreign aggression?

This communication, as well as the reply which you may make, will be considered by me as entirely confidential, not to be embraced in my regular official correspondence to my Government, but enclosed direct to the President of Texas, for his information. With assurances of my great regard, I have the honor to be Very Respectfully Your Ob[e]d[ien]t Serv[an]t, Isaac Van Zandt.

ALS in DNA, RG 59 (State Department), Notes from Foreign Legations, Texas, vol. 1 (T-809:1); PC in Senate Document No. 349, 28th Cong., 1st. Sess., p. 3; PC in House Document No. 271, 28th Cong., 1st Sess., pp. 88–89.

W[illia]m M. Blackford to Abel P. Upshur

Legation of U.S.
Bogota, Feb. 2d [18]44

Sir, In my Despatch No. 19, I had the honor to express the opinion that I should, in a short time, be enabled to bring the claim of the Brig Morris, to a satisfactory adjustment. Circumstances, which have led to some further postponement, but strengthen my hopes of ultimate success.

In an accompanying packet you will receive a copy of my detailed statement of the 16th Nov.—alluded to in my No. 19—a translation of the long and elaborate answer of the Secretary of Foreign Affairs [Joaquin Acosta], of the 11th of December; a copy of my reply of the 22d and a translation of his rejoinder of the 30th of the same month. A perusal of these documents will put you in possession of the merits of the case.

Our first conference was held on the 10th January. The evidence, on both sides, was produced and collated and many incidental points discussed and decided. I found the Secretary frank and liberal, and I am constrained to say that an examination of the evidence, contained in the original papers of the case, considerably modified the opinion I had formed upon the *ex parte* testimony in my possession.

I deemed it my duty to contend for the operation of the Treaty of Bogota, at the date of the capture of the Morris, and supported the position, in my despatch of the 22d of Dec[embe]r by such arguments as I could command. I confess, however, that I was not satisfied with my own reasoning, and had no authorities to cite in support of my doctrine. Acting in good faith, therefore, I abandoned the point insisted upon—viz. that the Treaty of Bogota should be considered in force from the date of its last ratification and not merely from the date of the Exchange of Ratifications. As the capture occurred upon the 12th & the Exchange of ratifications not until the 27th of May, 1825, the liberal provisions of the Treaty were consequently admitted to be inapplicable.

In the second conference, the question was presented, whether I would adhere to the judicial sentences in the case, or rely upon the general principles of the Law of Nations. In view of all the circumstances, I considered it to be safer to claim as a basis for the settlement, the first decision of the Admiralty Court of Puerto Cabello, pronounced on the 6th July 1825. This decision acquitted the Brig and the greater part of the cargo, as American property—upon the condition, however, that Captain [Henry H.] Williams should produce to the Court a certified copy of the clearance of the Brig, from the Custom House of St. Jago de Cuba. Within the time specified Williams presented a document of a character somewhat suspicious, certainly, but—which was pronounced by the Court to be satisfactory. The condition of the Sentence of the 6th July 1825 having thus been fulfilled, the Brig and the acquitted part of the cargo should at once have been restored to the owners. It was not, however, until the 12th of January, 1826 that the court declared itself satisfied and decreed restitution.

Unfortunately, Williams appealed from this last sentence because no damages had been awarded to him. The captors also appealed, on account of supposed partiality of the Judge, and on the further ground of the alleged spurious character of the document from the St. Jago de Cuba Custom House. This appeal of Williams—which is no where mentioned in his various statements—is the fact, upon which the Secretary bases his resistance to the claim for Demur[r]age, and led me to put down that item smaller than I should otherwise have done. I do not know that a claim for Demur[r]age could justly be demanded at all, but for the fact, which, I think, is sufficiently proven, that the clearance—the want of which prevented the Brig & neutral part of the Cargo from being unconditionally acquitted by the Sentence of the 6th July '25—had been given by Capt. Williams, with the rest of his papers, to the commander of the Privateer & was by the latter suppressed or destroyed.

Having failed to cover the case by the provisions of the Treaty of Bogota, as heretofore stated, I could not deny that the capture of the Morris was not in violation of the Laws of Nations. This admission, of course, implied a surrender of all claim to the Spanish property & money on board, and likewise for Freight. There were circumstances of subsequent outrage on the part of the Captors, and vexatious delays in the adjudication of the case. The whole of the judicial proceedings—conformable as they may have been to the Constitution and laws of Colombia—appear strange when compared with the administration of Justice in our own country. On the other hand, it must be admitted, that the conduct of Capt. Williams, at the time of the capture & subsequently, was somewhat calculated to excite suspicion. In more than one instance, during the progress of the Trial, and especially by his appeal from the sentence of 12th Jan[uar]y 1826 he seriously compromised his interests. He seems to have been badly advised.

Taking into consideration every circumstance connected with the case, and having reference to the deplorable state of the finances of New Granada—to the probable temper of the two Houses of Congress—and to the obstacles which each succeeding year added to a satisfactory adjustment of the claim, and believing that the present favorable dispositions of the Executive afforded an opportunity which might not speedily again present itself, I determined to present a modified demand for indemnity as follows.

1.	For value of Brig	$6,000
2.	For value of owner's part of cargo, as per Invoice	6,982.07
3.	For value of Backers' part of cargo as p[e]r Invoice	7,530.88
4.	For Demur[r]age, one year	5,000.00
		$25,512.95
5.	Interest at 6 p[e]r cent from 12th Jan[uar]y 1826 til paid say 18 years	27,554.59
		$53,067.54

The proportionate part of this Government being one half, the amount she would have to pay, at this time is about $26,533.77.

I am fully aware that this is an amount much below what the

17

parties interested have, heretofore, claimed and may be less than that, to which in strict justice, they are entitled. In offering to receive it, I acted for the best interests of the claimants—to have demanded more I believe would have led to the rejection of the whole claim. My instructions leave the management of the whole affair to my discretion and I have, to the best of my ability, followed the dictates of that discretion. I trust the Department, on a review of all the circumstances, will be pleased to approve of my conduct.

On receiving the above statement, the Secretary expressed great surprize at the amount demanded and endeavored to obtain a reduction. He, at length, promised to submit it to the President [Gen. Pedro Alcantara Herran] & give me a definitive answer on the following Saturday.

Instead of the answer I had a right to expect, I received, on that day, a note requesting another conference, which took place on 24th ultimo.

The Secretary began by expostulating with me upon the amount of the demand, and expressed his fears that, anxious as the Government was to settle the claim, it could not stipulate for an indemnity so much beyond, what in its opinion, was justly due. He proceeded to state that there was a cabal in the Senate, hostile to the Administration & to himself personally—that these gentlemen would oppose whatever he did in the matter—that he feared he should not be able to defend, successfully, a convention, which provided for so large an indemnity—that he had written, some weeks ago, for authentic information, as to the clearance of the Brig from St. Jago de Cuba—that if the evidence went to prove the neutral character of the Brig, he could the better defend the Convention from the attacks of his enemies—that he expected the information, within a month at farthest—and, finally, asked as a favor, that I would not press for a decision, until its arrival.

I answered that if, as I had a right to infer from his remarks, the Executive was determined not to accede to my proposition—which would not be abated in the least degree—there was no use in further delay—and that I should prefer to close the negotiation at once, however much I might regret its unsuccessful issue.

He replied that I had misapprehended him on this point—that he was not authorised to say the Government would not agree to my proposition—that the delay asked was for the purpose of enabling him the more certainly to induce the Chambers to vote the sum stipulated by the Convention, which we might make.

I said, with this understanding, I could not object to the postponement—as there would still be abundant time to conclude a Convention before the adjournment of Congress—and that if signed now, the probability was it would be acted upon no sooner than if signed six weeks hence. A postponement was then agreed upon—with a stipulation that final action should be had, in full time to allow any Convention which might be made, to be acted upon by Congress at its next session.

Two distinguished Engineers—despatched by the French Government—are now engaged in surveying the Isthmus of Panama, with reference to the practicability of constructing a Canal. I have not been able to ascertain the circumstances which have induced this movement. It must have been resolved upon anterior to the Circular note of the Granadian government—a copy of which I had the honor to transmit with my No. 16.

I have the honor to enclose the receipt of Mr. [Joseph] Gooding for the 5th Instalment of the By-Chance money and also duplicate receipts of the 3rd & 4th Instalments.

You will also find herewith his Receipt for a portion only of the 6th Instalment. The amount of the residue—as per statement enclosed—will be remitted, in gold, by the Brig Chaires, which is expected to sail, from Carthagena, about the 15th of next month, to Messrs. Prime, Ward & King, of New York, on account of the Department. This sum is the amount due to Alexander Ruden, Jr. for money and property taken from the "By Chance."

I wrote to Messrs. Prime, Ward, & King, on the 12th ultimo, requesting them to effect insurance upon about one thousand dollars, and advise you of the same.

The last mail brought intelligence of the appointment of Gen. O'Leary—at present Consul in Puerto Cabello—as H.B. Majesty's Chargé d'Affaires near this Government. This gentleman was distinguished as a soldier, in the War of Independence—was attached to the personal staff of [Simon] Bolivar and zealously supported all the political views of the Liberator. He participated actively in the party movements & civil wars of the country. His countrymen here who are personally acquainted with him, speak highly of his talents. His past connexion with Colombian and Granadian politics, in some degree, justifies the undisguised dissatisfaction with which the authorities of New Granada regard the appointment. This dissatisfaction is not diminished by the fact that he is married to a sister of Gen. [Carlos] Soublette the President of Venezuela, and from this and a long residence there, is suspected of strong predilections for that Republic. We have no reason to regret any circumstances, which may render his influence, with this Government, less than that of his predecessor.

I again earnestly and respectfully request to know the views of the President [John Tyler] upon the suggestions I had the honor to make, touching a modification of the instructions upon the subject of a Commercial Treaty. Maturer reflection & fuller information serve but to strengthen my conviction of the opinions heretofore expressed. The present is a favorable moment for negotiation, and, though I should not expect to obtain the abolition of all discriminating duties, I think some very advantageous concessions could be had. Congress meets on the 1st of next month. In the absence of any information from you, on the subject of the Treaty, I shall use all the influence I can command to effect the passage of those meliorating regulations, relating to our trade, which were proposed last year, but were lost from the want of time to act upon them.

The country remains in a state of tranquillity. Some of the persons implicated in the late attempt at insurrection, have been shot. The affair has greatly strengthened the administration.

I have dates to the 6th of December, and, of course, the President[']s message. My latest Despatch received is your No. 13. I have had no letter from my family of a later date than the 2d September. I have the honor to be, with high respect, Your ob[edien]t S[ervan]t, Wm. M. Blackford.

P.S. Since the above was written I have had the honor to receive Despatch No. 15 and enclosure. No. 14 has not come to hand. I am yet without a line from my family.

ALS (No. 20) with Ens in DNA, RG 59 (State Department), Diplomatic Despatches, Colombia, vol. 10 (T-33:10, frames 126–185), received 3/30; PEx in Senate Document No. 339, 29th Cong., 1st Sess., p. 5. NOTE: Blackford (1801–1864), a Fredericksburg, Va., lawyer and newspaper editor, was appointed Chargé d'Affaires to New Granada by John Tyler in 2/1842.

WADDY THOMPSON [JR.] to A[bel] P. Upshur

Legation of the U.S. of A.
Mexico [City], Feb. 2, 1844

Sir, I received some time since from Mr. [Joaquin] Harmony, an American citizen residing in San Luis Potosi, an application for my official interposition in two cases: the one a loan of $1000 or $1500 made to this Govt., and the other relating to an order, which had been issued by the Governor of that Department, requiring all persons under a certain penalty to receive the provisional dollar, which is of less value by one & a half per cent than the Eagle dollar, in which Government dues are payable. I of course could not interfere in either case, and addressed to Mr. Harmony a letter [of 1/20/1844], a copy of which I send you, marked No. 1. An express arrived from Guaymas [Sonora] on the 20th of last month, which Mr. John A. Robinson had sent to inform me that the Governor of that Department was about to enforce the collection of the Guia duties, claimed of his nephew, Mr. Bowers, as well as similar duties in cases in which Mr. Robinson had acted as the agent of others. About the same time Mr. [James G.A.] McKennay, an American citizen resident in the new Department of Chiapas, arrived in this city to ask my protection against the seizure by the collector of the Customs of $3400, belonging to him ["see note No. 2" *interlined*; of 1/19/1844]. I asked an interview of the minister of Foreign Affairs [José M. de Bocanegra], which was conceded me the next day. He also summoned to this conference the Ministers of the Treasury and of Justice. The result was entirely satisfactory to me, as you will see by the notes of Mr. Bocanegra, nos. 3 & 4 [both of 1/22/1844], and my reply no. 5 [of 1/27/1844]. Mr. Robinson was discharged from all liability on account of the Guia duties and an immediate investigation ordered of the charges against the custom house officer in Chiapas, which was all Mr. McKennay desired. I availed myself of this conference to bring up and have settled the claim for a balance of indemnity due certain Americans, who had been expelled from California in 1840. This claim was also adjusted, as you will see by note, no. 4. I have the pleasure to inform you that the claim of the American Insurance Company of New York was also settled. It is to be paid in two equal annual instalments from this date: the interest, at 6 per cent, being first computed, and all to bear interest from the date. I send you (No. 6) a copy of the remonstrance [of 1/26/1844], which I have addressed to the Minister of Foreign Affairs against the order prohibiting foreigners from engaging in the Retail trade.

I am not aware of any single matter now pending in this Legation, with the exception of the prohibitory orders of August & September last, and I have reasons to believe that both of these will be materially modified; and I am happy to be able to say that, excepting these two cases (which do not involve our interests exclusively, but equally interest all countries), I have made no official demand of this Govt., since I have been here, and scarcely an unofficial application, which has not been granted.

About half of the instalment due on the 30th ult. has been paid, and I am assured that the remainder will be paid in a few days.

Gen[era]l Santa Anna is still at his country residence [Manga de Clavo] near Vera Cruz. Gen[era]l [Valentín] Canalizo has been elected President ad interim until his return. The new Congress has exhibited some evidences of a disposition to resist and put an end to the absolute Dictatorship, which he has exercised for more than two years past. If they persist in them, he will come up with nearly all the army, which he has quartered in his neighbourhood, and dissolve them. He is very far from being popular, but he is feared by all. His great security consists in the divisions amongst those opposed to him, and their want of a leader, who could command general confidence. The army is in his interest, and so are the clergy generally. The former, as in all similar cases, of which history informs us, will remain faithful, as long as he can pay them, which it seems to me impossible that he can do much longer, without encroaching on the property of the latter. So that I think there is good ground to believe that before very long he must lose one or the other. It is hard to say, which of the two (the army or the church) is the strongest.

I am informed that the negotiation with Texas for peace is not only broken off, but that the armistice has also been suspended. You will remember that, from the beginning of this matter, I expressed the opinion that nothing would come of it. It was only a device, on the part of Santa Anna, to relieve him from the difficulty, in which he had involved himself by his threats and promises of reconquering Texas, which he knows perfectly well is impossible. There may be other marauding forays, like that of Gen[era]l Wool [*sic*; Adrian Woll], retreating more rapidly than they advanced. But as to any regular and reasonably sufficient force invading the country, the thing is impossible and will not be attempted. They cannot raise money to support such an army two months.

My own opinion is, notwithstanding all their vaporing & gasconade, that the most agre[e]able thing to Santa Anna would be an authoritative interposition of our Govt. to put an end to the war, as he would then say that we were too strong for them to contend with.

I have seen or heard nothing (although I have copies of all Capt. Elliott's [*sic*; Charles Elliot's] correspondence with the Texan Govt.) to justify the suspicion that G[reat] Britain has made the abolition of slavery in Texas the condition of her interposition, however desirable that object may be with England. There is no power on Earth, with which Mexico would not rather see Texas connected than with England, either as a colony, or upon any other footing of dependency or union, political or commercial; and in this I think they show more than their usual wisdom. I have the honor to be Very Respectfully, Y[ou]r ob[edien]t Serv[an]t, Waddy Thompson.

LS (No. 40) with Ens in DNA, RG 59 (State Department), Diplomatic Despatches, Mexico, vol. 11 (M-97:12), received 3/12; PEx in Senate Document No. 341, 28th Cong., 1st Sess., p. 85; PEx in House Document No. 271, 28th Cong., 1st Sess., pp. 84–85. NOTE: Thompson was a former Representative from S.C. and had been appointed Minister to Mexico by John Tyler in 2/1842.

STEWART NEWELL to A[bel] P. Upshur

United States Consulate, Port of Sabine
Texas, February 12th 1844

Sir, Your Letter of Jan[uar]y 18th, enclosing Letter from Hon. Secretary of the Treasury [John C. Spencer], dated December 11th 1843, I had the Honor to receive, and regret, that the Hon. Secretary, could not meet the views expressed in my Letter No. 4 to the Hon. Secretary of State, and most respectfully beg leave, to refer the Hon. Secretary, to my above named No. 4, and upon reviewing it, and by a comparison, with the circumstances that have arisen since at Sabine Pass, perhaps he may be induced to change his views upon the subject.

I had the Honor to address a Letter No. 6, dated Febr[uar]y 9th inst[ant], to the Department, relative to a difficulty on Sabine, and will now detail, some of the circumstances, and forward a full copy, of my record, of proceedings in the case, to the Department, and trust should it be ["deemed" *interlined*] necessary, that very full instructions will be afforded me to enable me, to meet other and similar cases.

The Merchandize on board Keel Boat, refer[r]ed to, was shipped by a highly respectable Firm, well known to me, in New Orleans, forwarded by American Sch[oone]r Louisiana, to Sabine Pass, on the Louisiana side. She, arrived, and was met by the Keel Boat, loaded with Cotton. The two vessels exchanged Cargoes, in Sabine Lake, about 1½ Miles from the Texas side. The Keel Boat belonged, to the Master ["of the" *changed to* "Jesse"] Wright, and was built by him, on Sabine River, on an outer bank, of said River, from the Texas side, and in ordinary stages of Water, completely overflowed. Said Wright, has not changed his Citizenship, nor does he consider himself, a Citizen of Texas, nor his Boat a Texian Bottom. The Cotton carried by him, was taken on board, at Sabine Town, on the Texas

23

side of the River, placed on board the Louisiana, and by her carried to New Orleans, and as I am informed, entered as Texas Cotton. The Texian Collector [William C.V. Dashiell], went on board the Keel Boat, and made such enquiries, as are contained in his Letter ["No. 1" *interlined*] addressed to me, and contained in copy of record annexed, upon which representations, I proceeded up Sabine River to Greens Bluff, about 35 Miles from Sabine Pass, there found U.S. Revenue Schooner Vigilant, W[illia]m B. Taylor Esq[ui]r[e] Commanding. A note was addressed by me to Cap[tai]n Taylor, requesting a detail of the circumstances, with a view of having both sides, of the question, before, entering upon an investigation of the matter, and beg leave to refer the Hon. Secretary, to the correspondence accompanying this Letter, for all the particulars, in relation to the whole matter. The Texian Collector, claiming the right, to enter upon any, and all, vessels, arriving within the limits of the Sabine Pass, Lake or River, to ascertain for himself, if any property on board, was intended to be smuggled, or introduced clandestinely into Texas, with a view to defraud the Revenue of Texas. I objected to the exercise of such authority, and shall continue to do so, until further directed by the Department.

Another claim set up by the Texian Collector, (whether by order of his Government or not I do not know) but which I shall feel it my duty, to resist, It is as follows, that all vessels, American or others, except Texian vessels, shall be compelled to come to the Texian Custom House, on the West Bank of Sabine Pass, and there Enter, and clear and pay *Tonnage* duties, to Texas, if bringing Cargo intended for Texas, or taking on board Texian Produce, for the U. States, or Europe, and this, is claimed, whether the Cargo is landed, or taken in, on the Louisiana side, or not, which if permitted, will present the singular anomaly, of a National vessel, taking in or landing cargo, in her own waters, and paying Tribute to a Foreign Country, without a Treaty, or other specific arrangement that I am aware of, to create such an exercise of Foreign jurisdiction, over American vessels, and which to me, would appear to be, humbling the Proud and daring Stripes and Stars, into submission, to a power, less than the smallest, with which they ever contended.

The American Schooner Louisiana, is now here, and taking in Cargo of Texas Cotton, for New Orleans, determined to resist the payment of Fees, to the Texian authorities, who have declared thier intention, to capture said vessel, should she attempt to leave Sabine for New Orleans, without reporting to the Texian Custom House, and pay the charges claimed by the Collector aforesaid, and to enforce which, the Texian Revenue Cutter, a private owned vessel, or Schooner of 40 Tons, hired by the Texian Government, for Revenue service, and armed with one Gun, on a Pivot, which said vessel, together with Two or three more Cannon, now on board said vessel, and intended to be landed, at Sabine Pass, are to be, by order of the Texian Government, placed at the disposition, *and under* the orders, of the Collector, for the purposes of compelling all, and any Boats, and vessels, navigating the Sabine Waters, to answer *his* enquiries, or demands. This may I hope, prove sufficient, to show the necessity of some more definite arrangement, for the protection of our Property, Citizens & Flag, from the illegal attacks of a Government, or its officers, particularly, when the latter, is governed by the effects of a free use of Intoxicating drink, more than good judgement, or proper discretion, and I trust that no more serious matter, may occur, at this place, to justify the apprehensions expressed by me, in Letter No. 4 to the Department. The U.S. Sch[oone]r Vigilant, intended to cruise between Sabine, and Pascagoula [Miss.], when here, her aid will be valuable, but the duties assigned her, being so various, she cannot be at this place, as frequently, as requisite. Of her Commander, I cannot speak, nor can the Government appreciate too highly, for Skill, Ability, Courage, and devotion to the trust reposed in him. Also his Son, now acting as his Lieutenant, whose management, and daring, under the circumstances which the Keel Boat was seized, by him, as Officer of the Boat, strongly reccommend him to the particular notice of the Govt. and with a full Commission under the guidance of his present Commander will not disgrace the Flag of his Country, in the Revenue or Regular Service. I have the Honor to be Most Resp[ectfull]y Your Ob[edien]t Ser[van]t, Stewart Newell.

ALS (No. 7) in DNA, RG 59 (State Department), Consular Despatches, Texas, vol. 1 (T-153:1), received 3/10.

Geo[rge] W. Slacum to Abel P. Upshur

Consulate of the United States
Rio de Janeiro, 12th February 1844
Sir, I have the honor to transmit herewith, a Deposition in the [African slave trading] case of the Brig "Hope" of New York, [Cornelius F.] Driscoll Master.

The deponents are now on board the United States Ship "Columbus"; and it is my intention to send them home as Witnesses, in the event of the arrest of Driscoll, who left this place clandestinely a few days since, in the Barque "Hebe" for Baltimore, where he has a family. The Brig "Duan" of Beverly Mass[achuset]ts alluded to in the deposition, and mentioned in my former despatches, also landed a Cargo of Slaves to the Southward of this port.

The "Porpoise," a small Brig belonging to Brunswick, State of Maine, brought back the Masters, and part of the Crews of the "Hope" and "Duan," and is a regular *Tender* to the Slave dealers. She is said to be *chartered* for Twelve months. The papers of both the "Hope" and "Duan" have been returned to me and cancelled.

The "Porpoise" sailed again yesterday for the [African] Coast, I suppose to bring back the Crews of the "Ganneclifft" and "Monte Video"; the former having sailed from this port a short time since: the latter sailed Yesterday. I also transmit a Copy of the shipping Articles of the "Duan," by which it appears that the voyage had its *"incipiency"* in the United States.

These cases require no comment, and I feel that I discharge my duty by laying the facts before you. I have the honor to be Sir Your most obed[ien]t Serv[an]t, Geo. W. Slacum, Consul U.S.A.

LS (No. 74) with Ens in DNA, RG 59 (State Department), Consular Despatches, Rio de Janeiro, vol. 7 (T-172:8), received 4/16; PC with Ens in House Document No. 43, 29th Cong., 1st Sess., pp. 25–28. NOTE: Among the documents found in Calhoun's papers at ScCleA that were inherited from Upshur is a letter dated on the same day as the above, in which Upshur informs John Tyler of the involvement of U.S. citizens in the slave trade to Brazil (of which he had, then, already learned) and asks whether the matter ought to be brought before Congress. In the same letter Upshur also tentatively suggests Cornelius P. Van Ness as the next Minister to Mexico.

ANSON JONES to the Secretary of State

Department of State
Washington [Texas,] February 15th, 1844

Sir, The President of the Republic of Texas [Samuel Houston], having thought proper to appoint General J. Pinckney Henderson, Special Agent from this Government to the Government of the United States, I have the honor of announcing the same to your Excellency, and of praying you to give Credence to whatever he shall say to you on my part. He knows the concern our Republic takes in the interest and prosperity of the United States, Our strong desire to cultivate its friendship, and to deserve it by all the good Offices which may be in our power. He knows also my Zeal to promote these by whatever may depend upon my ministry. I have no doubt that General J. Pinckney Henderson will so conduct himself as to meet your confidence, and I avail myself with pleasure, of this Occasion to offer you assurances of my high and distinguished consideration. Anson Jones [Secretary of State of the Texas Republic].

LS in DNA, RG 59 (State Department), Notes from Foreign Legations, Texas, vol. 1 (T-809:1), received 4/1.

W[ILLIAM] S. MURPHY to A[bel] P. Upshur

Legation of the United States
Washington, Texas, 15th Feb[ruar]y 1844

Sir, I have the Honor to inform you, that, on the 5th Inst[ant] I received your despatch requiring me to repair to the seat of Government, and present to His Excellency President [Samuel] Houston, the weighty considerations, which had induced the Government of the United States to propose to that of Texas, the annexation of the latter to the former country.

In obedience to that request, I arrived here on the 10th Inst[ant] and it affords me the most exquisite pleasure, to announce to you, the complete accomplishment of your wishes. The Government of Texas will invest Gen[era]l J. P[inckney] Henderson, with full powers, as Envoy Extraordinary, & Minister Plenipotentiary, to proceed to Washington City, with all possible despatch, for the purpose of ["Treating" *canceled*] negociating with the Government of the United States, a Treaty for the complete transfer of the public domain, and ["the" *interlined*] annexation of Texas to the United States.

This was concluded upon last evening by the President & his cabinet, on the part of Texas, & the undersigned, on the Part of the U. States. The powers to be given to Gen[era]l Henderson, are to be of the fullest & most complete character, so that no impediment shall be found requiring further, or other powers, or further, or other instructions. But inasmuch as the commissioners of Texas now in Mexico, in treaty, or negociation touching an armistice, are supposed not to have concluded their labors—and it is clear to the President of Texas that as soon as this negociation, in relation to annexation is known to the Government of Mexico, all negociation on that & all other questions between Texas & Mexico will cease—and that the President of Mexico [Santa Anna] will instantly commence active Hostilities against Texas, which Texas is wholly unprepared by Sea or Land to resist. It is understood, that the Government of the United States, having invited Texas to this negociation, will, at once, & before any negociation is set on foot, place a Sufficient naval force in the Gulf, to protect the coast of Texas—and hold a sufficient force of Cavalry, or other description of mounted Troops on the South Western border of the U. States, in readiness to protect or aid in the protection of Texas, pending the proposed negociation for annexation. I trust my Government will, at once see the propriety of this course of policy. For I found it impossible to induce, this government to enter heartily into the measure of annexation, without an assurance that my government ["would" *canceled*] would not fail to guard Texas against all the evils, which were likely to assail Texas, in consequence of her meeting & complying with the wishes of the U. States. And I took occasion to assure the President, that the Honor of my Government, was more than a sufficient guarantee to Texas that she should not suffer from any act, done in conformity with the advise [*sic*], & desire of my Government.

I gave these assurances, to secure the object my Government has in view. I took upon myself a great responsibility—but the case required it—any [*sic*; and?] you will, I hope justify me to the President [John Tyler].

I write in great haste—sending this note by Express to Galveston, to be forwarded to you at the earliest possible moment—and in 5 or 10 days after you receive it, Gen[era]l Henderson, the Texan Minister, will be with you.

I shall soon repair to Galveston, & the President will go to Houston, in order to be nearer each other, & where we can have the readiest intercourse with the U.S. Your ob[edien]t Serv[an]t, W.S. Murphy.

ALS (No. 20) in DNA, RG 59 (State Department), Diplomatic Despatches, Texas, vol. 2 (T-728:2, frames 280–282), received 4/16; PC in Senate Document No. 349, 28th Cong., 1st Sess., pp. 6–7; PC in House Document No. 271, 28th Cong., 1st Sess., pp. 92–93. NOTE: Murphy was a native of S.C. but had long been a lawyer and politician in Ohio when he was appointed Chargé d'Affaires to Texas by John Tyler in 1843 during the recess of Congress.

W[ILLIAM] S. MURPHY to A[bel] P. Upshur

Executive Offices of the Govt. of Texas
[Washington,] 15th Feb[ruar]y [18]44

The President of Texas [Samuel Houston] begs me to request you, that no time be lost, in sending a sufficient fleet into the Gulf, subject to my order, to act in Defence of the Texan Coast, in case of a naval descent by Mexico—& that an active force of Mounted men, or Cavalry be held ready on the line of U.S. contigeous to Texas, to act in her defence by land—for says the President—"I know the Treaty will be made—& we must suffer for it, If the U. States is not ready to defend us—" do comply with his wishes immediately.

Yours truly, in great Haste—as the Express is ready[,] mounted & waiting at the Door. W.S. Murphy.

ALS (Confidential) in DNA, RG 59 (State Department), Diplomatic Despatches, Texas, vol. 2 (T-728:2, frame 279).

D[ABNEY] S. CARR to A[bel] P. Upshur

Legation of the U.S.
Cons[tantino]ple, 16th Febr[uar]y 1844

Sir, I have the honor to enclose you herewith statements A & B—the former shewing the number of vessels which arrived at this port during the past year, the amount of their tonnage and the nations to which they belonged, and the latter, showing the present Naval Armanent of the Sublime Porte. For these statements I am indebted to Mr. [John P.] Brown, the First Drogoman of the Legation here, whose good standing and friendly relations with the Officers of the Porte and of the several Legations here, have enabled him to procure them. And this reminds me to say, that I have found Mr. Brown all that I could wish him and entirely worthy of the confidence and esteem expressed in your letter of 23d Oct. 1843. We are happily in advance of the other Governments who have diplomatic representatives here, in having for the important and confidential office of Drogoman a native of the country whose interests must, in all intercourse with the Turkish Government, be so entirely entrusted to him, in so far as correct interpretation is concerned. The British and other Governments represented here, becoming aware of this, are educating, at considerable expense, several young gentlemen, natives of their respective countries, for the offices of Drogoman.

You will perceive from the statement A the insignificant amount of American and the very large amount of British Tonnage, engaged in trade to this port. I have taken steps to procure a knowledge of the amount and value of the British trade here and of the character and denominations of the articles which compose it. When obtained, I will forward it to the Department. I am strongly under the impression that our trade with this place may be made of considerable value. The British send here large quantities of cheap coarse cottons, and the first thing which attracted my attention in Constantinople was the cry of *"Americana Campagna,"* which on inquiry, I found to proceed from Jews, who carried, on their backs, bales of Cotton and other goods, and that they were *English* instead of *American* Cottons. Recurring to the fact that the British had resorted to the same trick to sell their Coarse Cottons in the South American markets, when they found the Cottons of the U. States prefer[r]ed to them, I thought it worth while to pursue the inquiry. The result of this inquiry is that formerly all the Cottons brought to this place were *American.* The article becoming a favorite with these people, the English entered into the trade, sending their Cottons here, and as ["it" *interlined*] was known only by the name of American, they still sell under that name, by which it was first known here. The opinion has been expressed to me that the real American Cottons—of which for some years, there have been none in this market—would not now be as saleable as the English, which have taken their place, the latter being prefer[r]ed because of their being lighter. If this be so, I presume our people could easily accom[m]odate themselves to the taste here and make the greater profit by it. There are large quantities also of cheap cotton prints or calicoes of flashy and gaudy colors, brought here from England. A large portion of these, as well as of the plain cottons I have mentioned, find their way from here into Persia, where they meet a ready market. Merchants come, annually from Persia to this place from thence and many go up the Black Sea to Trebisond and thence to the interior of Persia. I cannot but believe that we might come in for a share of this trade both in Constantinople and Persia. There are other articles of trade too, which I incline to think we may enter with a fair prospect of successful competition. Shoes, I think, might be sent here from Massachusetts, where the manufacture of them is so immense and so cheap. I am led to believe too, that the famous Yankee clocks would meet a ready and profitable sale here, the signs of the hour being made *à la Tur-que*—and there are hundreds of "Yankee notions," which are finding their way now into England itself, that, I doubt not, might be sent here with profit.

I have been curious to learn why it has been, that our vessels, even if they could not bring out any profitable cargo to these regions, have not engaged in the carrying trade of the Black Sea—seeing that a very large amount of tonnage and a good deal of it too, *British*—is employed in carrying wheat from that quarter to the different parts of the Mediterranean &c., I learn that it has been because the small vessels of the Mediterranean, sailed by crews of Greeks, Genoese &c., who live on a few olives and a *little* bread and oil, can be sailed so much cheaper as to exclude all competition on our part—especially when we bring out no cargo, and earn no *outward* freight. If they got no cargo from here or from Persia, in Exchange, they might afford to take back wheat to the Mediterranean as cheap as the vessels of the Levant. If the English can do it, I can see no reason why we should not; particularly as our vessels make much quicker voyages than theirs. The article of coarse wool will always furnish a return cargo.

If there be any value in these suggestions, the next subject which will be found worthy of the Consideration of our Government will be that of establishing relations with that of Persia. We have no Treaty with that Power, and I think many considerations make it desirable that we should have. I am led to believe that a Treaty might easily be formed with it, on the ["footing of the" *interlined*] most favored nations. Such have been formed by almost all the other Powers with it, and England is now deriving the benefit of its Treaty with that power. Being as it were, comparatively speaking, on the spot, I should be most happy to be commissioned and empowered to make a similar one on the part of the United States. A few thousand Dollars—not more than five or six, including the *necessary* presents— would Cover the expense. This would—even though we should derive no Commercial advantages from it—be a cheap price to pay for the protection of our Citizens already residing within the jurisdiction of Persia. At present they are entirely without any, we having no Consular or other Agent in the Country. If you should deem well of this suggestion and empower me to carry it out in the shape of a Treaty, I would go up to Trebisond and thence, with one of the great Caravans to Teheran, the Capital of Persia and, I have no doubt, in two or three months, be back at my post here and you might have the Treaty to submit to the Senate at its next meeting. I have the honor to be With great respect Your ob[edien]t Serv[an]t, D.S. Carr.

ALS (No. 4) with Ens in DNA, RG 59 (State Department), Diplomatic Despatches, Turkey, vol. 10 (M-46:12), received 4/22. NOTE: Dabney Smith Carr, whose father Peter Carr had been Thomas Jefferson's nephew and secretary, was a Baltimore merchant and newspaper editor and had been appointed Minister to Turkey by John Tyler in 1843.

W[ILLIAM] S. MURPHY to A[bel] P. Upshur

Legation of the U. States
Washington Texas, 17th Feb[ruar]y [18]44
Sir, I take pleasure, in introducing to your acquaintance, Mr. [Washington D.] Miller, of this place, for many years the Private Secretary, and Confidential Friend of President [Samuel] Houston.

He is a gentleman every way relyable, and he can give you much useful information, of the past & present political events in Texas. I have the Honor to be Your ob[edien]t Serv[an]t, W.S. Murphy.

ALS (Private) in DNA, RG 59 (State Department), Diplomatic Despatches, Texas, vol. 2 (T-728:2, frame 282), received 4/1.

W[ILLIAM] S. MURPHY to A[bel] P. Upshur

Legation of the United States
Washington Texas, 19th Feb[ruar]y 1844
Sir, Your confidential note by Capt. Todd [*sic*; John G. Tod], accompanied with duplicates of your Despatches [*sic*] No. 14 was handed to me by Capt. Todd today. And I fondly repeat what I have already written to you, that your wishes have been fully accomplished—and that Col. [J. Pinckney] Henderson as Minister with full & ample power to treat for the annexation of Texas to the U. States, left here 4, Days ago, & is now on his way to Washington City. It now depends upon my own Government, to accomplish the great & highly important measure of annexation. As soon as I return to Galveston, where my Records are, (for [I] could bring nothing with me but a bag of Cloaths behind my Saddle, so bad were the roads) I will give you a more complete account, from my memorandas of

32

the various conversations[,] Letters &c &c occur[r]ing between myself & Pres[iden]t [Samuel] H[o]uston, prior, & leading to, the final determination on his part to accede to the views & wishes of my Government.

A rumour had reached me just before I left Galveston for this place, on the 6th Inst[ant] by merchants & their agents from Corpus Christie, that the British Minister [to Mexico, Charles Bankhead] then soon expected at Vera Cruz, was charged by his government with, demanding of Mexico the Cession of all that tract of Country Lying between the Rio Grand[e] and the Neussus [*sic*; Nueces] Rivers, including the vast & inexhaustable Lakes of Salt, or Salt Lakes, which lie about 30 miles from the Lagoon del Madre & 50 or, 60, miles west of Corpus Christie. The value of these Salt Lakes, cannot be estimated in money. I aver to you Sir, that it is past all human calculation to estimate their value to the Southern region.

On mentioning this Subject to Gen[era]l H[o]uston, this evening, he told me that he had long looked for an Event of this kind—and that he had no doubt of the truth of the report—and he added, that the Southern country would be diminished in value to the U. States, more than one half, if our Government did not hold on to all the territory embracing these Salt Lakes. That the Rio Grand[e] was the only true Boundary of South Texas—and that to that River the U. States should by all means assert her claim under the Treaty of annexation soon to be made. In great Haste, Your ob[edien]t Serv[an]t, W.S. Murphy.

[P.S.] The Gentleman who takes this leaves immediately for Galveston, & the U.S.

ALS (Private & Confidential) in DNA, RG 59 (State Department), Diplomatic Despatches, Texas, vol. 2 (T-728:2, frames 283–284), received 4/1.

STEWART NEWELL to A[bel] P. Upshur

United States Consulate
Port of Sabine, February 20th 1844

Sir, I beg leave to forward to the Department, a Copy of Consular record, relative to Keel Boat New Era, and trust the length of my letters, Nos. 7 & 8, accompanying it, may be excused, by the Department, when a desire only to know, and do my duty, prompts an extension of my communications, at this time. The variety of circumstances occurring, on a border, such as this Consulate happens to be connected with, neccessarily gives rise to many questions, that have been entirely settled, by Law, and Usage, when occurring in the interior of a Country.

At this time, two Steam Boats, one of which, is commanded by a Man, who some months since, was making an arrangement to introduce Slaves, from the West Indies, are engaged in trading upon the Sabine Waters, and have, or intend to take out, Texian Licence, and perhaps, change thier Flags, from the U. States to Texas! ! Are such required to pay Ton[n]age, or other dues to the U. States. If so, how are they to be collected! ! The Masters or owners, being, or becoming, Texian Citizens.

Permit me to ask also, if vessels belonging to, and from the U. States, are required, to deposit thier Ship Papers, with the Consul at this Port, although they may not, enter or clear from the Texian Custom House, but be over on the Louisiana side, of the Sabine Lake, or Pass, and discharge, and receive, their cargoes to, and from, Texas, Keel and Flat boats from the Texas side, being used, to receive from, and take to them, Texian cargoes, and if engaged in delivering or receiveing, Texian Cargoes, are said vessels, to be considered as in a Texian Port, although not attached to the Texas side.

A day or two since, a White man, has been discovered lying in the Water, some Miles above this place, who has been recognised, as one of the hands employed, on board one of the Steam Boats, now up Sabine River, and from circumstances stated to me, leaves great room, to fear his Death, has been caused by violence, upon him, while so employed on board, said Boat, and upon return of which, I shall examine into the matter. This circumstance alone, is sufficient in my opinion, to found apprehensions of violence, frequently, on such, and other vessels, in these Waters, as sufficient authority does not exist here, to arrest, or Punish, any illegal or violent acts, on the part of offenders, and this, I trust will meet the serious consideration, of the Government, to prevent, rather than, to remedy, evils, so likely to arise.

The former boarding Officer, at this place, has a good Boat, Arms & Flag, for the Boat, which at present, is useless, and liable to injury, for want of use, or if used, can only be used by him, for private purposes. Therefore, should it meet the views of the Department, to order the Boat, Arms & Flag, to be delivered to the Consul, at this place, to be taken care of, and used as emergency may require, it would be preserveing the Public property, and place the Consul, in a position, to perform his duties promptly, and arrest offenders, on the Water, when necessary. Said Boat &C is now about 8 Miles, from this place, and in charge of former, boarding Officer, resideing on Sabine Lake, and when the Govt. should determine to appoint, a boarding Officer at Sabine Pass, said Boat, Arms &C to be delivered to him.

The U.S. Schooner Vigilant, being required to inspect Light Houses, and perform various Revenue duties, along the whole Coast, of Louisiana, from Sabine, to Pascagoula, near Mobile, the Department will readily perceive, that these various duties, will neccessarily, keep her frequently, a long time out, from Sabine, during which times, outrages may be committed, and perhaps, these particular times, selected to perpetrate them, or should a seizure be made, of a vessel, or persons, found violating our Civil, Criminal, or Revenue Laws, how would it be possible, to apprehend, and secure them, until the arrival of a Revenue vessel, at this place.

I beg leave to ask the Department, for a duplicate answer, from Department, to my No. 4, relative to the etiquette, of useing the Consular Flag &C the original received by me, having been destroyed by accident.

An early reply from the Department to the foregoing No. 7 & 8 will be duly appreciated by Most Respectfully Your Ob[edien]t Servant, Stewart Newell.

[P.S.] Annexed is Copy of a new Revenue Law of Texas.

ALS (No. 8) with En in DNA, RG 59 (State Department), Consular Despatches, Texas, vol. 1 (T-153:1), received 3/15. NOTE: A Clerk's EU reads: "Respectfully submitted for the perusal of the Sec[re]t[ar]y of the Treasury. State Dept., Ap[ri]l 10, 1843 [*sic*]."

ISAAC VAN ZANDT to A[bel] P. Upshur

Legation of Texas
Washington D.C., February 21st 1844
Sir, The Undersigned Chargé d'Affaires of the Republic of Texas has the honor to acknowledge the receipt of the two communications of Mr. Upshur, Secretary of State of the United States, of the 29th of December, last, and of the 16th ["19th" *interlined*] ultimo, submitting in reply to a letter of his of the 10th of November, last, the views at present entertained by the Government of the United States in relation to certain outrages complained of by the Government of Texas, and inviting any further suggestions which the Undersigned might think necessary to elucidate the subject.

The Undersigned is gratified to be informed that the Honorable Secretary of State by direction of the President of the United States [John Tyler] readily disclaims any intention on the part of his Government to violate the territory of Texas—that Captain [Philip St. George] Cooke had no instructions which would ["have" *interlined*] authorized him to violate any right of Texas or her people, and that directions have been given to the Secretary of War to order a Court of Inquiry upon that officer—also, that the arms taken from the Texian troops will be restored, or compensation made for them, and that "such further steps will be taken upon the report of the Court of Inquiry as may seem to be necessary in order to render full justice to Texas and her people."

Under these assurances, and until the result of the Court of Inquiry, and the action of the Government of the United States thereon, shall be made known, the Undersigned deems it only necessary to notice the principal grounds which appear to be set up in justification, or extenuation of the extraordinary conduct of Captain Cooke.

The first is, that the Texian forces were ["found" *interlined*] in the territory of the United States. Captain Cooke attempts to prove this, First, By "actual observations, which" as appears from his diary show the transaction to have occurred in the 94th degree of West Longitude. As to the correctness of these "observations" let us examine the facts. The town of Independence, Missouri, from which the traders set out, is within a short distance of the western boundary of that State, which as delineated is in ["West" *canceled*] longitude ["west" *interlined*] 94 degrees and thirty minutes. The course of the road from Independence to Santa Fe is a few degrees south of west. The distance from the former place to the point on the Arkansas river where the occurrence took place must be four hundred miles, or more, and consequently several degrees west of the longitude named in the diary of Captain Cooke. Again, by an examination of the most authentic maps to which the Undersigned has been able to refer, it appears that Walnut Creek, (a tributary of the Arkansas) mentioned by Captain Cooke, is west of the 98th degree of west longitude. From this he had continued his march with the traders eight days. The Undersigned is not informed of the usual distance of a days' march under such circumstances, but believes it reasonable to suppose that they must have reached a point west of the 100th degree of west longitude. These facts show conclusively that the observations made as stated in the diary of Captain Cooke are wholly erroneous and unworthy of reliance. Secondly, Captain Cooke says that "the line was understood by all to strike at least fifteen miles higher up than

where they then were." This assertion though not directly contradictory of the observations mentioned in his diary, at least exhibits
a great discrepancy between them. But to whom does he allude
when he says it was "understood by all"? He of course did not mean
to include the forces of Texas, for their commander protested to the
contrary, but must be understood as intending to convey the idea
that it was a kind of general understanding or impression with his
own party. In some instances general understandings and impressions are entitled to much weight, but in cases of unmarked boundaries experience has shown that they merit but little consideration,
and more especially when the understanding (I care not how general
it may be) is confined to one of the interested parties. Previous to
running the boundary between the two countries from the Sabine to
the Red River the general impression existed in the United States that
the line would strike the latter river much higher up than where it
actually did when run. This impression was so strong that the State
of Arkansas attempted and for some time exercised jurisdiction as
high up as Jonesboro. By the authority of the United States a portion
of the same territory was surveyed and sold as United States land
and the proceeds applied to their use. When Texas proposed to open
her land office in the county of Red River, the seat of justice of which
is forty five miles west of the ascertained boundary line, Mr. [John]
Forsyth, then Secretary of State by direction of the President, threatened the Texian authorities with military force, if they did not desist.
The Undersigned does not state these facts with a design to impute
to the Government of the United States an undue desire for the extension of its jurisdiction, but only for the purpose of showing how
little importance is due to the argument or assertion of Captain Cooke
that it was so "understood by all."

On the other hand Major [Jacob] Snively states that he took up
his line of march from Georgetown and proceeded one hundred and
fifty miles west to where he crossed Red River. Georgetown is reputed to be about two hundred miles west of the point where the
boundary line heretofore run from the Sabine to the Red River,
strikes the latter, which by reference to the report of the Commissioners, is shown to be west of the 94th degree of west longitude.
The course of Major Snively's march from where he crossed Red
River was North 20 degrees west, and the distance to the Arkansas
about two hundred and seventy five miles. From these calculations
there is every reason to believe, that the point at which the Texian
forces reached the Arkansas and at which they were encamped was
within the territory of Texas.

Captain Cooke next alledges that the Texian forces were engaged in the attempt to interrupt the lawful trade between the United States and Mexico and that he had the right to disarm so as to take from them the power of molesting the citizens of the United States and of Mexico engaged in that trade. Now how are the facts of the case? The Texian force was strictly of a partisan character and directed against such Mexican traders as might be found within the limits of Texas. Such were the objects set forth in the order of the War Department of Texas directed to Major Snively, a copy of which was given to Captain Cooke at his request. The same objects were avowed by Major Snively to Captain Cooke, and there is nothing shown which manifests a different purpose. Captain Cooke, it is true, does say, that when at Walnut Creek he received intelligence that Major Snively had avowed that he would attack the caravan whenever he *found it unprotected*, that he had made threats against the American portion, and that three of the Texian spies had been reconnoitering in the territory of the United States. From whom this intelligence was derived is not stated. The presumption is that the name of the author could give it no additional force and that it was gotten up like the many false rumours that are frequently circulated upon the border. But admit that Captain Cooke did believe the intelligence when he received it, in his interview with Major Snively he must have discovered its falsity, for Major Snively states that he did not march to the river until the 29th of June, seven days after Captain Cooke had heard that his spies had previously been in the territory of the United States. This, with the assurances of Major Snively personally given, and the exhibition of his orders before alluded to, must have proven to him that there were no good grounds to apprehend an attack upon the caravan while it was protected by his superior numbers and arms, or so long as it was confessedly within the territory of the United States, which it then was, (being on the north side of the river). But to return to the objects of the forces of Texas—Were they not lawful and proper? As one of the attributes of sov[e]reignty Texas had the undoubted right to regulate her internal commerce and trade; and to take the necessary steps to guard and protect herself against the violation of those regulations. For her own security and preservation against her enemies she had the right in all cases to seize upon their persons and property wherever found without the limits of a neutral's territory, and especially within her own. The goods of the Mexican and American portions of the caravan, were designed to be smuggled through the territory of Texas, in evasion and violation of her revenue laws, and intended for the use of her enemies, and consequently would have been liable to seizure had they entered her territory; and such act of seizure would have furnished no good grounds of complaint on the part of the United States. The Undersigned knows of no rule, or principle of right which would authorize the United States to attempt the protection of her own citizens, who might be found within the limits of Texas engaged in such illicit traffic, much less the Mexican enemies of Texas, who in their manner of warfare have never hesitated to violate the sacred rights of humanity and the usages of civilized nations.

From the foregoing these conclusions may be deduced—That the the [*sic*] objects of Major Snively's expedition were lawful and proper—That though the boundary line had not been run, he had every reason to believe, he was within the territory of Texas, the worst that could be said of it was that the jurisdiction might be doubtful—in either case he had the right to be there. That he was there, evidently not for the purpose of attacking the caravan within the known limits of the United States, but to await its progress to the south side of the River, within the limits of Texas, and that Captain Cooke had no good reasons to apprehend danger to the caravan at the time, nor was his course necessary to its protection, in any portion of the United States, to the line of which he was to furnish the escort, and consequently that he was wholly unjustifiable in disarming the forces of Texas.

Captain Cooke next asserts that "he used no harshness nor more force than was necessary to accomplish the object." From this it is infer[r]ed that having falsely considered he had the right to disarm, he likewise holds the monstrous doctrine that all means are lawful which he may have deemed necessary to effect his object. Having shown that he had no right to molest the Texian force, it appears equally plain from his own admissions that the manner of doing so was both wanton and inexcusable. In proof of this the attention of the Honorable Secretary of State is invited to the following facts drawn from the two statements of Major Snively and Captain Cooke. When Captain Cooke's forces approached in sight of the Texian camp a flag of truce was hung out at the latter, which was recognized by him, sending at the same time a trumpeter and flag to the camp of Major Snively and offering him a safe conduct over and back. Under this assurance he visited Captain Cooke, where (without going into all the details) he was detained until the forces of Captain Cooke had crossed the river—formed the line of battle, and with port fires lighted demanded of the Texian force to lay down their arms. Thus violating the flag of truce and the assurances given by himself, both of which would have been held dishonorable in all ages and by all nations even between enemies, much more between friends.

The Undersigned will not enlarge upon this subject and the subsequent inhuman treatment extended to the Texian force. In his former note he took occasion to characterize the conduct of Captain Cooke in terms of strong reprobation. On farther examination he can see no cause to lessen or modify their character. He therefore confidently believes, and his Government expects, that upon the report of the Court of Inquiry Captain Cooke will be dismissed from his command, with that censure which his conduct so eminently merits.

In regard to the letter of Brevet Major General [Edmund P.] Gaines, the Undersigned has been unable to discover the grounds of the interpretation given it by the Honorable Secretary of State when he says that "it is not of an official character." The letter is dated at "Headquarters, St. Louis, Missouri," signed "Edmund P. Gaines Major General U.S. Army commanding" and directed to "Brig. Gen. Z[achary] Taylor, Com[manding] the 2d Dept. Fort Smith, Arkansas." It treats of the military operations of his Department, and in the opinion of the Undersigned has all the necessary requisites to give it the force, and attach to it the responsibilities of an official act.

The Honorable Secretary of State further remarks that it has not been communicated to any Department of this (his) Government by the writer. The Undersigned does not conceive it very material whether it was communicated by the writer or someone else. Previous to the receipt of the communication of the Honorable Secretary of State the Undersigned was informed through the courtesy of the late Secretary of War of the United States, that the letter alluded to had been communicated to his department, and certain orders or instructions had been given to the Major General of the United States Army concerning it.

The Undersigned believes it due to the Government of Texas that it should be informed whether or not, any order countermanding or disapproving this act of Brevet Major General Gaines, has been issued from the proper Department of the Government of the United States, and also whether any steps will be taken for ["the" *interlined*] punishment of that officer.

In Governments constituted like that of the United States the acts of their Officers must in some degree be considered as indicative of the disposition of those Governments. If this be true, and an officer of the high rank of Brevet Major General, shall acting in his official capacity write and *publish,* as in the instance complained of, his inflammatory orders traducing the forces and calumniating the people of Texas, and such act be suffered to go uncensured and its author unpunished, it may exert a most deleterious influence upon those amicable relations which have so happily existed between the two countries, and which it is the interest and must be the sincere desire of both to foster, preserve and perpetuate.

The Government of the Undersigned will receive with satisfaction the disclaimer made by the Honorable Secretary of State for his Government of so much of the letter of Brevet Major General Gaines as claimed the right to operate to the Rio Grande.

On the 8th of August, last, the Undersigned had the honor to communicate to the Honorable Secretary of State information which he had received of an assault upon a revenue officer of Texas, and the rescue of certain goods from his lawful possession, by citizens of the United States, who it is alledged were aided or countenanced by Officers of the United States Army. On the 10th of the same month the Undersigned received the note of the Honorable Secretary of State in reply, acknowledging the fact of the assault and rescue, and transmitting certain documents in relation thereto, giving at the same time an assurance that immediate measures would be taken to inquire into all the circumstances of the case and the result of the inquiry made known to the Undersigned. Since the date of the note last alluded to no communication has been received from the Honorable Secretary of State touching this subject. The Undersigned avails himself of this occasion to again invite his attention to it, and to request that it may receive the early consideration of the President of the United States. At the date of the former note of the Undersigned upon this subject he had not then received and was consequently unable to transmit an estimate of the goods, wares and merchandize rescued from the Collector. He has since been informed by his Government that the supposed amount is Seventy thousand dollars, for which sum he has been instructed to make a demand of the Government of the United States, which he now does, and to renew the request for proper satisfaction, for the insult given to the Government of Texas, in the person of its officer, and the grievous personal injury sustained by *him.*

The Undersigned seizes with pleasure this occasion to renew to the Honorable Secretary of State assurances of his distinguished consideration. Isaac Van Zandt.

ALS in DNA, RG 59 (State Department), Notes from Foreign Legations, Texas, vol. 1 (T-809:1); PC in Senate Document No. 1, 28th Cong., 2nd Sess., pp. 104–

109; PC in House Document No. 2, 28th Cong., 2nd Sess., pp. 102–106; PC in Crallé, ed., *Works*, 5:399–408. NOTE: Calhoun replied to the above on 8/14/- 1844. Van Zandt's penultimate paragraph refers to a dispute which took place in 1843 between James Bourland, a Texas Collector of Customs on the upper Red River, and certain citizens of Arkansas trading along that river to the U.S. Indian Territory.

W[ILLIAM] S. MURPHY to A[bel] P. Upshur

Legation of the United States
Washington, Texas, 22nd Feb[ruar]y 1844

Sir, I wrote to you on the 19th Inst[ant], by Mr. [Washington D.] Miller, acknowledging the receipt of your communication by Capt. Todd [*sic*; John G. Tod] and informing you, that some days before his arrival, I had agreed with the Government of Texas, upon the terms, upon ["which" *interlined*] a special minister, was to go out, from this Govt., to that of the U. States, with full powers to Treat for the annexation of Texas, to the United States. And ["that" *interlined*] Col. [J. Pinckney] Henderson, the minister appointed by this Government, for that purpose, had set out for Washington City, some days, before the arrival of Capt. Todd. It being the intention of Capt. Todd, to return immediately to Washington City, I avail myself of his politeness, to communicate to you, the Correspondence between this Government, and the Undersigned on the part of the U. States, which led to the appointment of Col. Henderson, with the authority above mentioned.

Enclosed, I send also, the copy of a *"secret order"* to Com[man]-d[an]t [John A.] Davis, of the U. States Schooner Flirt, which was given at the earnest solicitation of Gen[era]l [Samuel] Houston, and consonant to my own opinion of the propriety of the measure, as one of forecast & precaution.

And I trust, that the President [John Tyler], as well as the Department of State will not only approve of it, as such, but will give it immediate Cooperation, & Effect, by sending a fleet of greater force into the Gulf with as little delay as possible. It would be verry advisable, if a War Steamer, drawing not more than 12 or 13 feet water, could be sent to Galveston. One of that class could enter that Port with safety; & would be verry Efficient, on that account.

It is not less important, that a body of light troops, and a few hundred heavy Infantry, should be held in readiness on the line of Texas, and subject to my order, in their after movements. The

President [Samuel Houston] and myself, having agreed to go to Houston & Galveston, in order to facilitate our correspondence with the Government of the U. States, and at the same time, receive the Earliest notice of the movements of the Mexican forces, will leave this place in 8 or 10 days, where we hope to hear from you as soon as Col. Henderson arrives at Washington City. You will perceive it to be our opinion, that the appearance of an imposing force in the Gulf, will check any movement on the part of Mexico against Texas. And it will be far better, to check a movement of Hostility—than to oppose it, even successfully after it has moved. The first check, is not an act of open war. The Second, is.

Besides, we can alledge, that the Proclamation issued by the Texan Government, of a cessation of Hostilities, without limit of time, having been induced, as understood, by the mediation of England & the U. States; Both are bound in good faith, to take care, that no violation of this proclamation, be made by either party, without ["the" *interlined*] previous notice, required by the laws of nations, as well as by the principles of Justice & Common sense. No such notice has been given by Mexico to Texas—and until it is given, both England & the U. States are bound in good faith, to resist any sudden invasion of Texas, by Mexico, opposing even force to force.

Is it not Proper, that the Mexican Government be apprised of this, in due time—If the view is correct? And is it not best, that an imposing force, be kept at Vera Cruz, to check a movement by Land, or Sea, against Texas? For Mexico will not even attempt an invasion by land, if she sees it is to be resisted, upon the principles above mentioned, by an immediate attack upon Vera Cruz, by water. You will see, that I am anxious to check by the appearance of an imposing force, even the incipient steps of any hostile invasion of Texas by Mexico; because it will be so much more easy, to heal the wound, inflicted on Mexico, by the severance of her Texan Territory, and its annexation to the U. States, if it is not accompanied with the effusion of Blood. Nor can there be, the least pretext for the angry grumbling of other powers, if there is no open war, for them to interfere in.

Permit me Sir, to congratulate you, the President, and my beloved Country, upon the almost inevitable success of this great measure of annexation; The Happy termination of so many impending difficulties, and the great, and most brilliant success, of the administration and of the Department, under your more immediate controul. Whatever can be done, to ensure your final success in this measure, fraught with countless, and almost inconceivable, blessings to my Country, has already been done here: The rest, must be done at Washington

City. A Treaty made there, will be received and Ratifyed here, with loud shouts and acclamations, by the People—and the Government here, will heartily participate, in the general joy.

Let there be no unnecessary delay, on the part of my Government, in the final adjustment of this measure. Urge upon all concerned, the absolute necessity of dispatch, and the evils of delay. Dispatch will secure a peacible acquisition of this, almost invaluable Country. Delay may bring on a war, immensely expensive, in Blood & Treasure; and result in the loss of all, sought, to be gained.

May I ask of you, Sir, to present my congratulations, and most profound respect, to His Excellency the President of the U. States, and to those great & good men, associated with you, in the councils of my Country? Whilst I tender to you, the assurance, of my highest veneration and Esteem. Your ob[edien]t Serv[an]t, W.S. Murphy.

[Enclosure]

Anson Jones to W[illia]m S. Murphy

Department of State

Washington [Texas], Feb[ruar]y 14th 1844

Sir, The Undersigned, by desire of the President, has the Honor to communicate to Gen[era]l Murphy Charge d'Affaires of the U. States, that having received assurances from his government, that the annexation of Texas to the United States should take place, and having maturely considered the reasons adduced, for the adoption of such a measure, he entertains no disinclination to taking up the subject, & giving it the consideration which its importance demands.

It is proper to remark, prior to investing the proper persons with full powers for final negociation thereupon, that the peculiar situation and relations of this country, should be taken into view. Engaged, as this Government is, in negociations, with Mexico, under a suspension of Hostilities, it is but natural that it should desire to be fully prepared for the unfavorable termination of those negociations. Were Texas to commence negociations with the United States, in relation to annexation, and they should, from any cause be protracted, or ultimately result in failure, it would not only render our position in regard to Mexico, peculiarly hazardous, but place us in a delicate attitude with *other powers*. If Mexico, were to apprehend such a state of affairs it would provoke immediate hostilities against us, and if an armistice were even concluded, the President is satisfied, that it would be immediately violated by Mexico. Hence it becomes necessary that this Government should be prepared for these contingencies.

If therefore, Gen[era]l Murphy will, on the part of his Government give assurances to this, that the U. States, shall assume the attitude of a defensive ally of Texas, against Mexico, that the U. States, will maintain a Naval force in the Gulf of Mexico, subject to his orders, able suc[c]essfully to oppose the marine of Mexico, and also a disposable force on our Eastern & north Eastern frontier of 500 Dragoons with 1000 Infantry at some southern station of the U. States, whence they may be conveniently transported to our shores, in the event of necessity, the President, will have no hesitation in forthwith despatching a minister with ample powers, to the Govt. of the U. States, to cooperate, with our minister now there [Isaac Van Zandt], in negociating for the annexation of Texas. In the event of a failure of the Treaty of annexation, it is also necessary, that this Government should have assurance or, guaranty of its Independence by the U. States.

The Undersigned avails himself of this occasion to offer to Gen-[era]l Murphy the assurances, of the high consideration, with which he has the Honor to be his most faithful and ob[edien]t Servant, Anson Jones.

[Enclosure]
W[illiam] S. Murphy to Anson Jones

Legation of the U. States

Washington Texas, 14th Feb[ruar]y 1844

Sir, The Undersigned, charge d'affaires of the United States, near the Government of this Rep[u]b[lic] has the Honor to acknowledge the receipt of your note of this day, representing to him the delicate situation, in which the negociations pending between Texas and Mexico, would place the Government and People of Texas, in case a negociation for the annexation of Texas to the United States, should be set on foot, and ultimately fail of its object. And that even the progress of such negociation between Texas and the United States, when known to Mexico, would, in all probability, provoke immediate Hostilities on the part of Mexico against Texas and which Texas (I am well aware) is illy prepared to resist.

You therefore ask of me, some pledge for the security of Texas, pending such negociations, previous to the appointment of a special minister to act with Mr. [Isaac] Van Zandt your charge d'affaires near the Govt. of the U. States, in opening and conducting that negociation at Washington City, for the annexation of Texas to the United States.

Sir, I have no hesitation in declaring, on the part of my Government, that neither Mexico nor any other power, will be permitted to invade Texas, on account of any negociation which may take place,

45

in relation to any subject upon which Texas, is, or may be invited by the United States to negociate. That the United States having invited that negociation, will be a guaranty of their Honor, that no evil shall result to Texas, from accepting the invitation—and that active measures will be immediately taken by the United States to prevent the evils you seem to anticipate from this source.

As far therefore as my power and authority may go, I will take care, that my Government is speedily apprised of your views and wishes; and that a sufficient naval force shall be placed in the Gulf of Mexico, convenient for the defence of Texas in case of any invasion which may threaten her sea-board pending such negociation. Also, that measures shall be taken as required by you to repel any invasion by Land of a like character.

The Undersigned is aware, that in the event of a failure of the present proposed negociation, and for some time thereafter, it would be reasonable to expect, that Texas, should have an op[p]ortunity to place herself in an attitude of defence, in case her negociation with the United States on the subject of annexation, should provoke an attack from Mexico. He therefore feels no reluctance in assuring Mr. Jones, that the United States would not hastily withdraw her protection, even if the negociation should fail of its object. And he concieves that the High Honor of his country may well be rely'd upon, for such protection, to an extent, that shall leave no just cause of complaint.

The Undersigned would also inform Mr. Jones that the United States have now, a naval force in the Gulf, which the Undersigned believes to be vastly an overmatch for any naval force, Mexico can command at Sea. But he is not so fully advised of the amount of Land forces, on or near the South and Southwestern border of the U. States.

He will assure Mr. Jones however, that no time will be lost in giving to Texas ample assurance of her safety, whilst acting upon this subject, at the instance of the United States. And the Undersigned will fully advise his Government of all the circumstances of the case, without delay and press upon their consideration its vast importance to Texas.

With regard to the assurance, or guaranty of the Independence of Texas by the United States, in the event of the failure of the proposed negociation for the annexation of Texas to the United States, the Undersigned, has no authority from his Government to make such assurance or guaranty; But he proposes to Mr. Jones, that the minister of Texas shall be fully satisfied on this subject, by the Government of the United States, after he shall arrive at Washington City, and before entering upon such negociation.

The Undersigned takes great pleasure on this occasion, in renewing to Mr. Jones, the assurance of his great respect and high consideration. W.S. Murphy.

[Enclosure]

Anson Jones to W[illiam] S. Murphy

Department of State

Washington [Texas,] 15th Feb[ruar]y 1844

Sir, The Undersigned, Sec[re]t[ar]y of State of the Republic of Texas, has the Honor, to acknowledge the receipt of the note of Mr. Murphy Charge d'affaires of the United States to this Government of yesterday[']s date, in reply to the note of the Undersigned of the same date. The assurances given by Mr. Murphy, on the part of his Government are of so satisfactory a character, that the President has concluded to despatch without delay a Special agent, (the Hon[ora]bl[e] J. P[inckney] Henderson,) to the City of Washington with full powers, in conjunction with our Charge d'Affaires now resident at that court, to enter into negociations, and to conclude, and sign a Treaty with the Government of the United States, for the annexation of Texas to that Country.

The Undersigned avails himself, with much pleasure, of this occasion, to renew to Gen[era]l Murphy, Charge d'affaires of the U. States, the assurance of his highest consideration and respect. Anson Jones.

[Enclosure]

"Secret order" by W[illiam] S. Murphy to Lt. J[ohn] A. Davis, "Commanding U.S.S. Flirt"

Washington, Texas, 19th Feb: 1844

Sir, You will sail without delay to Vera Cruz, remaining there so long only as to ascertain if any expedition by land or sea is meditated or in progress against Texas by Mexico.

It is very desirable also, that the officer commanding such American Vessels of War as may be lying at Vera Cruz, or that you may fall in with on your cruise, should know that their presence in the Gulf at Vera Cruz, or at Galveston, or on the line of sailing between those two ports is very necessary at this time, and that if they have not orders to that effect, they will soon receive such in all probability. And that the Naval force of the U. States will be required to prevent any invasion of the Texan Coast which may be meditated by Mexico, or by any other power giving her aid & assistance for that purpose.

If Gen[era]l [Waddy] Thompson [Jr.] should arrive in Vera Cruz whilst you are there offer him a passage to Galveston in the Flirt where I wish much to see him whence he can go to the U. States on a steamer.

You will return to Galveston as quick as possible, two or three days only being allowed you for the above purpose at Vera Cruz. Yours &c, W.S. Murphy.

ALS (No. 21) with Ens in DNA, RG 59 (State Department), Diplomatic Despatches, Texas, vol. 2 (T-728:2, frames 285–292), received 3/9; PC with Ens in Senate Document No. 349, 28th Cong., 1st Sess., pp. 4–9; PC with Ens in House Document No. 271, 28th Cong., 1st Sess., pp. 93–95 and 89–91.

W[ILLIAM] S. MURPHY to A[bel] P. Upshur

Legation of the U. States [in] Texas
Washington, 22nd Feb[ruar]y [18]44
Sir, Since writing my despatch of this day, Capt. Todd [*sic*; John G. Tod], called at my office, and informed me, that Anson Jones Esq[ui]r[e], Sec[re]t[ary] of State, has just rec[eive]d letters from Capt. Cha[rle]s Elliot, Her Maj[esty']s Chargé d'Affaires, to this [Texas] Govt. now in N[ew] Orleans, in which he assures Mr. Jones, that the Senate of the U.S. will not Confirm, or ratify a Treaty for the Annexation of Texas, to the U. States. Mr. Todd, will give you the particulars of this matter. I only mention it, to shew how deep an interest, England takes in the subject—and How anxious Capt. Elliot is, in giving this information, to prevent this Government, from offering to treat on the Subject. I am well convinced, nay I feel assured, from all I can learn, see, or hear, that every thing depends upon the success of this measure at this time, and at the earliest possible moment of time, in which it can be brought about.

If it fail now, Texas is lost to our Country, & it may be, (for events look dark[e]ning that way), that our union is lost to our children, and Liberty consequently lost to mankind.

Gen[era]l [Samuel] H[o]uston & myself are Invited to a Public Dinner, given by the People to me, in Honor of the U.S. on the 24th Inst[ant]. We go. Invitations of this kind flow in upon us, all on account of the Hope the People have, of the Success of the great measure of annexation.

Let Col. Todd inform Senators of this new interfereance of Capt. Elliot in behalf of his government, in the affairs of Texas. Surely, if they feel for themselves & their country, as they ought, there can be but one voice amongst them—one loud long cry for annexation, to prevent annihilation.

I fear I trouble you too much, with repeating my views, on this most important subject—But you know how to Excuse me. Your ob[edien]t Serv[an]t, W.S. Murphy.

Note. The arrival of Capt. Todd, even after the appointment of Col. [J. Pinckney] Henderson, was nevertheless a happy circumstance—inasmuch, as the confirmation of all your communications, with many interesting particulars of the state of things at Washington City, strengthened the resolutions of the President and have had a salutary effect upon the Sec[re]t[ary] of State, who had been rather coerced into favorable action, by the President & myself.

Yet he is cool, on the subject—and I fear entertains the hope (tho feint) of the unfavorable result of the measure of annexation.

Capt. Todd, will also be enabled, by his speedy return to Washington City, to render the cause Essential service, in many ways. He is much respected here—and is, most unquestionably entitled to implicit credit, as well as great praise, for his arduous travel, & active exertions.

I hope he will not be forgotten at Washington City. Your ob[edien]t Serv[an]t, W.S. Murphy.

ALS (Private) in DNA, RG 59 (State Department), Diplomatic Despatches, Texas, vol. 2 (T-728:2, frames 292–294), received 3/9.

Richard H. Belt to A[bel] P. Upshur

U.S. Consulate, Matamoros
Mexico, 23rd February 1844

Sir, In accordance with my instructions I herewith apprize you of my arrival in the Sch[oone]r Emblem, to officiate as U.S. Commercial Agent at this port.

Business is exceedingly dull owing to no alteration having been made in the Tariff laws since the communication to the Department of my predecessor Mr. [Isaac D.] Marks.

There is no probability of any favorable change taking place as long as the present laws remain in force. As they now exist they approximate to a prohibition. At this time there is but one American vessel in port, and she will leave in a day or two.

The Texian Commissioners [to Mexico] are hourly looked for in this City; for several months past they have been waiting at Sabinas;

the head quarters of the Mexican army, in this Department, in expectation of receiving despatches from the Mexican government. But as far as I can ascertain nothing definite has resulted from their mission.

It is the impression of some of our well informed citizens that ere long, hostilities will be again renewed by Mexico. I remain with respect y[ou]r ob[edien]t S[ervan]t, Richard H. Belt.

ALS in DNA, RG 59 (State Department), Consular Despatches, Matamoros, vol. 4 (M-281:2, frames 357–358), received 3/25.

R[ICHARD] PAKENHAM to Abel P. Upshur

Washington, February 24, 1844

Among the matters at present under the consideration of the two Governments there is none respecting which the British Government are more anxious to come to an early and satisfactory arrangement with the Government of the United States than that relating to the Boundaries of the Oregon or Columbia Territory.

The Undersigned Her Majesty's Envoy Extraordinary and Minister Plenipotentiary has accordingly been instructed to lose no time in entering into communication with the Secretary of State of the United States upon this subject.

In fulfilment then of the commands of His Government the Undersigned has the honour to acquaint Mr. Upshur that He will be ready to confer with Him, with a view to ulterior negotiation on the subject in question, whensoever it shall suit Mr. Upshur[']s convenience.

The Undersigned is happy in taking advantage of this opportunity to offer to Mr. Upshur the assurance of his high consideration. R. Pakenham.

LS in DNA, RG 59 (State Department), Notes from Foreign Legations, Great Britain, vol. 22 (M-50:22); PC in Senate Document No. 1, 29th Cong., 1st Sess., pp. 140–141; PC in House Document No. 2, 29th Cong., 1st Sess., pp. 140–141; PC in Crallé, ed., *Works*, 5:418–419.

C[ALEB] CUSHING to A[bel] P. Upshur

U.S. Ship Brandywine
Macao Roads
Feb[ruar]y 26th 1844

Sir, I have the honour to inform you that the Brandywine cast anchor in Macao Roads on the twenty fourth instant.

The Brandywine must of necessity repair immediately to Hong-Kong to take in supplies and to make other arrangements preparatory to continuing her voyage towards Peking; by all which she will be detained several weeks on this part of the coast of China.

Of course, as neither of the other vessels of the Squadron has as yet arrived, I cannot immediately proceed to Peking, unless the Chinese Government should invite me to go thither by land.

Beside which during the winter season and until the change of the monsoon in April, it is hardly practicable and would not be wise, or safe, to attempt to make the voyage from Macao to the mouth of the Pih-ho under canvass.

In this, as in other respects, the want of a steam vessel here belonging to the United States is a very sensible inconvenience.

I have concluded to pass this period of delay at Macao, rather than at Hong-Kong between which alone the choice seems to be.

To proceed to Victoria and remain there might, in the eyes of the Chinese, if not of my own country men, wear the appearance of more intimate relation between the British authorities and myself, than seems to me convenient or desirable, considering the very recent termination of the war between Great Britain and China.

On the other hand, to land at Macao and remain there a short time will be a proceeding open to no such objection. Though in point of strict right, perhaps Macao is still subject to the sovereignty of China, yet it is, to most intents, a Portuguese settlement, and wholly neutral so far as regards the present question. In this view each of the successive British diplomatic Agents in China, Lord Macartney, Lord Amherst, Lord [William] Napier, Capt. [Sir Charles] Elliot and Sir Henry Pottinger have deemed it not improper to be temporarily at Macao, whether before, or after, or pending their official connection with China.

And such has been the conclusion touching this point of propriety adopted in practice by the diplomatic Agents of other governments.

I might, it is true, repair immediately to Canton but I do not think it suitable or judicious to do so at present unless by previous invitation of the Chinese authorities.

51

Meanwhile there is opportunity to employ these few weeks of sojourn at Macao, to the greatest advantage, in conferring with the many intelligent Americans whom objects of commerce or of religion have drawn to this neighborhood; in examining into the practical working of the new system of intercourse with China introduced by England, and seeing wherein it requires to be modified; in ascertaining the intentions of the Chinese Government towards the United States, and in completing the organization of the Legation.

I shall accordingly land at Macao to-morrow, and shall continue to communicate to you every important step in my further proceedings, day by day, as they occur. I am, with the highest respect y[ou]r ob[edien]t Ser[van]t, C. Cushing.

LS (No. 31) in DNA, RG 59 (State Department), Diplomatic Despatches, China, vol. 1 (M-92:2), received 7/30. NOTE: Cushing was a prominent Mass. lawyer, scholar, and politician and one of the few Whig leaders who had supported John Tyler. He had left the U.S. in 1843 as Commissioner to negotiate a commercial treaty with the Chinese. He proceeded aboard U.S. warships by way of the Mediterranean and Indian Ocean and wrote lengthy and informative reports of every place he passed en route.

A[bel] P. Upshur to RICHARD PAKENHAM

Department of State
Washington, 26th Feb[ruar]y 1844

The Undersigned, Secretary of State of the United States, has the honor to acknowledge the receipt of the note dated the 24th instant from Mr. Pakenham, Her Britannic Majesty's Envoy Extraordinary and Minister Plenipotentiary, in which he states that he will be ready to confer with the Undersigned, with a view to ulterior negotiation, on the subject of the boundaries of the Oregon or Columbia Territory, whensoever it shall suit his convenience.

In reply, the Undersigned has the honor to inform Mr. Pakenham that he will receive him for that purpose, at the Department of State, to-morrow, at eleven o'clock, A.M.

The Undersigned avails himself with pleasure of the occasion to offer to Mr. Pakenham assurances of his distinguished consideration. A.P. Upshur.

FC in DNA, RG 59 (State Department), Notes to Foreign Legations, Great Britain, 6:322–323 (M-99:35); PC in Senate Document No. 1, 29th Cong., 1st Sess., p. 141; PC in House Document No. 2, 29th Cong., 1st Sess., p. 141; PC in Crallé, ed., *Works*, 5:419.

R[ICHARD] PAKENHAM to A[bel] P. Upshur

Washington, 26 February 1844

Sir, In compliance with your request to that effect I have the honor herewith to transmit to you a copy of the Despatch from Her Majesty's Principal Secretary of State for Foreign Affairs [Lord Aberdeen], which I had the honor to read to you on Saturday last. I have the honor to be, with high consideration, your obedient Servant, R. Pakenham.

[Enclosure]

Lord Aberdeen to Richard Pakenham

Foreign Office, [London,] December 26, 1843

Sir, As much agitation appears to have prevailed of late in the United States relative to the designs which Great Britain is supposed to entertain with regard to the Republic of Texas, Her Majesty's Government deem it expedient to take measures for stopping at once the misrepresentations which have been circulated, and the errors into which the Government of the United States seems to have fallen, on the subject of the policy of Great Britain with respect to Texas. That Policy is clear and simple, and may be stated in a few words.

Great Britain has recognised the independence of Texas, and, having done so, she is desirous of seeing that Independence finally and formally established, and generally recognised, especially by Mexico. But this desire does not arise from any motive of ambition or of self-interest, beyond that interest, at least, which attaches to the general extension of our Commercial dealings with other Countries.

We are convinced that the recognition of Texas by Mexico must conduce to the benefit of both these countries, and, as we take an Interest in the well-being of both, and in their steady advance in power and wealth, we have put ourselves forward in pressing the Government of Mexico to acknowledge Texas as independent. But in thus acting we have no occult design, either with reference to any peculiar influence which we might seek to establish in Mexico, or in Texas, or even with reference to the Slavery which now exists, and which we desire to see abolished, in Texas.

With regard to the latter point, it must be, and is well known both to the United States and to the whole World, that Great Britain desires, and is constantly exerting herself to procure the general abolition of Slavery throughout the World. But the means which she has adopted, and will Continue to adopt, for this humane and virtuous purpose, are open and undisguised. She will do nothing secretly, ["or" *interlined*] under-hand. She desires that Her motives may be generally understood, and Her acts seen, by all.

With regard to Texas, we avow that we wish to see slavery abolished there, as elsewhere, and we should rejoice if the recognition of that Country by the Mexican Government should be accompanied by an engagement on the part of Texas to abolish Slavery eventually, and under proper conditions throughout the Republic. But although we earnestly desire, and feel it to be our duty to promote such a consummation, we shall not interfere unduly, or with an improper assumption of authority, with either Party in order to ensure the adoption of such a course. We shall counsel but we shall not seek to compel, or unduly controul, either Party. So far as Great Britain is concerned, provided other States act with equal forbearance, those Governments will be fully at liberty to make their own unfettered arrangements with each other, both in regard to the abolition of Slavery, and to all other Points.

Great Britain, moreover, does not desire to establish in Texas, whether partially dependent on Mexico, or entirely independent, which latter alternative we consider, in every respect, preferable, any dominant influence. She only desires to share Her influence equally with all other nations. Her objects are purely commercial, and she has no thought or intention of seeking to act, directly or indirectly, in a political sense, on the United States through Texas.

The British Government, as the United States well know, have never sought in any way to stir up disaffection or excitement of any kind in the slave-holding States of the American Union. Much as we should wish to see those States placed on the firm and solid footing which we conscientiously believe is to be attained by general freedom alone, we have never in our treatment of them made any difference between the slave-holding and the Free States of the Union. All are, in our eyes, entitled, as component members of the Union to equal political respect, favour, and forbearance, on our part. To that wise and just Policy, we shall continue to adhere; and the Governments of the slave-holding States may be assured that, although we shall not desist from those open and honest efforts which we have constantly made for procuring the abolition of Slavery throughout the World, we shall neither openly nor secretly resort to any measures which can tend to disturb their internal tranquillity, or thereby to affect the prosperity of the American Union.

You will communicate this Dispatch to the United States Secretary of State, and, if he should desire it, you will leave a copy of it with him. I am &c (signed), Aberdeen.

LS with En in DNA, RG 59 (State Department), Notes from Foreign Legations, Great Britain, vol. 22 (M-50:22); PC with En in Senate Document No. 341, 28th Cong., 1st Sess., pp. 48–49; PC with En in House Document No. 271, 28th Cong., 1st Sess., pp. 97–98; PC with En in Crallé, ed., *Works*, 5:330–333.

EDWARD EVERETT to A[bel] P. Upshur

London, 27 February 1844

Sir, By the last steamer I acknowledged the receipt of your number 69, dated 28th November last, which reached me on the 31st of January. I lost no time in asking an interview with Lord Aberdeen, for the purpose of conferring with him on the subject of the despatch.

Considering the importance and delicacy of the subject, I thought I should best fulfil your intentions, by reading to Lord Aberdeen your despatch *in extenso*. After I had read the despatch, to which Lord Aberdeen listened closely, he asked me what was the precise point to which I wished to call his attention. I replied that my government wished to be informed, whether, since the ratification of the treaty [of Washington], any instructions had been sent to the Governors of Her Majesty's colonies in the West Indies, relative to cases like those of the Creole; and if so, I should be glad to be furnished with a copy of them, to be transmitted to Washington. Lord Aberdeen said that such instructions had been sent and he would apply to the colonial office for a copy. He did not say expressly that he would furnish a copy to me, and seemed to reserve that point for further reflection.

Assuming however that a copy of the instructions would be furnished to me, I observed that when I received them, I should be able to judge what further step it would be my duty to take, in pursuance of your instructions. This would depend upon the fact whether the instructions given to the colonial authorities enjoined them to adopt a course in reference to such cases as those of the Creole, in conformity with those views of the law of nations applicable to the subject, which were maintained in your despatch. To this remark Lord Aberdeen replied that he doubted if this would be found to be the case—that it was impossible for Her Majesty's Government to make the slightest compromise on the subject of Slavery—and that when slaves were found within the British jurisdiction, by whatever means or from whatever quarter, they were *ipso facto* free.

I observed in reply, that it would not follow from this principle, even if its conformity with the law of nations were admitted, that

Her Majesty's authorities could be warranted in possessing themselves of American vessels driven by stress of weather or by mutiny into the ports of the British colonies, and exerting what Lord Ashburton called "officious interference" to liberate the slaves on board. He did not deny this, but said it was difficult to say what would constitute such interference.

I then called Lord Aberdeen's attention to the purport of Lord Ashburton's correspondence with Mr. [Daniel] Webster and to your remark, that but for the assurances given by his Lordship that a course of policy in conformity with his explanations would be pursued by Her Majesty's government, it was doubtful whether the treaty would have been ratified by the Senate. Lord Aberdeen said that this circumstance was entitled to very great consideration; and repeated the remark relative to the unavoidable difference of opinion as to what constituted "active interference."

Some further conversation ensued as to the discrepancy in the accounts given by the colonial authorities at Nassau and the officers of the "Creole" and the American consul at Nassau, which is not material to be repeated. Should I receive the instructions above alluded to, I shall lose no time in transmitting them to Washington; and if, after a reasonable interval, I do not hear from Lord Aberdeen, I shall again call his attention to the subject. I am, sir, with great respect, your obedient servant, Edward Everett.

LS (No. 90) in DNA, RG 59 (State Department), Diplomatic Despatches, Great Britain, vol. 52 (M-30:48), received 3/25; FC in MHi, Edward Everett Papers, 48:278–281 (published microfilm, reel 22, frames 1185–1186).

GEORGE H. PROFFIT to A[bel] P. Upshur

Legation of the United States
Rio de Janeiro, Feb[ruar]y 27th 1844
Sir, I have received no further Communication from Mr. [Hamilton] Hamilton [British Minister to Brazil] on the subject of the use of the American flag in the Slave Trade. It is surprising that he should have called my attention to a letter so entirely devoid of information as that of H.M. Vice Consul at Santos, when it was in his power by very slight enquiry to cite me many cases of almost open and avowed Slave traffic under the American flag. I regret to say this, but it is a fact not to be disguised or denied, that the Slave Trade is almost entirely carried on under our flag and in American built vessels sold

here, chartered for the coast of Africa & there sold, or sold here deliverable on the coast of Africa to Slave Traders. Indeed the scandalous traffic could not be carried on to any extent were it not for the use made of our flag, and the facilities given by the Chartering of American Vessels to carry to the coast of Africa the outfit for the trade and the materials for purchasing slaves. There have been landed on this coast between Bahia & Santos at least Ten Thousand slaves from Africa within the last four months, and in consequence of this large importation the price of Slaves has fallen from Seven hundred to Four hundred Milreas. The case of the Brig "Hope" [Cornelius F.] Driscoll Master is an exemplification of the manner in which our flag is used and disgraced by American citizens. I mention this case because affidavits have been forwarded to the department of State by our Consul here [George W. Slacum], signed by four ["out" *interlined*] of five of the crew, the other sailor having left this port immediately after his arrival. The men who swore to the Statement called upon me, and after a very close cross questioning I was perfectly satisfied of the truth of their story. I found them quite intelligent for men of their class & their statement was corroborated by the facts of the absconding of Driscoll & that the Brig Hope was then at Cape Frio, nearly a useless piece of property, having lost her American ["fl" *erased*] character & therefore valueless as a Slave trader. But this case is but one out of many that could be instanced of the desecration of the American flag; and what is still if possible more disgraceful, eight out of ten of all the vessels employed in this nefarious traffic are from Beverly, Salem [Mass.] and other eastern ports of the United States, where the people profess to be opposed to anything approaching involuntary servitude and are constantly interfering in the domestic institutions of the Southern States of the Union. With all due defference, I think that the President of the United States [John Tyler] has been incorrectly informed as to the efficiency of the American Squadron on the Coast of Africa in suppressing the Slave trade as stated by him in his message to Congress at the opening of the present session of Congress. The slave traders laugh at our African squadron and more than one Trader to the coast has openly avowed that he could Sail round the Frigate Macedonian three times in three miles, that they would not care if there were twenty such Frigates on that coast, that they have never yet seen one of the American squadron although they have visited the coast for hundreds of miles & that the only cruisers they meet with are British, and to them, they have but to display American colors. One fact alone, speaks too plainly to be misunderstood—Let there be two vessels for

57

sale in this or any neighbouring port, one English and the other American, both equally fast sailers, equal in equipment & in real value as Merchant vessels—The American will sell as an African trader for double the amount of the English. The difference in value is the price of the flag.

The American Naval Officers here inform me that their instructions as regards the Slave trade are so extremely limited that they are nearly to all intents & purposes a dead letter. This lamentable state of things exists, notwithstanding a law of the Union declaring the slave trade piracy and the punishment death. Under these circumstances the situation of a Diplomatic agent is any thing but pleasant, liable as he is to have these cases of slave trade brought to his notice at any moment, and subject under the Treaty of Washington to have his discretion severely taxed by a call of the British Minister to join in a remonstrance to this Government as to the prosecution of the Slave trade by Brazilian Subjects. A nation which subjects itself to ["such" *canceled*] the possibility of such a call, at least should have its own character above suspicion of laxity in the suppression of a prohibited traffic. It gives me pain as an American to be compelled to write thus to my Government; but duty & honor & humanity & a regard for the National character leaves me no alternative but to write these painful truths or by a culpable silence to leave the Government in ignorance of the disgraceful state of things at present existing. You Sir, will judge from what I have here reluctantly said, from the depositions transmitted by the Consul here to the State Department and from information easily obtained from the Commander of our Squadron here, whether some new law, instructions or regulations are not necessary to prevent the disgraceful use of our flag by Slave traders.

I shall in a few days give you my views respecting the negotiation of a treaty with this country. At present I will only say that there is not the slightest doubt of our obtaining one equal to the most highly favored nation & that, at an early day after the expiration of the British Treaty. I am Sir, Your Obedient Servant, George H. Proffit.

ALS (No. 9, Duplicate) in DNA, RG 59 (State Department), Diplomatic Despatches, Brazil, vol. 12 (M-121:14), received 5/29. NOTE: Proffit, a former Representative from Ind., was appointed Minister to Brazil in 1843 by John Tyler. On 1/11/1844 the Senate had rejected his nomination by a vote of 8 to 33.

EDWARD EVERETT to A[bel] P. Upshur

London, 28 February 1844

Sir, A few days since Mr. M[anuel M.] Mosquera, minister of New Grenada at this court, requested of me an interview, in order to confer with me on subjects of importance to the two countries, under the instructions of his government.

The first subject to which he called my attention was the purpose entertained by his government of endeavoring to effect the construction of a ship canal across the Isthmus of Panama, by the joint action of the United States, Great Britain, and France, in conformity with the provisions of a treaty or treaties to be negociated for that purpose. I understood Mr. Mosquera to say, that a proposal had already been made at Washington on behalf of New Grenada, that the United States should unite in this enterprize, and that their minister at this court should be instructed to treat with him on the subject. On my informing him that I had received no instructions to this effect, he said he would address me an official note, enclosing a *projet* of the convention which New Grenada was desirous of concluding with the three powers, and desiring me to transmit it to Washington.

I have accordingly received from him such a note with the document alluded to, setting forth the leading principles on which the Government of New Grenada wishes to conclude treaties with the powers above named for the construction of the canal. This note and the projet in question accompany the present despatch.

It is not necessary that I should enter into the consideration of the importance of the contemplated enterprize, or of the preliminary questions which would present themselves, in reference to the competency of the United States to participate in it. I have thought it my duty to a most respected colleague, the representative of a sister American Republic, to lose no time in complying with his request.

The other subject of conversation between M. Mosquera & myself, on the occasion alluded to, was the alleged encroachments of the Government of Great Britain, on the territorial rights of New Grenada in the Isthmus of Panama. Mr. Mosquera thought that the principles involved in the course which the British colonial authorities were pursuing in that quarter, under the sanction of the home government, were of common interest to all the States of the American continent. On this subject, Mr. Mosquera said he would address me a confidential note; and as the subject is one of some delicacy, I reserve the farther consideration of it, till the receipt of the proposed communication. I am, sir, respectfully your obedient servant, Edward Everett.

Documents accompanying despatch 91.

1. Mr. M. Mosquera to Mr. Everett, 26 February 1844 (in Spanish)
2. Projet of a treaty for the construction of a canal across the Isthmus of Panama enclosed in the preceding (in Spanish)
3. Mr. Everett to Mr. Mosquera, 29 February 1844.

[Enclosure]

M.M. Mosquera to Edward Everett, *"Translation"*

London, February 26, 1844

The Undersigned, Chargé d'Affaires of New Grenada, in compliance with the orders of his Government has the honor to address the Hon. Mr. Everett, Envoy Extraordinary and Minister Plenipotentiary of the United States of North America, at this Court with the object which he proceeds to unfold.

The Executive of New Grenada, issued on the 15th July 1843, a Decree, whereby it declared, that the privilege granted to a company of undertakers, to open a communication between the two oceans, through the Isthmus of Panama, by the Legislative Decrees of June 6, 1836, and May 30, 1838, had become void. The Granadine Undertakers, possessing the privilege have agreed to this declaration, admitting that they had not fulfilled the conditions to which they had bound themselves.

Agreeably to this and to the Legislative Decree of the 1st of June 1842, the Executive is to make a new call on the capitalists who may wish to undertake this important enterprise, at the present time, under a new charter. But the experience acquired in this business has convinced the Executive, that a new contract with private undertakers, would have the same results, as those already concluded, and being desirous, to carry into execution a work of such interest to the commerce of all nations, it has determined to adopt a more efficacious and secure method. This is to unite the Governments of the United States, France, and Great Britain, to the conclusion of a treaty with the Government of New Grenada, whereby the contracting Governments should pledge themselves, to undertake and to carry through this important enterprise, and to assure to the commerce of the whole world, under liberal conditions, the new route opened through the Isthmus of Panama.

The Granadine Government has extended its invitations directly to the Government of the United States, and conceiving that they will be met in a manner proportional to the high interest, which the commerce and navigation of the United States must have in the enterprise, it has urged that Government at the same time to appoint a Plenipotentiary on its part, to treat with those of France and Great Britain at this court, and with the Undersigned, for the conclusion of such a treaty. The Undersigned is furnished with full powers and instructions, which his Government has been pleased to issue to that effect; and has entered into communication with Her Britannic Majesty's Secretary for Foreign Affairs, and with the Ambassador of His Majesty, the King of the French.

The Undersigned hopes that the Hon. Mr. Everett will please to inform him whether he has received instructions from his Government on this matter; and in case he should not have received them to ask for them as soon as possible.

The Undersigned avails himself &c, M.M. Mosquera.

[Enclosure]
"Cutting a Canal across the Isthmus of Panama,"
"Translation"

London, February 26, 1844

The Government of New Grenada proposes to the Governments of the United States, of France, and of Great Britain, to undertake to open a ship canal, between the two oceans; taking upon themselves the whole expense, for which they are to be indemnified by receiving during a period to be stipulated, the whole of the duties of transit (tolls) collected on the canal—the right of dominion over the Canal to be reserved to New Grenada; to which is also to be reserved, a portion of the said duties whilst the Governments undertaking the work are in the enjoyment of them; and the whole of the duties, on the expiration of the prescribed period, when the Canal returns to the Republic.

The contracting Governments are to bind themselves, to maintain the neutrality of the canal and its ports, and to promote the conclusion of treaties with the other Governments, to the same effect.

The Governments of the United States, France and Great Britain, to guaranty the dominion of New Grenada in the territory of the Isthmus which belongs to it.

The use of the canal to be free to all the nations of the earth, not at war with New Grenada.

The passage of letters through the canal to be entirely free, and not subject to the Post Office Regulations of the Republic.

During the time in which the three contracting Governments are in possession of the right to receive the products of the canal, the

Government of New Grenada is not to lay any duties on any foreign goods or merchandize passing through the Canal; nor to exact any right of passage or passport from passengers.

The Government of New Grenada is to give up as much as a hundred thousand *fanegadas* of vacant lands, for the execution of the canal, and for all the works connected with the use and service thereof; and as much as two hundred thousand *fanegadas* of the same vacant lands, which shall be distributed amongst the strangers, who may desire to fix themselves in the Republic.

The Government of New Grenada will place at the disposal of the contracting Governments, the forests, quarries, and coal mines belonging to the nation which may be within fifteen leagues on either side of the line of the canal, in order that the materials required may be taken from them.

In case the said treaty should not be concluded, and the enterprise should be entrusted to private undertakers, with whom the Government of New Grenada should contract, it is proposed that the Governments of the United States[,] France and Great Britain should conclude another treaty in order to guaranty the neutrality of the canal[,] the dominion of the Republic over the Territory of the Isthmus which belongs to it, the maintenance of peace in the said territory, the fulfilment of the concessions and agreements made by the Government to the undertakers and the restitution and delivery to the Republic of the canal and the other works connected with it to be made by the undertakers at the proper time according to the contract.

[Enclosure]
Edward Everett to M.[M.] Mosquera, *"Copy"*
Grosvenor Place [London], 29th February 1844
The Undersigned, Envoy Extraordinary and Minister Plenipotentiary of the United States of America, has the honor to acknowledge the receipt of a note of the 26th instant from Mr. M.[M.] Mosquera, chargé d'Affaires of New Granada, transmitting the *projet* of a treaty to be concluded between the Government of New Granada and those of the United States of America, Great Britain, and France, on the subject of constructing a ship Canal across the Isthmus of Panama.

The Undersigned has already had occasion in a personal conference to inform M. Mosquera, that he has not as yet received any instructions from his Government on this interesting subject. But the Undersigned will lose no time in transmitting to Washington, for the information of the President of the United States, the projet of the Convention received from M. Mosquera, which will not fail to be considered by the Government of the United States, with all that attention which is due to the importance of the proposed enterprize and to the Government of New Granada.

The Undersigned avails himself of this opportunity to tender to M. Mosquera the assurance of his most distinguished consideration. (Signed) Edward Everett.

LS (No. 91) with Ens in DNA, RG 59 (State Department), Diplomatic Despatches, Great Britain, vol. 52 (M-30:48), received 3/25; FC in MHi, Edward Everett Papers, 48:286–289 (published microfilm, reel 22, frames 1189–1190); CCEx with Ens in ScCleA.

H[ENRY] WHEATON to [Abel P. Upshur], "Private"

Berlin, 1 March, 1844

My dear Sir, Among the difficult questions involved in our controversy with G[reat] Britain relating to the Oregon territory is one which ["involves a qu" *canceled and* "embraces a" *interlined*] principle of public law of the highest importance, & which, as they pretend, has a direct bearing on the case.

The British claim, as stated by them, is not to the *exclusive* dominion & property of the Territory in question, but only to a right to settle in places not already occupied, a right which they acknowledge belongs equally to us, & the temporary mutual enjoyment ["of which" *interlined*] has been regulated by the Convention of 1827. We claim the whole territory on several grounds, & among others as the assignee of all the rights, claims, & pretentions of Spain north of the 42d parallel of Latitude. G[reat] Britain does not deny the justice of our claim to all that was the exclusive property of Spain, but she contends that by the Convention of the Escurial concluded in 1790 between her & Spain, the latter Power reserved nothing more than the same rights secured equally to G[reat] Britain, namely the right to "navigate & carry on their fisheries in the Pacific ocean, or in the South Seas, or in landing on the coasts of those Seas in places not already occupied, for the purpose of carrying on their commerce with the natives of the Country, or of making settlements there."

The conclusion, therefore, is that the United States possess only the same rights within the territory in question which are common to ["her" *canceled*] them with G[reat] Britain.

I am not informed whether any, or what *official* answer has been given by our Government to this argument, unless it be that which is stated by Mr. [Robert] Greenhow in his Memoir, &c. that the Convention of the Escurial was annulled by the breaking out of war between Spain & G[reat] Britain in 1796, & not having been renewed *specifically*, subsequently to the reestablishment of peace between those two Powers, was not in force at the date of the Florida treaty by which the rights of Spain were ceded to the U. States.

I perceive it stated in the January No., 1844, of the *"British & Foreign Quarterly Review,"* ["the" *canceled*] p. 577, that "if Mr. Greenhow were as good a lawyer as he is an historian, he would have known that the Convention of the Escurial is one of those national compacts called *transitory conventions*; that such conventions are not put an end to, or even necessarily suspended by war; but that if suspended, they revive as a matter of course on the restoration of peace, without any express stipulation. There is no difference on this head among the best authorities in international Law. We shall content ourselves with citing a modern authority, which we are sure will be respected in the United States."

The writer then quotes the passage from my *Elements of International Law*, beginning with the words: "General compacts between nations, &c." (Part III, ch. 2, Sec. 7). He adds the Preamble to the Convention of the Escurial, to show that it is one of those treaties which are only suspended in case of war, & revive, without any express stipulation, on the return of peace.

I recommend the entire Article in the Review to your attentive perusal, & invite you to a careful examination of this question of international Law, which is one of the most important & difficult points of the controversy.

Wishing you a happy issue out of this & all your other official perplexities, I remain, my dear Sir, ever truly yours, H. Wheaton.

ALS in ScCleA; PEx (as to Calhoun) in Boucher and Brooks, eds., *Correspondence*, pp. 211–212. NOTE: This letter, found among Calhoun's papers, contains no address leaf, and no other obvious indication of its intended recipient, who must, apparently, have been Upshur.

C [ALEB] CUSHING to A[bel] P. Upshur

Macao, March 2d 1844

Sir, Mr. [Paul S.] Forbes, the Consul of the United States at Canton has placed in my hands copies of such correspondence as passed between him and the Imperial Commissioner Ke-ying, whilst the latter was at Canton; and has also communicated to me such of his correspondence with the Department of State as appertained to the same subject.

The Commissioner, it appears, on the conclusion of his negotiation with Sir Henry Pottinger, returned to Peking.

It is understood that some instructions have been left with the authorities of Canton in reference to my Mission, but the nature of those instructions has not yet transpired.

As Mr. Forbes had, under the instruction of the Department, given notice to the Imperial Commissioner, and through him to the Chinese Government of the intention of the Government of the United States to send a Minister to China it seemed to me desirable that he should have it in his power to give to the Chinese authorities official notice also of the arrival of the Mission.

In this view I addressed to him a communication, a copy of which is annexed hereto.

I annex also a copy of the reply given by the Imperial Commissioner to the note of Mr. Forbes, notifying the intention of the American Government.

You will perceive that this reply, while it seems, impliedly, to deprecate the proposed Mission, yet is conceived throughout in the most friendly spirit towards the United States, and tends in no degree to throw doubt over the prospect of the ultimate success of the Mission.

The Commissioner dwells on the fact that by the treaty between the Chinese and English Governments and the regulations thereupon adopted by the former, the ports of China are open to the ships and citizens of the United States. But when I shall have laid before you the details of these regulations, which I shall do with all possible despatch, it will be seen that the British treaty, although it provides for opening the ports; yet instead of thus preventing the occasion of a treaty with China on our part, does but render it the more indispensably necessary. I am, very respectfully Y[ou]r ob[edien]t Ser[van]t, C. Cushing.

LS (No. 33) with Ens in DNA, RG 59 (State Department), Diplomatic Despatches, China, vol. 1 (M-92:2), received 7/30. NOTE: Cushing enclosed an English translation of a note dated 10/12/1843 from Ke Ying, Imperial Commissioner, and Ke Kung, Governor of Canton, to Paul S. Forbes. Without being requested to do so, Chinese authorities have extended to the U.S. trade privileges equal to those granted to the British in the recent past. They request that the U.S. Consul "intercept and stop" Cushing, the U.S. Minister Plenipotentiary, from traveling directly to Peking. Ke Ying and Ke Kung have been ordered to meet Cushing before determining to conduct him to the capital.

W[ILLIAM] S. MURPHY to A[bel] P. Upshur

Legation of the U. States
Houston, Texas, 4th March 1844

Sir, I arrived here, from Washington[-on-the-Brazos], evening before last: and last night, Mr. [Lewis S.] Coryell arrived, here from Galveston, and handed me your note of the 12th Feb[ruar]y. Capt. [John A.] Davis, Com[man]d[an]t of the U. States Schooner Flirt, also arrived here with Mr. Coryell. I learn from him, that there is no reason to apprehend any hostile movements on the part of Mexico against Texas by Sea, at least for some time to come. I beg leave to call your attention, and that of His Excellency the President, to this Efficient and talented officer. He is certainly entitled to your especial notice, for all those qualities, that unite the able Seaman to the accomplished gentleman & gallant officer.

Mr. Coryell and Capt. Davis return to Galveston today and Mr. Coryell will proceed to the U. States in the Steamer, in which he came out. I have nothing new to impart to you, except to confirm & reassure you of my firm belief, that if the present effort on the Part of Texas, to gain a place in our union, shall fail, Texas is lost to us forever. She will, from the most urgent necessity, form a league with Great Britain, embracing, protection against Mexico, in some form, or other, and all the interests of commerce & navigation. Nay Sir, even whilst I am now writing this hasty note, I learn that a public meeting of the People is in progress, to express their approbation of this view of their case.

Is it possible, that my government can hesitate, as its true policy in relation to this subject? The Proce[e]dings of this meeting I will obtain before I close this Paper, & enclose them to you.

["1 o'clock P.M. The projected Public meeting has not been held as was proposed. But you will hear(?) from Mr. Coryell, the" *canceled.*]

I have the Honor also to inform you that President [Samuel] Houston will be here in 8 or 10 Days, by agreement between him & myself. After an interview with him, I will write to you. I have the Honor to be Your ob[edien]t Serv[an]t, W.S. Murphy.

[Enclosure]

At a large and respectable meeting held in the City of Houston on the Second day of March 1844 being the anniversary of Texian independance the following Preamble and Resolutions were after long debate by a respectable majority adopted.

Whereas the bright prospect of annexation to the United States

66

so lately placed before us has measurably disappeared, leaving in its stead gloom and disappointment and whereas the probability of an[n]exation is now full as remote as it ever was before, and whereas imperious necessity requires that Texas should take immediate steps for a certain termination of the difficulties in which she is involved— thereupon in view of the facts—

That Texas has for seven years been a suppliant to the United States for annexation—and thus far without success—

Resolved that it is the duty of our government to terminate forever the question—by requiring a final and prompt answer to our ["present" *interlined*] application.

Whereas the hope has been long and anxiously cherished that annexation would take place—by reason of which the people of Texas have not permitted themselves to indulge in the contemplation of any Union or arrangement with any other power, and whereas our salvation requires that ["we" *canceled*] some immediate steps should be taken by our government in the event that an[n]exation fails, to place Texas in alliance with some other power—and whereas it is very certain that if an[n]exation does not take place, that we cannot reasonably expect any considerable emigration from the United States— and whereas our very existence as a nation depends on a speedy settlement of our extensive domain and whereas we are principally of Anglo Saxon origin, speaking the English language and having the common law of England as the fundamental law of Texas—and whereas the importations into Texas from England have ap[p]roximated to Two Millions of Dollars while from the United States they have only equalled one hundred and Ninety thousand Dollars—and whereas the largest portion of the emigration to this country for the last Two years has been transatlantic and whereas England has been the only power that has apparently taken any interest in our Destiny and whereas we have positive information that propositions of a most highly advantageous nature has by Great Brittain been made to our government within a few days past—and whereas necessity will compel us to an Union with some power therefore

Be it Resolved That it is the duty of the government of Texas— to come to a decissive understanding with the Government of the United States on the subject of annexation and should the result be unfavorable to enter at once into an arrangement with England— having for its object the protection of that power on the basis of mutual benefit.

Resolved that while all our wishes have been and still are for annexation to the United States yet necessity knows no law and while

we would in anguish of spirit seperate forever from all political connection with that people—["still" *canceled*] we will yet know and
feel that we have been forced ignominiously so to do—and that Justice
to ourselves and our posterity requires the course we shall pursue.

Resolved that these proceedings be published and that the Citizens of the various counties take this measure in hand immediately
in order that the government of Texas may be fully informed of the
wishes and desires of the people.

Resolved that a Committee of Corresp[ondence] of Five persons
be appointed to correspond with the various counties of the Republic
in relation to this matter. A.C. Allen, Chairman. Francis Prentiss,
Secretary.

ALS (Confidential) with En in DNA, RG 59 (State Department), Diplomatic
Despatches, Texas, vol. 2 (T-728:2, frames 294–297), received 4/1.

Rob[er]t Monroe Harrison to A[bel] P. Upshur

American Consulate
Kingston Jam[aic]a, March 5th 1844
Sir, I have the honor to inform you that intelligence has just arrived
here of a second revolution having broken out in Saint Domingo; the
Senate having been fired on, and several members killed.

Application has been made to the [British] Admiral on the Station
Sir Charles Adam for assistance. With the greatest respect I have the
honor to be Sir Your very ob[edien]t & most humble serv[an]t, Robt.
Monroe Harrison.

LS (No. 274) in DNA, RG 59 (State Department), Consular Despatches,
Kingston, vol. 8 (T-31:8), received 4/5.

A[rchibald] M. Green to A[bel] P. Upshur

Consulate of the U.S. of America at Galvezton
Repub[lic] of Texas, 7th March 1844
Sir, I have the honor to acknowledge the recei[p]t of your communication under date the 10th Ult[im]o with its accompanying letter
from the Navy Dept. for which I am obliged to you. I take the

liberty of forwarding this communication to you by Mr. Lewis S. Coryell who is going direct to Washington and will hand you this in person and I avail myself of the present moment to enclose copies of ["two" *canceled and* "one" *interlined*] acts of the late Congress of this Republic, that will affect the commercial interest of our government; at the present time Ton[n]age duty on Steam Boats is only imposed according to the carrying capacity of the vessel and not according to the Register Tonnage of the vessel. Sail vessels have to pay one dollar p[e]r Ton according to Register Tonnage. The trade with Europe is daily increasing and I may add diminishing with our own Govt. & greatly as to what it has been.

I send you papers and a few paragraphs that are marked for your particular observation. I have the honor to be Sir most Respectfully y[ou]r ob[edien]t S[ervan]t, A.M. Green.

ALS (No. 28) with En in DNA, RG 59 (State Department), Consular Despatches, Galveston, vol. 2 (T-151:2), received 3/27. NOTE: The enclosed certified copy of a bill approved by the Texas Congress on 2/5/1844 sets a duty of $1 per ton on cargo of all vessels from nations trading with Texas and having no treaty stipulating otherwise. The law also states that all coasting trade will be handled by vessels under the Texas flag and will not be subject to tonnage duties.

W[ILLIA]M M. BLACKFORD to Abel P. Upshur

Legation of U.S.
Bogota, Mar[ch] 8th [18]44

Sir, In my despatch No. 12, I mentioned that the Granadian Government declined entering upon any arrangement, with respect to the transportation, across the Isthmus, of the mails carried to Chagres, by the American Packets, until the result of a negotiation, then in progress in London, between its Chargé d'Affaires [Manuel M. Mosquera] and the British ministry, should be known. A short time since, in answer to an inquiry touching the issue, or progress, of this negotiation, I was informed by the Secretary of Foreign Relations [Joaquin Acosta], that it had entirely failed, in consequence of the unreasonable demands of the British Government, and that he was now ready and anxious to receive any overture, I might feel authorised to make on the subject.

The despatch of the Department of the 4th March last, being far from explicit in its terms, I felt somewhat at a loss to know what answer to make to this invitation. Impressed with the importance of securing, upon equitable terms, the agency of the Granadian Post in carrying our mails, and believing that the present was a favorable moment, for the attainment of this object, I determined, after mature reflection, though not specially instructed to do so, to enter upon the negotiation. I therefore presented a memorandum of an agreement on the subject. It was considered fair and liberal and was acceded to without any alteration, and upon its basis a Convention—which I have the honor herewith to transmit—was framed, and signed on the 6th Inst.

The sum, stipulated to be paid for the transportation of each mail, is less than that which it would cost to despatch it by a special messenger—and even if it were not, the convenience and greater speed and safety of transmission by the Post, would be more than equivalent to the additional expense. In no country, is the mail considered so sacred as in this—nor, having respect to the physical obstacles, is there any in which it is carried with more regularity. Though large sums, in specie, are constantly remitted, there has never occurred but one instance of robbery of the mail, and that was perpetrated by a Guerrilla chief, at the head of a military corps.

You will observe that the bag is not to be opened by the Granadian authorities, but to be handed to the Consul, or other agent of the United States, and that the agency of the Post is confined to its transportation from Chagres to Panama and from Panama to Chagres. The maximum weight stipulated is, perhaps, sufficient to cover any amount of correspondence which may occur for some time. Should it not, however, I have provided that the excess shall be charged at a very moderate rate.

Aware that the establishment of a line of Packets, by the Government, was not with a view to profit, and that the vessels to be employed would be ships of war, I had no hesitation in agreeing that the Granadian mails should be carried from one port of this country to another, or to the United States, free of charge. This liberality—whilst it will be attended with no inconvenience on our part—is highly appreciated by this Government, inasmuch as a Postal Convention, just concluded here by the Chargé d'Affaires of France, stipulates that the French Packets are to receive half the rates of the Postage now established, for carrying letters between the ports of the country. By the same Convention, it is provided that a postage of one Real—or twelve and a half cents—is to be charged on each single letter, contained in the French mail, carried across the Isthmus by the

Granadian Post. I need not indicate to you, the greater liberality of the provisions of the Convention enclosed.

The President [Gen. Pedro Alcantara Herran] and Secretary of Foreign Relations have both manifested the most lively solicitude that the Packets should touch at Carthagena, before proceeding to Chagres, and I most respectfully, but earnestly, renew the recommendation to that effect, which I took the liberty heretofore to make.

The very little additional time, which this enlargement of the plan will require—the advantages which a regular communication with the United States will afford to persons in trade, in the opportunities of a safe and direct transmission of letters and specie—and the importance of counteracting the injurious influence, which the monthly communication afforded by the Steam Packets of England and France, cannot fail to exert upon our commerce with New Granada—are considerations, which, without a conscious dereliction of duty, I cannot omit, upon all proper occasions, to press upon the attention of the Department.

I would respectfully suggest that the Packets should sail, at least once a month and on a stated day, that the time of their arrival at Carthagena might be anticipated with some degree of certainty.

In order to save time, I have stipulated, in case the Government at Washington approve of the Convention, that its provisions should go into effect so soon as that fact is communicated to the Governor of Panama, by the Consul of the United States for that Port. This arrangement will give efficacy to the Convention some months sooner, than if the approval were required to be first communicated to the authorities here.

I feel conscious that I have assumed some responsibility in thus concluding a Convention, in the absence of specific instructions upon the subject. But I am equally convinced that I have made an arrangement as favorable to the United States, as could be expected or desired. I have endeavored to carry out what I inferred to be the wishes and designs of the Government, in the best manner possible, and I hope my proceedings in the premises will receive your approbation—or, at least, that my motives will be properly appreciated.

I could have wished, that the arrangement had been of a less formal character—but, according to the views of the Secretary, it could be effected in no other way than by a Convention.

I have the honor to enclose Mr. [William] Gooding's Receipt for the Seventh Instalment of the "By Chance" Indemnity, and also Duplicates of his receipts for the 5th & part of the 6th Instalments.

By the Post of this day, I have remitted to Mr. [Ramon Leon] Sanchez, Consul of the U.S. at Carthagena, with instructions to forward it to Messrs. Prime, Ward & King, New York, the sum of $912—in Gold—the nett amount of $987.90, in currency, as per statement herewith sent—being the amount of the claim of Alexander Ruden, Jr. for money and goods taken from the "By Chance."

Congress met on the 1st Inst. and was organized by the election of Mr. Marquez, as President of the Senate, and Mr. Rojas as President of the House of Representatives. The Message of the President was transmitted the same day. A copy of this Document as well as of the Report of the Secretary of State for Foreign Affairs, is herewith sent. I refer you to the 8th page of the letter, for what is said about the claim of the "Morris" and the relations of this country with our own.

There seems to be, in both of the Chambers, a strong feeling of hostility against the Secretary of Foreign Affairs—which I much regret, as I fear it may operate to the prejudice of any Convention, he may sign, in relation to the claim of the "Morris."

On perceiving this feeling, the Secretary tendered his resignation—which the President refused to accept. So violent are the prejudices against this gentleman, that it is believed an attempt will be made to legislate him out of office, by repealing the act of last session, which created a distinct Secretaryship for Foreign Affairs, or if this fails—as I think it will—to refuse the appropriation for his salary.

Under these circumstances, prudence dictates that I should not press to an immediate conclusion the convention in the case of the "Morris." I feel assured, if now laid before the Chambers, it would not be ratified. A delay of some days, therefore has been agreed upon. In the meantime, at Colonel Acosta's request, I am endeavoring to enlist the support, of some influential members, by demonstrating to them the justice of the claim, and the moderate amount of the Indemnity asked.

I am endeavoring to obtain some authentic information with respect to the efforts which the Government of Great Britain is silently, but successfully, making to obtain a present influence, and ultimate footing, upon the long reach of Coast, extending from the north-Western extremity of this Republic to Cape *Gracias a Dios.* Whether the contemplated improvement of the Isthmus be made between Panama and Chagres, or by the Lake Nicaragua, the vast advantage which the power, holding the Mosquito Shore, must have over all other nations, is equally apparent. It is beyond all doubt, that the

British Government—with its usual far-sighted policy—has an eye upon this important position. In fact the whole coast is now virtually under its influence—as the nominal sovereign—the King of the Mosquito Shore, as he is called—is an Indian, educated in Jamaica, devoted to the interests, and in the pay, of the British Government.

Though, I presume, these aggressive movements have not escaped the attention of the several Agents, despatched by the Government of the U.S. to Central America, I shall, on a future occasion, do myself the honor to make them the subject of a communication to the Department.

I lost no time, on the meeting of Congress, in endeavoring to impress upon the minds of some of the leading members the injustice of the United States, and the impolicy—so far as New Granada is concerned—of the existing discriminating duties. I succeeded in convincing a Representative from the South—heretofore in favor of them—who, on the second day of the session, introduced a Bill, abolishing *all* discriminating duties whatever, and putting the flags of all nations on a footing of equality with the Granadian. It was discussed several days, but I am pleased to say was, yesterday, passed in the House of Representatives, by a very large majority. Its fate in the Senate I consider very doubtful—though I have assurances from some prominent Senators that it will receive the sanction of that body. Should the Bill become a Law, the great obstacle to making a Treaty will be removed, and I think I can negotiate one, in time to be submitted to the Chambers, at their present session.

I have seen announced, in the [Washington] Madisonian, the appointment of Mr. [Bladen] Forrest, as Consul at Chagres, but have not yet received his Commission. I have the honor to be, with high respect, Your Ob[edien]t Ser[van]t, Wm. M. Blackford.

ALS (No. 22) and duplicate with Ens in DNA, RG 59 (State Department), Diplomatic Despatches, Colombia, vol. 10 (T-33:10, frames 188–202), received 5/1.

ALLEN A. HALL to A[bel] P. Upshur

Legation of the United States
Caracas, March 8th, 1844

Sir, I have the honor to inform you, that since preparing my despatch of the 2nd inst., I have received a letter from Mr. [William M.] Blackford, in which he states, that he has virtually concluded a Convention with the Government of New Granada, in the case of the Morris, which he has no doubt will be carried into effect. It is upon the following basis:

Value of Brig	$6,000.00
Owners' part of cargo	6,982.07
Backers' do do	7,530.88
Demurrage	5,000.00
	25,512.95
Int[erest] 18 years @ 6 per cent	27,554.59
	$53,067.54

This you will perceive is ten thousand dollars less in the aggregate, than would be afforded under the arrangement I have effected here. Under Mr. Blackford's arrangement, Venezuela[']s proportion would amount to $15,124 instead of $18,000 (the sum it has already agreed to pay)—New Granada's proportion to $26,533, instead of $31,500, and Ecuador's to $11,409, instead of $13,500.

Mr. Blackford further states, that "there is nothing in any instructions to his predecessors which deprives ["him" *interlined*] of plenary authority to act in the case to the best of his judgment—still less in those to him personally." Having been possessed of "plenary authority," the Convention he has concluded will, I presume, be binding upon the Government of the United States, and that circumstance will probably induce you to sanction at once the arrangement I have effected with this Government, whatever you may think of its merits.

I am apprehensive that the Venezuelan Government, upon hearing of what has been done at Bogota, will complain of having to pay more in proportion than New Granada, and that the Venezuelan Congress may refuse to appropriate more than its proportion of the general aggregate amount agreed upon by Mr. Blackford. Much as this discrepancy was to be deprecated, I do not well perceive how it could have been avoided. Although we have kept up an unreserved correspondence, it was impossible for either of us to foresee the controlling considerations which might present themselves at the turning point of the negotiation.

Were it practicable for Mr. Blackford and myself conjointly to give these claims a thorough examination at Bogota, where the papers all are—to agree upon a course of action in each case and the amount of indemnity that should be inflexibly demanded—to report the result of such examination to you, with a statement of the facts as established by the evidence, in every case, and receive in return specific instructions from you, the whole of these claims could be satisfactorily settled in a year.

Although the arrangement concluded at Bogota be not so advantageous to the claimants as that effected here, I have not a doubt that it was the very best, that, under the circumstances, could have been accomplished. Mr. Blackford in his letter to me, after stating the amount he had agreed to accept, proceeds to say:

"I am well aware this is much below what the claimants have hitherto demanded and expected, and led the Government to demand and expect. It is less than in strict justice they ought to receive, but I am persuaded it is all that can be obtained—if indeed I may obtain it. The finances of this Government are in an exceedingly low condition, and to have asked more would but jeopard the whole. I have acted for what I believed the best interests of the claimants and I am sure they ought to be satisfied. I was induced to make the modification from a knowledge of the deplorable condition of the revenue—the indisposition of the two houses to vote money for satisfying old claims, as shown in the By Chance case—a conviction that each succeeding year only made a settlement more difficult, and that the present favorable disposition of the Executive ought not to be neglected."

In any instructions you may think proper to give Mr. Blackford and myself, having for their object the preservation of future concert of action between us, the wide difference in the financial condition of the Governments to which we are respectively accredited, will, I doubt not, be taken into consideration by you. Venezuela, though owing a considerable public debt, pays the interest upon it with scrupulous fidelity, and possesses both means and credit. The knowledge of this fact exercised an important influence on the course I pursued in the recent negotiation, and I am free to say, that had the same state of things existed in this country that is represented by Mr. Blackford to exist in New Granada, I should have been in favor of accepting—provided nothing more could have been obtained—a much less sum from Venezuela as its proportion of indemnity in the case of the Morris, than the eighteen thousand dollars which it has stipulated to pay.

I hope to have the pleasure of announcing to you in the course of a fortnight the conclusion of a very favorable arrangement of the claim of Commodore Daniels [*sic*; John D. Danels]. I have the honor to be, Sir, with great respect, Your obedient Servant, Allen A. Hall.

ALS (No. 32) in DNA, RG 59 (State Department), Diplomatic Despatches, Venezuela, vol. 2 (M-79:3), received 4/13. NOTE: Hall, from Nashville, Tenn., had been appointed Chargé d'Affaires to Venezuela by William Henry Harrison in 1841 when Daniel Webster was Secretary of State. He subsequently held other federal appointments under Whig administrations, including that of Assistant Secretary of the Treasury, and was a Unionist during the Civil War.

ROB[ER]T MONROE HARRISON to A[bel] P. Upshur

American Consulate
Kingston, Jamaica, 8th March 1844

Sir, Herewith I have the honor to enclose you a Newspaper, from which you will learn the wretched state to which this fine Colony is now reduced by pseudo philanthropists.

Every exertion of persons in and out of the House [of Assembly], who have mostly contributed to this state of things, has been made by them to prevent the truth from being made known to the British Government or people, in consequence of which Mr. Spalding who moved an enquiry into the state of the Colony, has experienced all sorts of annoyances, so much so, that it has been put off to the next session although the Committee was appointed in November.

Mr. Spalding was the owner of several fine Estates, a man of honor and most benevolent feelings, but now almost ruined. "Osborn" is a woolly headed Mulatto, and with his partner "Jordon" (a Quadroon) are members of the Legislature, Editors of the paper herewith enclosed; and have contributed as much to the ruin of this Colony as any man living! "Sanguinetti" is a Bankrupt Jew looking out for some appointment, and who failed as a shopkeeper the other day, and took in all his creditors.

I am induced to mention these persons to shew you, what kind of Legislators we have here as also Judges of the Courts of Common pleas as well as Magistrates, the above mentioned persons being invested with these Offices as well as members of the Legislature! ! !

Under these circumstances you may form some idea of the Maladministration of Justice which often occurs in this place by persons without honor and deficient in education. With profound respect I have the honor to be Sir Your Ob[edien]t and most humble Servant, Robt. Monroe Harrison.

P.S. The enclosed Price Current will shew you that Our market is completely glutted with all Kinds of American produce.

LS (No. 274 [*sic*]) with Ens in DNA, RG 59 (State Department), Consular Despatches, Kingston, vol. 8 (T-31:8), received 4/7.

F[RANCIS] M. DIMOND to A[bel] P. Upshur

United States Consulate
Vera Cruz, March 9th 1844

Sir, I last had the honour to address you on the 27 ult[imo] and my last dates from the Department of State was to the 13th Dec.

The Law respecting retail seems to create in the public mind considerable excitement, the time is at hand when the Law unless repealed goes into effect, on the 23 inst[ant].

The French minister [to Mexico, Baron Isidore Alleye de Cyprey] has instructed his Consul to detain the French man of war now at Sacrificios. The Law will effect that Nation more than any other they having in the City of Mexico about 5000 retailers[,] the Spanish about 3000 and English about 1000 and of the U. States in the republic about 800.

The U.S. Brig Bainbridge arrived at Sacrificios yesterday from Pensacola touching at Tampico. She will wait the instructions of Gen[era]l [Waddy] Thompson [Jr.] who most likely will return to the U. States in her.

The English Minister [Charles Bankhead] has not arrived but is no doubt on board a Frigate which made her appearance off this port a week ago, and put to sea on account of a norther. She will no doubt be in in the course of to day as a ship is signalized.

The Four men who came out from New Orleans some four months since to dig for money on Gen[era]l Santa Anna['s] place and who were taken up on suspicion of attempting to assassinate his Excellency have been tried and ordered to leave the country and sail this day for New Orleans. One of the number is a Capt. Bredell a naturalized citizen of the U. States and with the others had permission to seek for the money by the President himself. I have the honour to be Sir most Respectfully, your Ob[edient] Se[rvan]t, F.M. Dimond.

ALS (No. 214) in DNA, RG 59 (State Department), Consular Despatches, Veracruz, vol. 5 (M-183:5), received 3/29. NOTE: Dimond, a Rhode Islander, had been appointed to the important Consulship at Vera Cruz by John Tyler in 2/1842. He was notable during the Mexican War for assisting General Winfield Scott with information about the defenses of Vera Cruz and later became Governor of R.I.

R[ICHARD] PAKENHAM to John Nelson, [Secretary of State ad Interim]

Washington, March 9, 1844

By the 8th Article of the Treaty between Great Britain and the United States signed at Washington on the 9th of August 1842, it is provided that copies of the orders given to the Squadrons maintained by each government on the Coast of Africa to enforce separately and respectively the Laws, Rights, and Obligations of each of the two Countries for the suppression of the Slave Trade are to be communicated by each government to the other respectively.

In accordance with the stipulations of that article and in fulfillment of the Instructions of His Government the Undersigned, Her Britannick Majesty's Envoy Extraordinary and Minister Plenipotentiary, has the honor to transmit to the Secretary of State of the United States the accompanying copy of Instructions which have been recently issued by Her Majesty's Government to the Senior Officer of Her Majesty's Ships and Vessels on the West Coast of Africa.

The Undersigned takes advantage of this opportunity to renew to Mr. Nelson the assurances of his high consideration. R. Pakenham.

LS with En in DNA, RG 59 (State Department), Notes from Foreign Legations, Great Britain, vol. 22 (M-50:22). NOTE: The enclosure, dated 12/12/1843, signed by J.G. Cockburn and W.N. Gage, is addressed to Capt. John Foote and directs him and other British officers commanding vessels in the British Naval squadron off the coast of Africa to cooperate with vessels of the U.S. squadron in suppressing the slave trade. The officers of both squadrons are to engage in a mutual exchange of information. Joint cruises are to be undertaken when deemed advantageous. If a vessel bearing a British flag is suspect, any U.S. vessel participating in a joint cruise is to be invited to join in the search and detention of the vessel. This right is to be reciprocal only insofar as vessels are suspected of dishonestly displaying the U.S. flag. "The Commanding Officers of Her Majesty's Vessels on the African Station are to bear in mind that it is no part of their duty to capture, or visit, or in any way to interfere with vessels of the United States, whether those Vessels shall have slaves on board or not . . ." If the U.S. flag is displayed honestly and properly, no further action should be taken by British officers. Force is to be used to detain a vessel only when absolutely necessary and when just cause for suspicion of the national character of the vessel is had. When a vessel is unjustly boarded to ascertain her national character, the boarding officer is to file a report with the British Admiralty and to note on the vessel's log the details and reason for the boarding. In the case of a vessel found to be displaying a fraudulent flag, the British officer boarding her is to "deal with her as he would have been authorized and required to do, had she not hoisted a false Flag."

HENRY WHEATON to A[bel] P. Upshur

Berlin, 10 March, 1844

Sir, Further reflection has convinced me that it is most expedient to conclude the proposed Arrangement with the *Zollverein* in the form of a Convention or Treaty, to be submitted to the Senate for its advice and consent to the ratification. Indeed I have some doubts whether such a contract with a foreign Power can be constitutionally made by the President in any other form, unless indeed it had been previously authorized by a law, or joint resolution, of the two Houses of Congress.

The power of the President, by and with the advice and consent of the Senate, to make treaties, appears to be an *exclusive* Power. It has been questioned how far the concurrence of the legislative power of Congress is necessary to carry into effect the treaties thus made, unless where some new legislative provision, or alteration in the existing laws, becomes necessary for that purpose. But the power itself is exclusively vested in the President and Senate.

The only examples, which I recollect, of contracts being entered into by the President with foreign nations in any other form, than that of a treaty or convention submitted to the Senate for ratification, are the following:

1st. The Arrangement made between the U. States and G[reat] Britain in 1809, by which the British Orders in Council relative to neutral trade were to have been repealed, so far as respects American commerce, on certain conditions. This arrangement was made in consequence of a *previous* authority vested in the President by act of Congress, authorizing him in case the orders and decrees ["of" *interlined*] either of the belligerent Powers should be thus repealed, to declare the renewal of commercial intercourse with that Power which had been suspended by the Non-Intercourse Act.

2d. The second instance of such an Arrangement was that made by Mr. Maclane [*sic*; Louis McLane] with the British Government in 1830 relating to the Colonial trade. This was also made under a *previous* Act of Congress passed in May of that year, authorizing the President, whenever he should receive satisfactory evidence that the British Govt. would open its ports in the West Indies &c. to the vessels of the United States, on certain specified terms, to issue his Proclamation declaring that the ports of the U. States were opened to British vessels coming from the Colonies on similar terms. (See Laws of the U.S. Vol. 3, p. 368.)

79

It will be perceived that these two cases are to be considered as examples of the exercise of the ordinary legislative power, made to depend upon the contingent action of a foreign Govt., rather than as instances of the exercise of the treaty-making power properly so called.

The President might certainly have gone to Congress for previous authority to enter into the proposed Arrangement with the *Zollverein,* and he might have been empowered by an Act, or joint resolution of Congress, to declare by Proclamation that whenever it should appear to him that the *Zollverein* would reduce the duties on our tobacco, &c. to certain rates, that the duties imposed on certain productions of the *Zollverein* States by our present Tariff laws should be reduced in certain proportions. But as the President has not thought proper so to do, it appears to me that this negotiation presents the ordinary case of the exercise of the treaty-making power by the President, subject to ratification by the advice and consent of the Senate.

There are innumerable examples in our diplomatic history of the exercise of the treaty-making power by the President and Senate in respect to conventions of navigation and commerce affecting the existing legislation of Congress in respect to trade and revenue. No doubt has ever been suggested of the constitutional power of the executive to make such treaties. The question has always been whether a treaty thus made, which the Constitution declares to be "the supreme law of the land," binds Congress to pass the laws necessary to carry it into effect, as it binds the other Departments of the Govt. to execute it; or whether Congress has a discretion, as in the exercise of other legislative powers, to give or withhold its sanction to that which the public faith is already pledged to carry into effect. On either supposition it will be necessary that the proposed Convention, if ratified, should be subsequently laid before the two Houses in order to enable Congress to conform its legislation to the stipulations of the treaty. I have the honour to be with the highest respect, Sir your ob[e]d[ien]t servant, Henry Wheaton.

LS (Duplicate, No. 241, Private) in DNA, RG 59 (State Department), Diplomatic Despatches, Germany, vol. 3 (M-44:4), received 5/8.

John Nelson to W[ILLIAM] S. MURPHY

Department of State
Washington, 11th March, 1844

Sir: Your despatch No. 21 [of 2/22/1844], with the accompanying correspondence with the Secretary of State of the government of Texas [Anson Jones], the copy of your order to Lieutenant [John A.] Davis, in command of the "Flirt," and your private letter of the 22nd of February, were received by the hands of Captain [John G.] Tod, on Saturday night.

Of the anxiety of the President [John Tyler] to provide for the annexation of the territory of Texas to that of the United States, you have been heretofore apprised, and of his readiness, by negotiation, promptly to effectuate this desire, you are well aware. He regards the measure as one of vital importance to both parties, and as recommended by the highest considerations of a sound public policy.

Entertaining these views, The President is gratified to perceive in the course you have pursued in your intercourse with the authorities of Texas, the evidences of a cordial coöperation in this cherished object of his policy: but he instructs me to say, that whilst approving the general tone and tenor of that intercourse, he regrets to perceive in the pledges given by you in your communication to the Honorable Anson Jones, of the 14th of February, that you have suffered your zeal to carry you beyond the line of your instructions and to commit the President to measures, for which he has no constitutional authority to stipulate.

The employment of the army or navy against a foreign power with which the United States are at peace, is not within the competency of the President, and whilst he is not indisposed, as a measure of prudent precaution, and as preliminary to the proposed negotiation to concentrate in the Gulph of Mexico and on the southern borders of the United States, a naval and military force to be directed to the defence of the inhabitants and territory of Texas at a proper time, he cannot permit the authorities of that government or yourself to labor under the misapprehension that he has power so to employ them at the period indicated by your stipulations.

Of these impressions, Mr. [Isaac] Van Zandt, the Charge d'Affaires of the Texan government has been, and General [J. Pinckney] Henderson, who is daily expected here, will be, fully advertised. In the mean time the President desires that you will at once countermand your instructions to Lieutenant Davis as far as they are in conflict with these views. In any emergency that may occur, care will be

81

taken that the commanders of the naval and military forces of the United States shall be properly instructed. Your request that they may be placed under your control cannot be gratified.

I am happy, however, to believe that no exigency, requiring the use of force by the United States against Mexico or any other power, is likely to result from the negotiation with Texas. The annexation I trust may be speedily and peacefully accomplished.

Advices of a late date from Mexico authorize the belief that the negotiation between that power and Texas has been broken off and that the armistice has been suspended. If this be so, it will render immediate annexation most important to Texas, since the power of Mexico, if at all to be dreaded, can in that event only be paralized by the prompt execution of our common purpose. But we have good reason to believe that no such dread need be entertained and that in the present embarrassed condition of her finances she has the ability neither to equip, nor for any continuous period, to sustain a hostile force, within the limits of Texas.

In the actual condition of our relations with Texas it will occur to you as being altogether important that the favorable tendencies of that government should be fortified and strengthened, and that you should avail yourself of all proper and suitable occasions to impress its authorities with a strong sense of the earnest desire of the President to introduce them into the privileges of our Union, and of his fixed purpose to exert his whole authority to carry out this desire, and in the mean time extend to Texas every protection that his constitutional power may enable him to afford. I have the honor to be, very respectfully, Sir, Your obedient servant, John Nelson, Secretary of State ad interim.

FC (No. 15) in DNA, RG 59 (State Department), Diplomatic Instructions, Texas, 1:88–90 (M-77:161); PC in Senate Document No. 349, 28th Cong., 1st Sess., pp. 10–11; PC in House Document No. 271, 28th Cong., 1st Sess., pp. 95–96.

J[OSEPH] C. LUTHER to A[bel] P. Upshur

Port au Prince, 14th March A.D. 1844

Sir, I have the honor to inform you that, in consequence of a revolt in the south-eastern portion of this Island, embraced in the original Spanish Territory, and now occupied mostly by a Spanish creole population, The Government of Hayti has seen fit to declare the port of the City of San[to] Domingo closed to all foreign vessels. I have the honor to be very respectfully Your obedient Servant, J.C. Luther, United States Commer[cia]l Agent.

ALS in DNA, RG 59 (State Department), Consular Despatches, Port-au-Prince, vol. 2 (T-346:2), received 4/6.

W[ILLIAM] S. MURPHY to President John Tyler

Legation of the United States
Galveston, 16th March 1844
Sir, I take the liberty of addressing this note to Your Excellency, be-cause I know not, as yet, who will succeed the Lamented [Abel P.] Upshur, in the Dept. of State. And because, the only information it imparts, is founded on a private letter, which is herewith enclosed, calculated, to give impressions, erroneous to those not conversant with the entire public & private correspondence, heretofore had between this Legation, & the Dept. of State.

Mr. M[osely] Baker the writer of this Letter is a gentleman of high Integrity, moral & political. He is well known to, Mr. [Arthur P.] Bagby of the Senate [from Ala.] & Messrs. D[ixon] H. Lewis, James Dellett, & J[ames] E. Belser of the H[ouse] of Rep[resenta-tives, from Ala.] of the Congress of the U.S. now in Session. I refer you to these Gentlemen for his worth & credability with great pleasure.

I desire to say to you, and to impress you with a belief of the fact, that President [Samuel] Houston and his Cabinet, as well, as all his leading confidential friends are, secretly opposed to annexation. That He & they have apparently entered into the measure heartily, in con-sequence of the undivided & overwhelming sentiment of the People in its favor. The President, having been much influenced by the urgent Letters of Gen[era]l [Andrew] Jackson lately written to him in favor of the measure.

And although as between the President and myself, the most friendly intercourse private and official, has ever preva[i]led—and although, I would be loath, to impute improper, or unworthy motives to him in this matter—and would not by any means do so—yet I feel it my duty to put you, & my Government, on every guard necessary, to protect the interests of the U. States.

The President & the Govt. of Texas certainly has the right, to hear, and decide every proposition, which may be made to Texas—in relation her national Independance, or national Interests—whether these propositions come from England, Mexico, or from the U.S. That such propositions, as those contained in Mr. Baker[']s letter to me, will soon be made, I can have no doubt. I infer[r]ed them, & so stated the facts, in some of my former despatches to the Dept. of State, in commenting upon the correspondence which occur[r]ed in June & July last between Mexico & Texas through the British Govt. here. But it has appeared to me, that the Dept. of State did not draw the same inference or conclusion from that correspondence. And it has given me some uneasiness. For certainly, these propositions, (and you may rely upon it) are to be made for the pu[r]pose of changing, if possible, the tide of popular sentiment, in this Country. The number of English agents, crowding, Galveston, & Houston, would astonish you—Secret, dark, and diligent, in something or other, which men known, or suspected, to be friendly to annexation cannot find out.

Spies & informers, are all around me—and I am under the necessity, and have been for some time so, of denying the ordinary introductions of every body, by every body, (so common here) to me.

I rec[eive]d a letter from the President yesterday in which he says—That "He will be here to join me on the 20 or 23 if the roads are passable by that time."

The Boat that takes this out, to N[ew] O[rleans], is about Starting. I ["have" *interlined*] written hastily. But will enlarge upon the subject, as soon as I receive notice official of the new Sec[retary] of State. Your ob[edien]t Serv[an]t, W.S. Murphy.

[Enclosure]

M[osely] Baker to W[illia]m S. Murphy

Houston, March 15th 1844

Dear Sir, Your untiring vigilance—as a Minister from the United States is so well known and appreciated here, that I do not presume I can drop you any hint that will be new to you. In a recent conversation with a gentleman closely connected with the President of this Country—I learn that a proposition will be made from Mexico to Texas through the medium of the British Minister to this effect.

1st Texas shall acknowledge for her Western Boundary The Neueces—and her Northern Boundary shall not include any portion of Santa Fee proper.

2nd In consideration of the portion that Texas ought to pay of the Mexican debt due Great Brittain—she will with the consent of Mexico relinquish to Great Brittain the country between the Neueces & Rio Grande.

3rd These conditions being agreed to Mexico will acknowledge the Independance of Texas.

4th If not agreed to a renewal of hostilities will commence—In which event it is intimated that Great Brittain will consider herself bound to side with Mexico—at least so far as maint[a]ining the possession of the Country between the Neuces & Rio Grande & so far as the pe[a]ceable possession by Mexico of Santa Fe is concerned.

I understand that this proposition is to be submitted to the people of Texas simultaneous with the proposition of annexation, should the same be ratified by the U. States Senate.

If annexation is rejected by the U. States Senate then I understand that the whole influence of the government will be thrown into the scale to bring about the consent of the people to the Mexican proposition of Boundary & Independance.

This may not be so but I am strongly inclined to think that I have not been misinformed.

What has produced the sudden and extraordinary change in the public mind about annexation? Op[p]osition to the measure is daily making its appearance in quarters least expected. New English faces are seen in different parts of the country. English policy & English power & grandeur are triumphantly spoken of in our City. Some of the presses evidently are leaning in that direction. Persons connected with the government openly advocate an alliance with England and in almost every circle into which you go a comparison of the advantages of annexation to the U. States or an alliance with Great Brittain is made. One month since you saw nor heard none of this & what has produced it? There is evidently an under current at work and the British gold now so current in the country has told its tale—what may not the next month tell? Whether or not there is any cause for alarm I do not pretend to say—but I do believe that an influence is at work which requires to be watched & to be checked. How it is to be done your sagacity will readily determine. I have thought it my duty to present this matter to your attention & beg that you will not regard me as officious. Respectfully yours, M. Baker.

ALS (Confidential) with En in DNA, RG 59 (State Department), Diplomatic Despatches, Texas, vol. 2 (T-728:2, frames 297–301), received 4/1.

G[EORGE] F. USHER to Abel P. Upshur

Commercial Agency of the U. States
Cape Haytien, 16th March 1844

Sir, I have the honor to inform You, that the Eastern, or Spanish population of this Island, has revolted against the present constituted Authorities; and the whole Army kept up by [Jean Pierre] Boyer, and which has been recently disbanded, is now being collected, & soldiers have been coming in to this City from the adjacent country for several days, preparatory to marching against the City of St. Domingo.

There appears to be more alarm, generally, for the safety of persons & property, by the best informed Haytiens, at the present disturbed state of affairs, than during the late Revolution, that drove Boyer from the Presidency.

All Haytiens, with few exceptions, from fourteen to sixty years of age, are now required to join the Army. Fifteen hundred Soldiers left here for the East on Wednesday, the 13th, & three thousand five hundred more Yesterday, the 15th Inst. This is termed the division of the Department of the North; will number about sixteen thousand men, & is under the command of Gen[era]l [Jean Louis] Pierrot, one of [Henri] Christophe's old officers.

The first Object of this division will be to attack St. Jago, a large, inland, Spanish City, about Eight days march from the Cape, and which, it is said, is strongly fortified, and will be vigorously defended.

The whole Army will number some forty thousand men when concentrated at a point this side of the City of St. Domingo, & will there be commanded by President [Charles Aimé] Herard.

Previously to this revolt, there was evidently a disaffection of the military Officers towards the newly constituted Civil Authorities: and the municipality here, deemed it prudent, from anonymous letters to the mayor, to suspend all Civil proceedings for some ten days: but present disturbances have diverted their attention to other objects, and the Civil, City government is again resumed.

Monday the 18th.

Yesterday, a Danish Brig arrived here from Port Plate, loaded with passengers, including the French Haytien Officers in command there, & women & children. That City having declared in favour of the Spaniards. The American Citizens there, I am informed, have hoisted the American Flag, as a kind of protection, & to manifest their neutrality.

Should any thing of interest further occur, I will avail myself of the earliest opportunity to acquaint you with it. I have the honor, Sir, to be, with the highest consideration, Your Very Ob[edien]t S[er]v[an]t, G.F. Usher, U.S. C[ommercial] Ag[en]t.

ALS in DNA, RG 59 (State Department), Consular Despatches, Cap Haitien, vol. 7 (M-9:7, frames 130–131), received 4/11.

F[RANCIS] M. DIMOND to the
Secretary of State

United States Consulate
Vera Cruz, 20th March 1844
Sir, Since I had the honour to address you the British Minister [Charles Bankhead] has arrived and landed with the usual Civilities; immediately on his arrival he went out to Manga de Clavo and after an interview with Gen[era]l Santa Anna he returned to this City and is now in Jalapa. All appears quiet about the insulted Flag.

The Law respecting retail will go into effect on the 23 inst[ant]. I have recommended the few retailers here (by the advice of General [Waddy] Thompson [Jr.]) to take a fair account of their stock before good witnesses and shut up their stores; there are but two or three retailers in this place.

The French Minister [Baron Isidore Alleye de Cyprey] I understand has despatched his Secretary to this point to embark immediately for France with dispatches.

The U.S. Brig Somers arrived yesterday and Mr. [Peyton A.] Southall will take the next Stage up [to Mexico City].

Gen[era]l Thompson is at Jalapa and expected down to embark in the Bainbridge. I understand he has procured the release of the Bexar Prisoners. I have the honour to be Sir very Respectfully your Ob[edient] Serv[an]t, F.M. Dimond.

ALS (No. 215) in DNA, RG 59 (State Department), Consular Despatches, Veracruz, vol. 5 (M-183:5), received 4/11.

D[ANIEL] JENIFER to A[bel] P. Upshur

Legation of the United States
Vienna, March 20th 1844
Sir, With my last despatch of the 18th February I forwarded to the Department a copy of a note I addressed to Prince Metternich, on

the 2d February, calling his attention to the Message of the President of the United States to Congress at the commencement of its present Session and the Report of the Secretary of State in relation to the Zoll-Verein or States of the Customs Union, at the same time suggesting that the articles proposed to be exchanged between the United States and the States of the Zoll-Verein, were similar to such as might be advantageously exchanged between the United States and the Austrian Empire. On the 29th of February Prince Metternich replied to my note and I now forward a [French-language] copy of his answer with a translation of the same. Although in my note it was merely intimated that a reciprocal exchange of articles of Commerce might be of advantage to both nations by a modification of duties upon those specified—the reply would indicate that a *proposition*, to that effect, had been made, which is evidently not the fact by the terms of the note.

It appears that the difficulties to the abandonment of the Tobacco Monopoly are at the present time insuperable. The immense revenues derived from that source, with other reasons not alluded to, induce the Government to be cautious in the extreme in touching the existing system, least any modification, however apparently beneficial, might in its operation prove injurious. It is constantly urged also that the duties and restrictions upon Tobacco in Great Britain and France are equally, if not more, onerous than in the Austrian Empire; whilst those Nations derive, each, far greater advantages from the trade with the United States than Austria.

The discontented and excited state of Hungary from whence the greater portion of the Tobacco trade is supplied—the large loans of money which have been recently effected by the Government of Austria through the Bankers who have the contracts for the supply both of the Hungarian and foreign Tobaccos—to whom, or to whose agency, the Government is indebted for the numerous and extensive sums annually borrowed, are reasons, though not expressed, too cogent not to have a controlling influence.

Prince Metternich, as also the Minister of Finance, continues to express opinions in favour of modifications and seem to entertain enlarged views upon this subject and commerce generally, but are over-ruled by the Council of State, to which all matters of this nature are submitted. The duty upon imported Rice is, as stated, much less than that of the Zoll-Verein, and that upon Cotton has been reduced to *1 florin 40 kreutzers* per Quintal. Thus in regard to those two Staples of the United States there is not much reason to complain.

I also transmit a Report from the Consul of the United States at

Vienna in answer to the Resolution of Congress of 3d March 1843. This delay has been owing to the difficulty of obtaining minute information upon the articles required, when but little direct trade exists between this city and the United States. With high respect, Sir, Your Obedient Servant, D. Jenifer.

LS (No. 19) with Ens in DNA, RG 59 (State Department), Diplomatic Despatches, Austria, vol. 1 (T-157:1, frames 246–251), received 4/24.

J[OSEPH] C. LUTHER to A[bel] P. Upshur

Port au Prince, March 20th 1844

Sir, Allow me the honor to express to you my opinion that, the interests of American commerce at this port, require the presence of an American man-of-war to be stationed within this Bay; and particularly is it demanded for the protection of American vessels and the rights of their officers and seamen trading here. My own official interposition against the numerous incursions upon our vessels and their officers, by the inhabitants and authorities of this Government, is, in the nature of my position, powerless, as I cannot be known to either, in an official capacity; and the acts of oppression and injustice which almost daily occur, of these sable officials and citizens, upon American captains, seamen and vessels, can only be repelled by threats of defence and force of arms.

During my short residence here, several cases have occurred where officers of American vessels have been arraigned before the government tribunals to answer as criminals to charges prefer[r]ed against them for merely defending their lives, property and honor on board their own vessels, against the unprovoked assaults and depradations of the numerous depraved wretches who watch their oppertunity for pillaging and ["a" *canceled*] insulting the officers and seamen of our vessels; and when repelled by force, have only to report, in their own way, their case to the City Authorities, and their chief object is at once obtained by by [*sic*] the unjust extortion of money from their innocent victims. The almost entire absence of any American naval force in this place for many months, emboldens them to these repeated acts of insult, which are sure to result in gain to the prosecutor; for it is in vain to attempt to establish the innocence of an American white Citizen, against the testimony of a Haytien, however false the accusation. The internal wars which are now raging in the Island with much vigor present, in my opinion, strong additional reasons why a naval force should be placed here. I beg therefore the honor, respectfully to suggest to the Department, the propriety of causing a man-of-war of a small class, to be stationed at this point to protect the rights of suffering Americans and their interests. All of which is respectfully submitted, with the hope that it will merit the desired action. I have the honor to be very respectfully your obedient servant, J.C. Luther, United States Commercial Agent.

ALS in DNA, RG 59 (State Department), Consular Despatches, Port-au-Prince, vol. 2 (T-346:2), received 4/27. NOTE: A State Department Clerk's EU reads "Respectfully submitted for the perusal of the Secretary of the Navy [John Y. Mason]." Another EU reads "Perused and returned."

From A. A. FRAZAR

Boston, March [*ca.* 21,] 1844

Dear Sir, In the case of the Brig "Douglas" taken possession of by a British Cruiser on the Coast of Africa I beg leave to call your attention to, In the President's last message he says the British Government have agree'd to pay me an indemnity & after Mr. [Edward] Everett had got the business in a fair way of adjustment, Mr. [Daniel] Webster writes him he need not trouble himself farther in the case of the Douglas, & I am inform'd by Mr. Everett that my only remedy is now *at Washington*. I reference to the documents in your department you will find that Mr. Everett had convinc'd the B[ritish] Govt. that they had *no* right to detain the "Douglas" & I do think I have a right to know *why* Mr. Webster gives my claim the *gobye*. But I trust the rights of our citizens will be better guarded under your Administration & although a few brawling politicians would make us beleive that your politicks are not so orthodox, allow me to *assure* you my Dear Sir that although there are some differing interests between the North & South, that the majority of the N.E. people have both confidence & respect for a character that shines as bright as that of John C. Calhoun of S.C. With great respect, A.A. Frazar.

(please over).

[P.S.] 22d. The Steamer has just arrived & in a letter from Mr. Everet[t] he says he has no directions from Washington about the "Douglas."

ALS in DNA, RG 59 (State Department), Miscellaneous Letters (M-179:104, frames 115–116).

J. M. MACPHERSON to the Secretary of State

Pontotoc Miss[issip]pi, 22 March [18]44

Sir, The letter of the late lamented Secretary of State [Abel P. Up-shur] accompanying a Commission as Commercial Agent to the Republic of Paraguya reached me yesterday.

When I learnt that the Gentlemen of the Mississippi Delegation had had the kindness to apply in my behalf for this appointment, I lost no time in signifying to them that I could not accept it. My letter however had not reached Washington in time to prevent the Commission being made out. I now return it together with the Documents which accompanied it, and Sir I have to request that you will do me the favor to make known to the President my grateful acknowledgements for his kindness in acceding to, the wishes of those friends who addressed themselves to him on my behalf. And I further request that you will inform the President, that my reason for declining the appointment is the Insular Situation of Paraguya, which must necessarily cut it off from all *direct* foreign commerce, and consequently deprive a Consul or Commercial Agent of the means of support arising from Fees of Office, or doing a Commission business.

From a small Map now before me it appears that Assumption the Capital of the Republic cannot be less ["that" *altered to* "than"] six hundred miles in a direct line inland from Buenos Ayres, through which place, altho under a different Government, it communicates for commercial purposes by the river Paraguya in small Boats propelled against the stream by poling.

My long residence in Carthagena New Grenada has given me some insight into the South American character, and to set a just value upon their inflated language. I therefore look with suspicion upon the verbal communication made to our Consul ["at Buenos Ayres" *interlined*] by the Minister of Paraguya then in that City. That Paraguya is a Country rich in soil with a fine climate we knew previously; but within twenty days sail from the shores of the United States are two Countrys, namely, New Grenada & Venezuela, the soils and Climates of which are unsurpassed on Earth, and yet the amount of Exports from those Republics proves how unavailing such natural advantages are without a secure government and an industrious population. I have the honor to be Sir Your Ob[e]d[ien]t Servant, J.M. Macpherson.

ALS in DNA, RG 59 (State Department), Consular Despatches, Asuncion, vol. 1 (T-329:1).

From AMBROSE BABER

Washington, 24th March 1844

Sir, One may be pardoned the expression of their confidence in the good fortune to the Country in your acceptance of the appointment to which you have been invited with so much unanimity.

Injustice would be done to the magnanimity characteristic of an American gentleman to suppose for a moment, that a difference on some constitutional questions, and also some leading subjects of national policy, could in any manner diminish your willingness to examine and promptly determine a matter of national right, etiquette and courtesy, notwithstanding the affair was officially communicated to the department prior to your appointment.

The subject to which your attention is respectfully requested can be more correctly understood by refference to a correspondence with the Sardinian Government (to which I had been accredited as chargé d'affairs[)], and this Department. The correspondence commences Sept. 1st 1843 and ends Jan. 10th 1844. The opinion given at the time of my recal[l] *was formed without a knowledge of the Circumstances* and I have now no means of ascertaining whether the opinions as expressed by the late Mr. [Abel P.] Upshur is still retained after the communication of a full statement of the circumstances connected with the occurrence.

It may not be improper for me to remark that I have been informed through a private channel that the subject has been refer[r]ed by the Sardinian Government to the several Courts of Europe & my recal[l] happening so soon after the occurrence to which attention has been invited may confirm the impression that the United States Government have condemned their agent regardless of the opinion of their own tribunal solemnly expressed on similar subjects. If on the statement communicated the opinion given should be found unjust, the Country, and it may be added with respect the agent are entitled to a reversion of that decision and the Sardinian Government should be distinctly notified of the views entertained on this subject.

I leave this communication in the hands of Mr. A[bsalom] H. Chappel[l] one of the Representatives from Georgia, who will receive and transmit to me any communication you may be pleased to make. I have the honor to be Very Respectfully Y[ou]r ob[e]d[ie]nt Serv[an]t, Ambrose Baber.

ALS in DNA, RG 59 (State Department), Diplomatic Despatches, Sardinia, vol. 4 (M-90:5).

PEYTON A. SOUTHALL to the Secretary of State

Jalapa, Mexico, 24th March 1844
Sir, I have the honour to report my arrival at this place on yesterday, and finding here the Hon[orab]l[e] Waddy Thompson [Jr.], Minister of the United States, delivered to him the [proposed] Treaty and despatches in obedience to my orders.

I have received from Mr. Thompson the Treaty and despatches for Mr. [Ben E.] Green, the Charge des Affaires of the U. States at Mexico [City], and shall proceed in the morning for the purpose of delivering them to him and shall await his orders. I have the honor to be Sir Very Respectfully Your Ob[edien]t Ser[van]t, Peyton A. Southall, Bearer of Despatches.

ALS in DNA, RG 59 (State Department), Letters from Bearers of Despatches, received 4/22.

F[RANCIS] M. DIMOND to the Secretary of State

United States Consulate
Vera Cruz, 25th March 1844
Sir, I last had the honour to address the Department of State under date of the 20th ins[tant] by the U.S. Brig Somers.

General [Waddy] Thompson [Jr.] has not yet reached here from Jalapa, the U.S. Brig Bainbridge is waiting for him.

Those Texan Prisoners taken at San Antonio Numbering 36 were to be released by order of Gen[era]l Santa Anna yesterday.

By the mail of this morning from Mexico, we learn that the vote in the Chamber of Deputies on the repeal of the retail Law was 40 in favour and 12 against the repeal.

The French Brig of War Mercure sailed this morning for France with the French Secretary of Legation with despatches. I have the honour to be Sir most Respectfully Your Ob[edient] Servant, F.M. Dimond.

ALS (No. 216) in DNA, RG 59 (State Department), Consular Despatches, Veracruz, vol. 5 (M-183:5), received 4/9.

WADDY THOMPSON [JR.] to the
Secretary of State

Legation of the United States Mexico
[Jalapa,] March 25th 1844

Sir, I have the honor to send you herewith a copy of a circular [of 3/1/1844] which I have addressed to each of our consuls in Mexico on the subject of the order prohibiting to foreigners the privilege of the retail trade. I have been making great exertions to obtain a modification of the order so as to exclude from its operation such persons as were engaged in that business at the date of the order without in any degree yielding the question as to those who may hereafter come to Mexico. This would have prevented much individual suffering as well as heavy reclamations against the Mexican Government. I have reasons to believe that I should have succeeded in this if it had not been for a very harsh & menacing note upon the subject which the French minister [Baron Isidore Alleye de Cyprey] felt it to be his duty to address to the Minister of Foreign Affairs [José M. de Bocanegra]. I had yesterday a long and interesting interview with President Santa Anna, who is at present at his country seat [Manga de Clavo] near this place (Jalapa). I found him very much excited by the course pursued by the French Minister and I saw that it was in vain to attemp[t] any thing at that interview. But I do not despair of the order being modified as to other nations if not as to the French. Although I am entirely satisfied that these prohibitive orders are violations of our Treaty and eminently impolitic and must involve very serious consequences, yet I assure you that he discoursed upon them with so much of patriotism and zeal for the interest of his country as to make me respect even his erro[r]s and I have not often listened to higher eloquence that the proud and indignant terms in which he spoke of the menaces of the French Minister. In one of my first despatches I said that I considered him

94

the first man that these Southern Republics have produced; all that I have since seen of him has confirmed this opinion. You must not judge him by the state of things in our own country. The condition of Mexico is anomalous and a Government such as ours would be for Mexico no Government at all.

At the close of the interview, I asked General Santa Anna for the release of the Texans made prisoners at San Antonio de Bejar, he replied in the promptest manner "A negotiation is now going on with Texas and until that is ended, I had not intended to release any of these men, but, Sir, as an evidence of my respect for you personally and for your official conduct since you have been in Mexico I will release them to you and you shall take them home with you.["] Nothing could have been more handsome than the manner in which this was done and I am sure that I have never experienced a more heartfelt pleasure. I regret to have to inform you that General Santa Anna has since excepted George Van Ness from the list of these liberated upon the ground that he was heretofore released upon his parol[e] of honor and that he even took an oath never again to return to Texas. But I have made another application for his release and hope yet for a favorable result. Indeed I am assured that he will very soon be released.

In a subsequent interview with him he has promised me to modify the prohibitory order of August last as to the only point upon which I objected to it, that is the reexportation of goods already imported. He says that as to the Menudeo order it was issued when under the bases of Tacubaya he had the power to do so, but that now as the Constitutional Government is installed he has no power to change it, but that the whole matter will be submitted to Congress for its consideration. I think that it will be repealed or modified. I have addressed a letter [of 3/25/1844] on the subject which I send you No. 2.

In one of my interviews with him he told me that the new English Minister, Mr. [Charles] Bankhead has assured him that if our Government attempted the annexation of Texas that England would have a hand in the matter. I told him that England had had two wars with us on her own account and that I did not think that the result of either had been such as to induce her to desire another. But that so far from such a threat inspiring us with fear that it would be a strong inducement to do it. That our Government was not to be intimidated by the threats of any power and that we would like nothing better than an opportunity to show to England that we would not permit the interference of any European power in the affairs of this Continent.

Mr. [Peyton A.] Southall arrived here last night with the despatches from the Department on the subject of the last convention. I had said in my despatch of the 23d November last, that it was absolutely necessary that I should visit the U. States early in January and requested that a successor might be appointed. Hearing nothing on the subject, although there have been repeated opportunities and my last despatch being directed to Mr. [Ben E.] Green, in the event of my absence, I thought that the Government contemplated my departure. On meeting Mr. Southall at Jalapa, 200 miles from Mexico [City], although the most imperious circumstances require that I should visit the U. States, I should have returned to Mexico [City] but for the following reasons. The first and most important of which is that I am physically unable to do so, and I do not see any good that I could accomplish there. Aided by the full argument which has been sent by the Department in support of the proposed amendments to the Convention, Mr. Green will be able to accomplish all that I could and probably more, as my having agreed to these articles was an admission of my opinion that they were just. But I have not the remotest hope that Mexico will consent to the changes proposed. The place of meeting was conceded in *consideration* of the concession made to me of naming the arbiter. The arguments urged by the Secretary of State against this are in my judgement more specious than solid. I say so in all deference, ["as" *interlined*] I do not regard this objection as originating with the Secretary but that he has been called on to find arguments to support the decision of the Senate. It is not true that this new commission is a continuance of that which met in Washington; that was confined to claims of American citizens against Mexico. This embraces the claims of the Government and Citizens of Mexico against the U. States. It is assumed (upon what authority I know not) that no such claims exist. This is not true, there are such claims to a large amount whether just or not I do not pretend to decide. This com[m]ission therefore can only be regarded as a continuation of the old one as to the cases submitted to the arbiter and not acceded by him, and four other small claims amounting to less than $200,000. As to the first class of cases it cannot be important where the commission meets, for these cases are not to be submitted to the Commission but directly to the arbiter; as to the others it could scarcely have been necessary to have established a commission for them.

There then only remains the case of Mr. J[ohn] Parrot[t] and the Texas land claims. As to Mr. Parrot[t]'s case all the evidence exists in Mexico and not in the U. States and so in a great degree as to the others. As to all these I must again repeat the opinion heretofore expressed. I do not doubt that the course of the Senate will be cause of regret to all who have just claims, particularly those whose cases were referred to the arbiter. It is possible that the prospect of collision with France may cause Mexico to yield this point, but I have not the slightest hope of it. As to the other point the Secretary of State says:

"Let it be distinctly understood that in rejecting the 16 articles no censure is intended to be cast upon the Plenipotentiary who concluded this Convention, and that this Government takes its full share of the error which has been committed." Certainly no portion of the responsibility for that error (if error it be which I do not think) can attach to me. The article in the projet sent me by the Department of State *expressly* and *in terms* submitted to the arbiter to be appointed claims involving the national honor. All the alteration which I made was to limit this submission to the umpire to claims of a pecuniary character: a limitation abundantly sufficient if executed in good faith and not in a cavilling spirit. I find in another part of the despatch just received these words. "In my despatch I commented upon the difficulty of carrying into execution the 6 articles of the Convention of 1843 relative to the claims of the 2 Governments upon each other. That article containing as it did an express agreement upon this subject induced the Government to incorporate a similar provision in the convention. This has been stated in former despatches and I had supposed that I had satisfactorily explained that it was a mistake. There is no provision whatever in the convention of 1843 to submit the claims even of Individuals to a commission, still less to submit those of the Government against each other. It is provided that a new Convention shall be entered into, not that a new Commission shall be established, two things totally different. I did not know that my Government should consent to a new Commission even for individual claims nor did I believe that it would as to the claims of the two Governments. I am very far from desiring to make an issue upon this point with the Government, still less with my distinguished and lamented friend the late Secretary of State [Abel P. Upshur], but I only desire to relieve myself from a responsibility that is not properly mine. But I freely admit that I think the 16 clause of the Treaty guarded as it is, in every point of view just and proper. I can see no good reason why if the Government submits claims of its citizens of a pecuniary character to arbitration it should not also submit to the same tribunal its own claims and claims against it, and the more especially being a strong Government dealing with a weak one. Any such claims as that for example growing out of aid furnished the Texans would not have been submitted, because it involves the national honor. It is not all claims of a pecuniary character which are to be submitted, for such as also involve the National honor are excluded. The claims for a Mexican vessel seized & carried into New Orleans or for damages for the invasion of California by Commodore [Thomas ap C.] Jones would have been submitted because they were for damages only, and if one Government demands reparation for such injuries and the other refuses it what other mode is there of settling it but by reference to an umpire. I wish that Mexico may yield these points, but my firm conviction is that she will not. I repeat that I regard this issue not as between me and the Executive which has approved the Convention, but with the Senate which has disapproved it. [*Marginal interpolation*: "I do not desire that this portion of this despatch should be published. If any blame attaches to this article I prefer bearing it myself to wishing any portion of it upon Judge Upshur the more particularly as my own judgment entirely approves it."]

I send you No. 3 my note [of 3/9/1844] to the Minister of Foreign Affairs on my leaving the city of Mexico and No. 4 his reply [of 3/9/1844].

I have the pleasure to inform you that I have obtained the consent of this Government to the reopening of the Santafe Trade. The close of that trade did not originate in any degree in ill feelings towards us, but from the fact that the Governor of that Department appropriated all the duties to himself and paid nothing to the Government. It seems that an armistice has been concluded with Texas. General Santa Anna tells me that he has no hope whatever of a favorable result and said with great indignation that at the very moment they were treating with him for reannexation they were making proposals to be annexed to our Government. He declared with great earnestness that he would not even treat upon any other basis but that of reannexation to Mexico. I told him that I thought the great difficulties in the way of that result would be the grants of land made by Texas and the slavery question. He replied that he would never consent to recognize those grants, as to slavery he said they were concluded by an article of the Treaty with England and could not admit slavery in any part of the Mexican Territory. This treaty he said was made when they were muchachos, muchachitos, (children, little children) and that he was sorry for it. For there was a large portion of the Mexican Territory, and his own very large Estates particularly that could only be cultivated by slave labor and that his visit to the U. States had dispelled all his prejudices on that subject, that he found our slaves a contented, happy people more so than the African race anywhere else. He added that he was willing to say nothing about the matter in the Treaty with Texas and thus to wink at the toleration of Slavery (his own words). I have no expectation whatever of any favorable result, but if Texas could be reannexed to Mexico with the toleration of Slavery and a merely nominal supremacy of Mexico I do not see any cause of regret on our part.

I send you a pamphlet in which you will find the argument on the side of the Government of Guatamala as to the contest with Mexico as to the right to the Department of Chiapas.

The last instalment of the indemnity which has been paid is now in Veracruz and the vessel will sail in two or three days for the U. States. It was nearly all paid at the day when it was due and as an escort could not be obtained for some two weeks afterwards, I did not press for the remaining few thousand dollars until the escort left, it was then all paid. I feel some pride in the Convention of 1843 and in no article of it more than in that which requires the payments to be made quarterly instead of annually. This Government never has and never will have Six Hundred Thousand Dollars at any one time, but it can always raise a Hundred or a Hundred & Fifty Thousand. There was some doubt as to this last payment being made and although, as I wrote you, I had intended to have left here in January, I felt it to be my duty to wait until the instalment become due. I think with prudence and a little forbearance on the part of the head of this Legation the other payments will be made. I am much indebted for the punctuality in the two last payments to the untiring efforts of Mr. Voss the partner of Mr. Hargous resident in Mexico and to the great influence which he has with the Mexican Government, and the aid which he is able to give the Government in negotiating loans for the balance of the instalment which they may need.

I would beg leave in conclusion to say that I regard this as one of the most important of our missions and I hope that my successor will be one who possesses ["prudence" *interlined*] and ability and a thorough knowledge of the laws of nations. The records of this Legation since I have been here will show an extraordinary accumulation of intricate and important principles which have been involved.

I shall visit Washington very shortly when I will communicate fully with the Government on all subjects upon which it may desire information. I have the honor to be very Respectfully, Waddy Thompson.

LS with Ens in DNA, RG 59 (State Department), Diplomatic Despatches, Mexico, vol. 11 (M-97:12), received 4/22; PEx in Senate Document No. 81, 28th Cong., 2nd Sess., pp. 12–13; PEx in House Document No. 144, 28th Cong., 2nd Sess., p. 13.

HENRY WHEATON to the Secretary of State

Berlin, 25 March, 1844

Sir, I have now the honour to inform you that I have this day concluded and signed a Convention with the Germanic Association of Commerce and Customs in pursuance of the instructions contained in your Despatches No. 51 and 52.

I beg leave to refer to my previous Despatches No. 201, 202, 203, 205 and 237, with their respective enclosures, as being essentially necessary to explain the origin and progress of the negotiation, and the nature of the arrangement in which it resulted.

Much of the delay and difficulty which have occurred in the final conclusion of this arrangement must be attributed to the variety of conflicting interests of the different States, not less than 19 in number, composing the Association, all of which require protection for these interests at the hands of their respective Governments. The proposed reduction of the present duties on the importation of Tobacco affects both the revenue and the cultivation of the native plant in several of the States which have little or no interest in the concessions in favour of German manufactures proposed to be made on our part; and as absolute unanimity is required to the consummation of such conventional arrangements with foreign Powers, the Prussian Government has encountered considerable difficulty in obtaining from its Allies the necessary authority to conclude this Convention in the name of the entire League.

I trust the arrangement will be found, on careful examination, not to affect injuriously any existing interest of our national industry, which has been hitherto deemed entitled to incidental protection in framing the laws for the collection of revenue; whilst, if carried into effect, it will prove of the highest advantage to the agricultural, commercial, and navigating interests of the community, as well as the general interests of the great body of consumers. The principal branches of woolen, cotton, glass, and leather manufactures, as well as those of iron and other metals, protected, or intended to be protected by our present tariff, are, with the exception of a few unimportant articles, untouched by the proposed Arrangement. Unless therefore, it be our policy to force into existence by artificial means new branches of national industry, which are not already established, and for which the Country has no peculiar aptitudes, at the expence of every other branch and of the general interest of the consumers, it is not perceived what possible objection can be made to the proposed mutual reductions in the respective tariffs of the two Countries, unless it be the loss which may possibly be occasioned thereby to the public revenue. But if it be true, as we have always insisted, that the reduction of the present duties levied on the importation of Tobacco into the States of the *Zollverein* would be attended with a correspondent increase of consumption, as experience has shown to have been the case with the article of Rice, so that no considerable loss to the revenue will probably be occasioned by the proposed reduction, may not the same result be expected from a reduction of the duties levied by our present Tariff on linens, silks, and the other goods included in the proposed Arrangement? And even supposing that some loss should actually be occasioned in the revenue arising from those particular articles, will not this loss be compensated by the increase accruing to other branches of revenue, in consequence of the increased activity communicated, both to the direct and indirect trade between the two countries, and to the navigation employed therein, by more liberal provisions to regulate their mutual intercourse?

If however the question be examined from a higher point of view than that of mere fiscal considerations, if it be considered as regarding the general prosperity of the Country, which must be affected by the number and value of the commercial exchanges which take place with other Countries, it will be perceived that the proposed Arrangement proceeds upon the broad and liberal basis of a reduction of duties on such articles the produce or manufacture of each Country, which the soil, climate, social condition, and general circumstances of the other do not enable it to produce or fabricate so advantageously. This is conceived to be most strikingly the case between the United States and Germany in respect to our agricultural staples of cotton, tobacco, rice, &c. on the one hand, and of their wines, linens, silks, &c. on the other. A wise and bountiful Providence has dispensed the blessings of various soils and climates among the different nations of the earth, doubtless with the view of exciting the industry of man to produce various objects of commercial exchange between

different regions, and thereby ["prosecuting" *changed to* "promoting"]
a pacific and friendly intercourse among the various members of the
great human family dispersed over the globe. A very inadequate
idea of the extent and importance of the commercial intercourse already carried on between the United States and the German States
associated in the *Zollverein* is to be formed from official returns
merely, which have reference only to the direct intercourse between
the two Confederations. The Germanic Association has, at present,
no sea ports except on the Baltic. Its commercial intercourse with
the transatlantic world is for the most part maintained, not directly
through the Prussian ports of the Baltic, but circuitously through
those of the Hanse towns, Holland and Belgium on the Northsea,
and even through the port of Havre in France, from which last
mentioned place considerable quantities of German goods are exported to the United States; so that the actual amount of exchanges
between the two Countries is vastly greater than the statistical tables,
which merely refer to the ports of the Association itself, would lead
us to infer. Having myself diligently explored every State, and every
province comprehended in the Association, with the view of studying
their economical resources, I have been forcibly struck with the vast
variety of rich productions with which Heaven has endowed this
beautiful and highly favored land. The fields teem with luxuriant
harvests of grain and fruit, the hill-sides are clad with vineyards
yielding the most exquisite wines, the mountains contain inexhaustible treasures of useful minerals—whilst the vallies are filled with
health-giving fountains of salubrious waters. When we add to these
productions of nature, and of agricultural labour, the vast variety of
useful and ornamental fabrics furnished by the patient and persevering industry of the German people, and their extensive consumption
of the peculiar staple productions of the new world, we must be convinced of the great and increasing importance of the constituent elements of German commerce, of the valuable exchanges it offers to the
trade of other Countries, and of the benefits which may be derived to
our own Country from cultivating and extending the commercial
relations between the United States and Germany.

The obstacles which have hitherto retarded the complete developement of the commercial capacities of Germany have been effectually removed by the formation of the Custom's Association
under the wise and beneficent councils of Prussia. A vast home
market has been opened for the products of national industry, the
barriers to internal intercourse between the different States have
been removed, and their commercial intercourse with foreign nations

greatly facilitated and improved. The relative situation of the different German States anterior to the formation of this League may not inaptly be compared to that of the United States previous to the adoption of our present federal Constitution, when the want of a common authority to regulate the commerce, the currency, and the Customs revenue of the Country was felt as the greatest of political evils, and as the prolific source of weakness, disorder, and poverty.

Without dwelling upon the political and fiscal advantages which have flowed from the institution of the *Zollverein,* it is sufficient to indicate its effects upon the general prosperity of the people, upon production and consumption, and the new elements it has furnished for the extension of foreign commerce. From the official statements which have recently been published of the total amount of importations into the Association, from 1834 to 1842 inclusive, it results that this total amount has increased at the rate of 113 per centum of the gross amount; whilst the population has only increased during these nine years at the rate of 17 per centum. The gross amount of duties received on importation has increased at the rate of 55 per centum. The amount of duties collected on our principal staples has increased as follows. The duties on *Cotton* have increased at the rate of 139 per centum; on *Rice* at the rate of 165 per centum; and on *Tobacco* at the rate of 60 per centum.

The quantity of *Rice* imported into the Zollverein in 1839 was 90,702 centners which paid a duty of 3 thalers per centner, whilst in 1842 (the duty having been in the mean time reduced to 2 thalers per centner), the amount imported was 212,315 centners. There can be no question that a similar result will be produced on the amount of *tobacco* imported, should the proposed Convention be ratified, by which the present duties are to be reduced from 5½ thalers per centner, to 4 thalers on *Leaves* and 3 thalers on *Stems.* The distinction which is now, for the first time, to be made between Leaves and Stems, will also obviate in a great measure the objection heretofore made by us to the unequal operation of the duties being imposed by weight on all kinds of tobacco without regard to its quality and value. Custom has rendered the use of tobacco almost universal among the various classes of society in Germany, not merely as a luxury, but as an article of comfort and a solace for the cares and anxieties of life. As the American tobacco is principally wanted to mix in the manufacture with the native plant, of an inferior quality, we may reasonably conclude that the consumption must be greatly increased by the diminution of duties, whilst the *Zollverein* will become a vast entrepôt for this article from which it will find its way into the ["other" *interlined*] countries of central Europe, where its introduction is now impeded by excessive duties or fiscal monopolies.

The consumption of *Cotton,* which is to remain free of duty by the proposed Arrangement, cannot fail also to increase within the *Zollverein* with the extension of the manufactures of that article, especially should the existing duties on *Cotton Twist* be augmented, for which Germany now pays such an immense annual tribute to G[reat] Britain.

It is also stipulated that the duties on *Rice* are not to be increased beyond their present rate; whilst the duties on *Lard,* a very important article of exportation from our western States, and of extensive consumption in Germany, are to be reduced from 3 to 2 thalers per centner.

If the present Tariff of the Germanic Association be compared with the fiscal systems of the other great commercial Countries of Europe, such as Great Britain, France, Austria, and Russia, in respect to its operation upon our staple productions, it will be found to be moderate and liberal; and in framing the proposed Convention the difficulty has been to find any article, the growth, produce, and manufacture of the United States, except *Tobacco,* on which a reduction of the present duties could fairly be demanded as an equivalent for the mutual reductions to be made by us. Even the present duty on the importation of that article into the *Zollverein* is vastly less than that imposed in Great Britain and Russia, whilst in France and Austria a monopoly of the trade and manufacture of tobacco is vested in the *Regie,* which takes, in each of these Countries, only a very limited quantity of American tobacco, whilst the sale to private parties is entirely prohibited. The same observation will apply to the Articles of Cotton and Rice. *Cotton,* the most important agricultural production of the United States, is charged with heavy duties on its importation into every considerable Country of Europe except the German States associated in the *Zollverein,* whilst upon Rice duties are every where imposed far more onerous than those collected in the *Zollverein.*

So long as the Tariff established by the Compromise Act of 1833 remained in force, our argument in favour of a reduction of the duties levied in the *Zollverein* States on the importation of American tobacco and rice was irresistible, as being founded upon the then existing fact of several principal articles imported from those states, such as linens, silks, worsteds, &c. being entirely free from duties in the United States, whilst the moderate duties imposed on other articles were constantly diminishing at the rate of ten *per centum ad valorem* ["bienally" *changed to* "biennially"], until they should all be reduced in 1842 to the nominal rate of twenty *per centum.* But this state of things was entirely reversed when heavy duties were imposed by the Tariff Act of 1842 upon the principal articles manufactured in Germany, whilst the duties on the importation of Rice into the *Zollverein* had been in the mean time considerably reduced. It then became evident that we must renounce all expectation of securing the admission of our Tobacco into the States of the *Zollverein* on more favorable terms, unless we should be prepared to make some equivalent concessions for a reduction of the duties on that article, and for the advantages to be stipulated in favour of our other principal staples.

The Germanic Association can derive no other considerable advantage from its commercial relations with the United States than that flowing from an exchange of the productions of the two Countries; whilst the United States may secure the additional advantage of carrying much the greater portion of the productions of both Countries in their own shipping which exceeds twenty times in amount of tonnage that of Prussia. Even at present a very large proportion of the sugar, coffee, tea, spices, dye-woods, and other productions of the tropical countries of the globe consumed in the States of *Zollverein,* is furnished by our enterprizing and industrious ship-owners and navigators, who pursue the carrying trade between the East and West-Indies and the ports of Germany on the North-sea. The ability of the German consumers to purchase these articles will be increased by the extension of our direct trade with this Country, and by the increased amount of its productions and manufactures which we shall take at reduced rates of duty. The exchanges between the two Countries will thus be multiplied with the extension of the direct and indirect commercial intercourse between them.

These will again be increased with the increase of population, of production, and of consumption in both countries; and, above all, by the probable ultimate extension of the present *Zollverein* to all the States of the Germanic Confederation—to the whole of that great and enlightened nation speaking the German tongue. If such are the present vast elements of commercial intercourse between the United States and the *Zollverein* with its 27 millions of population, what will be their extent when it comes to embrace the whole Germanic race consisting of 40 millions of industrious people? The importance of this consideration is greatly enhanced by the fact that Germany will ever have the deepest interest in maintaining the freedom of neutral commerce during any war in which we may be engaged with other

European Powers; and that no possible state of things can be imagined in which she can ever become the enemy of the United States.

The 5th article of the Convention is intended to limit the special advantages, secured by it in favour of the productions and manufactures of the two Countries, to such goods only as are imported in the vessels of either Party, or in the vessels of those States which are placed on the footing of national vessels, and coming *directly* from the ports of the other Party. For this purpose the Germanic Association of Customs and Commerce reserves the right of considering all the ports on the North-sea, from the Elbe to the Scheldt inclusive, as ports of the Association. As the Association has, at present, no sea-ports ["of Germany" *canceled*] except those of Prussia on the Baltic, it is necessarily compelled to use the ports of Germany, Holland, and Belgium as the natural outlets and inlets of its commerce by sea with foreign nations. A similar stipulation will be found to be contained in the Convention of Commerce concluded in 1841 between the Germanic Association and G[reat] Britain. (See Mr. Secretary [Daniel] Webster's Report of the 24th May, 1841, Doc. No. 1, 1st Session, 27th Congress.)

The effect of the entire article will be to confine, as much as possible, consistently with existing treaties the commercial intercourse between the two Countries to the direct trade carried on in the vessels of one or the other. A very large proportion of the freight will thus be secured to the navigation of the United States, whilst the manufacturers of the Germanic Association, instead of seeking their supplies of raw cotton and tobacco in the ports of Great Britain, will derive them from a direct intercourse with the United States. The direct trade between the two Countries will thus be greatly increased, and its profits confined exclusively to them, instead of being shared with other rival nations. Should the present duty on the importation of Cotton-Twist into Germany be increased, as there seems to be no doubt it will be, the demand for our raw cotton in this country will be proportionally increased by the establishment of new spinneries, whilst the consumption of Tobacco must be augmented by the reduction of the duties. The ship-owner and planter will thus both participate in the advantages of the Arrangement, whilst the increased importation of our agricultural staples into Germany will augment the means of paying for the amount of German manufactures taken in return. The commercial exchanges between the two Countries will thus be multiplied, and the prosperity of both greatly promoted. I have the honour to be with the highest respect, Sir your ob[edien]t Servant, Henry Wheaton.

LS (Duplicate, No. 242) in DNA, RG 59 (State Department), Diplomatic Despatches, Germany, vol. 3 (M-44:4), received 5/8; FC in DNA, RG 84 (Foreign Posts), Germany, Despatches, 4:78–90.

From JOHN BALDWIN

New Orleans, March 26th 1844

Sir: My friend Mr. Leonard R. Almy was duly appointed Consul of the United States for the Port of Laguna de Terminos & Island of Carmen in the Republic of Mexico. He repaired to his Consulate in July last and immediately remitted his Commission to the Minister of the U. States in Mexico through the Consul at Vera Cruz. His communication to Gen[era]l [Waddy] Thompson [Jr.] remained many months without answer and sometime previous to the decease of your lamented predecessor [Abel P. Upshur] I called his attention to the subject, and informed him that the interests of American Citizens was suffering in that Port for want of Consular protection which the incumbent was prohibited from extending to them in consequence of not having received his exequatur from the Mexican Government.

I received from the Consul a few days since the enclosed letter from Mr. Thompson covering a copy of a communication from the Mexican Secretary dated in October last[,] three months after Mr. Almy[']s arrival at his Consulate. Perhaps the multifarious and more important duties of our Minister is in his own opinion a sufficient reason for not replying more opportunely to the numerous letters written to him by the Consul.

The commercial house of Guttierez at Laguna was exceedingly anxious to have one of their clerks appointed to the Consulate, and have no doubt intrigued with their own Government to have an exequatur denied to Mr. Almy under the expectation that their desire might hereafter be consummated whilst in the mean time they would get rid of a person whose business qualifications might make him a dangerous competitor in the commerce of that Port which they now monopolize.

It may be possible however that the Mexican Minister has taken a retrospective view of Mr. Almy[']s conduct whilst a resident in the Northern part of the Republic where he became by his industry the proprietor of a magnificent landed property which he was peac[e]-ably cultivating and improving at the period when St. Ana [that is, Santa Anna,] conceived the idea of destroying the Constitution of his country and [to] deprive the individual States of their Sovereignty. The Governor of the State of Coahuila in which Mr. Almy then resided called on all the inhabitants to rally around his standard and sustain the integrity of the States. Mr. Almy although a civilian joined the Governor and astounded the despot & his satellites by his valour & intrepidity; but his efforts to sustain the constituted authorities of the country were unavailing. The Governor succumbed and fled to the United States and Mr. Almy was oblidged to abandon the cause and the country and take refuge in the U. States, his property was confiscated and from princely wealth he was reduced to beggary. Without any hope of again acquiring possession of his estate which had cost him many years of toil, he felt desirous of again commencing a mercantile career and if possible by industry to acquire a decent competence. If you will call for his vouchers of character you will be satisfied that he is a gentleman of high toned feeling & honour and in every way well calculated to discharge the duties of his office with credit to himself & honour to his country.

I have advised Mr. Almy to await your instructions, and if it is the policy of the Government of the United States to submit to the indignity of having one of its officers unrecognized you will of course order him home & appoint one of more congenial taste to the Mexican Government. In which case I hope the President [John Tyler] will, in order to allay in some degree the mortification that Mr. Almy must feel, order a vessel of War to bring him home having first received him on board in the Port of Laguna with Consular honours. Very respectfully your Ob[e]d[ien]t S[ervan]t, John Baldwin.

ALS with Ens in DNA, RG 59 (State Department), Consular Despatches, Ciudad del Carmen, Mexico (M-308:1).

PETER HARMONY to the Secretary of State

New York [City,] March 26th 1844
Sir, Having observed in the News Papers lately that a Treaty of Indemnity has been made & ratified between the United States & Peru, and being one of the largest claimants against the Government of Peru for the unlawful seizure & Condemnation in 1825 of the Ship General Brown of this Port and her valuable Cargo, I would Respectfully suggest an early appointment of Commissioners to apportion

the amount of said Indemnity according to the merits & amounts of the Respective Claimants, and as the apportionment would be greatly facilitated by the appointment of Commissioners already conversant with the Claims, I would most Respectfully recommend the following Eminent Citizens, Mr. [Samuel] Larned of Rhode Island, who devoted much time in Peru in arranging and presenting said Claims, Mr. [James C.] Pickett, late Charge des Affaires, who concluded the arrangement, and the Honorable David B. Ogden of New York who prepared the Documents to sustain the part of said Claim. It will be of great importance to the Claimants that a Respectable & Responsible person, be appointed who may reside in Lima to receive from the Peruvian Government the Instalments and Interest as they shall fall due & remit the amount in Specie or Bills to the United States.

Stanhope Prevost the present Consul for the U.S. in Lima is eminently qualified for this duty[;] he is well known as a Gentleman of large Responsibility[,] strict Integrity & highly respected among the influential Classes in Lima. With great Respect Your Ob[e]-d[ien]t Serv[an]ts, Peter Harmony [signed] By his att[orne]y Leonard S[?]. Juarez[?].

LS in DNA, RG 59 (State Department), Applications and Recommendations, 1837–1845, Ogden (M-687:24, frames 418–420).

W[ILLIAM] S. MURPHY to
[the Secretary of State]

Legation of the United States
Houston, Texas, March 26th, 1844
Sir, The rage of Speculation, in Texas Lands, Texas Bonds, Texas Stocks, Texas notes &c &c now rife in Galveston & New Orleans, has given rise to various reports, some of which, occasionally find their way into the Newspapers of N[ew] Orleans & Texas; and many of those speculators, do not Scruple to invoke my name, as authority for their reports.

I have been greatly annoyed, of late with these reports, and so far as some of them, reach the Public press, they may have given some uneasiness to my Govt. In this view of the matter, I felt bound to publish, in the Paper [*not found*] enclosed to you herewith, *a card*, relieving myself from such imputations.

I trust my Govt. will know how to appreciate these reports. I anxiously wait, to hear from you. Your ob[edien]t Serv[an]t, W.S. Murphy.

P.S. Gen[era]l [Charles F.] Mercer, has made a contract with this Govt. for a large tract of Land—and I learn that he is in New Orleans, endeavouring to Sell Shares &c &c.

I met him, for the first time in my life, at Houston, on my way to Washington, last month. The value of his contract depends wholly, on the annexation of this country to the U. States. It was made this last winter—and I think, closed in the Early part of Feb[ruar]y—or last of Jan[uar]y whilst Congress was in Session.

I can[']t account, for the publication in the N[ew] Orleans Rep[u]b[lican]. Yours, W.S. Murphy.

ALS (Private) in DNA, RG 59 (State Department), Diplomatic Despatches, Texas, vol. 2 (T-728:2, frames 301–302), received 4/9.

A. G. & A. W. B E N S O N to John Tyler

New York [City,] March 27th 1844

Sir, Enclosed we have the honor to hand you some extracts from a letter just received from our agent in Oregon by which it appears that the Hudson[']s Bay Company are extending their settlements even South of the Columbia River and that their agent Dr. Mc-Laughlin [*sic*; John McLoughlin] has seized upon the most valuable tract of land in the territory around the falls of the Wilhamette [*sic*; Willamette River] & is selling out lots to citizens of the U. States. We are Very respectfully Your ob[edient] Ser[van]ts, A.G. & A.W. Benson.

LS with En in DNA, RG 59 (State Department), Miscellaneous Letters (M-179: 104, frames 95–97). NOTE: The Bensons enclosed extracts from a letter to them from F.W. Pettygrove, dated 7/31/1843 at Willamette Falls. Pettygrove describes the colonizing activities of Dr. John McLoughlin on behalf of the Hudson's Bay Company and states that American settlers, barred from using Hudson's Bay Company vessels, require a brig to ship their produce to markets.

A[RCHIBALD] M. GREEN to the Secretary of State

Consulate of the U.S. of America at Galvezton
Republic of Texas, 28th March 1844

Sir, By the Steamer New York this morning I again write to the Department in regard to the duty and restrictions imposed on Texas Cotton introduced into the United States from this port.

At the present time American vessels would have cargos to the ports in the U. States, but for the restrictions, and whilst they exist, it is depriving our vessels from having the carrying trade and it necessarily prevents a great number of manufactured articles from being imported direct from the U. States to Texas—Articles of manufacture that must be consumed in this Country for a long time to come.

I am aware of the fact, of American merchants, having written to their friends in the various commercial cities in the U. States not to send vessels to Texas so long as this duty and the heavy exactions are made on Texas Cotton imported into the States. Let this duty be taken off, our trade will increase and our vessels will have freights and employment.

If the Texas Cotton is to be consumed in a European market, I ask does it matter whether it is carried there by way of N[ew] York or shipped direct from the ports of Texas, so far as the growers of that article are concerned in the United States. If a surplus was not raised in the U. States it might cause some difference, and just grounds, for imposing the duty.

Our shipping would have the carrying trade of this Cotton both to the U.S. & Europe for it would become mixed and mingled with Cotton the growth of the U.S. and it could not be distinguished—merchandize would be exchanged for the Cotton and it would be a fair exchange of the raw material for the manufactured articles.

A bill was introduced into the Congress to take off this duty; but it may be some time before this is done and in the mean time the vessels now in this trade may be driven off in search of another market.

And it is respectfully asked of the dept. if this duty will be required should a cargo of Cotton be shipped to the United States? It is one means which the Texans have of paying their liabilities, which are heavy; and would it not be better to facilitate that object rather than widen the breach?

I send you a paper containing a list of vessels in this port on the 23rd Inst[ant] and the nations to which they belonged.

These suggestions are made in no manner intending to be presuming but merely to suggest what I thought would serve to add greatly to our commerce and benefit. I have the honor to be most Resp[ectfull]y y[ou]r ob[edien]t S[ervan]t, A.M. Green.

ALS (No. 30) in DNA, RG 59 (State Department), Consular Despatches, Galveston, vol. 2 (T-151:2), received 4/8.

E DWARD K ENT to the Secretary of State, "(Private)"

Bangor (Me.), March 28th 1844

Sir, At the request of the signers, I enclose to you a memorial on the subject of the recent movement in New Brunswick in relation to the duty on American timber. A few copies have been printed, and the original is now forwarded to you in that form, as probably preferable to a manuscript and also a copy of the same.

I am requested also to state to you, that the American Consul at St. John [Israel D. Andrews] will, in a few days, forward to you a statement of facts, which will substantiate the material allegations in this memorial.

The course proposed by the Provincial authorities is unexpected, and, as it seems to me, indefensible. Certain I am, that it is contrary to my understanding of the objects of both parties to the treaty. The word "free" was understood by us all, as expressing in a single word what it was at first thought might require more minute specification, and as conferring absolute right of exemption from tolls, duties or impositions. I will not detain you by here repeating what is contained in the argument herewith submitted, but will merely remark that, having on this subject particularly had a minute and accurate knowledge of the views of those who framed and of those who assented to the treaty, I feel a perfect conviction that the views set forth in the enclosed paper are in consonance with the true intent & meaning of the treaty. I cannot doubt that the English Government upon representations from the proper authorities at Washington, will desist from the commencement of a system, which must lead to constant trouble, vexation & resistance, and excite anew feelings of hostility & ill will, which, happily, since the treaty, have in a great degree subsided. I think I am not mistaken in saying that the people & governments of Maine and Massachusetts will not quietly submit to the proposed exaction, which they deem but the commencement of a system of injuries & injustice and opposed to the letter & spirit of the treaty.

I beg leave to add, that those who are interested have a perfect confidence that the subject will receive your early and due attention, and that all proper measures will be taken to bring this matter to the attention & consideration of her Majesty's Government. Very respectfully your obedient servant, Edward Kent.

ALS with En in DNA, RG 59 (State Department), Miscellaneous Letters (M-179:104, frames 98–106); CC with En in DNA, RG 84 (Foreign Posts), Great Britain, Instructions, 8:171–210; PC with En in House Document No. 110, 29th Cong., 1st Sess., pp. 4–14. NOTE: Kent was a former Governor of Maine and had been a member of the commission appointed by the Maine legislature to confer with the State Department on the Webster-Ashburton treaty at the time of its negotiation. He enclosed a printed memorial signed by seventy individuals and companies protesting the imposition by New Brunswick of a 20 cents per ton export duty on lumber passing through New Brunswick ports and, in effect, upon American lumber traffic down the St. John River. The memorialists contend that the duty, imposed in late 1843, violated article three of the Treaty of Washington.

T[HOMAS] M. RODNEY to the Secretary of State

Consulate of the United States of America
Matanzas [Cuba, March 28, 1844]

Sir, The enclosed copy of a letter from the Governor of Matanzas in reply to a note of mine of this date I have already forwarded to the Collector of the Customs of Charleston S.C. to be published for general information.

The Department will observe that heretofore persons of colour arriving here have been permitted to remain on board their respective vessels on giving bonds of security, but here after they will be placed in confinement immediately on their arrival and detained until the vessels to which they belong are ready for sea.

If what I learn of the investigations going on in relation to the late conspiracy on the part of the blacks and mulattoes, and which is attributed to the agency of Mr. [David] Turnbull, formerly the British Consul at Havana, be true, they show a mighty plot, well arranged and organized and extending perhaps throughout the Island to make a desperate effort for the possession of the Country. Officers

113

from the Executive Council down to Captains of Companies had already been appointed among them and they only waited the appointed day to commence a general slaughter of the whites but thro' a mercy we have been preserved from the fangs of infuriated negroes.

All, I understand has been discovered and the retribution will be appalling[;] forts, jails, prisons all are full and arrests still going on. It is generally supposed that the free mulattoes and blacks engaged in this affair, and it seems they are all engaged without an exception, will either be executed or driven from the Island, the slaves will be dealt with severely but only the prominent leaders executed.

This state of affairs has given much trouble to our shipping interest, for the stevedores have all been arrested and vessels loading have great difficulty in obtaining hands to stow cargo. I have the honor to be sir your ob[e]d[ien]t S[ervan]t, T.M. Rodney.

ALS with En in DNA, RG 59 (State Department), Consular Despatches, Matanzas, vol. 4 (T-339:4), received 4/10. NOTE: Rodney enclosed a communication, dated 3/28, from Antonio Garcia Oña, Governor of Matanzas, announcing new restrictions on "foreign seamen of colour" in Cuba. Henceforth Matanzas authorities will enforce regulations "of like operation with that of the slave holding States of the American union"; that is, black seamen will be incarcerated in local jails while their vessels are in port.

EDWARD EVERETT to John Nelson

London, 30 March 1844

Sir, I enclose herewith a copy of a note of 8th instant from Messrs. G. and H. Davis & Co., Tobacco brokers of this city, with the printed statement accompanying it; together with the last business circular of those gentlemen.

The committee of the House of Commons alluded to by the Messrs. Davis has since been granted on the motion of Mr. [Joseph] Hume, which was expressed in the following terms: "Mr. Hume moved for a select committee, to examine into the present state of the Tobacco Trade, and to enquire what effects have been produced by the changes in the laws relating to it; and whether any and what legislative measures, compatible with the general interests of the country, may be advisable, in order to promote the trade or to check smuggling in tobacco, and to report their observations thereupon to the house."

I had some conversation with Mr. [William E.] Gladstone, the

President of the Board of Trade, shortly after the granting this committee by the house, in which he expressed himself rather more favorably on the subject of the reduction of the duty, than he had done in my former conversations on this subject, without however giving encouragement, that any thing important would at present be done. He said there was no doubt that a reduction of the duty to one shilling per lb. would materially increase the entire consumption. Unless this should be the result, the measure would produce no benefit to the United States. The only point remaining to be settled by the government, in order to induce them to lower the duty, is the effect of the reduction in wresting the trade from the smuggler. In granting Mr. Hume's committee, they seem to give a pledge of their intention to take this point into serious consideration. The trade, I believe, is unanimously of opinion, that with a duty not exceeding one shilling per lb. smuggling would cease.

I have received from Mr. [Henry] Wheaton, by a letter dated 20th March, the agreeable intelligence, that there is now a fair prospect of his negotiation resulting in the conclusion of a commercial convention with the Zollverein on the principles indicated in the notes exchanged between himself and the Prussian Minister in October last. Should this prospect be realized, and the convention be ratified by the President [John Tyler] and Senate, it would have a powerful effect on this government. I am well informed that it has watched with great interest the progress of this negotiation. I am, sir, with great respect, your obedient servant, Edward Everett.

Documents transmitted with Despatch 104.
1. Messrs. G. & H. Davis & Co. to Mr. Everett 8 March 1844, with a printed enclosure.
2. Circular of Messrs. Davis [dated 4/1/1844].

LS (No. 104) with Ens in DNA, RG 59 (State Department), Diplomatic Despatches, Great Britain, vol. 52 (M-30:48), received 4/24; FC in MHi, Edward Everett Papers, 48:393–396 (published microfilm, reel 22, frames 1242–1244).

From RICHARD S. ROGERS

Salem [Mass.] March 30 1844

Sir, I have the honor of laying before you a memorial with sundry other papers in relation to a claim on the British Government, growing out of an illegal and unjust imposition of duties levied on a large quantity of American Rum, exported to and landed at the Island of New Zealand.

A communication in regard to this matter was made in a letter dated June, 1842, and addressed to the Honorable Leverett Saltonstall, then member of Congress from this district, and by him transmitted to the Department of State. You will observe by a copy of a letter in August, 1842, and herein enclosed, from the Honorable Daniel Webster (then Secretary of State) that the subject of this memorial, was, at that time, to be submitted to our Minister at London, since then I have heard nothing definite on the subject, excepting in an interview which I had with the late Secretary of State, Mr. [Abel P.] Upshur, the day previous to the lamentable accident on board the Princeton, that terminated his life. On that occasion he informed me that the subject had been brought to the notice of the American Minister at London, Mr. [Edward] Everett, and that he was in daily expectation of hearing from him. Will you be pleased to inform me if the Department has received, since that time, any thing in relation to it.

Never before having presented this matter in the shape of a memorial, I have thought proper to do it at the present time, and have, accordingly, put together such facts as seemed most important and necessary, to justify the claim now made for the injury sustained by this high handed measure of the Legislative Council of New Zealand.

I therefore ask your kind assistance in this business and the interference of the Government of the United States, that justice may be rendered who have been so unjustly and severely dealt with in this matter. It will readily occur to you, Sir, that claims of this sort, unless promptly settled, easily pass out of the notice of the Department, to whose jurisdiction they belong, and, therefore, that unless speedy justice is obtained it is little likely to be obtained at all. I therefore take take [*sic*] the liberty to solicit such action in relation to this matter, as will be most adapted to obtain the result desired. With consideration of high respect, Your obedient Servant, (Signed) N.L. Rogers & Brothers by Richard S. Rogers, duly authorised.

CC with Ens in DNA, RG 84 (Foreign Posts), Great Britain, Instructions, 8:74–85; CC with Ens in DNA, RG 76 (Records of Boundary and Claims Commissions and Arbitrations), Miscellaneous Claims Records: Great Britain, Convention of Feb. 8, 1853.

From N[ATHANIEL] L. ROGERS & BROTHERS

[Salem, Mass., *ca.* March 30, 1844]
Respectfully represent Nathaniel L. Rogers and Brothers, native citizens of the United States, and Merchants of Salem in the State of Massachusetts—

That for many years previous to the year 1841 they were largely engaged in Commerce with the native ports of New Holland, New Zealand, The Fegee and Sandwich islands, and had carried on their trade with the natives in those places, and with the citizens of other states residing there, subject to no other regulations than such as were mutually established between their masters and factors, and the persons with whom they traded, and without any interference or claim of right to levy duties or impose restraints of any kind on the part of the officers of any foreign power whatever.

That among other settlements their vessels had visited and traded at a place called the Bay of Islands in New Zealand, and sold and bought merchandize there without the payment of any duties, or any forms of a Custom House, or any other claim to collect imposts from the goods and merchandize they landed there.

That in September 1840 their Ship "Tybee," Capt. J.H. Millet landed at that port 22 casks of New England Rum; and in October of the same year Capt. I[saac] N. Chapman of their Brig "Nereus" landed over 90 casks of the same merchandize there, and a quantity was also landed there about the same time by Capt. Hooper of their bark "Shepherdess" the whole amounting to about 18,646 gallons, and the same was delivered to William Mayhew Esq[ui]r[e] a Commission Merchant then doing business there, in whose warehouses the same was placed. That at that time there was no Custom House at the Bay of Islands, there were no forms of entry, making reports or other formalities required of masters of vessels, but they entered and departed from that port in the same way they entered and left any other port or place belonging to the natives in any part of the world, over which no civilized nation had exercised or asserted any jurisdiction.

That at that time the said Mayhew did not know or suspect, and no one at the Bay of Islands knew or suspected that the British Government claimed any right to impose duties upon imports, or assumed to regulate or interfere with, the commerce of other nations at this port or place; and as late as March 1841, Captain [William H.] Cross in the Ship "Lydia" belonging to your memorialists was at the Bay of Islands in said ship, and at that time there were no duties there, and although in the month of April 1841, when he left that port, it was reported that the British Colonial Government of New Holland intended to levy duties on Imports, yet up to the day of his sailing no such duties had been laid;

And your memorialists further represent that long after the landing of the goods aforesaid, their said Agent was called upon by certain officers of the colonial government of New Zealand to pay a duty of Five Shillings per gallon, sterling, upon all said spirits in his possession, under the pretence that the government had laid that duty upon all Rum imported into that place. That their said agent who was one of the oldest residents in the place, and then acting as the Deputy of the United States' consul at New Zealand, protested against the imposition of this duty as amounting to an actual confiscation of the property of the citizens of a friendly nation, and as wholly without precedent in American or British Legislation; but still under his protest and without his consent the property was removed to the Government Stores, in which process the casks were very much injured and large quantities of the rum were lost by leakage, and the expenses incurred for exorbitant charges for storage and other extortion so much reduced the value of the property, that to prevent a total loss by the accumulation of these oppressive exactions, and the continued leakage and theft, that their agent was at last obliged to sell the whole for a very small consideration, which has as yet never been paid; by means of all which your memorialists have incurred a loss upon the merchandize aforesaid of at least the sum of Ten to Eleven thousand dollars.

Inasmuch then as this injury has been suffered without any fault of their own, or any violation or attempt to violate the laws of their own or of any other government; inasmuch as ["under" *interlined*] the pretence ["under" *canceled and* "by" *interlined*] which their property was taken from them it would be in the power of any government to confiscate the property of the citizens of a friendly nation by encouraging its importation into its ports of merchandize free of duty, and then subjecting it to an impost of a greater amount than the whole value of the property, which was the actual operation of this ex post facto duty, upon the merchandize of your memorialists, they humbly submit that they are entitled to reparation and redress.

They therefore most respectfully ask the interference of the Government of the United States in their behalf to procure them such relief in the premises from the British Government, as right and justice, and the protection which all american citizens are entitled to, and the honor and dignity of our own Government, seem absolutely to require. N.L. Rogers & Brothers, by Rich[ar]d S. Rogers, duly authorized.

CC with En in DNA, RG 84 (Foreign Posts), Great Britain, Instructions, 8:79–85; CC with En in DNA, RG 76 (Records of Boundary and Claims Commissions and Arbitrations), Miscellaneous Claims Records: Great Britain, Convention of Feb. 8, 1853. NOTE: The enclosure is an undated statement of loss incurred in the transaction described in the memorial; the amount of loss is $9,565.63 before interest is added.

PEYTON A. SOUTHALL to the Secretary of State

City of Mexico, 30th March 1844

Sir, I have the honour to report my arrival here on the evening of the 28th inst[ant] and the safe delivery of the Treaty and Despatches, entrusted to my care as Bearer of Despatches, to Mr. [Ben E.] Green, Chargé des Affair[e]s of the United States at Mexico. I have the honor, to be Sir, Very Respectfully Your Ob[edien]t Serv[an]t, Peyton A. Southall, Bearer of Despatches.

ALS in DNA, RG 59 (State Department), Letters from Bearers of Despatches, received 5/6. NOTE: The "Treaty" which was delivered by Southall was doubtless the 1843 convention between the U.S. and Mexico, which had been ratified by the Senate, with amendments, in January.

From J[OHN] C. SPENCER

Treasury Department
March 30th 1844

Sir, I have the honor to enquire in view of a call made upon this Department, whether any change should be made in the estimate of the Expenditures under the direction of the Department of State during the present fiscal year, which was furnished, and laid before the House of Representatives at the commencement [in 12/1843] of the present session of Congress? Very respectfully your obed[ien]t Serv[an]t, J.C. Spencer, Secretary of the Treasury.

LS in DNA, RG 59 (State Department), Letters Received from the Fifth Auditor and Comptroller, 1829–1862; FC in DNA, RG 56 (Treasury Department), Letters to Cabinet and Bureau Officers, Series B, 4:341.

From A[RTHUR] P. HAYNE, "Private"

Maryetta Plantation near Georgetown
So[uth] Ca[rolina], March 31/44

Dear Sir: I avail myself of the present occasion, to congratulate you, and the nation, on your acceptance of the State Department, especially, as you have done so, at a period, when so many great, and important questions, agitate the public mind—questions of vital importance, the wise and judicious settlement of which, cannot fail to produce the happiest effect, upon the prosperity of the whole Country. Your decision, in consenting to take office, dictated, as your friends know, by the most elevated principles of patriotism, is approved of by all—for all concur in the fact, that your selection is the very best Mr. [John] Tyler could have made—and that your great abilities emphatically pointed you out, as the peculiar instrument in the hands of the *Almighty*, for the accomplishment of the greatest good to the people of the United States. Happy, indeed, am I Sir, to see you, at a *Crisis* like the present, in the station you now occupy— and I hope, and trust, you will tend to receive, the honorable, and proper rewards, which your long, and valuable services, your virtues, & your eminent abilities, so fairly entitle you to, in the opinion, of all the good, & patriotic minds in the Country.

I have always felt a deep interest in your prosperity, & happiness, personal, & political—and will only add, the kind & friendly manner, in which you have always been pleased to appreciate my military services, commands, & ever will receive, my warmest, & most heartfelt gratitude.

With the respectful & friendly salutations of my family, & best wishes for your happiness & health, I subscribe myself, Dear Sir, your friend, & ob[edien]t, A.P. Hayne.

P.S. My Sister in law, Mrs. Rob[er]t Y. Hayne requests, that you will send on to Charleston So[uth] Ca[rolina], *a Passport*, for her second Son, Doct[or] Arthur P. Hayne, who leaves for Paris, in in [*sic*] April, to complete his medical education. A.P.H.

ALS in DNA, RG 59 (State Department), Passport Applications, vol. 30, no. 1952 (M-1372:14).

APRIL 1–15, 1844

⑪

John C. Calhoun, who appeared, doubtless with punctuality, to take charge of the State Department of the United States on Monday, April 1, had recently observed his sixty-second birthday. He was no stranger to the duties of a Cabinet officer and head of an executive department—something to which he had devoted more than seven of his early middle years—though that period had ended nineteen years before.

The new Secretary was besieged, both by correspondence and in person, by well-wishers, office seekers, and persons with claims to press. There had been only an interim administration for over a month, and it was necessary to get a handle on both the day-to-day and the long-term affairs of the Department. This was complicated by the fact that Congress was at that point in its session where it was really beginning to seriously consider appropriations and new legislation; by the fact that the President and Calhoun's predecessor had made many appointments in his department (including that of Governor Wilson Shannon of Ohio to be the next Minister to Mexico) some of which were yet to be confirmed by the Senate; and that troubles were evident along the Maine-New Brunswick border where some of the issues incorporated in the treaty of 1842 were still to be worked out in detail. Calhoun's administrative labors were facilitated by the arrival from Virginia about April 10 of a trusted intimate, Richard K. Crallé, to take over the duties of Chief Clerk, the nearest thing to an Assistant Secretary in that day.

The most urgent business facing Calhoun was that of Texas. The initiative for annexation negotiations had been launched by Calhoun's predecessor, and Texas, independent for eight years, had, with considerable misgivings on the part of at least some of its leaders, agreed. The urgency rested, in Calhoun's opinion, on two factors. The treaty had to be concluded and ratified while the Senate was in session; otherwise Texas would be left vulnerable to a new invasion by Mexico that might be provoked by the annexation negotiations. Secondly, Texas, if not bound to the Union of the States soon, might seek support from some foreign imperial power, even at the price of its independence.

Much of the Secretary's first two weeks in office was spent with the Texan representatives, Van Zandt and Henderson. They reached final agreement on a treaty, already largely outlined by Calhoun's predecessor, signed by Calhoun for the United States on April 12. A special messenger was sent off the next day to carry the treaty and other information to the Texas government and to the United States representative in Texas, both of which were standing by in Galveston to receive the earliest possible word. Calhoun wrote to William S. Murphy, the American Chargé d'Affaires in Texas, that he expected the treaty to be ratified by the Senate. "The voice of the Country, so far as it can be heard, is so decidedly in favour of annexation that any hesitancy on the part of the doubtful will probably give way to it," Calhoun thought. It was a poor prophecy indeed, and by no means the only time that Calhoun underestimated the capacity of politicians to undermine and evade public opinion.

〚〛

CIRCULAR [to Representatives of the United States Abroad]

Department of State
Washington, April 1st 1844

Sir, I have the honor to inform you that the President [John Tyler], by and with the advice and consent of the Senate, has appointed me Secretary of State, of the United States, and that I have this day entered upon the duties of that office. I am, Sir, &c., J.C. Calhoun.

FC in DNA, RG 59 (State Department), Consular Instructions, 11:225. NOTE: This circular was sent to American Ministers, Chargés d'Affaires, Commissioners, Consuls, and Commercial Agents. LS versions (recipient's copies) are found in DNA, RG 84 (Foreign Posts), in many files, and also in many collections of private papers.

CIRCULAR [to Foreign Representatives in the United States]

Department of State
Washington, 1st April, 1844

The Undersigned, having been appointed to the office of Secretary of State, has the honor to inform [*name and title*] that he will be happy to receive any communications which the [*title and name*] may have occasion to address to him in that capacity.

The Undersigned avails himself of this occasion to offer to the [*title and name*] the assurance of his high consideration. J.C. Calhoun.

LS (with name and title filled in) in DLC, John G. Hülsemann Papers, Toner Collection. NOTE: From replies which appear below in this volume and from notations which appear in DNA, RG 59 (State Department), Notes to Foreign Legations, various files, it appears that letters similar to the above were addressed to the Ministers or Chargés d'Affaires of Austria, the Netherlands, Spain, Belgium, Denmark, France, Great Britain, Sardinia, Portugal, Russia, the Argentine Republic, Mexico, and Brazil, thirteen of the sixteen countries then represented at that level in Washington. The Prussian legation was vacant, Calhoun had already met in person the representatives of the Texas Republic, and, inexplicably, no record of this letter to the Swedish Minister has been found. The above transcription is generalized from an LS addressed to the Austrian Chargé d'Affaires.

From S[TEPHEN] H. BRANCH, "Private"

Cincinnati, Ohio, April 1, 1844

My Dear Sir: I have just received your very kind letter. A friend in New York [City] enclosed it to me. Will you please to inform me if your family accompanied you to Washington? If not, I will go to Fort Hill, if agreeable to you. If I come to W[ashington], I shall come as a devoted friend, to teach the highest objects of your affections, and not as a selfish applicant for office. *The humble Teacher of your children* is the proudest name I desire to leave behind me. Your intellect and public virtue have nourished and made me happy since I first began to read, in the pleasing transports of childhood, while in the halls of literature, and by the noble forest streams of Rhode Island. And *they* have nourished and sustained the nation, through its darkest perils, which the people, at length, I am pleased to find, begin to understand and truly appreciate. It is for this that

I admire you above all other men, and for which I am so very solicitous to express my gratitude beyond mere words.

Your morning and meridian sun, as refulgent as they were, were not more resplendent than the brilliant and glorious sunset that awaits you. Unsullied virtue and distinguished intellect, combined in any one man, and consecrated, through a long life, to the public good, must command the admiration of mankind, and ever elicit the highest favor of our God. With profound respect, S.H. Branch.

ALS in ScCleA.

To R[obert] P. Dunlap and Joshua Herrick, [Representatives from Maine], 4/1. Calhoun acknowledges their letter of 3/29 [*The Papers of John C. Calhoun*, 17:903–904] recommending Jeremiah O'Brien of Brunswick, Maine, for a Clerkship. "Should a vacancy occur, it will receive the most respectful consideration." FC in DNA, RG 59 (State Department), Domestic Letters, 34:112 (M-40:32).

From H[enry] L. Ellsworth, [Commissioner of the] Patent Office, 4/1. Ellsworth asks for "but a few moments" of Calhoun's time in regard to a case of a requested patent extension. (Clerks' EU's indicate the replies to this request. One reads: "The Secretary directs me to inform you that in consequence of a previous engagement ["for" *interlined*] to morrow he will be unable to see you on the business referred to in your note of this morning." Another EU reads: "Will see him at 12 o'clock, 4th April [18]44." ALS in DNA, RG 59 (State Department), Miscellaneous Letters (M-179:104, frames 124–125).

From George Evans and John Fairfield, Senators, and R[obert] P. Dunlap, Joshua Herrick, H[annibal] Hamlin, L[uther] Severance, and F[reeman] H. Morse, Representatives [from Maine], 4/1. They inform Calhoun that appropriations made by Congress to compensate the State of Maine under the treaty [with Great Britain] of 1842 have fallen short by about $80,000. They refer Calhoun to claims and accounts presented by Samuel L. Harris and ask that the State Department "furnish an estimate, to the appropriate committee of Congress" of additional appropriations needed. PC in House Document No. 242, 28th Cong., 1st Sess., p. 2.

From EDWARD EVERETT

London, 1 April 1844

Sir, On the 16th of March I had an interview with Lord Aberdeen at my request at his dwelling house. My immediate object was to make a personal communication to him of the mournful intelligence, which had just been received of the disaster of the 28th of February. This communication he received with expressions of unaffected and respectful concern.

The conversation then turned upon the reception of Mr. [Richard] Pakenham, of which that gentleman seems to have written home very satisfactory accounts, as of the purport of his first conversations with the late Secretary of State [Abel P. Upshur], on the principal objects of his mission, and especially upon the Oregon question. I availed myself of this opportunity, as I have of every other which has presented itself, to enforce upon Lord Aberdeen the extreme reasonableness & moderation of the terms, upon which the United States had repeatedly offered to settle the boundary. I told him that he would have it in his power to see, in a very distinct manner, how reasonable these terms are, if he would cause a map of the entire country to be prepared, on which the portion already conceded by both parties to Russia should be indicated by one color; the region between the forty second and forty ninth degrees of latitude by another color; and the remaining portion from the fortyninth degree to the Arctic Ocean by a third color. This last would be the portion of the territory which the United States had offered to leave to England. I thought it could not be less than twice or thrice as large as the share of the United States; and though the latter would have the advantage perhaps in point of climate; the region lying for eight or ten degrees north of 49° would possess the climate of Great Britain, and would enjoy advantages for navigation quite superior to those of the region reserved to the United States, in which there was but a single port, while the shores of Quadra & Vancouver's Island and of the continent opposite to it were full of bays and inlets. Granting this to be a true state of facts, and I thought it could not be disputed, it would follow that even on the admission to its full extent of the British claim vizt. that the country is equally open to both parties, we certainly offered very equitable terms of partition. While the principle of running the fortyninth degree of latitude to the sea and leaving to each party West of the Rocky Mountains the continuation of its territory East was, in all other respects, the most natural and equitable basis of settlement.

I had on previous occasions pursued substantially this line of argument with Lord Aberdeen, and I received from him now the same answer to it as formerly, vizt. that Great Britain could not now accept terms which she had distinctly refused before; that he felt that we were under the same necessity; that he did not expect the United States to agree to what they had already rejected; and that consequently it must, he thought, be assumed as the basis of negotiation that something must be yielded on each side. To this, I replied, that though as a general principle of negotiation under such circumstances this might be admitted, it was impossible to leave out of view the substantial character of the former propositions on either side; and that in proportion as he (Lord Aberdeen) should, on reconsidering the subject, be inclined to think that the offer formerly made by the United States to continue the forty ninth parallel to the Sea was an equitable offer, and one founded on natural and reasonable principles of adjustment, he ought to be satisfied with but a moderate departure from that proposal; particularly if such a modification, without involving a great sacrifice to us, were eminently advantageous to them. In fact, such a modification was the only one which the United States could, in my opinion, be brought to agree to. The modification which I had formerly suggested, vizt. that the United States would waive their claim to the Southern extremity of Quadra & Vancouver's Island, which would be cut off by the fortyninth degree of latitude, was precisely of this kind. It could be of no great importance to us to hold the Southern extremity of an Island of which the main portion belonged to England; while the entire possession of the Island and consequently the free entrance of the straits of Fuca would be a very important object to Great Britain. I repeated what I had often observed before, that I had no authority to say that this modification would be agreed to by the United States, but that I thought it might.

Lord Aberdeen did not commit himself on the point, whether or not this proposal, if made by the government of the United States, would be accepted. He however stated (as I understood him) that he had caused a map to be colored as I suggested; that he was desirous to go as far as possible for the sake of settling the controversy; that Mr. Pakenham's original instructions were drawn up in this spirit and that since he left home, he (Lord Aberdeen) had enlarged his discretionary powers. I confess from these facts, vizt. that Lord Aberdeen does not expect us to agree to the Columbia as the boundary, not even with the addition of Port Discovery and an adjacent tract of country within the straits of Fuca (which we refused in 1826); that he has never negatived the idea of the fortyninth degree with the suggested modification; that he has uniformly said that he did not think there would be great difficulty in settling the question, and this although I have as uniformly assured him that, in my opinion, the United States would not stop short of the 49th degree except in the point above stated, I draw the inference that this proposal would in the last resort be accepted.

I am satisfied that the Ministry sincerely wish to settle the controversy, and are willing to go as far as their views of consistency and the national honor will permit to effect that object. They do not, therefore, I imagine[,] much regret the agitation of the subject in the United States, and are willing we should advance a claim to the 54° 40′. Such a course, on our part, will make it easier for them to agree to stop at 49°. While therefore it cannot be denied that the Nootka sound convention impairs the strength of our claim beyond the fortyninth degree, which rests principally on the Spanish title, I conceive it to be good policy to make the most of that title and of our own as derived from it. At the same time, if, (as I infer from the instructions to myself contained in the despatch of the late Secretary of State Nro. 62) it is proposed by the President [John Tyler] to adhere to the basis of settlement which has been hitherto uniformly tendered by the United States, vizt. the 49th degree, care must be had, not to state our right up to 54° 40[′] so strongly, as to put ourselves in the wrong in receding from it. Fortunately the facts of the case are in harmony with the course which prudence dictates. Spain had not a perfect, but she had a respectable title to an indefinite extent of coast, founded on discovery & partial occupation. This title was somewhat weakened by non-user [*sic*], by the insignificant character of the occupation, and seriously shaken by the Nootka sound convention. That convention it is true, is of doubtful interpretation, and we deny that it had more than a temporary object. But we cannot expect to compel the opposite party to accept our interpretation. We gave up, without a struggle, to Russia a very large territory, to which our title was as good as to any other part of the coast north of the 49th degree, & the same motives which justified that arrangement, would fully warrant the present administration, in adhering to terms twice offered by Mr. [James] Monroe and once by his successor [John Quincy Adams]. I am, sir, with great respect your obedient servant, Edward Everett.

P.S. I transmit a copy of a pamphlet entitled "claims to the Oregon Territory considered by Adam Thom Esq[ui]r[e], recorder of Rupert's Island." It displays but moderate ability, and has no pretensions to the character of an impartial view of the subject. This opinion of it I expressed to Lord Aberdeen, in the course of my interview on the 16th instant. He had not read it.

LS (No. 106, Confidential) in DNA, RG 59 (State Department), Diplomatic Despatches, Great Britain, vol. 52 (M-30:48), received 4/24; FC in MHi, Edward Everett Papers, 48:398–405 (published microfilm, reel 22, frames 1245–1248). NOTE: This despatch was addressed to John Nelson as Secretary of State ad interim.

From FRANKLIN GAGE

Consulate of the United States of America
Cardenas [Cuba], 1st April 1844
Sir, An alarming & extensive Servile Insurrection has just been discovered in this neighbourhood & many persons have been implicated both Black & White. Several Foreigners and among others some American Citizens have been arrested & placed in close confinement merely on the Single accusation & extorted confession of the Slave.

I desire to ask the Department for early & definite instructions as to the course to be pursued in regard to our Citizens who are at the mercy of the local Government & whose arbitrary power is extended alike over the Black & White.

Those who have been thus far arrested are Engineers and Mechanics employed on the Plantations, & we have every reason to believe them entirely innocent of any intention to infringe the laws of the Island.

The most trifling conversation at the present Crisis, or the least suspicious act is sufficient to send one to prison. American & other Citizens when called upon as *Evidence* merely are bound with cords & indignantly treated without regard to their character or the country from whence they come. They are placed in Stocks & allowed no assistance from their Countrymen or the consolations or sympathies of their friends.

I am well aware that the U.S. Government affords no protection to any of its Citizens who may be guilty of any infraction of the laws of the Country in which they reside, but I have yet to learn whether it will suffer them to be disgraced and punished until they are proven guilty.

Trusting to the Department for early instructions on this Subject I have the honor to be with great Consideration Your mo[st] ob[edien]t Serv[an]t, Franklin Gage.

ALS (No. 5, Duplicate) in DNA, RG 59 (State Department), Consular Despatches, Cardenas, vol. 20 (T-583:1), received 4/25. NOTE: Gage was a native of Maine and a physician and was already a resident of Cardenas when he was appointed Consul by John Tyler in 1/1843.

From Samuel L. Harris, Washington, 4/1. Harris is agent for the State of Maine "to present to the General Government, for liquidation, the claims of that State for expenses incurred in the protection of her northeastern frontier, the reimbursement of which was made one of the conditions of the treaty of Washington . . . ." Accounts and vouchers are now in preparation for submission showing expenses of *ca.* $85,000 in excess of the $206,934.79 appropriated by Congress in 1843. So that these claims can be finally settled during the present session of Congress, he requests the Department of State to prepare and communicate to Congress "an estimate of the amount of the appropriation required." PC in House Document No. 242, 28th Cong., 1st Sess., pp. 2–3.

From Paul K. Hubbs, New York [City], 4/1. Hubbs congratulates both the country and Calhoun on his appointment as Secretary of State. He requests a passport and, if possible, an appointment as bearer of dispatches to Europe for "my partner in commerce," John Buzby. "Since I had the pleasure of passing part of an Evening last winter with you in Company with Mr. [Dixon H.] Lewis and Mr. Gen. [George M.] Keim, I have established a commercial house" in New York City. ALS in DNA, RG 59 (State Department), Passport Applications, vol. 30, no. 1942 (M-1372:14).

From W[illia]m Mayhew

Consulate of the United States of America
Bay of Islands New Zealand, April 1st 1844
Sir, I have the honor to inform you of the departure hence of J[ohn] B. Williams Esq. Consul on February 17th last for the United States and that on my arrival here from New South Wales in March last I found that he had appointed me Vice Consul and Mr. H[enry] G. Smith to act during my absence, and I learn also that it is not his intention to return here.

Deeming it necessary that the duties of the Office be fulfilled, I have acted as Vice Consul but as my sojourn here is very uncertain,

I shall on my departure hand the Seals and Archives to Mr. Henry Green Smith an American Citizen who purposes to reside here for some years and whom I have the honor to recommend for the appointment of Consul.

I have also to inform you that, application having been made from this Consulate, the Governor of this Colony has been pleased to permit American Whale Ships to land their Cargoes of Oil in the Ports of New Zealand for exportation either to England or the United States, thereby giving the Ships an opportunity of refitting here without the delay or expence of returning to the United States. I have the Honor to be Sir Your most Obedient Servant, Wm. Mayhew.

ALS in DNA, RG 59 (State Department), Consular Despatches, Bay of Islands and Auckland, vol. 1 (T-49:1), received 7/25. NOTE: A State Dept. Clerk's EU referring to the last paragraph, reads "Published in the Madisonian."

From A[lphonse] Pageot, [French Minister to the U.S.], 4/1. He acknowledges today's circular announcing Calhoun's appointment as Secretary of State and assures Calhoun of his high consideration. LS (in French) in DNA, RG 59 (State Department), Notes from Foreign Legations, France, vol. 12 (M-53:8, frames 696–697).

From GEO[RGE] W. SLACUM

Consulate of the United States
Rio de Janeiro, 1 April 1844

Sir, I have the honor to transmit herewith, duplicate Deposition in the [illegal slave trading] case of Cornelius F. Driscoll, late Master of the Brig "Hope"; duplicate Despatch No. 74—and Copy of my letter to the [U.S.] Marshal for the New York district.

I would here observe, that the Deponents of their own accord, gave the information upon which the Deposition is founded; and I would hope that no unnecessary restrictions may be put upon them. They have had liberty on shore frequently, and are quite willing to appear as Witnesses in behalf of the United States. I have the honor to be Sir Your most obed[ien]t Serv[an]t, Geo. W. Slacum, Consul U.S.A.

LS (No. 75) with En in DNA, RG 59 (State Department), Consular Despatches, Rio de Janeiro, vol. 7 (T-172:8), received 5/30; PC with En in House Document No. 43, 29th Cong., 1st Sess., pp. 28–29. NOTE: Slacum enclosed a copy of his letter of 4/1/1844 to the U.S. Marshal at New York City requesting him to receive custody of Joseph Carroll, David Henderson, James Lewis, and Abrah Post from Capt. [B.] Cooper of the *Columbus*. The seamen are to be kept in "safe custody" until the Marshal receives further information from Washington. Slacum addressed this despatch to Abel P. Upshur.

From W. W. T. SMITH

Consulate of the U.S., Port La Vaca
Matagorda Bay Texas, April 1st 1844
Hon. Sir, The last Congress of the republic of Texas enacted a law laying a Tonnage duty of one dollar per ton on all vessels entering her ports belonging to nations between whom and her no treaty exists. Believing that this law will bear very heavily on our commerce with this country I call your attention to the subject. Hon. Sir I am very respectfully your obedient servant, W.W.T. Smith, U.S. Consul.

ALS (No. 9) in DNA, RG 59 (State Department), Consular Despatches, Texas, vol. 1 (T-153:1), received 10/21. NOTE: This despatch was addressed to A[bel] P. Upshur.

From ISAAC VAN ZANDT

Legation of Texas
Washington, D.C., April 1st 1844
The Undersigned chargé d'Affaires of the Republic of Texas has the honor to announce to Mr. Calhoun[,] Secretary of State of the United States, the arrival in this City of Gen[era]l J. Pin[c]kney Henderson, who has been appointed by the President of Texas [Samuel Houston] a "Special Agent" to act in conjunction with the Undersigned in the conclusion of a treaty of annexation, in pursuance of the negotiations heretofore commenced betwe[e]n the late Secretary of State Mr. [Abel P.] Upshur and the Undersigned.

The Undersigned requests to be informed at what time it will be convenient for Mr. Calhoun to receive him for the purpose of presenting his colleague, that he may deliver his letter of credence.

The Undersigned avails himself of this occasion to offer to Mr.

Calhoun assurances of his very distinguished consideration. Isaac Van Zandt.

ALS in DNA, RG 59 (State Department), Notes from Foreign Legations, Texas, vol. 1 (T-809:1); FC in Tx, Records of the Texas Republic Department of State, Letters and Dispatches Sent by the Texas Legation in Washington, 1:481–482; FC in Tx, Records of the Texas Republic Department of State, Copybooks of Letters Received from Texan and Foreign Representatives, vol. 2-1/98, p. 492; CC in Tx, Records of the Texas Republic Department of State, U.S. Diplomatic Correspondence.

From [Levi Woodbury, Senator from N.H.], 4/1. Woodbury encloses a letter to himself dated 3/20 from [Jeremiah] O'Brien, who requests Woodbury's support in application for a Clerkship. Woodbury would be pleased to "see Mr. O'Brien succeed in his wishes." ALU with En in DNA, RG 59 (State Department), Applications and Recommendations, 1837–1845, O'Brien (M-687:24, frames 366–369).

From [the Count de] Zabielo, [Russian Chargé d'Affaires in the U.S.], 4/1. He acknowledges today's circular announcing Calhoun's appointment as Secretary of State. ALS (in French) in DNA, RG 59 (State Department), Notes from Foreign Legations, Russia, vol. 3 (M-39:2).

From J[uan] N. Almonte, [Mexican Minister to the U.S.], 4/2. He acknowledges the circular announcing the appointment of Calhoun as Secretary of State and in the future will address his official correspondence to Calhoun. LS (in Spanish) in DNA, RG 59 (State Department), Notes from Foreign Legations, Mexico, vol. 4 (M-54:2).

From Fidericio Bourman, [Spanish Chargé d'Affaires in the U.S.], 4/2. He acknowledges the circular of 4/1 announcing Calhoun's appointment, is ready to correspond with Calhoun about official business, and offers his respects. LS (in Spanish) and translation in DNA, RG 59 (State Department), Notes from Foreign Legations, Spain, vol. 11 (M-59:13, frames [964–966]).

From Charles Gould, New York [City], 4/2. Gould recommends that Joseph R. Curtiss be appointed the U.S. Consul at Marseilles in place of the incumbent, [D.C.] Croxall. Croxall, Gould contends, "does not sustain a reputable position." ALS in DNA, RG 59 (State Department), Applications and Recommendations, 1837–1845, Curtiss (M-687:7, frames 303–304).

From WASHINGTON IRVING

Legation of the United States
Madrid, April 2nd 1844

Sir, It was some time after the date of my last despatch, before the hurried state of the Spanish Cabinet incident to the return of the Queen Mother, permitted me to have an interview with Mr. Gonzalez Bravo, Minister of State. When I had such opportunity I took occasion, according to my instructions from the Department, to express in the strongest terms the high estimation of the government of the United States for the public and private character of the Chevalier [P.A.] D'Argaiz, and the regret with which the president [John Tyler] had received the letters of his recall; And in eulogizing the vigilance and ability with which the Chevalier had availed himself of the favorable interests of the United States, I alluded especially—as I was instructed—to his conduct on a recent occasion with regard to the island of Cuba.

And here, I cannot but notice how illy I was prepared by the Department to discuss this delicate point. I was instructed to dwell strongly on the eminent services rendered to his Country by the Chevalier; "especially on a recent occasion when this government had an opportunity of manifesting the sincerity of its friendship for Her Catholic Majesty, with reference to the Island of Cuba; not without some sacrifice on its part, which the importance of the crisis seemed to demand." Now with respect to all this important and delicate transaction, thus vaguely alluded to, this legation has hitherto been left by the department completely in the dark; and all that it knows respecting the application of the Chevalier to our Government for assistance and the consequent manifestations of friendship on our part, was communicated by *a member of the French legation at Madrid.*

In reply to my observations, Mr. G. Bravo, after admitting the general good character and good conduct of the Chevalier D'Argaiz, observed that, in the affair of Cuba, that gentleman had acted without especial, and quite beyond the limits of his general instructions. That he had been precipitate and indiscreet, and had unnecessarily run the risk of compromising his government with the government of another nation; his application to the government of the United States having become known in the Island and having filled it with rumors of armed intervention on our part, and awakened the jealousy of the British Consul.

As I have observed, the vagueness of my information on this topic left me at a disadvantage in discussing it; I however made the best defence of the conduct of the Chevalier that my materials permitted, and dwelt on the unequivocal manifestations of active and effective friendship on the part of the government of the United States which his application had called forth, and which, I observed, ought to be highly satisfactory to Her Majesty's Government, as well as conducive to the tranquility of the Island.

Mr. Gonzalez Bravo made very full acknowledgements on this head, and assured me that the government was perfectly satisfied of the patriotism and good intentions of the Chevalier D'Argaiz and would give him convincing proofs to that effect on his return home.

From the course of my conversation with Mr. Gonzalez Bravo on this, and on a former occasion and from all that I have been able to collect elsewhere, I am satisfied there is no ground for "uneasiness" or "suspicion" as to any sinister influence of England in the recall of the chevalier D'Argaiz. I apprehend that it has been contemplated ever since the downfall of [Baldomero] Espartero, of whom he was considered a partizan; and was a part of the general turning out of the office holders under the regency, to provide for adherents to the dominant party; and I think it highly probable that he would have been recalled, had the affair of Cuba not occurred.

I repeat what I expressed in my last despatch, that I am satisfied nothing is to be apprehended in this quarter at present, from any machinations of England with regard to the island of Cuba. I do not apprehend any pecuniary pressure that would induce this government to concede to her a control over that Island: Indeed, any measure of the kind would be one of the most unpopular expedients the government could adopt, both from the jealousy of the public with regard to English interference of all kinds, and from the sensitive pride of the Spaniards respecting the few but precious relics left of their once splendid American domains.

With respect to the case of Mr. Maximo de Aguirre, our Consul at Bilbao, I find there is no need of any further application in his favor, as I learn from him, that, by an order of the Spanish government, the whole of the fines extorted at Bilbao by Generals Alcala and Zurbano, are to be refunded in monthly payments out of the revenue of the custom house of that city.

I have had a tedious correspondence with Mr. Aguirre, having had to explain to him, what had repeatedly been explained to him before, the peculiarities of his case as a Spanish subject officiating as a foreign consul; and proving to him that, in all respects where his consular privileges had been interfered with, Mr. [Aaron] Vail had promptly and effectually remonstrated in his *official* capacity; but had properly made only *informal* representations where the circumstances of the case concerned the allegiance of Mr. Aguirre to the Spanish government.

Mr. Aguirre is at length brought to unwilling conviction on this head; but, finding the privileges and immunities of the consulship so short of his original conception, expresses his wish to resign the post, observing "that the United States offer no encouragement to consuls thus placed to display much zeal in their service." He adds however that he will continue his official assistance to Masters and Mariners until the American government finds opportunity to appoint a more Suitable servant in his place; but intimates an intention to persevere in a course which he has observed ever since the indignities he experienced in his consular character in 1841; viz, "to decline all invitations to public ceremonies; and to cease the visits and courtesies to military and superior authorities in company with the consuls of England, France, Holland & Belgium."

I trust the government may be able to find a successor to Mr. Aguirre willing to fulfil these more important duties of his office. I cannot but observe, however, the swelling ideas which foreign functionaries of this class are apt to entertain; and how difficult it is to make them understand that after all, a consul is but a mortal man, and subject to mortal laws.

Since my last notice of public affairs, the Queen Mother [Maria Christina] has arrived and taken up her residence in the Royal palace. It was apprehended that her return would produce great changes in the Cabinet; and the Capital has of late days been full of rumors to that effect; but, I understand she expresses herself satisfied with the conduct of the present Ministers, and well disposed to give them time to carry out their plan of policy. The latter have certainly acted with unwonted energy and hardihood, and aided by martial law, have carried into operation measures which less daring and more scrupulous statesmen would not have ventured to propose: They have altered the law of Ayuntamientos, or municipalities, disarmed the militia, reorganized the army; formed a civil guard similar to the gendarmerie of France; effected great financial contracts, and are now contemplating, it is said, the formation of a royal body guard of ten thousand men, similar to that disbanded by Espartero; the establishment of a censorship of the press; and the convocation of "Cortes constituyentes" for the modification of the Constitution!

The insurrections of Alicant and Carthagena are at an end, and Boné and many of his fellow insurgents have paid for their treason with their lives; still, martial law continues and will probably be kept up until the Ministers have carried all their bold schemes into operation. There has lately been a sudden talk of a war with Marocco to avenge the death of a Spanish Consular Agent: The Ministerial papers were for a time vehement and voluminous on the subject, though it did not appear that they had clearly ascertained the circumstances of the case, or the gravity of the offense. It is thought the Ministry were glad of something to occupy the public mind, and to find distant occupation for dangerous spirits of the army; who were growing factious in idleness. France, it is said, encourages this martial project; as it would favor her African enterprize; and prevent a more dangerous European neighbour on the Barbary Coast. The french papers have even talked of the policy of giving the Spaniards military aid in this new Crusade; pretending to feel aggrieved by the death of the Spanish Consul; he having been by birth a French Man.

This war talk, however, though furious for a time, has rather cooled for some days past; there being doubts of the safety of detaching a large military force to a distance, under the command of ambitious officers; lest it might produce another military revolution. I am Sir very respectfully Your Ob[edien]t Serv[an]t, Washington Irving.

LS (No. 38) in DNA, RG 59 (State Department), Diplomatic Despatches, Spain, vol. 34 (M-31:34), received 5/22; LS in DNA, RG 84 (Foreign Posts), Spain, Despatches, 2:58–63; PC in Ralph M. Aderman et al., eds., *Letters of Washington Irving*, 3:713–716.

From W[ILLIAM] W. IRWIN

Legation of the United States
Copenhagen, 2 April 1844

Sir; Last month, an article appeared in the "Times" a journal published at Cologne, intimating the immediate design of our government to resist the further payment of the "Sound Dues" by the employment even of force if necessary, and to send, with that intent, a formidable fleet as a Convoy for the American Merchant Vessels now preparing to sail for the Baltic.

The fact that a rigid censorship is established over the press throughout Prussia, and the impression that such an article could not have appeared in the Cologne paper, without the knowledge at least, if not the sanction of that government, connected with the dissatisfaction supposed to exist both in Prussia and the United States, with regard to this exaction, have given rise to much conversation, in the diplomatic circle at this court, although no one professes to give any credence to the story. The publicity, however, given to the statement by the Danish provincial papers, and its appearance in the Hamburg "Börsen-Halle" of the 19th ultimo have so annoyed the Danish government as to call forth a formal contradiction. This contradiction appears in the "Berlingske-Tidende" (the official Government journal, printed at Copenhagen) of the 28th ultimo, a translation of which, and of the article in the Hamburg paper is herewith annexed. It will be observed that the Danish paper cites an extract which it alleges is from an official communication of Mr. [Daniel] Webster of the 27th June 1842, in which he expresses his satisfaction at the arrangement made in the Tariff of 1841 relative to the Sound Dues. Never having seen Mr. Webster's communication, I cannot vouch for the fidelity of the translation into the Danish language. The re-translation of the paragraph from the Danish into English will probably alter its original phraseology, and may somewhat impair its true meaning.

I will further observe that no remark has been made to me, in reference to this matter, by any person in authority, although I have quite recently conversed with his Danish Majesty's Minister of Foreign Affairs. Of course, I did not deem it proper to introduce the subject. I have the honor to be Sir, very respectfully Your obedient servant, W.W. Irwin.

LS (No. 21) with Ens in DNA, RG 59 (State Department), Diplomatic Despatches, Denmark, vol. 3 (M-41:5), received 5/20; FC with Ens in DNA, RG 84 (Foreign Posts), Denmark, Despatches, vol. 1843–1847:117–[123a]. NOTE: Irwin was a former Representative from Pa. who had been appointed Chargé d'Affaires to Denmark by John Tyler in 3/1843.

From [Gaspar José] de Lisboa, [Brazilian Minister to the U.S.], 4/2. He acknowledges the circular of 4/1 announcing Calhoun's appointment as Secretary of State. ALS (in French) in DNA, RG 59 (State Department), Notes from Foreign Legations, Brazil, vol. 2 (M-49:2).

From R[ichard] Pakenham, [British Minister to the U.S.], 4/2. He acknowledges receipt of the circular announcing Calhoun's appointment. "The undersigned feels great pleasure in thus finding Himself placed in Official Relation with Mr. Calhoun, and He takes advantage of this opportunity to offer Mr. Calhoun the assurance of

His high consideration." LS in DNA, RG 59 (State Department), Notes from Foreign Legations, Great Britain, vol. 22 (M-50:22).

From FRANCIS W. SCOTT and Others

Caroline County Virginia, April 2, 1844

Dear Sir, The undersigned have been appointed a committee by the Caroline Democratic Association to invite you to a public dinner to be given on Thursday the 18th inst[ant] to our late Representative the Hon. R[obert] M.T. Hunter at the Golansvill[e] precinct in this County about four miles from Chesterfeild Depot on the R[ichmond,] F[redericksburg] & Potomac Rail Road. The Association earnestly hopes that it may suit your pleasure & conveniance to partake with them the festivities on that occasion and we take great pleasure in conveying to you their hearty and cordial invitation. Permit us to add our own individual desire that you will favor us with your company on that day, and accept the assurance of our best wishes for your health and happiness. Very Respectfully Y[ou]r most ob[edien]t S[er]v[an]ts, Francis W. Scott, James B. Thornton, James D. Coleman, James Chapman, Samuel C. Scott, Fred[erick] W. Coleman, Thomas L. Scott, William P. Taylor, George Fitzhugh.

N.B. Conveyances will be at the Chesterfeild Depot to carray such Gentlemen as may come on the [railroad] Cars to the Dinner. Those coming from the North can come down to the Junction House 7 miles below where ample accommodations can be had and return to C[hester]field Depot next morning.

LS in ScCleA.

From T[homas] L. Smith, [Register of the U.S. Treasury], 4/2. "Thinking that it might be agreeable to you to see our revenue prospects, I have the honor to send you the above statement. The receipts in this quarter will be more than $8,000,000." Smith appended a table showing customs receipts at various U.S. ports in the first quarter of 1844. ALS in DNA, RG 59 (State Department), Miscellaneous Letters (M-179:104, frame 129).

From Antonio de Aycinena, Washington, 4/3. He requests recognition by the U.S. as Consul General for Guatemala and encloses his commission and a letter from his government. LS with En in DNA,

RG 59 (State Department), Notes from Foreign Legations, Central America, vol. 2 (T-34:2).

From Steen Bille, [Danish Chargé d'Affaires in the U.S.], 4/3. He acknowledges the circular of 4/1 and congratulates Calhoun on "the universal approbation, with which his appointment has been hailed by the whole country." LS in DNA, RG 59 (State Department), Notes from Foreign Legations, Denmark, vol. 2 (M-52:2, frames 92–93).

From Henry Dammers, New York [City], 4/3. Dammers inquires if there is a vacancy in the State Department for a translator and presents his qualifications for such a post. He congratulates Calhoun on having been appointed, as he richly deserved to be, Secretary of State. ALS in DNA, RG 59 (State Department), Applications and Recommendations, 1837–1845, Dammers (M-687:8, frames 62–64).

From CH[ARLES] AUG[USTU]S DAVIS

New York [City,] 3 Ap[ril] 1844
My D[ea]r Sir, I venture to wait on you in this form with renew'd assurances of my high regard & esteem—but not to impose on your valuable time (occupied as you must be) than merely to ask your acceptance of these assurances.

I was unfortunately present at that appalling scene on board the Princeton, but escaped with only a slight injury on the lip and a hole in my hat and my head somewhat disturbed by the concussion—and returned home the next day with melancholy feelings. I almost began to think that amid the conflict of parties and threatened convulsions that this was only the beginning of a *blow up*—and that it would be follow'd by others. And I found the most of our citizens here indulging in awful forbodings—stock falling—and people looking confounded.

But in a few days a new and cheering light broke in upon us. Your nomination and unanimous confirmation was rec[eive]d here with one spontaneous approval. And so striking was this that I could not refrain from addressing a Letter to the President [John Tyler] and so stating it to him—not doubting that it w[oul]d gratify him. And I always like to communicate agre[e]able intel[l]igence.

The fact is there is only one point on which any number of our people North & East differ with you in opinion—and on this of late many of them begin to think you are more than half right & they more than half wrong so I suppose in good time public sentiment (guided by public practical intel[l]igence) will settle down on a line satisfactory to all parties. I allude ["to" *interlined*] the *Tariff*—which has heretofore been regarded as *the only means* of developing and advancing home industry. They begin to find now by late investigation that a Tariff alone had been and would continue to be a most *oppressive nul[l]ity*—if it had not been for the introduction of a system of artificial channels of intercourse at home—developing our sources of production and cheapening the cost of transit from points of production to points of consumption. This is clearly shown in a warm controversy now going on between the Ultra Tarif[f]ites and the *Rail road interest* which latter finds itself tax'd by a duty of $2,000 p[e]r mile on an article our Iron makers can't make yet and need not so long as they are unable to supply the home demand for all other kind[s] of Iron. And it is shown now that instead of "a Tariff for protection" being *primary*—and internal channels of intercourse being *secondary*—it is exactly the reverse—and as a proof [of] it—it is demonstrable that if our present roads & canals (tho' only begun as it were) were removed every mine of coal & Iron w[oul]d close and every factory and Water fall cease their labor. Even if we had a Tariff higher than the present—it w[oul]d fail to accomplish its design of *protection* to the leading branches of labor against the diminish'd prices of Europe.

It is an important feature—tho' not new to you—yet it strikes many minds here with conviction that[,] 1st. without cheap transit at home no *source of production* at home can be developed and unless developed—may as well be on the moon. 2nd. That a Tariff *alone* did not and never could accomplish this.

But I will not trouble you further than to repeat my thanks that you were induced to sacrifice the quiet enjoyments at home to the labor and anxieties of public duties at Washington—and to assure you of my profound respect[,] esteem & regard, Ch: Augs. Davis.

ALS in ScCleA; PC in Boucher and Brooks, eds., *Correspondence*, pp. 218–219.

From EDWARD EVERETT

London, 3 ["March" *canceled and* "April" *interlined*], 1844
Sir, Passing by the Foreign Office at a late hour yesterday afternoon, I called without appointment on Lord Aberdeen. In the course of our conversation some remarks fell from him, which I think it my duty to report to you. In reference to the convention negotiated by Mr. [Henry] Wheaton with the German Zoll verein, (of which Lord Aberdeen had received information, and which was brought by Mr. [Theodore S.] Fay from Berlin and left at my office yesterday), Lord Aberdeen asked what was to be its effect on the commercial relations of Great Britain and the United States. I told him we should be glad to admit British manufactures on as favorable terms as German; but of course on the same conditions. He said he conceived that by the Convention of July 1815 we should be bound to admit British fabrics on paying the same duties as German, without any such condition on their part. By that Convention, he continued, the two Governments have reciprocally stipulated, in unqualified terms, that no higher duties shall be imposed on articles imported from either country into the other than are imposed on the same articles from any other country. In concluding this Convention, unless you intend at the same time to put an end to that of 1815 between the United States and Great Britain, you violate this stipulation, and do what you charge us with doing in reference to the admission of Rough Rice free of duty from Africa.

I, of course, denied the similarity of the cases; and urged that the reduction of duties on certain articles of German manufacture was not a matter of favor but a mere exchange of equivalents, which we were ready to make with any other power: that if we made the reduction for Great Britain without the equivalents, we should place them not on the footing of the most favored nations which we were bound to do, but on a footing of greater favor than any other nation, which we could not do, without giving other nations ground of complaint.

He said they had, in some of their Commercial Conventions, introduced a clause to warrant such special arrangements to be made with other powers, but there was no reservation of the kind in the convention between the United States and Great Britain of July 1815; and in conversing with Mr. [William E.] Gladstone on the subject he said, that he too was under the impression, that the United States must intend, in concluding the treaty with the Zollverein, to announce the purpose of putting an end to the Convention with Great Britain.

I told him we had made a similar special agreement with France in 1832, and that the right to do so was so plain to my mind, that I felt some surprize at hearing it questioned. He said that their understanding to the contrary was so clear, that in their Cabinet conferences on the subject of a convention with Brazil, they had always taken it for granted, that on whatever terms Brazilian Sugar was admitted into Great Britain, the Sugar of Louisiana must be admitted on the same terms; although they were aware that, in the ordinary course of trade, Sugar was not exported from the United States.

Although I felt myself authorized, by the manner in which this subject is alluded to in the report to the President [John Tyler], by the late Secretary of State [Abel P. Upshur] of 24th November 1843, in advancing the general views above intimated, I did not of course feel myself called upon to pursue this discussion, into which we had fallen unexpectedly on both sides. Should it appear to me, on reflection, that such a step would be beneficial, I may address a note to Lord Aberdeen on the construction which he seems disposed to place on the Convention of July 1815; the principle of which was raised and thoroughly discussed between France and the United States as far back as 1817. I am, Sir, with great respect, Your obedient Servant, Edward Everett.

LS (No. 109) in DNA, RG 59 (State Department), Diplomatic Despatches, Great Britain, vol. 52 (M-30:48), received 4/24; FC in MHi, Edward Everett Papers, 48:415–419 (published microfilm, reel 22, frames 1253–1255). NOTE: This despatch was addressed to John Nelson as Secretary of State ad interim. This dateline was corrected by someone other than the writer of the despatch.

From [J.C.] de Figaniere e Morão, [Portuguese Minister to the U.S.], 4/3. He states the long-standing objection of Portugal to the imposition of ad valorem duties on the wines of that country imported into the U.S. and claims a refund of excess duties on the ground that they conflict with a U.S.-Portuguese treaty ratified in 1841. Past efforts to settle this claim have resulted in a bill (No. 118) before the House of Representatives to carry the treaty into effect and to refund excess duties charged heretofore. De Figaniere e Morão asks Calhoun's help in the effort to end the unjust duties so long charged on Portuguese wines. ALS in DNA, RG 59 (State Department), Notes from Foreign Legations, Portugal, vol. 3 (M-57:3, frames 514–517); CC in DNA, RG 233 (U.S. House of Representatives), 28A-F1; PC in House Document No. 224, 28th Cong., 1st Sess., pp. 1–3.

From Robert Grieve, [U.S. Consul], Leith, [Scotland], 4/3. He acknowledges a copy of a bill of 2/21/1844 to remodel the Consular establishment. One provision of the bill states that "no person shall be appointed Consul, Vice-Consul, or Commercial Agent who is not a citizen of the United States." Having served as U.S. Consul for many years and being almost 84 years old, Grieve asks that this provision not be applied to him. ALS (No. 99) in DNA, RG 59 (State Department), Consular Despatches, Leith, vol. 2 (T-396:2), received 5/8.

From C[OLIN] M. INGERSOLL, "Private"

New Haven, Ap[ri]l 3d 1844
Dear Sir, You have doubtless heard the result of the recent election in this State and perhaps, knowing as you did the conduct of Mr[. Martin] V[an] Buren[']s friends in our State convention, it was such as you anticipated. Our defeat cannot be ascribed to the apathy of your more prominent friends in Connecticut, for never have they done their duty more faithfully than during the campaign which we have just come out of, but in a great measure to the want of that enthusiasm throughout the State which the nomination of our Middletown Convention failed to inspire. For the past five weeks I have been traversing this and the adjoining counties and addressing our friends. I had an opportunity of knowing something of the feeling which pervaded the State, and I found many a warm hearted man supposed by the "wire pullers" to be strong for the *restoration*, actually condemn the nomination of our Convention, they try however to keep cool and are in fact the most radical and determined Democrats we have. The vote of the State shows, as any one will perceive who will examine it, that where we have proclaimed our choice for President to be another than Mr[.] V[an] Buren, the Democracy have done well. New Haven County which went nearly unanimous for yourself in the Convention shows a good vote, while Hartford Co. from whence the order for the Nom[inatio]n of Mr[.] V[an] Buren went forth to our convention, has fallen in the rear. The city of N[ew] Haven has increased her Dem[ocratic] vote about 150 from last year, and Hartford where the leaders, whose pet Mr[.] V[an] Buren is, reside, has not come up to her vote of last year! Another circumstance might also be mentioned; notwithstanding the Federal-

ists previous to the election had raised the cry of "Free trade and direct taxation," and appealed to the manufacturing towns to sustain the present tarriff [*sic*], the result of the election shows that the manufacturing towns have done as well as the farming towns, and in some instances better. Our opponents [the Whigs] had the aid of about one half I should think of the Abolitionists in the recent election. I never knew them so active and unscrupulous in their means before, money was poured out like water, and many instances of open bribery have come to my knowledge recently. Their victory however is not a great one, their Governor [Roger S. Baldwin?] probably falls short of an election by the people and they have both branches of the Legislature who will elect the Governor. Had our friends been united we should have secured the Legislature. So small are most of the federal majorities, that I have no doubt two hundred votes properly distributed would give us the Legislature and as a consequence State offices and an U.S. Senator.

With a candidate for the Pres[idenc]y who carried with his name a degree of popular enthusiasm I think we might carry the State at the fall election. With Mr[.] V[an] Buren[']s name we can do nothing. I do hope that the Nat[iona]l Convention will yet look to the interests of the people rather than to the interests of mere party leaders. I have the honor to remain Truly Y[ou]rs, C.M. Ingersoll.

PC in Jameson, ed., *Correspondence*, pp. 944–945.

To J[ames] I. McKay, [Representative from N.C. and] Chairman of the House Committee on Ways and Means, 4/3. "I have the honor to transmit to you, to be laid before the Committee, copies of letters [of 4/1] from the Senators and Representatives of the State of Maine, and Mr. Sam[ue]l [L.] Harris, Agent of that State, in relation to the necessity of a further appropriation to satisfy the claims" under the Treaty with Great Britain of 1842. LS in DNA, RG 59 (State Department), Accounting Records, Miscellaneous Letters Sent, 1832–1916, vol. for 2/1–9/30/1844, p. [84]; PC with Ens in House Document No. 242, 28th Cong., 1st Sess., pp. 2–3.

To D[aniel] Raymond, Cincin[n]ati, 4/3. Calhoun acknowledges Raymond's letter of 3/29 [*The Papers of John C. Calhoun*, 17:904–905]. The President [John Tyler] does not "encourage the appointment of foreign Consuls to reside in the inland cities" of the U.S. Therefore, Raymond's request [that the U.S. indicate to Bavaria that the appointment of Michael Dumbroff as its Consul in the U.S. northwestern States would be agreeable] cannot be granted. FC in DNA, RG 59 (State Department), Domestic Letters, 34:120 (M-40:32).

To Robert Semple, Alton, Ill., 4/3. Calhoun acknowledges Semple's letter of 3/22 [*The Papers of John C. Calhoun,* 17:883] and replies that "should a vacancy occur in any of the [South American] consulates ... your application will receive respectful consideration." FC in DNA, RG 59 (State Department), Domestic Letters, 34:120 (M-40:32).

From Ch[arles] Serruys, [Belgian Chargé d'Affaires in the U.S.], 4/3. He acknowledges the announcement of Calhoun's assuming the office of Secretary of State and congratulates the U.S. "more than Mr. Calhoun himself upon the appointment." ALS in DNA, RG 59 (State Department), Notes from Foreign Legations, Belgium, vol. 1 (M-194:1).

To J[OHN] C. SPENCER, Secretary of the Treasury

Department of State
Washington, 3d April 1844

Sir, I have had the honor to receive your note of the 30th Ultimo, in which you enquire "whether any change should be made in the estimate of the expenditure under the direction of the Department of State during the present fiscal year, which was furnished, and laid before the House of Representatives at the commencement [in 12/-1843] of the present session of Congress."

I have the honor to inform you that appropriations for Outfits will be required, in addition to those embraced in the estimate referred to, for Ministers to Mexico and Brazil, and for Chargés d Affaires to Sardinia and Chile, amounting to $27,000. Also, that the item in the estimate for the "salaries of the Commissioner [Albert Smith] and clerk appointed to mark the [northeastern] boundary line between the United States and Great Britain, and for other expenses of the Commission, including the purchase and repair of instruments, wages of persons employed and other contingencies," will require to be increased from $15,000 to $43,000, being amount to defray arrearages on the last season's operations, $8,000[;] To carry on the work the ensuing season, [$]35,000. I have the honor to be, Sir, Your obedient servant, J.C. Calhoun.

LS in DNA, RG 56 (Treasury Department), Letters Received from Executive Officers, Series AB, 1844, No. 13; FC in DNA, RG 59 (State Department), Accounting Records, Miscellaneous Letters Sent, 1832–1916, vol. for 2/1–9/30/-1844, pp. [86]–87; PC in House Document No. 242, 28th Cong., 1st Sess., pp. 3–4.

From [Isaac Van Zandt and J. Pinckney Henderson]

[Washington, April *ca.* 3, 1844]

The undersigned &c &c beg leave to remind Mr. Calhoun Sec[retar]y of State of the U.S. that they are fully empowered by the Government of Texas to enter into a Treaty annexing Texas to the Government of the U.S. and request Mr. Calhoun to inform them whether he is authorized and prepared on the part of the Government of the U.S. to take up the subject and if so they request Mr. Calhoun to inform them at what time they can have the honor to see him in conference on the subject. The undersigned also beg leave to assure Mr. Calhoun that it is the wish of the President of Texas [Samuel Houston] and every department of their Government to annex Texas to the Govt. of the U.S. and that the people of Texas by almost an unanimous vote at the time of the ratification of their Constitution expressed their wish to accomplish this great object and the undersigned can assure Mr. Calhoun that no changes has [*sic*] since taken place in Texas adverse to that expression of the opinion of the People of Texas. The undersigned &c &c.

Transcript in TxU, Isaac Van Zandt Papers, vol. II.

From John Carroll Walsh

The Mound, Harford Co[unty] Md., 3d April 1844

My dear Sir, Enclosed their [*sic*] is a communication addressed to the President [John Tyler], which I would be pleased for you to lay before him, and at the same time say a kind word in favor of the petition. It would take a long letter to give you an entire account of my nephew's case, one which I could not think of asking you to take the time to peruse, knowing how little time you will now have to devote to such matters.

A few days since I received a letter from our mutual and respected friend Judge [Richard M.] Young of Illinois, in answer to one I had occasion to address him, in which I expressed my mind freely in regard to the Presidential question. An extract from the letter of the Judge I cannot refrain from making. He says, "I think with you that no man living would fill the office of Chief Magistrate with so much ability, honesty of purpose, and true gentlemanly dignity as Mr. Calhoun. I know him intimately, and can truly say that he is less a time serving man, than any one I ever saw. I am gratified to find you so much attached to him, as he is every way worthy of your highest regard."

I was not sorry to see your letter to your friends withdrawing from the anticipated Convention as from its "materiel" we had but little to hope for. The leading politicians of the party, or rather a number of them, may say what they please, but Mr. [Martin] Van Buren is not the choice of the *people*, they may respect him, but he is entirely devoid of personal popularity, and if elected it will be owing to divisions in the ranks of our opponents, which from present appearances does not appear likely to be the case.

In this county the really intelligent portion of the Republican party are decidedly your warm, and devoted friends and I have every reason to believe that with you for our Candidate we would have had a bright prospect of carrying this State, which never has I believe, cast her vote for a Republican candidate for the Presidency.

With my former communication to the President I sent a letter which I had received from Mr. [Joel R.] Poinsett when he was Secr[etar]y of War, it was sent as a voucher in part of the statement I then made to the President, they were both enclosed in a letter to the late Hon. A[bel] P. Upshur in which I requested that Mr. Poinsett[']s letter might be returned to me. This has not been done, as I would wish this letter, if it has not been mislaid, I would be pleased to get it again.

As it is not mail day from my nearest office "Franklinville," this will be sent from another office. Any communication that may be addressed to me in reference to the subject of my letter to the President I would be pleased to have it directed to *"Franklinville Md."* Permit me to renew my highest considerations of respect and esteem. Very faithfully Your friend & Servant, Jno. Carroll Walsh.

ALS in DNA, RG 59 (State Department), Miscellaneous Letters (M-179:104, frames 131–133). NOTE: A Clerk's EU reads "Informed, April 4th, that the letter from Mr. Poinsett, referred to within, was enclosed to ["him" *canceled and* "Mr. Walsh," *interlined*] at 'The Mound, Harford County Md.' on the 12th ult[im]o."

From A[sbury] Dickins, [Secretary of the U.S. Senate], "Unofficial," 4/4. "By a Resolution of the Senate of the 23d February 1843, the President [John Tyler] was requested to send to the Senate at the Commencement of the present Session, a Catalogue of the Books &c. &c. in the several departments. That for the State Department has not been received. The matter was mentioned in the Senate today; and I undertook to call your attention to it, ["informally" *interlined*] and to enquire when the Catalogue will be sent." (A Clerk's EU indicates that this letter was answered on 4/5.) ALS in DNA, RG 59 (State Department), Miscellaneous Letters (M-179: 104, frame 136).

From F[ranklin] H. Elmore, Columbia, [S.C.], 4/4. Elmore introduces "my young friend" W. Pinkney Starke, "a son of Maj. Wyatt W. Starke who I believe is well known to you." The younger Starke, a recent graduate of South Carolina College, is on his way to Europe, and Elmore, "in common with many of your friends, will feel obliged by any assistance & attention you may extend to him." ALS in DNA, RG 59 (State Department), Passport Applications, vol. 30, no. 1993 (M-1372:14).

To George Evans and John Fairfield, Senators, and R[obert] P. Dunlap, H[annibal] Hamlin, J[oshua] Herrick, F[reeman] H. Morse, and L[uther] Severance, Representatives [from Maine], 4/4. In reply to their letter of 4/1, Calhoun states that "this Department did not submit the estimate upon which the former appropriation was made, nor has it now data upon which to found one for the unsettled claims." He has therefore referred their letter to the House Committee on Ways and Means. LS in DNA, RG 59 (State Department), Accounting Records, Miscellaneous Letters Sent, 1832–1916, vol. for 2/1–9/30/1844, p. 88.

To Samuel L. Harris, 4/4. "Your letter of the 1st instant, informing me that the State of Maine has a further claim for expenses incurred on account of the Northeastern Boundary, has been received; and a copy of it has been transmitted to [James I. McKay] the Chairman of the Committee of Ways and Means of the House of Representatives." LS in DNA, RG 59 (State Department), Accounting Records, Miscellaneous Letters Sent, 1832–1916, vol. for 2/1–9/30/-1844, p. [89].

From Rob[er]t Monroe Harrison, Consulate of the United States, Kingston, 4/4. Harrison has learned that [James] Semple [Senator from Ill.] has introduced a bill to remodel the U.S. Consular service. One of the provisions of this bill would increase consular bonds from $2,000 to $10,000. Harrison hopes that this provision will not pass. Such a law would mean that Harrison, a public official "off and on since the time of the elder Mr. [John] Adams" would "become a pauper in a foreign land, because I know not to whom to apply for Security." He believes that consular bonds are no longer necessary and that they "degrade them [consuls] in the eyes of foreigners." He asks that this letter be presented to President John Tyler for his information. LS (No. 277) in DNA, RG 59 (State Department), Consular Despatches, Kingston, vol. 8 (T-31:8), received 5/2.

To J. Pinckney Henderson and Isaac Van Zandt, [Texan Commissioners to the U.S.], 4/4. "The Secretary of State presents his compliments to Messrs. Van Zandt and Henderson, and will be glad to see them at the Department at one o'clock this day." FC in DNA, RG 59 (State Department), Notes to Foreign Legations, Texas, 6:69 (M-99:95).

From SIMEON HUBBARD

Norwich Conn., Thursday ev'ning 4th Ap[ri]l, [18]44
Mr. Calhoun: it is now *dusk* & I am just home from a day[']s fatigue without *meat or drink*; yet I am constrained to address you for *the special benefit of the President* [John Tyler]. And on a subject worthy a *leisure-hour[']s* consideration.

But, to the point. I was accosted, *short of ten minutes ago*, thus; "You will be at the *Tyler meeting* this evening[.]" I have heard of none. "It is advertised in *our* paper" "and there is out a *special invitation for you*[.]" I shall not go. "Why?" Because I will not favour the imposition upon the President. Adding, *you* know what I mean. *You know*, as well as I know, the business of this contemptible clique of imposters. This was said to the real, tho a stipend[i]ary editor of the *Norwich News*, himself a reporter of speeches never made, but designed to mislead the President & his friends in Wash-[in]g[to]n. The *proprietor* of that paper, with this *Tyler postmaster* so called, and one other, formed a meeting (the base trio) of themselves only—*organized*—*past resolutions*—deputed the *news-men* to attend a Tyler meeting in N[ew] York (this was sometime ago) and it was asserted that our Governor [Chauncey F. Cleveland] gave 10 dollars towards defraying the expenses of the mission—which materially lessened his popularity *here*, although he *denied it*. And it was in his office (Cleveland and Hoveys[?]) that the base transaction was disclosed to me; soon after making the bonds for the P[ost] O[ffice]. I was *enraged*, & *demanded his answer*; whether so or not; and [*Enoch C.*] *Chapman*, himself, the *hottest of red hot V[an] Burenites*, ["& who was educated in Tammaly Hall" *interlined*] in reply, said it was. But it was to oppose [*William*] *L'Hommodieu* (the old V[an] B[uren] postmaster) who was intriguing for a *reappointment*. It was then and there said, by an *official*, that "John Tyler is a *consummate fool* (the very words) who can be made to believe any thing and every thing said by those who flatter his vanity by exciting his hopes of a nomination." Yes, these were the very words of a V[an] B[uren] leader; whose actions plainly discovered that it ["*was*" *interlined*] a manoeuver of a clique of V[an] Burenites to bring the president into contempt by the folly of buying up his enemies. And so it did; and was a no small means of achieving the late [*Henry*] *Clay victory*—which was also aided by the assertion (passed about) that a certain *boisterous V[an] Burenite*, who had been a constant utterer of *philip[p]ics against Calhoun*, and a contemptuous declaimer against John Tyler, had, through [*George S.*] *Catlin*, caused his name to be presented the president for a nomination to the post office; *if Chapman should be rejected!* I afterwards told him it was conjectured he was seeking for office of the President. He replied with a *sarcastic sneer*, "*I* shall not ask John Tyler for office *at this late day*[.]"

I mentioned this *denial*, incidentally, in the P[ost] O[ffice]. *Chapman* said, "He has applied for the office." "And *I know it*."

For God[']s sake save the President from the poisonous fangs of these *reptiles*; (for so I call them *to their heads*—and *that in truth*) who inundate Washington with their spurious letters of recommendation.

Mr. Calhoun, I *ask it not*. Yet I am anxious to know your *true position*. And this as a means of enabling me to shape my *own* course in the coming contest. Yours &c, Simeon Hubbard.

[P.S.] I entertain no fears, on your account, in the tilting-match between yourself and the *Red-cross knight*. S.H.

[April 5.] Notwithstanding my *hurrying*, I found myself a few minutes too late for the last night[']s mail; and will now make some further remarks.

Faulkner himself, on his return from a trip (of which I had not heard) to Wash[in]gt[o]n (whither he said he had been at the expence of Charles Lester (collector N[ew] London) to prevent his being ousted) observed to me "Let it go with *Enock* and *Lester*, as it may; I am secure in my office (inspector) as long as John Tyler is in power[.]" Exultingly adding *"The President knows his friends*—and he *will stick by 'em".* And, some days after the senatorial rejection of *Chapman*; he called out aloud to a *Clay-man* at the door "You won[']t get rid of this *Coon* so easily, I can tell you; I calculate to keep this office, at least, till April 1845." *This,* I heard myself; and I had before heard that he thus boasted; *having assurances that there would be no other nomination made.*

Measures have been taken by both as I hear, to reenter the V[an] B[uren] ranks *publickly* when the time comes (looked for by all intriguers) that the President, though his eyes may be opened, will himself be powerless from lack of time for *vengeance.* Nay, I was told by one, who from his situation must know their secrets, that Faulkner would have doffed his Tyler flag some weeks since, but that he was told in *conclave "do it now, and you will loose your office instantly."* The result of the late election, so *anti-V[an] Buren,* seems to have encouraged him to hold on upon the "Captain[.]" I have seen *plain* indications of a *traiterous* use of the P[ost] O[ffice] to favour the V[an] B[uren] interest. *I am sure that I can not be mistaken[.]*

It would doubtless be for the president[']s interest *here,* to denounce conventioning, and rely solely upon his own acts for a reelection by the people. I cannot say how it might be in other States. But this I *will* say; that, in no other State would his chance be bettered by a convention, except where party corruptions have wrought more of degradation than *with us*—where, God knows, it is low enough.

One word of *Catlin.* He is from a village in an adjoining county, and a stranger *here.* I saw him but once before his election. He was pointed out to me as a *reformed inebriate.* The announcement awakened a *kindly-feeling,* as it ought to. I had, in *two articles,* denounced *our own,* & all other gregarious assemblages of intriguers in cities; and exhorted the district to leave *us* and go into the country. Which it did, and I was *cursed* therefor (what did I care?). *Catlin* came down—I saw him at his quarters in a *temperance tavern* (where liquors were kept *sub-rosa*) with this Chapman, and several others; his own face *too rosy*[.] I shuddered with an involuntary *apprehension.* What was then *apprehension,* became *conviction,* when it was known that on that evening a letter was wrote recommending *Enoch C. Chapman for postmaster*—and signed *Geo*[*rge*] *S. Catlin member of Congress elect*! I immediately called at the Governor[']s office, and in his absence said to his Secretary (an intimate of C[']s) *Catlin must have been drunk.* Exhort him; *I fear that we shall all be degraded*! He was exhorted *fervently,* and promised to be on his guard in Washingt[o]n.

His vote was *astonishingly large*; although it had been anticipated the *tetotallers* would mostly support him. *Since*; it has been said there was an understanding between him, or his friends, and the *abolitionists.* This accounts for it.

If *Faulkner,* and *Chapman* (and Catlin too if it pleases the P[resident]) shall continue to be the acknowledged friends of the President; *John Tyler sinks no more to rise in Connecticut.* No, nor in any other State where *their* history is known in connection with the manner in which the friendship was brought about by a negotiation in which a Washington reptile bore a no small part[.]

Mr. Calhoun—there will be a more urgent call upon your *sagacity & skill* to meet these cursed *office-craving* rascals, than you will have occasion for in your negotiation with the *Petticoats representative* [Richard Pakenham]. What there is in the foregoing of the confidential, you will readily perceive. And also, in the graphic sketch a picture of the deceptive rascallity with which you disposers of office are continually besot. S.H.

ALS in ScCleA. NOTE: Found among Calhoun's papers at ScCleA is an earlier letter written by Hubbard on 2/27/1844 which had first been addressed to Abel P. Upshur and then readdressed to "the Secretary of State," the writer having learned of Upshur's death before it was mailed. In that letter Hubbard discussed at length his opinions in favor of farmers and planters and against banks and capitalists. George S. Catlin was a one-term Representative from Conn. and in 1848 unsuccessful Democratic candidate for Governor.

From GEO[RGE] H. JONES, "Private"

Petersburg [Va.,] 4th Ap[ril] 1844

Dear Sir, Enjoying the pleasure of a slight personal acquaintance, together with a long *political* one, must plead my excuse for addressing you. Circumstances over which I had no control, aided by the operations of Mr. [Henry] Clay[']s *Bankrupt Law*, has reduced me & family from comfort to want; in this situation I am prompted to ask the kindness of you to confer with Hon. J[ohn] Y. Mason [Secretary of the Navy,] and endeavour if possible to get me a pursership in the Navy or some other appointment, that will give me the means of supporting a family of 4 little children. In asking you to confer with Mr. M[ason] I take great pleasure in saying he has known me from my youth & has always been a *friend & Father* to me.

I presume it is needless to remind You, that I am one of your earliest & greatest admirers and for my sincerity, I refer You to several of my letters to you while in the Senate of the U.S. & particularly to the one I wrote just on the eve of Your leaving that body. I read with more than ordinary pleasure, your letter to the [Calhoun] central Committee of your State, urging your objections to the mode of appointing delegates to the Baltimore convention. They were so conclusive to my mind that I am one of those of your friends, who has nor will not [*one word altered to* "pledge"] himself, to the support of the nominee of that convention. I feel like one entirely at sea & having every Confidence in you I should be highly flattered if You would on the re[ceip]t ["of this" *interlined*] advise me what course to pursue in the coming contest & rest assured every thing shall be *strictly confidential*—as your Zealous advocate, I desire to do every thing that will promote Your Int[erest] and not any thing ["that" *interlined*] will operate against your prospects. Y[ou]r friend Mo[st] Sincerely, Geo. H. Jones.

P.S. I shall expect y[ou]r early reply. I would ask the assistance of my representative Gen[era]l [George C.] Dromgoole, but I am inclined to think, he does not fancy me, since I voted in the district convention (being a delegate to select a candidate) for our friend W[illia]m O. Goode over himself.

ALS in ScCleA. NOTE: An AEU by Calhoun reads "Mr. Jones ["See Mr. Mason" *canceled*] Wants a pursership in the Navy. See Mr. Mason."

From Edw[ard] Kent, Bangor, Maine, 4/4. He encloses a newspaper [from Fredericton, New Brunswick] "containing a debate on the subject of the tax on lumber in the Provincial Parliament; which confirms the facts stated in the memorial from the citizens of Bangor" which he sent to Calhoun on 3/28. ALS in DNA, RG 59 (State Department), Miscellaneous Letters (M-179:104, frames 137–138); CC in DNA, RG 84 (Foreign Posts), Great Britain, Instructions, 8:219.

M E M O R A N D U M "Communicated by the
Texan Ministers to Mr. Calhoun"

[*Ca.* April 4, 1844?]
The following is communicated to Mr. Calhoun [by Isaac Van Zandt
and J. Pinckney Henderson], confidentially.

Extract from a note ["(private)" *canceled*] of the Hon. Ashbel
Smith, Chargé d'Affaires of Texas at London and Paris, to Hon. Anson
Jones, Secretary of State of Texas, dated Legation of Texas, Paris,
July 31st, 1843[:]
"Previously to leaving London, I had a long interview, on the
20[t]h inst[ant], with the Earl of Aberdeen, Sec[retar]y [of State]
for the Foreign Department, concerning the affairs of Texas. I think
it proper here to state that I had reason to be pleased with the full
and frank manner in which his Lordship discussed the affairs in question. As a matter of course he treated the subject mainly and almost
exclusively in reference to British policy and interests. Some time
before this interview with Lord Aberdeen, Mr. S[tephen] P. Andrews,
whom I have mentioned in former despatches as being in London, on
an abolition mission, requested me to present him to Mr. [Henry U.]
Addington [Under Secretary of State for Foreign Affairs]. After
some reflection, I consented to do so—the introduction being in no
degree official as I stated to Mr. Addington, and as this course put me
fairly in possession of the abolition schemes, which had already been
presented to the British Government. On this occasion I expressed
my utter dissent from and opposition to all operations then carrying
on in London, having for their object the abolition of slavery in
Texas. In my interview with Lord Aberdeen on the 20[t]h inst[ant],
I stated that Mr. Andrews' coming to London about abolition was
his individual act, wholly unauthorised by the Government or citizens
of Texas—that though there might be some individuals in our country
disposed to abolish slavery, I had no reason to believe they were numerous; but on the contrary that I had reason to think no disposition
to agitate the subject existed either on the part of the Government or
any respectable portion of the citizens of Texas. I also stated to
Lord Aberdeen that I was informed representations would be sent
out to Texas, ["based" *canceled*] based on statements made by members of the Antislavery convention, who had called on his Lordship
touching this matter, to the effect that Her Majesty's Government
would afford in some way the means of reimbursing or compensating

the slave holders, provided slavery were abolished in our country. I enquired what grounds there was for these assertions. His Lordship replied in effect: That it is the well known policy and wish of the British Government to abolish slavery every where—that its abolition in Texas is deemed very desirable, and he spoke to the point at some little length, as connected with British policy and British interests and in reference to the United States. He added that there was no disposition on the part of the British Government to interfere improperly on this subject, and that they would not give the Texian Govt. cause to complain. He was not prepared to say whether the British Govt. would consent hereafter to make such compensation to Texas as would enable the slave-holders to abolish slavery. The object is deemed so important, perhaps they might, though he would not say certainly. ["I here" *canceled.*]

["]Lord Aberdeen also stated that despatches had been recently sent to Mr. [Percy W.] Doyle, the British Chargé d'Affaires at Mexico, instructing him to renew the tender of British mediation based on the abolition of slavery in Texas and declaring that abolition would be a *great moral triumph for Mexico.* Your Department will not fail to remark that ["the" *altered to* "this"] despatch to Mr. Doyle appears to introduce a new and important condition into mediation.

["]The British Govt. greatly desire the abolition of slavery in Texas, as a part of their general policy in reference to their colonial and commercial interests, and mainly in reference to its future influence on slavery in the United States."

Extract from a private note of the Hon. Ashbel Smith to Mr. [Isaac] Van Zandt, dated Paris, Dec. 28[t]h, 1843[:]

"You have probably received before this time a letter I sent by the Count de Saligny, together with some documents concerning the efforts making in England for the abolition of slavery in Texas. Since the date of the letter just alluded to, I have received another communication from Mr. [Edward] Everett, American Minister in London, in which he states that Lord Aberdeen had informed him he had given no countenance whatever to the proposition made by the committee of the Antislavery Convention, to wit, that the British Govt. should guarantee the interest of a loan to Texas for effecting abolition. Mr. Everett uses the following language. 'I had an interview and a long conversation with Lord Aberdeen on the general question: and he mentioned to me of his own accord that the proposal of a loan for the purpose specified, received no countenance whatever from him but was promptly rejected.'

["]The committee of the Antislavery Convention drew a different conclusion from his Lordship's observations. The extracts from my despatches above mentioned contain full details of my interview with Lord Aberdeen on this subject. The reply which Lord Aberdeen may or may not have made to the committee of the Antislavery convention regarding a loan, is in my opinion of a very secondary importance. In his answer to a note of mine, a copy of which has heretofore been transmitted to you, Lord Aberdeen declares that there is a 'continued anxiety['] of Her Majesty's Govt. to see slavery abolished in Texas. The instructions from the British Govt. to Mr. Doyle in Mexico to present again the 'mediation' of England, connected with the abolition of slavery in Texas, and the order to state to the Mexican Govt. that this would be a 'great moral triumph for Mexico,' as well as numerous other facts with which you are acquainted, show a practical purpose to accomplish this object of their 'continued anxiety.'

["]I regret to see the subject of our annexation to the American Union discussed, as I am convinced it would be imprracticable [sic], and its discussion harms Texas in Europe.

["]I transcribe for you the following extracts from a letter addressed by Mr. Thomas Clarkson to Gen. Santa Anna, dated Oct. 6[t]h, 1843. He speaks in the name of the Antislavery convention: 'They are most deeply penetrated with the desire that no arrangement shall be made with Texas on the part of Mexico, which shall in any manner sanction the continuance of slavery, but on the contrary that the present most favorable occasion should be seized to impose terms on that country which shall result in its immediate and total abolition.' This desire to renew a war unless slavery be abolished, sounds well in the mouth of a philanthropist by excellence and a quaker! He adds: 'Such an event, the abolition of slavery, would be hailed with the utmost joy by all the friends of the slave in every part of the world, not only from considerations connected with the personal liberation of those now held in bondage, but from the immense influence which it would exert upon the continuance of slavery in the United States themselves. Instead of Texas then becoming, as has been feared by the committee, and intended by the slaveholders, a new and extended theatre for the employment of slave labor and for carrying on the nefarious traffic in human beings, it would[,] as a country enjoying free institutions, such as Mexico has proclaimed to the world, become the source of a most powerful counter influence upon the very borders of the slave region, threatening the speedy downfall of the system even there.'

["]The conversation on the 18[t]h August last in the British House of Lords, between Lords Brougham and Aberdeen, cannot have escaped your attention; wherein the former said he 'looked forward most anxiously for the abolition of slavery in Texas, as he was convinced it would ultimately *end in the abolition of slavery throughout the whole of America*'; and the latter reiterated his 'anxiety to see the abolition of slavery in Texas.'

["]These quotations and thousands of others which might be cited, betray the real purpose of the machinations in England to abolish slavery in Texas. It is as the entering wedge to abolition in the United States. *The final object is the destruction of the agricultural productions of the Southern States and the commerce and manufactures of the whole Union, as far as these are dependent on the former.* The productions and prosperity of Texas for a long time to come would, in this event, follow those of our nearest neighbors on the North. I am thoroughly convinced, that in the motives for abolition there is and has been no more humanity than there would be in cutting the hamstrings of your neighbors' horses. The masses in England who think little about abolition and know less, may be honest in their opinion—among the leading men the motives are sordid. Let Texas beware of their interested gifts.

["]I am happy to see from the tenor of a note of Mr. [Edward] Everett's to me, as well as to learn from other sources, that the British Govt. disclaim any disposition to interfere too promptly in our affairs. You may be sure, however, that they have had a full understanding with the abolitionists of the Antislavery convention on this subject and to a certain extent have cöoperated with them.

["]I need not mention the angry spirit roused in England by the supposed project for annexing our country to the Union, as you will see all this in their newspapers. Our affairs attract from time to time considerable notice."

Extract from a despatch of the Hon. [Anson Jones], the Secretary of State of Texas, addressed to [Isaac Van Zandt,] the Texan Chargé d'Affaires at Washington City, dated January 27[t]h, 1844[:]

"No proposition for a treaty of alliance has yet been authorized to be made to any other Govt., but as our negotiations with Mexico may be abruptly terminated, it becomes the duty of this Govt. to be prepared for such an emergency. It is, therefore, of the utmost importance that the views of the United States on the subject should be immediately known and communicated by you to this Department, in order that the President [of Texas, Samuel Houston], in the event of an unfavorable answer, might take prompt action, in reference to it, with some other Govt. whose friendly disposition can be relied upon."

ADU in ScCleA; PEx (under date of 7/31/1843) in Jameson, ed., *Correspondence*, pp. 866–868. NOTE: This memorandum is in an unknown hand. An EU, not by Calhoun, reads "Extract of a note from the Hon. A[shbel] Smith, Chargé de Affaires of of [*sic*] Texas ["Communicated to Mr. Calhoun" *canceled*]." Another EU, in a different hand, reads "Communicated by the Texan Ministers to Mr. Calhoun." Smith's letter to Anson Jones of 7/31/1843 and that of Jones to Van Zandt of 1/27/1844 are published in Garrison, ed., *Diplomatic Correspondence of the Republic of Texas*, 3:1116–1117, and 2:248–251, and an FC of the letter of 7/31/1843 is found in TxU, Ashbel Smith Papers. The memorandum is undated, and on what date it was presented to Calhoun is conjectural. However, the most likely time would seem to be in early April, 1844, during the drawing up of the treaty of annexation, because the document refers to "Texan Ministers." Texas was represented by only one Minister until Henderson arrived to join Van Zandt in Washington on 3/27/1844.

From A[lphonse] Pageot, [French Minister to the U.S.], 4/4. Pageot informs Calhoun that the King [Louis Philippe] has ratified the U.S.-French convention for the extradition of criminals which was concluded in Washington on 11/9/1843. The King proposes an additional article covering persons charged with robbery and burglary. LS (in French) and translation in DNA, RG 59 (State Department), Notes from Foreign Legations, France, vol. 12 (M-53:8, frames 697–700); CC of translation in DNA, RG 46 (U.S. Senate), 28B-B5.

From R[ICHARD] PAKENHAM

Washington, 4 April 1844

Sir, With reference to a letter which I had the honor to receive from Mr. [John] Nelson, while temporarily in charge of the Department of State, upon the subject of "the grants made by the British Government within the Territory which has heretofore been in dispute within the State of Maine," of which Grants it is desired that authenticated Copies should be procured, with a view to the fulfilment of the provisions of the 4th Article of the Treaty of Washington, I have the honor to inform you that on the 14th of last month I forwarded to the Lieutenant Governor of New Brunswick a copy of the application which was addressed on this subject to Mr. [Henry S.] Fox on 19 June 1843, requesting that the information desired by the Department of State might be transmitted to this Mission with the least possible delay.

I hope, therefore, to be able in the course of a few days to answer in a satisfactory manner the application which has been received from the Department of State upon this subject.

I take this opportunity also to acquaint you, Sir, that I have been in correspondence with the Government of New Brunswick upon another matter connected with the fulfilment of the Treaty of Washington, viz: the Disputed Territory fund, upon which subject I hope in like manner to be enabled within a short time to furnish the desired information. I have the honor to be, with high Consideration, Sir, your obedient Servant, R. Pakenham.

LS in DNA, RG 59 (State Department), Notes from Foreign Legations, Great Britain, vol. 22 (M-50:22); PC in House Document No. 110, 29th Cong., 1st Sess., p. 32.

From Charles Rogers, [Representative from N.Y.], 4/4. On behalf of the House "Committee on the Expenditures in the State Department," he encloses a resolution of 4/2 and asks that the "information sought [on contingent expenditures during 1841–1844] may be furnished . . . by the Department over which you preside, in order to enable" the committee to report to the House. ALS in DNA, RG 59 (State Department), Miscellaneous Letters from Congressional Committees, 1801–1877; PC of En in House Report No. 484, 28th Cong., 1st Sess., p. 1.

From THOMAS SCOTT

Chillicothe [Ohio,] April 4th, 1844

Dear Sir, The announcement, in the papers just received, that you had arrived in the city [of Washington] and entered upon your official duties, has been read with sincere pleasure by your friends here, as it assures them that our Western interests are now confided to safe hands. We consider these interests as identified with the interests of the South and therefore go Heart and Soul for the annexation of Texas and securing every foot of land west of the Rocky Mountains to which we can assert a just claim. These acquisitions instead of weakening will strengthen the chain which unites us as a nation. The whole country drained by the Gulf of Mexico from the Sabine to the Rio del Norte is essential to the perfect security of Western and

Southern interests and those interests will be greatly promoted by the establishment of our title to the country west of the Rocky mountains [*one word canceled*] to such an extent along the shores of the Pacific Ocean as will secure a sufficient number of good Harbors on that Ocean and the shortest and best route by land and water from thence east to different parts of the country drained by the Gulf. The tide of emigration is still rolling on towards that Ocean and at no distant day will spread along its shores for hundreds of miles. That country when once thoroughly explored may be found to be much more valuable for agricultural purposes than it is generally represented to be, and it may possess treasures of incalculable value to the nation. ["And" *canceled*] It will, at no distant day, be intersected with roads and canals connecting with the Mississippi val[l]ey. These roads and canals at the same time that they extend will strengthen the chain of the union. And although there may and necessarily will, at times, be some little confliction of interests, yet as the different sections of the union will find that each will derive advantages from keeping up a friendly intercourse and exchange of commodities with the others, it is believed that these conflicting interests would eventually be compromised and settled. But should it so happen in the course of human events, that the chain which so happily binds us together as a nation be rudely severed, it requires but little foresight and sagacity to perceive that a re-union of two separate and distinct Confederacys could never be formed, one on the one side, and ["the other" *altered to* "another"] on the other side of the line which seperates the slave holding from the non-slave holding States. On the happening of such an event the whole country drained by the Gulf would find it necessary to unite in a confederacy in order to protect each other, and your own State would soon perceive that her true interest would be promoted by joining that Confederacy. On the question of slavery the South & Southwestern States have nothing to fear from the States west of the Alleghenie mountains. Ninety nine hundredth[s] of the people of these States, you may depend upon it, are sound to the core on that subject. You may therefore look well to and confide in the people of the west. If the South and west would unite and draw together, the interests of each would be greatly promoted and they would have no cause to fear the power of any adversary. Your friends here would be extremely gratified to see you amongst them as early as practicable the present season as on you now rests the last hopes of the democracy, at least for a season. It is now apparent that Mr. [Martin] Van Buren cannot unite the scattered forces of the democratic Party and that if he be nominated by his friends in the Baltimore Convention this and most of the Western States will cast their votes for Mr. [Henry] Clay. The prospects of President [John] Tyler in this section of the state are not as good now as they were several months since. The friends who from principle heretofore sustained the measures of his administration finding themselves abandoned by him and that his patronage, for the last six months, has been bestowed in Ohio in such a manner as to streng[t]hen the forces of Mr. Van Buren, have become discouraged and laid down their arms. They think there is a principle of reciprocity which extends through all the ramifications of Society, and that he who disregards it, casts from him an anchor which, in the event of an unexpected storm, he may greatly need. The nomination of Governor [Wilson] Shannon [as Minister to Mexico] produced much surprise, as it is well understood here that General [Lewis] Cass is his favorite candidate for the presidency, and that General Cass (in case he cannot obtain the nomination of the Baltimore Convention) and his friends intend to cast their votes for Mr. Van Buren. It will be extremely difficult to produce a reaction in favor of President Tyler in this section of the State. This State of feeling has been produced by the continuous vacil[l]ation in the appointments made by the Executive of Whigs and Loco's, to the almost entire neglect of the friends who have uniformly sustained him. Taking into view the existing divisions in the democratic party in connexion with the circumstances just hinted at, together with these other facts, that South Carolina is justly entitled to the next president— that your claims to that exalted Station surpass that of all the candidates named and that the popular current is at this time setting in more strongly in your favor than it has ever done since the unfortunate rupture between you and General [Andrew] Jackson, the conclusion at which I have arrived is, that the Democracy can be more readily brought to unite in your support as a candidate for the next presidency than on any ["another" *altered to* "other"] man. If the South will give you its undivided support we can carry your election— and heal up the breaches which now unhappily divide the party. If you will consent, at this late period, to ["have your" *canceled*] a nomination, it will afford me great pleasure to bring you forward in this State—to procure for you a full representation at the Baltimore Convention and afterwards advocate your election. Your friends and the friends of Mr. Tyler must draw together and which ever of you can command in that convention the greatest number of votes must receive the nomination & support of the democratic party. Much will therefore depend in that convention on the course which the South may take. I would not have troubled you with this communication but from the fact that, Ohio has not a single officer in any of the departments at Washington with whom I could correspond freely and confidentially on these interesting suggests [*sic*]. I am Sir with the highest respect Your friend & Ob[edien]t Serv[an]t, Thomas Scott.

ALS in ScCleA; PEx in Boucher and Brooks, eds., *Correspondence*, pp. 220–221.

To Thomas L. Smith, Register of the Treasury, 4/4. "In order to enable me to answer an inquiry made by the [House] Committee on Expenditures of this Department, I have to request you to furnish a statement of the balances remaining in the Treasury on the 4th of March 1841, and the 1st of December, 1843, of the appropriations for Contingent Expences of the Department of State, including publishing and distributing the laws, and for Contingent Expences of Foreign Intercourse." FC in DNA, RG 59 (State Department), Accounting Records, Miscellaneous Letters Sent, 1832–1916, vol. for 2/1–9/30/1844, p. 90.

From J[ohn] C. Spencer

Treas[ur]y Department
April 4th 1844

Sir, The attention of this Department having been specially directed to the extensive system of smug[g]ling heretofore existing on the Canadian Frontier, it has been suggested, that among the most efficient means of checking illicit traffic, would be an arrangement with the Governor [General] of Canada by which it should become the reciprocal duty of the Officers of the revenue on either side of the line, to furnish immediate information of any known intention to engage in unlawful trade. It is not doubted that the Canadian Authorities would be ready to unite cordially with the Government of the United States to the measure proposed, which, while it guarded the revenue on either side, would be calculated to promote friendly feeling between the Revenue Officers of the respective Governments, and to prevent the recurrence of incidents of an unpleasant character such as recently took place in the seizure of the Canadian Steamboats The Admiral and the America.

Believing the subject deserving the attention of the Department of State, I have the honor to submit the proposition to your consideration. With great respect, I have the honor to be Your Obed[ien]t Serv[an]t, J.C. Spencer, Sec[retar]y of the Treas[ur]y.

FC in DNA, RG 56 (Treasury Department), Letters to Cabinet and Bureau Officers, Series B, 4:348.

By an UNIDENTIFIED GERMAN

United States of North America

Washington, 4 April [1844]

The president has made an excellent choice: he has called Mr. John C. Calhoun of South Carolina to the Department of State and appointed Mr. [John Y.] Mason of Virginia Secretary of the Navy. Of John C. Calhoun I often told you, that he is the most exalted statesman in the Union, and I have since had no cause, to alter my opinion. Besides he is also the most honest politician, which may account for it, that he can not succeed to ["gain" *canceled and* "form" *interlined*] for himself a party proper. He was no longer than two years ago the most prominent Candidate for the Presidency, but he has heretofore been entirely driven from the field by the friends & followers of Martin Van Buren. Nevertheless he entertains the classical idea, that a great man of the republic of the nineteenth *Century* like Cincinnatus on his rural retreat may quietly wait the time, when the State will call him to the helm. But this is a great mistake. In Rome there were no newspapers, consequently no privileged manufacturers of public opinion and no standing ["army" *altered to* "armies"] of voters. ["These are" *canceled*.] In these armies there are those who lead a squadron, others who command a regiment or a division, and at last a very small class, who understand to manage a campaign, that is: a presidential election. The world is not, as Shakespeare thinks, divided into good and bad actors merely; but into people, who are on the stage and play comedy, and ["in" *canceled*] spectators, among whom, of course, are also comprehended the Critics. The latter write the history, which is learned by heart ["at school" *interlined*] by the youths of later centuries, and on which poets and authors make their glossaries. In our active public life here—as long as the State is young and healthy—no body will remain long a spectator, ["whether" *canceled*] no matter whether he be in the pit, box or gallery; all press upon the stage, every one ["de" *canceled*] longs to play the part of a hero, and as those, who have not the strength or courage to ["jump" *canceled*] leap over the orchestra, strive to avenge themselves by hissing and shouting, it certainly requires a peculiar talent, to play the stage manager or ["even" *canceled*] to become the director ["even" *interlined*] of the ["theatre" *canceled*] whole. Mr. John C. Calhoun is a classic actor, he understands the piece eminently well, but not the "ensemble" and the spectators. As Secretary of State he will render the country distinguished services; but whether hereby he ["can" *altered to* "will"] attain to the Presidency ["in 1848" *interlined*], is doubtful. In spite of all efforts of the friends of free trade the tarif[f] still remains as it was. All that ["since" *canceled and* "for" *interlined*] three years has been heard about it in the House of Rep[resentative]s and Senate, belongs merely to the intrigues for the Presidency. The country is prospering too well with the present tarif[f], to admit of the success of any efforts to abolish it. Money is abundant, and all kinds of State securities are rising. The year 1845 will be one of great importance to us.

Ms. in ScCleA. NOTE: This handwritten document found among Calhoun's papers is labelled: "From the Augsburg [Bavaria] Gazette of May 10th 1844." The author has not been identified with certainty. However, in a letter to Calhoun of 6/25/1844, Alfred Schücking identified the Augsburg *Gazette* as a paper in which his family was involved, and the ms. translation is in Schücking's hand.

From [ISAAC VAN ZANDT and J. PINCKNEY HENDERSON]

Legation of Texas
Washington D.C. April 4th 1844

After the very satisfactory preliminary interviews had with him, the Undersigned &c, &c, &c, beg leave to inform Mr. Calhoun, Secretary of State of the United States, that they have been fully empowered by the President of Texas [Samuel Houston], and are now ready to proceed with him, whenever he shall be likewise empowered by the President of the United States [John Tyler], to the final arrangement of the terms of a treaty of annexation.

The Undersigned therefore respectfully request that Mr. Calhoun (Should the same meet his concurrence) would appoint a time, and place, when, and where they may have the honor of an interview for this purpose, and the exchange of their respective "full powers."

Transcript in TxU, Isaac Van Zandt Papers, vol. II.

From JAMES T. AUSTIN

Paris, 5th April 1844

My dear Sir, I beg to assure you of the universal satisfaction with which the information is received here that you have accepted the situation of Secretary of State of the U.S. In the state of the relations between our Country and Europe the accession of your character to the administration gives it a weight and efficiency which gratifies every American feeling.

I am here on a visit, for relaxation and improvement; but I shall be most happy to make a tour of pleasure one of business if there is any service in Europe with which you would do me the honor to charge me. With the highest respect and esteem Your personal friend, James T. Austin of Massachusetts.

ALS in ScCleA. NOTE: Austin was the son-in-law of Vice-President Elbridge Gerry and had been Attorney General of Mass. during 1832–1843.

COMMISSION Empowering Calhoun to Conclude a Treaty of Annexation with Texas

[Washington, April 5, 1844]

John Tyler[,] President of the United States of America, To all whom these presents shall concern—

Greeting—

Know ye that I have given & granted and do hereby give & grant to John C. Calhoun, Secretary of State of the United States, full power & authority & also present & special command to meet & confer with Isaac Van Zandt & J. Pinckney Henderson, Ministers accredited to the Government of the United States from the Republic of Texas, being furnished with the like full powers of & concerning the annexation of Texas to the said United States, and to conclude a treaty upon that subject and all others connected with it, for the final ratification of the President of the United States, by & with the advice & consent of the Senate thereof, if such advice & consent be given.

In testimony whereof I have caused the seal of the United States to be hereunto affixed. Given under my hand at the City of Washington, the fifth day of April eighteen hundred & forty four & of the Independence of the United States the sixty-eighth. [Signed:] By the President, John Tyler. Secretary of State[,] J.C. Calhoun.

DS in Tx, Records of the Texas Republic Department of State, U.S. Diplomatic Correspondence.

To Henry Dammers, New York [City], 4/5. To Dammers's letter of 4/3 Calhoun replies that the State Department is "provided with" a translator, "but, should it hereafter be in want of one, your application will receive respectful consideration." FC in DNA, RG 59 (State Department), Domestic Letters, 34:125 (M-40:32).

From J A M E S G A D S D E N,
"Private & Confidential"

Charleston S.C., 5 April 1844

My Dear Sir, I cannot sufficiently express my regret at not having a personal interview with you on your recent journey to Washington. You anticipated by 24 hours my calculation of your movements. Rail Road duties required my presence at Columbia on the opening of the Court on Monday & I had arranged to leave on Wednesday with the certainty of intercepting you at Branchville, or of meeting you at Hamburg. You passed on however on Tuesday & it was impossible for me to overtake you before your departure from Charleston. I had much to say to you which cannot be embraced in the compass of a letter. The correspondence I had had with you, had conveyed my ideas on recent events. Subsequent occurrances have confirmed me in the opinions then expressed; *that our principles had been compromitted by politicians.* They have succeeded & whether the position you are now placed in, will enable us to retrace our steps, & recover the ground lost, time alone can develop. I fear however we have not time & the contest left between Mr. [Henry] Clay & [Martin] Van Buren may in the issue inculcate a lesson of reproof stronger than that which [William Henry] Harrison's triumph spoke. Individually I trust such may be the result; for although I acquies[c]ed in the course of my friends when they accorded him ["V(an) B(uren)" *interlined*] a magnanimous support, I never was reconciled to it, having been always distrustful of one whose whole course of life has been non Committal & treachery. He has played his game to defeat those who had, in trying times, come to his rescue, and I fear was well understood by many who moved the springs in this State. I shall await events & should be happy to hear from you & to lend my exertions to a cause in which you must be persuaded I feel a common interest with you. Any communications in confidence will be received and so far, as my ability goes, acted on.

In relation to myself & to that position, in which circumstances, contrary to my wishes, have placed me I have a few words to say & possibly you may, without detriment to the public interests, enable me to gratify my long cherished desire, at the same time that I may render a service, in the position in which I am now placed. It has long been my anxious wish to pay a visit to Europe, & had I not under a Carolinian[']s excitement, committed myself & resources on those great [railroad] projects, which it was thought, would operate to Carolina's prosperity, I should long since, with my private means, have been enabled to gratify my wishes. But the interest which I have manifested & taken in these great designs superadded to some private obligations, on which I have been committed, leaves me no hopes, unless as a Public functionary, I can gratify my private feelings in the public service. A visit to Europe, at this time, to examine the Rail Roads, & manufacturing establishments connected with them, would no doubt enable me to do much for the Road which I now manage. Many think the [South Carolina Railroad] Company ought to send me, & I would cheerfully go myself if I could conveniently command the means. Our Company however has been so imposed on & has suffered so deeply, that I could not propose myself or permit my friends to suggest my going abroad at the Company[']s expense. An idea has struck me that in the progress of your negotiation with the British Minister, or under some other arrangement, connected with the public interest in the State Department, you could send me as a special messenger, merely paying my expenses. Emolument is not the object, but if my expenses could be paid it would be highly gratifying to me to execute your orders, with the permit to remain a few weeks to examine the public improvements, manufactures &c &c. You know by what means I was deprived of a Commission in the army & after having spent some 12 & 14 years of my life in the service forced from a profession to which I was attatched & compelled to try my fortunes in other pursuits. I was greatly wronged & the only return for the wrong is now to gratify me in the wishes now expressed. I should be happy to hear from you in anticipation on this subject, so that I might make the necessary arrangements in time should you have it in your power to gratify me. In candor I have been exposed the last 3 years to so many trials & vexations, that I feel as if my mind requires, not rest, but relaxation in change, and desirous as I now am to devote myself to the Great work in Carolina, which is to connect us with the Mississippi, I feel as if I would return to the operation with renewed energy & zeal, could I but have the opportunity of seeing what others have done and are doing & thus profiting from their experience, transfer their superior management &c to our benefit. Among the other applications of new powers, I feel very desirous of ["looking" *canceled*] looking into the Atmospheric Rail Way, impressed as I am, that it may be applied successfully to our Inclined Plane, which presents, at present, the greatest obstacle or impediment to the Trade between Charleston & Augusta. Let me hear from you soon on this application ["for to" *canceled*]. To leave would require some weeks of preparation.

In carrying out our grand design of a connection, through Georgia, with the Mississippi, I greatly regret that it will not be in your power to attend the contemplated convention at Huntsville [Ala.], to be held on the 20th proximo & to which you were invited. The Spirit is up in that quarter & the times are propitious to fill up the connections. The renewal of the duty on Rail Road Iron however is not so great a drawback as the exorbitant addition—$25 a Ton for an article which cost but $25–100 per c[en]t—is an outrage on common sense. Could you not exert your influence on this occasion & if the Duty be not remitted, at least have it reduced. We had to pay recently for the Geo[rgia] Rail Road $16,000 duty on Two Cargoes the first Cost of which did not exceed $15,500, and this too in the face of the fact, that the same Iron, for we tried the market, could not have been contracted for less than $50,000 or $70 per Ton for what exclusive of duty cost in England but $23. Our Road continues to have an increasing business—and it is difficult to speculate on what may be the operations on it when the contemplated connection with the Tennessee [River] is consummated. It will be one of the finest & most profitable Roads in the world. Yours Truly, James Gadsden.

[P.S.] Mr. [Thomas G.] Clemson passed up to day on his return home.

Should Mr. [Wilson] Shannon[']s nomination to Mexico be rejected—as has been intimated, I wish you would consider [Isaac E.] Holmes'[s] claims. There are many reasons for his friends wishing him at present to go abroad & it is understood that both [Abel P.] Upshur & [Thomas W.] Gilmer favored his appointment, but that the influences in favor of Shannon prevailed. If you can gratify me in my wish I should not care to leave here before the Steamer of 20 June or 11 July as I wish to close the first 6 months of 1844 & make a report.

ALS in ScCleA.

From Tho[ma]s D. Hailes, Grand Cane, DeSoto Parish, La., 4/5. Hailes solicits "the Appointment of a consular vacancy that may occur at any Southern Port" and indicates that he has the support of Representatives [John] Slidell and [Pierre E.] Bossier of La. and [Isaac E.] Holmes of S.C. ALS in DNA, RG 59 (State Department), Applications and Recommendations, 1837–1845, Hailes (M-687:14, frames 94–95).

From F.L. Lance, Charleston, 4/5. "I am sorry to trouble you so soon after your arrival [in Washington]. I am anxious to obtain a Lt. appointment in the Revenue Service. Will you be so kind as to apply for me. I can assure [you] that your exertions for me will be greatly appreciated." ALS in DNA, RG 59 (State Department), Applications and Recommendations, 1837–1845, Lance (M-687:19, frames 22–23).

From SETH T. OTIS

United States Consulate
Basel (Switzerland), April 5th 1844
Sir, I have the honor to inform You of my safe arrival here, of the immediate granting of my Exequatur by the Swiss Government, and of my having entered upon the duties of my office the 3rd inst[ant].

I regret to inform the Department that I find the affairs of this consulate in a very bad condition. I am informed that my Predecessor (Mr. Stephen Powers) upon leaving here January 6/[18]42 appointed as Vice Consul one Mr. Walter Merian, who continued to discharge the duties of the office until the 15th Sept. last, when he became Bankrupt, & all the property of the consulate was taken possession of, for the benefit of his creditors, by a "Notary" of this city. But at the same time, the Government of this canton, permitted or authorised one Mr. John Steigmyer to continue the business of the consulate in his own name, & to take so much of the property of the consulate as he deemed indispensable for that purpose. This he continued to do until the 3rd inst[ant], when upon my application, he promptly delivered to me such of the effects of the consulate as was in his possession. I have *demanded* in the name of my Government from the "Notary" above alluded to, the balance of the Books &c belonging to this Consulate. & at his request, have consented to wait *one week* for his Decision. These two Gentlemen (Merian &

Steigmeyer) are both natives of Switzerland, cannot speak a syllable of English, and the latter personage keeps an ordinary "Intelligence office," and the business of the *American* Consulate has been transacted at his *official Bureau of intelligence.*

Duty to my Government compels me to state, that I am informed by some of the most respectable citizens of this City, that Mr. Powers whilst here, conducted himself in a manner wholly unbecoming to the character of a representative of a Great Nation. That he neglected in a shameful manner the duties of his office, that he was notoriously *Indolent, Dissipated* and *Dishonest*. And that he posses[s]ed all the minor bad traits of character usual[l]y attendant upon those I have named. I of course know nothing of this, only from Reports given me, but justice to my own feelings, & those of my Young Family (who accompany me) compel me to add, that Every day we are here we see, & *painfully feel*, the light estimation in which an American Consul is regarded in this community.

A hasty inspection of such of the Books of the Consulate as have come into my possession shows either unpardonable neglect or wilful misrepresentation in the Entries of the same by Mr. Powers. Knowing as I do that no returns from this Consulate have been received at Your department for more than two Years, I shall as soon as possible *make an Effort* to give You the proper returns for that time, but am fearful from the bad state of the Books that nothing like accuracy can be arrived at.

This city contains about 30,000 Inhabitants, is the largest but one (Geneva) in Switzerland, is particularly noted for its Extensive manufactories of Silk Ribbons & other Goods of similar descriptions, and is the main outlet for all the products of Switzerland destined for the U. States. The trade with the United States at this time, although quite Extensive, is by no means as great (as I am informed) as it was previous to the high duties imposed by our Government upon the principal manufactures of this Country. This fact will Commend itself to the attention of the department in connexion with the Tariff.

The U.S. Government has within the last few months created in this Confederacy a new Consulate at the city of Zurich. And [Henry Mahler] a native Swiss (but resident for some Years in New York) has been appointed Consul. Strenuous opposition was made by the merchants & manufacturers of that city, to this Governments confirming his appointment. They believing, & alledging, that he still retained an Interest in a large Commercial House in the U.S. as also in another House at Lyons in France, & they did not wish to be compelled to submit their Invoices for legalization to a rival in business.

And I am credibly informed that this Government only granted him his Exequatur from feelings of Amity towards the United States.

Believing as I most sincerely do, that the office at Zurich is quite unnecessary in the present condition of our trade, and that the present Incumbent holds it to subserve his own purposes more than that of the United States—And that the fees from both offices if *united* (*being only about $800.00*) will illy support *one* Consul—and that my Government will from the best of motives (when consistent) give its offices and grant its favors to *True & Native Americans*—I Respectfully & Earnestly request the Department to take into consideration the propriety of abolishing the office at Zurich, And having the entire Consular business of this small Confederacy now as heretofore transacted at Basel. But I do not ask them to do it until such times as I lay before them additional information of the amount of trade fees &c &c, which I intend to do as soon as I receive an answer to my demand for the Effects of this Consulate, before alluded to. I am Sir Very Respectfully Your Ob[edien]t Serv[an]t, Seth T. Otis, *Consul.*

[P.S.] The writer of this learned only a few days since of the sudden & awful Death of the Hon. A.P. Upshur. Not Knowing his successor in office, he leaves the name blank. He has noticed the President[']s request to wear mourning & has complied with the same. He sincer[e]ly mourns the loss of such a man as the Hon. Abel P. Upshur.

ALS (No. 4) in DNA, RG 59 (State Department), Consular Despatches, Basle, vol. 1 (T-364:1), received 6/1.

To Alphonse Pageot, [French Minister to the U.S.], 4/5. Pageot's note of yesterday "has been duly submitted to the President [John Tyler], who directs me to inform you, that, upon the receipt of the ratification [of the extradition convention] to which you refer, it is not apprehended that there will be any serious difficulty in meeting the wishes of His Majesty [Louis Philippe] the King of the French in regard to the proposed additional article." FC in DNA, RG 59 (State Department), Notes to Foreign Legations, France, 6:79–80 (M-99:21).

To A[lexander] H. Tyler, U.S. Consul at Bahia de San Salvador, [Brazil], 4/5. "The Returns and Statement of Fees, from your Consulate for 1843 have not been received, nor has any letter, since your No. 17 of the 29th March 1843. The Department expects a full compliance with all the requisitions contained in the General Instructions to Consuls, and you are requested, upon the receipt of this, to furnish it with an explanation of your having thus omitted to conform to them." FC in DNA, RG 59 (State Department), Consular Instructions, 11:227.

From CALEB ATWATER

Washington, April 6, 1844

Dear Sir, Permit me to recommend to you, in the strongest terms, Messrs [Charles H.] Winder and [William] Carroll of your Department. The first, is the son of Gen. [William H.] Winder, and the second, is the descendant of Daniel Carroll of Dud[d]ington, a signer of the Declaration of Independence [*sic*; the Constitution]. They were the confidential clerks of my lamented freind [*sic*] Judge [Abel P.] Upshur. They well deserve *all your confidence*, and, they do not know that I write this note—they never will know it from me.

I wish to say, also, that I expect not even the smallest favor from this administration—for myself, or, for my friends; and so you see, I have no selfish motives in what I say to you. I have entertained, perhaps, wrong ideas as to the feelings of S.C. towards the Union, if so, I wish to know it, the sooner the better. I had been led to believe, that a monarchy was contemplated by the Southern Nullifiers, to be, under the protection of England and the Holy Alliance. I am a republican from principle. To set up this form of government, my immediate relatives died in battle, to the number of six, and my own father, shed his blood freely in battle. Should a war come with England, I am ready to march in the ranks to oppose the enemy. I will not plead my age to shield me from military duty.

Born during our revolutionary war, and trained up under these free institutions, I feel in duty ["bound" *interlined*] to defend them, by my pen, and if necessary, by the rifle and the sword. If I have done your Southern people any injustice, even in my thoughts, I wish to know it, and to correct any error into which I may have innocently fallen. I will, seek the very first opportunity, I can find, to see the South Carolina people, now near me, at Mrs. Hill[']s [Hotel]—the old capitol, perhaps.

Although I shall always be happy to see you, yet, unless specially invited to call on you, I have no business of an official nature with you, and cannot trespass on your time and attention.

I am labouring every moment, which my health permits me to

use, to place before the people, my views of the men now in power, in this city. I shall neither extenuate nor set down aught in malice. I wish to do good by correcting even my own previously conceived opinions, on every subject which I discuss. From this administration I have rec[eive]d no favors, and, I expect none, and they, have none to expect from me, or the people. In this free country, I shall exercise all the rights of a freeman. Towards yourself, I have not one unkind feeling, and only regret that our old friendship was broken off, by circumstances, over which, I had no control. The distance between us, prevented my knowing your exact opinions, objects and aims. I am, too, just descending into my grave, and wish to die, in peace with all the world. Adieu, Caleb Atwater.

P.S. What I have written of you, I will read to Mr. [James A.] Black, of your State, and to your son [Patrick Calhoun], if he will call on me and see it. I say this, in justice to myself, and not because I suppose you care about it. I shall never see you again, I presume, and you will never see my book, nor myself.

Of the four volumes of which I am the author, two of them are easily found by either Mr. Winder or Mr. Carroll. Judge Upshur read them attentively as well as my other volumes. Those returned by him to me, are marked by his pen, and my History of Ohio, has papers in it, where he laid any stress on my opinions.

His death changed my destiny and threw me [on] my present position, from which, nothing [can] move me, until a change of Administration, shall effect a change in my position, towards those in power.

ALS in ScCleA. NOTE: Atwater had published *A History of the State of Ohio, Natural and Civil,* in 1838, and other works on education and archaeology. In his *Mysteries of Washington City, during several months of the Session of the 28th Congress. By a Citizen of Ohio* (Washington: G.A. Sage, 1844), pp. 169–176, he described a visit to Calhoun in his office on 4/5/1844, which included an hour's conversation before Calhoun invited Atwater to his residence that evening and left to confer with the Texas representatives. Atwater wrote in vividly immediate and highly complimentary terms about Calhoun's conversational charm, talents, public ethics, private character, and enthusiasm for his home near the mountains.

To [J.C.] de Figaniḛe e Morão, [Philadelphia?], 4/6. Calhoun acknowledges his letter of 4/3 concerning high tariff duties on Portuguese wines and will refer it to the Chairman of the House Committee on Foreign Affairs [Charles J. Ingersoll] with a request for prompt attention. FC in DNA, RG 59 (State Department), Notes to Foreign Legations, Portugal, 6:73 (M-99:80).

To Charles J. Ingersoll, Chairman, House Committee on Foreign Affairs, 4/6. Calhoun transmits to him a letter of 4/3 from [J.C. de Figaniere e Morão] the Portuguese Minister at Washington asking that high tariff duties on Portuguese wines be discontinued. LS with En in DNA, RG 233 (U.S. House of Representatives), 28A-F1; FC in DNA, RG 59 (State Department), Domestic Letters, 34:126–127 (M-40:32); PC with En in House Document No. 224, 28th Cong., 1st Sess., pp. 1–3.

From Louis Mark, Bamberg, 4/6. He has received exequaturs from the Prussian and Bavarian governments as U.S. Consul. Since he must be absent for some time while engaged in business for [Henry] Wheaton, [the U.S. Minister to Prussia], he has appointed agents for Munich, Bamberg, and the Rhine provinces. ALS ("Copy") with En in DNA, RG 59 (State Department), Consular Despatches, Munich, vol. 1 (T-261:1), received 5/11.

From R[ICHARD] PAKENHAM

Washington, April 6, 1844

Sir, In the letter which I had the honor to address to you on the 4th of this month in answer to one which I had received from Mr. [John] Nelson upon the subject of the grants of land made by the British Government within that portion of the Territory formerly in dispute, which now belongs to the State of Maine, I mentioned that I had taken measures to obtain from the Governor of New Brunswick the information desired by the Government of the United States upon this subject.

I have now the honor to acquaint you that I have this morning received a Dispatch from His Excellency Sir William Colebrooke, in which He tells me that He has given directions that copies of the grants with the diagrams may be forthwith prepared in the Surveyor General's Office to be transmitted to Washington with the least possible delay.

I take advantage of this opportunity to renew to you the Assurance of my high consideration. R. Pakenham.

LS in DNA, RG 59 (State Department), Notes from Foreign Legations, Great Britain, vol. 22 (M-50:22); PC in House Document No. 110, 29th Cong., 1st Sess., pp. 32–33.

From LEMUEL SAWYER, [former Representative from N.C.]

New York [City], April 6, 1844

Dear Sir, Allow an old friend to throw in a few words on the negotiation which I presume is going on between yourself & Mr. [J. Pinckney] Henderson on the subject of the annexation of Texas. Two of your immediate predecessors have had the question of recognition, of the right of title in the Rio Grande & Texas land company, on the part of the government of Texas, & we have had an agent, a Mr. [Stephen H.?] Everitt at the seat of government there, to press our claim upon the administration. It remains still undecided. Our title is sustained by documents which I presume may be seen in your office, but I will forward to you in a day or two, a pamphlet, containing a condensed view of our claim, the opinion of the late Judge John Woodward of this city. There can be no question as to our right to a number of citios [*sic*; sitios, or cattle ranches], amounting to near half a million of acres, of prime lands in fee, lying about the middle region, on the Nueces river, & purchased by our agent in 1832, from actual settlers, who held by grants from the government of Mexico. In addition to this is our empressario grant to Doc[to]r John C. Beale, a citizen of Mexico, of a tract on the Rio Grande of more than 8 millions of acres, conditional upon colonization, which condition we have only fulfilled in part, by settling a colony in 1832 at Dolores, which is a town on the Moros Creek, near the R[io] G[rande] river founded by us at great expense & settled by 40 families, with considerable improvements in mills & other buildings. We were not able to complete the empressario contracts, on account of the civil war, which arrested the tide of colonization, after we had engaged several hundreds of families at Bremen & other hanse-towns, where we had agents employed to engage imigrants. In fact we have expended $60,000 in endeavouring to settle & improve the grant. But for want of protection, we learn that our colony at Dolores is dispers[e]d, our stock carried off by indians & our improvements gone to ruin. Had it not been for the revolution in Texas we should have enjoyed an undisturbed possession, & an undoubtful title to our grants under the ceding power [of] Mexico. But we have aided the Texans in their struggle for independance, by loans in money & stores, to her commissioners here, Col. [Samuel M.] Williams & others, (besides gratuities) to the amount of thousands, & I have contributed $150 out of my own pocket towards the equipment of one of their cavalry officers here, a L[i]eut. Hitchcock, for which I have received no acknowledgment even, tho the fact is known to George G. Sickels Esqr. of Nas[sau] Street in this place, who was the agent for the officer.

Myself & many others here, are the innocent purchasers of stock in the company, & I hold 28 shares, some of which cost me $500 in 1832 but owing to the failure of Texas to do us common justice by acknowledging our title or offering us a fair compromise, the shares are fallen to a mere nominal price, & we are reduced to poverty. I for one therefore do hope & trust that no treaty for annexation will be entered into, unless as a condition precedent, the title of the Rio Grande & Texas land Company be admitted, or a liberal compromise offered, upon our relinquishing all our cl[aim] of title, or a specific sum proposed, by way of indemnification for our losses by delays & vexations on the part of the Texian government. What sum we might think a fair offer, I will not presume [to] hint, but if $100,000 were proposed by Texas, on stock at par, or enough at the present rates to bring it to par, with provision for the payment [of] interest, at suitable periods, it would be a very cheap considerat[ion] for so large & valuable a tract, but which, rather than continue to encounter such difficulties & delays, our ["government" *canceled and* "company" *interlined*] would no doubt agree to accept.

Beleiving this matter could not be placed in better hands than yours, we are willing to leave it there—And conclude with assurances of our high & respectful considerations, Lemuel Sawyer, Secretary to the Riogrande & Texas L[an]d Co.

ALS in DNA, RG 59 (State Department), Miscellaneous Letters (M-179:104, frames 143–144).

From HENRY R. SCHOOLCRAFT, "Private"

Washington, April 6th 1844

Sir: In the spring of 1841, I was removed ["from office" *canceled*] by Mr. [John] Bell, [Secretary of War; "from an office I held under gover(n)ment," *interlined*] on the ground, stated to me by him, that I was a democrat, and had exerted my official influence, in an improper manner. The former assertion was true; the latter untrue; but it suited the purposes of those who wished to succeed me, to make the assertion, & Mr. Bell acted on it, without hesitancy & without reference. I have never made an effort, written a letter, or uttered a word, to any man in authority, from that day to this, to regain the place [in the Office of Indian Affairs], or to obtain office under the gover[n]-ment, ["in any shape" *interlined*] with the single exception of a note [of 3/2/1842] which I addressed to you sir, while ["you were" *interlined*] in the Senate of the U. States, in the winter or spring of 1842, just previous to my embarkation on a visit to Europe. I believed, that my experience and observation on the character & resources of a very wide and varied country, endowed by nature for great purposes, would enable me to serve the country in some humble capacity abroad. With this exception my remark is strictly ["just" *canceled*] true.

I have never entered the noisy area of politics, nor do I wish to do it now. Nothing is farther from the tenor of my feelings or ambition, while ["at the same time," *interlined*] I entertain a strong feeling, with which I was born & shall die, in favour of those institutions, securing to all the exercise of simple republican rights & franchises, guarded & defined, for which America first raised the flag of rebellion to Great Britian [*sic*]. One word more, on this head, is essential. My father (the late Col. Lawrence Schoolcraft of Albany) was one of the first men, who in '76 joined the standard of his country at the age of 17, and served it well, through many trying scenes. It is from the fire side relations of this conflict, that I learned the true principles of the contest. My ta[s]tes, studies & inclinations, have not, however, lead [*sic*] me ["to" *interlined*] tread ["either" *interlined*] the ["bloody" *canceled*] path of war, or the vista of politics. In the ["marked" *interlined*] movement of 1840, it happened that the place I occupied was filled by a foreigner, [Robert Stuart, born in Scotland] whose countrymen had ["been" *interlined*] the most inveterate of the foes we had to contend with, in 1776—He was a person too, who, had spent his life in amassing a fortune by trade with the Indian tribes, over whose ["affairs," *interlined*] in violation of, at least, the *spirit* of an act of Congress, he was appointed to preside.

It is my impression, that were these facts made known to Mr. [John] Tyler, he would direct a reversal of the decision, thus hastily made by Mr. Bell ["in 1841" *canceled*]. And it is with this view, that I ["have the honor to" *canceled*] address you the present note. My feelings & judgment alike impel me to it, ["and if I err, I trust you will pardon the error" *interlined*.] I have the honor to request, ["therefore," *interlined*] that you will accord me, an interview ["on this subject" *interlined*] on ["Monday next, or" *interlined*] at your earliest convenience, ["in reference to this subject" *canceled.*] I am aware, that the ["matter" *canceled*] situation alluded to, pertains to another department; but this department, must necessarily, ["in some cases," *canceled*] be ["subject" *canceled*] open, ["in some cases" *interlined*] to Executive suggestion, and I am mistaken, if there are not some ["peculiar"(?) *canceled*] features in ["the" *canceled and* "my" *interlined*] statements ["made" *canceled*], to justify it.

As this note is designed to give information, on a topic, in which your friendly interposition, is ["asked" *canceled*] solicited, I deem it proper to add, ["that" *canceled*] as I have lived at a remote point [Mich.], & with but few opportunities of seeing you, ["in the course four & twenty years," *interlined*] that my present residence, & for the last three years, my home has been in the city of New York. ["Having" *canceled and* "In the journey of life, I have" *interlined*] passed the age of 50, ["and I am" *canceled and* "For two years I have been" *interlined*] a widower. I have two children, a son & daughter, both promising, ["& just" *canceled and* "who are fast" *interlined*] approaching the threshold of active life; and it cons[t]itutes my chief & highest object, to fit & prepare them, by a thorough education, for usefulness & honor in life. My heart is devoted to their interest, and this application, which is rather wrung from me, is ["to" *canceled and* "made, that I may" *interlined*] have the ["continued" *interlined*] means of attaining an object so momentous to me & to them. I am Sir, with regard, faithfully & truly Y[ou]rs, Henry R. Schoolcraft, Miss Polk's[,] Penn. Avenue.

Autograph draft in DLC, Henry Rowe Schoolcraft Papers.

From T[homas] L. Smith, Register's Office, Treasury Department, 4/6. "I have the honor to enclose a Statement of the balances of the appropriations, and at the periods indicated by your letter of the 4th Ins[tan]t." The enclosed statement shows, among other things, that as of 12/1/1843 there were unexpended balances of $15,003.45 for the contingent expenses of the State Department, "including publishing and distributing the Laws," and of $46,393.94 for its contingent expenses "of Foreign Intercourse." LS with En in DNA, RG 59 (State Department), Letters Received from the Fifth Auditor and Comptroller, 1829–1862.

From A[RCHIBALD] M. GREEN

Consulate of the United States at Galvezton
Republic of Texas, 7th April 1844

Sir, I have the honor to communicate to the Department the fact of the Texan Commissioners having returned from Mexico, and are now gone to Washington[-on-the-Brazos] to see the president [Samuel Houston] and make their report.

No treaty I understand had been made with that Government, and only an extension of an armistice, & neither party to renew hostilities without giving to the other six months previous notice. This much I learn from one of the Commissioners and an *opinion* is expressed by them that Mexico would acknowledge the independence of Texas, provided the latter would remain a separate, free, and independent Government, & with a condition not to annex herself to the United States, also as another requirement Texas shall pay a due proportion of the Mexican debt.

The prospect of this country being annexed to the United States has cheered its inhabitants on to great activity, and beginning industry, a people naturally active, and energetic, with a good soil, and mild climate, are great advantages to a country like this, which is capable of producing every thing necessary to the wants and comforts for its inhabitants, besides a large surplus; yet when nature does so much, men seem ordinarily to do less than is naturally expected, and until now, industry and enterprize have been much neglected. And when the government has given its people quiet and security in their persons and property, it has done most that can be expected of it; And their own enterprise, industry, and intelligence, will it is to be expected doubtless do the rest.

There is ["nearly" *canceled*] always a constant cool breeze from the ocean and prairie, which purifies the air, and tempers the heat of the Sun. There is a clearness in the whole Atmosphere and in the heavens that is but rarely seen in any other Country, & it seems as if nature had selected her choicest beauties and greatest excellences & blended them into one scene.

At this season of the year but little sickness exists in the Country and the season is regarded as being very propitious towards the agricultural and farming interests and with the usual blessings of providence the crop of this year will greatly exceed that of the last.

By this mail I send you some papers. Already the length of my letter being much greater than contemplated and fearing, I may be intrusive, I beg leave to subscribe myself your most obedient Servant, A.M. Green.

ALS (No. 31) in DNA, RG 59 (State Department), Consular Despatches, Galveston, vol. 2 (T-151:2), received 4/19.

From BENJAMIN HALE

Newburyport Mass., April 7th 1844
Permit us dear Sir to call to your notice the case of the Seisure of the "Brig Retrieve" by the gover[n]ment of Texas in 1844 [*sic*] for the purpose of transporting Troops, for the particulars of this outrageous transaction reference to the papers, accompanying our claim now in the Dept. will more fully explain.

Hon. D[aniel] Webster acknowledged the receipt of the claim, with the assurance it would be urged to the fullest extent. The Hon. A[bel] P. Upshur his successor, entering on his official duties, wrote us that the Papers still remained in the Dept., that he had caused them to be copied at our expense, and had forwarded them to our Charged de Affairs at Galveston to be urged for Settlement.

Will the Dept. have the goodness to inform us if there is any prospect of the claim being adjusted, as it is confidently beleived that negotiations are progressing towards uniting both gover[n]-ments. This claim being of a character leaving us no alternative but that of seeking redress through our own Gover[n]ment, we confidently hope and beleive for the honour of the nation they will not loose sight of this most insolent and outrageous transaction without a full indemnity. Although comparatively small in a national point of view it is a very important and serious matter to us. The perplexity and trouble growing out of this transaction was no doubt the cause of the death of the Capt. of the Brig before he was able to reach home, and I am fearfull it may follow me to the grave unsettled. Any assistance your Honour may render us in bringing this business to a close will be greatfully appreciated. With Sentiments of high esteem beleive us truly your Ob[e]d[ient] Servants, Benjamin Hale for himself & Moses E. Hale.

ALS in DNA, RG 59 (State Department), Miscellaneous Letters (M-179:104, frames 145–147).

To "Col." Antonio de Aycinena, 4/8. "I have the honor to acknowledge the receipt of your letter of the 3rd instant . . . requesting your recognition by this Government" as Consul General for Guatemala in the U.S. "The corresponding Exequatur of the President of the United States [John Tyler] is accordingly herewith transmitted . . . ." FC in DNA, RG 59 (State Department), Domestic Letters, 34:134–135 (M-40:32).

From BEN E. GREEN

Legation of the U.S. of A.
Mexico [City], April 8th 1844

Sir, I have the honor to inform you that Gen[era]l [Waddy] Thompson [Jr.] left here on the 9th ultimo. Mr. [Peyton A.] Southall arrived on the 27th. On the 28th I addressed the note, marked no. 1, to the Minister of Foreign Affairs [José M. de Bocanegra]. Well knowing that the object of this Government would be to temporize and delay, I was anxious to get them committed at once by the appointment of Plenipotentiaries to treat upon the subject. On the 29th I called to see Mr. Bocanegra, who told me that nothing could be done, before hearing from Gen[era]l [Juan N.] Almonte. I endeavoured to urge upon him the propriety of giving at least an immediate hearing to what the U.S. had to say. He assured me of his desire to do so; but said that all he could do would be to inform me, as soon as he heard from Gen[era]l Almonte. On the 30th I addressed him, *unofficially*, the private note (no. 2). I was in hopes that this would have the desired effect; but on the 1st inst[ant], I received the note (no. 3), giving the same excuse for delay. I know that this is a mere pretext to secure the delay of another year; and I thereupon addressed to him the note [of 4/2] (no. 4), with copies of the Resolutions of the Senate and of Mr. [Abel P.] Upshur's despatch (no. 55). In the latter I omitted the paragraph, beginning: "But let us suppose that a case is made out, & reparation only demanded" &c. I thought it best to do so, because it seemed to be the wish of Mexico, in framing this Convention, to make the 16th art[icle] as comprehensive as possible. Here was the whole struggle. The Mexican Plenipotentiaries were anxious to throw all international claims into the hands of the umpire; and the argument here used would be with them an additional incentive to insist upon doing so; in as much as they would probably infer from it, that the U.S. feared an unfavorable and exorbitant award against them.

It will be very difficult to induce them to yeild these points, however clear the propriety of doing so may appear to you. The fact is that Mexico, ever since her revolution of independence, has been the prey of mal-administration & corruption. She is now completely exhausted. Any proposition to pay money at all, and particularly to foreign claimants, is extremely unpopular. The Convention of '39 was used by those now in power to throw odium on the administration of [Anastasio] Bustamante. To divert attention from themselves, they have fed the popular prejudice with the cry that foreigners were impoverishing the country by draining it of its specie. They have thus raised a spirit, which they are now afraid to cross; and the question for them to solve is whether they can with more impunity risk their uncertain popularity at home, or offend the U.S. They can not, and do not, deny the justice of our claims, nor the evident propriety of having those claims adjusted by a commission to sit in Washington. But the words of the Minister of Hacienda, to Gen[era]l Thompson, were: "We must satisfy our people; and to do so, we must make them believe that we too have claims upon the U.S." It was for this reason that the convention was framed in reference to the settlement of *mutual* claims, when in fact Mexico had no claims upon us; and for this reason they positively refused to treat on any other condition than that the Commission should sit in Mexico. You will thus readily see the difficulty to be encountered in effecting what you desire. I will continue to press the subject, respectfully but urgently; and perhaps may succeed. I am far from being sanguine of success. At this moment they are afraid to do any thing to weaken their popularity, and their object will be to delay as long as possible, and to wait the course of events.

Permit me, sir, to suggest that the mild tone of conciliation adopted in Mr. Upshur's Despatch, no. 55, is lost upon these people, and in confirmation, to refer to Gen[era]l Thompson's various despatches. Friendly argument is unheeded by them; and language, stern and positive, alone commands their respect and attention.

The menudes law has not been repealed, notwithstanding the united remonstrances of all the foreign Ministers. What is most singular is that it should be persisted in, when all intelligent Mexicans are now of opinion that it can not but be injurious to Mexico, by driving so much capital & industry out of the country, apart from the prospect of a collision with France. The French Govt. has taken the most positive ground, and no doubt is entertained here that its action will be as positive as its words. The Secretary of the Legation left here on the 20th ult[imo], with despatches for his Govt. on the subject; and France having committed herself so far, not only by the speech of Mr. [F.P.G.] Guizot in the Chambers, but by her instructions to [De Cyprey] her Minister here (which I learn are of the strongest character), another blockade of the ports may be expected.

What makes the matter worse is that licenses to continue business have been sent, *unsolicited*, to most of the English retailers. On the other hand, the French have been treated with rigour, & compelled to conform to the strict requirements of the Decree. This conduct can not but exasperate France and render an amicable settlement more difficult.

Certainly if ever a country needed quiet and a peaceful Govt. Mexico needs them now. Santa Anna, however, said to Gen[era]l Thompson, and says openly, that Mexico needs a foreign war to *develope her resources*! It is the general opinion here that he really seeks to involve his country in war, with a view to the reassumption of the Dictatorial power, which he held under the 7a base of Tacubaya. If it is possible to learn his character aright from common report, one might believe that he looks to even more than the "facultades estraordinarias" of the 7a Base, and that he seeks to place upon his brow the imperial diadem, which cost [Agustin de] Iturbide his life.

The Congress has adjourned, and the trial of strength between it and Santa Anna has resulted in favor of the latter. The former began by proposing to annul many of his decrees; but adjourned without doing so in any one instance. He is still near Jalapa, and delays coming to Mexico [City] to take the oath of office. 'Tis generally thought he avoids taking the oath, until events ripen for his purposes. The new British Minister [Charles Bankhead] arrived some weeks since, and was received as the best of friends. The best feeling seems to prevail between him and this Govt., and it is evident that Santa Anna seeks a difficulty with France, while he cultivates the most friendly relations with England. The quarrel with France will throw every thing into confusion, and furnish the favourable opportunity; and England will, doubtless, be well pleased to see Mexico settle down quietly under his despotic sway. Unfortunately there are many Mexicans, who honestly believe that to be the best remedy for the evils they now suffer.

I send you the "Siglo XIX," [newspaper] of the 5 inst[ant] in which Santa Anna's ambitious views are hinted at, and condemned. This is an opposition paper, but dares not speak very openly. In the Diario [official newspaper] of the 6th I have marked the place, in which the "Siglo" is warned of the punishment of traitors.

I deem it proper to inform you in advance that the payment of the next instalment is extremely doubtful. The last was paid with much difficulty. They could pay but $60,000 on the day; with the greatest difficulty the balance was raised, and the whole was not paid until the 1st March. Before Gen[era]l Thompson left, he heard from a quarter, not to be neglected, that the next would probably not be paid. There is scarcely a dollar in the Treasury; and now that preparations must be made for the anticipated difficulty with France, their ability to pay becomes even more questionable. For the sake of the claimants, I hope it may be paid, and for the sake of Mexico herself, it is to be hoped that our difficulties with her may be speedily and amicably arranged. She has much to lose; but we have nothing to gain by quarrelling with her unless indeed we should end by gaining possession of California, and thereby secure a harbourage for our shipping on the Pacific, and one of the finest countries on the Globe.

You will see by the copies (nos. 6 & 7) of the notes of Mr. Bocanegra of the 26th and 30th March, that the period, fixed by the Decree of the 14 Aug[us]t last for the sale or reembarcation of prohibited goods, has been extended to three years. I have the honor to be Very Respectfully Your ob[edien]t Serv[an]t, Ben E. Green.

ALS (No. 1) with Ens in DNA, RG 59 (State Department), Diplomatic Despatches, Mexico, vol. 12 (M-97:13), received 5/11; FC in DNA, RG 84 (Foreign Posts), Mexico, Despatches, pp. 484–489; draft in NcU, Duff Green Papers (published microfilm, roll 5, frames 357–368). NOTE: In addition to the enclosures mentioned by Green, a copy in Spanish of a letter of 4/6 from de Bocanegra to Green and an English translation are enclosed. Upshur's despatch No. 55, dated 2/9/1844 and addressed to Waddy Thompson, [Jr.,] can be found in DNA, RG 59 (State Department), Diplomatic Instructions, Mexico, 15:275–288 (M-77:111). Ben E. Green was one of the many children of Duff and Lucretia Maria Edwards Green and an 1838 graduate of Georgetown College, D.C. He was practicing law in New Orleans in 12/1843 when he was appointed by John Tyler to be Secretary of the U.S. legation in Mexico. On the departure of the Minister, Waddy Thompson, Jr., he became acting Chargé d'Affaires.

W[ILLIAM] S. MURPHY to
President [John Tyler]

Legation of the United States
Galveston Texas, 8th April 1844

Dear Sir, I had been at Houston 3 weeks, waiting the arrival of Pres[i]d[ent] [Samuel] Houston. He arrived there 3 Days ago; and we came here together yesterday.

Her Brit[annic] Maj[e]st[y's] Chargé d'Affaires [Charles Elliot] and the Texan Commissioners [to Mexico] had arrived here some time before.

I learn that the Commissioners had suspended further negociations for the Present, But the armistice is to continue—and the Commissioners are to meet again, and resume negociations, as soon as Her Brit[annic] Maj[e]st[y's] Minister, at Mexico [Charles Bankhead], shall have arranged & settled, with the Mexican Govt. the, New Policy, in the arrangement of which, the affairs of Texas, are to bear a conspicuous part.

The President of Texas, has rec[eive]d by the Neptune, a dispatch from Mr. [Isaac] Van Zandt, in which he says, my stipulations, touching the negociation of a Treaty of annexation are disavowed by my Govt.—And the President, informs me, but a few moments ago, that he sends a dispatch, by the Neptune (now on the eve of departure) to Gen[era]l [J. Pinckney] Henderson not to move, in the negociation, unless such pledges and assurances, are again renewed, by my Govt.

I rec[eive]d a letter from Capt. [John G.] Tod, by the Neptune dated at Washington City 15th March, in which he informs me, that a Similar disavowal of my Conduct, had been, or would be transmitted to me. If such be the fact, I shall Certainly receive it, by the New York Steamer, which is looked for tomorrow, or next day.

I lament, all these occurrences, but I hope, that a Treaty will have been concluded before these instructions, from President Houston, reach Washington.

The Flirt was sent out, merely for the purpose of obtaining information. But, on the 3d day after her departure, she returned to Port, under stress of weather, where she has been ever since.

Nothing has occur[r]ed, or [is] likely to occur for a long time, to disturb the peace of Texas—or lead in any event to Hostilities between Texas & Mexico—and you will allow me to say, that no inconvenience can possibly ensue, from allowing the Negociations to proceed, under the assurances I made.

185

But I will obey any order given me, as I have hitherto done, with all diligence & alacrity. I have written in great haste, & must close—the Boat is about to leave the wharf. With Sentiments of the most profound respect & high esteem, Your ob[edien]t Serv[an]t, W.S. Murphy.

ALS (Private & confidential) in DNA, RG 59 (State Department), Diplomatic Despatches, Texas, vol. 2 (T-728:2, frames 303–304), received 4/19.

From A[lphonse] Pageot, [French Minister to the U.S.], 4/8. He has received from his government the ratifications of the U.S.-France extradition treaty. On what day would it be convenient for Calhoun to exchange them for those of the U.S. government? LS (in French) in DNA, RG 59 (State Department), Notes from Foreign Legations, France, vol. 12 (M-53:8, frames 701–703).

To Charles Rogers, [Representative from N.Y.], 4/8. In reply to Rogers' note of 4/4 enclosing a House resolution of 4/2, Calhoun refers Rogers to several printed reports concerning State Department finances and adds manuscript statements reporting balances totaling about $90,000 as of 3/4/1841 in two contingent accounts and about $75,000 in the same two accounts as of 12/1/1843. FC in DNA, RG 59 (State Department), Accounting Records, Miscellaneous Letters Sent, 1832–1916, vol. for 2/1–9/30/1844, pp. 93–95; PC with Ens in House Report No. 484, 28th Cong., 1st Sess.

To N[athaniel] L. Rogers & Brothers, Salem, Mass., 4/8. Calhoun acknowledges the receipt of their letter of 3/30 concerning a claim they have against the British government for charging a duty on a large quantity of American rum exported to and landed at New Zealand. In reply Calhoun encloses a copy of a note of 2/10 from "Her Britannic Majesty's Principal Secretary of State for Foreign Affairs" to the U.S. Minister at London, "showing the present state of your Claim, which you are assured will not be lost sight of by this Department." FC in DNA, RG 59 (State Department), Domestic Letters, 34:130–131 (M-40:32).

From R. H. Weyman

Charleston, April 8th 1844

Respected Sir, This package will be handed you by our well received & distinguished friend Mr. Henry Clay, and from the station you now occupy, I feel assured an immediate demand will be made on the government of Columbia [*sic*] for just satisfaction of my claim. Mr. Beaufort T. Watts arranged the papers for me, when acting as charge des affaires in that Republic.

An early attention to this matter, & an acknowledgement of the receipt of these papers will greatly oblige Y[ou]rs with sentiment of high regard, R.H. Weyman.

P.S. I beg further to remark that the papers are legally recorded both in Maracaybo & Bogota. R.H.W.

ALS with En in DNA, RG 76 (Records of Boundary and Claims Commissions and Arbitrations), Miscellaneous Claims Records: Colombia, 1818–1825. NOTE: Weyman enclosed a 70-page memorandum and chronology, in Spanish, of his claim. A State Dept. Clerk's EU reads "Rejected for want of proof. Feb. 17/[18]66."

To [Alphonse] Pageot, [French Minister to the U.S.], 4/9. "The Secretary of State presents his compliments to Mr. Pageot, and will be happy to see him at the Department of State to-day or to-morrow, at such time as it may suit his convenience to call." FC in DNA, RG 59 (State Department), Notes to Foreign Legations, France, 6:80 (M-99:21).

To Lemuel Sawyer, [former Representative from N.C.], New York [City], 4/9. "I have to acknowledge the receipt of your letter of the 6th instant, relative to the claim of the Rio Grande and Texas Land Company, and to inform you in reply that the suggestions which it contains shall be taken into respectful consideration." FC in DNA, RG 59 (State Department), Domestic Letters, 34:129–130 (M-40:32).

To George W. Summers and Augustus A. Chapman, [Representatives from Va.], 4/9. Calhoun informs them that their letter to the President [John Tyler] on 4/4 was referred to him. In answer, he states that the U.S. Minister to Mexico has been instructed to do all that lies within his power to effect the release of Ezekiel Smith, the Texan prisoner on whose behalf they wrote. FC in DNA, RG 59 (State Department), Domestic Letters, 34:130 (M-40:32).

From H[UGH] J. ANDERSON, [Governor of Maine]

State of Maine
Executive Department
Belfast, 10th April 1844

Sir, I have recently received a copy of a Memorial addressed to the President of the United States [John Tyler] by a large number of respectable citizens of the City of Bangor in this State, representing, that the Provincial Government of New Brunswick has passed an Act imposing an export duty of twenty cents per ton upon all timber shipped from any port in that Province. As this Act of the Provincial Government makes no exception in favor of timber cut upon territory belonging to this State, and indeed, is supposed to have been adopted specially for the purpose of taxing the produce of our soil & industry, it has occasioned no little uneasiness & alarm.

By the third article of the Treaty of Washington, the people of this State had supposed the free & unrestricted use of the river St. John, for the purposes therein specified was explicitly guaranteed to them; and they perceive with surprise & indignation a disposition evinced by the authorities of New Brunswick and countenanced by the British Government, to impose such conditions & restrictions, as will render this important article of the Treaty wholly nugatory.

In behalf of the people of this State, who are deeply interested in a scrupulous fulfilment of the terms of the Treaty, I respectfully request your attention to this matter. I have the honor to be with great respect Your obedient Servant, H.J. Anderson.

LS in DNA, RG 59 (State Department), Miscellaneous Letters (M-179:104, frames 156–157).

To [Richard K. Crallé], 4/10. "I hereby appoint Richard K. Cralle of Virginia, to be Chief Clerk in the Department of State, during the pleasure of the Secretary of State for the time being, with a salary at the rate of two thousand dollars per annum. [Signed:] Secretary of State, J.C. Calhoun." LS in ScCleA.

To Edward Everett, London, 4/10. Calhoun encloses five documents related to the claim of N[athaniel] L. Rogers & Brothers of Salem, Mass., against the British government for duties levied in New Zealand. He refers Everett to instructions sent in 1842 about pursuing settlement of the claim. LS (No. 82) with Ens in DNA, RG 84

(Foreign Posts), Great Britain, Instructions, 8:57–92, received 5/21; FC in DNA, RG 59 (State Department), Diplomatic Instructions, Great Britain, 15:189–190; CC with Ens in DNA, RG 76 (Records of Boundary and Claims Commissions and Arbitrations), Miscellaneous Claims Records: Great Britain, Convention of Feb. 8, 1853.

From Sam[ue]l A. Hale, Tuscaloosa, [Ala.], 4/10. Hale encloses to Calhoun a petition asking for the release from prison in Mexico of a young man named [William F.] McMath. McMath's father "will feel very thankful at learning from the Department of State that the petition has been forwarded." ALS in DNA, RG 59 (State Department), Miscellaneous Letters (M-179:104, frames 158–159).

From ROB[ER]T MONROE HARRISON

Consulate of the United States
Kingston Jamaica, 10th April 1844
Sir, I have merely time to inform you that two American vessels have just arrived here from Aux Cayes, from the vengeance of the Negroes, who had declared a war of extermination against the Browns.

The masters of these vessels report to me, that several others may be expected here in a day or two with other Emigrants, and amongst whom, will be our Commercial Agent [William B. Gooch] with his family. It is deeply to be regretted that none of our Men of War seldom or ever come here, as our Commercial Agent at Port au Prince is most anxious for one to protect American interest at that Place, and has written me to that effect.

I have been for some time expecting the "Preble" from Carthagena, where she has been on shore (but said to have received no damage) and when she arrives, I shall recommend the Commander to proceed to Aux Cayes. With great respect I have the honor to be Sir Your Ob[edien]t and most humble Servant, Robt. Monroe Harrison.

LS (No. 280) in DNA, RG 59 (State Department), Consular Despatches, Kingston, vol. 8 (T-31:8), received 5/7. NOTE: A State Dept. Clerk's EU, dated 5/7, reads "Respectfully referred to the Sec[re]t[ar]y of the Navy [John Y. Mason,] for perusal."

From DAVID HAYDEN

Washington, April 10th 1844

Sir, The following Estimate of the Imports and Exports of what is called *"Eastern Texas"* do not find a place in the commercial Statistics of Texas, and are therefore to be added, to any such Statistics.

For the Year 1843

Jefferson & Jasper	Counties	Export	6000	Bales	Cotton
Sabine County	County [*sic*]	"	6000	"	do
San Augustine	do	"	8000	"	"
Nacogdoches	do	"	8000	"	"
Shelby	do	"	8000	"	"
Bowie	do	"	6000	"	"
Red River, Fannin & Lamar		"	10,000	do	do
Harrison County		do	8,000	do	do
		Total	60,000	Bales	

60,000 Bales @ $40.00 gives $2,400,000 as the Value of the Exports of Eastern Texas [along the La. border] alone. The imports from the United States, into Eastern Texas, will amount to as much as the Exports, $2,400,000. The reason why the Commercial Statistics of Texas do not show, this importation from the United States, is found in the fact that the people of Eastern Texas pay no duties upon the produce and Merchandise introduced through the frontier.

The reason why the United States commercial Statistics do not show this import of Texas Cotton, is because ¾ths of all the Texas Cotton passing down Red River goes as the produce of the United States. The ratio of increase of the Culture of Texas Cotton in Eastern Texas, has for the last three years been as 2 to 1. $1\%_{0}$ths of the Imports from the United [States] into Eastern Texas are the produce & manufactures of the United States. You may rely upon these statements as not being far from the truth. I am Sir Very Respectfully Your Ob[edien]t Servant, David Hayden.

ALS in DNA, RG 59 (State Department), Miscellaneous Letters (M-179:104, frames 153–155). NOTE: Hayden was an official in the New Orleans Customhouse.

From W[ILLIA]M HOGAN

Washington, 10 April 1844

I have the honor, Sir, of enclosing to you, my account [*not found*] for services rendered on my late Private Mission to Mexico and Cuba[.] Very respectfully your ob[edien]t Servant, Wm. Hogan.

ALS in ScCleA. NOTE: An endorsement on this letter reads: "Mr. Hogan's acc[oun]t for Secret Service." See below Hogan's letter of 5/9 and the undated letter from Charles H. Winder placed at the end of April. Found among Calhoun's papers at ScCleA are four documents pertaining to Hogan dated before Calhoun entered the State Department. The most important of these is a long letter from Hogan, Mexico [City], 2/3/1844, to Abel P. Upshur. In this letter Hogan expounded at length on the "views & desighns [*sic*] of the Mexican Government & its ecclesiastical establishment, on the Institution of slavery in the United States, Texas, &c." These designs were being aided by the "Irish Clergy" and British agents. Hogan's conclusions were based upon conversations with high ranking members of the Catholic hierarchy and the government. He added that he had learned that U.S. civil and military officers in Mexico had been giving away secrets to persons met socially who were actually spies for Santa Anna. Also among Calhoun's papers are letters from Hogan, Boston, 9/15/1843, to Upshur, pursuing appointment as U.S. Consul at Lyons, France; from Upshur to Hogan, 11/1/1843, giving permission to deviate from the agreed upon route to Cuba; and from Joshua R. Sands, Commander, U.S. Navy, Havana, to Hogan, 1/11/1844, concerning Hogan's transportation to Mexico. Found among the papers of Richard K. Crallé, Calhoun's Chief Clerk, at ViU (Crallé-Campbell Papers) are six more Hogan documents, dated from 7/17/1843 to 11/29/1843, mostly letters between Hogan and Upshur concerning Hogan's seeking an appointment by the State Department. In 1843 Upshur did appoint Hogan as U.S. Consul for Nuevitas and Cienfuegos, Cuba. Hogan (1788–1848) was a native of Ireland and a former priest who was well-known as a leader of the ultimately unsuccessful but widespread effort in the American Catholic church to increase the power of parish laymen against the bishops.

From [Johann Georg, Chevalier von] Hülsemann, [Austrian Chargé d'Affaires in the U.S.], 4/10. He acknowledges the announcement of Calhoun's appointment as Secretary of State. ALS (in French) in DNA, RG 59 (State Department), Notes from Foreign Legations, Austria, vol. 1 (M-48:1).

From J[abez] W. Huntington, [Senator from Conn.], and Levi Woodbury, [Senator from N.H.], 4/10. They introduce E. Champion Bacon of Litchfield, Conn., "a gentleman of the highest respectability, of perfect integrity, & of great moral worth. . . . He is about to visit Europe, & we shall feel obliged, if you can confide to his care despatches for our minister at London, or will furnish him with a travelling passport." LS (in Huntington's hand) in ScCleA.

From THOMAS O. LARKIN

Consulate of the United States of America
Monterey California, April 10, 1844

Sir, I have the honor to inform you that I have received my commission of Consul for this Port, also the corresponding Exequatur from Mexico [City], under date of December 2d 1843. The acknowled[g]ment of my commission has also been made by Don Manuel Micheltoreno Gov[erno]r General of this Department of California, as by his letter to me of yesterday.

I observe that my appointment was to hold only untill the end of the next Session of the Senate. I shall at this distance hardly know in time whether the appointment was ratified by the Senate or not.

As I am the first United States Consul who has entered upon the duties of his Office in California (the English Vice Consul took office here a few months ago) I am without Seal, Stamp, press, Books, flag or coat of Arms. By applying to Messrs. William Appleton & Co. or B.T. Read Esq. Merchants, Boston, information can be obtained when a Vessel leaves Boston for this coast, by their Vessels any thing from the Depart[ment] of State can be sent to me.

I have signed my Bond for the Office of Consul, and ["sent" *interlined*] it to the United States to be filled up. I have the honor to be with much respect your most Obedient Ser[van]t, Thomas O. Larkin, Consul.

ALS (No. 1) in DNA, RG 59 (State Department), Consular Despatches, Monterey (M-138:1), received 6/19; FC in CU, Bancroft Library, Larkin Collection; PC in Hammond, ed., *Larkin Papers*, 2:91. NOTE: An AEU by Larkin on the FC reads "Answer dated June 24, 1844. Rec[eive]d May 2, 1845."

To J.M. Macpherson, Pontotoc, Miss., 4/10. "Your letter of the 22nd Ult[im]o resigning the office of Commercial Agent for the Republic of Paraguay, and returning the certificate of appointment &c sent to you, has been received, and your resignation accepted." FC in DNA, RG 59 (State Department), Consular Instructions, 11:228.

From GEO[RGE] W. SLACUM

Consulate of the United States
Rio de Janeiro, 10th April 1844

Sir, I have the honor to acknowledge the receipt of your letter under date 10th of January in which you inform me "that the President has appointed George W. Gordon Esq. to succeed you as United States Consul at Rio de Janeiro"; and you request me to deliver over to him the Archives of the Consulate, and all other property in my possession belonging to the United States.

Mr. Gordon presented your letter yesterday and the moment he is recognised by this Government, your Instructions shall be complied with. I have the honor to be Sir Your most obed[ien]t Serv[an]t, Geo. W. Slacum.

LS (No. 76) in DNA, RG 59 (State Department), Consular Despatches, Rio de Janeiro, vol. 7 (T-172:8), received 5/30. Note: This despatch was addressed to Abel P. Upshur.

From J[ohn] C. Spencer, Secretary of the Treasury, 4/10. In reference to a letter of 3/30 from C[laudius] Crozet to Calhoun [*The Papers of John C. Calhoun,* 17:905–906], Spencer informs Calhoun that Manuel Simon Cuculla has already been appointed to the office [Collector of Customs at New Orleans] sought by Crozet. LS in DNA, RG 59 (State Department), Miscellaneous Letters (M-179: 104, frame 155); FC in DNA, RG 56 (Treasury Department), Letters to Cabinet and Bureau Officers, Series B, 1842–1847, 4:349.

From HENRY WHEATON, "Private"

Berlin, 10 April, 1844

My dear Sir, You will not doubt that I learnt through the Newspapers of your appointment as Secretary of State with the highest satisfaction. I trust that in consideration of the critical state of our public affairs you will not ["acce" *canceled*] hesitate to accept this post in which it may be in your power to render most important services to the Country. I saw your retirement from the Senate with regret, & shall be much gratified to learn that you have determined again to participate in the public councils.

Anticipating that this will be the case, I take the freedom of an old friend in calling your attention to the results of my recent commercial negotiations here.

I was authorized by the President's [John Tyler's] instructions, communicated through our late lamented friend Mr. [Abel P.] Upshur, to conclude an Agreement with the German Zollverein for a mutual reduction of Tariffs in respect to certain articles, either in the form of an Arrangement to be submitted to Congress for its approbation, or of a Treaty to be laid before the Senate for its advice & consent to ratification. My reasons for adopting the latter mode of proceeding are stated in my Despatch, No. 241, dated the 10 March, addressed to Mr. Upshur, & marked *private*. I have good grounds for believing that he would have approved of my determination.

The grounds upon which the Convention already transmitted for ratification was concluded are fully stated in my official despatches accompanying and preceding it. Should it be approved & carried into execution, some of the most objectionable features of our present exaggerated Tariff may be effaced, & at the same time great advantages secured to our staple articles of Cotton, Rice, Tobacco, & Lard in the extensive & increasing markets of Germany. I do not know what may be your opinion on this point, but it appears to me that the most advantageous mode of effecting modifications in our present Tariff is by diplomatic Arrangements with other nations, since we thereby secure equivalent concessions from them; whereas if the duties of importation be reduced by legislation, independant of the action of foreign Powers, we obtain nothing from them in return, & they will not even thank us for the boon.

You will perceive that the reductions stipulated on our part by the Convention are principally applied to those articles which ["are" canceled] were left *free* by the Compromise Act of 1833, & which were subsequently burthened with excessive duties, which duties are now proposed to be reduced to 10, 15, & 20 per cent ad valorem. I do not see how the manufacturing States of our Union can reasonably refuse such a concession to the agricultural States of the South & West, especially when their own commercial & navigating interests will be essentially promoted by such an Arrangement. I should think a strong appeal might be made on this ground to the sense of justice & wisdom in the North. Whatever may be thought of the policy of *protecting*, by duties carried beyond the point of what is necessary for revenue, branches of manufacture which already exist, & might perish for want of that protection, it surely cannot be ["necessary" canceled] deemed wise to force into existence by artificial means new branches, at the expence of the agricultural, navigating, & commercial interests of the Country, as well as the more general interests of the great body of its consumers.

You will observe that both the contracting Parties are left perfectly at liberty to grant similar concessions to other States, with or without equivalents, & either by special Arrangements or by general modifications of the respective Tariffs. The only qualification of this reserve is that favours granted to others shall immediately be extended to each Party, gratuitously if gratuitous, & on giving the same equivalent if conditional, & that such general modifications shall not exclude either Party from participating in the common benefit of reductions made by legislative Acts. Even should the Germanic Association exercise this reserved power by extending to *all* foreign Tobacco the reductions of duties on *our* Tobacco stipulated by the Convention, our object would still be in a great measure attained, as it is principally North American Tobacco which is now, & will continue to be, consumed in Germany. We should still continue to profit by the reduction on Tobacco in proportion to the quantity we imported into the ports of the *Zollverein,* whilst the stipulations against increasing the present duties on *our Rice* & exempting *our Cotton* from all duties whatever would still remain in full force. On the other hand, if we should exercise the reserved right by extending the reductions stipulated in favour of the silks, linens, &c. of Germany to the same productions of any & all other nations, there would in my opinion be no harm in it; and it might even be attended with great benefit, if we should thereby obtain equivalent concessions from others in favour of our principal agricultural productions. Indeed it is in this point of view that I regard the Treaty as most valuable. Its importance ought not to be measured merely by the extent of the concessions obtained from Germany, but by its value as an instrument of negotiation by which the admission of our agricultural staples into the other European markets may be secured on terms equally favorable, & as the first step towards a more liberal commercial intercourse between the different nations of Europe & the United States. It is in this point of view that it is regarded in Paris, London, & Vienna, where the progress of the negotiation has been watched, & the conclusion of the Treaty has been looked at with the most intense anxiety, & with a view to ward off its consequences upon the manufacturing & commercial interests of France, G[reat] Britain, & Austria.

There are several other subjects connected with our foreign commercial concerns to which your official attention will necessarily be called. These are

1. The Danish Sound duties.

2. The duties collected by the Hanoverian government at Stade on the river Elbe.

3. Our existing reciprocity treaties of Navigation with Denmark, the Hanse towns, & other States of northern Europe.

On these different subjects my views, the result of much consideration, were fully explained to the Department in my Despatches,

No. 173, dated 10 March, 1841, No. 187, dated 8 Sept. 1841, No. 188, dated 24 Sept. 1841, and No. 239, dated 21 Feb. 1844. Whenever you can find time to take up these subjects, I respectfully request you to read these Papers. In respect to the question of the treaties of Navigation, I would, at present, merely observe that, in my opinion, very different considerations of policy ought to be applied in negotiating for a revision of these Treaties with States such as the Hanse towns & Denmark, which have no back country & a comparitively small number of consumers, from those which are applicable to the German Zollverein represented by Prussia, which has equivalent commercial advantages to offer for the largest concessions in favour of its ["navigat" *canceled*] shipping interests. In respect to the former, I consider our treaty with Hanover as affording the proper measure of concessions, whilst in respect to Prussia, I think the existing treaty of 1828 may be suffered to continue without inconvenience.

I wrote Mr. Upshur in February [*sic*; March 1] a private Letter, of which I have kept no copy, relating to one of the questions of public law involved in the negotiation respecting the Oregon territory, which I have already desired might be delivered to his successor in office, & to which I ask your attention.

I also wrote the President on the 27 March stating the expediency of revising our existing treaty of Commerce & Navigation with France, with a view of obtaining from that Power concessions in favour of our agricultural staples similar to those contained in the proposed Convention with the Zollverein. I also stated the urgency of commencing the negotiations for that purpose with the least possible delay, in order to be able to lay the results before the Senate at the opening of the next Session of Congress, & that if it was the President's intention (as I had been informed by Mr. Upshur) to nominate me for the mission to Paris, no time should be lost, & none need be lost on account of our affairs here, in making the appointment, as should the Convention with the Zollverein be ratified, the ratification could be exchanged by the Secretary of this Legation, & the other minor business committed to my charge here would all be finished in the month of May.

I shall sometimes take the liberty of writing you in this form, but must request that my Letters marked *private* may be considered as strictly so, & not in any case to be placed on the official files of the Department. This suggestion is, of course, not intended to prevent you from communicating this, or any other of my Letters on public affairs, to the President whenever you may think fit.

I most sincerely sympathize with you in the sudden & violent death of our excellent friend [Virgil] Maxcy. In him you have lost a constant, disinterested, & enlightened friend, & his family their ornament, stay, & support. I pray you, should an opportunity occur, to make known to the ladies of his bereaved family—bereaved of such a husband & father—all my regret at the inestimable loss we have all sustained. I have already written to Mr. [Francis] Markoe on the sad subject. I am, my dear Sir, ever truly your obliged friend, Henry Wheaton.

ALS in ScCleA. NOTE: Wheaton (1785–1848) had been a Republican newspaper editor in New York City during the War of 1812 period and was of considerable note as an author and scholar. He had held many public offices, including reporter to the U.S. Supreme Court, 1816–1827, and Chargé d'Affaires in Denmark, 1827–1835. In 1835 he was appointed Chargé d'Affaires to Prussia, and two years later was upgraded to Minister.

From HENRY WHEATON

Berlin, 10 April, 1844

Sir, I have the honour to enclose two Conventions concluded with the Kingdom of Wurtemberg and the Grand Duchy of Hesse, in pursuance of Instructions contained in Mr. Secretary [Abel P.] Upshur's Despatch No. 50, for the mutual abolition of the *Droit d'Aubaine* and *Droit de Detraction* between those Governments and the United States.

The stipulations incorporated into these Conventions have been principally taken from our existing treaties with Prussia, Austria, the Hanse Towns, and Hanover. The motives for concluding such Arrangements with the different German States will be found fully explained in Mr. Secretary Upshur's Report of the 24 Nov., 1843 (Congress Documents, No. 1, pp. 13, 19) and in my Despatch, No. 226, dated the 14th June last.

Similar Conventions with the other German States enumerated in the above Despatch of Mr. Upshur are in train of negociation, and will be communicated to the Department as soon as concluded. I have the honour to be, with the highest consideration, Sir, your ob[e]d[ien]t servant, Henry Wheaton.

LS (No. 244) in DNA, RG 59 (State Department), Diplomatic Despatches, Germany, vol. 3 (M-44:4), received 5/8; FC with En in DNA, RG 84 (Foreign Posts), Germany, Despatches, 4:102–106. NOTE: This letter was addressed to John Nelson. The enclosed conventions were ratified by the Senate on 6/12.

To AMOS ABBOTT, [Representative from Mass.]

Department of State
Washington, 11th April 1844

Sir, The Secretary of the Treasury [John C. Spencer] has referred to this Department the letter which you addressed to him under date the 9th instant, accompanied by one from Mr. J.P. Frothingham to you, containing an enquiry relative to the claim upon the Mexican government in the case of the schooner Eclipse. Mr. Frothingham is mistaken in supposing that any new Convention upon the subject of claims has been completed between this government and that of Mexico. The business is still pending but, it is expected, will soon be brought to an issue which will be published for the information of claimants upon that Government generally. Mr. Frothingham[']s letter is herewith returned. I have the honor to be, Sir, Your Obedient Ser[van]t, John C. Calhoun.

FC in DNA, RG 59 (State Department), Domestic Letters, 34:136–137 (M-40:32).

From Col. J[OHN] J. ABERT

Bureau of Topographical Eng[inee]rs
Washington, April 11th 1844

Sir, In obedience to directions some time since received from the War Department, we have compiled in this Office, for the State Department, a map of Texas, which I have the honor of sending to you by Lieut. [William H.] Emory, by whom the work was done.

In the course of tomorrow, his statement of the authorities consulted in the compilation will be made out and transmitted, in order that you may judge of the confidence to which the map is entitled. Very respectfully Sir Your Ob[edien]t Serv[an]t, J.J. Abert, Col. Corps [of] T[opographical] E[ngineers].

LS in DNA, RG 59 (State Department), Miscellaneous Letters (M-179:104, frame 160); FC in DNA, RG 77 (Records of the Office of the Chief of Engineers), Letters Sent by the Topographical Bureau, 7:200 (M-66:7, frame 109).

From J[ames] E[dward] Boisseau, New York [City], 4/11. He recommends John A. Mitchell, "a respectable citizen regularly bred to business, of excellent moral character," for appointment as Despatch Agent of the State Department at New York City, if the office "is vacant, or you should conceive it desirable to make a change. . . ." ALS in DNA, RG 59 (State Department), Applications and Recommendations, 1837–1845, Mitchell (M-687:23, frames 311–312).

From John M.S. Causin, T[homas] A. Spence, and J[ohn] P. Kennedy, [Representatives from Md.], 4/11. They recommend to Calhoun's "favorable consideration" William H. Dunkinson of Md. "We can most confidently guarrantee that any trust, which it may be in your convenience to confide to him, will be ably & honorably discharged." LS in DNA, RG 59 (State Department), Applications and Recommendations, 1837–1845, Dunkinson (M-687:9, frames 603–604).

ANNA [MARIA CALHOUN CLEMSON] to Pat[rick Calhoun, Washington]

Canebrake [Edgefield District, S.C.] April 11th 1844
Dear Pat, As you are determined to drop our correspondence I will make another effort to recall myself to your remembrance. Seriously tho' I have been a little surprised at not hearing oftener from you but have taken it for granted that the mail not yourself was in fault for I should be sorry to think that even the fascinations of Washington & the ladies could drive me from your mind especially when you remember how far from all other amusements I am & therefore how much dependent on my friends for all that passes in the world. However I will not scold you because in the first place I am not sure as I said that it is not the mail & in the next I know that my correspondence affords so little pleasure from the dullness of my letters that it makes but little compensation for the amusement I receive that I don[']t wonder after all at persons not writing—but enough on this *interesting* subject & if you set down & write me a nice long letter we will start a new score.

I have been gadding about wonderfully for me. In the first place I went to Edgefield expecting to remain only a few days but Mr. [Thomas G.] Clemson paraded off to Washington & I of course staid at Edgewood till he came back. Then he took me to Augusta but we only staid a day but all this took time & we have only returned to the Canebrake a few days & I am once more at hard work which father [John C. Calhoun] will tell you agrees with me wonderfully.

I saw mother [Floride Colhoun Calhoun] in Edgefield. She looks particularly well & is in good spirits but she is constantly tied down to your aunt Maria [Simkins Colhoun] & cannot leave her long enough even to come here. I am sorry to say that I think Maria really in a dangerous condition & fear that she ["will" *interlined*] go off as all the rest [of the Simkinses] have done. You will of course be careful how you write about what I say to mother for Maria might get hold of the letter & it would be injurious to her you know. I think she is consumptive. She spits blood & mother writes me be [*sic*] Tom to-day that she threw up a good deal. I would not of course leave her if I thought her in any immediate danger ["I would not leave her" *canceled*] but I fear she may fall into permanent ill health & finally go off in a decline.

Cousin Francis [W. Pickens] has become the greatest beau & gad-about you ever saw. He dresses a great deal & is I think crazy to be married & least that is the general opinion I believe.

Poor Arthur [Simkins] lost his only son [Arthur Pickens Simkins]— a fine promising little fellow a week or two ago. It is a great blow to them. They were perfectly devoted to him.

My children [John Calhoun Clemson and Floride Elizabeth Clemson] are I am happy to say well & improving in sense & appearance. I think you would be amused with Calhoun now he is such a smart little rascal but in spite of me he is pretty bad. When John [C. Calhoun, Jr.] first came he called him "uncle Paddy" constantly which proved he remembered you for you know there is considerable general resemblance between you. About John's health I don[']t know what to say—sometimes I think him better & then again I fear not. Mr. Clemson says undoubtedly his lungs are affected & that he scarce thinks the disease can be rooted out but that whatever means are resorted to for that purpose should be used speedily as every day renders the disease more confirmed. He is really a most estimable young man & it is a pleasure to have him with us. I am only sorry I can do no more towards his recovery.

I hope father is well & pleasantly settled. How agreeable it is both ["for" *interlined*] you & ourselves that you & he are together. Write me all about your "*fixins*" &c. Give my best love to father & tell him I will write him shortly & in the meantime he must consider this letter to both of you. Beg him if he has no time to write to *make you write often.* I must stop. It is late but I was anxious to send this letter by Tom to be mailed in Edgefield. I fear you will find it dull for I am so tired at night I can scarce keep my eyes open. Truly your sister, Anna.

[P.S.] Mr. Clemson & John desire to be remembered to you. Mr. C[lemson] wrote father from Augusta.

ALS in ScCleA. NOTE: This letter was mailed to "Hon. J.C. Calhoun" at Washington and carries John C. Calhoun's AEU: "Anna." Maria Simkins Colhoun, wife of James Edward Colhoun, died on 4/17/1844.

From JAMES GADSDEN

Office of the S.C. R[ail] R[oad] Company
Charleston So[uth] Carolina, April 11, 1844

Dear Sir, It affords me a high gratification (by a Resolution of the Board of Directors unanimously concurred in) to be the Organ through whom is tendered a Free Travelling Ticket for Life on the South Carolina Rail Road. Your name will be registered at the Different Depots, and the officers will receive instructions to permit you to pass free of charge, at all times and on all occasions, in any of the Travelling Trains. Respectfully your ob[edien]t S[ervan]t, James Gadsden.

[P.S.] The above was communicated to our agent at Hamburg on your late expected visit to Charleston, but was not received in consequence of your coming via Aiken. I was gratified however to hear that our agent at Aiken carried out in part the intention of the Resolution.

ALS in ScCleA. NOTE: An AEU by Calhoun reads: "Col. Gadsden, Informs me that the railroad has granted me the right of ["free" *canceled*] passage free."

From W[illia]M B. GOOCH

U.S. Commercial Agency
Aux Cayes, April 11, 1844

Dear Sir, I would inform you that this Island is again engaged in Civil war—the contest is now between the mulattoes & blacks. This city is in possession of the blacks with most of the South part of the Island. They entered this place on the 3d inst. It was heart rending to witness hundreds & hundreds of the coloured population, rushing to the sea side to go on board the vessels in the harbour for protection from the Negroes.

Three American vessels, two of them had commenced loading, were chartered by the inhabitants to transport them & their effects, (what they had saved;) to Jamaica.

I considered it my duty to retire with my books and papers on board an American vessel during the excitement. The Brittish Vice Consul with all Foreigners embarked on board the Shipping & went into the outter harbour.

The most that we feared on account of our selves, was plunder & burning of the city.

I remained on board four nights but was on shore most of the day. The commanding officers of the blacks assured me every assistance & protection I might wish for my self and all Americans in the place. I believe the officers sincere in their professions of attachment & friendship; but the most to be feared that they have not power over an infuriated mob of blacks, eight thousand of them now hovering in & around the city demanding pillage.

I do not consider the place in Safety until the troop retires from this city, & subburbs. The officers informed me that they were to march some days since for Port au Prince, but I have just learned that it will [be] some time before they will march. I consider all hope of their again having a settled government futile. It is but the commencement of their difficulties. Should the excitement continue I must consider it duty to return to the U. States & relinquish the office which I have held for two years with little pecuniary benefit to my self, but I trust, with honour to my Government.

You will excuse my not writing a formal letter to the State Department, not being prepared, not thinking it my duty to remove my books & papers from the vessel. I am Sir, with high esteem your devoted & obedient Servant, Wm. B. Gooch.

ALS in DNA, RG 59 (State Department), Consular Despatches, Aux Cayes, vol. 2 (T-330:2), received 5/27. NOTE: This letter was addressed to Abel P. Upshur.

To A[RCHIBALD] M. GREEN, U.S. Consul, "Galvezton"

Department of State
Washington, April 11th 1844

Sir, Your letters from No. 21 to No. 28 inclusive, with their respective enclosures, have been received.

Your No. 22 has been referred to the Secretary of the Treasury, and the information contained in No. 27, respecting the increased duties imposed on Sail Vessels and Steamboats, published. I am, Sir, Respectfully Your Obedient Servant, J.C. Calhoun.

LS in DNA, RG 59 (State Department), Drafts of Domestic Letters Sent, 1801–1877; FC in DNA, RG 59 (State Department), Consular Instructions, 11:229.

From BEN E. GREEN, "Private"

Mexico, April 11th 1844

Dear Sir, I learn, by the newspapers, the sad death of Judge [Abel P.] Upshur, and your appointment to the State Department, with a view to the Oregon and Texas questions. My position here has given me an insight into the condition of Texas, California and Oregon; and as it may be of some importance to you in the anticipated negotiations at Washington, I deem it proper to give you all the information I possess.

That information is chiefly derived from a Mr. [Lansford W.] Hastings, of Ohio, who, some two years since, led a party of emigrants from the West to Oregon, and past through this city about three months ago, on his return to the U.S.

He describes Oregon as a fine country; but chiefly valuable for its fisheries and fur trade. The salmon of Columbia river is unrivalled in quality, & inexhaustible in number. In an agricultural point of view, the country is important; but much less so, in comparison with the rich soil and more attractive climate of the adjoining Californias.

The political state of those countries is very interesting to us. Mr. Hastings told me, *in confidence*, that California is on the point of following the example of Texas, and of declaring her independence. The whole project has been well digested, and reduced to a systematized plan. The province of California is far distant from the seat of the Mexican Govt.; which has neither soldiers to send there, nor money to support them. Michael Torrena [Micheltorena], the Mexican Commandante General, has but two hundred vagabond soldiers to oppose the movement, and has no resources within himself, being destitute both of talents and courage. The military strength is in the hands of the foreigners, and the natives in their favor. A German, named [John A.] Sut[t]er, is at the head of the movement, and the execution of their designs is only delayed for the return of Mr. Hastings, with a reinforcement of settlers.

The settlers in Oregon have already a legislative council and governor: & while Mr. Hastings was in Oregon, they were debating the propriety of declaring their independence of the U.S., and of forming a separate Republic on the Pacific coast, in conjunction with the Californias. They do not wish to do so, however, if they can obtain protection and encouragement from home.

Nor is California the only portion of Mexican territory in danger. Sonora has been for two years the theatre of civil war, and will probably join in with the movement in California. The provinces, bordering on Texas, have long envied the freedom from forced loans & martial rule, enjoyed by their neighbours. New Mexico has been on the eve of a revolution ever since the Santa Fé trade was closed, and there is reason to believe that even Tamaulipas, were it not for her exposed condition would at once throw herself into the arms of Texas. Santa Anna is trying to provoke a war with France. His object is believed to be to take advantage of the confusion & excitement of an invasion, to make himself Emperor; trusting to the English mediation to pacify France, as soon as his object is accomplished.

If France refuses to be pacified, her Minister here [De Cyprey], if he advises well, will advise that the attack should be made through Texas, and upon the discontented provinces. It is by no means improbable that the result will be the annexation of those Departments to Texas. With that addition of Territory, Texas would no longer desire admission to our union, but on the contrary would prove a dangerous rival both to the cotton interests of the South, and the manufactures of the North. I have the honor to be Very Respectfully Your ob[edien]t Ser[van]t, Ben E. Green.

ALS in ScCleA; draft in NcU, Duff Green Papers (published microfilm, roll 5, frames 380–381); PC in Jameson, ed., *Correspondence*, pp. 945–947.

To Benjamin Hale, Newburyport, Mass., 4/11. Calhoun acknowledges Hale's letter of 4/7 concerning a claim against the Texas government in the "case of the Brig Retrieve." He assures Hale that the papers in this case were transmitted to Texas by his predecessor "with an instruction." No news has been received "of the adjustment of the business," but the question will receive "due attention." LS in ScU-SC, John C. Calhoun Papers; FC in DNA, RG 59 (State Department), Domestic Letters, 34:138 (M-40:32).

From C[HARLES] J. INGERSOLL, [Representative from Pa.]

Ap[ri]l 11, [18]44

Dear Sir, To enable me to move effectually in the endeavour to get an appropriation for an assistant Secretary of State, which I will attempt by an amendment of the Civil and Diplomatic appropriation bill, it will be important that some one whom you may set to that matter, in your Department should furnish me with suggestions & views in some detail of the necessity and advantages of the proposition.

I do not need a formal or official communication, unless you prefer that method, but merely a full memorandum.

And I will thank you to let me know whether you think the Assistant Secretary should be a presidential appointment thro' the Senate or only by the Secretary of State. I am very sincerely and respectfully Y[ou]rs, C.J. Ingersoll.

ALS in DNA, RG 59 (State Department), Miscellaneous Letters (M-179:104, frame 161).

From W. Cost Johnson, [former Representative from Md.], Washington, 4/11. He introduces to Calhoun's "friendly acquaintance" [William H.] Dunkinson of St. Marys County, Md., "a gentleman of high respectability and great worth and worthy of any confidence." ALS in DNA, RG 59 (State Department), Applications and Recommendations, 1837–1845, Dunkinson (M-687:9, frames 601–602).

From THOMAS O. LARKIN

Consulate of the United States of America
Monterey California, April 11, 1844

Sir, I beg leave to inform you that as I am the first United States Consul who has taken office in the Department of California, that this consulate is entirely destitute of every thing. I can obtain no Books to guide me in my office nor can I obtain any advise from any quarter in this vast and distant region, and for me to fulfill my duties as I wish to do, it[']s of the greatest consequence that I should receive Books and instruction in full from your Department.

I am also distitute of Seal, Stamp, press for the latter, flag and coat of arms. By applying to Messr[s]. William Appleton & Co. or B.T. Reed Esq. Merchant of Boston Mass. & Traders on this coast, information can be obtained when vessels are loading in Boston for Monterey of which one leaves this Summer, by these vessels any thing can be sent to me from the Department.

There has within three years past been appointed two or three Gentlemen as Consul for this Port and San Francisco—neither of whom I believe accepted office. There are laying in different offices and private houses in this country for them from the Department of State, several letters. I wish'd to be informed if I am to take them out pay the postage and open them for the use of my office.

There have arrived in California, several Citizens of the United States by land with their Families. I expect the number to increase yearly. There has already been married by a Californian Magistrate some of these People. We suppose the marriage not legal by the laws of Mexico, as the ceremony is always performed by a Catholic Priest, and he will not marry Protestants. I look for application from some of these new Settlers to preform the ceremony of matrimony between them, and beg leave to ask from you if I can preform it legally.

Correct and prompt information on this subject, is of the most importance to many young Americans who may come to California to settle and want to marry on their arrival. I speak w[h]ere both parties are American.

Letters to me from the Department ["to me" *canceled*] will reach in due time if sent to John Parrott Esq. U.S. Consul, Mazatlan, also as before mentioned. I am with high esteem and great consideration your obedient Servant, Thomas O. Larkin.

ALS (No. 2) in DNA, RG 59 (State Department), Consular Despatches, Monterey (M-138:1); slightly variant FC in CU, Bancroft Library, Larkin Collection; PC in Hammond, ed., *Larkin Papers*, 2:92–93. NOTE: An AEU by Larkin on the FC reads "Answer dated Washington June 24, 1844. Received May 2, 1845."

"Memorandum" [from Alphonse Pageot?, French Minister to the U.S., *ca.* 4/11]. "The following Resolution was adopted by the House of Representatives in the 2d Session of the 27th Congress. [']Resolved that the President of the United States be requested to cause to be prepared & reported to the House by the Secretaries of State & Navy, at the commencement of the next session of Congress, a plan for the establishment in concert with the Government of France of a line of weekly steamers between the ports of Havre & New-York, together with estimates of the expense which may be required to carry the said plan into effect.['] This resolution has not yet been acted upon ["by" *interlined*] the Executive, & the proposition of the French Government remains unanswered." ADU in DNA, RG 59 (State Department), Notes from Foreign Legations, France, vol. 12 (M-53:8, frames 703–705).

To STEWART NEWELL, U.S. Consul, Sabine

Department of State
Washington, April 11th 1844

Sir, Your letters Nos. 6, 7, 8, 9 & 10 have been received with their respective enclosures.

As requested in your No. 8 [of 2/20/1844], I enclose a duplicate of the reply to No. 4, dated on the 7th December 1843.

Your letters Nos. 8 & 9 have been referred to the Secretary of the Treasury for his perusal. I am Sir &c, J.C. Calhoun.

FC in DNA, RG 59 (State Department), Consular Instructions, 11:230.

To FRANCIS W. SCOTT and Others, [Caroline County, Va.]

Washington City, April 11, 1844

Gentlemen: I have just received your polite letter, dated April the 2nd, inviting me in the name of the Caroline Democratic Association, to partake of a public Dinner to be given on Thursday, the 18th instant, to your late representative, the Hon. R[obert] M.T. Hunter.

I need not assure you how agreeable it would be to my feelings to meet and unite with you on the occasion referred to. My respect for you and those you represent, as well as my high regard for the distinguished gentleman whom you propose to honor, alike prompt me to accept your friendly invitation; but the pressing demands of important public business will not allow me to indulge such inclination. I am sure I need not add any thing further to secure your indulgence. With grateful acknowledgment for your kindness, I am, gentlemen, Your obedient servant, J.C. Calhoun.

PC in the Richmond, Va., *Enquirer*, May 17, 1844, p. 1. NOTE: During the dinner on 4/18, Calhoun was honored in a toast "Sent, by a Lady," as follows: "John C. Calhoun: His private character is as unblemished as his talents and political honesty are conspicuous."

To WILSON SHANNON,
Governor of Ohio, Columbus

Department of State
Washington, 11th April, 1844

Sir: I have the honor to inform you, that the President, by and with the advice and consent of the Senate, has appointed you Envoy Extraordinary and Minister Plenipotentiary of the United States to the Mexican Republic. If you accept the appointment, it is desirable that you should repair to this City without any delay which can be avoided, for the purpose of receiving your credentials and instructions. I have the honor to be, Your Excellency's obedient servant, J.C. Calhoun.

FC in DNA, RG 59 (State Department), Diplomatic Instructions, Mexico, 15:292 (M-77:111).

To I[SAAC] VAN ZANDT and J. P[INCKNEY] HENDERSON, "Ministers from the Republic of Texas"

Washington City, April 11th 1844

Gentlemen: The letter addressed by Mr. Van Zandt to the late Secretary of State, Mr. [Abel P.] Upshur, to which you have called my attention, dated Washington 17th of January 1844, has been laid before the President of the United States [John Tyler].

In reply to it I am directed by the President to say that the Secretary of the Navy [John Y. Mason] has been instructed to order a strong naval force to concentrate in the gulf of Mexico, to meet any emergency; and that similar orders have been issued by the Secretary of War [William Wilkins] to move the disposable military forces on our Southwestern frontier for the same purpose. Should the exigency arise to which you refer in your note to Mr. Upshur, I am further directed by the President to say that, during the pendency of the Treaty of Annexation, he would deem it his duty to use all the means placed within his power by the Constitution to protect Texas from all foreign invasion. I have the honor to be &c. &c., J.C. Calhoun.

LS in DNA, RG 84 (Foreign Posts), Records of the Texas Legation; FC in DNA, RG 59 (State Department), Notes to Foreign Legations, Texas, 6:69 (M-99:95); FC in Tx, Records of the Texas Republic Department of State, Letters and Dispatches Sent by the Texas Legation in Washington, 1:491–492; CC (marked "Confidential") in Tx, Records of the Texas Republic Department of State, U.S. Diplomatic Correspondence; FC (marked "Confidential") in Tx, Records of the Texas Republic Department of State, Copybooks of Letters Received from Texan and Foreign Representatives, vol. 2-1/98, pp. 492–493; CC in TxU, Anson Jones Papers; CC in Tx, Samuel Houston Papers; PC in House Document No. 271, 28th Cong., 1st Sess., pp. 96–97; PC in Senate Document No. 349, 28th Cong., 1st Sess., p. 11; PC in *Congressional Globe*, 28th Cong., 1st Sess., Appendix, p. 572; PC in the Washington, D.C., *Daily National Intelligencer*, June 3, 1844, p. 2; PC in the Washington, D.C., *Daily Madisonian*, June 3, 1844, p. 2; PC in the Washington, D.C., *Globe*, June 20, 1844, p. 2; PC in *Niles' National Register*, vol. LXVI, no. 15 (June 8, 1844), p. 232, and vol. LXXII, no. 2 (March 13, 1847), p. 26.

To Leonard R. Almy, Laguna, Carmen Island, Mexico, 4/12. Calhoun informs Almy that the Mexican government has refused to grant an exequatur to him as U.S. Consul. He will therefore cease to perform the duties of that office. FC in DNA, RG 59 (State Department), Consular Instructions, 11:232.

From A[LEXANDER O.] ANDERSON, [former Senator from Tenn.]

Washington City, April 12th 1844

My Dear Sir, I herewith recommend to you Mr. W[illia]m H. Dunkinson of Maryland as a gentleman of ["good" canceled] high character, great fidelity, and one who may be trusted in whatever is confided to him. He is a gentleman well qualified for business, has been a member of the Maryland Legislature, & can be again whenever he chooses. I recommend him to your favorable notice for your patronage. He is personally my friend & may be relied upon as a man of faith & integrity. Yours truly, A. Anderson.

LS in DNA, RG 59 (State Department), Applications and Recommendations, 1837–1845, Dunkinson (M-687:9, frames 605–607).

Commission from John Tyler, President, 4/12. Tyler grants to Calhoun "full power and authority, and also general and special command," to negotiate, conclude, and sign a treaty or convention of extradition with [Alphonse] Pageot, the French Minister Plenipotentiary. CC in DNA, RG 59 (State Department), Credences.

From Geo[rge] William Gordon

Rio de Janeiro, April 12th 1844

Sir, I have the honor to inform the Department of my arrival at this port, in the frigate "Raritan," on the 5th inst. after a passage of forty five days from New York. My Commission has been sent in to the Brazilian Government by Mr. Proffitt [*sic*; George H. Proffit, U.S. Minister], and I only await the receipt of my Exequatur to assume the duties of the Consulship at this place. I have the honor to be, with great respect, Your Obedient Servant, Geo. William Gordon.

ALS (No. 1) in DNA, RG 59 (State Department), Consular Despatches, Rio de Janeiro, vol. 7 (T-172:8), received 5/29. NOTE: This despatch was addressed to A[bel] P. Upshur.

From Tho[mas] D. Hailes

Grand Cane, Parish of DeSoto
Louisiana, April 12th 1844

Sir, I congratulate my fellow citizens on your consenting to assume the duties of the Dep[ar]t[men]t of State; and have the honor to inform you that, through the intermediate recommendations of my Friends in Congress, Messieurs. [Isaac E.] Holmes of So[uth] Carolina and [John] Slidell and [Pierre E.] Bossier of Louisiana, I applied to the lamented [Abel P.] Upshur for a Consulship, attended with active duties, at a Southern Port. With sentiments of respect I beg leave to renew the application I then made, for the favorable consideration of his distinguished successor. I have the honor to be Sir Your obedient Servant, Thos. D. Hailes.

Two slightly variant ALS's in DNA, RG 59 (State Department), Applications and Recommendations, 1837–1845, Hailes (M-687:14, frames 87–88 and 91–92).

To WILLIAM R. KING, [Senator from Ala.]

Department of State
Washington, 12th April, 1844

Sir: I have the honor to inform you that the President [John Tyler], by and with the advice and consent of the Senate, has appointed you Envoy Extraordinary and Minister Plenipotentiary to France, and wishes you to proceed on your mission without unnecessary delay. Should this appointment be agreeable to you, you will acquaint me with your acceptance of it, and in that event your instructions will be immediately prepared, and delivered to you with your commission, &c., when you are ready to take your departure. I am, Sir, with great respect, Your obedient Servant, J.C. Calhoun.

FC in DNA, RG 59 (State Department), Diplomatic Instructions, France, 15:[1] (M-77:55).

From THOMAS O. LARKIN

Consulate of the United States
Monterey California, April 12, 1844

Sir, I have the honor to inform you, that on the second of this month I received a letter from Don Agustin Sutter, Alcalde of the new town of New Helvetia of which the following is an extract. It may be proper to say that Mr. Sutter is a Swiss, and now Citizen of Mexico, and obtained from this Government a large [tract] of Land on which he is establishing a Town having already a Fort to protect him from the Indians. This Fort or Town is ["up" *canceled and* "situated on" *interlined*] the River Sacramento one of the branc[h]es of San Francisco about 175 or 200 miles from the entrance of the Harbour of San Francisco. All Parties by land from the Oregon or from the United States, to California touch at this Establishment first, most of the Emigrants over land from the States since 1840 have settled near Mr. Sutter. Some of them having become Citizens of this Republic have six or eight leagues of land given them by this Government.

[John A. Sutter to Thomas O. Larkin]
New Helvetia, March 28/[18]44

Sir, On the 6 instant Lieut. J[ohn] C. Fremont of the U. States exploring expedition arrived here in distress, having been forced to

211

deviate from his course on account of deep snows, loss of Animals and want of Provisions. He informed me of having left the Columbia River a short distance above Fort Vancouver, with the intention of crossing to the head waters of the Arkansas River eastward through the lower or Southern part of the Oregon Territory, but finding a succession of high mountains covered with snow which with the distressed condition of his company, forced him to abandon his route and strike for the settlements of California, refit and cross the mountains farther to the South. On the morning of the 25 instant he left here direct for the U. States, his party consisted of twenty five (25) men.

The visit of this Exploring Expedition I attribute entire to accident, for a month previous to their arrival, the Company had subsisted entirely on horse and Mule flesh. The starvation and fatigue they had endured rendered them truly deplorable objects. Signed, J.A. Sutter.
Thomas O. Larkin, Esq.
U.S. Consul
Monterey California

On my hearing from the Govonor of California (in Monterey) of the arrival of Lt. Fremont, I addressed a Note to Mr. Sutter to offer to Lt. F[remont] any assistance I could afford him. He was gone on the arrival of my letter. I believe he obtained the Supply of Horses, Mules and provisions he wanted. Hoping this information may be of some service, I have the honor to subscribe myself your most obedient Servant, Thomas O. Larkin.

ALS (No. 3) in DNA, RG 59 (State Department), Consular Despatches, Monterey (M-138:1); FC in CU, Bancroft Library, Larkin Collection; PC in the Washington, D.C., *Daily Madisonian*, June 19, 1844, p. 2; PC in the Washington, D.C., *Globe*, June 24, 1844, p. 3; PC in Hammond, ed., *Larkin Papers*, 2:93–94. NOTE: A Clerk's EU reads "Respectfully submitted to the Secretary of War for his perusal & return. Dept. of State, June 19/[18]44."

To HENRY LEDYARD, [Paris]

Department of State
Washington, 12th April, 1844
Sir: I have the honor to inform you that the President [John Tyler], by and with the advice and consent of the Senate, has appointed

William R. King, Esq[ui]re, [native] of North Carolina, Envoy Extraordinary and Minister Plenipotentiary of the United States to France, and that this gentleman will probably leave this country for Paris about the beginning of May next. I make this communication to you that you may be enabled by it to regulate your movements and arrangements for your return home, with a view to your own convenience; and at the same time to request you to deliver over to Mr. King, upon his arrival at Paris, all the books, records, archives, &c., of the Legation.

Dr. J[ohn] L. Martin has been nominated to succeed you as Secretary of the Mission, and will probably reach France in company with Mr. King.

In making the above communication, I feel authorized to assure you that your conduct as Acting Chargé d'Affaires, as well as in the character of Secretary of Legation, has been satisfactory to the President. I am, Sir, respectfully, Your obedient Servant, J.C. Calhoun.

FC (No. 28) in DNA, RG 59 (State Department), Diplomatic Instructions, France, 14:322 (M-77:54); CC in DNA, RG 84 (Foreign Posts), France, Instructions.

From J[acob] W. Miller, [Senator from N.J.], 4/12. "I have the honor to enclose a letter from a widowed mother to her son now a prisoner in Mexico unless very lately released, with a request that it may be forwarded with the government despatches to Mexico." ALS in DNA, RG 59 (State Department), Passport Applications, vol. 30, unnumbered (M-1372:14).

From the Count de Montalto, [Sardinian Chargé d'Affaires in the U.S.], New York [City], 4/12. He congratulates Calhoun upon his appointment and regrets that his absence from Washington prevents a personal call. ALS (in French) in DNA, RG 59 (State Department), Notes from Foreign Legations, Sardinia (M-201:1).

To Z[adock] Pratt, [Representative from N.Y.], 4/12. In reply to a request to the State Department on 3/22, Calhoun reports the names and salaries of 11 extra Clerks who were employed by the department during the first quarter of 1844. FC in DNA, RG 59 (State Department), Accounting Records, Miscellaneous Letters Sent, 1832–1916, vol. for 2/1–9/30/1844, pp. 102–[104].

From Catharine S. Raguet

Philadelphia, April 12th 1844

Sir, I recur with pleasure to the remembrance of your intimate acquaintance with my much lamented husband [Condy Raguet], who would have been one of the number of your many friends in rejoicing at your acceptance of the high station assigned you.

Relying on your friendly feelings, I take the liberty of requesting your ["friendly" *canceled*] favorable consideration of a Claim on Government drawn up by Mr. Raguet, a copy of which I have sent to the Hon. C[harles] J. Ingersoll [Representative from Pa.] & is now before Congress. My husband in his last illness desired this claim not to be neglected. About the time of his arrival at Rio de Janeiro as Consul [in 1822], a change had taken place in the Government; no official Agent being there Mr. Raguet was applyed to by the Americans then in that country to redress their wrongs, and he rendered many important services to them and to our Govt. as will appear by refer[r]ing to his correspondence in the Department of State. With what zeal and interest he embarked in this undertaking, I will not say to you who are so well acquainted with ["his" *interlined*] indefatigable exertions in the cause of the South [during the nullification controversy] which he maintained for several years.

He considered himself entitled to remuneration for services during a period of ten months—the Consulate fees being then so limited that he was compelled to live with the strictest economy.

Allow me, Sir, again to offer you many apologies for the liberty I have taken, & for intruding myself upon you at this most important moment. I am very respectfully Y[ou]rs &c, Catharine S. Raguet, No. 183 Spruce St.

ALS in DNA, RG 59 (State Department), Miscellaneous Letters (M-179:104, frames 167–168).

From John C[alhoun] Sterling

Watertown N.Y., April 12 1844

Respected & D[ea]r Sir, My father and your friend M[icah] Sterling is no more. He expired yesterday about 6 o'cl[oc]k P.M. For two or three years past, as you are probably aware his health has been feeble, yet he has had no severe sickness until that which preceeded his death. His disease was the scarlet fever—and in addition to this an affection of the lungs. He suffered very little pain during his sickness, and expressed himself as ready to depart, if such was the Lord's will. It is a great consolation to us that his last hours were so tranquil and free from pain.

It was one of the parting requests of my father that I should write to Mr. Calhoun informing him of his death, and that Mr. C[alhoun] was remembered by him on his dying bed. He wished me also to say, that he trusted Mr. C[alhoun] would enter upon the duties of his office with a firm determination to do that which was just & right without reference to party.

It gives me pleasure to think of Mr. Calhoun as an early and lasting friend of my father, and the only one, with one or two exceptions whose correspondence has ["been" *interlined*] continued since you were associated together as College Classmates. Truly & Respectfully Yours, John C. Sterling.

ALS in ScCleA.

A Treaty of Annexation, Concluded Between the United States of America and the Republic of Texas

[Washington, April 12, 1844]
The people of Texas having, at the time of adopting their constitution, expressed by an almost unanimous vote, their desire to be incorporated into the Union of the United States, and being still desirous of the same with equal unanimity, in order to provide more effectually for their security and prosperity; and the United States, actuated solely by the desire to add to their own security and prosperity, and to meet the wishes of the Government and people of Texas, have determined to accomplish, by treaty, objects so important to their mutual and permanent welfare.

For that purpose, the President of the United States [John Tyler] has given full powers to John C. Calhoun, Secretary of State of the said United States, and the President of the Republic of Texas [Samuel Houston] has appointed, with like powers, Isaac Van Zandt and J. Pinckney Henderson, citizens of the said Republic: and the said plenipotentiaries, after exchanging their full powers, have agreed on and concluded the following articles:

Article I.

The Republic of Texas, acting in conformity with the wishes of the people and every department of its government, cedes to the United States all its territories, to be held by them in full property and sovereignty, and to be annexed to the said United States as one of their Territories, subject to the same constitutional provisions with their other Territories. This cession includes all public lots and squares, vacant lands, mines, minerals, salt lakes and springs, public edifices, fortifications, barracks, ports and harbours, navy and navy-yards, docks, magazines, arms, armaments and accoutrements, archives and public documents, public funds, debts, taxes and dues unpaid at the time of the exchange of the ratifications of this treaty.

Article II.

The citizens of Texas shall be incorporated into the Union of the United States, maintained and protected in the free enjoyment of their liberty and property, and admitted, as soon as may be consistent with the principles of the federal Constitution, to the enjoyment of all the rights, privileges, and immunities, of citizens of the United States.

Article III.

All titles and claims to real estate, which are valid under the laws of Texas, shall be held to be so by the United States; and measures shall be adopted for the speedy adjudication of all unsettled claims to land, and patents shall be granted to those found to be valid.

Article IV.

The public lands hereby ceded shall be subject to the laws regulating the public lands in the other Territories of the United States, as far as they may be applicable; subject, however, to such alterations and changes as Congress may from time to time think proper to make. It is understood between the parties that if, in consequence of the mode in which lands have been surveyed in Texas, or from previous grants or locations, the sixteenth section cannot be applied to the purpose of education, Congress shall make equal provision by grant of land elsewhere. And it is also further understood, that, hereafter, the books, papers and documents of the General Land Office of Texas shall be deposited and kept at such place in Texas as the Congress of the United States shall direct.

Article V.

The United States assume and agree to pay the public debts and liabilities of Texas, however created, for which the faith or credit of her government may be bound at the time of the exchange of the ratifications of this treaty; which debts and liabilities are estimated not to exceed, in the whole, ten millions of dollars, to be ascertained and paid in the manner hereinafter stated.

The payment of the sum of three hundred and fifty thousand dollars shall be made at the Treasury of the United States within ninety days after the exchange of the ratifications of this treaty, as follows: Two hundred and fifty thousand dollars to Frederick Dawson, of Baltimore, or his Executors, on the delivery of that amount of ten per cent. bonds of Texas [*blank space*]; One hundred thousand dollars, if so much be required, in the redemption of the Exchequer bills which may be in circulation at the time of the exchange of the ratifications of this treaty. For the payment of the remainder of the debts and liabilities of Texas, which, together with the amount already specified, shall not exceed ten millions of dollars, the public lands herein ceded and the nett revenue from the same are hereby pledged.

Article VI.

In order to ascertain the full amount of the debts and liabilities herein assumed, and the legality and validity thereof, four commissioners shall be appointed by the President of the United States, by and with the advice and consent of the Senate, who shall meet at Washington, Texas, within the period of six months after the exchange of the ratifications of this treaty, and may continue in session not exceeding twelve months, unless the Congress of the United States should prolong the time. They shall take an oath for the faithful discharge of their duties, and that they are not directly or indirectly interested in said claims at the time, and will not be during their continuance in office; and the said oath shall be recorded with their proceedings. In case of the death, sickness or resignation of any of the commissioners, his or their place or places may be supplied by the appointment as aforesaid or by the President of the United States during the recess of the Senate. They, or a majority of them, shall be authorized, under such regulations as the Congress of the United States may prescribe, to hear, examine and decide on all questions touching the legality and validity of said claims, and shall, when a claim is allowed, issue a certificate to the claimant, stating the amount, distinguishing principal from interest. The certificates so issued shall be numbered, and entry made of the number, the name of the person to whom issued, and the amount, in a book to be kept for that purpose. They shall transmit the records of their proceedings and the book in which the certificates are entered, with the vouchers and documents produced before them, relative to the claims allowed or rejected, to the Treasury Department of the United States, to be deposited therein; and the Secretary of the Treasury shall, as soon as practicable after the receipt of the same, ascertain the aggregate amount of the debts and liabilities allowed; and if the same, when added to the amount to be paid to Frederick Dawson and the sum which may be paid in the redemption of the Exchequer bills, shall not exceed the estimated sum of ten millions of dollars, he shall, on the presentation of a certificate of the commissioners, issue, at the option of the holder, a new certificate for the amount, distinguishing principal from interest, and payable to him or order, out of the nett proceeds of the public lands, hereby ceded, or stock of the United States, for the amount allowed, including principal and interest, and bearing an interest of three per cent. per annum from the date thereof; which stock, in addition to being made payable out of the nett proceeds of the public lands hereby ceded, shall also be receivable in payment for the same. In case the amount of the debts and liabilities allowed, with the sums aforesaid to be paid to Frederick Dawson and which may be paid in the redemption of the Exchequer bills, shall exceed the said sum of ten millions of dollars, the said Secretary, before issuing a new certificate, or stock, as the case may be, shall make in each case such proportionable and rateable reduction on its amount as to reduce the aggregate to the said sum of ten millions of dollars, and he shall have power to make all needful rules and regulations necessary to carry into effect the powers hereby vested in him.

Article VII.

Until further provision shall be made, the laws of Texas as now existing shall remain in force, and all executive and judicial officers of Texas, except the President, Vice-President and Heads of departments, shall retain their offices, with all power and authority appertaining thereto; and the courts of justice shall remain in all respects as now established and organized.

Article VIII.

Immediately after the exchange of the ratifications of this treaty, the President of the United States, by and with the advice and consent of the Senate, shall appoint a commissioner who shall proceed to Texas, and receive the transfer of the territory thereof, and all the archives and public property and other things herein conveyed, in the name of the United States. He shall exercise all executive authority in said territory necessary to the proper execution of the laws, until otherwise provided.

Article IX.

The present treaty shall be ratified by the contracting parties and the ratifications exchanged at the City of Washington, in six months from the date hereof, or sooner if possible.

In witness whereof, we, the undersigned plenipotentiaries of the United States of America and of the Republic of Texas, have signed, by virtue of our powers, the present treaty of Annexation, and have hereunto affixed our seals respectively.

Done at Washington, the twelfth day of April, eighteen hundred and forty-four.

J.C. Calhoun   (seal)
Isaac Van Zandt   (seal)
J. Pinckney Henderson (seal.)

DS in DNA, RG 11 (General Records of the United States Government), Unperfected Treaties, R-3; PC in Senate Document No. 341, 28th Cong., 1st Sess., pp. 10–13; FC in Tx, Records of the Texas Republic Department of State, Letters and Dispatches from Washington, 1:493–500; PC in House Document No. 271, 28th Cong., 1st Sess., pp. 5–8; PC in the Washington, D.C., *Spectator*, April 28, 1844, p. 3; PC in the Charleston, S.C., *Courier*, May 2, 1844, p. 2; PC in *Niles' National Register*, vol. LXVI, no. 10 (May 4, 1844), pp. 149–150; PC in the London, England, *Times*, May 16, 1844, p. 6; PC in Crallé, ed., *Works*, 5:322–327.

ISAAC VAN ZANDT and J. PINCKNEY HENDERSON to Anson Jones, [Texan Secretary of State]

Texian Legation, Washington City, April 12[t]h, 1844

Sir, We have the honor herewith to transmit to you, a copy of the treaty which we have this day signed, with Mr. Calhoun, the Secretary of State of the United States. We do this hastily, as this Government will, on Sunday, despatch an express to Texas to convey this and other important intelligence to our Government.

The treaty we have agreed upon, you will readily see, is not precisely such an one as we expected to make or had a right to wish. But, after consulting the wishes and views of all parties concerned, we agreed to it as the best we could frame with the prospect of its ratification by the Senate of the United States. Had we been left to consult the wishes and disposition of the President [John Tyler] and Cabinet of the United States, we could and would have concluded a treaty much more favorable to Texas than the one we have signed. But such was not the case. We have been compelled to consult the views and wishes of the two great leading parties in the United States—avoiding on the one hand the very liberal terms which the Southern politicians would have been willing to grant us and the restrictions which the North would wish to impose.

Texas has in this case consulted, through her agents here, as far as she could understand and reconcile them, the wishes of all parties in the United States. Upon examination, reflection and consultation, we concluded that the best mode of our admission was as a territory. Consequently, we did not hesitate to agree to come into the United States in that way. By the terms of the treaty, you will see that we have the right to claim the preservation of all of our property as secured by our domestic institutions as well as to claim admission into the Union as a State or States, under the provisions of the Federal Constitution of the United States.

We have felt ourselves obliged to avoid any allusion, directly, either to slavery or boundary, leaving the one to the future negotiations of this Government, and the other to be governed by that clause of the treaty which secures to us the right of property, &c., which we understand to include our right to slaves, as the constitution of the United States recognizes that species of property. Indeed, we have, as nearly as we could, followed the language of the treaties ceding Louisiana and Florida to the United States, in order that those precedents might be referred to, to justify the language used in the present treaty. The manner in which our present debt is to be paid, too, did not entirely meet our sanction; especially as there is no distinction made by the treaty between debts due to speculators and the debts due to our own citizens, for civil, military and naval service, or to persons who generously furnished money and supplies for our army and navy when we most needed them. But it was deemed best to accede to the terms agreed upon, in order to obviate objections. The only inquiry with us was: What will the Senate of the United States agree to? and not, What can we get from the Executive of the United States? We very much wished to have this Government pay the dues to our army, navy, civil officers, &c., but we feared the consequences of such a provision; and therefore we agreed to the terms inserted in the treaty on that subject. The additional excuse is, that our people will be in a great degree repaid by the additional security given to them by the contemplated annexation.

We fear, too, that the President [Samuel Houston] expected us to make better provisions for Texas on the subject of public schools, internal improvements, &c., &c.; but we are sure that he would have been well satisfied of the impropriety of inserting any better terms, had he been present here.

You will herewith receive the reply [of 4/11] of Mr. Calhoun, made at our request to a note addressed by your undersigned representative, I. Van Zandt, to Judge [Abel P.] Upshur, upon the subject of the assurance of protection to Texas by the United States, during the pendency of the treaty negotiations. We have no doubt that the President of the United States will act on this subject in a way that will fully meet the views and wishes of the President of Texas. We have strong assurances of this. The main body of the army designed for the protection of Texas, we have agreed, shall be concentrated and stationed at Fort Jesup [La.]. Those already at Fort Towson [in Indian Territory], New Orleans, and other places, near Texas, will remain where they now are; and it is understood and agreed that the President of Texas shall at once open communications with the commanding officers at each station, so as to give them the earliest possible news of any hostile demonstrations on the part of Mexico. The Secretary of State of the United States will superintend the issuance of orders to the different officers in command at the several stations above alluded to; which instructions we are assured will be such as to meet the wishes of our Government fully.

As it is not certain that the Senate of the United States will ratify the treaty which we have signed, the President of the United States assured us, before we agreed to sign and submit it, that he would, immediately upon its rejection by that body, should it be so disposed of, send to both Houses of Congress a message, recommending to them, in the strongest terms, the passage of a law annexing Texas as a State, under that provision of the constitution of this Government, which authorizes Congress to admit new States into the Union. The history of the debates and proceedings of the convention which framed that constitution prove beyond doubt that Congress has such power. And it is confidently believed by the friends of Texas in the Congress of the United States, that such a law can be passed. It was under this view of the case that we agreed to frame the treaty and submit it to the Senate of the United States, under such doub[t]ful chances for its ratification by that body, believing that this course will be fully approved by the President of Texas.

You will observe that we have fixed the time in which the exchange of the ratifications of the treaty is to be made, at six months, which will render it necessary for the Senate of the United States to act definitely on it during the present session of Congress, and not leave them at liberty to delay that action until next winter, which many of the Senators wish to do, and probably would do, if the time given by the treaty permitted it. We would respectfully suggest to you and through you to the President, the propriety of delaying any action on the part of our Senate, until after the treaty shall have been ratified on the part of the Senate of the United States, as there is some doubt of its ratification here.

[*The following passage was revised and then entirely canceled*: "Since writing the above, we have had an interview with Mr. Calhoun, at his request, during which he informed us that the President of the United States had directed him to ("make a" *interlined*) more full verbal assurance ("in regard to the required protection" *interlined*) that his Government would grant to Texas the protection required than he would like to make in writing; and as the reasons he assigned were satisfactory, we concurred in his views in that regard." *canceled and* "In addition to the foregoing," *interlined and then canceled.*]

The assurance ["was then" *altered to* "has been"] given to us by Mr. Calhoun, verbally, which we reduced to writing in his presence and by his consent and then read them over to him. They are as follows, to wit: A powerful naval force, to consist of ten or twelve vessels, will be ordered to the gulf of Mexico, the commander of which, Capt. [David] Conner, will, upon any serious demonstration being made by water by Mexico against, ["Texas" *interlined*] inform the Mexican commander that any attack upon Texas will be considered as a hostile act, and the Executive will feel himself bound to use every means to repel it—that the old division as established by Mr. Calhoun as Secretary of War, extending from Florida Point to the Southern extremity of Lake Michigan, has been restored, and Gen. [Edmund P.] Gaines been put in command ["of the western Division" *interlined*] and ordered to take up his ["position" *erased*] head quarters at Fort Jesup, who will receive similar orders as to any demonstration by land, to those given to the naval commander as to a demonstration by sea, and that he and the Chargé d'Affaires will keep up an active correspondence with the President of Texas; and if they should receive any communication from him which he conceives threatens any serious intention upon the part of Mexico to invade Texas by land, they or either of them shall forthwith despatch the same to Washington City, by express—that the President will in that event send a message to Congress, informing them of the fact, and request Congress to adopt, as speedily as possible, such measures as may be necessary for the defence of Texas; and if the emergency should require it, to say in his message that he would in the mean time consider it his duty to defend Texas against aggression, and will accordingly do so.

In addition to the above, we received the accompanying answer from Mr. Calhoun to the communication above alluded to; which is communicated confidentially.

Mr. Calhoun expressed to us the wish of the President of the United States, that we should inform the President of Texas that it is his desire that Texas shall herself repel any light attempt on the part of Mexico to make war upon her frontier, and not call on the United States to render the promised aid unless the demonstration made by Mexico should be such as Texas could not easily repel. This we promised to do, and at the same time assured Mr. Calhoun, that the wishes of the President of the United States would be complied with by the President of Texas.

Much more passed between Mr. Calhoun and ourselves on this subject, calculated to assure us that everything would be done by the United States to protect Texas from the aggressions of Mexico, but which we cannot now mention.

Gen. Gaines will soon be at Fort Jesup, ready to receive any intelligence which the President of Texas may have to communicate in regard to the movements of Mexico, and to move into Texas at any time, by the permission of the President of Texas, when it may be deemed advisable. We have the honor to be your ob[edien]t serv[an]ts, Isaac Van Zandt[,] J. Pinckney Henderson.

P.S. That portion of the foregoing despatch which is obliterated was done by the request of Mr. Calhoun upon the same being read to him by us. I.V.Z.[,] J.P.H.

LS with En in Tx, Records of the Texas Republic Department of State, U.S. Diplomatic Correspondence.

From Silas Wright, [Senator from N.Y.], 4/12. Wright transmits a letter to himself from E[dward] C. Delavan and would appreciate Calhoun's compliance with Delavan's request [which was for the Secretary of State to furnish Lewis Weld with letters of introduction to U.S. representatives in Great Britain stating that Weld will be in that country to obtain information on institutions for the deaf and blind]. ALS with En in DNA, RG 59 (State Department), Miscellaneous Letters (M-179:104, frames 163–167).

From A[LEXANDER] H. EVERETT, "Private & Confidential"

Washington D.C., April 13, 1844

Dear Sir, I transmitted to your predecessor, Mr. [Daniel] Webster, some months ago, for the information of the President, a letter that I had received from a source of the highest authority in Cuba upon the subject of the present political situation and relations of that island.

The writer has since passed some months in the United States, and during the greater part of the time resided at Philadelphia. While there he wrote to me several other letters on the same subject, from which I herewith send you a few extracts, as a sort of supplement to the details given in the first. You would oblige me by bringing them to the notice of the President. If they do not add any thing to the information already in possession of the government, they may serve to confirm the corresponding accounts, that may have been received from other quarters. At all events, I have thought it due to the high character of the writer, and ["high" *canceled*] his evident predilection for the United States to comply with his request, that his suggestions might be made known in the quarter, where only they can be acted on.

Soon after the date of the last of these letters the writer sailed for Europe. I had an interview with him at New York, before his departure, and conversed with him very fully on the whole subject. As a proof of the reality of the plan of insurrection and emancipation, described in his letters, and of the correctness of his information, he mentioned, that he had himself been invited by the persons most actively concerned in it to take a military command in the contemplated army. I am, dear Sir, very truly your obed[ien]t ser[van]t, A.H. Everett.

[Enclosures]

I.

Translation of part of a letter, written in Spanish under date of Philadelphia, May 12, 1843.

The situation of Cuba is the most precarious that can well be imagined. At a considerable personal sacrifice I have succeeded in defeating the plans of one of the Agents of the British Abolitionists, who was particularly known to me & have induced him to leave the island. But this partial success is of no importance to the tranquillity and security of the island, so long as the slave trade continues to be carried on, as it is now with unblushing perseverance. This traffic is the source of all our evils, and as there is too much reason to fear, will be that of our ultimate ruin. General Valdez [*sic*; Jeronimo Valdes] is a Castilian cavalier of irreproachable character and the utmost disinterestedness: but his good qualities are purely passive. He does not, like his predecessors, levy a doubloon a head upon every negro clandestinely imported into the island, but he connives at the trade, because he has been made to believe that the Island will be ruined, unless there is a fresh importation of eight or ten thousand blacks every year.

II.

Translation of part of a letter written in Spanish under date of Philadelphia, Aug. 10, 1843.

I learn from your letter the steps you have taken in reference to the unfortunate island of Cuba in consequence of my preceding one, & regret that they have been attended with so little success. The person on whose aid I place the strongest reliance is Mr. Calhoun, from his character and position as the leading representative of the Southern interest. The answer of Gen[era]l [Vincente] Sancho, was characteristic. He is, like all the members of the violent party in Spain, utterly regardless of the true interest of the island of Cuba, which they consider as a mere sugar-plantation, to be carried on for the benefit of the mother country. He is also individually a decided opponent of the introduction of liberal institutions in Cuba, takes no interest in her future fortunes, and would feel little or no regret, if England, the protectress and ally of his party in Spain, should succeed in her projects upon Cuba.

What surprises me most is the opinion expressed by your brother, Mr. Edward Everett, that England is not likely to entertain projects of this description, because she is aware of the determination, that has been expressed by the government of the United States not to permit the island to pass into the hands of any foreign power other than Spain, and of the forcible opposition that would be made, in concert, by those governments to an invasion by Great Britain. Your brother surely cannot be ignorant that the British Government are not obliged or likely to proceed in the way of an open invasion ["by he"(?) *canceled*] with a naval and military armament, in carrying into effect their plan of obtaining the control of Cuba, the other West Indian islands, and, through them, the Southern States and Florida. It is only necessary to employ two or three active and skilful private agents to foment an insurrection of the blacks & thus carry desolation and slaughter through our fertile plantations, without committing, in any way, the name of England. The insurgents might be supplied, in an underhand way with arms and ammunition, and a few small armed vessels by the English authorities in Jamaica and at New Providence, who are always ready, when called on to aid in stirring up rebellion in Cuba. Finally they have only to introduce from Haiti the elements of confusion and disorder, that are so abundant there, in order to produce an insurrection at once. When this object is effected, it becomes, of course, a perfectly natural thing for a great and powerful nation which has important interests to look after & numerous subjects to protect in the West Indies, to station one or two ships of the line, and a few frigates on the coast of Cuba and in the principal harbors—recognise the *black flag* as that of an independent nation, and then, without any breach of the received principles of public law, conclude a treaty of peace and amity and commerce with the new power, so nicely accommodated to those principles that Puffendorff himself [that is, Samuel Pufendorf] would find nothing to add or take away. What would France or the United States have to say against such transactions between two independent nations? Non intervention in such cases is the strict rule of international law.

That you may be able to form an opinion of the correctness of the reports made to the British Foreign Office upon the state of the Island of Cuba I add an extract from a letter, that I received from my brother-in-law Miguel Aldama, under date of the 24th of July.

"The slave trade is carried on here with a shameless publicity characteristic of our nation. New slave ships are constantly being fitted out: the barracoons (slave markets) are full, and slaves are now being sold as low as $200. Add to this that the Government is throwing obstacles in the way of the Company, that has been formed to colonise the island with white laborers, so that we are going on from bad to worse. A few planters have determined to send to Cuba for laborers; and orders have been already transmitted for 500, in addition to those of the Colonisation Society."

The result of the new revolution in the [Iberian] Peninsula (the fall of [Baldomero] Espartero) is of very little importance to Cuba.

All parties in the mother country agree in regard to the policy to be pursued towards the island. The only hope that we have ["for" *canceled*] of bringing about a better state of things is founded in the probability, that the Congress at Madrid may perhaps attempt to emancipate the slaves in the colonies, were it only for the purpose of imitating the English and the French. The passage of a law to this effect would be the signal for Independance. The planters of all classes would then unite in favor of it, and the Colonial authorities ["would place" *interlined*] themselves at the head of the movement. *All would, of course, resort, at once for aid, and protection to the great North American Confederation.*

III.

Extracts from a letter, written in Spanish under the date of
Philadelphia, Dec[embe]r 9, 1843

My intelligence from the Havana is exceedingly unpleasant. You will have seen in the newspapers the accounts of the rising of the negroes on a plantation near Matanzas. I have received from several correspondents the following additional particulars on the subject.

Don Gaspar de Betancourt, an inhabitant of Puerto Principe, and one of our most eminent citizens, both as an ardent patriot, and a distinguished periodical writer, informs me, under date of the 11th of November: "In the night of the 5th the negroes rose on the sugar estate of Don Julian Alfonso. The lancers were immediately called in, and succeeded in quelling the insurrection. Fifty of the blacks were killed, and sixty seven taken prisoners, most of them having been previously wounded. Several have been condemned to death by the military commission and a number have hung themselves. What with the slave-traders on one side and the negroes on the other, we are in a pretty condition. ["There" *canceled*] It is said that Alfonso loses more than $80,000. Incidents of this kind have now occurred at short intervals at Santiago, Trinidad, Bemba, Cardenas and Matanzas. The slave-trader fills his pockets, and leaves us the precious cargo, to be made food for powder. The sugar planter pays all expenses—A pleasant state of things truly! The fact is that we are rapidly following in the tracks of St. Domingo. Yet these demons in human shape (the slave-traders) are constantly sending out their ships to Africa, and another set of demons are buying the return cargo, in order, apparently, to have the pleasure of seeing them hung or cut to pieces a few weeks afterwards."

Mr. de Betancourt has been long labouring by his eloquent writings in the Puerto Principe Gazette, and by his more persuasive example, to shew the practicability & expediency of introducing free labor in the island. On his plantation near Puerto Principe he employs a great number of natives of the Canary Islands, who work in the field as vigorously as the blacks.

My mother, under date of the 21st of November gives a still more particular account of the same catastrophe.

"On the night of the 5th all the blacks upon the *Triunvirato*[?] rose, and proceeded at once to Acaña (an estate belonging to D[on] Joseph E. Alfonso) where they attempted to induce the blacks to join them. Failing in this, they set fire to the negro huts and surrounded the house of the Inspector, where the whites had taken refuge with their wives and children. They next fired the house, when the whites, being reduced to the alternative of being assassinated, or burnt to death, opened their doors. The blacks entered and killed three women, two men & one child. They then marched successively to the neighboring plantations of Conception, San Miguel and Lorenzo, where they obtained a few recruits. It was now three in the morning and at this time they were attacked by a guard of twenty men from Sabanilla, whom they succeeded in repulsing. At six in the morning the blacks, who now amounted to three hundred, including many women with their babies on their backs, reached the plantation of San Rafael, and were about setting fire to it, when they were encountered in the public square by a squadron of horse from Matanzas including the twenty men from Sabanilla, who had joined them on the road. On being summoned to surrender, the blacks defied the troops, and a battle took place which lasted two hours. The negroes were finally routed with the loss of fifty four killed and sixty seven prisoners. Thanks to the rain, the damage sustained by fire has not been very considerable; two hundred soldiers have been quartered in the neighborhood, and at the last accounts all was again quiet."

My brother-in-law Miguel gives me a similar account, and adds: "Five hundred and fifty negroes arrived this week from Africa. It is understood that [Gen. Leopoldo] O'Donnell connives at the trade and takes the half ounce of gold ($8) a head."

My brother-in-law Gonzalo, a young man of one and twenty, in concluding his narrative, exclaims with the warmth natural to his age: "This was not the worst: while the battle was raging, seven hundred negroes were being landed from a slave trading vessel on the neighboring coast. Thus our condition is constantly growing worse & worse, while the infamous Spanish government gives itself no trouble whatever about the matter."

The Civil Engineer, D[on] Manuel Carrera, who built the railroad to Cardenas, and is the only Spaniard, who has ever undertaken a work of that kind, writes to me in a different strain, but agrees fully with my other correspondents in regard to the facts. "Our board of directors," says he, "are thinking of purchasing some negroes to employ upon the road, and regret very much that they lose a favorable opportunity for this purpose, which occurred in the *fortunate* arrival the other day of a cargo of eight hundred at Matanzas. I tell them that they need not be uneasy, that other cargoes will arrive, and that there will be no want of merchandise in the slave-market. Thus you see that the apprehensions, which were entertained that the island would suffer for want of hands are not likely to prove well founded, for there are now more negroes coming in than ever before, and no obstacle is thrown in the way by any one."

Excuse me for troubling you with these communications but it is a satisfaction to me to make known my feelings to one, who I am sure, sympathises with me & regrets, as every good American must, to see this beautiful island, which was intended by nature to be a flourishing State, connected in the strictest bonds of amity, as well as neighborhood with the Union, condemned by the stupidity and barbarism of its tyrants to be converted into another Haiti.

ALS with Ens in DNA, RG 59 (State Department), Miscellaneous Letters (M-179:104, frames 169–180). Note: On a cover sheet appended to this letter an endorsement in an unidentified hand reads "There is [in] these letters some evidence to warrant the belief that England Connives at the Slave Trade with Cuba; and that the Spanish authorities divide the profits. The Inference that England desires to reduce Cuba to the condition [of] Haiti, or St. Domingo, with the view of obtaining a Controul of the Island through Commercial stipulations deserves to be considered. The facts in regard to the Slave Trade are startling—but the source of the evidence is suspicious—inasmuch as the author obviously leans to the policy *of introducing free labour in the Island.*" Alexander H. Everett, a brother of Edward Everett, had been U.S. Minister to Spain during 1825–1829 and then editor of the *North American Review.*

From C[HARLES] J. INGERSOLL, [Representative from Pa.]

Ap[ri]l 13, [18]44

Dear Sir, The Oregon letter & tract herewith may perhaps be of some use to you.

They were handed to me to day by Mr. [Osmyn] Baker [Representative from Mass.] from whose district they come.

Mr. [Robert] Greenhow of the State Department says that the writer of them is unworthy of credit.

But I consider him and so does Mr. Baker a man of information [and] enthusiast about Oregon. I am very truly y[ou]rs, C.J. Ingersoll.

[Enclosure]
Hall J. Kelley to Osmyn Baker, Washington
Three Rivers, Mass., April 10, 1844
Sir, I received on the 30th inst[ant] a letter from Mr. Henry Hatch of Boston, son of the late Crowell Hatch, one of the owners of the ship Columbia which entered the mouth of the "Oregon" river in 1792. Ill health has prevented an earlier answer. He desires me to reply to a request made to him to send to some committee in Congress (what com[mittee] he does not say) *the log book and papers* of the above ship. He states that many years ago, all the papers important to the interests of the general government were sent to the State Dept. and that nothing remains in his hands. Every fact, as I conceive, necessary ["for the" *canceled*] to show the consummation of the Am[erican] title to the Oregon country has been given to the public. As early as the year 1818 I commenced enquiries after historical facts concerning that territory. Perhaps there is no important items of information about the discoveries, or any of the acts performed on the N[orth] W[est] Coast, by persons of any civilized country effecting the great questions of title and boundary, which in the course of my devotion to the subject has not been acquired, and, under a sense of duty, sent to the proper Dept. of the general government.

My communications may have been deemed unworthy a place in the national archives, and may be found only on my own records; for indeed, the style and slovenly dress of my language may have rendered them objectionable. Having been made the victim of books and publications of every kind, I am now called upon to state, and respectfully as well as explicitly would I state, that much of the knowledge in the possession of the public concerning the history of Oregon has been furnished directly or indirectly by me; and the credit of commencing the colonization of that territory, and of instituting christianity in it is manifestly my due. I ask pardon for this digression, and return to the request of my friend Hatch.

The log book of the Columbia is not in existance. Some years ago it was destroyed with other books and papers, supposed to be of no value, by the family of Capt. Atkins of Boston. ["Charles Bulfinch Esq(ui)r(e) in his memoir" *canceled.*] In 1828 or 9 I made such extracts from it, as I thought would be desirable for Congress to know. They are to be found in the document I herewith send, entitled "Discoveries, Purchases of lands &c. on the North West Coast." Also, in the Doc[ument] No. 43 Ho[use] of Rep[resentative]s 26 Cong., 1st Session.

For several months in the year 1829, I had the loan of Capt. [Robert] Gray's journal kept by [John] Hoskins the clerk of the ship. In it are recorded all the interesting things mentioned in the log books. This journal I am informed was in the hands of a committee of Congress of which the Hon. Francis Bayl[i]es [of Mass.] was chairman. It is, probably, at the present time, in the keeping of some one of the heirs of the owners of the ship. To the truth of the above statements I am ready to testify under oath.

I consider the Am[erican] claim to be well founded to all the territory on the ["Western" *canceled and* "Pacific" *interlined*] shore, between the Mexican and Russian boundaries. The land purchases made by Capt. J[ohn] Kendrick of native chiefs consummate the title to Quadra's Island and to a large extent of country south of DeFuca's sea. They were unquestionably valid—made at a time and place, when and where, the parties were free to exercise their natural rights in buying and selling of property of any description.

I will forward to you in a few days a map shewing the exact situation and limits of Kendrick's lands; which map, I wish when you return from Washington, you would bring with you, or if you please, return it by mail. Yours—very respectfully, Hall J. Kelley.

ALS with En in ScCleA. NOTE: An AEU by Calhoun on the address leaf of the En reads: "Mr. Kell[e]y, relates to Oregon."

From CALVIN J. KEITH

New Orleans, Ap[ri]l 13, 1844
Sir, I am the Agent of all the Heirs of the late Samuel Elkins, & as such presented a claim before the Commissioners under the late Treaty with Mexico, which claim was in the hands of the Umpire at the time said Commission was closed & returned by him undecided. I have been informed that a Treaty has been made with Mexico for a new Commission & I have been requested to sign a remonstrance against the ratification of the treaty, upon the grounds that the Com-

missioners are to meet at Mexico. Now if there are no other or stronger objections to said Treaty than the meeting of the Commission in Mexico (if the wishes of the Claimants are to be considered) I, as the representative of about one seventh of the Claims returned undecided by the former Umpire, hope said treaty may be ratified. Give me the Commission I care not where it meets. I am with Great Respect Your Ob[edien]t Serv[an]t, Calvin J. Keith.

ALS in DNA, RG 59 (State Department), Miscellaneous Letters (M-179:104, frames 181–182).

To W[ILLIAM] S. MURPHY, [Galveston]

Washington City, April 13th 1844

Sir: I have to inform you that a Treaty for the purpose of annexing the Republic of Texas to the United States was signed in this city on yesterday by the Plenipotentiaries on the part of that Republic and myself. The Instrument will be sent to the Senate as soon as the Documents relating to it can be prepared; which will probably be by the middle of next week. I entertain little doubt of its approval by that body. The voice of the Country, so far as it can be heard, is so decidedly in favour of annexation that any hesitancy on the part of the doubtful will probably give way to it.

The Messenger who takes this despatch is also the bearer of the Texan duplicate of the Treaty.

It is the President's [John Tyler's] intention to exert all his Constitutional power to defend Texas against Mexico, should this latter Power make an attack pending the Treaty. An assurance to this effect is given in the note [of 4/11] from this Department to Messrs. [Isaac] Van Zandt & [J. Pinckney] Henderson, a copy of which is herewith transmitted.

To enable this Government to accomplish the purpose referred to, a large Naval force will be ordered to rendezvous in the Gulf of Mexico, under the command of Captain [David] Conner, who is now the Commander on that station. The whole military force of the Western Division will also be put under the command of General [Edmund P.] Gaines, who will be ordered forthwith to Fort Jesup as his head quarters.

You will keep up a constant correspondence and the most intimate relations with the Texan Authorities, and especially with President

[Samuel] Houston. Should you receive any information from him going to show that Mexico meditated any serious attempt to invade Texas, you will promptly communicate the information to General Gaines and Captain Conner. These Officers are authorized to inform the Commander of the Mexican force that the President would regard an attack upon Texas, during the pendency of the Treaty before the Senate, as an act of hostility towards the United States, and would exert all the force which he may possess to repel it.

You will lose no time in communicating to this Department the information referred to; and you will transmit with your despatch upon the subject, a copy of the note from the Texan Government, conveying the information. You will, however, consider the authority to employ an express as limited to the case where a serious attempt to invade Texas is indicated by Mexico.

You will continue to be watchful for the purpose of discovering any thing which may affect the interests of the United States. Your attention will be particularly directed to the proceedings of the Agents of other Powers in Texas; and ["you will" *interlined*] keep this Department apprized of all such facts and circumstances as may seem to you of interest to the Government and Country; particularly of the state of public opinion in Texas in regard to annexation. I am, Sir, your ob[edien]t Ser[van]t &C. &C., J.C. Calhoun.

LS in DNA, RG 84 (Foreign Posts), Records of the Texas Legation; FC in DNA, RG 59 (State Department), Diplomatic Instructions, Texas, 1:91–92 (M-77:161); CCEx in Tx, Andrew Jackson Houston Papers; CCEx in Tx, Records of the Texas Republic Department of State, Letters and Dispatches Sent by the Texas Legation in Washington, filed in vol. 1.

From T[homas] M. Rodney

Consulate of the United States of America
Matanzas [Cuba], April 13th 1844
Sir, I have the honor to enclose herewith copies of letters passed between this Consulate and the governor of Matanzas, in relation to Christopher Boone a Citizen of the United States, cruelly maltreated and confined in prison fifty one days on the declaration of a negro; and released therefrom yesterday. The Department will perceive that according to the opinion of the consulting judge of the military commission, endorsed, by the act of ["their" *canceled and* "its" *interlined*] transmission through the governor that it is not deemed proper

or admissable that this Office should ask for information touching the arrest, imprisonment and cruelty practiced against a citizen of the United States.

But if the views of the Department have undergone no change since 1842, it will not be necessary for me to trouble it with a recital of similar cases in future; in that year (June 30) I addressed a letter to the Department in relation to certain American citizens imprisoned here, and then in confinement about two years, suggesting "the propriety of a communication from the Department direct to the Governor and Captain General *asking* their speedy *trial* or enlargement." On the 18th of October following the Department wrote me in reply "that it is one properly to be decided by the laws of Matanzas to which these persons have voluntarily subjected themselves and with which the Department can in no manner interfere." Of these prisoners two died in jail, and two were released, pending trial, after having been confined three years and a half.

If this were a government of laws and speedy justice, the views of the Department would have been perfectly correct—but this is a military despotism—the law, the will of the Government in all political cases, where tho' the semblance of trial is given the lingering process drags its slow length along thro' months and years of protracted imprisonment, and where to be suspected is sure to bring with it long and tedious Spanish confinement costs, and all the effects of conviction.

The same negro who made his voluntary declaration against Mr. Boone also declared against four others, planters of the first respectability, who have also been imprisoned, tho' treated with more consideration than Mr. Boone. Three of these are French and I am given to understand that the Consul of their nation, who has manifested a warm interest in their behalf, has made it a matter of serious correspondence and one requiring ample indemnity.

I am perfectly aware that in the present state of things in this Island energetick measures are required, but it does seem most strange and unnatural that the testimony of a single black man of bad character should be taken against persons of the first respectability, whose interests are identified with the Island and whose general character is above suspicion further than that they are foreigners.

The examination of the Blacks and mulattoes whether slave or free is conducted with a cruelty that savours of the Inquisition. They are questioned under the lash and numbers have died under the operation, and as leading questions are put it is easy to see that the most innocent may be criminated, for under the exquisite torture the poor wretches are willing to say any thing that will relieve them from present suffering, and it will be a matter of no surprise if others of our citizens are brought into the custody of the military commission.

Our Government may rest assured that something of efficient action is required to stay the abuses practised on our citizens and that the perem[p]tory exaction of indemnity in a single case would do more the [*sic*] check these things than quires of diplomatic correspondence.

I am on the best personal terms with the authorities here, and have every reason to be satisfied with their courteous conduct in my intercourse with them. It therefore give[s] me no pleasure to be obliged to call the attention of the Department to matters of this kind. I have the honor to be Sir, your obedient S[ervan]t, T.M. Rodney.

ALS (No. 17) with Ens in DNA, RG 59 (State Department), Consular Despatches, Matanzas, vol. 4 (T-339:4), received 4/29. NOTE: Rodney transmitted four Ens with this despatch. They were: a note from himself to Antonio Garcia Oña, dated 4/8, reporting particulars of the Boone case; an English translation of Oña's reply of 4/13; a letter, dated 4/13, from Rodney to President John Tyler, sending a memorial from Boone; and Boone's autograph memorial, dated 4/13. In it, Boone states that he had been arrested on 2/19/1844, kept in solitary confinement 14 days before being charged with having "in his possession, under a tree, three thousand stand of arms!!" His imprisonment totaled 49 days and he seeks "an honorable and adequate indemnity."

To Isaac Van Zandt and J. Pinckney Henderson, Texan Commissioners to the U.S., 4/13. "Mr. Calhoun presents his compliments to Mr. Van Zandt and General Henderson, and would be glad to see them at the Department of State as soon after the receipt of this note as they can make it convenient to call." FC in DNA, RG 59 (State Department), Notes to Foreign Legations, Texas, 6:70 (M-99:95).

[To ISAAC VAN ZANDT and J. PINCKNEY HENDERSON]

[Washington, *ca.* April 13, 1844?]

Inquiries propounded by the Secretary of State of the United States to Messrs. [Isaac] Van Zandt & [J. Pinckney] Henderson.

First—Under what authority was the vote of the people of Texas taken on the question of annexation to the United States, at the time of the adoption of the Constitution?

Second—How many votes were in favour of annexation and how many against it?

Third—What evidence is there that the people of Texas are equally unanimous now in regard to the same question?

Fourth—What evidence is there that the Government of Texas is also unanimous in all its departments?

Fifth—In what do the debts and liabilities consist and on what data is the estimate of $10,000,000 based?

Sixth—What amount of lands in acres is there estimated to be in Texas?

Seventh—What portion of this amount is covered by grants, patents and other legal claims under the laws of Texas?

Memorandum in Tx, Records of the Texas Republic Department of State, Letters and Dispatches Sent by the Texas Legation in Washington, 1:501. NOTE: The date of this memorandum made by or for Van Zandt and Henderson is conjectural.

From W[illia]m Bevan

Bridgeton [N.J.], April 14, 1844

Sir, I have take[n] the liberty of writing to you stating that in February of 1843 the Schooner Vigilant commanded by Capt. Barber & principally owned by me was captured by the *Mexicans* & taken to Verricruse supposing that she had munitions of war on board but her cargo was hoisted out a[t] Verricruse & found to consist whol[l]y of Corn & flower so wrote the A[merican] Council of Verracruise [Francis M. Dimond] in March of 1843 to Capt. Barber's *Father*. It is reported that the Schooner was given up to the A[merican] C[onsul] at Verracruse for the benefit of the owners & that she now is running from thence to N. Orleans.

If I am ["informed" *interlined*] the late Secratary [Abel P. Upshur] wrote to Verracruise to the Consul for a statement of facts but has had no answer returned to the office. I wish you if you pleas[e] to enquire of Gen[era]l [Waddy] Thompson [Jr.] our late Minister if he can give the facts of the case &c &c. If the Gen[era]l does ["not" *interlined*] posses[s] the information please to write for information to the A[merican] Council at Verracruise please to assertain the facts for me so that I can try to get pay for the vessle and detention &c &c.

236

Sir you will do me great service by putting me in a way to get pay. Please write to me or inform the Hon[orab]l[e] L[ucius] Q.C. Elmer [Representative from N.J.] so that that [*sic*] I can go ahead. Yours &c, Wm. Bevan.

ALS in DNA, RG 59 (State Department), Miscellaneous Letters (M-179:104, frames 184–185).

From WILLIAM R. KING, [Senator from Ala.]

[Washington] April 14th 1844
Sir, I have the honor to acknowledge the receipt of your Note of the 12th Inst. informing me that the President, by and with the advice of the Senate, has appointed me Minister Plenipotentiary to France. I accept of the Situation thus conferred on me, and will be prepared to take my Departure, whenever required by the President. With the highest respect I am your ob[edien]t Ser[van]t, William R. King.

ALS in DNA, RG 59 (State Department), Diplomatic Despatches, France, vol. 30 (M-34:33).

From W[ILLIAM] S. MURPHY

Legation of the United States
Galveston Texas, 14th April 1844
Sir, Your despatch No. 15 of the 11th March, was received on the 11th April and on the day following, the Undersigned addressed a note, to the Sec[re]t[ary] of State of the Rep[u]b[lic] of Texas [Anson Jones]; a copy of which is herewith enclosed.

The United States Schooner Flirt, was absent from this Port only 4, Days under the order, to which you allude. She was driven back, by adverse winds. The object of sending her out, was purely to obtain information &c &c. I have the Honor to be Your ob[edien]t Serv[an]t, W.S. Murphy.

[Enclosure]

W.S. Murphy to Anson Jones

Legation of the United States
Galveston Texas, 12th April 1844
Sir, The Undersigned, charge d'affaires of the United States, near the Government of the Republic of Texas, has the Honor of inform-

ing Mr. Jones, that whilst his government approves of the general tone and tenor of his intercourse, with the Government of the Republic of Texas, a regret is felt, in perceiving, that his Zeal for the accomplishment of objects, alike beneficial and interesting to both countries, have led him beyond the strict tone of his instructions; That the President of the United States, considers himself restrained by the Constitution of the Union, from the employment of the Army and Navy, against a foreign power, with whom the United States are at peace; And that, whilst the President of the United States is not indisposed, as a measure of prudent precaution, and as preliminary to the proposed negociation, to concentrate in the Gulf of Mexico, and on the Southern borders of the United States, a sufficient naval and military force, to be directed to the defence of the inhabitants and Territory of Texas at a proper time: He is unwilling that the authorities of Texas should apprehend, that He has power to employ this force, at the period indicated in my note to you of the 14th of February last.

In making this communication to the Government of Texas, the Undersigned is gratified at being enabled to assure Mr. Jones, that no possible evil, can, or will ensue to Texas, from this determination of his Government. Mexico is not in a condition, if it was her present purpose, to move hostilities against Texas; and no such movement can be reasonably apprehended.

Mr. Jones is well advised, by the official report of the Texas commissioners, who have lately adjourned their negociations with the commissioners of Mexico, to a distant day; that the armistice, heretofore proclaimed by this Government, between Texas and Mexico, is yet in full force, and will continue, by express agreement, until they meet again, to resume negociations. Long before that time can arrive, the great question of annexation will doubtless be settled, and the just wishes of the people of Texas, and those of the United States, the Undersigned, fondly hopes, will have been consummated.

The Undersigned, congratulating Mr. Jones upon the probability of this great event—an event, so full of interest, and pregnant of results, at once glorious and beneficial to both countries, renews to Mr. Jones the assurance of his most sincere respect, and high consideration. Your ob[edien]t Serv[an]t, W.S. Murphy.

ALS (No. 22) with En in DNA, RG 59 (State Department), Diplomatic Despatches, Texas, vol. 2 (T-728:2, frames 302 and 305–306), received 4/30; FC in DNA, RG 84 (Foreign Posts), Records of the Texas Legation; PC with En in Senate Document No. 349, 28th Cong., 1st Sess., pp. 11–12; PC with En in House Document No. 271, 28th Cong., 1st Sess., pp. 97–98; PC with En in the Washington, D.C., *Daily National Intelligencer,* June 3, 1844, p. 2; PC in *Niles' National Register,* vol. LXVI, no. 15 (June 8, 1844), p. 232.

From I[saac] C. Bates, [Senator from Mass. and Chairman of the Senate Committee on Pensions], 4/15. Bates submits for Calhoun's consideration a letter from the Commissioner of Pensions [James L. Edwards] and a resolution [of 3/6 concerning the proposed transfer of the "Washington Papers" from the custody of the State Department to that of the Pension Office]. ALS in DNA, RG 59 (State Department), Miscellaneous Letters (M-179:104, frames 188–189); PC of enclosed resolution in *Senate Journal,* 28th Cong., 1st Sess., p. 150.

From W[alter] T. Colquitt, [Senator from Ga.], 4/15. Colquitt introduces "Col." —— Russell, who "was acquainted with you some years ago; but may perhaps be forgotten. He brings high testimonials of character, family and standing, and desires to obtain some appointment. . . . Your polite attention will be remembered by your friend, W.T. Colquitt." ALS in DNA, RG 59 (State Department), Letters of Introduction to the Secretary of State, 1820–1849.

To WILLIAM CRUMP, Powhatan Court House, Va.

Department of State
Washington, 15th April, 1844
Sir: I have to inform you that the President [John Tyler], by and with the advice and consent of the Senate, has appointed you Chargé d'Affaires of the United States to the Republic of Chile. If you accept the appointment, you will notify this department to that effect and state when you will be ready to set out on your mission, so that your credentials and instructions may be prepared in season. I am, Sir, your obedient Servant, J.C. Calhoun.

FC in DNA, RG 59 (State Department), Diplomatic Instructions, Chile, 15:49 (M-77:35).

From R[ICHARD] H. DANA, JR.

Boston, April 15, 1844
Sir, In sending the accompanying document, I deem it my duty to state that the character of some of the petitioners & their connexions

in life are highly respectable; & that all necessary evidence can be procured in such manner as the Department may require.

The petitioners have requested me to receive any communication from the Department in their behalf. Y[ou]r ob[edien]t Se[rvan]t, R.H. Dana, Jr.

ALS in DNA, RG 59 (State Department), Applications and Recommendations, 1845–1853, De Silver (M-873:23, frames 39–40). NOTE: The document submitted by Dana was apparently the memorial immediately below from James Gale Hubbell and others.

From JA[ME]S GALE HUBBELL and Others

[Boston, *ca.* April 15, 1844]

We the undersigned believing that the Government at Washington will not uphold their Agents in acts of abuse and oppression towards American citizens in foreign lands, beg leave most respectfully to state the following facts. That they are all citizens of the United States, and shipped as such on board the Ship Hibernia and sailed from the port of New Bedford [Mass.] in June 1842. That after a lapse of 15 months the said ship having procured nearly a full cargo of oil went into Port Louis in the Isle of France [Mauritius, a British colony]. While there the undersigned together with several others comprising a large majority of the crew wrote to [William H.] Hollier[-]*Griffiths* a subject of Great Britain and Commercial Agent for the United States at that place, stating that the said ship was not seaworthy, that we were afraid to proceed to sea in her without she was repaired, and asking him in respectful terms to order a survey to be held upon the ship. We afterwards went to Mr. Griffith's office and after being detained in the yard for half an hour while he and our Captain were within, we were allowed to enter. Mr. Griffiths then called over our names, asked us what we were, and *without inquiring what was our business with him*, proceeded to say that we were a pack of damned American cowards, and that if we did not go on board our ship to our duty, he would put us all in prison. We replied that we were afraid to proceed in the ship in her present condition, and asked him to order a survey to be held upon her. He said that he would not order a survey, and when some of our number in a respectful manner, attempted to explain to him the condition of our ship, he told us that he would not listen to us, and that if we did not stop talking he would commit us to prison for impertinence. We then

240

went on board of our ship and obeyed every order except lifting the anchor. The Captain attempted to force us to go to sea, but failing in that, applied to Mr. Griffiths, who sent a detachment of Police to the ship, took us on shore and lodged us in prison during the night. In the morning we were taken before Mr. Griffiths, and told by him that he should commit us to prison on a charge of mutiny and there keep us until he had an opportunity to send us to the United States for trial. He did not make the slightest inquiry into the affair, and would not listen to one word of explanation on our part. He said that he knew how to manage crews like us—that he had confined such men before, and after keeping them sixteen days upon bread and water, they were glad to write and beg his pardon.

He also said that he knew that our situation would be very painful, and that we would write to him for more bread but it would be useless as he should not listen to our complaints. We asked him for the clothing that belonged to us on board of our ship, and were told that we had forfeited all of it, and that we ought to be thankful that we were allowed to take what we had on our backs. We were then taken back to prison and for four days confined in a cell where we had nothing to sit or lay upon except stone. We were then removed to a smaller room where there was a wooden platform with room for about 15 to lay upon it—there was always more than that number confined in it, and sometimes as many as 27. This cell was partially underground, with but one window which opened into a recess and admitted very little light.

The weather was intensely hot and the atmosphere was suffocating.

In this condition we remained *thirty one days* with only half an hour outside during the twenty four—subsisting upon 1¼ lbs. of miserable bread each day, with not a rag to protect our aching limbs from the hard wood and stone. We had no change of clothing, and what little strength we had, was sapped by swarms of vermin of every species mentioned in the catalogue. Our sufferings from their attacks may perhaps be imagined but cannot be described.

After about two weeks had passed, one of our number obtained leave to go with a guard and ask Mr. Griffiths for more bread. He did so, and his answer was "Guard, take that man back—you have prisoners allowance, such as mutineers deserve." He also sent orders to the Police Office that we were neither to be allowed to come and see him any more, nor to have paper to write. Through the kindness of one of the Brigadiers of Police we secretly obtained a sheet of paper and a pen and ink, and wrote a letter to the English Governor stating our condition and that unless we had relief we should not survive many days.

He sent to the Prison to enquire into our situation, and as we were told and believe, through his orders on the 31st day of our confinement and during the remainder of our stay we were supplied with a dinner of meat and vegetables and 4 hours liberty of the yard each day. We considered that the Governor had saved our lives, but still our condition in consequence of having no change of clothing, was most miserable. We represented this to the Governor in another letter, and on the 43d day of our confinement we were each supplied with one shirt, a pair of trowsers and some soap.

On the 46th day we were taken out and placed on board of an English vessel bound to St. Helena. We were furnished with no more clothes nor any bedding, and as there was no place provided for us to sleep, the greater part lay upon deck during the 38 days passage to St. Helena.

When we arrived at St. Helena, Mr. [William] Carrol the Commercial Agent at that place [and former Governor of Tenn.] treated us very kindly, furnished us with necessary clothing and bedding and placed us on board the first ship bound to the United States.

We were in charge of the U.S. Marshal until March 29th when after a confinement of more than six months duration, we were arraigned before the U.S. Dist[rict] Court in Boston, where our conduct was fully investigated, and we were triumphantly acquitted of every charge brought against us.

Several of our crew were unwell during the entire passage home in consequence of confinement and starvation, from the effects of which they will probably never recover.

The undersigned feel confident that the Government will not sanction the conduct of one of their foreign agents in such oppressive treatment of American citizens, even if it was not also attended with an expense of several thousand dollars, employed needlessly and wrongfully to punish men whose acts have met the unqualified approval of a Jury of their countrymen. They also consider it due not only to themselves, but to the public at large, that such abuses of power should be made known to the proper authorities, in order that other American seamen should not undeservedly suffer by the oppressive acts of such unworthy representatives of their country. Jas. Gale Hubbell, William Lee[?] Irving[?], Cha[rle]s F. Hardie, Henry F. Givens (his mark), Alonzo Wood, William H. Dawson, Henry Dawson, John F. Crist, Jefry Slide, Joel H. Plummer.

[Appended:] Boston, Massachusetts, April 15, 1844. I hereby

certify that the above named persons have stated to me their belief of the above statement, & that they can procure all necessary evidence of the facts, if required by the Department. Rich[ar]d H. Dana, Jr., Jus[tice] of the Peace.

LS in DNA, RG 59 (State Department), Applications and Recommendations, 1845–1853, Griffiths (M-873:35, frames 307–310); variant LS in DNA, RG 59 (State Department), Consular Despatches, Port Louis, Mauritius, vol. 4 (M-462:2, frames 142–144), received 5/9. NOTE: On 3/23/1844 Acting Secretary of State John Nelson had written to Franklin Dexter, U.S. District Attorney at Boston, enclosing papers received at the State Department from representatives in Mauritius and St. Helena and suggesting the commencement of proceedings against the *Hibernia* "mutineers." FC in DNA, RG 59 (State Department), Consular Instructions, 12:73–74. Hollier-Griffiths was superseded by the appointment of a Consul at Port Louis in 5/1844.

From EDWARD EVERETT

London, 15 April 1844

Sir, On the 29th of May last I received a despatch from the Department numbered 42, transmitting an account of an outrage alleged to have been committed upon an American vessel called the "Roderick Dhu," on the coast of Africa on the 4th of January preceding. On the 5th of June I addressed a note to Lord Aberdeen representing the case, and requesting that it should be enquired into. In the answer from the Foreign Office dated 3d of July, I was informed that an investigation had been already ordered. On the 10th instant the result of this investigation was sent to me in the accompanying note, from Lord Aberdeen.

I hesitate somewhat as to the notice which ought to be taken of this explanation. On the one hand, it appears that the commanding officer of the British Cruizer, not having from some unexplained inadvertence received the instructions of Lord Aberdeen relative to vessels bearing the American flag, acted on those of Lord Palmerston. Such a case is very unlikely to happen again. The officer has farther been told that the government consider the grounds on which he detained the "Roderick Dhu" insufficient; the "serious displeasure" of Her Majesty's government has been signified to the Boarding Officer for a part of his conduct; and the sincere regret of this government is expressed by Lord Aberdeen to the government of the United States, that the visit ever took place.

Considering that the detention of the vessel lasted less than an hour and that no injury resulted, these explanations and expressions may perhaps be considered satisfactory.

On the other hand, the grounds assigned by Mr. Raymond the Boarding Officer for detaining the vessel appear to me not only "insufficient" but frivolous, and such as ought to have drawn upon him the censure of his government.

These considerations I think, authorize us to receive the note of Lord Aberdeen in such a manner as may, on other grounds, be expedient; either to regard it as satisfactory and so final, or to make the detention of the "Roderick Dhu" the subject of a farther remonstrance.

Whether it would be advisable to pursue the latter course is a matter exclusively for the President's decision, and would depend very much on the state of the negociations in train at Washington. I have accordingly thought it expedient to address a short note to Lord Aberdeen acknowledging the receipt of his communication and await your farther instructions. I transmit, at the same time, the draft of an answer to Lord Aberdeen, containing the view of the subject which appears to me to be warranted by the facts, should you think it advisable that the discussion should be pursued. I am, sir, very respectfully your obedient servant, Edward Everett.

Documents accompanying Despatch 112.

1. The Earl of Aberdeen to Mr. Everett, 10 April 1844.
2. Draft of a note from Mr. Everett to the Earl of Aberdeen, submitted for the President's consideration.
3. Mr. Everett to the Earl of Aberdeen, 16 April 1844.

LS (No. 112) with Ens in DNA, RG 59 (State Department), Diplomatic Despatches, Great Britain, vol. 52 (M-30:48), received 5/8; FC in MHi, Edward Everett Papers, 48:450–453 (published microfilm, reel 22, frames 1271–1272). NOTE: This despatch was addressed to John Nelson as Secretary of State ad interim.

From THEOPHILUS FISK

Washington, April 15, 1844

Sir, I beg leave, very respectfully to ask that that [*sic*] the Chronicle and Old Dominion at Portsmouth, Va.[,] may be allowed to publish the laws of the United States "by authority."

When Mr. [Daniel] Webster assumed the duties of the State Department, the proprietor of that paper declined the appointment of publisher of the laws—since which no other paper in that section of the State has been selected, so that no removal will be necessary. With perfect respect, Theophilus Fisk.

ALS in DNA, RG 59 (State Department), Miscellaneous Letters Received regarding Publishers of the Laws, 1789–1875.

From A[RCHIBALD] M. GREEN

Consulate of the U.S. of America at Galvezton
Republic of Texas, 15th April 1844
Sir, I beg leave to submit to the Department, the following question about which there seems to be much diversity of opinion—viz. "A British ship is chartered to sail for a foreign port, to take in a cargo of Cotton and return to England. The charterers, not being in a position to procure sufficient cargo, without heavy loss, desire to send the ship to the port of New Orleans to complete her lading. The ship in question having, say 200 Bales of Texan Cotton on board; said Cotton being taken in at Galvezton and there being no treaty at present subsisting between the United States and Texas, can said vessel, finish her loading in New Orleans without making the vessel liable under the revenue Laws of the United States?

Or would she only be regarded under the circumstances, as any other English vessel going to that port for the purpose of taking a cargo to England having at the same time the American consul[']s certificate, stating the quantity of Cotton on board designed for a European market and not for importation in the United States."

May I solicit an early answer. I have the honor to be most Respectfully y[ou]r ob[edien]t S[ervan]t, A.M. Green.

ALS (No. 32) in DNA, RG 59 (State Department), Consular Despatches, Galveston, vol. 2 (T-151:2), received 5/1.

I[saac] E. Holmes, [Representative from S.C.], to Thomas Ritchie, [Richmond], 4/15. Holmes informs Ritchie that an anti-tariff bill has just failed to be brought up for consideration in the House of Representatives by a vote of 95 to 84, with New York Democrats voting against it. He asks Ritchie, as the "Nestor of Democracy," what course Southern Democrats should now pursue. [This document, found among Calhoun's papers, is perhaps a copy sent by Holmes to Calhoun.] ALS in ScCleA.

From [William Hunter, Jr.]

[Washington, *ca.* April 15, 1844]

Memorandum. The claim in the case of the brig Morris is for the unlawful capture of that vessel and her cargo by a Colombian privateer in 1824.

The claim was presented to the late government of Colombia by the diplomatic agents of the U. States at Bogotá, but was not adjusted when, in 1829, that Confederacy separated into the three States of Venezuela, New Granada and Ecuador. These States subsequently entered into a treaty with one another for the purpose of determining the share which each should assume of the liabilities of Colombia. By this treaty, New Granada assumed fifty per cent of those liabilities, Venezuela twenty eight and a half and Ecuador twenty one and a half.

The diplomatic agents of the United States accredited to those States have been instructed that this government held those States jointly and severally accountable for claims of citizens of the United States, but that we would release them from any further accountability upon their paying the proportion of the claims or of any one of them as determined by the treaty above mentioned.

Mr. [Allen A.] Hall, the Chargé d'Affaires in Venezuela has accordingly effected an adjustment of the claim in the case of the Morris by an arrangement with the Minister for Foreign Affairs. His instructions, however, require him not to accept any particular sum in satisfaction of any one of the claims without previously referring the matter to the department for further instructions. This course he has accordingly pursued. He has acquainted the claimants with the terms of the adjustment, and they have written to the department expressing their approbation of them and requesting that they may also be approved by the Secretary as soon as may be convenient so that Mr. Hall may receive intelligence of that approval in season to obtain an appropriation at the present session of the Venezuelan Congress.

ADU in ScCleA. NOTE: This memorandum is in the hand of William Hunter, Jr., a Clerk in the State Department. On 4/13/1844 Hall's letter conveying information of this settlement was received at the State Department; on 4/25/1844 a letter from Calhoun to Hall directed him to accept the terms proposed.

From Aaron Leggett, Washington, 4/15. Leggett writes as representative of Mary Hughes, widow of George Hughes who suffered "abuse, robbery, false imprisonment and death" in Mexico and whose claim for indemnification was first made in 1834. In a 17-page letter Leggett discusses at great length what he considers the obstinate and treacherous conduct of Mexico toward the legitimate claims of U.S. citizens, while European claimants against Mexico are paid. He asks that Congress set the amount of compensation due to Mrs. Hughes and "enforce the payment thereof in a becoming & suitable manner." ALS in DNA, RG 76 (Records of Boundary and Claims Commissions and Arbitrations), Records of U.S. and Mexican Claims Commissions.

From Aaron Leggett, Washington, [*ca.* 4/15?]. "I believe the communication with the case I now present, worthy of your attention at this crisis. I called to have an interview with you but was disappointed. I will see you again about our Mexican affairs." [This undated document is tentatively dated by its possible relation to the letter from Leggett of 4/15 above.] ALS in ViU, Crallé-Campbell Papers.

To John Y. Mason, Secretary of the Navy, 4/15. Calhoun refers Mason to a letter of 2/20 from the State Department and asks that the information then requested [concerning the feasibility of a line of packets between New York City and Le Havre] be furnished with as little delay as possible. The French Minister [Alphonse Pageot] has recently repeated his interest in the information. LS in DNA, RG 45 (Naval Records), Letters from Federal Executive Agents, 1837–1886, 6:99 (M-517:2, frame 252); FC in DNA, RG 59 (State Department), Domestic Letters, 34:140–141 (M-40:32).

From FRED[ERIC]K SCHILLOW

Stettin, 15th April 1844

Sir, I have the honour to enclose returns of American ships arr[ive]d in the Ports of Stettin & Danzig since 1st July last & Statement of Fees, as also official lists of Imports & Exports of these ports & Königsberg.

The intercourse between this port & the United States, as I predicted some years ago, gradually increases. The number of American & foreign ships arr[ive]d last year amounts to twenty, laden with Oil, Rice, Rosin, Potashes, Logwood &c, value together $446,140 & I hope we shall have direct importation of tobacco, if the proposed new treaty between the U.S. & the Zollverein is confirmed, and also of

Cotton, if a better regulation of the [Danish] Sound Dues takes place. All negociations respecting the latter on the Part of Prussia have till this moment led to nothing altho' most liberal proposals have been made, such as to buy them off altogether, *or* to pay 1 p[er] c[ent] ad valorem, & this payment to be made in the Prussian ports for Danish Account, so that no detention take place in the Sound, *or* to fix the duty at the average rate of the last 10 years. It would certainly be of great importance if the U.S., would earnestly cooperate, as they are not bound by such considerations as the continental powers & I beg leave to refer to my reports No. 26 & 28—1841 on this subject, in which I submitted to authorize Mr. [Henry] Wheaton to negociate with Denmark.

The whole importation into this port amounts to $17,600,000 which is an increase of $2,800,000 upon the preceeding year.

The arrangement with [Friedrich Ludwig,] Baron von Roenne & the establishment of a new Council of Commerce & a board of trade, to consist of His Majesty [Frederick William IV] & 4 Ministers & a board of trade of which Mr. v[on] Roenne, is to be the president, seem at last to be completed. Mr. Wheaton has probably already made some confidential communication on this subject & may have informed you of the active & influential part, I have had in this matter, which is considered to be of the greatest importance to the Commerce of the Zoll Verein & all Germany, & no less so, I hope, to the U.S. as Mr. Von Roenne retains the greatest predilection for the Country, in which he so long resided & to which he owes all that information, which enables him to fill the Situation at the Head of the Commercial Department, now created for him, & will therefore no doubt forward in preference the commercial interest of the U.S. as far as it lays in his power. I have the honour to be most respectfully Sir your mo[st] obe[dien]t Serv[an]t, Fredk. Schillow [U.S. Consul].

ALS (No. 37) with Ens in DNA, RG 59 (State Department), Consular Despatches, Stettin, vol. 2 (T-59:2), received 6/3. NOTE: In the margin of this letter adjacent to the last paragraph Schillow added the AEU "Confidential."

From P. ROMAN STECK

Cumberland [Md.,] April 15, 1844
My dear Sir: As it is my intention to withdraw shortly from the editorial department of the *"Maryland Gazette,"* would you be kind

enough to use your influence, in procuring me a situation ["in" *canceled*] as clerk in one of the Bureaus at Washington? I can furnish unexceptionable references from distinguished men both of Baltimore and of this place—as well as [John C. Legrand] the Secretary of State at Annapolis, who is a warm political friend of yours. I am, Sir, most Respectfully, Your ob[edien]t Serv[an]t, P. Roman Steck.

ALS in ScCleA.

From BENJ[AMIN] TAPPAN, [Senator from Ohio]

Washington City, 15th April 1844

Sir, I wish to call your attention to some letters in your Department from Mr. [Amory] Edwards the consul at Buenos Ayres with regard to the "Herald." I believe that you will find that the conduct of the Consul in this matter is altogether correct & for evidence of his character I refer you to Capt. [Charles] Morris who has lately been at Buenos Ayres & ["whom" *altered to* "who"] if I am not mistaken is acquainted with the manner in which the Herald has been used to annoy our friends—it is important that a speedy decision of this case should be made & the vessel delivered up to the Argentine Republic if you agree with me in opinion that such course would be most correct.

I take the liberty of recommending to the government Mr. Edwards as a suitable person to be authorised to negotiate with the government where he has resided as consul for some years for a settlement of all American claims upon that government. Mr. Edwards is intimate with [Gen. Juan Manuel de] Rosas & is highly esteemed by him & in the expected event of the [Senate's] rejection of Mr. [Harvey M.] Watterson would supercede the necessity of appointing a Chargé. Very respectfully Yours, Benj. Tappan.

ALS in DNA, RG 59 (State Department), Consular Despatches, Buenos Aires, vol. 7 (M-70:8). NOTE: Edwards was a nephew of Tappan.

From ISAAC VAN ZANDT and J. PINCKNEY HENDERSON

Legation of Texas
Washington City, April 15t[h], 1844

The undersigned, &c. &c., in reply to the ["request" *canceled and* "inquiries" *interlined*; on 4/13?] of Mr. Calhoun, Secretary of State of the United States, have the honor to submit the following:

In 1836, after the declaration of the independence of Texas, in pursuance of the orders of the convention and the expression of the popular will, the President *ad interim*, by his proclamation, ordered an election to be held throughout the Republic, for the ratification or rejection of the constitution which had been adopted by the convention, and for the expression by the people of their wishes in regard to the Annexation of Texas to the United States. The result was, that upon a full poll but ninety three votes were given against the Annexation.

Following up this declared wish of the people, the first Congress that assembled, thereafter, passed an act empowering the President to appoint a minister to present the question to the Government of the United States. The proposition having been declined, it was deemed prudent, in order to facilitate negotiations with other countries, not to press the question of Annexation further, and therefore it was withdrawn.

Subsequently, in 1842, instructions were given for the informal renewal of the negotiations; which, not having been met, by a reciprocal action on the part of the United States, were, in August last, again withdrawn, and the attention of the Government of Texas directed to other objects calculated, in its opinion, to secure its safety and advance its prosperity—for the attainment of which reasonable assurances had been received.

Afterwards, on the 16t[h] October last, the proposition for the formation of a treaty of Annexation was made by this Government, through the late Secretary of State, Mr. [Abel P.] Upshur, to the Government of Texas. At that time—no arrangement having been concluded, inconsistent with such a step, and the Congress having expressed their approbation of the measure, and every expression of public sentiment fully indicating that the people of Texas were yet desirous to consummate a measure, believed to be promotive of the mutual welfare of both countries, and without which, from motives of policy or necessity, they might be compelled to adopt measures which, it is to be feared, would engender a feeling of unfriendly rivalship, productive of discord and strife and dangerous to their mutual peace and quiet—the President of Texas determined to accede to the proposition, and accordingly empowered the undersigned to adjust the terms of the treaty just concluded.

The undersigned have the most abiding confidence that, should the Annexation be consummated, the same will receive the hearty and full concurrence of the people of Texas. And believing that the fate of this treaty, be the decision whatever it may, will forever decide the question of Annexation—a question, the continued agitation of which has prevented their Government from pursuing vigorously any other policy—they feel the highest gratification that this opportunity has thus been offered. They will not anticipate nor speculate upon the consequences of a rejection. Satisfied, however, that the language, institutions and locality of the two countries have fitted them for becoming members of the same great political family, or fated them to a conflict of interest, which may result in evil consequences, they trust that it may be so determined as to secure the blessings of liberty to both and promote the happiness of mankind.

Upon the subject of the public lands, the undersigned submit a summary statement made from a late report of the Commissioner of the General Land Office to the President of Texas. He estimates the aggregate at 203,520,000 acres,
Lands appropriated at 67,408,673 "
Remainder, unappropriated, at 136,111,327 ".

In a report of a committee of the House of Representatives of the Congress of Texas, made to that body on the 12t[h] January, 1841, the debt and liabilities of the Republic are stated to be as follows:

Funded debt bearing 10 per cent. interest $1,650,000
Bonds sold and pledged, bearing 10 per cent.
    interest 1,350,000
Treasury notes without interest, 3,000,000
Debts of various descriptions, say
    audited drafts and other claims
    without interest 1,000,000
                Total $7,000,000.

This report includes the interest then accrued and a number of unaudited claims, supposed to be valid, which were not computed in the report of the Secretary of the Treasury to the same Congress, which report shows the public debt as less than five millions of dollars.

Since the date above referred to, no further general estimate has been made at the Treasury Department. It is known, however, that

251

the revenues of the Government have nearly equalled its expenditures. So that the debt has not been materially increased, except from the interest which has since accrued.

The undersigned avail themselves of this occasion to offer to Mr. Calhoun assurances of their distinguished consideration. Isaac Van Zandt, J. Pinckney Henderson.

LS in DNA, RG 59 (State Department), Notes from Foreign Legations, Texas, vol. 1 (T-809:1); FC in Tx, Records of the Texas Republic Department of State, Letters and Dispatches Sent by the Texas Legation in Washington, 1:502–506; CC in DNA, RG 46 (U.S. Senate), 28A-E3; PC in Senate Document No. 341, 28th Cong., 1st Sess., pp. 13–15; PC in House Document No. 271, 28th Cong., 1st Sess., pp. 13–14; PC in *Niles' National Register*, vol. LXVI, no. 11 (May 11, 1844), p. 163; PC in the Washington, D.C., *Daily National Intelligencer*, May 20, 1844, p. 1; PC in the Washington, D.C., *Globe*, May 22, 1844, p. 1; PC in Crallé, ed., *Works*, 5:327–330.

From Henry Wheaton, Berlin, 4/15. He encloses official letters from the Prussian Foreign Minister, [Baron Heinrich von] Bülow, and the Bavarian envoy at Berlin, Lerchenfeld, recognizing Louis Mark as U.S. Consul for the Prussian Rhine provinces and Bavaria. (Von Bülow's letter also suggests that a U.S. Consular agent be appointed for Creveld and Elberfeld.) LS (No. 248) with Ens (in French) in DNA, RG 59 (State Department), Diplomatic Despatches, Germany, vol. 3 (M-44:4), addressed to John Nelson and received 5/20; FC with Ens in DNA, RG 84 (Foreign Posts), Germany, Despatches, 4:117–123.

APRIL 16–30, 1844

Ⅱ

Though there was pressing business of all sorts to occupy the Secretary of State, the most important was Texas. The treaty of annexation that Calhoun had signed on April 12 was sent by President John Tyler to the Senate for its consent on April 22. The work related to this vital matter was just beginning. Calhoun had to prepare to answer the hostile inquiries that would without doubt come from enemies in the Senate. This hostility rested partly on Northern sectionalism and partly on fear of war with Mexico. But much of it rested on narrowly political grounds that were revealed on April 27. On that date were made public letters written shortly before by the titular leaders and acknowledged front-runners for Presidential nominations of both national political parties. In these letters Henry Clay and Martin Van Buren declared their opposition to the annexation of Texas, a stand that was bound to influence their numerous followers in the Senate.

Not only this internal hostility to the beleaguered administration's chief foreign policy goal had to be dealt with; it was necessary also for Calhoun to advise U.S. representatives abroad how this move on the international stage should be explained to foreign powers. The most important representative in this connection was undoubtedly the interim Chargé d'Affaires in Mexico City, who was Ben E. Green, son of Calhoun's old friend and kinsman Duff Green. On April 19 a special messenger, a trusted officer from the Navy Department, was dispatched to Green with official word of the U.S.-Texas treaty and with instructions upon how this sensitive matter was to be discussed with the Mexican authorities.

To the same end, Calhoun on April 18 had deliberately opened a correspondence with the British Minister in Washington on the subject of Texas, in which he put the blame for an urgent United States move toward annexation on the threat posed by the abolitionist face of British imperialism. This correspondence, when it was leaked to the press by a hostile Senator, became perhaps Calhoun's most controversial act since Nullification, but it was one he undertook deliberately. He thought that he would strengthen the case for an-

253

nexation, which had been hanging unresolved for nearly a decade. He also thought the issue he raised to be of great importance in that it was necessary as a matter of principle to refute British pretensions to regulate the morals and legal rights of American slaveholders.

Appointments, appropriations, and politics pressed upon Calhoun's attention. Word was received of outrages against American citizens in Cuba, where foreigners and other residents lived in a vise between potential slave revolt on one side and an arbitrary colonial government on the other. Calhoun was becoming aware of the many claims that individual American citizens and companies had pending against various Latin American states, often of long standing. The most numerous of these, of course, were against Mexico. A new convention for the settlement of Mexican claims had been agreed to in November, 1843. It had been ratified by the Senate in January, 1844, but with amendments that went out of their way to make it unpalatable to Mexico and discourage Mexican ratification. Calhoun, thus, could offer little comfort to those American citizens who were waiting for a settlement.

On April 23 the Secretary of State drafted instructions for the new Minister to France, his former Senate colleague William R. King of Alabama. And on April 29, the President transmitted to the Senate for its consideration another treaty, one concluded in March by Henry Wheaton, the U.S. Minister to Prussia, with the states of the German Zollverein or Customs Union. This provided for the lowering of duties on tobacco and other American agricultural products, and could be regarded as a step on the road toward free trade. This treaty, too, would run into difficulties in the Senate, its friends and enemies rather resembling the friends and enemies of Texas.

⬜

From Osmyn Baker, [Representative from Mass.], 4/16. Baker encloses a letter to himself [of 2/24] from [Edwards A.] Park [alleging failure of the government to compensate Dr. J(ohn) G. Flugel for his services as U.S. Consul at Leipzig]. If Calhoun can assist Flugel in any way, Baker will be gratified to communicate so to Park. ALS in DNA, RG 59 (State Department), Consular Despatches, Leipzig, vol. 2 (T-215:2).

R[ichard] K. Crallé, Chief Clerk, State Department, to Osmyn

Baker, Representative [from Mass.], 4/16. In reply to Baker's letter of today to Calhoun, Crallé states that [John G.] Flugel has been treated with lenity in the settlement of his accounts and not with harshness as he claimed. FC in DNA, RG 59 (State Department), Consular Instructions, 10:238–239.

To I[saac] C. Bates, [Senator from Mass. and] Chairman of the Committee on Pensions, 4/16. Calhoun has received Bates's letter of 4/15 concerning the transfer of "the Papers purchased of Gen. [George] Washington's heirs, or such portion of them as constitute evidence upon which claims to pensions are adjusted" from the State Department to the War Department. In reply, Calhoun refers Bates to a lengthy report made on the same subject on 2/18/1835 by Secretary of State [John] Forsyth. "The objections to such proposed transfer . . . are therein fully set forth," and Calhoun concurs with these objections. LS in DNA, RG 46 (U.S. Senate), 28A-D10.

To Edward Everett, [London], 4/16. Calhoun introduces Ker Boyce of Charleston, who is "one of our most respectable & wealthy [S.C.] merchants, & is an old friend & acquaintance of mine." Boyce "is accompanied by his two daughters, & is travelling for their health & pleasure." Calhoun will be grateful for Boyce's being provided with letters of introduction. ALS in MHi, Edward Everett Papers (published microfilm, reel 20, frames 499–500).

To Theophilus Fisk, Washington, 4/16. In reply to Fisk's letter of yesterday, Calhoun states that under a law of 8/26/1842 "it is made the duty of the Secretary of State to cause the Laws to be published in the newspapers only of this City." FC in DNA, RG 59 (State Department), Domestic Letters, 34:142 (M-40:32).

From BEN E. GREEN

Legation of the U.S. of A.
Mexico, April 16th 1844

Sir, I have the honor to send you herewith (no. 1) a note, dated Feb. 26th [18]44 from the Minister of Foreign Relations asking an explanation of the character and functions of Mr. [Richard H.] Belt, appointed "Commercial Agent" of the U.S. for the Port of Matamoros. No. 2 is a copy of my reply [of 4/16].

I have little doubt that I have properly represented the character of this "Commercial Agent." But, in as much as Gen[era]l [Waddy] Thompson [Jr.] was at a loss what answer to give to the enquiry of Mr. [José M. Ortiz] Monasterio, I should not have ventured to give this explanation, had I not received a letter from Mr. Belt yesterday, stating that there was business in Matamoros, requiring his prompt attention, & that he was very much in want of his exequatur. Our citizens at that port require a protector. Mr. Belt can not act without an execuatur from this Govt.; and rather than suffer our citizens to remain longer without protection, I have reluctantly taken upon myself to give this explanation. If I am wrong; and if it is intended to invest Mr. Belt with any other functions than those of a "consul," you will please inform me. I have the honor to be Very Respectfully Your ob[edien]t Serv[an]t, Ben E. Green.

ALS (No. 2) with Ens in DNA, RG 59 (State Department), Diplomatic Despatches, Mexico, vol. 12 (M-97:13), received 5/11; FC in DNA, RG 84 (Foreign Posts), Mexico, Despatches, p. 490.

To C[harles] J. Ingersoll, "Chair[ma]n of the Com[mittee] on For[eign] Affairs," 4/16. Calhoun transmits for the consideration of the House committee a communication of 12/26/1843 from the Sardinian Chargé d'Affaires, the Count de Montalto, concerning duties on certain articles imported into the U.S. FC in DNA, RG 59 (State Department), Domestic Letters, 34:144–145 (M-40:32).

From THOMAS O. LARKIN

Consulate of the United States
Monterey California, April 16, 1844

Sir, I have not had time or opportunity since I took office (this month) in Monterey as consul, to make any regular statements of Trade or Commerce in this Consulate, for the use of your Department.

Although my commission is given as for Monterey, I suppose in making official statements relative to American commerce, I must embrace the whole Department of Upper California which is from San Diego to San Francisco. Monterey is the only port of entry for Foreign Vessels, they are fined if touching at any other Port previous to their coming here and paying their duties. The Comma[n]dant

General and Gove[r]nor, Don Manuel Micheltoreno, his civil and Military Officers also reside in this town.

The law of Mexico does not allow coasting by Foreign Vessels. The California Government do allow it on this coast. This infraction of Law, is not noticed by the Supreme Gover[n]ment in Mexico. Its allowance is on very fluctuating terms by the local Authorities here. Most of the U.S. Vessels have a hide house in San Diego, where they always keep a Mate & some men to cure their hides as the[y] collect them from different Ports in California. There is no Foreigners belongs to San Diego nor many Natives. Our American vessels leave this part of the coast last, when bound home. Within three months 40,000 raw Hides have been exported from San Diego for Boston. Within the same time (55,000$) Fifty five thousand dollars has been paid in Monterey for duties on goods from Boston. There are Five American Ships now on the coast.

It was the opinion of many both Natives and Foreigners in 1842, that the taking of Monterey by Com[modore Thomas Ap Catesby] Jones would be of serious injury to his country in California, and leave a bad impression respecting our Gover[n]ment. I am happy to give as my opinion that the result has not been as anticipated, in fact I think its proved to the reverse. But a few days after Oct. 20, 1842, Com[modore] Jones and his officers were treated in a remarkable kind manner by all on ashore. This treatment towards me and my Countrymen has continued to this time in this Port. The Gover[n]-ment has allowed it as my right to hoist our Flag. Yesterday it was displayed at my house for the first time and was well rec[eive]d by the People, saluted by three American Ships at anchor, every Ship at anchor hoisting her colours including the Mexican vessels. A Collation of mine was attended by the Com[mandan]t Gen., all his officers off duty, and the principal Citizens of ["to" *canceled*] the Port. A very ["good" *interlined*] feeling appeared to subsist among all, towards Americans and our Gover[n]ment.

This account is of no service or interest within itself to your Department. I make it know[n] to you in order to do away any impression that may have arose in Washington (as I have heard there was such an idea) respecting the ill will of Californians towards Citizens of the United States. I am respectfully your obbedient Servant, Thomas O. Larkin.

ALS (No. 4) in DNA, RG 59 (State Department), Consular Despatches, Monterey (M-138:1); FC in CU, Bancroft Library, Larkin Collection; PC in Hammond, ed., *Larkin Papers*, 2:96–97. NOTE: An AEU by Larkin on the FC reads "Answer to this wrote June 24, 1844. Received May 2, 1845."

To Z. Collins Lee, U.S. District Attorney, Baltimore, 4/16. "I enclose herewith an extract of a letter [of 2/12/1844] received this day from the United States Consulate, at Rio de Janeiro, with the original deposition referred to, in the case of the Brig 'Hope' of New York, [Cornelius F.] Driscoll, master, [accused of African slave trading,] and request that you will cause the proper legal investigation to be had in the matter." FC in DNA, RG 59 (State Department), Consular Instructions, 11:233.

To N. Newton, Jr., Norwalk, Ohio, 4/16. Calhoun acknowledges the letter of 3/27 from Newton and others [*The Papers of John C. Calhoun,* 17:896–897] recommending B[enjamin] T. Brown for employment in the State Department. FC in DNA, RG 59 (State Department), Domestic Letters, 34:144 (M-40:32).

From R[ICHARD] PAKENHAM

Washington, April 16 1844

Sir, I have been instructed by Her Majesty's Government to endeavour to ascertain the terms upon which the Government of The United States are permitted to send their correspondence across the Isthmus of Panama.

Supposing this enquiry to relate to the transmission of Publick Mails made up in the United States for Countries situated beyond the Isthmus of Panama, and that the desired information may be easily obtained from the Post Master General [Charles A. Wickliffe], I take the liberty of requesting that you will be good enough to cause application to be made for it to that Department, in order to enable me to answer the enquiry of Her Majesty's Government in the most authentic form—and on the other hand in case the information which I have been directed to procure should relate to the transmission of the Despatches which the Government of the United States may have occasion to send to the publick Agents or Officers of this Country, stationed on the other side of the Isthmus, I shall also feel infinitely obliged to you for any information, which you may be pleased to communicate to me respecting the arrangements of the Government of the United States upon this subject. I have the honor to be, with high consideration, Sir, Your most obedient, humble servant, R. Pakenham.

LS in DNA, RG 59 (State Department), Notes from Foreign Legations, Great Britain, vol. 22 (M-50:22).

From RAMON LEON SANCHEZ

Consulate of the United States
Cartagena, April 16th 1844

Sir, The U.S. Schooner Phenix Li[e]ut. Comm[andin]g [Arthur] Sinclair having arrived yesterday at this port, on her return to Norfolk, enables me to address a few words to the Department respecting the expediency of including Cartagena in the route to be taken by the Chagres Packets on their return home.

All vessels from Chagres for the United States are obliged as I understand to run very near this port to take their departure for the Western Coast of Cuba, and if so, very little delay say of a few hours in this port, would enable me to transmit with regularity the Dispatches from the Chargé d'affaires at Bogota and would also be attended with favorable results, to our Commerce in this part of the Republic.

Our harbour is decidedly the best on this coast, being very capacious and well Sheltered. The Climate is also healthy during the year, excepting the months of August[,] September & October, which being wet and Sultry, causes malignant fevers to prevail, some Seasons. For the few hours delay of the Packets, to water, get fresh Provisions, And receive the mail if any, I donot think that any danger would be incurred by the Officers or crew, especially if some precaution is taken, to avoid the effects of the Sun and rain during the day, and dews, at night. I have the honor to be Sir Your most Obed[ien]t Serv[an]t, Ramon Leon Sanchez, U.S. Consul.

ALS (No. 35) in DNA, RG 59 (State Department), Consular Despatches, Cartagena, vol. 4 (T-192:4), received 5/7. NOTE: A State Dept. Clerk's EU, dated 5/8, reads "Respectfully submitted for the perusal of the Secretary of the Navy [John Y. Mason], with the request that it may be returned."

From W[ILLIA]M P[INKNEY] STARKE

Brown[']s Hotel[,] Wash[ington] City, April 16th 1844

Sir, I take the liberty of addressing a note to you on the subject of a Passport to Europe which I would like to procure as soon as possible. One of the ["principle" *altered to* "principal"] objects I had in view in stopping at Wash[ington] City, was the pleasure of your acquaintance, but your business is so pressing that I cannot prevail upon myself to intrude on you. I wished not simply ["for" *canceled*] an introduction, but an interview, in order to ["procure" *erased and* "obtain" *superimposed*] the advice of the Greatest Statesman of the age as to the subjects most worthy the attention of a young man desirous of giving himself a liberal Education & fitting himself for a moderate career of future usefulness to his Country—to which I felt that I had a title, as coming from the same State, from the known intimacy subsisting between my father & yourself, and from the remarkable influence you have without knowing it, exercised on my past life. My reverence & admiration for you commencing in early life continued to strengthen as I became more and more capable of appreciating the grounds upon which your great reputation rested. When I left home for College my pockets were crammed with your speeches and to the invigorating discipline afforded by a diligent study of these able treatises on Government, engendering besides a fondness for exact analysis which led me to the perusal of Clarke, Butler, Chillingworth—that I mainly owe my triumphs in the lecture room and debating club, my entire success in College which ["is" *interlined*] however ["is" *canceled*] but a starting point in life. I had then some Claims to your attention—but I will not intrude—for your intimate friends I understand are excluded. I beg you will excuse the length to which this *note* has almost imperceptibly extended and bear in mind that I am always, with the highest respect Yours &c., Wm. P. Starke.

P.S. I would be much obliged to Mr. Calhoun if he could have my Passport made between this and Thursday morning. W.P.S.

ALS in ScCleA. NOTE: Starke (*ca.* 1823–1886) was later author of an account of Calhoun's early life, a typescript of which survives at ScCleA and a condensed version of which is published in Jameson, ed., *Correspondence*, pp. 65–89. He was a graduate of South Carolina College in 1842 and spent 1844–1846 in Europe, Africa, and Asia. He was a lawyer, planter, a lifelong bachelor, took no part in the Civil War, and during 1874–1877 was a teacher of classics at Ohio University. He spent his last years living at Fort Hill with Thomas G. Clemson and working on the biography of Calhoun.

To [former Capt.] A[ndrew] Talcott, 4/16. "Your account, claiming a per diem allowance for performing the duty of Commissary and disbursing agent for the exploration and Survey of the N.E. boundary of the U.S., amounting to $1822, has been presented to me. This claim appears to have received the consideration of one of my predecessors, who expressed the opinion that the law of 1839 precluded the allowance. I do not find any reason to reverse the decision made by him. The account and accompanying papers are, therefore, returned herewith." FC in DNA, RG 59 (State Department), Accounting Records: Miscellaneous Letters Sent, 1832–1916, vol. for 2/1–9/30/-1844, p. 107.

To Benjamin Tappan, Senator [from Ohio], 4/16. Calhoun acknowledges Tappan's letter of 4/15 and its recommendation of [Amory] Edwards as a suitable person to negotiate with the Argentine government should [Harvey M.] Watterson be rejected by the Senate. Edwards's previous course in regard to the *Herald* was approved, as he was informed in a letter from the State Department of 12/13/1843. FC in DNA, RG 59 (State Department), Consular Instructions, 11:233.

From NATHANIEL CROSS

Matanzas [Cuba], April 17th, 1844
Sir, The Department will allow me again to call its attention to my truly unfortunate case. In 1841 while being in fact and of right the Consular Representative of our Government at this port, I was arrested upon the testimony of persons of vile character & subjected to an imprisonment of one hundred & forty seven days! Soon as I was arrested, I appealed to the Government for protection which was denied me. I appealed to Congress without success, and subsequently to the Executive through Mr. [Abel P.] Upshur, late Secretary of State.

Justice having long been delayed, I do now most earnestly solicit the attention of the Government to the case, respectfully referring the Department to the papers relative to it, now in its possession. I have the honor to be, Sir, with high regard, your most ob[edien]t Serv[an]t, Nathaniel Cross.

ALS with En in DNA, RG 59 (State Department), Miscellaneous Letters (M-179:104, frames 196–197), received 5/2.

From EDWARD EVERETT, "Private"

London, 17 April 1844

My dear sir, Although the newspapers leave scarce the possibility of a doubt that before this reaches Washington, you will have entered the Department [of State], yet as no official intelligence has reached us of that event, the despatches continue to be addressed to Mr. [John] Nelson [as Secretary of State *ad interim*]. I have already taken the liberty, in writing directly to the President [John Tyler], to express to him the sincere satisfaction I have experienced, in your being called to the first place in his administration at this important juncture. The unanimous confirmation of the President's choice by the Senate, which I take for granted no other nomination could have obtained, is a sufficient indication that, in the opinion of all parties, you bring to the all-important duties of the department at this moment, a capacity of usefulness possessed by no other individual. In this opinion I most cordially concur.

I have several times felt disposed, since I have been here, to address you confidentially on some very momentous questions of domestic and foreign politics, with the freedom warranted by our friendly personal relations, and in the hope of contributing my mite to induce you to take a position, in which your talents and weight of character would have full scope. I have been deterred from doing so by considerations you will readily appreciate.

By looking back to my despatches for the last year, you will become possessed of all the official information in my power to communicate in reference to public affairs. As they are furnished with marginal indications, and as each despatch is latterly devoted to a separate topic, the labor of looking over the mass will be materially lightened. I also in the course of the year have addressed several private and confidential notes to Mr. [Abel P.] Upshur, some of which contain important details. I have desired the President, (as Mr. Upshur's personal friend,) to receive these letters from his widow, and to hand over to you such of them as would be of interest to you, which I will request you when you have read to return to me.

I do not know that I have any thing of great importance to add ["to" *altered to* "on"] the matters of chief [*an illegible word altered to* "consequence"] treated in my communications to your predecessor. The despatches by this steamer will acquaint you with the state of the current business of the Legation.

With respect to a commercial treaty between the two countries, there has hitherto been a great disinclination on this side of the

water to attempt it. But Sir Robert Peel professes an entire willingness reciprocally to reduce duties, if it can be done in the way of independent Legislation. Mr. [Richard] Pakenham was instructed,
however, to receive any overtures which might be made on the subject: and I dare say the conclusion of the treaty with the Zoll-Verein
will cause the whole matter to be considered anew. My despatch
No. 109, by the last steamer will give you the first impressions of this
government on the subject of that treaty.

As to Oregon, *I think*, for the reasons set forth in my last letters
on that subject to Mr. Upshur, that they will agree to the 49th degree
of latitude as the boundary, provided we will give up the Southern
point of Quadra & Vancouver's Island, which that line would cut off.
Farther than that, I do not believe they will go, unless some entirely
new basis of negotiation be suggested. I do not mean that any such
new basis has been hinted at: but merely that if the negotiation is
taken up where it was left in 1826, some departure from what they
then rejected will be insisted on: and *I believe*, they will agree to the
smallest possible departure, which will enable them with truth to say
they have stood out for better terms.

In regard to Texas, as Mr. Pakenham, I understand from Lord
Aberdeen, made a communication to Mr. Upshur on the subject,
you are probably better acquainted with the views of this government than I am. You will perceive from my correspondence, that he
disclaimed with great emphasis all designs, on the part of this government, of acquiring that country for themselves, and though he had
admitted that they had advised Mexico to recognize the independence of Texas on the basis of the abolition of Slavery, he more than
once assured me, that this advice had not been pressed with any
urgency. In one of my private letters to Mr. Upshur I have made
some remarks on the degree to which the Anti-Slavery feeling prevalent in this country influences the policy of the government. To the
view of the subject there taken I still adhere.

I would observe in conclusion, as some of my private letters to
Mr. Upshur relate to the operations of General [Duff] Green in this
country last summer, that I have heard that the general has intimated, since his return to America, that, under the influence of personal jealousy of him, I refused to grant him facilities in my power
toward the accomplishment of the objects he wished to promote. I
think it quite likely that this is but a part of the groundless gossip of
the day and that nothing of the kind was ever said by General Green.
At all events, I cannot need to say to you, that I am incapable of such
a feeling; and that in the somewhat embarrassing position in which

I was placed by General Green's agency, I acted, as I endeavor always to do, with a single and inflexible regard to public duty. I am, dear sir, with the highest respect, sincerely yours, Edward Everett.

LS in ScCleA; FC in MHi, Edward Everett Papers (published microfilm, reel 22, frames 1288–1291). NOTE: On Duff Green's mission, see Everett's letters of 5/17/1843 to John Tyler and 5/18/1843 to Daniel Webster. FC's in MHi, Edward Everett Papers (published microfilm, reel 22, frames 610–614, 638–639). Everett had already been Professor at Harvard University and Representative from and Governor of Mass. when he was appointed Minister to Great Britain in 9/1841 while Daniel Webster was Secretary of State.

From JAMES GADSDEN, "Private"

Charleston S.C., April 17, 1844

My Dear Sir, I truly congratulate you on the success of one of the negotiations committed to you. I feel no apprehensions as to the Ratification. Even the Eastern States, with an instinct peculiar to them, know where their interests are. Indeed they are to profit from the annexation of Texas more than the South. The political question was important to the slave holding States—but I fear that their pecuniary interests are to be seriously affected.

If rumor is to be credited I fear the provision of leaving Texas in possession of her lands will be fatal for a time, to the value of landed property in the older Southern States & Territories. Indeed many of us who have paid government high prices for lands in Alabama & Florida, will be ruined if now forced to sell. I have been desirous to dispose of my estate in Florida & remove my negroes but this Treaty will effectually defeat that object. The losses which I have sustained, The depreciation of my lands ["in" *changed to* "&"] negroes in Florida, and the very large amounts unprofitably appropriated to Rail Road Building in my native State, with a hope of advancing the commercial prosperity of ["my" *changed to* "the"] City of my birth; all require some peculiar exertions & enterprise on my part to retrieve my losses & meet my obligations, before I am too old. In my present condition I am tied hand & foot & the excitement & labor of Rail Road management, in a community so peculiar as this, I fear is beyond my strength. Indeed it seems to me impossible for the energies of any man, to be long sustained under responsibilities, and obligations so trying as those which devolve on Rail Road Presidents.

I feel therefore disposed, I may say resolved, to try another occupation & the annexation of Texas has awakened new enterprises. If the Lands are not to be given to the new Territory but to remain as the lands in other portions of the Government Domains & to be surveyed & disposed of, I would be pleased to be made Surveyor General, & Commissioner for adjudicating the Land claims under the Texian grants—Or to adjust the Scrip &c. I feel resolved to go there or somewhere. I cannot remain (Indeed I could not long survive) in the laborious & thankless place in which the best feelings of my nature, has unfortunately placed me. I must change my occupation & this I cannot do without changing my location. I think I have some strong claims on the General Government. My early years were devoted to her service & at the moment when all my hopes & aspirations, in a profession to which I was attatched [*sic*], were on the eve of realization I was cruelly seperated from my profession & forced to seek my fortunes as chance would present objects. I see no prospect of being reinstated in the grade of which I was deprived (which I would prefer to any place in the gift of the Government) but this being impossible, I should be more than gratified in being placed in a situation to justify my leaving the place I now hold from necessity. Your friend, James Gadsden.

ALS in ScCleA. NOTE: Gadsden had left the U.S. Army in 1822 after a distinguished career when the Senate refused to confirm him as Adjutant General.

From D[ANIEL] JENIFER, "Private"

Vienna, April 17th 1844

Dear Sir, Information has been received at the Legation here of your appointment as Secretary of State, tho no official notice of your acceptance. I take this earliest moment to express my sincere wishes that you may have yielded to the desire of the President [John Tyler] and what appears also to be the general voice of the Country. I feel no delicacy in thus expressing my feelings to you, with a firm belief that no individual could have been called to that Department, who would have it so much in his power to influence and satisfactorily settle the delicate and important questions in which the U. States are at present involved and that none could carry to it a more singleness of purpose. With an ardent hope that you may be enabled to effect this desirable object and thereby calm the strong elements at work to distract and divide our common Country, I most sincerely trust that you will have accepted.

I turn with feelings of the deepest sympathy to the horrid catastrophe of the Princeton. In the death of so many talented and estimable men the Country has sustained a severe loss, their families an irreparable berievement. Most of those gentlemen were personally known to me, for all of whom I mourn; but the fact that my early and most esteemed friend [Virgil] Maxcy should have been one of the unfortunate victims has sadly afflicted me. I cannot express what I feel for his berieved wife and daughters, between whom there was such affectionate attachment. Their loss is heavy.

I will not intrude longer upon your time or feelings which I know are sensibly alive[?] to this dispensation of Providence. V[er]y sincerely, y[ou]r o[bedien]t s[ervan]t, D. Jenifer.

ALS in ScCleA. NOTE: A planter of Revolutionary family, Jenifer had been Representative from Md. during 1835–1841 and then had been appointed U.S. Minister to Austria by John Tyler. Apparently enclosed with this letter was an undated clipping from the [London] *Chronicle* commenting upon the appointment of the "moderate and able statesman" Calhoun as Secretary of State. Since Calhoun was one of America's "enlightened" rather than its "bigoted and ignorant minds," the remaining differences between Great Britain and the United States could be settled without serious conflict. "It is worthy of remark," continued the paper, "that, notwithstanding bluster and party, the Americans select their ablest men [such as Webster and Calhoun] to conduct a negotiation with us."

From Jos[eph] Michard, "Capitol Hill," 4/17. He asks for employment as a translator of Spanish and states that he is "personally known" to "Col." [Thomas H.] Benton and the late "Judge" [Abel P.] Upshur. [An enclosed business card indicates that "Professor" Michard was available as a teacher and translator of French, Spanish, and Italian on New Jersey Ave. "next to the Capitol Grounds."] ALS with En in DNA, RG 59 (State Department), Applications and Recommendations, 1837–1845, Michard (M-687:23, frames 2–3).

To Count de Montalto, [Sardinian Chargé d'Affaires in the U.S.], 4/17. Calhoun responds to a communication to the State Department of 12/28/1843 concerning "several articles of Sardinian merchandize, which you conceive to be almost excluded from the American market, by reason of the heavy duties laid upon their importation; and, suggesting whether it would not be more equitable to tax silks according to their value, and not their weight." De Montalto's letter has been sent to the Committee on Foreign Affairs of the House

of Representatives, from whom the subject will receive due consideration. FC in DNA, RG 59 (State Department), Notes to Foreign
Legations, Italian States, Greece, and Turkey, 6:66 (M-99:61).

From S[tephen] Pleasonton, [Fifth Auditor], Treasury Department, 4/17. He transmits claims from Alexander H. Everett, former
U.S. Minister to Spain, to more than $6,000 for office rent, for his
salary before the date of his departure, and for a differential in cash-
ing drafts. Everett's accounts were settled in 1830, and these claims
were then disallowed. He now urges them on the *ex post facto*
ground that later administrations have granted similar claims to
other diplomats. Pleasonton submits the matter to Calhoun: "you
cannot fail to perceive the momentous principle involved in their
allowance, it being no less than the right of one administration to
revise and reverse the acts of all preceding administrations, without
limit." LS in DNA, RG 59 (State Department), Letters Received
from the Fifth Auditor and Comptroller, 1829–1862; FC in DNA,
RG 217 (General Accounting Office), Fifth Auditor: Letters Sent,
5:116–117.

From WILSON SHANNON

St. Clairsville, Ohio
April the 17th 1844
D[ea]r Sir, I am in the receipt of your note of the 11th Inst. informing
me that the President by and with the advice and consent of the
Senate has honored me with the appointment of Envoy Extraordinary
and Minister Plenipotentiary of the United States to the Mexican
Republic. I do hereby accept the appointment and will leave this
place on Monday next for Washington City.

Expecting to have the pleasure of seeing you personally in a few
days I have the honor to be very respectfully Sir your obed[ien]t Ser-
v[an]t, Wilson Shannon.

ALS in DNA, RG 59 (State Department), Diplomatic Despatches, Mexico, vol.
12 (M-97:13).

——, Washington, to Richard K. Crallé, 4/17. This unsigned
letter, in reply to Crallé's inquiry of 4/16, states that [Gregory A.]
Perdicaris, U.S. Consul at Athens, is now in Cheraw, S.C., and is at-

tempting to obtain a situation teaching Greek on the faculty of "some one of our Colleges, especially the So[uth] Ca[rolina] College." "What are the expectations of Mr. Perdicaris in relation to returning to Greece, I am unable to say." ALU in DNA, RG 59 (State Department), Consular Despatches, Athens, vol. 1 (T-362:1).

From ROBERT I. ALEXANDER

St. Clairsville O[hio,] April 18, 1844

Dear Sir, I do not now write to you, expecting that you will trouble yourself with answering me, Knowing the extent of the labours of your present station, but merely to say to you that your friends in this region of Country, & who are rapidly increasing, are well pleased with your entire course in relation to the contest, if I might so call it, for the Presidential nomination, and especially with the frank, just & indisputable view presented by you in your late letter to your friends on the subjects of the Tariff, Abolition & the organization of the so called national democratic nominating convention to be held next month in Baltimore. However some of your friends doubt the propriety of entirely withdrawing your name from the list of Presidential candidates.

I can also assure you that your friends in Ohio are much gratified that you accepted of your present place in the cabinet, and when all things are considered we believe that much good may result to the country from your labours in that situation.

As to the next Presidential election the opinion is very general that Mr. [Martin] Van Buren cannot in any event obtain the electoral vote of this State, & but few electoral votes in the Union, though Mr. [Henry] Clay is undoubtedly very unpopular. There appears to be but very little enthusiasm indeed with the mass of the people to restore the possession of the Government to Mr. Van Buren, & the old horde of office holders who have heretofore so successfully and unscrupulously plundered the public treasury, & who have lately literally packed conventions to bring about a "Restoration": and in fact it would be very strange if there should be, when it is so evident that the result would be to replace & perpetuate in power an old selfish proscriptive & rotten dynasty. It appears sometimes even to me that it would be almost sinful to aid in such an enterprize, and that there is no remedy adequate to the curing of the disease unless it is an entire & thorough breaking up of the old corrupt organization, and this

I am lead to believe would prove ineffectual if left to be performed solely by the whig party. I do not by this mean that we should aid the whigs, but that in some way we ought to stand at least indifferent—making principles & not party our motto, as of old.

We are also much, very much gratified with the nomination & confirmation of our friend and fellow-citizen Gov[erno]r [Wilson] Shannon as Minister to Mexico. The solution was I think a fortunate one as he may be relied on & is right on all questions now existing in reference to our relations with that Republic.

The Gov[erno]r will leave here on Monday next for Washington City, & I hope you will form a more thorough acquaintance with him, as you can confidently rely on him as your friend, & if the Governor had but remained the fast friend of a "Restoration" rely upon it he never would have been villified by some selfish aspirants of our State, & through them even by the [Washington] Globe, and even now he can wield a greater influence with the democracy of Ohio, than any other man within her borders.

Hoping that you may have great success in your present situation, and that our old fashioned republican principles, and a strict integrity & accountability in the administration of our public affairs may soon regain complete & permanent ascendency I remain yours &c., Robert I. Alexander.

ALS in ScCleA; PC in Boucher and Brooks, eds., *Correspondence*, pp. 221–222.

From Fidericio Bourman, [Spanish Chargé d'Affaires in the U.S.], 4/18. He has a letter from his Queen announcing to the President [John Tyler] the death of her aunt and wishes to know when the President will receive him so that he may present the letter in person. LS (in Spanish) and translation in DNA, RG 59 (State Department), Notes from Foreign Legations, Spain, vol. 11 (M-59:13, frames 973–974).

From JOHN CAMPBELL, [Representative from S.C.]

Washington, Ap[ri]l 18th 1844
Dear Sir, You probably remember to have seen Mr. W[illia]m Bryan, a son of Mrs. Pages [sic], when we boarded with that lady. Previous to your coming on, he requested me to recommend him to you as bearer of despatches, or for some other temporary employment, if

more permanent could not be obtained. I told him that I could not take the liberty of making recommendations to you in the discharge of your duty, but that after your arrival, I would take some opportunity of mentioning his name to you, with my opinion of his qualifications. He is a young man of excellent sense, great prudence, intelligent, industrious, and of business habits. By profession, a civil Engineer, but now out of employment.

The fever still adheres to me. With sincere Esteem Y[ou]rs &c, John Campbell.

ALS in DNA, RG 59 (State Department), Applications and Recommendations, 1837–1845, Bryan (M-687:3, frames 556–557).

From C[ALEB] CUSHING

United States Legation
Macao, 18 April 1844

Sir, In my despatch of the fifteenth instant numbered fifty-one, I had the honour to transmit to you certain documents communicated to me by the Governor General of the two Kuangs, to wit, the Supplementary Treaty between China and Great Britain, the late articles of convention between China and Portugal and a paper purporting to be the Treaty of Kiang Nan [that is, Nanking].

Herewith I transmit sundry documents supplementary to that despatch, the knowledge of which may be of service to the Government. No. 1 is a complete copy of the Treaty of Kiangnan [of 8/29/-1842], in Chinese, with an English translation.

This is an important document, it being the only complete copy, within my knowledge, of any Chinese Treaty, that is, the only copy embracing the formal parts of preamble and so forth, as well as the articles of convention.

It does not come to me through an official channel, but I have good reason to believe that it is in substance a genuine copy of the Treaty.

No. 2 is the only document published by Sir Henry Pottinger, as and for the Treaty of Kiangnan. You will observe that it professes to be but an abstract and it turns out to be an abstract of but certain of the articles.

This appears from document No. 3 [dated 12/28/1842] which consists of three certain articles of the Treaty subsequently published by Sir Henry Pottinger *in extenso,* and one of which is numbered ten (10) although the previously published abstract embraces but eight articles.

No. 4 is the Supplementary treaty [of 10/8/1843] as published by Sir Henry Pottinger, this being in like manner an abstract only. To this I have appended the [published] Tariff and the Commercial Regulations, which seem to derive their efficacy from and to be essential parts of the Supplementary Treaty.

A careful comparison of this document with the Supplementary Treaty entire, as communicated by me in the despatch above referred to, exhibits some discrepancies which have been the subject of much remark in Hong-Kong and Macao.

It is also worthy to be observed that in the Chinese originals the things done are styled *grants,* or acts of favour from the Emperor, and not stipulations between China and England.

No. 5 is the publication made at Macao [on 10/3/1843], by the Portuguese authorities, of and for the late articles of convention transmitted to the Department by me in the before mentioned despatch.

No. 6 is a translation from the Chinese of the pre-existing articles of Convention [made in 1749] between the Portuguese of Macao and the Chinese Government.

No. 7 is the abstract of the same, as published by the Portuguese.

Neither of the Portuguese documents, it may be observed purports to be a Convention between Sovereign and Sovereign, but on the contrary they are conceived in the style of concessions made by the local authorities at Canton to the local authorities at Macao.

To these documents I subjoin two others, which, with those previously given, constitute all which I have seen of the diplomatic compacts between China and the various powers of Europe.

No. 8 is a translation of the Treaty of Peace concluded between China and Russia in sixteen hundred and eighty nine.

No. 9 is what I have been able to obtain of a second Treaty between Russia and China negotiated in seventeen hundred and twenty eight by Count Vladislawitsh.

I shall take occasion in another letter to enter into some details concerning the diplomatic intercourse of the European powers and China, especially that of Portugal, Russia and England. I have the honour to be, very respectfully Your obedient servant, C. Cushing.

LS (No. 53) with Ens in DNA, RG 59 (State Department), Diplomatic Despatches, China, vol. 1 (M-92:2), received 10/23. NOTE: This despatch was addressed to A[bel] P. Upshur.

To R[ichard] H. Dana, Jr., Boston, 4/18. Calhoun acknowledges receipt of Dana's letter of 4/15, transmitting the complaints by seamen of the American ship *Hibernia* against the U.S. Commercial Agent at Port Louis. If Dana will send evidence to corroborate the complaints, they will be investigated. FC in DNA, RG 59 (State Department), Consular Instructions, 12:77–78.

From W[illia]m H. Dunkinson, Washington, 4/18. He submits letters of recommendation [from W. Cost Johnson, dated 4/11; from three members of the Md. Congressional delegation, dated 4/11; and from A(lexander O.) Anderson, 4/12]. "I shall be greatly obliged, and shall not forget the favor, if you can make it suitable to your views to give me some employment. I should be gratified to be the bearer of Despatches to any of our Foreign Ministers . . . ." ALS with Ens in DNA, RG 59 (State Department), Applications and Recommendations, 1837–1845, Dunkinson (M-687:9, frames 599–607).

To Peter Force, Washington, 4/18. Calhoun directs Force to furnish the Secretary of the Senate and the Clerk of the House of Representatives with 693 copies of "the 4th and 5th volumes of the Documentary History of the American Revolution, and the Clerk of the House of Representatives with 368 additional copies of the same, as soon as they are ready." LS in DLC, Peter Force Papers, vol. 19; variant FC in DNA, RG 59 (State Department), Domestic Letters, 34:145–146 (M-40:32).

From Ben E. Green, Mexico [City], 4/18. He asks that $1,027 be paid to Messrs. Hargous and Bros. of New York [City] for his salary as Secretary of Legation and Chargé d'Affaires ad interim. Two ALS's (retained copies) in NcU, Duff Green Papers (published microfilm, roll 5, frames 402–404).

To John F. McGregor, U.S. Consul at Campeche, 4/18. "Your letter No. 5 [of 1/20/1844] enclosing a copy of the Treaty between the Government of Yucatan and the Mexican Republic has been received." The State Dept. has not received any Consular returns or statements of fees from McGregor; blank forms are transmitted to him and he is instructed to "follow them closely" in transmitting the returns as required in future. FC in DNA, RG 59 (State Department), Consular Instructions, 11:236.

To J[OHN] L. MARTIN, [Washington]

Department of State
Washington, 18th April, 1844

Sir: The President of the United States [John Tyler] having, by and with the advice and consent of the Senate, appointed you Secretary of the Legation of the United States at Paris, I now transmit to you your commission, your printed personal instructions, and other papers therein referred to—the receipt of which you will be pleased to acknowledge. In signifying your acceptance of this appointment, you will also acquaint this Department with the name of the State or country in which you were born. The salary of Secretary of Legation commences from the date of the commission. I am, Sir, your obedient Servant, J.C. Calhoun.

FC in DNA, RG 59 (State Department), Diplomatic Instructions, France, 15:[1]–2 (M-77:55). NOTE: Martin was a Washington physician and druggist who had been something of a social companion of Calhoun. He was a former Clerk in the State Department and, like his chief, William R. King, newly-appointed Minister to France, was a native of N.C.

To RICHARD PAKENHAM, [Washington]

Department of State
Washington, 18th April, 1844

The Undersigned, Secretary of State of the United States, has laid before the President [John Tyler] the note of the Right Honorable Mr. Pakenham, Envoy Extraordinary and Minister Plenipotentiary of Her Britannic Majesty, addressed to this Department on the 26th of February last, together with the accompanying copy of a despatch of Her Majesty's Principal Secretary of State for Foreign Affairs to Mr. Pakenham.

In reply, the Undersigned is directed by the President to inform the Right Honorable Mr. Pakenham that, while he regards with pleasure the disavowal of Lord Aberdeen of any intention on the part of Her Majesty's Government "to resort to any measures, either openly or secretly, which can tend to disturb the internal tranquillity of the slave-holding States, and thereby affect the tranquillity of this Union," he, at the same time, regards with deep concern, the avowal, for the first time made to this Government, "that Great

Britain desires, and is constantly exerting herself to procure the general abolition of slavery throughout the world."

So long as Great Britain confined her policy to the abolition of slavery in her own possessions and colonies, no other country had a right to complain. It belonged to her, exclusively, to determine according to her own views of policy whether it should be done or not. But when she goes beyond, and avows it as her settled policy, and the object of her constant exertions, to abolish it throughout the world, she makes it the duty of all other countries, whose safety or prosperity may be endangered by her policy, to adopt such measures as they may deem necessary for their protection.

It is with still deeper concern the President regards the avowal of Lord Aberdeen of the desire of Great Britain to see slavery abolished in Texas; and, as he infers, is endeavoring, through her diplomacy, to accomplish it, by making the abolition of slavery one of the conditions on which Mexico should acknowledge her independence. It has confirmed his previous impressions as to the policy of Great Britain in reference to Texas, and made it his duty to examine with much care and solicitude, what would be its effects on the prosperity and safety of the United States should she succeed in her endeavors. The investigation has resulted in the settled conviction that it would be difficult for Texas, in her actual condition, to resist what she desires, without supposing the influence and exertions of Great Britain would be extended beyond the limits assigned by Lord Aberdeen; and that, if Texas could not resist, the consummation of the object of her desire would endanger both the safety and prosperity of the Union. Under this conviction, it is felt to be the imperious duty of the Federal Government, the common representative and protector of the States of this Union, to adopt, in self-defence, the most effectual measures to defeat it.

This is not the proper occasion to state at large the grounds of this conviction. It is sufficient to say, that the consummation of the avowed object of her wishes in reference to Texas, would be followed by hostile feelings and relations between that country and the United States, which could not fail to place her under the influence and control of Great Britain. That, from the geographical position of Texas, would expose the weakest and most vulnerable portion of our frontier to inroads, and place, in the power of Great Britain, the most efficient means of effecting in the neighboring States of this Union, what she avows it to be her desire to do in all countries, where slavery exists. To hazard consequences which would be so dangerous to the prosperity and safety of this Union, without resorting to the most effective measures to prevent them, would be, on the part of the Federal Government, an abandonment of the most solemn obligation imposed by the guaranty, which the States, in adopting the Constitution, entered into to protect each other against whatever might endanger their safety, whether from without or within. Acting in obedience to this obligation, on which our Federal system of Government rests, the President directs me to inform you that a treaty has been concluded between the United States and Texas, for the annexation of the latter to the former, as a part of its territory, which will be submitted without delay to the Senate for its approval. This step has been taken as the most effectual, if not the only, means of guarding against the threatened danger, and securing their permanent peace and welfare.

It is well known that Texas has long desired to be annexed to this Union; that her People, at the time of the adoption of her constitution, expressed by an almost unanimous vote, her desire to that effect; and that she has never ceased to desire it, as the most certain means of promoting her safety and prosperity. The United States have heretofore declined to meet her wishes; but the time has now arrived when they can no longer refuse consistently with their own security and peace, and the sacred obligation imposed by their constitutional compact, for mutual defence and protection. Nor are they any way responsible for the circumstances which have imposed this obligation on them. They had no agency in bringing about the state of things which has terminated in the separation of Texas from Mexico. It was the Spanish Government and Mexico herself which invited and offered high inducements to our citizens to colonize Texas. That, from the diversity of character, habits, religion, and political opinions, necessarily led to the separation, without the interference of the United States in any manner whatever. It is true, the United States, at an early period, recognised the independence of Texas: but, in doing so, it is well known, they but acted in conformity with an established principle to recognise the Government *de facto*. They had previously acted on the same principle in reference to Mexico herself, and the other Governments which have risen on the former dominions of Spain, on this continent. They are equally without responsibility for that state of things already adverted to as the immediate cause of imposing on them, in self-defence, the obligation of adopting the measure they have. They remained passive, so long as the policy on the part of Great Britain, which has led to its adoption, had no immediate bearing on their peace and safety. While they conceded to Great Britain the right of adopting whatever policy she might deem best, in reference to the African race, within her own possessions, they, on their part, claim the same right for themselves. The policy she has adopted, in reference to the portion of that race in her dominions, may be humane and wise; but it does not follow, if it prove so with her, that it would be so in reference to the United States and other countries, whose situation differs from hers. But, whether it would be or not, it belongs to each to judge and determine for itself. With us, it is a question to be decided, not by the Federal Government, but by each member of this Union for itself, according to its own views of its domestic policy; and without any right on the part of the Federal Government to interfere, in any manner whatever. Its rights and duties are limited to protecting, under the guaranties of the Constitution, each member of this Union, in whatever policy it may adopt, in reference to the portion within its respective limits. A large number of the States has decided, that it is neither wise nor humane to change the relation, which has existed from their first settlement, between the two races; while others, where the African is less numerous, have adopted the opposite policy.

It belongs not to this Government to question whether the former have decided wisely or not; and if it did, the Undersigned would not regard this as the proper occasion to discuss the subject. He does not, however, deem it irrelevant to state, that, if the experience of more than half a century is to decide, it would be neither humane nor wise in them to change their policy. The census and other authentic documents show that, in all instances in which the States have changed the former relation between the two races, the condition of the African, instead of being improved, has become worse. They have invariably sunk into vice and pauperism, accompanied by the bodily and mental inflictions incident thereto—deafness, blindness, insanity and idiocy, to a degree without example; while, in all other States which have retained the ancient relation between them, they have improved greatly in every respect—in number, comfort, intelligence, and morals, as the following facts, taken from such sources will serve to illustrate.

The number of deaf and dumb, blind, idiots and insane, of the negroes in the States that have changed the ancient relation between the races, is one out of every ninety-six; while in the States adhering to it, it is one out of every six hundred and seventy-two—that is seven to one in favor of the latter as compared with the former.

The number of whites, deaf and dumb, blind, idiots and insane, in the States that have changed the relation, is one in every five hundred and sixty-one; being nearly six to one against the free blacks in the same States.

The number of negroes who are deaf and dumb, blind, idiots and insane, paupers, and in prison in the States that have changed, is one out of every six; and in the States that have not, one out of every one hundred and fifty-four; or twenty-two to one against the former as compared with the latter.

Taking the two extremes of North and South, in the State of Maine the number of negroes returned as deaf and dumb, blind, insane and idiots, by the census of 1840, is one out of every twelve; and in Florida, by the same returns, is one out of every eleven hundred and five; or ninety-two to one in favor of the slaves of Florida, as compared with the free blacks of Maine.

In addition, it deserves to be remarked, that, in Massachusetts, where the change in the ancient relation of the two races was first made, (now more than sixty years since,) where the greatest zeal has been exhibited in their behalf, and where their number is comparatively few, (but little more than eight thousand in a population of upwards of seven hundred and thirty thousand,) the condition of the African is amongst the most wretched. By the latest authentic accounts, there was one out of every twenty-one of the black population in jails or houses of correction; and one out of every thirteen was either deaf and dumb, blind, idiot, insane, or in prison. On the other hand, the census and other authentic sources of information establish the fact, that the condition of the African race throughout all the States, where the ancient relation between the two has been retained, enjoys a degree of health and comfort which may well compare with that of the laboring population of any country in Christendom; and it may be added, that in no other condition, or in any other age or country has the negro race ever attained so high an elevation in morals, intelligence, or civilization.

If such be the wretched condition of the race in their changed relation, where their number is comparatively few, and where so much interest is manifested for their improvement, what would it be in those States where the two races are nearly equal in numbers, and where, in consequence, would necessarily spring up mutual fear, jealousy, and hatred, between them? It may, in truth, be assumed as a maxim, that two races differing so greatly, and in so many respects, cannot possibly exist together in the same country, where their numbers are nearly equal, without the one being subjected to the other. Experience has proved, that the existing relation in which the one is subjected to the other in the slave-holding States, is consistent with the peace and safety of both, with great improvement to the inferior; while the same experience proves, that the relation which it is the desire and object of Great Britain to substitute in its stead, in this and all other countries, under the plausible name of the abolition of slavery, would, (if it did not destroy the inferior by conflicts to which it would lead,) reduce it to the extremes of vice and wretchedness. In this view of the subject, it may be asserted that what is called Slavery, is, in reality, a political institution, essential to the peace, safety, and prosperity of those States of the Union in which it exists. Without, then, controverting the wisdom and humanity of the policy of Great Britain, so far as her own possessions are concerned, it may be safely affirmed, without reference to the means by which it would be effected, that, could she succeed in accomplishing in the United States, what she avows it to be her desire, and the object of her constant exertions to effect throughout the world, so far from being wise or humane, she would involve in the greatest calamity the whole country, and especially the race which it is the avowed object of her exertions to benefit.

The Undersigned avails himself of this occasion to renew to the Right Hon[ora]ble Mr. Pakenham the assurance of his distinguished consideration. J.C. Calhoun.

FC in DNA, RG 59 (State Department), Notes to Foreign Legations, Great Britain, 7:[1]–8 (M-99:36); CC in DNA, RG 84 (Foreign Posts), Mexico, Instructions, vol. 5.I; CC in DNA, RG 46 (U.S. Senate), 28A-E3; PC in Senate Document No. 341, 28th Cong., 1st Sess., pp. 50–53; PC in House Document No. 271, 28th Cong., 1st Sess., pp. 50–53; PC in the New York, N.Y., *Evening Post*, April 27, 1844, p. 4; PC in the Washington, D.C., *Daily Madisonian*, May 2, 1844, p. 2; PC (dated 4/13) in the Charleston, S.C., *Courier*, May 7, 1844, p. 2; PC in *Niles' National Register*, vol. LXVI, no. 11 (May 11, 1844), p. 172; PC in the Washington, D.C., *Spectator*, May 13, 1844, p. 3; PC in the Washington, D.C., *Daily National Intelligencer*, May 20, 1844, pp. 1–2; PC in the Washington, D.C., *Globe*, May 22, 1844, p. 1; PC in Crallé, ed., *Works*, 5:333–339. NOTE: The interviews between Calhoun and Pakenham that surrounded this correspondence are described by Pakenham in despatches to Lord Aberdeen on 4/14 and 4/28, copies of which are found in the Aberdeen Papers, British Museum, folios 68–70 and 74–76 and in the British Public Record Office, Foreign Office Papers, American Series, 404.

278

From R[ICHARD] PAKENHAM

Washington, April 18 1844

The Undersigned, Her Britannick Majesty's Envoy Extraordinary and Minister Plenipotentiary, has the honor to submit for the consideration of the Secretary of State of the United States, the inclosed copy of a Memorial [of 6/23/1843] which has been addressed to the Lieut[enant] Governor of New Brunswick [Sir William M.G. Colebrooke] by the Hon[ora]ble W[illiam] Black, President of the Legislative Council of that Province, relative to certain lands situated on the Aristook which were purchased by Him in 1824, in His Title to which He claims to be confirmed under the Treaty of 9th August 1842.

It appears to the Undersigned that in this Memorial a clear case is made out of "equitable possessory claim" according to the terms of the Treaty, and under this impression He begs leave to recommend Mr. Black's application for the confirmation of His Title to the early attention of the Government of the United States.

The Undersigned takes advantage of this opportunity to renew to The Hon[ora]ble John Calhoun the assurance of His High Consideration. R. Pakenham.

LS with En in DNA, RG 59 (State Department), Notes from Foreign Legations, Great Britain, vol. 22 (M-50:22); PC with En in House Document No. 110, 29th Cong., 1st Sess., pp. 33–34.

To S[tephen] H. Weems, U.S. Consul at Guatemala, 4/18. "A letter from Mr. H[enry] Savage, dated 29th September 1843 (No. 11) has been received, enclosing a Copy of a memorandum relating to the Lake of Nicaragua, and the line of the projected canal, surveyed by Mr. John Baily. These papers were referred to the President [John Tyler], and were read by him with much interest." Also received at the State Dept. were Weems's unnumbered despatches of 12/15/-1843. FC in DNA, RG 59 (State Department), Consular Instructions, 11:234.

From ROBERT B. CAMPBELL

United States Consulate, Havana
April 19th 1844

Sir, I have delayed giving you an account of a brutal outrage committed on the person of an American Sailor belonging to the Brig Mary Pennell, recently arrived from New York. The delay has arisen from an anxiety to avoid unnecessary excitement, hoping that each day by by [*sic*] its events would enable me in the same communication, to acquaint you with the circumstance, and the condemnation and execution of the offender. The trial has been so procrastinated, and the issue appearing uncertain, I do not feel justified in longer with[h]olding a statement, which you will perceive is ex parte, although in my mind there is no doubt of its truth in all essential parts. The Brig Mary Pennell arrived here on the evening of the 8th inst. On the following morning the master came on shore to attend necessary business. Ordering the crew ["consisting" *canceled*] of his boat consisting of [Michael] Murphy and [John] Scott to have the boat at the only landing place permitted boats of foreign merchant vessels (this place is called the Steps) and being narrow, boats are required to draw off as soon as passengers are received or landed. In obedience to the order received by the men the boat was brought to the steps a few minutes before 12 M. The Master on reaching the wharf (called Key) was detained a short time in conversation with Mr. Churchill, which caused some detention of the boat, and during this short detention Murphy was inhumanly murdered by a sentinel on a corporal[']s order. From all that can be discovered it was a wanton and unnecessary order eminating from an Official menial under the combined influence of drunkenness and brutal passion. As I did not see the occurrence, you are referred to the accompanying affidavits made before me, by these it will appear that an unoffending youth, of good character and steady habits, has at mid day, in the most frequented part of the City, been deliberately shot, to gratify the brutal rage of a fellow, whose only claim to character or authority was the worsted [insignia] upon his shoulders. It has not appeared, that any offence was committed by Murphy, unless it be offence, not to understand a gesture, or a language which in all probability he had never before heard spoken. There is however no offence which could justify the act, if he had offended, nothing was easier than his arrest, and punishment should have followed trial.

From the prom[p]t attention which the former & the present Capt[ai]n Gen[era]l [Leopoldo O'Donnell] have always given my requests, and the disposition at all times to enquire into and redress grievances of all kinds, I do not despair of obtaining justice ultimately. The laws of the land however not permitting my presence and aid in the prosecution, by adducing the best evidence I could find, or confuting that which might be untrue, leaves the investigation in hands who however justly disposed, may fail in eliciting the testimony which would ensure conviction. Should the Corporal be found guilty of Murder, and shot, we must be content, and do justice to the Government for its impartiality, how[ever] we may deplore the death of an innocent youth. Should he however escape punishment, and the Gov[erno]r makes his justification less than certain, every citizen of our Country abroad, will feel himself humbled & degraded if this Government is not compelled by the U. States through the intervention of Old Spa[in] to make the most ample atonement. The death of Murphy has produced here an excitement which is said to have had no paral[l]el, the flags of a[ll] the foreign Merchantmen were at half mast for three days including our own, English, Russian, Germ[an] and all others except the French which were partially taken down under an order from an officer of a man of war of that nation accidently in Port.

Accompanying this communication you will receive the copies of a correspondence with the Cap[tain] General carried on immediately after the death of Murphy, the first letter being in fact written by me the moment I heard he was dead, but before he actually was so. Should it meet your approbation it is all I desire, disconnected with this Govt. Two of my letters will perhaps need explanation. That which asks for the embalmment of the body & that which speaks of a meeting having been advertised by the American Masters. The first, was in compliance with the wish of all the Ship Masters as the body could not be embalmed, and sent home, as they desired, but upon express permission. The other became necessary in consequence of an Advertisement against the law requiring every thing published to undergo the examination of the Government. And I had every disposition to keep ourselves in the wright. I have the honor to be Y[ou]r Most Ob[edien]t Serv[an]t, Robert B. Campbell, U.S. Consul Havana.

ALS with Ens in DNA, RG 59 (State Department), Consular Despatches, Havana, vol. 19 (T-20:19), received 5/4. NOTE: Campbell was a former Representative from S.C. and "Nullifier." He had been appointed Consul at Havana by John Tyler in 9/1842. He was U.S. Consul at London during 1854–1861.

From A[RCHIBALD] M. GREEN

Consulate of the U.S. of America at Galvezton
Republic of Texas, 19th of April 1844
Sir, With great reluctance and much regret I resolve on reporting the conduct of Gen[era]l [William S.] Murphy to the Department.

However great and important his services may have been to the Country, of which he is the representative yet a duty equally obligatory on myself requires that I should make known to the Department his improper conduct, conduct towards myself, highly unbecoming, and derogatory to himself as a gentleman.

In consequence of his harsh epithets applied to me, I have been under the disagreeable necessity of adopting a course towards him, far different from what I could have wished or expected and fear that I shall be driven to the further necessity of offering him an indignity, which by me was never before extended to any one.

As our conversation at one time occurred in the presence of Capt. [John A.] Davis of the U. States Sch[oone]r Flirt I deem it unnecessary to make any comment upon its nature; but if the Department think proper to make further enquiry into the matter I shall be gratified, for I flatter myself that my official and private conduct and deportment, since my residence amongst the people of Galvezton, will stand the test of scrutiny.

This is not the first time Gen[era]l Murphy has behaved indecorous and indecently towards myself and nothing but the station he occupies, has twice, saved him from the severest chastisement.

The language and conduct of Gen[era]l Murphy to a worthy and highly respected officer of the Navy (on board the United States Sch[oone]r Flirt, the son of late a distinguished officer of our Navy) when in company with a distinguished citizen of this Republic, whilst on an official visit to said vessel, was of so course [sic] and vulgar a nature as to elicit the profound contempt and disgust of all present and was totally unwarranted and without a parallel.

The station he occupied I presume was then the only shield which saved the representative of the United States from a personal difficulty.

These things would have been made known to the Department before; but as they were too forbid[d]ing to be placed on paper, they have been defer[r]ed until a proper representation could be made in person; but the conduct of Gen[era]l Murphy was of so injurious and insulting a nature as to forbid the ["language" changed to "long"] delay of this report.

Many things might be related to substantiate gross charges against the Ch[arg]e de'Affairs—for it is only for one to be present to see and know the vulgarity & egotistical conduct of the Representative of the United States. I have the honor to be most Respectfully y[ou]r Ob[edien]t S[ervan]t, A.M. Green.

ALS (No. 33) in DNA, RG 59 (State Department), Consular Despatches, Galveston, vol. 2 (T-151:2), received 5/1. NOTE: An AEU of 5/1 by a State Department Clerk referred this to the President "for his perusal." An AEI of 5/2 by Tyler reads "Green's charges are altogether vague. He should have descended to particulars. Gen[era]l Murphy's conduct has always been regarded as respectful to all around him, and he should not be condemned unheard."

To BEN E. GREEN, [Mexico City]

Washington, 19th April 1844

Dear Sir, This will be delivered to you by Col. Gilbert L. Thompson, Engineer in Cheif [*sic*] of the Navy Department, who bears dispatches from the State Department for you, in the absence of the Minister, the Hon. W[addy] Thompson [Jr.].

Col. Thompson is a gentleman of intelligence well acquainted with the affairs of Mexico and informed as to the views of the government, and with whom I wish you to converse & consult freely. With great respect I am & & &, J.C. Calhoun.

ALS in NcU, Duff Green Papers (published microfilm, roll 5, frame 413).

To BENJAMIN E. GREEN

Department of State
Washington, April 19th, 1844

Sir, A Treaty for the annexation of Texas to the United States, has been signed by the Plenipotentiaries of the two Governments; and will be sent by the President [John Tyler] to the Senate, without delay, for its approval.

In making the fact known to the Mexican Government, the President enjoins it on you to give it, in the first place, the strongest assurance, that in adopting this measure, our Government is actuated by no feelings of disrespect, or indifference to the honor or dignity of Mexico; and that it would be a subject of great regret, if it should be otherwise regarded by its Government. And, in the next place, that the step was forced on the Government of the United States in self-defence, in consequence of the policy adopted by Great Britain in reference to the abolition of Slavery in Texas. It was impossible for the United States to witness with indifference the efforts of Great Britain to abolish Slavery there. They could not but see, that she had the means in her power, in the actual condition of Texas, to accomplish the objects of her policy, unless prevented by the most efficient measures; and that, if accomplished, it would lead to a state of things dangerous in the extreme to the adjacent States and the Union itself. Seeing this, this Government has been compelled by the necessity of the case, and a regard to its Constitutional obligations to take the steps it has, as the only certain and effectual means of preventing it. It has taken it in full view of all possible consequences; but not without a desire and hope that a full and fair disclosure of the causes, which induced it to do so, would prevent the disturbance of the harmony subsisting between the two countries, and which the United States is anxious to preserve.

In order that the Mexican Government should have a just and full conception of the motives, which have compelled this Government to take the course it has, I enclose, by the direction of the President, a copy of the declaration of Lord Aberdeen, which Mr. [Richard] Pakenham, the British Minister, was instructed to read to the Secretary of State of the United States, and to leave a copy, should he desire it; and the answer to it on the part of our Government. The President authorizes you to read them to the Mexican Secretary of State, and to permit him to take memoranda of their contents, as you read, should he desire it; but not to leave copies, as they constitute a part of the documents which will be transmitted with the Treaty to the Senate.

You are enjoined, also, by the President to assure the Mexican Government, that it is his desire to settle all questions between the two countries, which may grow out of this Treaty, or any other cause, on the most liberal and satisfactory terms, including that of boundary. And with that view the Minister, who has been recently appointed [Wilson Shannon], will be shortly sent with adequate powers.

You will, finally, assure the Government of Mexico, that the Government of the United States would have been happy, if circumstances had permitted it to act in concurrence with that of Mexico, in taking the step it has; but with all its respect for Mexico, and anxious desire, that the two countries should continue on friendly terms, it could not make what it believed might involve the safety of the Union itself, depend on the contingency of obtaining the previous consent of Mexico. But while it could not with a due regard to the safety of the Union, do that, it has taken every precaution to make the terms of the Treaty as little objectionable to Mexico as possible. And among others, has left the boundary of Texas without specification; so that what the line of boundary should be, might be an open question to be fairly and fully discussed, and settled according to the rights of each, and the mutual interests and security of the two Countries. I have the honor to be &C &C, J.C. Calhoun.

LS in DNA, RG 84 (Foreign Posts), Mexico, Instructions, vol. 5.I; FC in DNA, RG 59 (State Department), Diplomatic Instructions, Mexico, 15:293–295 (M-77:111); CC in DNA, RG 46 (U.S. Senate), 28A-E3; PC in *Congressional Globe*, 28th Cong., 1st Sess., Appendix, p. 482; PC in Senate Document No. 341, 28th Cong., 1st Sess., pp. 53–54; PC in House Document No. 271, 28th Cong., 1st Sess., pp. 53–54; PC in the New York, N.Y., *Evening Post*, April 27, 1844, p. 4; PC in the Charleston, S.C., *Courier*, May 7, 1844, p. 2; PC in *Niles' National Register*, vol. LXVI, no. 11 (May 11, 1844), pp. 172–173; PC in the Washington, D.C., *Daily National Intelligencer*, May 20, 1844, p. 2; PC in the Washington, D.C., *Globe*, May 22, 1844, p. 1; PC in Crallé, ed., *Works*, 5:347–349.

From J[OSEPH] R. INGERSOLL, [Representative from Pa.]

House of Representatives, April 19, 1844
Sir, A letter from Freemantle, Western Australia was placed some time since in the hands of the President [John Tyler] by Colonel Samuel Moore of Baltimore. The object was to suggest the advantage which might be derived from the appointment of a Consul for the United States at the place where the letter is dated. Wool to a considerable extent is grown at and near the place and has been shipped to this country, and the Australians want tobacco[,] flour[,] furniture and other articles of American produce. The colony it is thought will succeed. No less than thirty two Whaling ships from this country are said to have visited the colony during the year, and much trouble was experienced from the conduct of their sailors who were not subject to the Consular control which is usually found in foreign Ports. The writer of the letter is Mr. Samuel Moore a native of Ireland. He has resided as a merchant in Australia for several years, and Expects to remain there with his family. He is a relation of Colonel Moore of Baltimore, who is a gentleman of the highest respectability, well known to the President, long resident in this country, distinguished and wounded as a gallant volunteer officer in the late war and in all particulars entitled to the utmost confidence. He strongly recommends his kinsman of the same name as worthy of the place of Consul.

A book of some interest has been placed in my hands by Colonel Moore "Ogle on Western Australia." It gives favorable accounts of the condition and prospects of the Colony. If citizens of the United States are frequently there in considerable numbers, if the ships of our country occasionally stop there in their whaling voyages and in pursuit of direct and useful trade, it may be worthy of the consideration of the Government whether an official representative of its mercantile interests should not be established permanently in this flourishing and growing Colony.

I take the liberty to submit to you the foregoing remarks with a view to bring the measure itself to the consideration of the President. I have the honor to be With great consideration[,] Y[ou]r ob[edient] servant, J.R. Ingersoll.

ALS in DNA, RG 59 (State Department), Applications and Recommendations, 1837–1845, Moore (M-687:23, frames 451–454), received 4/20.

From J[ohn] Y. Mason, [Secretary of the Navy], 4/19. "I beg leave to introduce to you the Rev[eren]d Mr. [Elias L.] Magoon, who [is] contemplating a visit to Europe and desires the necessary passports. He is a Gentleman of great worth, and your attention to his wishes as early as convenient" will oblige Mason. [Magoon was a Baptist clergyman and at this time pastor of a church in Richmond. He was the author of a number of books, including *Living Orators of America* (1849) which devoted a chapter to Calhoun.] ALS in DNA, RG 59 (State Department), Passport Applications, vol. 30, unnumbered (M-1372:14).

From R[ichard] Pakenham

Washington, April 19, 1844

The Undersigned, Her Britannick Majesty's Envoy Extraordinary and Minister Plenipotentiary, has had the honor to receive the Note which The Hon[ora]ble Mr. Calhoun, Secretary of State of the United States, was pleased, yesterday, to address to Him, containing observations on a Dispatch from Her Majesty's Principal Secretary of State for Foreign Affairs [Lord Aberdeen] to the Undersigned, of which the Undersigned had the honor at the request of the late Secretary of State, Mr. [Abel P.] Upshur, to furnish a copy, for the more complete information of the Government of the United States.

Mr. Calhoun at the same time announces to the Undersigned, by direction of the President [John Tyler], that a Treaty has been concluded between the United States and Texas, for the Annexation of Texas to this Country as a Part of its Territory, which Treaty will be submitted without delay to the Senate for its approval.

Mr. Calhoun, further takes occasion to enter into explanations as to the motives which have induced the Government of the United States to adopt their present policy with regard to Texas, and He concludes by presenting certain remarks, founded on statistical Information, *in defence* of the Institution of Slavery as now established in a portion of this Republic, and in proof of the necessity of taking measures for its preservation.

It is not the purpose of the Undersigned in the present communication to enter into discussion with Mr. Calhoun respecting the project thus formally announced on the part of the Government of The United States to annex Texas to the American Union—That duty will, if thought necessary, be fulfilled by higher Authority—Still less is the Undersigned disposed to trespass on Mr. Calhoun's attention by offering any remarks upon the subject of Slavery as expounded in Mr. Calhoun's Note—That Note will be transmitted to Her Majesty's Government by the earliest opportunity, and with this intimation the Undersigned would for the present content Himself, were it not for the painful impression created on his mind by observing that the Government of the United States—so far from appreciating at their just value the explanations furnished by Her Majesty's Government in a spirit of frankness and good faith well-calculated to allay whatever anxiety this Government might have previously felt on the particular points to which those explanations have reference, appear to have found arguments in that communication in favor of the contemplated Annexation of Texas, thus, as it were assigning to the British Government some share in the responsibility of a transaction which can hardly fail to be viewed in many quarters with the most serious objection.

All such Responsibility The Undersigned begs leave in the name of Her Majesty's Government at once and most positively to disclaim—whatever may be the consequences of that transaction, the British Government will look forward without anxiety to the judgement which will thereon be passed by the civilized World in as far as shall apply to any provocation furnished by England for the adoption of such a measure.

With the political Independence of Texas not only has Great Britain disavowed all intention to interfere, but it is a well known fact that Her most zealous exertions have been directed towards the completion of that Independence by obtaining its acknowledgment at the hands of the only Power by which it was seriously disputed.

Great Britain has also formally disclaimed the desire to establish in Texas any dominant influence, and with respect to Slavery, she is not conscious of having acted in a sense to cause just alarm to the United States.

From the avowed desire of Great Britain to see Slavery abolished in Texas it is inferred by The Government of the United States that England is endeavouring through Her Diplomacy to make the abolition of Slavery a condition to the acknowledgment of the Independence of Texas by Mexico. If Mr. Calhoun will have the goodness to refer once more to the copy of Lord Aberdeen's Dispatch which lies before Him, He will find the following exposition of the intentions of Great Britain on this point which the Undersigned flattered Himself would have been sufficient to forbid any such inference—"With regard to Texas we avow that we wish to see Slavery abolished there, as elsewhere, and we should rejoice if the recognition of that Country by the Mexican Government should be accompanied by an engagement on the part of Texas to abolish Slavery eventually, and under proper conditions throughout the Republic. But although we earnestly desire, and feel it to be our duty, to promote such a consummation, we shall not interfere unduly, or with an improper assumption of Authority, with either Party" (either Mexico or Texas) "in order to ensure the adoption of such a course. We shall counsel, but we shall not seek to compel, or unduly controul, either Party, so far as Great Britain is concerned, provided other States act with equal forbearance, those Governments will be fully at liberty to make their own unfettered arrangements with each other, both in regard to the abolition of Slavery, and to all other Points."

The Undersigned takes advantage of this opportunity to renew to The Hon[ora]ble Mr. Calhoun the assurance of his High Consideration, R. Pakenham.

LS in DNA, RG 59 (State Department), Notes from Foreign Legations, Great Britain, vol. 22 (M-50:22); CC in DNA, RG 84 (Foreign Posts), Great Britain, Instructions, 8:141–147; CC in DNA, RG 84 (Foreign Posts), France, Instructions, Jan. 29, 1843–May 20, 1846; CC's in DNA, RG 46 (U.S. Senate), 28B-B12; PC in Senate Document No. 341, 28th Cong., 1st Sess., pp. 63–65; PC in House Document No. 271, 28th Cong., 1st Sess., pp. 63–65; PC in the Washington, D.C., *Daily Madisonian*, May 20, 1844, p. 2; PC in the Washington, D.C., *Daily National Intelligencer*, May 20, 1844, p. 2; PC in the Washington, D.C., *Spectator*, May 21, 1844, p. 2; PC in the Washington, D.C., *Globe*, May 22, 1844,

p. 1; PC in the Charleston, S.C., *Courier*, May 25, 1844, p. 2; PC in *Niles' National Register*, vol. LXVI, no. 13 (May 25, 1844), p. 202; PC in Crallé, ed., *Works*, 5:340–342.

From H[UGH] J. ANDERSON, [Governor of Maine]

State of Maine
Executive Department
Belfast, 20th April 1844

Sir, During the last year several letters were addressed to the Department of State by my immediate predecessor Hon. Edward Kavanagh, asking the aid of the General Government in procuring from the Provincial Authorities of New Brunswick, copies of grants of land made by the British Government, within that portion of the late disputed territory, which, by the Treaty of Washington, falls within the limits of Maine.

In reply to one of those communications, the late Mr. [Abel P.] Upshur transmitted a copy of a letter from the British Minister, Mr. [Henry S.] Fox, in which he says "that he shall lose no time in forwarding the correspondence to the Provincial government of New Brunswick, and also to Her Majesties Government in England, in order that such measures may be taken to supply the information required, as may be found just & expedient."

This communication from Mr. Fox was under date of June 25th [1843], and though again addressed by Mr. Upshur on the 31st of October following, no information touching the subject has yet been received.

As the Commissioners appointed by this State to locate the grants referred to, in execution of the fourth article of the Treaty, are about to resume the prosecution of their duties, it is highly important that they should be possessed of copies of those grants, and the surveys, plans & allotments having reference thereto.

Authentic copies of those documents can be procured only from the records in possession of the proper authorities of New Brunswick, and in order seasonably to obtain them, the interposition of the General Government is again respectfully invoked. I have the honor to be most respectfully Your ob[edien]t Servant, H.J. Anderson.

LS in DNA, RG 59 (State Department), Miscellaneous Letters (M-179:104, frames 212–213).

To F[idericio] Bourman, [Spanish Chargé d'Affaires in the U.S.], 4/20. In response to Bourman's note of 4/18 Calhoun states: "If you will call at this Department on Monday, the 22nd Instant, at 1 o'clock, P.M., I will accompany you for the purpose indicated in your note, to the President's Mansion." FC in DNA, RG 59 (State Department), Notes to Foreign Legations, Spain, 6:109–110 (M-99:85).

From W[illia]m Crump

Powhatan C[ount]y Virginia, April 20th 1844
Sir, I have received your letter dated the 15th of this month, informing me that the President by and with the advice and consent of the Senate, has appointed me Charge d Affairs of the United States, to the Republic of Chile.

In obedience to your request contained in your letter, I hereby inform you that I do accept the appointment. I expect to be enabled to leave home and enter on the voige to engage in the dutys of my mission about three weeks from this time, say about the 15th or 20th of May. I am Sir Very Respectfully Your Ob[edien]t S[er]v[an]t, Wm. Crump.

ALS in DNA, RG 59 (State Department), Diplomatic Despatches, Chile, vol. 6 (M-10:T6, frame 205).

From F[rancis] M. Dimond

United States Consulate
Vera Cruz, April 20, 1844
Sir, I have the honour herewith to transmit Despatches I received by this morning[']s mail from Mexico [City] and the Sandwich Islands.

I have nothing of importance to communicate from hence. Every thing is tranquil[.] Repairs are slowly go[i]n[g] on at the Castle.

Mr. Geo[rge] Van Ness has been liberated and returns to New York in the first Packet[,] which port has been designated by Gen[era]l Santa Anna.

On the 4th of this month I received as did the other Consuls a verbal order from the Prefecta to close the retail stores of our respective Countrymen. No attention however was paid to it, and they are with the exception of two French continuing without molestations. We have only one[,] the French about 30. I have the honour to be Sir most Respectfully your Ob[edient] Servant, F.M. Dimond.

ALS (No. 217) in DNA, RG 59 (State Department), Consular Despatches, Veracruz, vol. 5 (M-183:5), received 5/11.

To BENJAMIN E. GREEN

Department of State
Washington, 20th April, 1844

Sir: I transmit a petition addressed to President Santa Anna by respectable inhabitants of the County of Tuscaloosa in the State of Alabama, praying for the liberation of William F. McMath, a Texan prisoner represented to be confined in the Castle of Perote. If he should not have been released when you receive this letter, you will take all proper care that the petition reaches its destination and that the respectability of the signers is understood. I am, Sir, your obedient servant, J.C. Calhoun.

LS (No. 2) in DNA, RG 84 (Foreign Posts), Mexico, Instructions, vol. 5.I; FC in DNA, RG 59 (State Department), Diplomatic Instructions, Mexico, 15:295 (M-77:111).

To Samuel A. Hale, Tuscaloosa, Ala., 4/20. Calhoun acknowledges Hale's letter of 4/10 and the enclosed petition [concerning McMath, a prisoner in Mexico]. The latter has been transmitted to the U.S. representative at Mexico [City]. FC in DNA, RG 59 (State Department), Domestic Letters, 34:150 (M-40:32).

From JOHN HOGAN, "Private"

Utica [N.Y.,] April 20th 1844

Dear Sir, The [Martin] Van Buren party is all broken up[.] There is no confidence to be reposed in any ["other" *canceled and* "their" *interlined*] professions[.] At Albany all is confusion & chaos[.] Old Hunkers with [William C.] Bouck the Gov[ernor] at their head & the radicals or barn burners as they are called on the other. *Van Buren is loosing* [sic] *ground every day* & before one month the State

291

of New York will be out opposed to him[.] *What do you think of that*[?] Such a state of feeling prevales as to put the true construction on ["it" *interlined*.] So firm & decided a disposition to throw him off exists that should he be the Candidate he will be beaten in this State by 25,000 votes, but I do not apprehend any harm from him[.] He will be laid a one side[.] Now the next question that comes up is who will be the Candidate[;] this question should be looked too in time[.] Will it be Mr. [John] Tyler[;] will it be Gen. [Lewis] Cass[,] Col. [Richard M.] Johnson or who[?] Your friends ["will"? *interlined*] never consent to your being brought forward by a fraction of the party[.] If matters continue in the unsettled state they now are in[,] total prostration & defeat must be the result of the next Election[.] If the Country comes forward & with energy demands your being the Candidate depend upon it there will be no danger[.] Will I hear from you[?] I hope that your arduous duties will allow you time to write a few lines. The contest about Texas just begins[.] The Clay men are against the annexation of Texas[,] I was going to say to a man[.] Van Buren[']s followers are inclined that way but they are now changing ground[.] The Texas question will succeed in this State[.] Your friends stand firm on that question. I am Sir your Ob[edien]t Serv[an]t, John Hogan.

P.S. I hope you will not forget the Guatemala[?] question.

ALS in ScCleA.

From THOMAS O. LARKIN

Consulate of the United States
Monterey Calafornia, April 20, 1844
Sir, I have to day received a letter of which the following is a copy.

Mr. Thomas O. Larkin[,] United States Consul for the
port of Monterey

[Monterey, April 18, 1844]

Sir, I, Isaac Graham a citizen of the county of Lincoln, State of Kentucky, United States of America, Hereby represent to you as Consul of the said States, that you may represent the same to our Gover[n]ment.

That in the month of April 1840 I was forcibly attacked in my house in the vicinity of this town by armed officers and soldiers of

Mexico, wounded both by swords and pistols, Tied and brought to prison in this town, in company of other Americans. Here kept in irons several days. Then put on board a vessel ironed and carried to San Blas[,] Thence taken into the interior and again imprisoned and returned to this town after an imprisonment and absence of fifteen months.

When attacked as above stated I was in the peaceable pursuit of my business, and to this day know of no reason why I have been wounded and imprisoned; nor to this day have I ever received any compensation from Mexico for my imprisonment and losses.

At the time of my attack and during my absence I lost property to a large amount, which I claim from the Gover[n]ment of Mexico. Also fifteen hundred dollars per month for my lost time, and the sum of fifty thousand dollars for being attacked and wounded and imprisoned for so long a time. The justness of the latter sum I leave to the wisdom of my Gover[n]ment.

I have through the hands of John Black Esq. U.S. Consul at Mexico [City], and Com[mo]d[ore] Thomas Ap C. Jones sent to Washington a statement of my losses but to this day have had no information on the subject. Signed, Isaac Graham.

I think it of sufficient importance to inform you, that at the time of Mr. Graham[']s arrest and imprisonment, there were about one hundred English and Americans ["imprisoned" *interlined*] also, about one half of whom were shipped in irons to San Blas, thence taken into the interior and again imprisoned. Mr. Barron the English Consul of San Blas gave several of his countrymen and some of the Americans two hundred and fifty dollars each to release the Gover[n]ment of Mexico from farther claim respecting their false imprisonment. The same Gover[n]ment in 1841 sent the remainder to Monterey. I am of the opinion that Calafornia had no just cause for the arresting and shipping of these men. I am Sir with much respect and consideration your most ob[edien]t Servant, Thomas O. Larkin.

ALS (No. 5) in DNA, RG 59 (State Department), Consular Despatches, Monterey (M-138:1), received 6/19; FC in CU, Bancroft Library, Larkin Collection; PC in Hammond, ed., *Larkin Papers*, 2:100–101. Note: A State Dept. Clerk's EU reads "Write to him and tell him to furnish *authentic* proof of the outrage complained of by Graham, if it has not been sent."

From Thomas O. Larkin, Consulate of the United States, Monterey, 4/20. Larkin reports that his business ventures may require him to travel every two or three years to the Sandwich Islands or to

Mexican ports as far south as Acapulco. On these trips he will be absent from his post for two to five months. To apply for and receive permission for leave would require a year or more and would hamper his business interests. He therefore asks for permission in advance for such leaves with the provision that he appoint a Vice-Consul during his absences. ALS (No. 6) in DNA, RG 59 (State Department), Consular Despatches, Monterey (M-138:1); FC in CU, Bancroft Library, Larkin Collection; PC in Hammond, ed., *Larkin Papers*, 2:99.

From J[OHN] Y. MASON, [Secretary of the Navy]

Navy Department
April 20, 1844

Sir, I have had the honor to receive your communication of the 15th inst[ant] calling my attention to the subject of a letter of the 20th of February last, addressed to this Department by Mr. [Abel P.] Upshur, late Secretary of State, on the subject of a Resolution of the House of Representatives, of the 27th July, 1842.

There is nothing on the files of this Department, on the subject "of *a plan* for the establishment, in concert with the Government of France, of a line of weekly steamers between the ports of Havre and New York."

The second branch of the Resolution, calling for a statement of the expense, which may be required to carry the said plan into effect, cannot be answered, until the data for estimates shall be furnished by the adoption of a plan, exhibiting the number and size of the steamers to be employed. I have the honor to enquire if any plan has been proposed by the Government of His Majesty [Louis Philippe] the King of the French, within the knowledge of the Department of State? and to enquire further, if it be the desire of the State Department, that this Department shall cause to be prepared the plan of such a line, as is contemplated by the Resolution, and to estimate its expense? I have the honor to be Very respectfully Y[ou]r Obed[ien]t Serv[an]t, J.Y. Mason.

LS in DNA, RG 59 (State Department), Miscellaneous Letters (M-179:104, frames 205–207); FC in DNA, RG 45 (Naval Records), Letters Sent by the Secretary of the Navy to the President and Executive Agencies, 1821–1886, 4:492–493 (M-472:2, frame 628).

From FRA[NCI]S B. OGDEN

New York [City,] April 20th 1844
Sir, I have the honor to present to you Mr. Tho[ma]s Petherick of Cornwall, England, with whom I had the pleasure of making a passage across the Atlantic and in whom I became highly interested from his great scientific & practical knowledge of Metal[l]urgy, to which he has given his attention for many years in that country. Mr. Petherick proposes visiting the mineral regions of the South, and having heard of the extraordinary productions of Gold[,] Copper &c in your State and of your personal interest in their development, he has solicited a letter of introduction to you, which I am much gratified in giving, confident you will be pleased with his information, and in the hope you may derive some benefit from his experience. I am Sir your obedient Serv[an]t, Fras. B. Ogden.

ALS in ScCleA. NOTE: Francis B. Ogden (1783–1857) was a noted engineer and U.S. Consul at Bristol, England, 1840–1857.

From G.W. Trueheart, Baltimore, 4/20. Trueheart asks for "any *certain intelligence*" concerning the release of Texan prisoners captured at San Antonio, especially his brother, James L. Trueheart. ALS in DNA, RG 59 (State Department), Miscellaneous Letters (M-179:104, frames 207–208).

From an UNIDENTIFIED TEXAN

Houston, April 20, 1844
You may rely upon the following as the necessary result of the rejection of the treaty:

1. That the negotiations between England and Texas will be immediately resumed.

2. That a free-trade treaty, giving great advantages to England, will be immediately concluded.

3. That England will guaranty the independence of Texas upon condition that we stipulate to remain an independent power.

Such are the propositions made by England, and they will be consummated so soon as the treaty is rejected. This is the determination of President [Samuel] Houston, and he is sustained by a secret act of Congress, passed with almost entire unanimity, providing for the contingency of the failure of annexation.

You may ask me, will the people of Texas consent to this? I answer, Yes; for the President and Congress have already assented; and the people will assent, when we are spurned and rejected by the Government of the Union.

This treaty and alliance with England, Captain [Charles] Elliot has long been endeavoring to effect; and it would have been closed ere this, but for the intervention of the present negotiation with the United States.

We are offered, also, almost unlimited loans of money in England, and the re-establishment of our finances upon mortgage of our public domain, which, we are encouraged to believe, would, soon after the treaty, be sold to English emigrants. The free-trade treaty with England would compel us to raise the duties to the very highest revenue standard upon all American products—such as beef, pork, lard, flour, &c.; and these duties, together with some small augmentation of the direct taxation now authorized by law, would support the Government when permanent peace was restored by the guaranty of our independence by England. We would then incur no expense for armies or navies, as the guaranty of England would stand in lieu of both.

I communicate these facts, to use as you think proper; and confer with our ministers, and you will find that they cannot deny them; but my name must not be divulged to them, unless in the event of the ratification of the treaty, which, from our information, is almost certain.

PEx in House Document No. 271, 28th Cong., 1st Sess., p. 103; PEx in the Washington, D.C., *Spectator,* July 16, 1844, p. 1. Note: This letter is known only in the form of a printed extract, and no earlier version has been found. Identified only as "Extract of a letter," it was one of six documents transmitted by Calhoun to President John Tyler on 5/16 in response to an official request for information on "what will probably be the Course of the Govt. of Texas, in the event that a treaty of Annexation should at this time fail." It is not even absolutely certain that the letter was addressed to Calhoun, though that seems fairly likely.

From [Jean Corneille, Chevalier] Gevers, "Chargé d'Affaires of His Majesty the King of the Netherlands," Washington, 4/21. Gevers informs Calhoun of a discrepancy in the tariff of 1842 which places a twenty per cent duty upon Java coffee imported into the U.S. from Holland. According to the tariff, the coffee is an item of indirect trade but "Holland forms in fact the depot and home market of Dutch colonial productions and as such the exportation of these products is unquestionably direct trade." The coffee duty also violates treaties of reciprocity between the U.S. and Holland. He recounts several concessions made to the U.S. in Dutch colonies and expresses the hope that the discrepancy can be remedied. Gevers also reports claims of some Dutch merchants that they have suffered from an erroneous imposition of the tariff of 1842 upon their cargoes, the customs rates having changed while their cargoes were in transport to the U.S. LS in DNA, RG 59 (State Department), Notes from Foreign Legations, Netherlands, vol. 2 (M-56:2, frames 166–169).

From S[tephen] Pleasonton, [Fifth Auditor of the Treasury Department], 4/21. He asks Calhoun to appoint the son of the late Rev. [Andrew T.] McCormick to a Clerkship in the State Department. Dr. McCormick was a Clerk in that agency for more than 20 years; he died in 1841, leaving his family in indigent circumstances. ALS in DNA, RG 59 (State Department), Applications and Recommendations, 1837–1845, McCormick (M-687:21, frames 233–234).

From J[uan] N. Almonte

Mexican Legation
Washington, April 22, 1844

The Undersigned, Envoy Extraordinary and Minister Plenipotentiary of the Mexican Republic, has observed, that the newspapers of this country, have studiously endeavoured to inculcate the idea, that he has declared, that his Government would conform to any explanation, or indemnification, which the Government of the United States might choose to give, to secure its assent to the incorporation of the Territory of Texas, with the U. States: and even in one newspaper, [the *Madisonian*,] well known in this City, as being semi-official, the same idea has been given out [in its issue of 4/19]. This is highly offensive to the dignity of Mexico; and the Undersigned, although he considers it as no other than a ridiculous invention, calculated only to deceive the vulgar, nevertheless believes it to be his duty, in order to avoid any doubt upon this subject, to address the Hon. Mr. Calhoun[,] Secretary of State of the United States, as he now does, with the object of making known to him, that he may communicate it to the President of the Republic [John Tyler], that neither the Government of Mexico, nor the Undersigned have any motive to change their resolution, as regards the protest which they addressed to the Government of the United States, on the 23d of August, and the 3rd of November of the year last past; against the annexation of Texas to the American Union.

The Undersigned avails himself of this occasion, to repeat to the Hon. John C. Calhoun, the assurances of his high consideration. J.N. Almonte.

State Department translation of LS in Spanish in DNA, RG 59 (State Department), Notes from Foreign Legations, Mexico, vol. 4 (M-54:2).

To Brig. Gen. Don J[UAN] N. ALMONTE

Department of State
Washington, 22nd April, 1844

The Undersigned, Secretary of State of the United States, has the honor to acknowledge the receipt of a note of this date from General Almonte, Envoy Extraordinary and Minister Plenipotentiary of the Republic of Mexico, and in reply thereto assures General Almonte that the statements and speculations to which he refers have never, directly or indirectly, received any authority or countenance from him. He doubts not that General Almonte has attributed their appearance to the true cause—to the common disposition of the Public Journals to speculate at pleasure on the course of public affairs.

The Undersigned takes pleasure in declaring that, in no conversation with which he has been honored by General Almonte has any intimation been given by him to the Undersigned, either that the Government of Mexico or himself entertained any motive or purpose to change the resolution already expressed in the protests of the 23d of August and the 3d of November, last, in regard to the annexation of Texas to the United States.

The Undersigned avails himself of the occasion to renew to General Almonte the assurance of his high consideration. J.C. Calhoun.

FC in DNA, RG 59 (State Department), Notes to Foreign Legations, Mexico, 6:182–183 (M-99:69); PC in Jameson, ed., *Correspondence*, pp. 578–579.

From Rich[ar]d H. Belt

U.S. Comm[ercia]l Agency, Matamoros
Mexico, 22nd April 1844

Sir, Annexed I have the honor to hand you an Inventory of the additions made to this Consulate since the one forwarded by the former Consul Mr. [D.W.] Smith in 1842.

This Consulate is very much in want of a flag, the one now in use is completely worn out. A coat of arms is also needed[;] the one belonging to the office was stolen several years since, the department was advised of the theft by Mr. Smith.

I herewith enclose you a Mexican paper containing a decree for the reopening of the ports of Taos &c; these are the ports of entry for the Santa Fee traders.

The law restricting foreigners in the retail trade has gone into effect in the City of Mexico and its vicinity, and will be in operation here next month. It appears to be the prevalent opinion that this law will virtually be annulled by the granting of permits to those who apply for them. An American house in this City has already obtained permission, but no particular length of time is specified.

The foreigners generally are making applications. There are but few of our citizens affected by the law within the jurisdiction of this Consulate.

Business still continues very ["dull" *interlined*;] there is only one American vessel in port. The Cotton and other crops of the Country promise an abundant yield, the weather has been unusually favorable.

I have received no advices relative to my appointment to the Consulship at this place. Should the department deem it fit, I should be pleased to receive a Commission.

I came here with the appointment of Com[mercia]l Agent, conferred upon me by the late Hon. Secretary of State [Abel P. Upshur] during the recess of Congress. I am engaged in no other business, and can give the office my exclusive attention.

I have drawn on the Department for $208.45 being the amount as per account rendered, of the expenses of the destitute mariners who were wrecked in the Schooner Clara Ann. I remain y[ou]r ob[edien]t S[ervan]t, Richd. H. Belt.

ALS (No. 2) with Ens in DNA, RG 59 (State Department), Consular Despatches, Matamoros, vol. 4 (M-281:2, frames 359–365), received 6/17.

To I[saac] E. Holmes, [Representative from S.C.], 4/22. Calhoun informs Holmes that "a nomination of Mr. F[rancis] M. Auboyneau to the Senate as Consul of the United States for the port of La Rochelle, was sent from this Department to the President on the 15th Instant." FC in DNA, RG 59 (State Department), Domestic Letters, 34:151 (M-40:32).

From J[OHN] H. HOWARD, *"Confidential"*

Columbus [Ga.,] April 22nd 1844

My Dear Sir, If you can snatch a moment from your duties I should be pleased to know if a proper effort was now made by your friends, whether it would avail in producing a larger concentration of the Democratic influence in your favor than in that of Mr. [Martin] Van Buren. I see there is an effort making to bring Mr. [John] Tyler forward in these diversities of opinion. May we not expect that it will result in greater concentration on yourself[?]

I am a member of the Baltimore convention & will call on you on my way thither. I shall not set out before the 20th May.

Be pleased to give me your views & prospects without delay at as full length as your other duties will allow. Write me fully ["the" *canceled*;] its confidential character will be properly regarded.

Will the treaty of annexation of Texas be ratified? We are all for it here. What course will Mr. [Henry] Clay & Mr. Van Buren take upon it? Respectfully &c, J.H. Howard.

ALS in ScCleA. NOTE: An AEU by Calhoun reads: "Col. Howard[,] answered."

From John Nelson, [Attorney General], 4/22. He encloses a note [*not found*] from a Mr. Reid, who "is a lawyer of accurate and strong views" and "a gentleman . . . every way qualified" for an unidentified position he is seeking. ALS in DNA, RG 59 (State Department), Applications and Recommendations, 1837–1845, Reid (M-687:27, frames 316–317).

To G[regory] A. Perdicaris, "now in Cheraw," S.C., 4/22. "Your leave of absence from the Consulate at Athens having expired long since, and no information having been received at the Department in relation to your departure for that post, I feel it to be my duty to inquire whether you intend returning, and, if so, at what time you design doing so." FC in DNA, RG 59 (State Department), Consular Instructions, 10:240.

From F[rancis] W. Pickens

Charleston, 22 April 1844

My dear Sir, I suppose you have heard of the dreadful affliction occasioned by the death of [my late wife's sister] Maria [Simkins Colhoun]. Cousin Floride [Colhoun Calhoun] & Anna [Maria Calhoun Clemson] were with her to the last and she had every thing ["done" *canceled and then interlined*] that could be. She suffered intensely but bore all with perfect resignation. Col. [James Edward] Colhoun is utterly overwhelmed. I did not think it would have overcome him so. Of course it is an awful blow to me & mine, as it leaves my little children without a female friend near & dear to council and advise them as they rise up into the sorrows and temptations of this life. I have come down to-day for Susan [Pickens] to take her home in our affliction, & will start up in the morning. Cousin F[loride] & the Col. are still at my house.

As to politics I have had no time to read even the newspapers. I have been entirely occupied in planting ever since you left my house. I arrived home a few days after you left. We have had a beautiful spring—dry & warm. I have a fine stand of cotton on 700 acres, & my small grain is beautiful. Our corn looks as good as can be so far—ploughed & hoed over all the first planted.

I suppose you are in the midst of business. I hope you will take the highest grounds on the Oregon question. It is the only question where we of the South have nothing to lose. It gives us the sympathy of the nonslaveholding States of the North-West & seperates them from the Middle & Northern States. Besides if it is to be settled up it drains the Middle & Northern States and does not weaken the slave States at all. The country is ours by all the laws of possession & settlement, and cannot be yielded to England without weakening our moral position before the world, particularly after the Ashburton Treaty. It seems to me that you might also keep open the question of the seizure of our slaves in the Bahamas & the W[est] Indies & the promise made by Ashburton on that point, so that if the negotiation is to be arrested let it be arrested on as many points as possible so as to keep the South at least united. And if it is to be unsettled at present let the highest grounds be taken upon all points, and let the next Adm[inistratio]n meet the questions in such a shape that they cannot sacrifice our honor or our interests.

As to the Texas question I fear you will be defeated on its ratification at present. If Mr. [Henry] Clay & the Whigs see it is to strengthen you they will do every thing to give it the go-by & they have the power in the Senate. Their struggle will be to let you do all the foundation work & incur all the odium that is to be incurred & then keep things in the hands of Clay as to the final action, supposing that he will certainly come in &c. Mr. Clay said in Columbia, so I hear, at a private table that the Texas question was exaggerated greatly—that the South expected too much from its admission & the North feared too much—that from his information the country would make but *two slave States* & *three free States*. So this is to be the policy—it speaks much as to the future. They will make the issue upon creating 3 free & 2 slave States.

I take it for granted nothing is to be done on the Tariff—& that it is uncertain who is to be President. But if Va. goes ag[ain]st [Martin] V[an] B[uren] how can he run?

I have troubled you on politics, and now may God grant that you may go through your complicated and difficult negotiations successfully. I fear your situation may end rather embarrassing—& that you may be disappointed in results. As to character & fame I know you can lose neither. Very truly & sincerely, F.W. Pickens.

ALS in ScCleA; PEx in Boucher and Brooks, eds., *Correspondence*, pp. 222–223.

From GILBERT C. RICE

New York [City,] 22 April 1844

Distinguished Sir, I wrote you a letter in behalf of the Irish Emigrant Society of N.Y. in or about August 1841[.] In your reply under date 13 Sept[embe]r [18]41 you say "I enclose $5 which the Society will please to regard as my annual subscription for the next five years[.]"

I would again solicit y[ou]r attention to the claims of the Society believing that apart from the aid of your munificence the expression of your good wishes & notice will subserve the interests of the Body[.]

I would not be importunate or over-tax your kindness. I simply wish to afford an *opportunity of good* to a man I really honour & at the same time do service to an association of merit[.] My health forbids me being a member any longer of the Executive Com[mittee] but still I endeavor to do the Society occasional service[.]

My Brother Purser [C.C.] Rice is at the moment in Washington, if he should call on you please regard him as the brother of Y[ou]r friend & Ob[edien]t Serv[an]t, Gilbert C. Rice, 14 St. & 6th Avenue, New York.

[P.S.] Your reply to this will be submitted to the Executive Com[mittee] of the Society and perhaps to the assembly at the quarterly meeting.

ALS in ScCleA. NOTE: An AEU by Calhoun reads: "Mr. Gilbert [*sic,*] Relates to my subscription to the Irish imigrating Society."

To President [JOHN TYLER]

Department of State
22d April, 1844

The Secretary of State has the honour to refer to the President a letter [of 4/19] from the Hon: J[oseph] R. Ingersoll [Representative from Pa.] in relation to the appointment of Mr. Samuel Moore as Consul of the United States at "Freemantle," in Australia or New Holland. It would seem that the interests of our commerce require a public agent at that port, but as we have at present two Consuls in Australia and it is desirable that the number of Consuls should not be unnecessarily increased, it is respectfully suggested, that the Consul at "Sydney," in whose district "Freemantle" lies, should be requested by the Department to appoint Mr. Moore his Consular Agent for that port; a Consular Agency it is believed, being quite sufficient for every purpose which the state of our trade with it will for many years at least, probably require. Respectfully submitted, J.C. Calhoun.

LS with En in DNA, RG 59 (State Department), Applications and Recommendations, 1837–1845, Moore (M-687:23, frames 448–454). NOTE: An AES of 4/22 by Tyler reads "The suggestion of the Secretary of State is approv'd. J. Tyler."

From ISAAC VAN ZANDT and J. PINCKNEY HENDERSON

Legation of Texas
Washington, April 22nd 1844

Sir, We have the honor to submit for your information a brief outline of some of the efforts which have been made by the British Government to effect a settlement of the difficulties between Mexico and Texas.

By a convention concluded between Texas and Great Britain on the 14th day of November 1840, the British Government agreed to offer its mediation for this purpose, conditioned that, if the mediation should succeed, the Republic of Texas would "take upon itself a portion, amounting to one million pounds sterling, of the capital of the foreign debt contracted by the Republic of Mexico prior to the 1st day of January 1835." This ["tender of this" *interlined*] mediation of Great Britain was rejected by Mexico and the Government of Texas notified of the fact.

Afterwards, in 1842, representations were made to the Governments of Great Britain, France and the United States, asking their joint cooperation and interposition for the termination of the war between Mexico and Texas. To this request France and the United States acceded with alacrity and friendly zeal, but Great Britain declined to be thus associated, suggesting, at the same time, that each should act separately. In the spring of 1843 the British Government again informed the Government of Texas that the mediation, as before pursued, was utterly hopeless; and that Mr. [Percy W.] Doyle, the British Chargé d'Affaires, in Mexico, had been instructed to propose a settlement, based upon the abolition of slavery in Texas, and directed to urge upon the Mexican Government as an inducement to its acceptance, that such a result would be a great moral triumph on the part of Mexico.

Shortly afterwards it was made known to the Government of Texas through Capt. [Charles] Elliot, the British Chargé d'Affaires in Texas, that Gen[era]l Santa An[n]a, upon certain representations being made to him by Mr. Doyle, had agreed to an armistice or cessasion of hostilities for the purpose of negotiating as to the terms of a final peace. It was in pursuance of this arrangement that the Texian Commissioners were ordered to Mexico. Pending their negotiations, the British Government invited France to unite with her in pressing upon Mexico the propriety of concluding a permanent peace with Texas. The reason of this invitation, by Great Britain, to France to unite with her in the mediation, to the exclusion of the United States, when it was known that the United States were equally desirous for a peace between Mexico and Texas, may be accounted for on the ground, that the British Government was satisfied that the United States would not cooperate with them upon the proposed basis of the abolition of slavery.

We communicate these statements confidentionally [*sic*] but you will be permit[t]ed to show the same to such gentlemen as you may deem prudent under proper injunctions, not in any manner to be made public.

We avail ourselves of this occasion to renew to you assurances of our high regard. Isaac Van Zandt, J. Pinckney Henderson.

LS in ScCleA; CC in Tx, Andrew Jackson Houston Papers; PC in Boucher and Brooks, eds., *Correspondence*, pp. 223–224. Note: An endorsement on the LS reads "Letter from the Texan Ministers to Mr. Calhoun, containing a brief history of the transactions of Texas with Foreign powers in regard to recognition." Found among Calhoun's papers at ScCleA is a 16-pp. undated ms. memorandum which seems possibly to be related to this LS. This document is headed "Correspondence between the Respective Governments of Mexico and Texas, through Captain Charles Elliot, H.B. Majesty's Chargé d'Affaires near the Government of the Republic of Texas in relation to a[n] Armistice between Texas and Mexico." It contains copies of the following documents: Charles Elliot to Anson Jones, 6/10/[1843]; Percy W. Doyle to Elliot, 5/27/1843 (extract); Jones to Elliot, 6/15/1843; [Mexican Gen.] Adrian Wool [*sic*; Woll] to Samuel Houston, 7/16/1843; G.H. [*sic*; George W.] Hill, Texas Secretary of War and Marine, to Woll, 7/29/1843; Elliot to Jones, 7/24/1843; Jones to Elliot, 7/30/[1843]; and Elliot to Jones, 7/31/1843.

From FRANCIS WHARTON

Philadelphia, April 22d, 1844

My dear Sir, You have probably already had your attention called to the consequences of Judge [Henry] Baldwin's death, and I make no apology, therefore, for saying one or two words to you on the subject of an appointment [to the U.S. Supreme Court] which is of such material interest to the bar of this district. A Lawyer of eminence, you are aware, is demanded for such a position, but there seems to be the falsest idea current away from here about who really *is* a lawyer of eminence among us. Mr. [Horace] Binney undoubtedly & incomparably is such, but in case of his non-appointment or non acceptance, allow me to mention to you the name of Chief Justice [of Pa., John B.] Gibson, a man of stupendous intellect, a great common law lawyer, and a Judge who by twenty years services has acquired what few ever acquire at all, a judicial mind. The wild action of our late constitutional convention has made even a Chief Justiceship but a poor shelter for a man of independence & energy, and I have no doubt that he would be willing to leave his present high station for the more secure seat opened by Judge Baldwin's death. For twenty years removed from party politics[,] he will go to the Supreme Court, if such should be the case, untrammelled by the partisan prejudices which infect almost every other great legal leader, and I cannot but say that from intellect, from character, from learning, and more particularly from a strong & sturdy devotion to the liberties of the common law, he is most qualified to do honour to a bench upon whose strict Constitutional purity so much depends.

Should you be able to let me hear from you it would do the greatest favour, to yours most faithfully, Francis Wharton.

ALS in DNA, RG 59 (State Department), Applications and Recommendations, 1845–1853, John B. Gibson (M-873:32, frames 232–234).

From JAMES WISHART, "Private"

St. Clairsville [Ohio,] April 22nd 1844

My Dear Sir, In reply to your letter of the 8th ult[imo], which reached me on the 23rd, I addressed one to you at Washington, on the 28th, which should have reached you three or four days after your arrival there. Its contents were such as I would have addressed to no one but yourself. I hope it has not fallen into other hands. Gov. [Wilson] S[hannon] leaves today for the City. He resigned his office as Gov. of the State and made his arrangements [to] leave for the east, several days before he received official notice of his appointment.

In addition to former points presented, I may observe that your withdrawal, by your friends, does not give you a stronger position with the friends of Mr. [Martin] V[an] B[uren] than if you had continued before the public, as I presume was the idea entertained by them, in the contingency of his withdrawal. In either case you would be their second choice, but not with a decided wish to elect you.

A southern whig is more congenial to a northern Van B[uren] democrat. Have the goodness to say my former [letter] reached you, and believe me as formerly truely your Friend, James Wishart.

ALS in ScCleA.

From P[ierre] E. Bossier, [Representative from La.]

Washington, April the 23d 1844

Sir, In transmitting you the letter [dated 4/5] of Mr. Thomas D. Hailes, I most earnestly solicit you, Sir, to exercise your generous influence in behalf of this worthy gentleman. He is an intimate acquaintance of mine, highly recommandable under every respect; and possesses to my judgment a great capacity for public business, and is able I think to fulfil the office he solicits extremely well, and much to the satisfaction of all. It is no exaggeration, Sir, on my part. I assure that Mr. Hailes is a thorough gentlemanly man under every respect.

I should feel myself, Sir, very ["much" *interlined*] honoured and under great obligations to you if you were so kind as to exercise your benevolent influence in favor of Mr. Thomas D. Hailes at the first vacancy of a consular dignity to some southern Port.

In the hope that these few lines in behalf of my friend will meet with a kind reception and benevolent ["reception" *canceled and* "attention" *interlined*] on your part, I remain, Sir, Your very obedient Servant, P.E. Bossier, By P.A. Buard.

Copy with En in DNA, RG 59 (State Department), Applications and Recommendations, 1837–1845, Hailes (M-687:14, frames 93–95).

From G[eorge] M. Dallas, [former Senator from Pa. and U.S. Minister to Russia], 4/23. Dallas asks that letters of introduction to U.S. representatives abroad be prepared for Dr. Samuel Jackson [of Philadelphia], a talented physician who has been forced by his health to "visit some of the milder climates of Europe." Dallas adds: "I am quite sure that you could not give your valuable sanction to a worthier man." (An EU indicates that the request was complied with.) ALS in DNA, RG 59 (State Department), Miscellaneous Letters (M-179:104, frame 220).

From Ed[mund] S. Derry and John Riker Brady

N[ew] Y[ork City,] April 23d 1844

Sir, The Undersigned respectfully recommend the appointment of George E. Baldwin Esq. as U.S. Despatch Agent for this City in place of Mr. [William Henry] Leroy who nows [*sic*] holds the station.

Mr. Baldwin has long been identified with our political movements in this City, and is qualified by character and education for the post. With high respect Your ob[e]d[ien]t Serv[an]ts, Ed. S. Derry, Chairman of N.Y. Calhoun Central Committee, John Riker Brady, Secratary of the Central Calhoun Com[mitte]e in New York.

LS in ScCleA. NOTE: William Henry LeRoy, the Despatch Agent at New York City, was the brother of Daniel Webster's wife.

From JOHN FAIRFIELD, [Senator from Maine]

Senate Chamber, Ap[ri]l 23d 1844

Sir, I take the liberty to enclose certain papers relating to the unjust ["& illegal" *interlined*] imprisonment & ["at Gonaives (Hayti) & illegal" *canceled*] detention of Sam[ue]l S. Thomas and Joseph R. Curtis[,] Master & Mate of the Brig Zebra at Gonaives (Hayti) during the year 1843. They consider that they have a just claim upon their own Government for its services in procuring from the Haytien government an indemnity for the suffering and expenses attendant upon their imprisonment.

I would refer you Sir, to representations now on file in the Department of State, made, I believe, by Capt. Thomas while in prison & by myself, for ["a" *canceled*] further particulars upon this subject.

Permit me to hope Sir, that your early attention to this subject may be secured, and that an immediate demand may be made upon the Hatien Government, for a full remuneration to Capt. Hill & Mr. Curtis. With high respect I am Sir Your most Ob[edien]t Serv[an]t, John Fairfield.

ALS with Ens in DNA, RG 76 (Records of Boundary and Claims Commissions and Arbitrations), Miscellaneous Claims Records: Haiti.

To George W. Gordon, U.S. Consul at Rio de Janeiro, 4/23. Several letters from G[eorge] W. Slacum, Gordon's predecessor, have been received at the State Dept. The papers concerning the brig *Hope* have been sent to the U.S. District Attorney at Baltimore [Z. Collins Lee] in order that "the proper legal investigation may be had in the matter." FC in DNA, RG 59 (State Department), Consular Instructions, 11:237–238.

From WASHINGTON IRVING

Legation of the United States
Madrid, April 23d 1844

Sir, Political affairs here wear a tranquil surface under the domination of martial law; a schism however, is taking place between the leaders of the party in power, which gives great solicitude to those who wish the continuance of the present government. Many of the older moderados, especially those of high aristocratic pride, are desirous of getting rid of Gonzalez Bravo, whose loyalty they distrust, and whose origin they despise. They would form a cabinet from men of their own *creed* and their own *caste*; and would give [Ramon M.] Narvaez a place in it as Minister of War; in which case he would probably have the control. Gonzalez Bravo, however, is not disposed to relinquish the post which has raised him to such importance, and in which he really has acquitted himself with great spirit and ability. He is endeavoring to organize a little party of his own, formed of what is technically called the "Young Spain," and to set up General [Manuel G.] Concha in opposition to Narvaez. Narvaez is in favor at the Palace, and by his past services has secured the good will of [Maria Christina] the Queen Mother; though she apparently countenances Gonzalez Bravo, who pays assiduous court to her; the latter has the support of the French Ambassador, who at present has great influence at Madrid.

As Narvaez and Gonzalez Bravo are the master Spirits of the actual government, an open ["rubture" *altered to* "rupture"] between them might shake the whole to its foundations; exertions therefore are made, by the considerate and experienced of the party to prevent such a catastrophe, but there are so many young and hot heads at present in power, and there are such rivalries and jealousies at work, that it is next to impossible to maintain that unity of purpose and of action requisite to carry out any great scheme of policy.

Since I last wrote to the Department the decree subjecting the press to great restrictions, has been promulgated, and has been received with silent acquiescence. Some of the opposition papers are preparing to resume publication, subject to those restrictions. A decree is also in existence restoring to the clergy such of their confiscated lands as have not been sold. This measure is said to have been dictated by the religious feelings of the Queen Mother; and to have been strongly objected to by part of the Cabinet; from the embarrassment it might give to the Treasury and the clamours it might awaken among the people. It is likely, therefore, to be held in reserve for the present.

Among the various reports got up by alarmists, is that of a combination forming between the Carlists and the liberals, to compel a match between the Young Queen [Isabella II] and the eldest son of Don Carlos; or to revive the pretensions of the latter to the throne. Numbers of Carlist *facciosos* have been arrested making their way into Spain from the French frontier; and some of them have been shot according to the prompt dispensation of martial law.

While jealousies and intrigues are fermenting in the Capital, and seditions have been but recently stifled in the provinces, the Court is projecting an expedition into Catalonia, on the 8th of next month, to give the Young Queen the benefit of a change of air, and a course of mineral baths, prescribed by physicians as necessary for the cure of a cutaneous malady with which she has long been afflicted. This project of the Court is regarded by many with great solicitude; apprehending that it may bring the present differences between the party leaders to a crisis and produce some explosion. They observe that it was precisely a journey of the kind, to the same region, and ostensibly for the same purpose (the health of the Young Queen) that preceded the abdication and exile of Queen Christina, and the downfall of the moderado party in 1840. Madrid, they say, is too dangerous a capital to be left to its own internal fires.

Mr. [Angel] Calderon de la Barca, recently appointed Minister plenipotentiary to our Government, has just left Madrid for his place of destination, via France and England. I was desirous of having some further conversation with the Minister of State on the subject of Cuba, prior to the departure of Mr. Calderon; but have repeatedly been disappointed in seeking an interview, Ministers being so much engrossed at present by their own immediate interests and concerns, and the struggle to maintain their places. Indeed, Mr. Calderon himself has been unable to have a full explanation with the Ministry and has departed without his written instructions, which are to be sent after him. A proof of how little clear knowledge prevails here with respect to our Country and its concerns is that in a conversation with the Minister Mr. Calderon was charged to inform himself diligently of occurrences in Cuba, from every vessel that arrived from that island at Washington; the Minister having supposed Washington a Sea-port, in frequent intercourse with Havanna!

With such ignorance respecting us, it would not be surprising if the expressions drawn from our government by the application of the Chevalier D'Argaiz, with respect to the island of Cuba, should have inspired the Spanish Cabinet with some distrust as to our real motives. I am persuaded some such distrust has been felt, and I am apprehensive it may be fomented by England and France; both of whom (but especially the former) are jealous of our designs upon the island. I shall endeavor, whenever an opportunity presents, to remove any such doubt from the minds of Ministers and to impress them with the sincerity of our wish and determination to maintain Spain in the possession of the island.

Information, derived from an intelligent Spaniard, commercially connected with the island of Cuba, gives an alarming picture of the state of affairs there.

It seems beyond a doubt that, under the new Captain General, [Leopoldo] O'Donnell, slaves are again admitted in great numbers. Under [Jeronimo] Valdes, the former governor, who faithfully carried into effect the laws and treaties for the suppression of the slave trade, the traffic in a great measure declined, and many abandoned it, discouraged by the difficulties and losses attending its prosecution. These men have returned, or are returning to it under the present governor.

It is argued that the plantations and factories of Cuba cannot be kept up without fresh importations of negroes; there not being a sufficient number born in the island to keep up the necessary supply; few women being imported excepting for household service. It is true, the introduction of a large number of Africain males in the present excited condition of the blacks is hazardous in the extreme; but the proprietors of the plantations and factories are chiefly Spanish Capitalists, and they reason on the selfish principle, that, if affairs continue as they are for a few years only, their fortunes will be made, and withdrawn from the island; with the fate of which they ["they" *canceled*] will then be disconnected.

The Government of Spain appears to close its eyes to these dangers; and indeed could not, without timely and very urgent notice of troubles, send any considerable force for the protection of the island. The troops actually there are said to be about 20,000 men; one half of whom are regulars; the rest Militia. The Naval force consists of half a dozen vessels of various rates; the most efficient being two small steamers built some years since in the United States.

There is a general impression, among the planters, that the partial insurrections which occurred lately near Matanzas, were the result of a plan which extended throughout the island; and which still subsists, awaiting a favorable opportunity to strike a decisive blow.

In concluding I must again express my regret that I have so little information from home to guide me in respect to this delicate and critical subject; and that I have been left entirely in the dark as to the circumstances of the negotiation of the Chevalier D'Argaiz, which seems to have been so fruitful of doubts and jealousies. I feel this especially, whenever I have to converse with the Ministry here on the matter; fearing they may impute to a want of frankness that vagueness and reserve on certain points, which results from a want of full and accurate information. I am, Sir, very respectfully Your Ob[e]d[ien]t Serv[an]t, Washington Irving.

LS (No. 39) in DNA, RG 59 (State Department), Diplomatic Despatches, Spain, vol. 34 (M-31:34), received 5/20; LS in DNA, RG 84 (Foreign Posts), Spain, Despatches, 2:64–69; FC in NN, Berg Collection, Washington Irving Letterbook; PC in Aderman and others, eds., *Letters of Washington Irving*, 3:730–733. NOTE: Irving made brief corrections in his own hand and signed this letter, most of which is in another hand.

To WILLIAM R. KING, "Appointed Envoy Extraordinary and Minister Plenipotentiary U.S. to France"

Department of State
Washington, 23d April, 1844

Sir: Having received your letter of the 14th instant, notifying your acceptance of the appointment tendered to you by the President [John Tyler], as Envoy Extraordinary and Minister Plenipotentiary of the United States at Paris, and signifying your readiness to proceed upon your mission, I have now the honor to transmit to you your commission in that character, and a credential letter addressed to His Majesty the King of the French [Louis Philippe], together with an open copy of the same for your inspection and use. In presenting your letter of credence, you will take advantage of the occasion to express to His Majesty assurances of the earnest desire by which the President continues to be animated, to maintain unimpaired, and to strengthen, if possible, the very friendly relations so happily subsisting between the United States and France; and to that end the President relies with confidence upon your general knowledge of the situation and position of the two countries with regard to each other, and upon your experience and discretion, for a judicious coöperation in the cultivation and improvement of this good understanding between the parties.

You will also receive with this letter,

A set of printed personal Instructions.

A printed list of our diplomatic and consular agents abroad.

A letter of credit on the Bankers of the United States at London, authorizing them to pay your draughts for $8500 (balance of outfit,) for your salary as it becomes due, and for the contingent expenses of the Legation, actually incurred. You will be careful, however, in availing yourself of this authorization, to conform with the established rules of this Department, as detailed in the accompanying printed personal instructions.

A special passport for yourself.

A printed circular establishing a rule respecting salaries of Diplomatic Agents absent from their posts on leave.

A circular relative to the form of draughts on the Foreign intercourse Fund.

Mr. J[ohn] L. Martin, as you are already aware, has received the appointment of Secretary of the United States' Legation in France; and his immediate predecessor in that office, Mr. Henry Ledyard, at present Acting Chargé d'Affaires, has been requested to deliver over to you, on your arrival in Paris, the Archives, documents, and books, of the Legation, now in his possession.

Your salary, as fixed by law, is at the rate of nine thousand dollars per annum, with an outfit equal to one year's salary and a quarter's salary for your return. By a general rule the compensation of Ministers to Foreign Courts is made to commence with the date of their commissions, if they quit the United States to proceed on their missions within thirty days from that date, and to cease on their taking leave of the courts to which they are accredited, after the receipt of orders or permission to return home. In your case, however, it will begin on the 15th of the current month, the day on which, it is understood, you quitted your seat in the Senate.

The instructions of this Department to your predecessors in the mission—to which you are referred as embodying the views entertained by the existing administration of this Government—together with the other records and papers belonging to the Legation, will give you an adequate idea of the state of the relations between the United States and France. These are at present, and have long been, of the most friendly kind; and in entrusting them to your immediate charge and superintendence, the President indulges the confident hope, as I have already intimated, that no efforts will be spared on your part, to strengthen and confirm the sentiments of mutual good understanding and respect, prevailing between the two Nations, and which are not less honorable to the character, than advantageous to the interests, of the parties. Special instructions upon important points at issue between the two Governments, will be transmitted to you from time to time, as occasion for them may arise.

During your residence in France, you may sometimes be applied to, to interpose in behalf of American citizens to obtain satisfaction for claims which they may have on His Majesty's Government, or the redress of grievances which they may experience in the course of their dealings and transactions. You will, in all such cases where the intervention of the Government may be proper according to the public law, afford such official aid as may appear to you likely to be useful, whether you have special instructions from this Department or not. I am, Sir, with great respect, Your obedient servant, J.C. Calhoun.

LS (No. 1) in DNA, RG 84 (Foreign Posts), France, Instructions, Jan. 29, 1843– May 20, 1846; FC in DNA, RG 59 (State Department), Diplomatic Instructions, France, 15:2–4 (M-77:55); CCEx's in DNA, RG 46 (U.S. Senate), 28A-E3; PEx in *Congressional Globe,* 28th Cong., 2nd Sess., pp. 61–62; PEx in Senate Document No. 13, 28th Cong., 2nd Sess., pp. 2–3; PEx in the Washington, D.C., *Globe,* December 23, 1844, p. 2; PEx in the Washington, D.C., *Daily National Intelligencer,* December 24, 1844, p. 2.

From S. A. LAURENCE

New York [City,] 23d April 1844
Dear Sir, The distribution of Circulars, pamphlets, and private letters by our Committee favorable to the district system, and your nomination, has failed to accomplish all the objects contemplated; yet those documents, spread as they have been all over the U.S., have done much to satisfy the people, of the "equal and exact justice" of the district system, and the moral impos[s]ibility of electing Mr. [Martin] Van Buren, should he be nominated by the Baltimore Convention. That Convention, being acknowledged illegal, will *injure,* rather than favor, his position with the democratic party; and yet it is the *sole* reliance of his friends! They are possessed of the same infatuation, and reckless spirit, which broke down the party in 1840, and should they persist, and run him again, a result more disastrous and fatal to the democratic party will be the inevitable consequence. Many of his strong friends understand this to be his position and prospects; they for[e]see, if he falls, they go down with him, and

evidently begin to *falter*—many of them, acknowledge that you would have been their first choice, had a majority of the delegates been for you; that all they want is to take the Candidate of the people! In reply, I have uniformly stated, that our friends proposed the district system as the best, if not only plan, of ascertaining the full and fair expression of the party! that with a Convention, thus constituted, all would have been satisfied, and the nominee elected; and that that Convention would clearly express the public sentiment, and you would unquestionably have received the nomination.

There is evidently a fluttering in the camp! The nominee of the Baltimore Convention is still uncertain! the *rise* or *fall* of the democratic party *rests* upon that nomination! and yet I hope such powerful considerations and influences, will be brought to bear upon that Convention, as will force them, to do you justice. Your nomination, and *yours alone*, will command and receive the entire democratic vote, and succeed.

Mr. [John] Tyler's friends are making great exertions, but his case is similar to Mr. Van Buren's in 1840—he has very little to rely upon but the *public patronage*! which could not save Mr. Van Buren, altho' held and exercised under much more favorable circumstances. It is a prevailing opinion here that if Mr. Tyler could get the Bal[t]imore nomination, he would not be elected! altho he would probably pole more votes, than Mr. V[an] B[uren]. Your nomination, in the opinion of a *majority* of our Citizens, is the only proper[?] means of sustaining the democratic party, in its purity and strength, and prevent the success of the Whigs at the ensuing election. Your Southern friends, by compromising with Mr. Tyler, and not backing our early efforts, made a great, if not fatal, mistake! But if they will still come to the rescue, and co-operate with us in pushing your interest at Baltimore, your nomination may yet be made by that Convention. But in order to accomplish it, all your friends must be active and true; and, as many as possible be in Baltimore on or before the day of the meeting of the Convention. We can, and shall go in force from this City. I wish to be distinctly understood, that I regard a nomination of the Baltimore Convention, *worthless*, except so far as it will satisfy some of our friends, who honestly differ with us as to its legality, and are strong advocates for party discipline, and will vote for the nominee.

In making an amicable arrangement at Baltimore for uniting the party in the support of *one candidate*, the friends of those withdrawn, will of course expect to participate equally in the honors and emoluments of Office.

I observe by the papers, Charles G. Ferris is nominated to the Senate for Collector of the Customs for this port, and Ely Mo[o]re for Surveyor. They are both popular, influential men well qu[a]lified for the Offices, and entertain right *views* of *men* and *measures*. These appointments will be favorably received by our Citizens generally, and greatly weaken the Van Buren interest. I hope therefore to see their nominations promptly confirmed; and, if consistent with your own views, that your countenance and support may be extended to them.

Our Committee addressed a Circular to the South Carolina Central Committee, a few days ago, on subjects connected with the presidential nomination.

I pray leave to tender (rather late, but not the less sincere) my congratulations on your appointment of Secretary of State; and more especially for the manner and character of the invitation. It is not considered by your friends in this quarter, a party measure, but a voluntary call elicited by the mass of your fellow-citizens! and this it is, that renders it so highly honorable to you, and gratifying to your friends. I hope the result of your Official labors will not disappoint the expectations of your fellow-citizens; but that they will prove successful, in securing the annexation of Texas, & the settlement of the Oregon boundary line: and finally that all the measures connected therewith, will terminate satisfactorily and honorably to the U.S., to Mexico, and to yourself. Very respectfully and truly, y[ou]rs, S.A. Laurence.

ALS in ScCleA.

To J[ames] I. McKay, Chairman, House Committee on Ways and Means, 4/23. Calhoun calls the attention of the committee to a request [made by Abel P. Upshur] in 12/1843 for an appropriation for contingent expenses of the State Department. Funds available are "wholly inadequate" for the purpose of preparing reports on the foreign commerce of the U.S. that are requested by the House and Senate. FC in DNA, RG 59 (State Department), Accounting Records: Miscellaneous Letters Sent, 1832–1916, vol. for 2/1–9/30/1844, pp. 117–118; PC in House Document No. 242, 28th Cong., 1st Sess., p. 4.

To [John Y. Mason], Secretary of the Navy, 4/23. Calhoun asks for estimates of the cost of two steam packets of 450 horsepower each, to carry passengers and freight between the U.S. and France. "The views of the French government in regard to this subject are developed in a note from the French Minister to this Department, dated 20th June, 1842, a translation of which is herewith enclosed." LS with En in DNA, RG 45 (Naval Records), Letters from Federal Executive Agents, 1837–1886, 6:108 (M-517:2, frames 269–271); FC in DNA, RG 59 (State Department), Domestic Letters, 34:165–166 (M-40:32).

From A[lphonse] Pageot, [French Minister to the U.S.], 4/23. He asks for copies of Treasury Dept. circulars of 1843 concerning tariff duties on iron and steel and information about a recent Treasury Dept. decision on duties on "mixed silk goods" under which some French merchants may be due refunds. Translation and LS (in French) in DNA, RG 59 (State Department), Notes from Foreign Legations, France, vol. 12 (M-53:8, frames 705–708); CC (translation) in DNA, RG 56 (Treasury Department), Letters Received from Executive Officers, vol. for 1844, no. 17.

From J[AMES] C. PICKETT

Legation of the U. States
Lima, April 23, 1844

Sir: I have the honor to enclose herewith, a copy of a letter addressed by me to Commodore [Alexander J.] Dallas, which I was induced to write, in consequence of the violent and arbitrary proceedings of Lord [George] Paulet at the Sandwich Islands, last year. The Commodore takes the same view of the subject that I do, ["and" *canceled*] which I suppose to be undoubtedly the correct one, and if it is, the commanders of British vessels of war in these seas, ought to be made to know, that when they choose to play the buccaneer, they are not to meddle in any way, with the persons, property or commerce of our citizens, as his lordship did—most unjustifiably, I think.

It appears that the British Government has disapproved Lord Paulet's conduct, which was rather too outrageous to be formally sanctioned. It is my opinion though, notwithstanding the disavowal, that the restoration of King Kamehameha is nothing more than a respite and that Great Britain will some day or other, seize the Sandwich Islands as a counterpoise to the recent acquisitions of the French in the Pacific, unless she shall conclude to look elsewhere for an equivalent—to the Californias, to Cuba or to the Isthmus of

Panama, which (the Isthmus) Sir Walter Raleigh called "the Keys of the world," about 250 years ago; but it certainly is not of importance enough in the present day, to be so considered, whatever it may have been then.

It is supposed that a decisive engagement has taken place before now, between the armies commanded by Generals [Manuel] Vivanco and [Ramon] Castilla. They were near each other, 15 or 20 days ago, about 300 miles from Lima, on the road to Cuzco. I have the honor to be, with great respect, Sir, Your Ob[edien]t Servant, J.C. Pickett.

ALS (No. 92) with En in DNA, RG 59 (State Department), Diplomatic Despatches, Peru, vol. 6 (T-52:6, frames 478–482), received 6/22. NOTE: This despatch was addressed to A[bel] P. Upshur. James Chamberlayne Pickett (1793–1872) was a Kentuckian and a veteran of the War of 1812. He had held several federal posts before appointment as Chargé d'Affaires in Peru in 1838.

From [FRIEDRICH LUDWIG, BARON VON] ROENNE

Berlin, April 23d 1844

My dear Sir, I cannot express to you the pleasure it gave me when I heard of your appointment as Secretary of State, I only regret that I shall not be benefitted by it, as I may now consider it as certain, that I shall not return to the United States, my appointment as President of the "Office of Trade" (Handels-Amt) being now determined upon. It would have been my greatest delight to transact business with you as Secretary of State, for you know how much I love and esteem you and how great a value I place upon the friendship you always honoured me with. I hope this will be but the forerunner of a still higher office and that the people of the United States will be wise enough to bestow the highest office in their gift upon one so eminently fit to fill it—it would certainly form an epoch in the history of the United States, if they would elect you President, you would by your enlightened views bring about a radical change and we should hear no more of bribery and corruption. I hope to God and for the United States, to which I feel a great attachment, that this will come to happen. I regret in a thousand respects, that I am not to return to the United States, but then the King [Frederick William IV] is so very kind to me, that it would be ungrateful in me not to accept the place he has expressly created for me. It is to be a Ministry of Commerce in every sense of the word, only it is not for the present to bear that name, but to go by the more modest name of "Office of Trade" in order to reconcile conflicting interests and to avoid jealousy on the part of others. There is to be besides a Council of Trade consisting of myself and a number of Ministers, in which the King himself is to preside and in which all measures prepared by the Office of Trade will be finally determined upon. You will perceive two new features in the new institution, 1st the entire separation of commercial matters from the Ministry of Finance with which they were hitherto connected and 2d the provision, that merchants and manufacturers shall always be consulted upon every measure of importance; this is the first instance of a popular element in our administration upon which I insisted as most essential, indeed as indispensable. I hope my new position will also enable me to promote our intercourse with your country; I regret the new Office did not yet exist when the treaty with the United States was concluded; but although I might have wished it different in many respects, I still hope it will be confirmed, as it is indeed the beginning of a new and more liberal system. Mr. [Henry] Wheaton has done every thing in his power to bring this matter to a successful result; he is, as you know, a most excellent and distinguished man, and sorry as I should be to lose him here, as his friend I can but wish that his great desire of being sent to Paris may be accomplished.

I conceive that it is almost asking too much to be occasionally favoured by a few lines from you, but I beg you to be assured that such a token of your continued friendship for me would render me most happy. Believe me, my dear Sir, with the highest regard and esteem your most obed[ien]t serv[an]t, Roenne.

ALS in ScCleA; PC in Gunter Moltmann, "Eine Deutschland-Korrespondenz John C. Calhouns aus dem Jahre 1844," in *Jahrbuch fur Amerikastudien,* vol. XIV (1969), pp. 161–162.

From FERNANDO WOOD, "Private"

New York [City,] April 23 1844
Dear Sir, Being established here in business again it would be of very great service to me to have the appointment of *Despatch agent* of your Department. It is now in the hands of a person [William Henry LeRoy] who at all times (as he is now) has ["the" *altered to* "been"] the most unqualified opponent of yourself—principles &

party[.] The office is one belonging particularly and exclusively to the Secretary of State and is made by him without consultation with either the President or Senate—if I am informed correctly. My pecuniary circumstances induces me to ask it from your friendship and generosity. My business would be in no way interfered with and its compensation would be of very great service at this time. Very Truly Yours, Fernando Wood.

ALS in ScCleA.

From CH[ARLES] AUG[USTU]S DAVIS, "Private"

New York [City,] 24 Ap[ril] 1844

My D[ea]r Sir, My House addresses you to day officially on a matter of *Barratry* committed under our flag—a crime so fatal to any flag—if suffered to go unvisited by Govt. leads us to call y[ou]r attention to it. We have already had some correspondence with the Treasury Dept. on this subject—but as our last Letters from England furnish us these additional documents and as our London Correspondents also inform us that the British Govt. had Communicated or w[oul]d soon Communicate with their Minister at Wash[ingto]n I concluded it was best to send you the documents sent to us—and to respectfully suggest for your Consideration the Expediency and Propriety of issuing a Proclamation. It w[oul]d do more good than many publications offering a reward by Private individuals—and altho this Capt. may Escape—it w[oul]d go far to deter others from a like offence. A whole Commercial marine feels exceedingly sensitive in cases of this nature—and would be thankful and grateful on seeing such a crime visited by the Promptest action of Govt.

I take this occasion to add that by the last Steamer I have a Letter from my friend Mr. [Edward] Everett ["our Minister" *interlined*] at London dated 3d inst. They had rec[eive]d the day before the announcement of your appointment which seems to have given as much Satisfaction in London as it did here. And he was indulging Every hope that the next arrival would announce your acceptance. He is a worthy and excellent character and sensitively alive to the best interest and honor of our Country.

It gave me great Pleasure to tell him at the Period of your appointment that in all this quarter the highest Satisfaction was manifested. I hope you may be induced to snatch a few days for recreation and make our City a Visit. It w[oul]d gratify all—and none more than Y[ou]r Ob[edien]t Ser[van]t, Ch. Aug[ustu]s Davis.

ALS in DNA, RG 59 (State Department), Miscellaneous Letters (M-179:104, frames 227–228). NOTE: This letter was accompanied by a letter of the same date from Davis, Brooks & Co. concerning Capt. Samuel Denison of the ship *O.C. Raymond.* This American ship had been engaged by a British mercantile house to transport a cargo of precious metal from Chusan to Macao in China. Capt. Denison absconded and was subsequently reported in the Sandwich Islands (Hawaii) and then at Valparaiso, Chile, where he left his ship. The case led to an extensive correspondence, not included herein, of the State Department with the British Minister in Washington, various U.S. representatives around the world, and other parties. The stolen cargo was evidently valuable enough for the London commercial house involved to offer a reward of $5,000 in the case. Davis, Brooks & Co. were apparently business associates of the London house.

To Charles J. Ingersoll, Chairman, House Committee on Foreign Affairs, 4/24. Calhoun encloses a copy of his letter of today to [James I. McKay], the Chairman of the House Committee on Ways and Means, stating the necessity of appropriations for outfits for certain newly appointed diplomats. FC in DNA, RG 59 (State Department), Accounting Records: Miscellaneous Letters Sent, 1832–1916, vol. for 2/1–9/30/1844, p. [124].

To J[AMES] I. McKAY, Chairman of the Committee of Ways and Means, House of Representatives

Department of State
Washington, 24th April 1844

Sir, Ministers having been recently appointed to replace Gen[era]l Waddy Thompson Jr. at Mexico, who has resigned, and Mr. G[eorge] H. Proffit at Brazil; and a Chargé d'Affaires to Sardinia to succeed Mr. [Ambrose] Baber, and to Chile, in the place of Mr. [John S.] Pendleton, resigned, I have the honor to invite the attention of the Committee of Ways and Means to the necessity of providing for their outfit, either by a special appropriation, or, by making an addition to the item of appropriation for outfit in the bill now before the House of Representatives, for that purpose. The amount will be $27,000. I have the honor to be, Sir, Your obedient servant, J.C. Calhoun.

FC in DNA, RG 59 (State Department), Accounting Records: Miscellaneous Letters Sent, 1832–1916, vol. for 2/1–9/30/1844, p. 125; PC in House Document No. 242, 28th Cong., 1st Sess., pp. 4–5.

From J[ohn] L. Martin, Washington, 4/24. "At the request of Mr. W[illia]m E. Stubbs, I take pleasure in stating that he was employed by the [State] Department when I was connected with it, and that he proved himself capable, faithful, & obliging." ALS in ViU, Crallé-Campbell Papers.

From J[ohn] Y. Mason, [Secretary of the Navy], 4/24. "I have the honor to inform you in reply to your reference, that there is at present no vacancy in the grade of pursers; but when one occurs, the application of Mr. [Francis S.?] Claxton will be respectfully considered." LS in DNA, RG 59 (State Department), Miscellaneous Letters (M-179:104, frame 229); FC in DNA, RG 45 (Naval Records), Miscellaneous Letters Sent by the Secretary of the Navy, 33: 371 (M-209:12).

From J[OEL] R. POINSETT

White house PeeDee, near Georgetown
So[uth] Ca[rolina], April 24th 1844
Dear Sir, I take the liberty to transmit herewith a letter from Mr. Isaac Stone addressed to me, and beg to say, that he is I have reason ["to know" *interlined*] a very honest man & perfectly capable of fulfilling the duties of the office he solicits. I am Dear Sir very respectfully Your Ob[edien]t Serv[an]t, J.R. Poinsett.

ALS with En in DNA, RG 59 (State Department), Applications and Recommendations, 1837–1845, Stone (M-687:31, frames 418–420). NOTE: The enclosed letter of 3/28 from Stone to Poinsett asks assistance in obtaining the appointment of U.S. Consul at San Juan de los Remedios, Cuba. Found among Calhoun's papers at ScCleA is a letter from Stone to John Tyler, dated 2/7/1844, concerning the same appointment. This earlier letter carries Tyler's endorsement, probably directed to Abel P. Upshur, stating that he has no objection to the appointment.

From [EDWARD STUBBS]

[State Department] 24 April 1844
From a report made to Mr. [Abel P.] Upshur in July 1843 it appeared that there were then four extra clerks employed in the Department,

and that if they were to be continued during the fiscal year the expenditure would far exceed the amount appropriated for that branch of the service, which could only be met by a transfer from other heads of appropriation.

They have been continued and ["six" *changed to* "seven"] more are now employed, making in all eleven. The annexed statement shows that the expenditure for extra clerk hire to the 31st March exceeds the sum appropriated by the sum of $3639
to which may be added the compensation of the
clerks now employed, for the quarter,   3042

making a deficiency of $6681.

The probable surplusses that may be transferred are, from the heads of,

Stationery &c	200
Labor &c	400
Printing & advertising	800
Miscellaneous	300
Books & maps	200
	1900

Leaving a probable deficiency of $4781.

In addition to the appropriations for the current fiscal year there was a balance of former appropriations remaining, not restricted to specific heads,
amounting to   6852.87
from which it is presumed the deficiency may be paid.

There may, also, be a surplus of the amount appropriated under the head of Publishing &c and packing and distributing laws &c, but, it is not possible to estimate at this time what that surplus may be. It is not considered safe to make any dependance upon it.

The present fiscal year is the first in which appropriations for the Contingent Expenses of the Department, including publishing and distributing the laws, have been subdivided into specific heads. They were previously made in one gross sum. Hence the difficulty of estimating correctly for each separate head of expenditure. This however is remedied by the power given of transferring the surplus in any one head to any other which may require it.

ADU with En in ScCleA. NOTE: Edward Stubbs was the Disbursing Agent of the State Department. The "annexed statement" is an enclosed table showing the amounts appropriated under nine categories of contingent expenses for the fiscal year ending 6/30/1844, with the amount already spent and that remaining to be spent in each category. Found among Calhoun's papers at ScCleA are two documents from Stubbs to Abel P. Upshur that are probably related to the above document. One, dated 7/31/1843, concerns the payment of part-time Clerks. The other, undated, itemizes projected contingent expenditures for the year beginning 7/1/1843. Also in the same collection is another document, undated and unaddressed, which is a memorandum discussing the contingent expenses of the department before and after 7/1/1843, which document is probably related to the others.

From HENRY WHEATON

Berlin, 24 April, 1844

My dear Sir, This Letter will be handed you by Mr. Louis Mark, our Consul for Bavaria & the Prussian Rhine Provinces. I have deemed it necessary to request Mr. Mark to proceed once more to Washington as bearer of despatches, & to give the necessary explanations respecting the late negotiations here, which he is perfectly competent to do from his practical knowledge of the commercial relations of the two ["Countries" *interlined*] & having personally attended at the different conferences which terminated in the conclusion of the Treaty of the 25 March.

As Mr. Mark did not determine to go until the last moment, & as he proceeded *directly* to London without coming here, it was not in my power to ["send" *canceled and* "give" *interlined*] him a Letter of introduction in time to take with him. I therefore send this by the first Steam-packet, begging to recommend Mr. Mark to your kind attentions & confidence. I am, my dear Sir, ever truly & respectfully your faithful friend & servant, Henry Wheaton.

ALS in ScCleA. NOTE: On 2/14/1844 Edward Everett had written to Secretary of State Abel P. Upshur concerning an earlier phase of Mark's activities as U.S. bearer of despatches, during which Mark had been detained by British customs officials at Liverpool. LS with Ens in DNA, RG 59 (State Department), Diplomatic Despatches, Great Britain, vol. 52 (M-30:48).

From W[ILLIA]M WILKINS, Secretary of War

War Department
April 24, 1844

Sir, I respectfully transmit, herewith, an extract of the proceedings, containing the opinion, of the Court of Inquiry held at Fort Leavenworth, Missouri, under the orders of the President [John Tyler], in the case of Captain [Philip St. George] Cooke of the U.S. Dragoons, in relation to the discharge of the duty assigned to him for the protection of the Caravan of Santa Fe traders over the territory of the United States to the Texan frontier in May and June 1843. Very respectfully Your ob[edien]t Serv[an]t, Wm. Wilkins, Secretary of War.

[Enclosure]

Adjutant General's Office

Washington, April 24, 1844

Extract of the proceedings of the Court of Inquiry held at Fort Leavenworth, Mo., in the month of April, pursuant to "General Orders" No. 6, dated February 28th, 1844, instituted by order of the President, "to examine into and report the facts respecting the manner in which Captain P. St. George Cooke, of the United States Dragoons, discharged the duties assigned to him for the protection of the caravan of Santa Fe traders over the territory of the United States to the Texan frontier in May and June, 1843—whether, in his march he disarmed the Texan force under Colonel [Jacob] Snively; if so, in what territory, and in what manner; and whether his conduct was harsh and unbecoming."

"The Opinion."

In view of the foregoing facts, the Court is of opinion, that Captain P. St. George Cooke, of the Regiment of United States Dragoons, on the 30th of June 1843, disarmed a Texan force under Colonel Snively, within the territory of the United States, by causing them to lay down their arms, under an appropriate exhibition of military force of United States Dragoons; and that there was nothing in the conduct of Captain Cooke that was "harsh and unbecoming." The Court is further of opinion that Captain Cooke did not exceed the authority for the protection of the lawful trade of the Santa Fe caravan, "derived from the Orders of the Secretary of War to the Commanding General of the Army, dated March 28th, 1843, and of the Adjutant General to Colonel Kearny, dated March 29th, 1843;" and that the confidence reposed in him by his government was not "in any degree misplaced."

The Court then adjourned sine die[.] (Signed) H[enry] S. Turner, 1 Lieut[enant] & Adj[utan]t Dragoons, Recorder of Court. (Signed) S[tephen] W. Kearny, Col. U.S. Dragoons, President of Court. True copy: R[oger] Jones, Adj[utan]t Gen[era]l.

LS with En in DNA, RG 59 (State Department), Miscellaneous Letters (M-179: 104, frames 232–234); FC in DNA, RG 107 (Secretary of War), Letters Sent Relating to Military Affairs, 1800–1861, 25:316 (M-6:25); CC with Ens in

Tx, Andrew Jackson Houston Papers; CC with En in Tx, Records of the Texas Republic Department of State, U.S. Diplomatic Correspondence; FC with En in Tx, Records of the Texas Republic Dept. of State, Copybooks of Letters Received from Texan and Foreign Representatives, vol. 2-1/98, pp. 526–527.

From J[oseph] A. Woodward, [Representative from S.C.], 4/24. Woodward asks that Calhoun give C[harles] P. Pelham [tutor in Classics at South Carolina College] letters to [Henry] Wheaton and [Edward] Everett, U.S. Ministers [to Prussia and Great Britain]. Pelham is going to Europe to pursue his studies of Greek and Roman literature. ALS in DNA, RG 59 (State Department), Miscellaneous Letters (M-179:104, frame 230).

To P[ierre] E. Bossier, [Representative from La.], 4/25. Calhoun acknowledges Bossier's letter of 4/23 and will give "respectful consideration" to Thomas D. Hailes for an appointment as U.S. Consul at some southern port. FC in DNA, RG 59 (State Department), Domestic Letters, 34:154–155 (M-40:32).

From Sidney Breese, [Senator from Ill.], 4/25. Breese asks Calhoun to place an enclosed letter among the despatches to [Wilson] Shannon, U.S. Minister [to Mexico]. The enclosed letter asks that Shannon attempt to obtain the freedom of a U.S. citizen [Pierre Menard Maxwell] imprisoned in the castle of Perote. ALS in DNA, RG 59 (State Department), Miscellaneous Letters (M-179:104, frame 237).

From EDWARD EVERETT

London, 25 April 1844

Sir, In my despatch No. 109, I reported to you the substance of a conversation which I had incidentally had with Lord Aberdeen, on the subject of the convention recently negotiated by Mr. [Henry] Wheaton with the Prussian government, on behalf of the German Zoll-Verein, from which it appeared that this government was disposed to consider, that, in virtue of the commercial convention of July 1815 between Great Britain and the United States, Great Britain would become entitled unconditionally to all the privileges stipulated by that convention to the Zoll-Verein.

The subject of Mr. Wheaton's convention was brought up last

evening in the House of Commons by Dr. [John] Bowring, who stated its provisions in substance, as they had been represented to him and enquired of the government, whether they had received any information as to the negotiation of such a treaty, "which," he added according to the report, "would exercise a most prejudicial effect upon the interests of British Industry."

Sir Robert Peel in reply to this enquiry said, that the information was substantially correct; but that the convention had not yet been ratified. It required the sanction of the Executive government of the United States and of two thirds of the Senate. Mr. [Henry] Labouchere observed, that he was under the impression that the United States could not, in conformity with their commercial convention with Great Britain, admit the products of any other country on terms more favorable than those on which the same articles are admitted from England. "If he was correct in this opinion," Mr. Labouchere is reported to have added, "any reduction of duties made by the United States in favor of the Prussian or German manufactures, must be equally extended to the manufactures of Great Britain."

Sir Robert Peel rose again and stated, that this question had been taken into consideration by the government; but since the treaty alluded to had not yet, as he had already observed, been ratified, he thought it advisable at present not to enter farther into details, but to content himself with stating, that the subject had not escaped his attention. He then added, according to the report in the papers, that there were two kinds of commercial treaties. Under one class it was agreed by one nation that another should be put on the footing of the most favored nation unconditionally and without any equivalent being given; and by another description of treaties it was stipulated, that this should be done freely, if the same concession were made freely to another country, and on allowing the same equivalent, if the concession were conditional. The treaty existing between the United States and Great Britain, he observed in conclusion, was of the former description.

Although the above report of what passed last evening on this subject is not probably exact to the letter; and although the morning papers, which I have seen, differ considerably as to the words used by Sir Robert Peel in his concluding remark, there is no doubt that he expressed himself substantially as I have stated. It is clear from what fell from him on this occasion, taken in connection with what was said to me by Lord Aberdeen as reported in my despatch 109, that this government is prepared to take the ground that, in virtue of the convention of July 1815, between Great Britain and the United States, the former is entitled to any reduction of duties, which we may stipulate by special agreement and on specific conditions to any other power.

Whatever countenance may be afforded by the letter of the convention of 1815 to this construction, it is of course entirely at war with its spirit. I shall be careful to keep you advised of any farther indications of the views here taken of this interesting subject; or the course which it may be in contemplation to pursue. I am, sir, very respectfully your obedient servant, Edward Everett.

LS (No. 115) in DNA, RG 59 (State Department), Diplomatic Despatches, Great Britain, vol. 52 (M-30:48), received 5/20; FC in MHi, Edward Everett Papers, 48:502–506 (published microfilm, reel 22, frames 1297–1299). NOTE: This despatch was addressed to John Nelson as Secretary of State ad interim.

To FRANKLIN GAGE, U.S. Consul at Cardenas, [Cuba]

Department of State
Washington, Ap[ri]l 25 [18]44

Sir: Your communication dated the 1st instant has been received at this Department.

In the present disturbed state of the Island of Cuba, it is more than probable that great outrages will be committed on the rights and liberties of the white residents, especially of our citizens. It is amongst your first duties to inquire into and report to this Department all such cases as may come to your knowledge, and to exert your full powers to protect those who are entitled to our protection. You should consult freely and frequently with the Consul of the United States at the Havana [Robert B. Campbell], who will be instructed to cooperate with you, and exert with him your united influence and authority to preserve uninjured, the persons and property of our citizens against all unlawful acts. Firm and resolute appeals to the civil Authorities, in all cases affecting the rights and liberties of neutrals, may not be without a beneficial influence. If these fail, you will report the matter fully to this Department, each case specifically, in order that it may direct its future action in regard to them. I am, Sir, &c, J.C. Calhoun.

FC in DNA, RG 59 (State Department), Consular Instructions, 10:240–241.

From Cha[rle]s Gould, New York [City], 4/25. Gould introduces Jed Frye to Calhoun. Frye is a very respectable member of P.J. Farnham & Co. of New York City. "His business is with the State Department—arising out of the seizure of his barque Jones by the English." ALS in DNA, RG 59 (State Department), Miscellaneous Letters (M-179:104, frames 235–236).

From BEN E. GREEN

Legation of the U.S. of A.
Mexico, April 25th 1844

Sir, I have the honor to send you a note [dated 4/13] of the Minister of Foreign Affairs [José M. de Bocanegra], in which he says that Mr. [J.F.] McGregor, recently appointed Consul of the U.S. for Campeche, being a Mexican citizen, the permission of the Mexican Congress is necessary, before an exequatur can be issued in his favor. As the Congress has now adjourned, and it is generally believed that Santa Anna will never suffer it to meet again, it may be some time before that permission can be obtained.

As yet I have not been able to do anything with the Convention. The Mexican Minister of Foreign Affairs has always some excuse for delay. The only way to bring them to the point is to fix a day for them to answer, definitively, whether they will agree to our propositions, or not. I have not, however, felt authorized to take so decisive a step on the eve of the arrival of the new Minister, & without instructions.

In addition to the difficulties mentioned in my despatch of the 8th inst[ant], the newspapers from the U.S. have of late come freighted with the subject of the annexation of Texas. Annexation is spoken of as the subject of serious deliberation with our Govt., and as a very probable event. While this subject is pending, this Govt. will not act upon the convention, unless forced to do so.

It has been rumoured for some time that Messrs. Trigueros and Bocanegra are to leave the Ministry; and that Gen[era]l [J.M.] Tornel is to go into the Foreign Office and D[on] Manuel Escandon into the Treasury. I hope this may not be so; for Gen[era]l Tornel hates us with a most envenomed spite, and Escandon is no friend to us; but a warm friend of England and her late Minister here, Mr. Packenham [*sic*; Richard Pakenham].

I send you files of the Diario, and the Siglo XIX of the 19th April, in which you will see an article upon Texas, & the condition of the northern provinces. The discontent in New Mexico has forced them to reopen the frontier trade. Taos, Paso del Norte, and Presidio del norte have been made ports of entry. I have the honor to be Very Respectfully Your ob[edien]t Serv[an]t, Ben E. Green.

ALS (No. 3) and En (with State Department translation) in DNA, RG 59 (State Department), Diplomatic Despatches, Mexico, vol. 12 (M-97:13); FC in DNA, RG 84 (Foreign Posts), Mexico, Despatches, pp. 491–492; draft in NcU, Duff Green Papers (published microfilm, roll 5, frames 438–441).

To ALLEN A. HALL, [Caracas]

Department of State
Washington, 25th April, 1844

Sir: Your despatches Nos. 31 and 32, have been received. The information which they communicate in regard to the adjustment of the claim in the case of the brig Morris, is acceptable and I lose no time in acquainting you that the terms of that adjustment are approved by the President [John Tyler]. They have also been approved by the agent of Mr. H[enry] H. Williams, who is understood to be the principal claimant in the case.

You will consequently inform the Venezuelan government that the government of the United States, actuated by a spirit of compromise and by a desire to bring this long pending subject to a close and thereby to remove one of our few causes of complaint against that government, is willing to receive the sum offered as a full indemnification on the part of Venezuela.

When the money is paid, if, from the papers and vouchers in your possession, you should be satisfied that Mr. H.H. Williams is in fact the principal claimant, and that in the prosecution of the claim he has represented the other claimants, you may remit the amount as he may direct, being careful, however, to require such acknowledgements from him as will secure the department from any future accountability in the matter. If, on the contrary you should doubt the propriety of paying the money at once to Mr. Williams or to his order, you will remit the same to the United States, either in good bills, payable to the order of the department, or in specie, to be deposited to the credit of the department at the port where the vessel which brings the specie may arrive. I am, Sir, your obedient servant, J.C. Calhoun.

LS (No. 19) in DNA, RG 84 (Foreign Posts), Venezuela; FC in DNA, RG 59 (State Department), Diplomatic Instructions, Venezuela, 1:47–48 (M-77:171); CC in DNA, RG 76 (Records of Boundary and Claims Commissions and Arbitrations), Miscellaneous Claims Records.

To [James H.] Hammond, Governor [of S.C.]

25th April [1844]

My dear Sir, I transmit the enclosed unofficial note [*not found*] of the British minister, merely as an act of courtesy without ["without" *canceled*] wishing the fact that it passes through my hand to have the least weight with you. I have complied with the request of Mr. [Richard] Pakenham only in reference to yourself. Truly, J.C. Calhoun.

ALS in DLC, James Henry Hammond Papers, vol. 11. NOTE: The subject of this letter is elucidated by later Calhoun-Hammond correspondence and by a despatch from Pakenham to Lord Aberdeen, the British Secretary of State for Foreign Affairs on 4/28. Pakenham wrote that in compliance with instructions he had "addressed a note to Mr. Calhoun requesting that the sentence of death, passed [in S.C.] on Mr. J. Browne supposed to be a British subject, for having aided in the escape of a Slave, might be reversed or commuted. Mr. Calhoun states he has no power to prevent such an execution, but will forward any letter on the subject, Mr. Pakenham may address to him, to the Gov[erno]r of the State, who alone possesses the power of preventing the sentence being carried into execution." FC in British Museum, Aberdeen Papers, folio 74.

From Rob[er]t Monroe Harrison

Consulate of the United States
Kingston Jam[aic]a, 25th April 1844

Sir, I do myself the honor to inform you that the United States Ship "Preble" Capt. [Thomas W.] Freelon arrived here on the 17th inst. and after receiving some supplies which she required, sailed from hence for Aux Cayes on the 23rd inst. inconsequence of the revolutionary State of the Island of San Domingo, where the property as well as lives of many of our fellow citizens are greatly exposed.

Vessels are constantly arriving from that unfortunate Island crowded with Refugees consisting mostly of white and brown persons.

By a private letter from San Domingo addressed to a friend of mine I understand that the French Brig of War Oriel was to sail from Port au Prince on the 24th with three members of the Haitians Legislature on board for the City of San Domingo probably bound on some political Mission in which the French are Concerned. With great respect I have the honor to be Sir Your Ob[edien]t and most humble Servant, Robt. Monroe Harrison.

LS (No. 281) in DNA, RG 59 (State Department), Consular Despatches, Kingston, vol. 8 (T-31:8), received 5/19.

From W[illia]m Kennedy, Philadelphia, 4/25. He asks Calhoun's assistance in securing an appointment for his son, David H. Kennedy, a civil engineer, as supervisor for a public work in Del. which is contemplated in an appropriation now before Congress. ALS in DNA, RG 59 (State Department), Applications and Recommendations, 1837–1845, Kennedy (M-687:18, frames 190–191).

From J[ohn] L. Martin, Washington, 4/25. He accepts appointment as "Secretary of the Legation of the United States at Paris," as offered in Calhoun's letter of 4/18. ALS in DNA, RG 59 (State Department), Diplomatic Despatches, France, vol. 30 (M-34:33).

From WILLIAM PAGE

Boston, 25th April 1844

It being intimated to me that it was thought a change would soon be made in the Office of the Consul at Paris—and that my own expectation of that appointment, in such an event, might be as reasonably entertained as that of any other person, but that it would be necessary a personal application therefor should be made to the Department of State over which you preside—I have the honor, Sir, to make this application to you for that appointment.

Such representations as may be expected to be produced I believe will be offered me by those who will cheerfully give me their assistance in this purpose when from any hope I may be allowed of its need, I may be encouraged to ask it of them. Yours Most Obediently, William Page.

ALS in DNA, RG 59 (State Department), Applications and Recommendations, 1837–1845, Page (M-687:25, frames 18–19).

From W[illia]m Parmenter, [Representative from Mass.], 4/25. He encloses a letter [*not found*] from William Barry of Framingham, Mass., a clergyman "of great respectability and of a high order of intellect," and endorses the wishes [for an appointment to office] expressed by Barry. ALS in DNA, RG 59 (State Department), Applications and Recommendations, 1837–1845, Barry (M-687:1, frames 897–898).

From S[tephen] Pleasonton, [Fifth Auditor], Treasury Department, 4/25. Albert Smith, the Commissioner for marking the northeastern boundary line under the Treaty of Washington, has submitted accounts that include more than $3,000 for the services in 1843 of three civilian engineers and of two commissaries. The statute of 3/-3/1843 called for the assignment of Army Topographical Engineers, not civilian engineers, to the task, and the former were made available in ample number; and the law did not provide for the employment of commissaries. Pleasonton declines to pay the account without "the sanction of the Secretary of State." LS with En in DNA, RG 59 (State Department), Letters Received from the Fifth Auditor and Comptroller, 1829–1862; FC in DNA, RG 217 (General Accounting Office), Fifth Auditor: Letters Sent, 5:120.

To James H. Williams, U.S. C[onsul], "Sidney," N[ew] S[outh] Wales, 4/25. In response to recommendations to the State Dept. that a Commercial Agent be appointed at Freemantle, on the western side of N.S.W. and that Samuel Moore, a merchant there, be appointed, Calhoun suggests that Williams appoint Moore unless there is some reason why he should not. FC in DNA, RG 59 (State Department), Consular Instructions, 12:79–80.

From G E O [RGE] M. B I B B,
[former Senator from Ky.]

Louisville, April 26, 1844

My dear friend, Since I heard of the unanimous approval ["of" *altered to* "by"] the Senate of your nomination as Secretary of State, & of your acceptance, various resolves have passed through my mind to write to you, to congratulate (not so much you personally, for under the existing state of political fermentations I am not prepared to say that you have done any more than to give another Evidence that with you love of country rises above all selfish considerations), my country that at a critical period of affairs, the president has selected a counsellor so sound in his feelings & so capable to advise for the best.

A chance, (which often decides the fate of mighty affairs,) has brought forth this letter, which [( ]not touching the great affairs of state) will inform you that I am ("Semper Eadem") unchanged in political opinions, and in no degree chilled in my feelings towards you. I labour in my office of Chancellor for ab[ou]t nine months in the year about fifteen hours out of the twenty four of each day, & for the residue of the year, upon a[n] average, about Eight hours ["for" *altered to* "of"] the day. This leaves me no time for, writing political essays, nor mingling in political discussions.

My brother in law Dudley Walker, who married Jane Ashton, the sister of Mrs. Bibb, suddenly made his appearance at my house, on his way to Washington; & had but a few hours to tarry. You knew him formerly, but as I did not know ["him" *interlined*] upon sight, after an absence of more than nine years, I resolved that I would give him a letter to you, knowing that his opinions & good wishes towards you fully corresponded formerly, as now, with my own.

What Matters of business take him to Washington I know not. But I can confidently recommend him to your civilities & notice as true & upright in his dealings, & worthy of your confidence.

I dare affirm that you are so well assured by past acts, that I have been in the habit of making my friends your friends, that to say so at this time, would lack the freshness of novelty.

If you will so manage as to annex Texas to the United States, either, by treaty approved by the Senate, or by the vote of the Congress of the U. States, which latter mode I think preferable, you shall be advanced, in my estimation, from "Magnus" to "Major" Apollo— And if in addition to that you can so manage as [to] allay the fev[e]rish temper in relation ["of" *altered to* "to"] Oregon, so as to give time & patience for future events; or adjust the question between the U. States & Great Britain by a treaty, you shall be "Maximus Apollo."

Whilst you remain the Secretary of the department of State & friend [John] Tyler Pres[iden]t, ["politics" *altered to* "political"] parties may rave, & roar, & whistle, I shall repose in confidence that no harm will be done. As ever your friend, Geo. M. Bibb.

ALS in ScCleA. NOTE: Bibb endorsed this letter "By Mr. Dudley Walker," who probably hand-delivered it to Calhoun. An AEU by Calhoun reads "Judge

Bibb." Within three months Bibb joined Calhoun in the Cabinet, as Secretary of the Treasury.

From STEEN BILLE

Philadelphia, 26th April 1844

The Undersigned Chargé d'affaires from Denmark, has been directed by his Government, with a view to the erroneous impressions, to which the report of the late Secretary of State, Mr. [Abel P.] Upshur, to the President of the United States, bearing date the 24th of Nov[em]b[e]r 1843, on the subject of the Sound Dues, and which was transmitted to Congress by the last annual message of the President might so easily give rise, and actually has done so, to express the deep regret, felt by His Majesty's Government, that Mr. Upshur should have made a report of the above description, so entirely at variance with the previous Note of the 27th of June 1842 on the same subject, addressed to the Undersigned by the Hon[ora]ble Daniel Webster as the then Secretary of State, without any regard whatever to those considerations, upon which a Government, entertaining the most friendly relations with the United States believed it had a fair and just right to calculate.

The Undersigned does not feel himself called upon to enter upon any discussion of the subject matter of the said report, and the less so, as his Government relies with the fullest confidence on the disposition, manifested in the Note of Mr. Webster, above alluded to, on the part of the United States Government, while the present Note, by the direction of His Majesty's Government, has for its sole object, to obviate any inference, that possibly might be drawn, though without any adequate cause, from any further silence upon the subject on its part.

In conclusion the Undersigned begs leave to observe, that in his Note to Mr. Webster of the 20th of June 1842, he expressly declared, that the lowering of topsails at the Castle of Cronborg, complained of by Mr. Webster, had been dispensed with, and a display of the national colours of the vessel only required, as both proper and expedient, referring at the same time, in corroboration thereof, to the 25 § of the printed Rules and Regulations of the Sound, as submitted to the Secretary of State of the United States at the time, and through him to the President; In the face of this declaration, so supported, Mr. Upshur has in his said report asserted it as a grievance against

Denmark, that the vessels of the United States still continued to lower their topsails at the castle of Cronborg, which is by no means the case; But from the positive manner, in which the assertion was made, the Undersigned deemed it proper, to refer the matter to his Government before he took up the subject, which, however, he has now the honor of doing, having been instructed by his Government, from an anxiety that such error should be corrected, to reiterate, in an unqualified manner, his former declaration to the effect above stated.

The Undersigned avails himself of this occasion to tender to the Secretary of State the assurance of his high and distinguished consideration. Steen Bille.

ALS in DNA, RG 59 (State Department), Notes from Foreign Legations, Denmark, vol. 2 (M-52:2, frames 93–95).

To R[OBERT] B. CAMPBELL, U.S. Consul, Havana

Department of State
Washington, Ap[ri]l 26 [18]44

Sir: I transmit to you a copy of a letter [of 4/1] received at the Department from Mr. [Franklin] Gage, U.S. Consul at Cardenas, together with a copy of one [of 4/25] in answer to it, in relation to a servile insurrection in that neighborhood.

The Department is confident that the advice and assistance which Mr. Gage is instructed to ask of you will be fully and freely given, and that no exertion on your part will be spared to protect the persons and property of our citizens in the Island. I am, Sir, &c, J.C. Calhoun.

FC in DNA, RG 59 (State Department), Consular Instructions, 10:241.

From SAM[UE]L HAIGHT

Consulate of the United States
Antwerp, April 26th 1844

Sir, I had the honor on the 4th of Jan[uar]y last to forward my semi annual Consular acc[oun]ts, which I trust have been duly received at the Department.

I deem it my duty at the present time very respectfully to call your attention to the great decrease of our Carrying trade with this Kingdom, which is now almost entirely monopolised by vessels of foreign nations, principally of Sweden and the Hanseatic Towns. From the commencement of the present year up to this time, out of nearly thirty Vessels which have arrived at this place from the various ports of the United States, only five, have been American the others were Hanseatic and Swedes. From this state of things it is but too apparent, that if our Government continues to permit the present reciprocal treaties with those Countries to remain in force, we shall not only lose, the entire carrying trade of Belgium but also that of Russia, Austria, and the different Governments, of the North of Europe. I have been recently informed by an intelligent merchant residing in Sweden that a very large number of vessels are now building in that Country for the purpose of taking advantage of our trade. They are built of large Capacity and in every respect similar to our ships, and from the cheapness of their mode of living and the extreme low wages, paid their Crews, they can afford to take freights at much less rates than our own vessels, and consequently will be enabled at all times to obtain business, whilst American vessels will be forced to lie idle in the docks.

I am further informed that not more than six vessels of our flag visit in the course of a Year the Ports of Sweden, whilst in the same period of time upwards of one Hundred Swedish Ships arrive in the different ports of the United States and are there loaded for Places principally out of their own Kingdom.

Trusting that these remarks may not be deemed inappropriate at this particular time, when the attention of the Government is being turned towards this subject, I submit them with great deference to your high consideration. I have the honor to be Sir, Your ob[e]d[ien]t Servant, Saml. Haight, U.S. Consul.

ALS in DNA, RG 59 (State Department), Consular Despatches, Antwerp, vol. 3 (T-181:3), received 5/20.

To J[oseph] R. Ingersoll, [Representative from Pa.], 4/26. In reply to Ingersoll's letter of 4/19, Calhoun states that it is not advisable for the U.S. to appoint another Consul in Australia, there being two there already. However, Mr. [Samuel] Moore will be appointed a Consular Agent if it is not deemed inexpedient by the Consul within whose jurisdiction Freemantle lies. FC in DNA, RG 59 (State Department), Domestic Letters, 34:155 (M-40:32).

From DANIEL P. KING, [Representative from Mass.]

House of Representatives, April 26, 1844
Sir, Will you permit me to ask your attention to the petition [of 9/-
1843] of many merchants of Massachusetts for the appointment of
Joseph Warren Fabens to the office of consul at Cayenne [French
Guiana].

The application is supported by the favorable representations of
the late Collector of the port of Boston, Mr. [David] Henshaw, and
of the present collector, Mr. [Robert] Rantoul [Jr.]. I have great
pleasure in being able to recommend Mr. Fabens as a gentleman who
by his habits, education and character is every way qualified for the
appointment. I have the honor to be With great respect Your obedient servant, Daniel P. King.

ALS in DNA, RG 59 (State Department), Applications and Recommendations,
1837–1845, Fabens (M-687:11, frames 20–21).

From W[ILLIAM] L. MARCY

Albany, April 26, 1844
Sir: Mr. Aaron Leggett one of the claimants before the late Mexican
Commission discovered after the award was made in his ["case" canceled and "favor" interlined] and after the commission had expired,
sufficient cause ["as he thought" interlined] for opening his case. It
was one of the most important that came before the board, and the
transactions involved in the investigation of it multifarious and complicated. He applied to the government to interpose in his behalf.
Judge [Abel P.] Upshur, your predecessor, thought Mr. Leggett had
made out a case which warranted the interference of the government. As I was quite familiar with the whole case Mr. Leggett prevailed on me to visit Washington last ["fal" canceled] November
["last" interlined and then canceled] to make some statements and
explanations in relation to his case to the then Secretary of State.

I am aware that the documents which Mr. L[eggett] has presented
to the department are very voluminous and I can hardly expect that
you will find leisure to examine them. The main grounds on which
Mr. Leggett rests his application and claims the interposition of his
government were disclosed in a paper which I in behalf of Mr.
L[eggett] presented to your predecessor. That is not long and will

show, though imperfectly, the views and wishes of the applicant. He is exceedingly desirous that you should look into his case and at his instance I have take the liberty to address you on the subject & invite your attention to it. Mr. Leggett was certainly a great sufferer by the misconduct of the Mexican authorities and the amount allowed by the Umpire was far short of that which the American Commissioners thought he was justly entitled to. He does not however seek relief on account of the inadequacy of the sum allowed, but on account of frauds and forgeries which he supposes produced this inadequacy and have been brought to light since the board was dissolved. I have the honor to be with great respect your Ob[edien]t Serv[an]t, W.L. Marcy.

ALS in DNA, RG 59 (State Department), Miscellaneous Letters (M-179:104, frames 238–239). NOTE: Marcy was a former Governor of N.Y. and had been a member of the expired Mexican Claims Commission.

To [RICHARD] PAKENHAM

Department of State
Washington, April 26, 1844

The Undersigned, Secretary of State of the United States, has the honor to acknowledge the receipt of a note addressed to him by the Right Honorable Mr. Pakenham, Envoy Extraordinary and Minister Plenipotentiary of Her Britannic Majesty, of date the 18th instant, with the accompanying copy of the memorial of Mr. William Black, President of the Legislative Council, addressed to His Excellency the Governor and Commander-in-Chief of the Province of New Brunswick.

The Undersigned has attentively considered the subject of the said memorial; and, without entering into the merits of the claim, begs leave to observe, that, by the fourth article of the treaty of Washington, claims of the character under consideration, when established according to the laws of the States wherein the property lies, are, in express terms, fully confirmed and quieted. The question seems to belong exclusively to the civil jurisdiction of the States; and all that appears necessary to be done on the part of this claimant is to produce the evidences of his title, before the proper tribunal in Maine, in order, under the treaty, to have such title confirmed to him in due form of law.

The Undersigned tenders to Mr. Pakenham the assurance of his distinguished consideration. J.C. Calhoun.

FC in DNA, RG 59 (State Department), Notes to Foreign Legations, Great Britain, 7:10–11 (M-99:36); CC in DNA, RG 76 (Records of Boundary and Claims Commissions and Arbitrations), Miscellaneous Claims Records: Great Britain, Convention of Feb. 8, 1853; PC in House Document No. 110, 29th Cong., 1st Sess., pp. 34–35.

To J[ohn] C. Spencer, Secretary of the Treasury, 4/26. He encloses to Spencer a copy of [Alphonse] Pageot's letter [of 4/23] and asks that the information he requested [concerning tariff duties on iron, silk, and steel] be furnished. LS in DNA, RG 56 (Treasury Department), Letters from Executive Officers, 1844, no. 16.

From ROBERT WALSH, "Private"

Paris, 26th[?] April 1844

Dear Sir, The letter which an Italian gentleman, Mr. Uzielli, brought to me from you, was doubly acceptable, as it was evidence of a personal recollection whereon I could scarcely count. This circumstance emboldens me to throw a few lines into the mass with which you must be nearly overwhelmed in the commencement of your official career. I do not present myself as an *applicant* for any share of patronage; but I may venture to suggest that to be in the Service of my country to whose interests I have always practised more or less of devotion without Seeking or desiring requital, would fulfil my final wish in life. The studies which I have pursued in Europe; the connexions I have formed; the various languages with which I am familiar; might seem particularly adapted to render me useful in Some modest position near the government at home, or in a central part of Europe. My correspondence with the Intelligencer conveys only a portion, & that not the weightiest, of the information political & Statistical, which it would be in my power to collect abroad, or digest in your Department. Impaired health, & pecuniary misfortunes, such as I may well style spoliations committed on the trust & absence of Mrs. [Anna Maria Moylan] W[alsh] & myself, have occasioned a Separation from most of my children, felt as the worst of my ills. To be able to rally Some of them again is naturally my constant & vehement aspiration. If you Should remain Secretary of State, you would, probably, welcome my views of the condition of American diplomacy

340

in Europe, a Subject which I have long & widely observed, & on which I have heard the opinions of Statesmen & travellers eminently ["qualified" *interlined*] to judge. I refer especially to what touches the peculiar dangers & exigenc[i]es of the Southern States of our Union. Altogether, Since the departure of General [Lewis] Cass, the representation or agency of American concerns has been inadequate here, & not a little wanting in other capitals requiring peculiar diplomatic character and influences, and very positive Sentiments and sensibility concerning the European crusade against American negro-Slavery. What I thus say does not originate, nor has it the least relation, with any aims, pretensions or chances of my own. My motive is entirely patriotic; and I should spare you the topic if it had not happened to me to See and learn more, I think, than has fallen to diplomatic opportunities and impulses.

Pardon this intrusion; the elevation and liberality of your spirit and your faculties and modes of appreciation, inspire me with a degree of confidence. Formerly, I dissented from your political doctrines & Some of your measures; my ideas on certain points of national economy may still diverge from those you so ably expounded in the Senate. There are cardinal matters on which, however, there must ever be a common feeling & decision. And, with regard to personal impressions, I am sure that I have always been, & must uniformly prove, Dear Sir, Your truly respectful & faithful Servant, Robert Walsh.

ALS in ScCleA. NOTE: Walsh (1784–1859), a Marylander, had been an active editor and author in Philadelphia and had lived in Paris since 1837.

From J[OHN] S. BARBOUR, [former Representative from Va.], "Private"

Catalpa [Culpeper County, Va.], April 27th 1844
My Dear Sir, If I have omitted for a time to write you it was solely because I had nothing agre[e]able to communicate.

At Richmond we were (in Feb[ruar]y last) reduced to a small minority and carried by the current with the party insisting on Mr. [Martin] Van Buren[']s nomination.

With that party as[?] offering to us a choice more congenial with our principles, we were driven into concert.

The Virginia elections are now over & without knowing more

341

than what is visible within my immediate horizon it is probable that the State is ["manifestly"? *canceled*] averse to Mr. V[an] Buren. In this County (ag[ains]t my remonstrance & ["entreaty" *canceled*] entreaty) my name was offered as a Candidate for the State Legislature. The majority of the Whigs at the last election was 106[;] it is now 110, although I obtained twenty or thirty Whig votes & as many others declined voting. But many of the friends of Mr. Van Buren ["voted" *canceled*] refused to vote for me. I was not in their words "Democrat enough for them." This number did not exceed as I think the number of Whigs voting for me or declining to vote in the election. Whilst some ["*few*" *interlined*] of your friends *proper* voted directly ag[ains]t me as they avowed to show the weakness of the democratic party under the auspices of Mr. V[an] B[uren]. I have not been familiar for years with the people & last winter could say very little of the relative strength of Mr. V[an] B[uren] & yourself. But it was vouched (& taken to be so,) that four fifths of the County were favourable to Mr. V[an] Buren. The result shows that this ["to have been" *interlined*] wholly erroneous and its reverse (& more) true. Other Counties may have been misrepresented to a greater extent. I give you what has now been disclosed in the election.

I did not get a dozen votes that will not sustain you ag[ains]t all opposition and I am persuaded that twenty votes will cover the retreating strength of Van Buren proper.

If the State has gone ag[ains]t him will the Convention press him on the Country in the face of inevitable defeat? The question is serious[?] & calls for sound deliberation and unflinching action.

What is to be done? We cannot go for Mr. [Henry] Clay. Mr. [John] Tyler is feeble though preferable to Clay. *We cannot carry him.* It is in vain to resist Mr. Clay with Van [Buren] or Tyler. In Rappahannock (a part of Culpeper under the old constitution) the Whig candidate excludes the democrat by 66 votes. Though last ["year" *interlined*] the Republican was elected *over the same Whig* by 30 votes. In Madison (another part of old Culpeper,) instead of a majority of 500 for [William F.?] Gordon, he receives only 385 & [William L.] Goggin will be returned to Congress. With all Respect Y[ou]rs Sincerely, J.S. Barbour.

ALS in ScCleA.

To Sidney Breese, [Senator from Ill.], 4/27. "Your letter of the 25th Instant has been received. The package which accompanied it

addressed to Pierre Menard Maxwell shall be forwarded to its destination. I cannot officially interfere in his behalf, but I will request
our Legation at Mexico to do anything which can with propriety be
done in an informal manner towards setting him free." FC in DNA,
RG 59 (State Department), Domestic Letters, 34:158 (M-40:32).

From D[ANIEL] C. CROXALL

U.S. Consulate, Marseilles, April 27th 1844
Sir, I have the honor to inform you that I have this day drawn on you,
at thirty days sight, in favor of Et[ienne] Gautier, (Merchant &
Banker of this place) for six hundred dollars, on acc[oun]t of disbursements for distressed seamen &c.

In consequence of the laws on imprisonment at New Orleans &
Charleston, many col[ore]d seamen, from neighbouring ports as well
as this, have been thrown on my hands during the last two years.
The Blacks on board of Vessels going hence to those ports refuse to
proceed, & ["as" *interlined*] they invariably have received a month's
advance in the U.S. & the voyage made in from 30 to 45 days, little
or nothing was due them on quitting the ship; & as most of our Vessels do not go *direct* to the U.S. the men are necessarily here for some
time before an opportunity presents to send them home. Respectfully I have the honor to be, Sir, y[ou]r ob[edien]t Ser[van]t, D.C.
Croxall.

ALS in DNA, RG 59 (State Department), Consular Despatches, Marseilles, vol. 4
(T-220:4), received 6/11.

From Asbury Dickins, Secretary of the U.S. Senate, 4/27. A
standing resolution of the Senate orders its Secretary to furnish to the
State Department "twenty five copies of all confidential papers, prepared by the Department of State, and ordered by the Senate to
be printed confidentially." Accordingly, Dickins transmits printed
copies of the treaty of annexation between the U.S. and Texas and
related papers. These papers are under "the injunction of secrecy
imposed by the rules" of the Senate. LS in DNA, RG 59 (State Department), Miscellaneous Letters (M-179:104, frame 250); FC in
DNA, RG 46 (U.S. Senate), 24D-A1, Letterbooks of the Secretary,
3:133–134.

From F[RANCIS] M. DIMOND

United States Consulate
Vera Cruz, April 27, 1844

Sir, I have the honour to acknowledge the receipt of your communication of the 21th ult[im]o, in which you have been pleased to grant me permission to visit the U. States, the conditions of which will be complied with.

Mr. [Ben E.] Green Acting Charge de Affair[e]s of the U.S. informs me he will have dispatches for Washington by the first of June. I shall therefore not embark for the U. States before that time.

This is forwarded by the Mexican Steamers of war Montezuma and Guadalupe which vessels are dispatched for New York either for repairs or to get them out of the way of the French squadron should that Government see fit to send a fleet down here.

I am glad to say that Gen[era]l Santa Anna has seen fit to release Mr. George Van Ness, and a Mr. [Patrick] Lusk, and I am inclined to believe that they will all be liberated soon.

Altho it is generally believed that Texas will be annexed to the United States little or no excitement is expressed on the subject.

Cap[t]. W[illia]m F. Martin who has been on trial for killing a seaman on board ship N. York in the month of October last has been liberated by the Court that tried him.

I have the honour to transmit the duplicates No. 204 and 206 as called for. I have the honour to be Sir most Respectfully Your Ob[edient] Servant, F.M. Dimond.

ALS (No. 218) in DNA, RG 59 (State Department), Consular Despatches, Veracruz, vol. 5 (M-183:5), received 7/1.

From Hooper C. Eaton, U.S. Consul at Lyons, 4/27. On 3/18 Eaton received his commission from the late [Abel P.] Upshur. "I now beg to announce to you my having been at my Port since the commencement of the month; of having presented the Exequatur of the King, to the Prefect of the Department of the Rhone & established the Consulate." ALS (No. 2) in DNA, RG 59 (State Department), Consular Despatches, Lyons, vol. 1 (T-169:1), received 5/20.

To Edward Everett

Department of State
Washington, 27th April, 1844
Sir: I have the honor to transmit to you, herewith, sundry additional applications received at this Department since the date of Mr. [John] Nelson's letter of the 27th ultimo, in behalf of American citizens now imprisoned in Van Diemen's Land for their participation in the revolutionary movements in Canada in the year 1838; and to bespeak your good offices in promoting the object of the petitioners. A list of the original papers sent is subjoined to this despatch.

In the cases of two of the individuals in favor of whom papers are herewith sent, vizt. Joseph Thompson and Robert Marsh, who are said to have been residents of Canada previous to the late disturbances there, proper measures have been taken, through the British Minister at Washington, to give notice to the Governor General of that province, with a view to the institution of the requisite inquiries on the part of His Excellency, of the intended application to Her Britannic Majesty's Government for the pardon of these men. I am, Sir, respectfully, Your obedient servant, J.C. Calhoun.

LS (No. 84) with Ens in DNA, RG 84 (Foreign Posts), Great Britain, Instructions, 8:108–137, received 5/15; FC in DNA, RG 59 (State Department), Diplomatic Instructions, Great Britain, 15:190–192 (M-77:74). NOTE: Enclosed are approximately 14 letters and memorials asking the release of George T. Brown, John G. Swanberg, Garret Hicks, John Cronkhite, Jacob Paddock, David House, Emanuel Garrison, Jr., Daniel D. Heustis, Leonard Delano, and Bemis Woodbury. Shortly before Calhoun entered the State Department, the British government had indicated that it would entertain individual petitions for pardon of U.S. citizens deported to Australia after the Canadian revolt. There is a great deal of correspondence between Calhoun and the relatives and Congressional representatives (chiefly from N.Y. and Ohio) of the prisoners which is not included herein. Additional petitions continued to be received and forwarded in batches. Most of Calhoun's considerable subsequent correspondence with Everett and with Richard Pakenham on this subject has also been omitted.

To Edward Everett

Department of State
Washington, 27 April, 1844
Sir: I herewith transmit to you, a copy of the Treaty concluded between this Government and the Republic of Texas, with the accom-

panying documents, which has been laid by the President [John Tyler] before the Senate for its approval.

I also forward you copies of a correspondence between this Department and Mr. [Richard] Pakenham, Her Majesty's Minister near this Government; to all of which I call your special attention.

The necessity of preparing these papers so as to have them ready for the steamer of the 1st proximo, with the briefness of the time allowed me before the mail which carries them closes, will ["not" *canceled*] allow but few remarks.

You will perceive that the measure which has been adopted was demanded by the condition in which the avowed policy of Great Britain as proclaimed in Lord Aberdeen's despatch, has placed the United States. This Government could not quietly fold its arms while a policy was avowed and measures adopted so fatal to the safety and prosperity of the Union. It is in this view of the subject that the Government, as you will perceive, has felt itself called upon to act, and in this aspect it is urgently addressed to your consideration. You will, in your correspondence with Her Majesty's Government fail not to vindicate the motives, and sustain the course of the President, by an appeal to the facts and arguments adduced in the correspondence communicated, and in temperate but firm language, make it to be understood that, reluctantly constrained, in self defence, to adopt the measure in question, the Government of the United States will shun no responsibility which justly attaches to her conduct.

I will, by the first opportunity, communicate with you further, and more fully, on the subject; and am, With high respect, Your obedient servant, J.C. Calhoun.

LS (No. 85) with Ens in DNA, RG 84 (Foreign Posts), Great Britain, Instructions, 8:138–155, received 5/5; FC in DNA, RG 59 (State Department), Diplomatic Instructions, Great Britain, 15:192–193 (M-77:74); PC in Jameson, ed., *Correspondence*, pp. 579–580.

From W[illia]m C. Hern

Pittsburgh, Apr[il] 27th 1844

Dear Sir, Having been out of buisness for some time, I want to procure a situation in one of the Departments at Washington if possible[;] if you could do any thing for me I would take it as a verry great favour. I can get recom[m]endations from all the influential Polititions in the City, and a number of buisness men having been engaged in the Post Office here for seven or eight years, and in the Post Office at Detroit and also Book Keeper at O[']Leary[,] Mulvany & Co. and I have now a pretty large family and it does not answer for me to be Idle. If I could procure a situation in Washington or in the Custom House at Philadelphia or New York for a while it would be a great assistance to me.

I hope yet to see you the Candidate of the Democratic Party for the Presidency, as you have been my only choice for the last eight years. I do not say so now becaus[e] I am an applicant to you for a situation as I stood alone for you here for a long time, but now we are increasing daily and I hope before long to show a pretty strong front[.] I remain Your Ob[e]d[ient] S[ervan]t, Wm. C. Hern.

ALS in ScCleA. NOTE: An AEU by Calhoun reads: "Hern's letter."

From CHARLES NICHOLS, "Private"

United States Consulate
Amsterdam, April 27th 1844

Dear Sir, My feelings of gratulation can scarcely be imagined with which I received the announcement of your acceptance of the compliment paid you by the President [John Tyler] in soliciting your eminent services, to become the head of his Cabinet at this important Crisis.

Allow me to say your favorable decision has been hailed in Holland with satisfaction and highly commended by the English Press. All eyes in Europe are directed to you as the conservator of peace. I further rejoice at this fortunate event for our Country, as directly tending to secure that Elevation of you (which is so much desired) to the highest Office in our Government; and which should have been done long since as a just reward for distinguished Public Services and a life devoted to the promotion of our national prosperity.

That this anticipation may be soon realized and you may enjoy uninterrupted health and success in the present most important negociations is the fervent wish of your Sincere Friend, Charles Nichols.

[Addendum:] Dear Sir, Allow me to improve the present moment to remark that your influence exerted to give Consuls a salary instead of the precarious support they now receive from the Fees of Office (with the exception of a small number) would enlist in your support the connections and friends of this class of our Public Officers. This being a Diplomatic Post it would be a great relief to be allowed an extra sum beyond what what [*sic*] may be allowed to those Consuls who have no such expenditure. For our Countrymen, unless they receive these Diplomatic Attentions, leave dissatisfied.

A strong feeling has now set in against our Country in consequence of the protracted Bad Faith of some of the States[.] The King of the Netherlands [William II] very recently asked for a Loan of 127 Millions of Guilders to meet the current expenses of the Gov[ernme]nt and to pay former Loans about maturing; which after great exertion was accomplished. Viz: By the acceptors of the Loan converting O[ld] 3 per Cents for the new Stock at its pa[*ms. torn*]. The Old Stock being at 70, the sacrafice submitted to by the Public Creditors is estimated at more than 12 millions of doll[ar]s American Currency. The population of the Kingdom is Two Millions Eight Hundred Thousand; and the previous Debt Twelve hundred Millions of Guilders or about £ 1 . . 3 . . 6 sterling per head on the whole population. In the hope the above may not be unacceptable I have the honor to remain Truly Yours, Charles Nichols.

ALS in ScCleA.

From R[ichard] Pakenham, Washington, 4/27. Pakenham protests the removal from Gonaives, Haiti, [by a U.S. warship] in 12/-1843 of two U.S. citizens accused of murdering a British subject at that place. The British government expects the U.S. to hold a "strict & formal trial" of the accused [Samuel S. Thomas and Joseph R. Curtis] and, if they are found guilty, to punish them accordingly, thus remedying the "irregularity in which the case is now involved by the removal of the Prisoners from the Jurisdiction to which their trial naturally belonged." LS in DNA, RG 59 (State Department), Notes from Foreign Legations, Great Britain, vol. 22 (M-50:22).

To R[ichard] Pakenham

Department of State
Washington, April 27th, 1844

The Undersigned, Secretary of State of the United States, has the honor to acknowledge the receipt of the answer which the Right Honorable Mr. Pakenham, Envoy Extraordinary and Minister Plenipotentiary of Her Britannic Majesty was pleased to make to his note of the 18th instant, relating to the despatch of Lord Aberdeen, of which a copy was left with the late Secretary of State[,] Mr. [Abel P.] Upshur, by his request.

He regrets that Mr. Pakenham has fallen into an error, in supposing that the Undersigned intended, by introducing the statistical facts in reference to the comparative condition of the African race in the States of this Union, where slavery has been abolished, and where it is still retained, with the accompanying remarks, was "to expound the subject of slavery," and to "defend it as it exists in the United States."

If Mr. Pakenham will have the goodness to recur to the note of the Undersigned, he will find, on a reperusal, that his intention in introducing the details, instead of being that which he attributes to him, was to correct what the Undersigned believed to be a misconception on the part of Her Majesty's Government, as set forth in Lord Aberdeen's despatch. His Lordship seems to be of the impression, that the objection of the United States was not to the policy of Great Britain, in reference to abolition as avowed by him; but to the means which might be resorted to for its accomplishment; and that if slavery should be abolished in the United States, by the influence and exertions of Great Britain, without using what he is pleased to call "secret," or "undue means," it would be an act of humanity to the African race, and, in its consequences, would neither "disturb the internal tranquillity of the States," where it exists, nor "affect the prosperity of the Union." The object of the Undersigned in introducing the statistical information referred to, was to correct this erroneous impression by showing from facts drawn from unquestionable sources, that the condition of the African race in the States which had abolished slavery was far worse than in those which had not; and that, of course, Great Britain could not consummate in the United States what she avows to be the object of her policy and constant exertions to effect throughout the world, without rendering the condition of the African race in the slave-holding States much worse than it is, and disturbing their "internal tranquillity and the prosperity of the Union."

That such was the intention of the Undersigned, he hopes will be evident to Mr. Pakenham on a reperusal of his note; and not as he supposes to "expound the subject of slavery," or to "defend it as it exists in the United States." He is the more solicitous to correct the error into which Mr. Pakenham has fallen, in this particular, because the intention which he attributes to the Undersigned would be incompatible with the principle which regulates the United States in their intercourse with the rest of the world; that is to leave all other countries without interference on their part to regulate their own internal relations and concerns as to each may seem best, without permitting any to interfere with theirs. He could not, consistently with this well-established principle of their policy, permit any question belonging exclusively to the internal relations or concerns of any of the States of this Union, to be brought into controversy between this and any foreign Government whatever.

The Undersigned regrets, that Mr. Pakenham should entertain the impression, that the Government of the United States did not appreciate at their full value the explanations of Her Majesty's Government on the subject of its policy in reference to Texas. He would repeat, what he had supposed had been explicitly stated in his note to Mr. Pakenham, the assurance that this Government fully appreciated the spirit of frankness and good faith, in which the explanations were furnished. If they have failed to allay the anxiety which it had previously felt on the subject to which they referred, it was because they were accompanied by an avowal, on the part of Her Majesty's Government in reference to the abolition of slavery generally, and to Texas in particular, calculated to defeat the object, which the explanations were intended to effect. It was not possible for the President [John Tyler] to hear, with indifference, the avowal of a policy so hostile in its character and dangerous in its tendency to the domestic institutions of so many States of this Union, and to the safety and prosperity of the whole. Nor could he abstain from declaring his regret at the avowal, consistently with that frankness and sincerity which have ever characterized the conduct of this Government in its intercourse with other countries.

The United States in concluding the treaty of annexation with Texas, are not disposed to shun any responsibility which may fairly attach to them on account of the transaction. The measure was adopted with the mutual consent and for the mutual and permanent welfare of the two countries interested. It was made necessary in order to preserve a domestic institution, placed under the guaranty of their respective constitutions, and deemed essential to their safety and prosperity.

Whether Great Britain has the right, according to the principles of international law, to interfere with the domestic institutions of either country, be her motives or means what they may; or whether the avowal of such a policy and the exertions she has made to consummate it in Texas do not justify both countries in adopting the most effective measures to prevent it, are questions which the United

States willingly leave to the decision of the civilized world. They confidently rest the appeal on the solid foundation, that every country is the rightful and exclusive judge, as to what should be the relations, social, civil, and political, between those who compose its population; and that no other country, under the plea of humanity or other motive, has any right whatever to interfere with its decision. On this foundation rest the peace and the harmony of the world.

The Undersigned has again referred, in conformity with the request of Mr. Pakenham, to the portion of Lord Aberdeen's despatch to which he has pointed his attention, with the view of rebutting the inference of the President, that Great Britain has endeavored, through her diplomacy, to effect the abolition of slavery in Texas, by making it one of the conditions on which Mexico should acknowledge her independence. He is constrained to say, on a careful reperusal, that he can discover nothing in it calculated, in any degree, to weaken the inference of the President. His Lordship avows that Great Britain wishes to see slavery abolished in Texas; that she would rejoice if the recognition of that country by the Mexican Government should be accompanied by an engagement on the part of Texas to do so; and that she feels it to be her duty to promote such a consummation. If to these emphatic declarations the fact be added, that Great Britain, at the very time they were made, was engaged in negotiating with the Mexican Government in order to obtain from it a recognition of the independence of Texas, and that she declined to unite with France and the United States in a joint effort for that purpose, it is surely not a forced or unfair inference to conclude, without calling in the aid of other evidence, that she used in conducting it all the legitimate means of diplomacy, backed by her great influence, to effect an object, in the accomplishment of which she acknowledges she took so deep an interest, and to which she obviously attached so much importance. Nor does the Undersigned regard the declarations of Lord Aberdeen, that Great Britain would not interfere unduly or with any improper assumption of authority; that she will counsel, but not seek to compel or unduly control either party, as, in any degree, weakening the inference of the President: nor does he consider the remarks of Mr. Pakenham as a denial of its truth.

The Undersigned avails himself of the occasion to renew to Mr. Pakenham the assurances of his distinguished consideration. J.C. Calhoun.

FC in DNA, RG 59 (State Department), Notes to Foreign Legations, Great Britain, 7:11–15 (M-99:36); CC in DNA, RG 84 (Foreign Posts), Great Britain, Instructions, 8:148–155; CC in DNA, RG 84 (Foreign Posts), France, Instructions,

Jan. 29, 1843–May 20, 1846; CC's in DNA, RG 46 (U.S. Senate), 28B-B12; PC in Senate Document No. 341, 28th Cong., 1st Sess., pp. 65–67; PC in House Document No. 271, 28th Cong., 1st Sess., pp. 65–67; PC in the Washington, D.C., *Daily National Intelligencer*, May 20, 1844, p. 2; PC in the Washington, D.C., *Daily Madisonian*, May 20, 1844, p. 2; PC in the Washington, D.C., *Spectator*, May 21, 1844, p. 2; PC in the Washington, D.C., *Globe*, May 22, 1844, p. 1; PC in the Charleston, S.C., *Courier*, May 25, 1844, p. 2; PC in *Niles' National Register*, vol. LXVI, no. 13 (May 25, 1844), pp. 202–203; PC in Crallé, ed., *Works*, 5:343–347.

From W[illia]m Parmenter, [Representative from Mass.], Washington, 4/27. Parmenter encloses a letter [of 4/25] to Calhoun from W[illia]m Page of Boston who seeks the appointment of U.S. Consul at Paris "in case a change should be made." ALS with En in DNA, RG 59 (State Department), Applications and Recommendations, 1837–1845, Page (M-687:25, frames 16–19).

To John M. Reed, Philadelphia, 4/27. "I have the honor to inform you, that the paper enclosed in your letter [*not found*] of the 24th instant, recommending the Hon: George M. Dallas for the office of assistant Justice of the supreme Court of the United States, has, agreeably to your request, been laid before the President" [John Tyler]. FC in DNA, RG 59 (State Department), Domestic Letters, 34:158–159 (M-40:32).

H[ARVEY] M. WATTERSON to [John Tyler]

Buenos Ayres, April 27th 1844

Dear Sir, Some two weeks since I conceived it my duty to write you certain facts in regard to the conduct of [Amory Edwards] the American Consul in this City in the settlement of the estate of the late Andrew Thorndike. The estate was worth at least twenty thousand Spanish dollars. Timothy Thorndike of Boston has been here more than two months endeavoring to procure from the Consul a statement showing how much the property of his brother had sold for and what amount of money was due the heirs. Despairing of success, on yesterday he proposed to the purchasers of the property and Mr. Edwards that he would take four thousand Spanish dollars and give them a clear receipt. The proposition was accepted and Mr. Thorndike leaves to morrow with four thousand dollars—out of an estate worth the sum specified. These are the facts and now it is for you to apply the corrective if in your judgment the case requires one. If Mr. Edwards is removed I have recommended to your favorable consideration J.M. Moss, late of Philadelphia and now a Merchant of this City. Mr. Moss is a gentleman of great intelligence and high respectability.

On the day before yesterday a battle was fought which resulted in the death of some three or four hundred men on each side (at Monte Video). No quarter was given. What a terrible war—but it can not continue many months longer. The Frenchmen under arms at Monte Monte [*sic*] Video, went through the farce, ten or fifteen days ago, of laying ["down" *interlined*] their arms as *Frenchmen* and taking them up as *Orientals. This satisfied the new French Admiral.*

The latest dates from the United States are up to the 15th Feb. I am truly gratified at the triumphant confirmation of Mr. [Henry A.] Wise [as U.S. Minister to Brazil]. I am in anxious suspense to hear what has been done with your humble servant. I must and will as long as I hold it, keep up the dignity and respectability of my present station, and to do that requires my entire salary. Hence my solicitude to be confirmed as Chargé De Affairs. I have been treated by Gov. [Juan M.] Rosas and all the officers of this Government with whom I have had any thing to do, with the greatest respect and kindness. They are desirous that the diplomatic relations between the two countries should be completely re-established. Rosas is a real General Jackson of a fellow if I may use the expression. He may be wrong and no doubt is in many things—but that he believes he is right, there is not the slightest question in my mind. I greatly admire his frankness. He has no concealment about him. "Sir, Said he to me the other evening, how much more manly is the conduct of your Government in its intercourse with foreign nations, than that of England & France. You determine what is right, then take your stand and maintain it with firmness—whilst England and France consult their interests, and their interests alone." I remarked to him that it seemed a little strange to me, that Commodore Purvis and Mr. Mandeville the British Minister, should be taking opposite sides in this contest—both professing to act in conformity with instructions from their government, and still both are retained in the service. With a significant shrug of the shoulders, he replied, "["that's" *altered to* "that"] *exactly verifies what I have been saying."* Set down Gov. Rosas as a great man—very great man—a man of the people—a man who understands human nature in all its various ramifications. He is one of natures ["nobleman" *altered to* "noblemen"] & a higher compliment I could not pay him.

I see the Democrats are going to the Devil & I am sorry for it.

Give my compliments to your two sons, Robert & John, & believe ["me" *interlined*] to be what is sincerely so, Your Friend, H.M. Watterson.

ALS in DNA, RG 59 (State Department), Diplomatic Despatches, Argentina, vol. 5 (M-69:6), received 6/25. NOTE: *Watterson was a former Representative from Tenn. and had been nominated as Chargé d'Affaires to Argentina by Tyler. The nomination was rejected by the Senate on 6/5 by a vote of 16 to 21.*

From John M. Wyse, Deer Park, near Pikesville, Md., 4/27. "The enclosed letter [*not found*] to Mr. [Richard K.] Cralle is the one, which you yesterday requested me to write in relation to my brother [Nicholas H. Wyse?]." *ALS in ScCleA.*

From L[ANSFORD] W. HASTINGS

New Madrid Mo., April 28, 1844

Dear Sir, I hope you will have the goodness to excuse the liberty which I take, in thus addressing you. I have not the honour of a personal acquaintance with you, yet I have ever been an ardent admirer of your political course, And I assure you Sir, that I am greatly gratified with the course you have pursued, and are pursuing, in reference to the annexation of Texas. I anxiously look for the consum[m]ation of that grand and important object.

But Sir, as the object of this communication is not, to enter into a review of our political [*one word altered to* "affairs"], you will excuse me, if I make no further reference to them, at present. The object of this, is merely, to request you to forward to me, at this place, the report of Lieut. [Charles] Wilkes of the exploring squadron, and also such other information as you may have in your possession, in reference to Oregon & California.

I am the more anxious to receive information in reference to those Countries, as I have but recently returned from Oregon (by the way of California & Mexico,) and as I hear various conclusions and remarks in reference to Oregon, purporting to have originated from reports &C. of persons who have been to that Country, I am extremely anxious to see those reports for myself. Will you have the goodness also to forward to me, the report of Dr. E[lijah] White, (Indian agent in Oregon)?

You will see the present condition of that country, from a brief letter which I wrote the Editor of the "St. Louis New Era," and which was published in the "St. Louis New Era" (daily) of the 25 Ult. and in the same paper (weekly) of the 30 Ult. You will there observe that our Citizens have organized a government. This became absolutely necessary. If I can add to your, already acquired information, in reference to that country I shall be very happy to do so.

The reason why I did not write to some member of Congress, from this State is, that I was of opinion, that Congress would most likely adjourn previous to the reception of this, which would defeat my object.

I hope sir, that the foregoing may afford a sufficient apology for my thus obtruding myself upon your notice.

With my best wishes for your health and prosperity, allow me to subscribe myself Dear Sir, Your most ob[edien]t humble Serv[an]t, L.W. Hastings.

ALS in DNA, RG 59 (State Department), Miscellaneous Letters (M-179:104, frames 251–253).

From ROBERT G. SCOTT

Richmond, April 28th 1844

Dear Sir, I beg leave to introduce to you, my son Robert G. Scott jr. esq[ui]r[e], who will hand you this. He will remain in Washington a few days, having taken a short trip, as a relaxation from business, from which his health has somewhat suffered.

I have just risen from the perusal of Mr. [Martin] Van Buren's letter, & also that of Mr. [Henry] Clay on the Texan question. They throw every thing into "confusion worse confounded." A storm will arise in the South, that will shake the pillars of the government, on this question, unless I greatly mistake the character of our people.

We are all for Texas. I mean the Democratic party here. A great proportion of the Whigs are with us; but follow Mr. Clay & will cast their votes for him now, without reference to any opinions he may entertain, or policy he may recommend. We have most probably lost our House of Delegates, & may be in a minority on joint ballot. With your name, ["before the people" *interlined*] we should have had 30 at the least of majority. With my best wishes I am yours with sincere & high regard, Robert G. Scott.

ALS in ScCleA.

From JAMES A. SEDDON

Richmond, April 28th 1844

Dear Sir, Relying on the kind consideration with which you have honored me I venture to introduce to your acquaintance my friend Mr. Jno. A. Caskin of this City who proposes to make a brief visit to Washington. I need not commend Mr. Caskin to your friendly consideration and confidence since the reputation which he has early won ["and" *canceled*] and the devotion which he has already manifested to our republican Cause and to its ablest exponent, the knowledge of which has no doubt reached you, will constitute more effectual recommendations. Mr. Caskin being fresh from the Scenes of recent political Struggle in this State and himself no unnoted Actor in them will be able to communicate to you the fullest results of our State Elections and the Causes which have operated in inducing them. He will also be able to give fuller information, than could be contained in a letter, of the State of the public mind in this State in relation to the all important Question of the annexation of Texas and of the possible influences which it may exercise on the approaching Presidential Canvass. Mr. Caskin has been fully possessed of the views entertained by myself and many Common friends in the State, and I confide to him with pleasure the office of explaining them to yourself and others of our Common friends in Washington. Most Cordially Y[ou]rs, James A. Seddon.

ALS in ScCleA.

To "R.J." [*sic;* Hugh J.] Anderson, Governor of Maine, Belfast, 4/29. Calhoun acknowledges Anderson's letter of 4/20, in which he repeated a request that he be furnished with copies of land grants made by the British government in that portion of the territory of New Brunswick that was, by the Treaty of Washington, placed within the boundaries of Maine. In response to renewed applications from the State Department, the British Minister in Washington, [Richard] Pakenham, has made arrangements for copies to be sent to Washington as soon as possible. FC in DNA, RG 59 (State Department), Domestic Letters, 34:162 (M-40:32).

From Daniel J. Desmond, Philadelphia, 4/29. Desmond informs Calhoun that he has been "duly elected an Honorary" member of "The Historical Society of Pennsylvania." ALS in ScCleA.

From Henry Dolliver, Somerville, N.J., 4/29. He asks if Wilson Shannon, U.S. Minister to Mexico, is empowered to negotiate a treaty with that government for the settlement of claims of U.S. citizens. Dolliver sailed to Mexico in 1828 with a cargo to be sold there, but the cargo was seized by Mexican authorities. He has never received compensation for this outrage, though he has applied to the State Department on previous occasions. He is old and unable to work and hopes that his claim will receive the attention it merits. ALS in DNA, RG 76 (Records of Boundary and Claims Commissions and Arbitrations), Records of United States and Mexican Claims Commissions.

From ROBERT L. DORR

[Dansville, N.Y.] April 29/[18]44

My Dear Sir, I received from the Commissioner of the Land Office, a communication in answer to mine, to you, written sometime since stating that Mr. [John] Williamson, of Penn[sylvania]; is the present incumbent of the Recorders Office, and that the compensation, as now provided by law, is $2000 per annum. I have heretofore requested you to make inquiries, if consistent with your feelings, as to the manner in which I discharged the duties of a small office in that Department in 1838 & 1839. I presume however that the multiplicity of your engagements, and their importance, have hitherto prevented you from satisfying yourself whether justice has been done, had you had the inclination so to do. I recollect well, however, that your letter in answer to mine was of a friendly character—that you did not wish to place yourself under any obligations to Mr. Tyler[']s Administration, and that it would be rather unusual for you to interest yourself in a matter beyond your jurisdiction, or out of your own State. I am by no means a lover of office. I have not asked nor sought it in this State since I left Washington, and had I done so, the ruling powers at Albany would probably never have granted it.

The only desire I have ever felt, was that ample justice might be done me at Washington, where, with the most honest intentions, and justifiable motives, I started to earn an honest fame, and [was] thwarted in it, only because I could not lick the sandaled feet of some great Master. I could witness, after two years of unremitting toil, only an impaired constitution and blasted hopes.

I have always been the subject of Federal[ist] hatred, and persecution, and never more so, probably, than at the present time. It would seem, that all the Abolition Federal forces, in this section of the State, were combining for my destruction. They lack no criminality in their persecution towards me, except the manliness of the *highwayman*. Lies, Slander, fraud, perjury, all have been brought into requisition to effect my ruin, and all because I have been attached to Southern men and Southern institutions, and have defended them when attacked. My Dear Sir, You cannot measure the extent of their wickedness, nor ["they" *altered to* "the"] injury they meditate inflicting upon me; and strange as it may appear, the principal representatives of the political power of the State, here, are the most active in endeavouring to effect my ruin.

They are constantly getting up unfounded and malicious prosecutions, and of a criminal nature too, to prejudice the public mind against me, hireing men to swear false—and thus swearing me out of my property and out of my reputation—and Oh shall I tell it, the infamous wretches declare that they will have me in State Prison. I have stood all their fires, and all their infamous proceedings, with a firmness and complacency of mind, that conscious innocence alone could produce.

This is *abolition* and if they effect my ruin you will see what Abolition, Federalism, and Rum[?] can do.

Under such circumstances it will be apparent to you, that a triumph over such wicked men, would indeed be a great satisfaction to me. But I cannot triumph over them, without the aid of others who may perhaps be able to appreciate my merits, and who, in consequence, may be anxious to rescue me from such a hell. To be placed beyond their reach, and rewarded by the wise and the good, would indeed be a great moral triumph, and the lesson that would be taught *them* and *me* would not soon be forgotten, nor lost in its beneficial effects.

Under no other circumstances would I ask you to interpose. Under no other circumstances would I desire an office at the hands of any power. You have never known me personally but you have otherwise. I cannot boast of of [*sic*] my virtues nor my qualifications. I have always endeavoured to be faithful and honest, and could I get the Recorders Office, it would be my greatest study to discharge its duties faithfully, and reflect honor upon the Administration that should bestow it. My gratitude would be ["as" *interlined*] lasting to you as my regard has been steadfast tho', comparitively a stranger.

If I cannot in this way, put down the most wicked men, I ever met, it then remains for me, to fight it out with them single handed, and alone, and if I fall I shall fall gloriously, and if necessary, as did the brave [Baron] De Kalb, or the youthful the brave the generous [Gen. Richard] Montgomery under the walls of Quebec. Yes, they want my blood and they want circumstances to justify them in taking it.

Should you feel disposed to favour me I can send on petitions. If you say so I will. Excuse the hasty manner in which this letter is written and believe me Sincerely Your Friend, Robert L. Dorr.

ALS in ScCleA. NOTE: An AEU by Calhoun reads "Mr. Dorr. Desires to be restored or appointed to office." The "Recorder" was an officer in the General Land Office of the Treasury Department.

To F[RANKLIN] H. ELMORE, Charleston

Washington, 29th April 1844

My dear Sir, This will be delivered to you by Mr. [Friedrich] Von Raumer of Berlin, the celebrated Historian of Germany. He visits the United States with the view of becoming better acquainted with the country, its inhabitants and the character of their institutions. He is desirous, on his visit to Charleston, to see, among other things, the mode of our cultivation, & for that purpose to visit some of our rice & cotton plantations.

I feel assured you will take pleasure in extending your kind attention to so celebrated a visitor, during his so [*sic*] sojourn in your city.

He is accompanied by his son. Yours truly, J.C. Calhoun.

ALS in ViHi, Wickham Family Papers.

From W[ILLIA]M B. GOOCH

U.S. Commercial Agency
Aux Cayes, April 29th 1844

Sir, It has been but a few days since I heard the mournful intelligence of the death of Mr. [Abel P.] Upshur, late Secretary of State.

I directed a private letter [of 4/11] to him via Jamaica, giving information that this city was in possession of the blacks.

All the south part of the Island, is now in their possession, and the Army marching for Port au Prince.

The French part of the Island, (so called;) will probably soon be under a black government. The Spanish will, I believe, establish a sepparate Government.

There are very few blacks capable of conducting the affairs of the Island, and by what I know of their character I have not a doubt that they will soon commence fighting each other & sepparate themselves into clans & become like Africa, and the navigation in the vicinity of the Island becom[e] dangerous to foreigners on account of piracy. Business is prostrated. There is a large amount of American produce in this city, remaining unsold, & must remain so, as they have no specie; & no produce is brought into the market and cannot be, so long as this war continues which will continue for months, if not for years.

All Americans who have arrived with cargoes since the chang[e] of government, I have advised to proceed to some other Island.

There are three Ships of war in the harbour, two English & one French for the protection of the property & lives of the inhabitants of those nations residing here; and one of the English Captains informed me, that if I considered the property, or lives of any Americans in danger, he would protect them.

As the U.S. has several Armed vessels on the West India station, I consider it important for some of them to call at different ports on this Island, as there is much American property and some lives unprotected. I am Sir with high esteem your obedient & devoted Servant, Wm. B. Gooch.

ALS in DNA, RG 59 (State Department), Consular Despatches, Aux Cayes, vol. 2 (T-330:2), received 5/20.

From Rob[er]t Monroe Harrison, American Consulate, Kingston, Jamaica, 4/29. "Herewith I have the honor to send you a Newspaper [the Kingston, Jamaica, *Royal Gazette* of 4/29] containing a Notification from the Senior British Naval Officer on the Station, declaring the Ports of St. Juan de Nicaragua and the coasts adjacent under Blockade." LS (No. 282) with En in DNA, RG 59 (State Department), Consular Despatches, Kingston, vol. 8 (T-31:8), received 5/19.

From I[saac] E. Holmes, [Representative from S.C., *ca.* 4/29]. Holmes encloses a letter from [Thomas D.] Hailes [to Calhoun, dated 4/12] and endorses Hailes's application for a Consul's appointment "if it can be consistently given . . . ." ALS with En in DNA, RG 59 (State Department), Applications and Recommendations, 1837–1845, Hailes (M-687:14, frames 87–89).

To W[illiam] L. Marcy, Albany, 4/29. Calhoun acknowledges Marcy's letter of 4/26 concerning Aaron Leggett's claim against the Mexican government and states in reply that Leggett is aware that the problem has been referred to [Henry] Wheaton, [U.S. Minister to Prussia]. Nothing can be done until the result of Wheaton's efforts is known. [The King of Prussia had been the neutral member of the U.S.-Mexican Claims Commission.] FC in DNA, RG 59 (State Department), Domestic Letters, 34:161 (M-40:32).

From W[ILLIAM] S. MURPHY

Legation of the United States
Houston Texas, 29th April 1844

Sir, Your despatch of the 13th Inst[ant] was delivered to me, on the 26th Inst[ant] at Galveston by R.C. Murphy who was also the bearer of the Texan duplicate of a Treaty annexing the Republic of Texas to the United States.

The President of the Rep[u]b[lic] of Texas [Samuel Houston], (by an arrangement between his Excellency and myself,) being in waiting at this City, for the earliest information on this deeply interesting subject, I thought it proper to accompany your messenger to this place, in order that I might have a personal interview with His Excellency after he should have received the duplicate Treaty.

The President was highly gratified, at my having done so—and gave to your messenger an expression of his approbation.

After his Excellency had fully examined the duplicate Treaty; and in conjunction with the Attorney General of the Republic, fully considered its provisions, in connection with all the Private letters, from the Texan Envoys on the same subject—he expressed to me his hearty approbation of every part thereof, and his high & sanguine hopes of the final success of this important measure. I then took occasion to make known to his Excellency, so much of the substance of your despatch to me, relating to the defence of Texas pending the Treaty of annexation, as I deemed useful, and proper to communicate: at which he rose to his feet, & gave utterance to his feelings of gratitude ["to" *canceled and* "towards" *interlined*] the President of

the United States [John Tyler] & yourself for this distinguished manifestation of the generous and noble policy, which ruled in the councils of my beloved Country.

His Excellency will remain near this Legation, until the ["news of
the" *canceled*] final, or definate action of my government, ["of" *canceled*] upon this Treaty is known ["here" *interlined*].

His Excellency finally pressed upon me the momentous consideration, of the utter hopelessness of ever effecting this great measure
of annexation, in case the present Treaty for that purpose should be
rejected by the Senate of the U. States.

I have so often & so earnestly labored to impress this truth upon
my government, that I am almost ashamed, to repeat it at this time.

You will have the goodness to excuse the haste with which this
brief despatch is drawn up, I have barely time to do it. Your messenger leaves here immediately ["for Galveston, that he may go"
interlined; "take" *changed to* "in"] the Neptune for N[ew] Orleans,
tomorrow. With great respect & esteem, I have the Honor to be
Your ob[edien]t Serv[an]t, W.S. Murphy.

Note. It is almost useless for me to add, that I am fully impressed
with the high responsability which your last despatch casts upon me.
And that I shall take care, to follow your instructions, with great
caution and [*one word changed to* "precision"]. W.S. Murphy.

ALS (No. 25) in ScCleA, received 5/13; variant copy in DNA, RG 84 (Foreign
Posts), Records of the Texas Legation; PC in Jameson, ed., *Correspondence*, pp.
947–948.

From W[illiam] S. Murphy, "Private"

Houston, 29th April 1844

Sir, I have not seen the Treaty—and as the President [Samuel Hous-
ton] did not offer it for my perusal, I thought it indelicate to ask for
it. Yet, I cannot doubt, but that my government has obligated the
U. States, to assume the payment of the Public debt of Texas. And
inasmuch, as the assumption of that debt, would create no greater
obligation on the part of the U. States, than that under which Texas
rests—It may not be unimportant to suggest, even now, that the Treasury Drafts of Texas, now outstanding were not issued for the amount
which appears up[on] their face. Some were issued as equivalent to
50 cents on the Dollar, some as equivalent to 25 cents &c. &c. and some
as low as 16 cents on the Dollar, and the Govt. of Texas was only

obligated to redeem them at the price, or value, for which they were issued.

The Govt. Records will shew, when compared with the date of the Drafts, for what equivalents they were issued. In great Haste, Yours Respectfully, W.S. Murphy.

P.S. I learn from the Auditor of the Treasury, who is here, that the Public Debt of Texas, when fairly audited as above will not amount to [$]5,000,000. W.S.M.

ALS in ScCleA; PC in Jameson, ed., *Correspondence*, p. 949.

From M [ILFORD] P. NORTON

Houston [Texas Republic,] Ap[ril] 29, 1844

Dear Sir, I write you at this moment because I am sure there is no one here will do it, as most of those in the confidence of the President here [Samuel Houston] are bitterly opposed to annexation. It is now *certain* that we can form such a commercial treaty with Great Britain as will insure our immediate independence. Gen. Houston had an interview with Capt. [Charles] Elliot [British Chargé d'Affaires in Texas] on the day he left Galveston for New Orleans. Mons[ieu]r [Alphonse de] Saligny the French minister is now at Galveston. The President is strongly urged & importuned to break off from the treaty with the U.S. & listen to their propositions. We are all prepared if we are spurned again from the Union to enter into a commercial *free trade* treaty with G[reat] B[ritain] & France on a guaranty of our Independence which we can *now* have & the advantages it promises us in the Cotton trade renders it very desirable. The enemies of annexation urge upon the President that we can not get as good terms after annexation ["fails" *interlined*] & that it is his duty now to receive propositions & I can assure you beyond a doubt that when it shall be known here that Gen. [J. Pinckney] Henderson shall have made his visit of leave at Washington that propositions will have been received & agreed to by us that will place annexation beyond all hope forever without a war with G[reat] B[ritain] and that such propositions will be gladly accepted by our Government & people. The President was strongly urged to consent to entertain the proposition when it was apprehended here that certain pledges made to us by Gen. [William S.] Murphy were to be disavowed. That apprehension is removed by Gen. Henderson's letter of 9th Ap[ril]. These

363

apprehensions were founded on a certain communication supposed to have been made by Mr. [John] Nelson to Gen. Murphy before your arrival. It is very important to the success of the measure that all the assurances made to the President by Gen. Murphy shall be carried out to the *letter* not so much from immediate of [*sic*] danger from Mexico as that the President may ["not" *interlined*] be induced to seize upon a breach of them to ["put" *canceled*] break off the treaty which it is urged here that he may do at any moment when he shall have received it without submitting it to the Senate. It is therefore of the utmost importance that no single assurance of Gen. Murphy be disavowed or left *unfulfilled*. I do not say these things because I have any want of faith in President Houston but because I know the almost overpowering influences that are brought to bear upon him. You will doubtless be furnished by this mail through Gen. Henderson with the evidence that the commission for an armistice was at once rejected by Gen. Houston when it reached him on the ground that we were treated in it as a department of Mexico & that the commissioners had not the slightest authority to treat upon that basis. In truth the Commissioners who are violently opposed to annexation are believed here to have entered into that agreement for the very purpose for which it will doubtless be used by Mexico & the opponents of annexation—to defeat the measure and there is great fear here that the disavowal by the President may not reach you in season to meet the objection as a copy of the instructions to the commissioners & the action of the President on the armistice will not reach here in season to go out by the Neptune. Gen. Henderson will have however a letter from the President which may have the same effect to a certain extent. Allow me to suggest that the commissioners to settle claims under the ten million allowance made for that purpose in the Treaty be allowed to sit at "Washington in Texas" *or such other place in Texas as they may themselves appoint,* as there are very serious objections to that place and that if any lesser sum than ten millions shall be likely to accelerate the passage of the Treaty that it had better be amended in the Senate even down to ["five"(?) *canceled and* "eight" *interlined*] if necessary as that change will not prevent its ratification by us. Most of these claims are held in the United States. It must certainly be desirable if you have a majority in the Senate but not two thirds, that you hold the Treaty up & not allow it to be *rejected* untill action shall have been had on the question on *affirmative* resolutions in the House as when these shall reach the Senate & the opponents shall see that we may be annexed by resolution they may be disposed to favor the treaty—besides if the Treaty shall be rejected you will no longer have any such hold upon the Government of Texas as may prevent the President ["the" *canceled*] from entering into negotiations that must greatly embarrass if not entirely defeat the measure for I am absolutely certain that this is the only treaty you can ever get and that propositions will be crowded upon us the moment the Treaty is rejected that will place the subject beyond your reach by peac[e]able means. There is no doubt entertained here that the English & French ministers at your Court have instructions to interpose their protest if they think such course may prevent & not accelerate the measure and may be the *only means* of preventing it. Such information has been received here from a quarter entirely to be relied upon at Paris—but the movements of those Governments with your own on that question is better known to you than to us.

I am not willing that this letter shall go on to the files of your department. I am not certain that you think the facts communicated of any importance or that you may not have them from other quarters on which you have more right to rely or that they may not be too late for any useful purpose. If annexation shall fail this letter might prove very injurious to me if known here. If the measure succeed I care nothing about it. I am known to Gen. Henderson & Messrs. [George] Evans and [John] Fairfield of the Senate [from Maine] and I refer you to them for the faith you can place in my statements. I am among the few friends of annexation who are so much in the confidence of the Executive as to know what movements are taken to favor or defeat the measure and I repeat, if I have said it before, that annexation can never occur peac[e]ably unless by the present movement, that it is not at all unlikely to be broken off from this quarter & that the line between Texas & the United States will form the *Slave line* within five years after a commercial treaty shall be formed with G[reat] B[ritain] and that too by our own free will and still sooner if we are left alone to take care of ourselves for we cannot go into another war with Mexico & leave our families at home exposed to the dangers of a slave population and we never *will* surrender the country to Mexico while one man is left to fight. Y[ou]rs Very Truly, M.P. Norton.

ALS in ScCleA; CCEx's in DNA, RG 46 (U.S. Senate), 28B-B12; PEx's in House Document No. 271, 28th Cong., 1st Sess., pp. 104–105; PEx's in the Washington, D.C., *Spectator*, July 16, 1844, pp. 1–2; PC in Jameson, ed., *Correspondence*, pp. 949–952. NOTE: Norton (1794–1860) was a native of Maine and a former member of the legislature of that State who had moved to Texas in 1839 to look after the large landholdings of his father-in-law. He was at this time Postmaster of Houston and editor of the Houston *Democrat*.

To STEPHEN PLEASONTON, Fifth Auditor [of the Treasury]

Department of State
Washington, 29 April 1844

Sir, I have received your letter of the 25th instant in which you inform me that the account of Mr. Albert Smith, Commissioner for marking the Northeastern Boundary line, contains charges for the services of three [civilian] Engineers amounting to $2135 and of a Commissary and Assistant Commissary, amounting to $1037.50; and, that as you cannot allow those charges without the sanction of the Secretary of State, they are referred for my decision thereon.

It appears that the law to provide for the survey &c. gives to the Commissioner a salary of three thousand dollars per annum. It also provides that the President should cause to be detailed so many officers from the [Army] Topographical Corps, as might be deemed sufficient to aid the Commissioner.

Under this latter clause five officers were detailed, and the inference is that this number was sufficient. There is no evidence going to prove that the number was unequal to the duty.

Under these circumstances, this Department cannot assume to itself authority to pass a judgment against the President and the Secretary of War, by allowing charges for other engineer services.

The third Section of the act aforesaid appropriates fifteen thousand dollars, for the payment of salaries, and other expenses of the Commission, including the purchase and repair of instruments, wages to persons employed and other contingencies.

No mention is made of a Commissary or Assistant Commissary, and the charges for such cannot be allowed without proof that such persons and services were necessary for the Commissioner. This is more especially requisite as to the Assistant. The per diem also must be shown to be reasonable. I am, Sir, Your Obed[ien]t Servant, J.C. Calhoun.

FC in DNA, RG 59 (State Department), Accounting Records, Miscellaneous Letters Sent, 1832–1916, vol. for 2/1–9/30/1844, pp. 133–134.

From [John Slidell, Representative from La.], 4/29. Slidell recommends to Calhoun's "favorable consideration" an enclosed letter [of 4/12 from Thomas D. Hailes to Calhoun]. ALU with En in DNA, RG 59 (State Department), Applications and Recommendations, 1837–1845, Hailes (M-687:14, frames 90–92).

From Lathrop J. Eddy, "Private"

New York [City,] April 30th 1844

Respected Sir, Enclosed I send you a recommendation for the appointment of Geo[rge] E. Baldwin Esq. as U.S. Despatch Agent in this City. Your friends in this City are all very anxious that this appointment should be made. Mr. Baldwin has always been one of your most active & influential friends, and his excellent character & qualities have endeared him to us all.

Your friends here are remarkable above all other politicians for their independent course, & disregard of official patronage, but there are many reasons why we are induced to urgently solicit this appointment for Mr. Baldwin. With great respect Your Ob[edien]t Serv[an]t, Lathrop J. Eddy.

ALS in ScCleA.

From Christopher Hughes, "Private"

The Hague—30th April 1844

My dear Sir, I have no *official* right to write to you—for as yet I have not received any authentic information of your having accepted the appointment of Secretary of State! All I know on the subject is derived from News Paper rumours—and these completely coincide with my own wishes—for nothing could give me greater pleasure, than to see you—My dear Mr. Calhoun—the Cheif of the Department—to which, I have so long belonged, and which I *have served* (I hope I may be allowed to say it) with—at least—indefatigable zeal—for now nearly Thirty years; or, in other words—for a little more than half of my life! C.H. Aetatis 58; "and yet no holyday have seen"; for "Holyday" read Promotion.

But if I had received regular advice of your acceptance—as I sincerely hope I shall do in a few days—I have nothing whatever of a publick or official character—to afford material for a Despatch; indeed—I rarely have; and I, therefore, write but very few *Despatches*; for I have long since adopted the system or practice—of neither writing nor speaking—unless I really have something to say. All I have to say—as regards our affairs & interests in this Country—can be summed up in the few words of stating that our concerns and relations in Holland are on the most easy[,] harmonious and satisfactory footing possible; the King and the Government are animated by the most perfect sentiments of good will & friendliness towards our country and people; and it is my constant study—and the object of all my wishes & efforts—to foster and preserve these favourable and friendly dispositions.   I doubt, if I should contribute to this—the great end & object of my residence here—by sending home frequent and long histories & compositions, called "Despatches"—there being really nothing of direct interest or importance *to us*—to write.   *Things are well*; and I shall endeavour *to keep them so*.

Almost the last act of the late estimable & lamented Mr. [Abel P.] Upshur—in which I was concerned—was an act of Kindness, amiable feeling & consideration for me!   Such had he always shewn himself to me.   He sent me—through my Friend Mr. Joseph R. Ingersoll—& in a letter addressed to Mr. Ingersoll the President's Permission to make a short visit to the U. States; leaving it to me, to decide, whether & when I should avail myself of this indulgence, seeing always, that the public interests did not suffer by my temporary absence from my Post.   Mr. Ingersoll sent me Mr. Upshur's Letter; and I consider myself as authorized by it, to come home, as I propose doing in the course of the Summer; it is, however, possible, that I may not find ["it" *interlined*] absolutely necessary to go home, this year.   In these circumstances, it seems proper that I should mention the subject to you; and, in doing so, I beg leave also to say, that I shall be very much obliged to you—if you will with the President's sanction—renew this permission so kindly granted by Mr. Upshur—allowing me to avail myself of it—or not—as the necessity of my private affairs may dictate to me! and I shall be exceedingly grateful for your *early* attention to my present request.

I am tempted to mention a little incident that occurred here, a few Evenings since, at my House; it may look a little—or rather—*not* a little—vain.   It had got out that I contemplated a visit to my country! & it seems the subject *must* have been discussed; for, a few Evenings ago—an address—of the most flattering & friendly kind—signed by 14 members of the Corps Diplomatique—was presented to me— imploring me not to leave the Hague: actually beseeching, entreating, imploring (strong words, Sir—but true;) me, not to go away; & "leave them all lamenting."   *Do* tell this to the President; it may amuse him; I am sure it will please him; as it will you, my dear Mr. Calhoun. The explanation of this charm—does not reside *in* me—it resides, however, *with* me; it is to be found in the gentle nature, manners & conduct of my darling little Daughter [Margaret Smith Hughes], & in the ease & grace, with which she does the honours of our simple, but hospitable little Salon! Our hospitality is limited to an amiable *welcome & Tea*! As to dinners; it is as much as we can do *to compass a* dinner for ourselves; & that of the most modest description, for this is the dearest place in Europe; not excepting London! It is certainly three times as dear as Baltimore. To give you an idea of the smallness of my house—it is *too* small *to invite* our friends to; if we *invited*—we must invite *all*; so, we have never invited any one. The fashion—on the Continent—is to visit in the Evening, & to remain—in the house—which is the most agreeable! In this way we live; & I assure you (and I *may* after such a testimonial) my Daughter[']s Salon—is voted to be the most agreeable—if not the *only*—Diplomatic Salon—at the Hague; and yet we have Ministers—English—Russian—Prussian—Hanoverian—living in Palaces & in Princely Style. I have written & I have bragged—up to the last moment for the English Post & Steamer of 4th May.

May I pray you—to frank the enclosed—my Daughter's & my family Letters—to Baltimore? I am—Respectfully & sincerely—Y[ou]r obed[ien]t Serv[an]t & Friend, Christopher Hughes.

[P.S.] My Compliments to the President. I was exceedingly pleased with his Friend—Mr. [Henry W.?] Hilliard; who passed a day here last week! an excellent & clever Man. C.H.

ALS in ScCleA. NOTE: Hughes (1786–1849), a Marylander, was one of the most experienced of U.S. representatives abroad and in 1842 had begun a second tour as Chargé d'Affaires to the Netherlands.

From David McDaniel, St. Louis Prison, Mo., 4/30. McDaniel, a native of Pickens District, S.C., states that he has been unjustly convicted in the U.S. Circuit Court of being an accomplice in the murder of Antonio José Chavis [on the Sante Fe trail in the unorganized territory of the U.S.]. He is scheduled for execution on 6/14. He asks that Calhoun obtain for himself and his brother, John McDaniel, a reprieve. McDaniel mentions his uncle, the Rev. Joseph Grisham of S.C., his parents with whom he "infers" Calhoun was acquainted, and David R. Atchison, Senator from Mo., to whom Calhoun is referred for information about the supposed murder. (A Clerk's EU reads "No action as yet on these papers.") ALS in DNA, RG 59 (State Department), Petitions for Pardon and Related Briefs, 1800–1849, no. 292A.

To R[OBERT] D[ALE] OWEN, [Representative from Ind.]

Department of State
Washington, April 30th 1844

Sir: Your note of yesterday was too late yesterday to admit of such inquiries as it called for—I have, however, caused some examinations to be made this morning, and find that you will probably meet with all the documentory evidence you desire in volumes 1 and 2 of the Democratic Review. The facts are embodied in a series of Papers purporting to be a *Retrospective Review of the South American States.* You will perhaps derrive more authentic information from this source than any one other. If the examination prove unsatisfactory, or the information imperfect—the defect may perhaps be supplied by reference to manuscript documents in this Department. With high regard, your ob[edien]t Serv[an]t, J.C. Calhoun.

LS in PHi, Dreer Collection, Presidents. NOTE: *Retrospective View* [*sic*] *of the South American States* was published in the *United States Magazine and Democratic Review* in 1838, 1:263–276, 369–380, 477–492, and 2:99–112. It was also issued separately at Washington in the same year and is attributed to Robert Greenhow, Librarian of the State Department.

From R[ICHARD] PAKENHAM

Washington, 30 April 1844

The Undersigned, Her Britannic Majesty's Envoy Extraordinary and Minister Plenipotentiary, has had the honor to receive the Note which The Hon[ora]ble John [C.] Calhoun Secretary of State of the United States, was pleased to address to the Undersigned on the 27th of this month in reply to the Note of the Undersigned of 18 [*sic*; 19] Instant, in answer to Mr. Calhoun's Note of the day proceeding [*sic*] relating to the Despatch of the Earl of Aberdeen, of which a Copy was delivered to the late Secretary of State Mr. [Abel P.] Upshur at His request.

Mr. Calhoun's Notes of the above mentioned dates have been transmitted by the Undersigned for the information of Her Majesty's Government.

The Undersigned avails Himself of this opportunity to renew to Mr. Calhoun the assurance of His high consideration. R. Pakenham.

LS in DNA, RG 59 (State Department), Notes from Foreign Legations, Great Britain, vol. 22 (M-50:22); CC in DNA, RG 46 (U.S. Senate), 28B-B12; PC in Senate Document No. 341, 28th Cong., 1st Sess., p. 68; PC in House Document No. 271, 28th Cong., 1st Sess., p. 68; PC in the Washington, D.C., *Daily National Intelligencer*, May 20, 1844, p. 2; PC in the Washington, D.C., *Spectator*, May 21, 1844, p. 2; PC in the Washington, D.C., *Globe*, May 22, 1844, p. 1; PC in the Charleston, S.C., *Courier*, May 25, 1844, p. 2; PC in *Niles' National Register*, vol. LXVI, no. 13 (May 25, 1844), p. 203; PC in Crallé, ed., *Works*, 5:347.

From R[obert] Rantoul, Jr.

Collector's Office, Custom House
Boston, Ap[ril] 30th 1844

Sir, While at Washington, lately, I had the honor to call your attention to the situation of the trade between this country and the port of Mansanilla, near the Island of Cuba. This port is one with which we have traded only about twelve or fifteen years, and the business was commenced and built up by the enterprise of Capt. Josiah Raymond, a citizen of Beverly, in this State.

The trade is mostly carried on with Boston, Salem and New York [City], and, though fluctuating, from one year to another, yet in the aggregate, is of considerable importance.

I enclose an Account of the Imports at Boston, from Mansanilla, since the first of January 1841. It will be perceived that the business of the present year nearly equals in the four months, thus far, that of all last year. The business last year was greatly diminished by the operation of the Tariff, as was our trade with most other ports of the world.

This port being on an Island by itself, and at a considerable distance from the residence of any Consul of the United States, the want of a Consul resident there (and with full powers), is continually felt. The certificates of resident merchants are a very ineffectual safeguard against frauds upon our revenue laws, and our vessels, property and seamen need the protection of an accredited representative of our Government.

Messrs. Homer & Sprague and others who have signed a memorial, desiring the appointment of Capt. Raymond, as Consul at Mansanilla, are the principal persons engaged in that trade. Their representations are worthy of entire confidence, and they are gentlemen of the highest respectability and standing as merchants.

I have known Capt. Raymond, for thirty years past. He is an

active, intelligent, faithful, and honorable man; and if appointed, would discharge the duties punctually and conscientiously, and do credit to the service abroad. I should esteem it as a personal favor, as well as a benefit to our Commercial Community, if he should receive the appointment asked for.

These sentiments, so far as I have been able to ascertain, meet with the concurrence of all parties concerned in the trade to the Island alluded to. I have the honor to be with the highest consideration, Your Obed[ien]t Serv[an]t, R. Rantoul, Jr., Collector.

ALS with En in DNA, RG 59 (State Department), Applications and Recommendations, 1837–1845, Raymond (M-687:27, frames 213–218). NOTE: An EU reads: "nomination to be made & carried up by myself to the Pres[i]d[en]t." The enclosure is a table indicating the respective value of the major imports from Manzanillo into Boston from 1841–4/30/1844. They include tobacco, palm leaf, honey, mahogany and other wood, molasses, dye wood, sugar, and other articles.

From R[obert] B[arnwell] Rhett, [Representative from S.C.], 4/30. Rhett asks Calhoun to "have dispatches prepared for Col. James M. Grimké to Rome and Naples." If no dispatches are available, Rhett requests that letters of recommendation be written for Grimké. "He will be in Washington tomorrow on his way to Europe." ALS in DNA, RG 59 (State Department), Miscellaneous Letters (M-179:104, frames 267–268).

From JOHN HEART, "Private"

Wednesday morning [April?, 1844]

Dear Sir, I embrace the opportunity of preferring a request to you which I would wished to have done personally but I fear that it would be intruding too much upon your time at a period when there are such demands upon it. I am unable to support myself by the paper [the Washington *Spectator*], and Mrs. Heart has requested me to ask for some copying from the State Department, if there is any given out to do. I can answer for her competency, & a compliance with her wish would afford her much gratification in enabling her to aid me in my struggle to get along, and would confer a great favor on myself. I remain With the highest respect Your ob[edien]t serv[an]t, Jno. Heart.

ALS in ScCleA. NOTE: This letter cannot be dated certainly except as falling between April and October, 1844.

From [JOHN R. MATHEWES]

[April, 1844]
Commenced in the Mountains [of Ga.]

My Dear Sir, By this time you are in the Arm (I will not say easy Chair) of State, and before long engaged in dangerous correspondence with the British Minister; by the by, is this the Son of Gen[era]l Packenham [*sic*] & who fell under the Watch word of "Beauty & Booty"? If so it is an omenous [*sic*] movement; such a one as when she sent Copenhagen [Sir George] Jackson to wind ["up" *interlined*] her hitherto professions of friendship, peace &c, into open & warlike demands.

I wrote you at Pendleton & hope you rec[eive]d my letter not for its value, but that I am opposed to the Paulpryism & suppression of the Post Office Genda[r]mes. In that letter I hastily & strongly urged upon your notice the *instability* of British diplomatic *professions* & this is to renew the subject in a more tangible & detailed letter.

In the first, ["place" *interlined*] (I believe I may have adverted to it in a former letter) that as long as England can keep up a Slave question excitement or a party call'd Abolition, of ["our" *altered to* "her"] *own fostering* and at nurse in *this* country—*no treaty honourable* or *abiding* can be made with her. She will hold the word of promise to the ear & break it to the sense. This I know is a twice told tale to you, but nevertheless if you keep it before your eyes during the whole negociation you will find at the end for weal or woe—that it has been the fulcrom [*sic*] upon which she rests ["of" *canceled*] her outrageous interference with the affairs & possessions of this Governm[en]t from Canada, Cuba, Gulph of Mexico, Pacific, Oregon, by land and water, to the *remotest corners of the earth*, where she is *blasting* our *character* upon the Subject of *Slavery* and *repudiation*; the former she well knows being the *only means* of paying our debts by its ["agency in an" *interlined*] *annually reproductive* essence ["(cotton)" *interlined*] from the Earth & she would rather lose our debt to her than not forever deprive us of this extraordinary ["& everlasting" *interlined*] *power of credit* in time of *War*. She is now retaliating our proposed conquest of the Canadas last war; by sustaining numerous presses ["at present" *interlined*] & expending sums in all of our States whose frontiers are widely open to her embrace. New Hampshire has got but a very small line[?] in her neighbourhood even near that no doubt are to be found the fiew [*sic*] abolitionists that are in that State. Main[e], Massachusetts & Rhode Island are one people. Maine has 3 out of her 5 sides exposed; thro' her is disseminated British intrigue into Massa[chuse]tts & Rhode Island and a portion of Connecticut; (see journals of last war for a similar movement of England on this portion of *New* England) Vermont[,] New York, Pen[n]sylvania (the quaker egg of this abolition feeling in the U. States) Ohio, Indiana are all contiguous to her influence and even Michigan begins to echo this British project for the downfall of a Republic: as you approach the Atlantic these dark shades of ultra abolition subside into indifference in these States. She uses in this country such instruments ["in this country" *canceled*] as J[ohn] Q. Adams & [Joshua R.] Giddings & whilst diverting the attention of other parts of the world on Negro *Corporeal* Slavery, she is ["at the same time" *interlined*] enslaving the White man[']s *mind* & Governm[en]t to her selfish Dogmas, to her aggrandizement[,] to her universal power & monopoly, thereby consolidating to her own uses & purposes the trade & wealth of all nations. From her Local and isolated position she is successful[l]y compell'd to cultivate the [phrenological] Bumps of *concentration* & acquisitiveness, at the same time endeavouring to obliterate them in all other nations by seeking out & using their most favourable Hobby for the promotion of civil War or Division—*peaceably* but as constantly is she pursuing this game towards this *republic* as she did against Napoleon[']s dynasty by *War* & *subsidizing* his *neighbouring States*[;] in place of war ["& subsidy" *interlined*] she is using moral influence with the World or religion or any thing else that will serve her purpose & to insure us a Waterloo defeat, in place of [Marshal] Grouchy, she has Jno. Q. Adams whose services in that line the last war, afford her sufficient evidence when he betray[e]d his Boston friends Rec[eive]d the thirty pieces of silver as Mr. [John] Randolph said in his appointment to an embassy which Jno. Adams (his father) attributed to "Aristides being banished because he was too just." Mr. Pickering (Timothy) says "That he can exhibit a temper which no candid, liberal & honourable mind w[oul]d indulge[,] manifesting a rancour alike unbecoming a Gentleman, a Statesman & Christian" &c &c. That he is in strict alliance with England in all her views towards the dismemberment & ultimate destruction of this her rival[;] it is only necessary to look at every movement of his life from the time that the father boasted "That there was not a pen in the U.S. of which the *Jacobins* were so much afraid as of my Son[']s"—his friendship & associations with the British Henry conspirators in Massachusets whom he denounced & rec[eive]d his consequent reward— *his leaving* out [of] the instructions to the comm[issione]rs [in] 1814 "the degrading practice, the impressm[en]t of Seamen must cease, ["the"(?) *altered to* "our"] *flag must protect the crew; or the U.S. can not consider themselves an independent nation"* and substituting therefor in the treaty with England an unauthorised & isolated article in this British treaty about the Slave trade which has been *since* made the Entering wedge to all of our Southern difficulties with that nation, permitting *her* to *meddle* with a question *our* Laws had already set at rest for ever, the cessation of the Slave Trade. He was after this made minister to England but am not certain. When Secretary of State he wrote an insulting ["letter" *interlined*] to the authorities of So[uth] Ca[rolina] which Gov[erno]r [John L.] Wilson communicated to the Legislature with the remark that they sh[oul]d form a rampart of their Bodies before this *British* interference with the rights of So[uth] Ca[rolina] sh[oul]d be submitted to. Georgia was threatened by him with the Bayonet of the U.S. for her unfriendly feeling towards the accustomed allies of the British when ["ever" *interlined*] at War with U.S. The Tomahawk & Scalping Knife. When war was proposed against *France* by Gen[era]l [Andrew] Jackson he was in favour of it *in Congress* but on his return home denied *this feeling* to his friends. This for a few Millions of Dollars—and his allies England & himself are ready to sacrafice ["not only" *interlined*] every dollar[']s worth of property south of the Potomac, but every life Black & White to accomplish her ["desired" *interlined*] destruction of this *republic.*

During the British Chinese Opium War he was delivering lectures in her favour saying that the sufferings of these unoffending people were right & just in furtherance of the views of God towards civilization. He is *now* horrified at the annexation of Texas when he in 1818 proclaimed that our Title to Texas "was established beyond the power of controversy" and at a subsequent period he was the cause of the Sabine ["line" *interlined*] in place of the Rio Grande being put in our Title from Spain. I believe (but will not be certain) that he slip'd over to England immediately previous to the World[']s [abolitionist] meeting held at London over which presided a superannuated co-temporary of J.Q. A[dams]'s—but to a more important subject—The Present treaty with England—permit me to repeat it. She will make none in sincerity with the U. States so long as she has hopes of producing disunion, civil war or any other means for the destruction of this Governm[en]t. She will say as in the Ashburton Treaty what Napoleon said at the time of his abdication to Caulincourt—"Make what treaty you please I shall abide by none." As long as she has her abolition party in this country doing her work for her she will be only true to that party, as in a similar case & conduct of hers she did with ["the" *interlined*] Erskine Treaty at Washington. In the Ashburton Treaty she has already decided that what is murder *north* of Mason[']s & Dixon[']s line is not murder *South* of it & quotes the action of her friend J.Q. Adams, & others of her party, in the Amistad case as authority for this monstrous assumption of *her* construing *alone* the merits of the treaty excluding the sacred Right of Property & Life at the Southern & Western points of the U. States and only recognizing ["them" *interlined*] at the North & East—*requiring us to give up* a woman which she has pronounced *innocent* of *Murder* & secreting the murderers of a whole family of Americans.

What if a ship load of *her impress[e]d* seamen were to enter ["a southern port" *interlined*] with one of *her* vessels of war *without* having *committed murder*, but merely securing their officers. Suppose that under sympathy for our Colour, language[,] Religion, relationship, our Southern citizens were with the expression of horror at the *greater crime of impressment worse* than *slavery* & which our Laws will never submit to; I say supposing we were to receive these seamen with open arms & send them to the West as a place of security as she did these pirates & these murderers in her West India Islands! ! She hangs her subjects for forgery—we do not—her game Laws would be ridiculed here—yet she demands & indiscriminate surrender of Criminals from us without a trial or hearing but before she will deliver up the convicted, aye self convicted, she must first enquire whether the treaty was intended for So[uth] or North of Mason & Dixon[']s Line of the *U. States* & if the case happens in the former she denies the existence of the Treaty towards that *section* of the *Union* & rejoices in the murder of our fellow citizens, on the Land & high Seas, receives the murderers with open arms & fraternizes with them in fellow citizenship. Did Robespierre, Danton or any other french Revolutionist come up to or exceed such cruel deception with fair promises—all compromising the Rights of the South[;] for Northern popularity has hitherto failed in sustaining the popularity of the negociator, & the validity of the Treaty. Gen[era]l Jackson[,] for deceiving the South was made LLD by Mr. [Daniel] Webster &ca. The latter in the Ashburton Treaty whilst forgetting to secure the South is now receiving his reward from Political friends & foes. Our friend Judge [Langdon] Cheves—leaving his rising & controuling star—the South—was sacraficed to make way for Mr. [Nicholas] Biddle—the one no ["more" *interlined*] like unto the other than Hyperion to a Satyr. If a Southern man wishes to retain his high & merited greatness, let him exercise his talents equally towards the security & promotion of the interests of the South & West as to any other part of the Union, but let him once be cozen[e]d into the honours & approbation of the most clamourous to the exclusion of the most unoffending, & silent—he will be soon mouthed & then swallow'd & sent home again to make way for a more favour[e]d occupant of his successful & honourable position. This has been the fate of all Southern Statesmen. Whenever they could[,] they ["northern Politicians" *interlined*] have showed their feelings in this way toward yourself—and nothing but the determination of Character with which you have hitherto withstood their smiles & Blandishments, their invitations to do as others have done; ["had you" *interlined*] turned your back ["& your thoughts away fo" *canceled*] upon the South & your thoughts & favourable feelings only upon them, ["or you" *interlined and then* "or" *canceled*] would long since have ["had" *interlined*] cast upon your shoulders the highest honours they could bestow as a voluntary gift & they would ["now" *interlined*] have been saved the present mortification of being *compelled* ["to do it" *interlined*] by your constancy to truth & principle at this crisis of danger when all false games must be losing to those who have been living by them; I say they ["have been" *canceled and* "are now" *interlined*] compell'd to render unto Caesar the things which are Caesar[']s.

Upon the subject of Texas—her annexation is "Caesar aut nullus" with the U.S. Let England get foothold there ["&" *interlined*] she will protect her present ally if not collony against all future attacks of ours by Land or Sea, and all our trade which is now said to be valuable by Land with Mexico will in peace as ["well as" *interlined*] war be subject to British surveillance. Texas as a part of the U.S. is a Sine Qua Non to the peace commerce wellfare & happiness of the U.S.; & ["the" *interlined*] preservation of British intrigue[,] meddling & wish to destroy this Gover[n]ment & a great proportion of its inhabitants. Where we know we are right she will only continue to make wry faces even if we perfect our intentions—but "let the gall'd jade wince so our withers are unwrung." Lord Aberdeen, in reply to Brougham on some question about the French Right of Search &c. said in Parli[amen]t the other day—"The *first* object of G. Britain must now be *the preservation* of *Peace* among the nations of Europe. They must not risque the first & greatest ["of" *interlined*] blessings for the sake of any work of supererogation or humanity. To do so would be the most preposterous attempt any great nation could engage in."

In all of our your [*sic*] plans[,] views & intentions upon the subject of negociation &c with this nation (England) permit me to add one or two suggestions which may appear at the first as unnecessary & too far from the ["subject" *canceled and* "consideration" *interlined*] of important subjects. The four walls of your bed chamber are not sacred from British espionage. Servants of every description in ["your employment" *interlined*] & way, within your hearing or presence have their ears, eyes, & guessing[?] faculties *in pay*. Your written views from friends or yourself no lock can secure from being copied & in possession of the British minister & they are always ready to be forewarned so as to be fore armed. Therefore your *own bosom alone* is capable of *suspending their knowledge* of *most important action*. These suggestions I speak advisedly of as when I was in England I was not only forewarned of the fact but had it demonstrated in the bed chambre of myself & friend in London. Napoleon said of the British—"their ministers never publish facts—a false account is sent to be submitted to the *public* and deposited in the archives; and a *secret* one *stating the* Truth for your *ministers themselves* to *act* upon, but *never* to be *produced*. So that your ministers upon an enquiry being made by Parliament, have a set of documents in the archives ready to submit for inspection; from whence conclusions are to be drawn & decisions made—everything appears satisfactory tho' the ground work of the whole is false. Nobody knows them better than I do. Your system is a compound of Lies & truth. In no other ministry in the world is there so much *Machiavelism* practiced; because you have so much to defend, and so many important points to contest against the rest of Europe & because you are obliged to enter into explanations with the [English] Nation." Now my dear Sir I could write a great deal more but I know you are if possible more fatigued than I am[;] yet you must excuse me. I write for my country, for wife[,] children & friends—for Posterity. Had England been met firmly as she ought to have been on the subject of her meddling with the concerns of this country 20 years ago, she would not now be whetting the knife of the African Race against the Throats of that part of the U. States which thro' her mouth ["piece" *interlined*] in this country she has dared to call in our Congress—Slave Breeders—but depend upon it you must first scotch the snake—Her abolition army in the U.S. before you can kill or in other words make a treaty of any kind or for any purpose with her. I shall not sign my name for Post Office reasons but it will be gratifying to me to hear that this & my former came safely to your hands. Mr. [Edward] Everett or any other New Englander who if not openly an abolitionist, his friends, relations or connexions most probably are will not do at the Court of St. James. As you progress an inch they will pull you back a foot in these negociations. See the unanimous & reiterated resolutions of

Massa[chuse]tts virtually carrying out the wishes of Old England[,] a dissolution of the Government of the U.S. There is more danger in the present state of things than we are willing to believe but with patience, prudence & PRECAUTION out of this Nettle danger we *can* pluck the flower safety. In the negociation, aim high and our object will be hit—by not aiming high we oftner [*sic*] undershoot the mark than hit it—and another thing—the British always endeavour to get ["first" *interlined*] the ["first" *interlined and then canceled*] full extent of our desires by claiming extravagancies. This inflames us—we pout—she pats us—kindly asks us what we wish. All yet may go well— we candidly tell. She apparently acceeds *unwillingly* to our *extraordinary* demands whilst laughing to think how easily she has obtained from us what she wished to know & how like a child we are satisfied with any other Toy than what at first we were determin[e]d to have. See the Treaty of Ghent—'twas thus she[?] serv[e]d Mr. [Henry] Clay—J.Q. Adams. We went to war for free trade & Sailors['] rights which was forgotten in the treaty when these Comm[issione]rs got alarmed at their opponents claims "Uti possidetis," the protection of Indian rights &c & J.Q.A. in his alarm in order to appease the Lion threw in the treaty the slave question. To reach England[']s feelings she must ["be" *interlined*] made to see the effect this conduct of hers w[oul]d produce were we to act the same to her & *her Laws* which are as repugnant to our feelings. *Impressment.* Slavery produces no paupers—no starvlings—it does not steal men to leave their families to be *shot at, maim'd or killed* never to see their Home again. Our jails are not filled with Slave criminals &c &c. Be careful of the cidivant Minister Mr. [Henry S.] Fox. I understand he has not been an idle looker on at Washington City. Such men as J.Q. A[dams] & co cannot reject his council & friendship. We rec[eive]d [Charles] Dickens here with open arms[;] he splintered us with touchwood. England cannot tamely look on & see us *grow* & manufacture Cotton whilst she has to *import* & manufacture this valuable production sought after by all the world from the Pallace [*sic*] to the humblest Shante [*sic*] with more avidity than gold & silver, & the poorer the house keeper the more anxiety to obtain Cotton. The longer the winter, the severer the climate the more valuable for indoor work & profit. England will be subdued only by the public reprobation of her *allies* in *this* Country—the leaders to be exposed by detection & a fearless exhibition to the people of the United States the insiduous and uprooting policy of a pretended, Philanthropic religious effort of Friendship & peace offering by a nation whose Arnolds & andres are

379

now within our peaceful & reposing citadel. There will be no rest for us 'till this *foolery & frivolity* is publickly exposed and forever put down.

Ended on the Seaboard [near Charleston].

[P.S.] Do not think I have an itch for writing. 'Tis done with pain & reluctance whenever I am compell[e]d to write & more especially uninvitedly but take the will for the deed.

ALU in ScCleA.

From J.H. Pillsbury and Eben[eze]r Webster, [Bangor, Maine?, *ca.* 4/———]. Pillsbury and Webster have been authorized since 1838 to cut timber on the Aroostook. In order to float their lumber down the St. John through the territory of New Brunswick, they have been obliged to pay a duty of 8 shillings 3 pence per ton. They have made payment bonds to New Brunswick of $11,827.20 and have paid five thousand dollars of the amount. They are presently being sued by New Brunswick authorities for the remainder. Pillsbury and Webster seek "justice" under the Treaty of Washington to have the suit stopped and the bonds canceled. LS in DNA, RG 76 (Records of Boundary and Claims Commissions and Arbitrations), Letters and Miscellaneous Documents Relating to the Maine-New Brunswick Boundary Dispute, 1824–1850, document 182; PC in House Document No. 110, 29th Cong., 1st Sess., pp. 77–78.

From CH[ARLES] H. WINDER, [Clerk, Department of State]

[Washington, April?, 1844]

Sir, In obedience to your directions, I wrote to George Upshur Esq[ui]re, the executor of the late Hon[ora]ble A[bel] P. Upshur, desiring him to forward to the Department all the letters and and [*sic*] papers, in his possession in relation to the mission of Mr. William Hogan to Mexico.

I have received from Mr. Upshur a reply, in which he informs me, that he had, before receiving my letter, received from the President [John Tyler] the Same request, and in compliance with it, he had forwarded to him two letters from Mr. Hogan to the late Secretary, being all that he could find.

In conformity with the desire you expressed this morning—that I would inform you of all that I knew in relation to the mission of Mr. Hogan—I have the honor to State, that in 1840 a Bull of the pope of Rome [Gregory XVI], appeared in this Country, Containing a deep Censure upon the institution of Slavery, and appealing to the Catholics to use their utmost exertions to destroy it. At least such was the Construction put upon it by the fanatics of the north & their worthy Coadjutor, Dan[ie]l O[']Connell.

This Bull was republished ["last" *canceled and* "this" *interlined*] year, & was wielded with ve[ry gr]eat effect by the enemies of the South.

The subject arrested the attention of Judge Upshur—he felt a great anxiety that the Catholic Church in the United States should disclaim, by Authority, the Construction put upon the Bull by the abolitionists. In a letter to Mr. William Carroll, a catholic, now attached to this Department, he says, "I can only repeat, it (the Bull) is likely to become a powerful weapon in the hands of the abolitionists. It ought in my opinion to be explained. I cannot pretend to say what Course the Church in this Country will feel itself Authorized to take; but suggest that the following is the *best* that ought to be done.

1. A declaration Should be published from the proper Authority, assuring the public that the Church here understands the Bull, only as referring to the African *Slave trade*, and not to the institution of Slavery as it exists among us.

2d. The Pope should be induced to Confirm this Construction by a new Bull."

Mr. Carroll had a conferrence [*sic*] with [Samuel Eccleston] the Archbishop of the Catholic Church [in Baltimore], and submitted to him Judge Upshur's letter. The Archbishop disclaimed to this gentleman the Construction put upon this Bull by the Abolitionists, but told him at the same time, that he would not be committed by any verbal Communication upon so important a subject, but that ["]if the Secretary would write to him either officially or unofficially, he would Cheerfully & promptly respond in the same way."

The Secretary of Course declined to enter into a Correspondence with the head of the Catholic Church, upon a subject that really required no correspondence. If the Bull was improperly construed, injustice was done to the Church, as well as injury to the south, and it became the duty of the archbishop spontaneously to repudiate this pernicious construction. This the archbishop would not do.

Judge Upshur from other information he had received, became keenly apprehensive of the designs, of the Catholic priesthood abroad, upon our institution of Slavery. It was to obtain authentic information on this subject, as well as of England upon Mexico & Texas, that Mr. Hogan was sent abroad.

I am not aware that any specific compensation was agreed upon, & I suppose from the nature of the case there could be none. I respectfully refer you to the accompanying letters belonging to the files of this Department. I have the honor to be very Resp[ectfull]y, Your ob[edien]t ser[van]t, Ch. H. Winder.

ALS in ViU, Richard Kenner Crallé Papers.

MAY 1–15, 1844

◫

Entering his second month in office, the Secretary of State continued to find the business of his department far-flung and complex. Attention had to be paid to affairs in the Caribbean. Appropriations and appointments took up much of his time. As to appointments, he was a member of an administration that, contrary to Calhoun's own well-known principles, was replacing many officers, and which was also losing many of its appointments in the Senate.

The Senate was still deliberating the Texas Treaty. Much of its time was not spent on the main issue, however, but rather on investigations designed to embarrass the administration and on detecting and censuring Benjamin Tappan, the Ohio free-soil Democrat who had violated the Senate's executive sessions by leaking documents to the press. By this time Calhoun had realized that the rejection of the annexation treaty in the Senate was a virtual certainty. He was convinced that the annexation of Texas was desired by a majority of the public and vital to the interests of the South. The problem was in translating public sentiment and urgent interest into accomplished fact, given the resistance of the established political leaders of both parties to allowing a new issue to upset their carefully laid calculations in regard to the Presidential election.

There was, of course, no hope from the Whigs, who convened in national convention in early May and, to no one's surprise, nominated Henry Clay for President (as it turned out, for the last time). The hope was in the Democratic party, where the Texas sentiment was strongest. With many others, Calhoun saw that this was the case, but could not foresee exactly how it would work out. He was willing to support any Democratic candidate who was pro-Texas. He thought that the Democratic National Convention and the friends of President Tyler, who were to meet in Baltimore at the same time in late May, ought to collaborate. Tyler should be considered as a Democratic candidate for the nomination along with others.

Calhoun himself was still looked to by some as a potential Presidential candidate. On May 10 in New Orleans, a place where he had never been particularly popular, a mass meeting nominated him for

383

President as an independent people's candidate—which showed the opinion of that greatest of Western cities of Calhoun's Texas treaty. But Calhoun sought no nomination for himself. He was willing to serve only in the unlikely event that no other pro-Texas candidate could be agreed upon.

◫

To R[OBERT] M. T. HUNTER, [Lloyds, Va.?]

Washington, May 1844

My dear Sir, Since you left here great changes have taken place. Every thing is in a state of confusion in the Democratick ranks. Mr. [Martin] V[an] B[uren]'s letter has completely prostrated him, and with him [Thomas H.] Benton, [William] Allen, [Benjamin] Tappan & [Silas] Wright have fallen. The annexation of Texas has become the absorbing question. It will probably control the presidential election. From present indications, there will be three candidates. Mr. [John] Tyler[']s & Mr. V[an] Buren[']s friends seem resolved to run them, and the friends of annexation, who are indisposed to rerun ["him" *canceled and* "the former" *interlined*] will start another. [Lewis] Cass, [James] Buchanan, [Charles] Stewart, [Richard M.] Johnson & [Levi] Woodbury are spoken of. The question of selection is to be decided at Baltimore, where the two conventions, Tyler's & the other, is to meet on the same day. The prospect is great confusion and difficulty in making the selection.

If the friends of annexation can agree on a candidate, the prospect is, that he would defeat both [Henry] Clay & V[an] B[uren], should they both run, and pretty certainly Clay should the latter not run. That he will withdraw or be dropt, I regard as ["prob" *canceled*] highly probable, so that the prospect is fair of success if concentration on any respectable and influential candidate can be ["rallied on" *canceled and* "had" *interlined*]. I prefer myself Tyler to any northern man. He will be the safest for the South; &, If he can be made the candidate, I will give him cheerfully my support, notwithstanding my objections to much of his administration. I am clearly of the opinion, that he ought to be treated as one of the candidates of the party, and that the two conventions, to preserve harmony & to obtain unity of action, ought, if possible, to be brought to act together, or at least to unite on the same individual. The success of the annexation question depends on it. In this state of things, it appears to me important, that little should be said about the candidates and the effort should be made to give the greatest impulse to the question of annexation. It is to the South & the Union the vital question. If the treaty should be rejected, which is now almost certain, I am under strong impressions, that the govt. of Texas will propose an alliance offensive & defensive to England, & France & the U. States or a guaranty of her independence, which in effect will be the same, in less than a month, unless such a demonstration shall be made in her favour, as to assure her, she will not be deserted by the South & West. The U.S. could not agree to such a treaty. It would ["be in fact" *interlined*] against themselves; but there is little doubt, the other two powers would & where would we be placed? Our condition never was so critical.

As to myself, I hold annexation to be the paramount question, more so than the presidential, except as the means of effecting it. I shall give ["it" *interlined*] my support ["to it" *canceled*], without becoming the partisan of any candidate; and I intend, that my position & course shall conform to that determination. I, of course, desire my friends to regard me wholly in the light of its honest & zealous supporter. Thus regarded, I do not think it would be advisable to present my name, as a candidate. It would give me the attitude of using the occasion to advance myself, and place me on the level of the others, who are striving to get the nomination. It appears to me, that there is but one possible occurrence, in which my name could be brought forward with propriety, or in conformity with the position, which I desire to occupy; and that is, in case I should be the only person on whom the ["parties" *canceled and* "friends of the several candidates" *interlined*] could be brought to unite at Baltimore. If such should be the case, I certainly would not decline to accept, and it is only, in that contingency, ["that" *canceled*] it would be advisable, that my name should be presented.

I take it for granted, that the friends of annexation will take care to make it a condition, that ["the" *canceled*] no one shall receive their support, who is not the friend of immediate annexation.

Under this aspect of things, in this unexpected turn of events, ["it is of the utmost" *canceled*] the proceedings at Baltimore will be of the deepest interest, and it is of the utmost importance, that there should be a full attendance, not only of its members, but that able & experienced men, who are not ["members" *interlined*] should be present. If you are not a member, I hope you will make it a point to be there. The safety of the South & the Union, may depend on its action. Truly, J.C. Calhoun.

ALS in DNA, RG 109 (War Department Collection of Confederate Records), Citizen File, R.M.T. Hunter.

From W[ILLIA]M M. BLACKFORD

Legation of U.S.

Bogotá, May 1st [18]44

Sir, I have the honor to inform you that on 22d ultimo I concluded with [Joaquin Acosta] the Secretary of Foreign Affairs a Convention of Indemnity for the claim of Captain John Hugg, a citizen of the United States, for losses sustained by him during the late civil war. The documents in this case were transmitted to me by the Consul of the U.S. at Carthagena. The amount of indemnity obtained is nearly as much as the claimant demanded. The price—fifteen cents—at which he had valued the cotton, was objected to as exorbitant. Upon enquiry, I found it was extravagant, and proposed to reduce the price to twelve and a half cents per pound, which proposition was agreed to. I transmit, herewith, a translation of the Convention. I do not apprehend any difficulty as to the appropriation of the money by Congress.

When I last had the honor of addressing you, I hoped, ere this to bring the claim of the Morris to a settlement. In this hope I have been disappointed.

As the time which I agreed to wait for the arrival of the document, expected by the Secretary, and by him deemed important to secure the concurrence of the chambers, had more than elapsed, I determined, early in last month to demand a definitive answer to the proposition, which, in a spirit of compromise, I had made in January last. Fortunately, the receipt of a letter from Mr. [Allen A.] Hall, our Chargé at Caracas, informing me of the offer, made by Venezuela, to pay Eighteen thousand Dollars, cash, in full of her part of the claim, enabled me to make the demand, with a stronger probability of receiving a favorable answer. I, accordingly, on the 12th ult. addressed to the Secretary a note, requiring an explicit acceptance or rejection of my offer, by the 17th of the month—beyond which day, I told him, I should not consider myself longer bound to abide by its terms. A copy of this note and a translation of the Secretary's answer are herewith transmitted.

You will observe the ambiguous character of his answer, and that, after explicitly stating the Granadian Government could not, consistently with duty, enlarge the offer which it had, heretofore made—an offer rejected by me as utterly inadequate—he trusts I will not lose the hope of a speedy settlement of the claim, which he says will not be deferred beyond one or two months.

I immediately waited upon him, and had a long conversation upon the subject. Persuaded of his and [Gen. Pedro Alcantara Herran] the President's desire that the claim should be settled, I inferred the obstacle to immediate action to be the uncertain fate of the Convention in the chambers. He admitted this to be the true reason. I pressed him to sign the convention at once—that the Executive would thus discharge its duty—that, if the chambers withheld the appropriation, the responsibility would rest upon them—and that, if the money were not voted at the present, it would probably be during the next, session. He replied that the Convention would, assuredly, be rejected by both houses, on grounds apart from its merits—and that the Executive had already sustained so many mortifying defeats during the present session, that it was unwilling to give the chambers an opportunity of adding to the list. I appreciated the force of these objections, and agreed with him in the opinion, that the Convention would be rejected, if now submitted to Congress, and that, practically, it was the same, whether it was signed now, or after the adjournment. But I pressed him to give me a distinct assurance, that it should then be signed—in which case, I told him, I would still regard myself as bound by my offer. He had many reasons to allege, why he could give no other assurance than that implied in his note of the 16 April, which he thought was sufficient to satisfy me as to the intentions of his Government. He went so far as to say that he saw no obstacle to a settlement of the claim, which the adjournment would not obviate.

I then said I must adhere to the resolution announced in my note, of the 12th ultimo—but that if, in the meantime, I received no instructions on the subject, I would, in the first week in June next, be still willing to make a settlement, on the basis of my proposition—and with this understanding the conference closed.

A sum proportionate to that granted by Venezuela, would considerably exceed that which I proposed to accept. It may be proper therefore, to explain why I am disposed, notwithstanding, to abide by the offer I have made.

That offer was made at a time, when the letters of Mr. Hall held out no hope of an adjustment of the claim by Venezuela, and when an elaborate discussion of its merits here had, apparently, produced no favorable impression upon this Government. I adhere to it now—1st.

Because the sum is, in my opinion, not a great deal below a fair indemnity, taking all the circumstances into view, and 2nd because, I have not the slightest hope, that this Republic can be brought to pay her proportionate amount, upon the basis of the Venezuelan settlement—unless the arguments of the Diplomatic agent here were enforced by a naval demonstration—and 3d because reference must of necessity, be had to the exceedingly embarrassed state of the finances of New Granada, as well as to the precarious duration of peace and order within its limits.

Ordinary prudence would suggest the expediency of receiving, at the present moment, the sum I have indicated, rather than to defer, for a year or two, the settlement of the claim, in the, perhaps, vain expectation of extorting three or four thousand Dollars more, from the unpopular Government of a country, in which a revolution occurs, on an average, once in about five years. I feel assured I shall consult the true interests of the claimants by bringing the case to a final adjustment upon the terms I have proposed, and which I consider to have been virtually acceded to.

Should the Secretary, after the adjournment, notwithstanding all that has passed, still refuse to conclude a Convention—which I do not, however, anticipate—I shall then, under a full sense of the responsibility, proceed to urge the adoption of measures, which, in my opinion, will be necessary to bring the case to a favorable issue and, at the same time, vindicate the rights and honor of our country.

I omitted to mention, in its proper connexion, that in presenting the claim of Capt. Hugg, I took occasion in my note of 4th April 1843, to state that Mr. [Ramon Leon] Sanchez, Consul of the United States at Carthagena, complained of want of courtesy, on the part of the Governor of that Province, in not answering his official letters upon the business. In a note of the 22d ult. the Secretary gave such explanations as the case admitted. A translation of his note and a copy of my answer are herewith transmitted.

The expectation, expressed in my despatch No. 22 that the feeling of hostility against the Secretary of Foreign Relations might lead the chambers to attempt to legislate him out of office, has been in part verified. They refused to repeal the law, creating a new Department of Foreign Relations, but withheld, some weeks since, the appropriation for the salary of the Secretary. Public sentiment did not sanction this movement, and, on reconsideration, last week, the salary was voted by the House, & will be by the Senate. The chambers persist, however, in refusing appropriations for all the Foreign missions—except the useless one at Rome—and, in consequence, the Chargés of the Republic have been recalled from London, Quito and Lima. The army has also been reduced from five, to three, thousand men, and other economical reforms effected, which, altogether will reduce the expenditures of the Government several hundred thousand Dollars. A favorite measure of the present administration was the subdivision of the Provinces into large Cantons. A bill for this purpose was introduced, and, after an animated and boisterous debate, rejected by the House by a large majority. During the recent Revolution Congress passed a law, giving extraordinary powers to the President & the Governors of the Provinces. The President, in his message at the opening of the session, recommended a modification of this Law—the crisis, which rendered it necessary, having passed. A Bill for its total repeal was passed in both Houses. The President vetoed it, and the chambers adhered, by a unanimous vote, to their opinion. The veto suspends the Bill until next session, when, if two thirds of both Houses sanction it, it becomes a law. In the mean time the chambers have passed another Bill, effecting, in another way, the same object. This will also, I presume, receive a veto. I learn that, in this event, still another bill will be carried, which, in like manner, the President will refuse to sign.

I have already informed you, that the Bill abolishing all discriminating duties, which had passed the House, was defeated in the Senate by a majority of one vote. In my last, I stated that a bill had been introduced into the Senate, placing the flag of the United States on the footing of the most favored nation. I regret now to have to inform you that it was lost in that body by the same vote. Nothing, in the shape of favorable legislation, need be hoped from the present session of Congress, so far as our commerce is concerned.

To appreciate fully the great reluctance of this Government to come to a settlement in the case of the Morris, it must be recollected, that it has never yet recognized any of the numerous claims, based upon spoliations committed on neutral commerce, during the existence of Colombia. It is true that, in the cases of the Josephine & Ranger, the Granadian Congress appropriated the money to pay its proportion of the Indemnity—but the Convention was made, ten years before, by the Colombian Government, before the dismemberment of the Republic. England & France have claims, to a large amount, of a character similar to those, the documents of which fill the archives of this Legation. The English & *French* Chargés d'Affaires here are patiently awaiting the issue of the negotiation in the case of the Morris. The Granadian Government, therefore, is reluctant to make a settlement, not only because the Treasury is in a wretched condition, and public credit so low that money is borrowed, for current expenses, at a rate of Interest, varying from one and a quarter, to two per cent, *per month*, but, because of the precedent which it will establish and the conviction that it will be promptly and vigorously urged to make like indemnity to the claimants of other nations.

The discrepancy, between the sum granted by Venezuela, and that which I have offered to receive, is to be regretted—but I do not perceive how independent negotiations, carried on at points so widely apart; with Governments differing so materially in their prosperity and ability to pay; and in the absence of all common & explicit instructions; could result in a nearer approximation of the amounts of indemnity obtained.

I have the honor to state that the Postal Convention, which I concluded with this Government, on the 6th March, and a copy of which I transmitted with my No. 22 has been ratified by both Houses of the Granadian Congress.

The uncertainty and tardiness of communication, between this Legation and Washington, induce me, thus earlier than I should otherwise do, most respectfully to ask the favor of a leave of absence for four or five months, for the purpose of visiting my family—the Leave to take effect at any time after the first of November of this year, when the business of the Legation—the state of the roads, river & weather—and the prospect of meeting a vessel for the United States— may concur to render it expedient to leave my post. I shall by that time have been resident here, considerably more than two years— during which, I trust, I have devoted myself zealously to the discharge of my official duties—with what ability or success the Department can best judge. My private affairs render my presence in the United States desirable, and I need not say how anxious I am to see my family. Under these circumstances, I hope the President will be pleased to regard my application in a favorable light.

As our cruizers now frequently visit the Ports of this Country, I am emboldened to ask the further favor, that a sloop of war may be ordered to touch at Carthagena, about the 15th December next, to convey me to some port in the United States. This is asked, in view of the uncertainty of finding any vessel bound homewards—when I reach the coast, and in the conviction that the favor may be granted without involving any inconvenience or expense—as the cruizer may, in the ordinary routine of service, convey me home.

I most earnestly request that I may be apprized, at the earliest possible moment, of the decision of the Department, with respect to both of these applications—that favorable or not I may make arrangements conformably thereto.

My No. 19, covering duplicates of Nos. 13 & 14 was entrusted, by the Consul at Carthagena, to Lieut. [Richard W.] Meade U.S.N. who sailed in the Brig America, on 18th January last. We have a rumor, that the Brig was wrecked and passengers and crew lost. The rumor I fear is but too well founded.

I again, respectfully, request that you will give positive orders that nothing, intended for me, may be forwarded to the Despatch Agent, N.Y. I have the honor to be, with high respect, Your Ob[e-dien]t Serv[an]t, Wm. M. Blackford.

ALS (No. 24) with Ens in DNA, RG 59 (State Department), Diplomatic Despatches, Colombia, vol. 10 (T-33:10, frames 205–220), received 6/22. NOTE: This despatch was addressed to A[bel] P. Upshur.

Henry Buckmaster, Wayne County, Ohio, to [President] John Tyler, 5/1. Buckmaster asks that the U.S. government seek "redress" and "justice" from the government of Mexico for incidents that occurred in 1840–1841 in connection with the sale of $7,000 worth of horses and goods to persons representing themselves to be officials of that government. He relates at length circumstances in which he was cheated of payment and his partner murdered and robbed, and then the murderers freed and his goods seized by the government. He encloses an affidavit by a witness. ADS with En in DNA, RG 59 (State Department), Miscellaneous Letters (M-179:108, frames 131–142).

From Edward Curtis, Collector [of Customs], New York [City], 5/1. He asks that passports be furnished for Gerard H. Coster, his wife Matilda, and their three sons. Coster will gladly take charge of any despatches due for Paris. ALS in DNA, RG 59 (State Department), Passport Applications, vol. 31, nos. 2090 and 2091 (M-1372: 14).

From F[RANCIS] M. DIMOND

United States Consulate
Vera Cruz, May 1d 1844

Sir, Since I had the honour to address you on the 30 ult[im]o, I have been credibly informed that the Two Mexican Steamers of War,

which left here on the evening of the 28th ult[im]o said to be destined
for New York, have actually been ordered to Tobasco, to protect that
place against the late Governor Semana [*sic*; Francisco Sentmanat],
this Government having received information from the Mexican
Consul at New Orleans, that General Semana was to embark from
that port with men destined for Tobasco; this General Semana
(formerly the Governor of Tobasco), rebel[l]ed against the supreme
Government and was d[r]iven with a few troops into Yucatan last
year, after which he went to Havana and over to New Orleans.   I
have the honour to be Sir most Respectfully Your Ob[edient] Servant, F.M. Dimond.

ALS (No. 220) in DNA, RG 59 (State Department), Consular Despatches, Veracruz, vol. 5 (M-183:5), received 5/21.

From EDWARD EVERETT

London, 1 May 1844
Sir, Since my despatch Nro. 115 was written, I have had another
conversation with Lord Aberdeen, on the subject of Mr. [Henry]
Wheaton's convention with the Zoll-Verein.   It arose in reference to
what passed in the House of Commons on the evening of the 24th.
With a view of ascertaining how far this government would be disposed generally to agree to a similar convention, I made the remark
that I supposed, that with the exception of Tobacco, there would be
no great difficulty in their coming to a similar arrangement.   Lord
Aberdeen said he did not know whether he was accurately informed
as to the provisions of Mr. Wheaton's Convention; but supposed in
the material points he was.   I offered to send him a copy of the German Memorandum, upon which the Convention was drawn up; but
he said he had already received it; I presume from Mr. [John] Ward,
a commercial agent of this government now in Berlin, with whom Mr.
Wheaton has been in communication.   Lord Aberdeen then said that
with reference to Cotton and Rice the question might be entertained,
but that no such reduction as that contemplated on Tobacco could
be thought of.   He then said, "besides, as I have already observed to
you, we consider that by our commercial convention with you, we are
entitled to send our fabrics to the United States, on the same terms on
which you receive articles of the same description from any other
country: that commercial treaties were of two kinds one which did

and one which did not stipulate, that this reciprocity should be conditional, and that ours was of the latter kind."

I replied that I was aware the British Government took this distinction, and that I had carefully adverted to what passed in the House of Commons on the 24th; that the American Government had taken a different view of the subject, and considered the conditional clause, which had latterly been introduced into reciprocity treaties, both by ourselves and other powers, as by no means intended to affect the reciprocity principle in its general character, but to make more clear, by positive reservation, a right which must always be supposed to exist; vizt., that of coming to specific arrangements with a third power, on conditions, which we are willing to extend to all other powers: that this right was in our view of the matter unquestionable, and had more than once been asserted & exercised by the United States. He said that their understanding was clearly to the contrary, & repeated the observation relative to their treaty with Brazil, which I have reported in a former despatch.

In the discussion which took place in the House of Commons on the 29th of April, on occasion of the annual financial exposition of the chancellor of the Exchequer, allusions were made by one or two speakers on the opposition side of the House, to the convention between the United States and the Zoll-Verein, but no direct notice was taken of these remarks by the Government. Mr. [Henry] Goulburn observed in reference to any arrangements relative to Brazilian sugar, that they should be very careful not to infringe the commercial treaty with us; but that no sugar was raised for exportation in the United States. Several speakers regretted that the government in abandoning the duty on Wool, had not made up their minds also to repeal the duty on Cotton. This sentiment was expressed with great emphasis by Mr. M[ark] Philips, the member for Manchester, where a public meeting has lately been held on the subject of this reduction.

You perceive from Mr. Goulburn's exposition, (of which the fullest report which I have seen is apparently that contained in the [London] Morning Chronicle of the 30th April), that he proposes to reduce about £400,000 of taxation, in consequence of the prosperous condition of the Treasury. Should this prosperity continue, Parliament will be called upon next year to decide upon the continuance of the Property tax and the repeal of a considerable amount of miscellaneous taxation. Should the latter course be preferred, which I am inclined to think it will be, I should have little doubt that Cotton and Tobacco would be at the head of the favored articles. The duties on both are of course purely revenue duties. There is a very strong manufacturing interest in favor of the total repeal of the Cotton duty; and the enormous extent to which Tobacco is known to be smuggled, constitutes a powerful motive for a great reduction in the duty on that article. This motive is counterbalanced only by the necessities of the Revenue, and the unwillingness to institute an experiment on so productive an item as tobacco. Should the state of the public finances admit the repeal of a couple of millions of taxes, this experiment I feel confident will be made. I am, sir, very respectfully, your obedient servant, Edward Everett.

LS (No. 117) in DNA, RG 59 (State Department), Diplomatic Despatches, Great Britain, vol. 52 (M-30:48), received 5/20; FC in MHi, Edward Everett Papers, 49:10–14 (published microfilm, reel 23, frames 5–7). NOTE: This despatch was addressed to John Nelson as Secretary of State ad interim.

To George W. Greene, U.S. Consul at Rome, 5/1. Calhoun introduces James M. Grimké, "who has been recommended to me by the Hon[ora]ble R[obert] B[arnwell] Rhett" of S.C. Grimké is about to visit Europe; Calhoun will appreciate any attention given him by Greene. FC in DNA, RG 59 (State Department), Consular Instructions, 10:243.

From ALEX[ANDE]R HAMMETT

Consulate of the U.S. of America
Naples, 1st May 1844

Sir, My different communications have always put in doubt a favorable result of the Treaty negotiations of England & France with this Country. Appearances seem now as strong as ever against it; at least the negotiation is here at an end, and if anything be effected hereafter, it will be at Paris. The Neapolitan Commissioners do not view in the same light their reciprocity principle (for there can be none, they say, where the parties are not balanced) and will only grant one specific advantage for another, of equal, or greater value, as their inferior position requires.

I have before taken the liberty of expressing my opinion, that our commercial relations with this Country would not be changed for the better, even had we a treaty on the footing of the most favoured nation.

As long as the flag of the Two Sicilies enjoys 30% reduction of the duties on Cargoes from America, our Citizens will be in some measure benifited by those shipped in the U.S., though our own flag be not available for the freight of such cargoes. For England, France and Holland are thereby deprived of half the supply of refined Sugars, Coffee &c. which they would regain, as soon as the Sicilian flag be precluded from the enjoyment of the aforesaid reduction, a necessary consequence of the contemplated Treaties, should they be ever agreed to.

An American Legation then at Naples is ridiculous, when there exist no political relations whatever, and but very few commercial between the two Countries; neither is it due to the dignity of our Government to keep it up with unnecessary expense when His Sicilian Majesty has never thought fit to appoint a correspondent one to reside at Washington. Indeed the report to the Senate for the first nomination was not warranted by the facts. I have the honor to be, Sir, very respectfully, your Obed[ien]t Serv[an]t, Alexr. Hammett.

ALS (No. 122) in DNA, RG 59 (State Department), Consular Despatches, Naples, vol. 3 (T-224:3), received 8/12.

To Lt. John M. Jones, [U.S. Revenue Cutter Service?], 5/1. Calhoun sends his respects "and accepts with pleasure the highly finished & beautiful walking stick" which Jones presented to him. ALU in PHi, Library Company of Philadelphia Papers, Breck Collection.

To [JOHN W. JONES], Speaker of the House of Representatives

Department of State
Washington, 1 May 1844

The Secretary of State in obedience to a Resolution of the House of Representatives, of the 26th of February, 1844, directing him to inform the House whether any gross errors have been discovered in the printed "Sixth Census or enumeration of the inhabitants of the United States, as corrected at the Department of State in 1843"; has the honor to report: That there was not any work bearing that title corrected at the Department of State in the year 1843. The correction of the returns of the census, made at the Department, were previous to the printing, in 1841, of the work, for the use of Congress. They were confined, principally, to clerical errors in relation to the additions and making up the aggregates. Such errors as were discovered in the printed copy previous to its delivery to Congress are noted in errata on the last page of the work.

The duties imposed upon the Secretary of State in relation to the Census having been performed by the delivery, to the Printers to Congress, of the copy of the corrected returns, there has been no subsequent examination made, nor have any gross or material errors been discovered in the printed copy. I have the honor to be &C. &C., J.C. Calhoun.

LS in DNA, RG 233 (U.S. House of Representatives), 28A-F1; FC in DNA, RG 59 (State Department), Accounting Records: Miscellaneous Letters Sent, 1832–1916, vol. for 2/1–9/30/1844, pp. 136–[137]; PC in House Document No. 245, 28th Cong., 1st Sess. NOTE: The House resolution of 2/26 to which this letter was a reply can be found in *House Journal*, 28th Cong., 1st Sess., p. 471.

From SAM[UE]L R. MACNEVEN

New York [City,] May 1, 1844

Sir, As a member of the Central Committee of your political friends in this State, I take the liberty of requesting your favourable consideration of ["a" *altered to* "an"] application made to you in behalf of George E. Baldwin Esq[ui]r[e] who desires the situation of U.S. dispatch agent at this place.

Mr. Baldwin is among the most active and influential of your friends in this section, and his selection for this station would be highly gratifying to them. With great respect Your ob[edien]t serv[an]t, Saml. R. Macneven.

ALS in ViU, Crallé-Campbell Papers.

From EDWARD JOY MORRIS, [Representative from Pa.]

Ho[use] of Rep[resentatives]
Washington, May 1st 1844

I take pleasure in introducing to your acquaintance Mr. Warder Cresson of Philadelphia, who desires an appointment as American Consul at Jerusalem in Palestine. Mr. [Jasper] Chasseaud resident at Beyrout in Syria has at present I believe the appointing power of Vice

Consuls in Syria & Palestine. Having recently travelled in the countries of the East I know the great conveniences of American Consulates in the interior of Syria & Palestine to the American & the protection & comfort that is often afforded to him by the Official representative of his country. Jerusalem is now much frequented by Americans. A consulate there will be of service to our citizens.

Mr. Cresson is a gentleman of capacity & probity & intends to make Jerusalem his place of residence. I have the honor to be Y[ou]r most Obedient Servant, Edward Joy Morris.

ALS in DNA, RG 59 (State Department), Applications and Recommendations, 1837–1845, Cresson (M-687:7, frame 155); PEx in Isidore S. Meyer, ed., *Early History of Zionism in America* (New York: Arno Press, 1977), p. 3.

From John T. Reid, Washington, 5/1. Because a new U.S. Minister [Henry A. Wise] is about to proceed to Brazil, Reid has "been requested by the gentlemen who were interested in the New York South American Steamboat association, to bring their claim against the Brazilian Government to your notice . . . ." Reid discusses in great detail the circumstances and legal considerations related to a claim for $150,000 with interest. In 1826, having been encouraged to do so by Brazilian officials, the association sent there a steamboat for navigation of the Amazon. They were prevented by the Brazilian government from undertaking the business for which the ship had been sent, and after nine months of fruitless negotiations, the vessel returned to the U.S. *"There has now been a denial of justice for fourteen years,"* and the Amazon steamboat investors "conceive that the Government of the United States may now with propriety put their claim on the proper footing, and urge its settlement with all the weight of their authority." CC with En in DNA, RG 76 (Records of Boundary and Claims Commissions and Arbitrations), Miscellaneous Claims, Brazil Convention of 1849; CC in DNA, RG 84 (Foreign Posts), Brazil, Despatches, 11:69–77.

From H[ENRY] S[T]. G[EORGE] TUCKER

University of Virg[ini]a, May 1, 1844

My dear Sir, I hope I shall not be considered as obtrusive in addressing this note to you on a subject on which many around me feel and express the deepest interest.

The recent elections in Virginia have brought conviction to the minds of many that the cause of the Democracy is desperate if the nomination of Mr. [Martin] Van Buren is still persisted in, and even before the intelligence of this morning, a general sentiment was beginning to prevail, of the necessity of giving him up and insisting once more upon the nomination of yourself. But since his Texas letter has made its appearance his warmest friends have openly declared their unwillingness to support him, and their earnest desire to have you selected as the candidate of the party. The object of this communication is merely to ascertain whether you will consent that your name shall be again presented to the public. It is by no means intended to commit you or even to communicate any answer you may give. We only wish to be assured that the efforts of your friends will not meet with your disapprobation and on receiving that assurance, some ["efforts" *canceled; sic*] will probably be made to give through the public prints some direction to public opinion.

Without intruding further on your valuable time I beg leave to offer you the assurance of the very great regard with which I am sincerely yours, H.S.G. Tucker.

ALS in ScCleA.

R[obert] J. Walker, [Senator from Miss.], to President John Tyler, 5/1. Walker asks that [David] Babe, sentenced to be executed for piracy, be given a reprieve for 30 days in order to "afford time for further developements." Babe's accomplice was recently acquitted of the same crime. The bench, bar, and legislature of New York have joined in asking that Babe be pardoned. An AEI by Tyler asks that Calhoun examine the papers in the case "or if it would be more agre[e]able to him refer the same to the Att[orney] Gen[era]l [John Nelson] and request his views on the propriety of a reprieve for 12 months or other time, and then a pardon." ALS in DNA, RG 59 (State Department), Petitions for Pardon and Related Briefs, 1800–1849, no. 6B.

From W[illia]m Wilkins, [Secretary of War]

May 1st [18]44, Wednesday morning

Dear Sir; Mr. [William R.] King, Minister to France, applied to me to have made for him a copy of the Map of Texas. I promised to comply with his wish.

Will you be so obliging as to give the Map to Mr. Emery [*sic*; Capt. William H. Emory] of the Topogra[phica]l Bureau for the purpose of having the copy made?

This request is made, but in no way intended to interfere with your wishes, or convenience. Very truly y[ou]rs &c, Wm. Wilkins.

ALS in ScCleA.

To Weston F. Birch, U.S. Marshal for Mo., Fayett[e], Mo., 5/2. Calhoun encloses a reprieve for 40 days signed by the President [John Tyler] for John McDaniel, a prisoner convicted of murder in the U.S. Circuit Court. If the date of McDaniel's execution is not within the 40 days allowed by the reprieve, the reprieve is not to be used; its sole purpose is to allow McDaniel time to find any evidence that may "be of use to him." FC in DNA, RG 59 (State Department), Domestic Letters, 34:168 (M-40:32).

From RUFUS CHOATE, [Senator from Mass.]

[Washington] 2 May 1844

Sir, I have the honor to ask your attention to the letter enclosed, & to say, that the writer is a respectable member of the legal profession. Of the facts, beyond his statement, which from my knowledge of him I fully believe, I know nothing personally. I have the honor to be Your obedient Servant, Rufus Choate.

ALS with En in DNA, RG 59 (State Department), Applications and Recommendations, 1837–1845, Fabens (M-687:11, frames 23–26). NOTE: An enclosed ALS of 4/21 to Choate from J.V. Williams asks that Joseph Warren Fabens of Salem, Mass., be appointed U.S. Consul at Cayenne, French Guiana. Fabens heads a commercial house at Cayenne and plans to return there shortly; he is the only U.S. resident at that place. A memorial sent to the State Dept. some time since asked that a U.S. Consulate be established at Cayenne and was signed by "all the most eminent merchants of Salem" because "all the regular trade with Cayenne is from" there.

From Edm[un]d S. Derry, New York [City], 5/2. "Representations have been made to several of our [Calhoun?] Committee in relation to a Mr. [Joseph A.] Binda now holding the Consulate at Leghorn [in Italy]. On their being heard by you and should you deem them to call for his removal, it would afford satisfaction to us all that you should remove from office him or any other person who may be found unworthy of such a post." (An AES by G[eorge] E. Baldwin states, "I freely coincide" with Derry's opinion. In the same file are depositions alleging that for the last three years Binda had been in New York engaging in the sale of fraudulent paintings while leaving the duties of the Consulate in the hands of an incompetent deputy.) ALS in DNA, RG 59 (State Department), Applications and Recommendations, 1837–1845, Binda (M-687:2, frame 326).

To John Fairfield, [Senator from Maine], 5/2. Calhoun acknowledges Fairfield's letter of 4/23 enclosing papers concerning a claim upon the government of Haiti stemming from the recent imprisonment of Samuel S. Thomas and Joseph R. Curtis, master and mate of the brig *Zebra*. The attention of the State Department will be given to this subject. FC in DNA, RG 59 (State Department), Domestic Letters, 34:169 (M-40:32).

To A[RCHIBALD] M. GREEN, "U.S. C[onsul,] Galvezton"

Department of State
Washington, May 2d 1844

Sir, Your letters to No. 33 inclusive have been received. In answer to your enquiry contained in No. 32 [of 4/15], whether a ship, having taken in part of her Cargo in a Foreign port, can enter a port of the United [States] to complete it, without the Vessel's being made liable under the Revenue Laws, I have to refer you to the following copy of the 32nd Section of the General Collection act of 2nd March 1799, as entirely applicable to the case presented.

"That it shall be lawful for any ship or Vessel to proceed with any goods, wares, and merchandise, brought in her, and which shall, in the Manifest first delivered to any officer receiving the same, be reported as destined, or intended for any Foreign port or place, from the District within which such ship or Vessel shall first arrive, to such Foreign port or place, without paying or securing the payment of any duties upon such of the said goods, wares, or merchandise, as shall be actually re-exported in the said Ship or Vessel accordingly, anything herein contained to the contrary notwithstanding." A proviso to this Section requires that the Master or person having the charge or command of the said Ship or Vessel, shall first give bond, conditioned that

400

the goods, wares and merchandise, or any part thereof, shall not be landed within the United States, unless due entry thereof, shall have been first made, and the duties thereupon paid or secured to be paid according to law. The fact that the Cargo is destined for another Country, you will perceive, must appear in the Manifest of the Ship's Cargo. The Consular certificate is not necessary, but if the Captain chooses to take it, the Department sees no objection to his doing so. A Consul has clearly no right to compel him to take it. Our officers of the Customs cannot act on it, but must look to the manifest alone.

Your letter No. 33 [of 4/19] has been submitted to the President for his perusal. I am, Sir, &c, J.C. Calhoun.

FC in DNA, RG 59 (State Department), Consular Instructions, 11:241–242.

From A[RCHIBALD] M. GREEN

Consulate of the U.S. of America at Galvezton
Republic of Texas, 2nd May 1844

Sir, I hope you will pardon me for again writing you on a subject which to myself is of great moment and likewise every American who wishes well to his Country.

On the 19th Ult[im]o I wrote the Department and in that letter I reported Gen[era]l [William S.] Murphy's conduct, no regular, formal ["specific" *interlined*] charges however were made—but his general conduct bad, & disreputable. Gen[era]l Murphy now insinuates that he had made confidential communications to *me* as one of the officers of our Government and that subsequently he had heard those very things repeated; thereby implying that I had been the one to communicate and make public the Correspondence from the Department of State—when in fact it is well known that after drinking of spirituous liquors, he kept nothing secret and it was a matter of notoriety that he would impart to *many* gentlemen the same information, Enjoining on each one secrecy; until he was told by some when he proposed to give information in confidence, that they would hear it if he had not, and would not, tell others, and that it was an insult to their understanding to communicate any thing that was secret and enjoin secrecy; and then in a few months to tell the same thing to half doz[en] others, either of whom might divulge the pretended secret, and thus cause the innocent to be censured. Information that has been given to me by Gen[era]l Murphy—I have been prudent not to speak of until it has been made public by others. And then, did I repeat it, only as coming from others or the purport of my own correspondence.

But to be candid with you & to make a full and faithful report I shall have to say, that Gen[era]l Murphy is now notorious for prevarication and falsehood. And for the verification of this charge and for the charge of vulgarity & indecency before gentlemen and Ladies, for blac[k]guardism, drunkenness and being disreputable to the Government which he represents—I refer to all who know anything of his character in this city.

He has made statements and then denied them—The proof of which can be established by many reputable and high minded Gentlemen. His conduct to a gentleman of high respectability of this City, no longer than yesterday was of such a gross and insulting nature as to cause that gentleman to *curse him.*

I am induced to believe that much of the information imparted to me by Gen[era]l Murphy was false—for instance, he represented to me, that there were 43 Senators in fav[o]r of annexation—that a vote had been counted on some test question in secret session ["in secret session" *canceled*] in the Senate. This was ["early" *interlined*] in February. Soon after, he told others the same thing, and he was the cause of several publications in the public Journals of this country in relation to this matter, the nature of which publications will be seen by reference to them.

He said that the President had informed him by letter, that if his rejection before the Senate took place, that he should most certainly be appointed Secretary of War & be a member of his Cabinet. In some short time that vacancy which occurred was filled and then he said that the President had informed him that he (Murphy) should at any time after his remaining twelve months as Ch[arg]e d'Affaires to Texas, have a full mission to the two Sicilys, And that the Pres[i]-d[en]t had told him that the present incumbent should be dismissed as soon as he left here, & was ready to go ["and that the President had said to him that Gen[era]l [Waddy] Thompson [Jr.] gave great dissatisfaction and had of[f]ered to him (Murphy) the mission to Mexico" *interlined*]. I know persons to whom Gen[era]l Murphy has made these last statements ["to" *canceled*]. And perhaps if enquiry was made, I could in a few minutes find persons who had heard the whole statement as I relate it—but really it made an impression on my mind because of the improbability of the statement from begin-[n]ing to end.

Gen[era]l Murphy[']s whole conduct, since his first arrival in the country has been undignified and ungentlemanly—highly censurable in a private gentleman & doubly so in a representative of a great nation. The first step which he took in reaching the country was to condemn and abuse the policy of the executive of this nation—openly telling the people, if they knew what was going on between Gen[era]l [Samuel] Houston & the British Minister, that they, the people would kick them both out of the country—That Gen[era]l Houston was a Benedict Arnold—His course was such that any other Government than this would have demanded his immediate recall. The president of this Republic did address a letter to Gen[era]l Murphy on the subject of his charges against him, which the Gen[era]l denied, altho the facts can be established by many.

I am aware that I have made heavy charges against the Ch[arg]e de'Affairs & knowing how matters stand here, I would not be doing a duty I owe to myself & to the Department, not to speak out. And if any enquiry is made and the charges cannot be verified, I will be the first to memorialize the Department to dismiss me from office instantaneously.

I beg leave to give a few references as to ["the gen(era)l conduct and demeanor of Gen(era)l Murphy to" *interlined*] persons, some of whom are personally known to the Dept. and ["the most" *canceled and* "many" *interlined*] of them by character, viz:

Maj[o]r John M. Allen, Mayor of the City of Galvezton

Maj. James H. Cocke Collector of Customs d[itt]o

Gen[era]l A[lbert] Sidney Johnston now in Louisville Ky.

Gen[era]l M[irabeau] B. Lamar now in Macon Georgia

Gen[era]l James Hamilton [Jr.] of Carolina

Gen[era]l Ch[arle]s F. Mercer of [*blank space*] U. States

General M[emucan] Hunt of Texas now in Galvezton

Colo[nel] James Love of Galvezton

Gen[era]l Hugh McLeod of d[itt]o

Colo[nel; *blank space*] Cazenove [*sic*; William L. Cazneau?] of the Senate of Texas ["in" *canceled*]

Judge Rich[ar]d Morris of Galvezton

Judge B[enjamin C.] Franklin of d[itt]o

Judge R[obert] D. Johnson of d[itt]o

Mr. J[ohn] P. Cole Att[orne]y at Law Galvezton

Dr. Levi Jones of Galvezton

All the merchants of d[itt]o

Every respectable & Intelligent man of the City.

I have the honor to be Sir most Respectfully y[ou]r ob[edien]t Serv[an]t, A.M. Green.

P.S. If it is deemed necessary that I shall be more specific in my charges & collect proofs to substantiate the truth of what I say; I will make them out and send you letters and aff[idavi]ts corroborating all that I say and more besides. A.M.G.

ALS (No. 34) in DNA, RG 59 (State Department), Consular Despatches, Galveston, vol. 2 (T-151:2), received 5/28.

From J[OHN] H. HOWARD, "Private"

Columbus [Ga.,] May 2nd 1844

I wrote to you but a few days since, which I hope you have rec[eive]d, & replyed to. This morning I have seen Mr. [Henry] Clay[']s letter in regard to Texas & look upon it under the circumstances as not only fully sustaining Mr. [Daniel] Webster[']s views, but having the merit of some peculiar follies in addition.

I have also heard that Mr. [Martin] Van Buren has written a letter identifying himself with the Northern prejudices against our institutions, in which he comes out distinctly against annexation. We have not yet seen the letter. It may not be so, or may be very much perverted, but if it has been correctly represented to us we *must* have a third candidate for the presidency. What say you to this proposition? We may be weak since Southern people will give up their interests when called upon by their party to do so for party purposes; yet I believe there are now a sufficient number of both parties to constitute a decided majority in this State in favor of the treaty, and that they would if an opportunity was afforded them, make annexation a sine qua non.

[John] Tyler will not in our judgement answer the purpose, but if you would consent to be brought forward, although I cannot flatter you, that you would succeed with certainty, yet I believe it would create a great diversion, and produce an excitement, that would place the election more upon principal [*sic*] & more upon measures than upon men. And I do hope the argument might be made strong enough & would be made strong enough to produce a happy result. I may have overrated the consequences of rejecting the treaty, but if I have not, ["if" *canceled and* "and" *interlined*] it be allowed to pass away without a strong manifestation of dissent by the Southern people to ["the" *interlined*] acction of the majority we had as well surrender at once. It is a surrender of all our rights, if we permit

Texas rejected because she is a slave holder. A third candidate might fail of success, or be crowned with success, as we cannot anticipate exactly the effects of the agitation of so great a question, but if a third candidate should be unsuccessfull he would do much good by breaking up in some degree the arrangements of parties for power.

I should be pleased to hear from you *in confidence* before I set out for Baltimore, which will be on the 19th Inst[ant]. I have written to [Walter T.] Colquit[t] today making the same suggestions. Yours, J.H. Howard.

ALS in ScCleA; variant PC in Boucher and Brooks, eds., *Correspondence*, pp. 224–225.

From Geo[rge] R. Ives, New York [City], 5/2. Ives recommends that Theobald C. Jung, a respectable and well-qualified citizen of New York, be appointed as a U.S. Consul in Bohemia. ALS in DNA, RG 59 (State Department), Applications and Recommendations, 1837–1845, Jung (M-687:17, frames 734–735).

From John McDaniel, St. Louis Prison, 5/2. He encloses to Calhoun two articles from the St. Louis *Missouri Republican* concerning "the injustice which has been done me by this court." McDaniel states that he is innocent of the crime for which he was convicted and asks Calhoun's "intercession with the President [John Tyler]" in his behalf. E[dward] Bates, McDaniel's attorney, has forwarded to Attorney General [John Nelson] a copy of the proceedings of his trial. ALS in DNA, RG 59 (State Department), Petitions for Pardon and Related Briefs, 1800–1849, no. 292A.

From G[regory] A. Perdicaris, Cheraw, [S.C.], 5/2. In reply to Calhoun's inquiry of 4/22, Perdicaris states that he wishes to return to his post as U.S. Consul at Athens "as soon as possible, but circumstances of a peculiar nature, will not I fear, allow me to leave the U. States during the present year, and I find myself under the necessity of again applying—not without reluctance—for a further leave of absence for twelve months." ALS in DNA, RG 59 (State Department), Consular Despatches, Athens, vol. 1 (T-362:1).

David Pingree, Salem, [Mass.], to President John Tyler, 5/2. "The enclosed is a correspondence from His Highness the Sultan of Muscat, now residing at his palace at Zanzibar. The two Arabian horses he shipped per Barque Eliza, for your Excellency, have been landed in good condition, and I have placed them in the stable of the

Essex House in this City, with the groom, to see they are properly taken care of, and to await the order of your Excellency. The Barque Eliza will shortly return to Zanzibar, and I shall be happy to forward anything by her that your Excellency may be pleased to send." LS in DNA, RG 59 (State Department), Miscellaneous Letters (M-179: 104, frame 277).

From G[ILBERT] L. THOMPSON

Steam Ship Poinsett
Navy yard Pensacola
May 2d 1844

I regret extremely to inform you that I found no U.S. Ship of war on this Station Com[mo]d[ore David] Conner having sailed. By the kind and prompt action of Com[modore E.A.F.] Lavalette he has commenced fitting out this vessel. Regardless of personal comfort I am determined to press on and execute my mission at all hazards. I am at home fortunately with a Steam ship[;] shall touch at the Balize and Tampico for Fuel. If successful in obtaining a sufficient quantity of Coal I shall make the voyage in less time than any other way. I am most respectfully Your Ob[edien]t S[er]v[an]t, G.L. Thompson.

ALS in DNA, RG 59 (State Department), Diplomatic Despatches, Special Agents, vol. 13 (M-37:13, frames 75–76). NOTE: A Clerk's EU reads "Entered June 25th."

To [JOHN TYLER]

Department of State
Washington, May 2d 1844

To the President of the United States.

The Secretary of State, to whom was referred the Resolution of the Senate of the 29th of last month, requesting the President to communicate to that Body a copy of the answer [of 2/2/1843] of the Secretary of State, to the letter of the Texan Chargé d'Affaires [Isaac Van Zandt] of the 14th of December 1842, of the letter of Mr. [William S.] Murphy of July 8th 1843, and of the communication of the Texan Chargé referred to in Mr. [Abel P.] Upshur's letter of January 16th ultimo, Showing that the proposition of this Government for the

Annexation of Texas had been for the present, declined, by the Government of Texas; has the honor to lay before the President, a copy of the two first mentioned papers, and of others connected with them.

There is not on the files of this Department any communication from the Chargé D'Affaires of Texas Showing that the proposition of this Government for the Annexation of that Country to the United States, was temporarily declined, nor anything to Show that such a communication was ever made, in writing to the late Mr. Upshur. All of which is respectfully Submitted. Jno. C. Calhoun.

FC in DNA, RG 59 (State Department), Reports of the Secretary of State to the President and Congress, 6:100; PC with Ens in Senate Document No. 341, 28th Cong., 1st Sess., pp. 68–74; PC with Ens in House Document No. 271, 28th Cong., 1st Sess., pp. 68–73; PC with Ens in the Washington, D.C., *Daily National Intelligencer*, May 22, 1844, p. 4; PC with Ens in the Washington, D.C., *Globe*, May 22, 1844, p. 1; PC with Ens in the Washington, D.C., *Daily Madisonian*, May 22, 1844, p. 2; PC in *Niles' National Register*, vol. LXVI, no. 13 (May 25, 1844), p. 195. NOTE: Tyler transmitted this report to the Senate on 5/6. The resolution to which the above letter is a reply can be found in DNA, RG 59 (State Department), Miscellaneous Letters (M-179:104, frame 265) and *Senate Executive Journal*, 6:264.

To [JOHN TYLER]

Department of State
Washington, 2nd April [*sic*; May], 1844
To the President of the United States.

The Secretary of State has the honor to submit the enclosed correspondence relating to the treaty recently concluded by the Minister of the United States at Berlin [Henry Wheaton], with the States composing the Zoll-Verein, with a recommendation that they be transmitted to the Senate, as an accompaniment to the Treaty, and the despatches already sent to that body. J.C. Calhoun.

LS with Ens in DNA, RG 46 (U.S. Senate), 28B-B11; FC in DNA, RG 59 (State Department), Reports of the Secretary of State to the President and Congress, 6:99–100. NOTE: Enclosed were copies of ten documents, correspondence between Wheaton and Secretaries of State Daniel Webster and Abel P. Upshur from 7/1842 to 1/1844. Though both copies of the above letter are dated 4/2, the date has been changed to 5/2 because, from the *Senate Executive Journal*, 6:262 and 267, it is evident that Tyler did not transmit the Zollverein treaty to the Senate until 4/29, and on 5/6, under a cover letter dated 5/3, he transmitted the additional documents referred to above.

From W[illia]m J. Armstrong, Secretary, American Board of Commissioners for Foreign Missions, New York [City], 5/3. He asks that the Rev. H[enry] M. Scudder be granted a passport to work in Ceylon as a missionary. Scudder was born in Ceylon in 1819 where his father [John Scudder] worked as a missionary. Armstrong hopes that Calhoun will set a precedent in recognizing Scudder as an American citizen by sending him a passport. ALS in DNA, RG 59 (State Department), Passport Applications, vol. 31, no. 2096 (M-1372:14).

D. FORBES CAMPBELL to an Unknown Person, "Copy," "Extract"

Colonial Bank
London, 3d May 1844

. . . . March & April have passed away, without your making your appearance in London as you intended & *promised.* As some time may yet elapse before we have the pleasure of seeing you here, I have resolved to write you, & communicate a bit of news which may prove acceptable.

On the failure of his negotiations with the Brazils, Sir Robert Peel turned his attention to Holland, and after a good deal of sounding & parleying, made something like the following proposition to the Cabinet of the Hague, vizt, To reduce the duty on *free labour* sugar, & also on Coffee, provided Holland would emancipate her slaves in the West Indies (making that a "sine qua non" to the admission of Java produce, at least from Holland, tho' not, if shipped direct from Java) and reduce, or rather repeal, the discriminating duties on English manufactures (at present Dutch pay 15 per cent & English 30%) in her East India possessions.

The boon offered to Holland is great, but our Cabinet, in furtherance of their Anti Slavery Policy, are set upon retaliating on Brazil, and anxious to *detach* Holland from the sort of *league* which may spring up between the great slave-holding nations viz. *The United States, Spain,* The Brazils & France.

Slave emancipation in Surinam would bring "the pressure from without" down to French Guiana, & might ultimately force France to follow the example of England & Holland.

My information is from a source worthy of credit, & is confirmed by what fell from the Chancellor of the Exchequer [Henry Goulburn], on last monday evening, in bringing forward the Budget. His Speech is very accurately reported in the Times, & merits perusal. He proposes to keep the duty on British plantation Sugar at 24/. p[e]r cwt. and reduce the duty on *free grown* sugar to 34/. p[e]r cwt. Such a change will prove a serious blow to our half ruined W[est] I[ndies] planters. The first West India Merchant of the City told me yesterday—"The only salvation for our W[est] I[ndies] Colonies is to produce *sugar as cheap as in the Slave Colonies*—for to that point they will have to come at last, *whether whig or Tory be at the head of the Government."* Their prospect of salvation seems to me a very uncertain one. Indeed it is still my opinion that the total *ruin* & abandonment of our Colonies will be the result[.]" Believe me Sincerely yours, (Signed) D. Forbes Campbell.

Ms. in ScCleA. NOTE: This document carries an AEU by Calhoun: "Mr. Campbell of London[,] relates to the views of the British Govt. in reference to the sugar duties."

From H[ENRY] L. ELLSWORTH, [Commissioner of the Patent Office]

Patent Office
May 3 1844

Sir, I notice a present to Congress of [George] Washington[']s camp chest, and that the same is deposited with the State Department. Permit me to say that there is a very convenient place for this relic, in the National Gallery beside the sword of Washington, the cane from [Benjamin] Franklin, and other articles entrusted to the care of the Commissioner of Patents as a branch of the State Department. I am most respectfully yours, H.L. Ellsworth.

LS in ScCleA.

From EDWARD EVERETT

London, 3 May 1844

My dear Sir, I beg to refer you to my despatches—six in number—for an account of the Public Business. I have nothing of a confidential nature to communicate. The despatches continue to be addressed to Mr. [John] Nelson, as we have no official intelligence of your having entered upon the discharge of the duties of the department. A portion of them are written on mourning paper, in obedience to Mr. Nelson's instructions, to take a proper notice of the melancholy event of the Princeton, during a period of thirty days, which commenced at this legation on the 26th April.

Lord Aberdeen told me, in conversation in his own house, on the Evening of the Queen's Birthday, that they should write to Mr. [Richard] Pakenham, remonstrating against the ratification of Mr. [Henry] Wheaton's Convention with the German Zollverein, as inconsistent with the Commercial Convention between G[reat] Britain & the U. States. There is undoubtedly some little embarrassment in the ground we take on this subject, in consequence of the strenuous manner, in which—in reference to the duties levied on Rough Rice & Exported Woolens, we have maintained the principle, that so soon as England, for any reason whatever, admits an article from a third country at a given rate of duty or grants any privilege in exportation from England to any third country, the same relaxation becomes *ipso facto* due to the United States, in virtue of our Convention.

In maintaining on our part the right to conclude a treaty like Mr. Wheaton's and in contesting this right on theirs, or rather claiming without equivalent the benefit of its provisions, there is on the two sides an apparent, & on theirs a real change of ground, each verging toward the line of argument hitherto pursued by the other. In our case the change of ground is rather apparent than real; but it will require some care in treating this subject, to avoid coming in conflict with a portion of what I have urged in reference to Rough Rice & the Export duty on Woolens.

Mr. Pakenham, as I have observed in previous despatches, is instructed to receive any proposals which you may wish to make toward a Commercial Convention. It will deserve consideration, whether, in any revision of the commercial relations of the two Countries which may take place, we should not endeavor to procure a stipulation on the part of England, corresponding with our Constitutional provision, that a Treaty is a law of the land, binding on the Courts. You will perceive by my notes on the Rough Rice & Woollens' duty business, that no treaty provision is effectual till re-enacted by parliament; & that though Parliament may enact a law notoriously at variance with a pre-existing Treaty, the Courts of justice will afford no redress nor permit the treaty to be pleaded.

So too in reference to such a case as the extradition of fugitives, the technical formalities which have hitherto prevented & threaten still to delay the surrender of [John] Clinton a notorious forger, who has passed half his life in our prisons, are purely matters connected with the statute which was enacted to carry the treaty into effect, but which in this signal instance has wholly defeated it. I am, Dear Sir, with the highest respect, faithfully Yours, Edward Everett.

ALS (Private) in DNA, RG 59 (State Department), Diplomatic Despatches, Great Britain, vol. 52 (M-30:48); FC in MHi, Edward Everett Papers, 49:27–30 (published microfilm, reel 23, frames 13–14). NOTE: An AEU by Calhoun on the ALS reads "Mr. Everett. States that Lord Aberdeen has instructed Mr. Pakenham to remonstrate against the Prussian Treaty. See his Remarks in reference to the ground taken on the subject of importing rough rice."

From JAMES GADSDEN, *"Confidential"*

Charleston, 3 May 1844

My Dear Sir, [Henry] Clay[']s & [Martin] Van Buren[']s letter[s] on Texas have created some excitement here, particularly that from the latter.

The first was expected. But the course of the latter was the reverse. It demonstrates most clearly what the influence of abolishionism is at the north in spite of declarations to the contrary.

I consider the annexation of Texas now that the views of Great Britain and the Northern States are not only disclosed, but openly avowed the most vital one which has occurred since the revolution. On it hinges the very existence of our Southern Institutions, and if we of the South now prove recreant, we will or must [be] content to be Hewers of wood & Drawers of Water for our northern Bretheren. There is much excitement among us, & many ready for immediate action. But what should be the action is the question with a very large portion of our Friends. Unity of action seems to be the difficulty. No inconsiderable portion of the Democracy are ripe for hoisting the [John] Tyler flag and of rallying under an Administration party to carry out the President[']s policy as explained in his message. Others however, and the decided majority of the Democrats, do not think Tyler equal to the crisis and still turn on & confide in you as our leader. Unwilling to have a split at a period when union is so important we feel much at loss untill we can be better instructed from Washington. Would you, in confidence communicate your views to me.

Your friends are all ready & anxious to raise a standard, which should never have been lowered, but they are unwilling to act precipitately and possibly against your judgement. If you think from indications at Washington that we should move—we will do so. But if you think delay preferable, or if you concur in bringing out Tyler, why we will be prepared to act. We all are resolved to hold communion with Van Buren no longer. For myself, who never did trust him, I feel gratified at the course he has pursued. Your friend, James Gadsden.

[P.S.] I have written to Gen[era]l [Andrew] Jackson & hope to bring him out.

ALS in ScCleA; PC in Jameson, ed., *Correspondence*, pp. 952–953.

From A[rchibald] M. Green, [U.S. Consul at] Galveston, Texas, 5/3. He acknowledges the State Department circular of 4/1 announcing Calhoun's appointment as Secretary of State and wishes him well in the office. He adds that "no one wishes more warmly the success of your good and well directed efforts to secure, and annex to the United States, this Republic, than" he does. ALS (No. 35) in DNA, RG 59 (State Department), Consular Despatches, Galveston, vol. 2 (T-151:2), received 5/28.

From William R. King, [*ca.* 5/3?]. He encloses a letter [to himself, dated 4/30] from F[rancis] S. Claxton. "He is a young gentleman of good education, and of the most exemplary conduct, & habits. The son of a gallant officer, and every way worthy of your kind consideration" [for an appointment as Clerk in the State Department]. ALS with En in DNA, RG 59 (State Department), Applications and Recommendations, 1837–1845, Claxton (M-687:5, frames 438–440).

From J[ohn] Y. Mason, [Secretary of the Navy], 5/3. Mason has entered the name of B.B.S. Heywood on the register of applicants for appointment as Midshipman. Heywood's claims will be given consideration should there be a vacancy, which is not likely. There is now an excess of about 40 Midshipmen above what is allowed by law. LS in DNA, RG 59 (State Department), Miscellaneous Letters (M-179:104, frame 282); FC in DNA, RG 45 (Naval Records), Miscellaneous Letters Sent by the Secretary of the Navy, 33:393 (M-209:12).

From J[OHN] MURPHY, "Private"

United States Consulate Office
Cove Cork [Ireland,] May 3, 1844

Sir, I have the honor to inform you that I have received two notes (with parcels) from a Mr. Thomas Fitnam who represents himself as holding a situation in the Department of State.

I have the honor herewith to hand you copies of the notes alluded to above, with the addresses on the parcels &c[,] those received with the first letter I delivered into the post office, but that latterly come to hand I consider myself justified in holding for your commands (I refer to that addressed to Dan[ie]l O[']Connell MP).

It is a matter of some surprise why Mr. F[itnam] should address me, or make me the medium of communicating with his political friends in this country, I neither interfere with the politicians, or the politics of Great Britain. I am not a native of this land (being born in Baltimore St[ate of] Maryland) and I do not imagine that I should be acting conscienciously were I to neglect putting you in possession of the enclosed particulars.

I would also remark that the first parcel was sealed with the seal of the Department of State, the E[n]velopes I still hold.

The new[s]paper (the ["]Nation") to which Mr. F[itnam] has alluded in his letter, is the leading organ of the Repeal party in this Country.

I have paid postage and other charges a/c of Mr. Fitnam[']s letters &c am[oun]t[in]g to about $6.00—please say shall I draw on the Department for that sum.

In addressing you on this subject I request my communications will be regarded as private & confidential & have the honor to be Sir Y[ou]r very ob[e]d[ient] Serv[an]t, J. Murphy, U.S. C[onsul].

ALS with Ens in ViU, Crallé-Campbell Papers. NOTE: Murphy enclosed with the above letter a list of letters and papers received from Fitnam in Washington, to be delivered to individuals, including Daniel O'Connell, in Ireland, and copies of letters from Fitnam to himself in which Fitnam discussed his attempts to mobilize Irish sentiment in the U.S. against Great Britain.

From John Nelson, [Attorney General], 5/3. He has examined the evidence sent by Calhoun's note of "this morning" concerning David Babe, convicted of piratical murder. His opinion is that the President [John Tyler] can "very properly interpose his authority to arrest the execution of the sentence pronounced by the Court" in this case. FC in DNA, RG 60 (Department of Justice), Opinions of the Attorney General, 1817–1845, F:183.

From H[ENRY] L. PINCKNEY and Others

Charleston So. Ca., May 3d 1844

The Memorial of the Undersigned respectfully sheweth:

That a wanton and unprovoked outrage on the Flag of the United States, was committed at the Port of Havana, in the Island of Cuba, on the 9th of April last, by the murder of Michael Murphy, a naturalized citizen of the United States, and one of the crew of the Brig Mary Pennell, of Brunswick, Maine, commanded by Captain Sylvester Merriman. From the testimony of several letters, and the certificates of Capt. Merriman, and others, and also from the statement of John Scott, another of the crew of the Brig Mary Pennell, and who was in the boat with the deceased, at the time of the murder, the facts of the case are substantially as follow:

Michael Murphy and John Scott were ordered to go ashore in the Boat, for the purpose of carrying Capt. Merriman off to the Brig. They were waiting at a part of the Key, near the office of the Captain of the Port, know[n] as the steps, where the boats of Foreign Merchantmen are permitted to land. They arrived at the steps about 15 minutes before 12 o'clock M[eridian] and found the place crowded with boats—some of the sailors were sitting on the steps, and others in the boats, waiting for their respective captains who were on shore. The Sentinel stationed there had ordered some of the boats off. He afterwards called the Corporal, who immediately on coming up, commenced using the most abusive language towards the seamen at the same time striking and kicking them indiscriminately. None of whom offered the least resistance. The deceased was one of those so abused and stricken. He laughed at the Corporal when he struck him on the back with his sheathed sword, which exasperated the Corporal greatly. The deceased and Scott then resumed their oars and commenced shoving their boat off. Thereupon the Corporal immediately drew his sword and seizing the blade of the oar in the hands of the deceased, made a cut at him, but the boat receding from the wharf under the impetus given by the oars used by Scott and the deceased in shoving her off, he did not succeed in effecting his object, and was dragged into the water. The water being shallow (not over three feet in depth) The Corporal continued to pursue the boat for about 12 or 14 feet, striking all the time with his sword at the deceased, when fearing he was about to escape his fury, he ordered the Sentinel to fire, who immediately obeyed and shot the deceased through the head, which caused his death in about an hour afterwards. The ball passed through his head from the front, and wounded the other sailor, John Scott, in the left side.

The above statement of the facts as they occurred, your Memorialists have every reason to believe is correct and true.

All the letters and certificates which your Memorialists have seen, represent the unfortunate deceased, as being of a good disposition and sober habits. He was about 23 years of age, and has been thus cut off in the bloom and vigor of manhood by an act disgraceful to humanity—one which must cast a stain on the country where it was perpetrated, and which should not go unpunished.

The body of the deceased was embalmed. The expense of embalming was defrayed by subscription of the Ship Masters in Port at the time, without distinction. The body was brought to this city on the 23 ult., on the Sch[oone]r Warrior, Captain E[dward] Griffiths. Arrangements were promptly made by the Charleston Marine Society, to have it conveyed to New York, where the deceased has a mother and sister. It was put on board the Packet Ship H. Allen, Capt. Wilson, which sailed for that Port on the 30th Ult., and was consigned to the charge of the Marine Society of that City.

Your Memorialists fear that the murderer has already escaped or will eventually escape the punishment due to his crime, as it is stated upon the best authority, that he was at liberty on the 17th ult. eight days after the perpetration of the barbarous act.

In addressing the department of State, on the subject of this most flagrant outrage, your Memorialists, while they feel that indignation, which every American should feel at an insult offered the Flag of their country, and the wanton and inhuman murder of a peaceful and unoffending fellow creature, console themselves with the assurance, that Government will not allow such an act to go uninvestigated, but will take measures to have it promptly, and if necessary, severely punished. The Undersigned in transmitting this Memorial, do not wish to be understood in the least, as desiring to prompt the Department to the performance of its duty, but simply to give expression to the high indignation they feel on the subject, and to furnish such facts as they have been enabled to collect, so as to facilitate the action of the Department in investigating and resenting the indignity offered our Flag, and the outrage on humanity which has been so wantonly, insultingly and cruelly committed.

415

All which is respectfully submitted. Signed by order, and in behalf of, a public meeting of the Citizens of Charleston held on the 1st of May 1844. H.L. Pinckney, Chairman, John C. Hoff, John Carnighan, G. Wilson, Wm. P. Lee, Sen[io]r, W.P. Rose, A.S. Halsey, W.L. Duval, W. Nason, W.H. Bartless, J.D. Yates, H.E. Vincent, Walter Finney, A. Chase, R.S. Ham[m]ett, Wm. S. King, R.W. Seymour, Tho[mas] D. Jervey, P. Cantwell, J. Goldsmith, C.D. Kanapaux, E.B. White, J.F. Gordon, Francis Middleton, Committee of the Public Meeting of the Citizens of Charleston, S.C.

LS with Ens in DNA, RG 59 (State Department), Miscellaneous Letters (M-179: 104, frames 285–297); PC with Ens in the Charleston, S.C., *Courier*, May 4, 1844, p. 2; PC with Ens in the New Orleans, La., *Courrier de la Louisiane*, May 10, 1844, p. 3. Note: Two Ens were statements by John Scott and Sylvester Merriman, relating to the killing of Murphy. Another En is a second copy of the memorial containing the signatures of 306 additional individuals.

To JOSIAH QUINCY, President of Harvard University, Cambridge, Mass.

Department of State
Washington, May 3rd 1844
Sir, By a letter [*not found*] recently received from the Rev[eren]d Allen Greely, Pastor of the Congregational Church, at Turner[,] Oxford County, Maine, I have been informed, that a Catalogue of the Library of Harvard College, has been published in five volumes; containing indications of many maps, Collections of Treaties, and other works, the examination of which might be useful to the Government, especially in its negotiations with Foreign Powers. As the copy of the catalogue in the Library of this Department is in four volumes, published in 1831, it appears, that either a supplementary volume, or a new edition of the whole, has since appeared.

Mr. Greely also informs me that there is in the Library of Harvard College a map with the following title "New and accurate map of North America (wherein the errors of all preceeding maps respecting the Rights of Great Britain, France, & Spain &c are corrected) by Heaske, Thomas Ritchen, Sculpsit, London 1775 [*sic*; John Huske and Thomas Kitchin, 1755]."

These Documents may serve to throw some light on the issues pending between this Government and Great Britain; and I should feel under many obligations to you, Sir, if they could, through your instrumentality, be procured for the use of this Department, under such conditions as you may think proper to prescribe. They might be forwarded by mail or otherwise at the expense of the Department. With very high respect I am Sir, Your obed[ien]t Serv[an]t, J.C. Calhoun.

FC in DNA, RG 59 (State Department), Domestic Letters, 35:78 (M-40:33); FC in DNA, RG 59 (State Department), Reports of the Secretary of State to the President and Congress, 6:126; PC in Jameson, ed., *Correspondence,* p. 580.

From Richard S. Rogers, Salem, [Mass.], 5/3. Rogers informs Calhoun that he is about to undertake a voyage to New Zealand, partly in the hope of obtaining evidence to support the claim of N[athaniel] L. Rogers & Brothers "for a loss by the exaction of illegal duties upon their goods in New Zealand." If Rogers can take any despatches to U.S. representatives in Hobartstown, Sydney, or New Zealand, he will be happy to do so. Rogers gives Rufus Choate [Senator from Mass.] and Nathaniel Silsbee [former Senator from Mass.] as references. ALS in DNA, RG 59 (State Department), Miscellaneous Letters (M-179:104, frames 283–284).

From C[HARLES] A. WICKLIFFE, [Postmaster General]

Post Office Department
May 3d 1844

Sir, I have read the communication of Mr. Packenham [*sic*; Richard Pakenham] to you, of the 15th April [*sic*; 4/16], making enquiry of you in order to ascertain "the terms on which the United States are permitted to send their correspondence across the Isthmus of Panama," which you did me the honor some days ago to transmit with a request to furnish you any information upon the subject in the possession of this Department.

I have the honor to state, in reply, that I have no information on the subject. The United States make up no mails to be sent to any point beyond the United States, except to the British Provinces of Canada and New Brunswick. Letters from the United States to foreign ports, (except such as go by the British Steamers) are usually delivered by Post masters at the port of departure to the masters of vessels sailing nearest the place addressed. It occurs to me that Mr.

[Abel P.] Upshur, while Secretary of the Navy, either made or essayed to make some arrangement with an Agent or through the Consul at Chagres [New Granada] for the transmission, across the Isthmus, of the correspondence of the Navy Department destined for the Pacific Squadron.

Mr. Packenham's letter is returned. Very respectfully Your Ob[e]d[ien]t Serv[an]t, C.A. Wickliffe.

LS in DNA, RG 59 (State Department), Miscellaneous Letters (M-179:104, frames 280–281); FC in DNA, RG 28 (Records of the Post Office Department), Letters Sent by the Postmaster General, M.2:433.

From Theo. Antry, New York [City], 5/4. He supports [William J.] Armstrong's request that Henry [M.] Scudder be granted a passport. Antry states that Scudder's father was abroad as an agent of the U.S. when Henry was born, and he therefore deserves recognition of U.S. citizenship just as is given to the children of official U.S. representatives born in foreign countries. ALS with En in DNA, RG 59 (State Department), Passport Applications, vol. 31, no. 2096 (M-1372:14).

From GEO[RGE] BROWN

Honolulu, May 4, 1844

Sir, I last had this honor on the 6th of March, when I enclosed my accounts for the year ending that day. On the 7th of that month I left this place for Maui on which island I remained about five weeks, principally at Lahaina, the present residence of the King. While I was in Lahaina, Mr. [Milo] Calkin our Vice Commercial Agent, was taken sick, and I rendered all the assistance in my power to his clerk, and for ten days had my hands full; at one time there were thirty six Whale ships in port. The list, I send with this, will give you the number of vessels which had touched at Lahaina, to the latest dates, and the paper also contains the number of those which have touched at this place. Almost all the whaling vessels which have touched at these islands this season have gone to the Northwest, sperm whales being very scarce. I also send you a paper with the Statistics of these islands.

I much regret to be obliged to relate an account of a horrid affair, that took place while I was at Lahaina. Capt. Greene of the Ship Ontario of Sag harbor [N.Y.], lost, by desertion three of his men, a few nights before he sailed, and the same evening, a boat was stolen from the beach. Capt. Greene was obliged to leave without his men.

On the 22d of March two of the deserters by the names of Walter G. Pike from Orange County State of New York, and Robert McCarty of the City of New York, were brought to Lahaina, from the neighboring island of Lanai, and on being brought before me, Mr. Calkin being still confined to his bed, acknowledged that they had deserted from the Ontario; on the night of the 15th, and after pulling untill about the 18th, they became exhausted, and were able to pull no longer. They left Lahaina without any water or provisions. On the morning of the 19th they drifted on the shores of Lanai, at a place surrounded with high precipices, which they were too weak to mount, and for the preservation of the lives of two it became necessary that one should die. They accordingly cast lots. The lot of death fell upon a colored man by the name of Jacob Van Clief of Middleton Point, New Jersey, whom the other two killed by beating him on the head with a stone. They then cut his throat, and his arms, and drank his blood, and ate a piece of one of his arms. After becoming strengthened, they were able to ascend the precipice, and in a short time met some natives, who gave them food, and brought them to Lahaina.

As the man was *killed on shore,* I considered that the affair came under the cognisance of the authorities of these islands and ordered them to be handed over to the Governor, who after examining them, sent them to prison to wait for their trial.

On the 27th of March they were brought before the Governor, and Paki, Judge of the Supreme Court, and a Jury of Foreigners nominated by myself, ["and" *canceled*] consisting of six American Ship masters and six residents on shore. After the evidence, was given in, and which coincided with the statements of the prisoners the Jury retired, and after being absent nearly an hour returned and brought in a verdict of acquittal, at the same time stating that had there been a law of these islands, making manslaughter a crime, they certainly should have unanimously brought the prisoners in guilty of that crime.

The prisoners were remanded to prison to be tried hereafter for stealing a boat, of which Crime they were tried and brought in guilty and sentenced to pay her value, which not being able to do they were ordered to work on the roads untill they had earned sufficient money to pay for her. I was present during the first trial, as council for the defendants, and Mr. Calkin having recovered, attended the second trial. When I left Maui the men were at work on the roads.

While I was at Maui, I received a letter from Mr. [William] Hooper our Commercial Agent at Honolulu, enclosing me copies of correspondence, between him and Dr. [Gerrit P.] Judd in relation to the sending on board American vessels, armed men, without due notice being given to the U. States representative here. As Mr. Hooper informed me that copies would be sent to your department I have thought it unnecessary to do more than merely refer to it. I approved of the course taken by Mr. H[ooper] as although this Government had a perfect right to take out a man by Habeas Corpus from a vessel of any nation, yet situated as they are, it is no more than proper, (and heretofore has always been done) to give due notice to the Consuls of the nation to whom the vessel belongs, before coercive measures were taken.

I have not thought it requisite to address Dr. Judd on the subject by note, but from conversation held with him, presume that it will not occur again.

You will see by the note marked "A" accompanying this despatch, which I received from Dr. Judd, that an Attorney General has been appointed. His name is [John] Ricord, from the State of New York, and with the exception of his bringing with him, a document, proving his admittance to practise in the Supreme Court of the U. States nothing appears to be known about him. He came here by the way of the Columbia River.

Previous to my leaving for Maui Dr. Judd consulted me, about giving him an appointment, and I strongly urged to the contrary, untill he knew something more about him, saying that it was very easy to *employ him* without giving him a *responsible situation*, or appointment.

Much to my surprise however, although Dr. Judd appeared to agree with me, I received, shortly after I arrived at Lahaina, the official notice of his appointment as Att[orne]y General. I also received as you will see by note marked "B" his first official "Law Notice," a copy of which I forward as requested by Dr. J[udd]; though I feel ashamed as an American that such a document should have issued from a department, at the head of which, a country man of mine is placed. There appeared to be but one opinion, among all respectable people here—that it was highly derogatory to a high officer of the crown, and evidently emanated, from at least a third rate lawyer. I find also since my return, that a long correspondence has taken place between Dr. Judd & the British Consul General [William Miller] in relation to a claim for land, made by him in behalf of Mr. Charlton, the former Eng[lish] Consul. The correspondence on the part of Dr. J[udd] evidently *written* by Mr. Ricord is in very bad taste, and has excessively annoyed General Miller, who certainly appears to wish nothing but what is right, and might have led to unpleasant consequences, had not efforts been made by myself and others to induce the General to defer, moving farther in the business, untill the return [from Europe] of Mess. [William] Richards and Haalilio, providing their return is not much longer delayed. I had previously advised Dr. Judd not to stir in the matter of Charlton, untill the return of Mr. Richards, but it seems that Ricord has the greater influence. All the friends of the Government here are very much opposed to the proceedings of the Sec[re]t[ar]y of State since the appointment of Mr. Ricord; but the return of Mr. Richards we hope will set matters strait.

You will perceive by the newspapers accompanying this, that the official announcement of the acknowledgement by France & Great Britain, of the Independence of these islands has been received and published here. I had ["been" *canceled*] some time previous to this, been shewn, by the Eng[lish] Consul General, a copy of the same document, which he had received via Mazatlan in February last. I trust these poor people will not again be annoyed, but suffered to pursue their march of improvement in peace.

While I was at Maui I visited the districts of Wailuku, Makawao and Kula. The first situated near the sea shore, the two latter much more elevated, and capable of producing wheat with all the fruits & vegetables of the temperate Zone, and admirably adapted to grazing. I ate bread made from Native wheat, fully equal to any I ever tasted. The Irish potatoes raised in the district of Kula cannot be surpassed for size and flavor. The ground is covered for miles with strawberry vines, and fruit bearing Shrubs. I am informed that the natives in these districts are more industrious than many of those in other districts, and I can readily believe it, as Mr. Greene the Missionary at Makawao, receives no assistance from the Society at home; and while I was at Wailuku, The Parishioners of Mr. Clarke had a meeting, at which they agreed to support him, which they are fully able to do.

Since I last wrote to the department, three vessels have arrived from the United States, and one from Mazatlan, by none of which have I received any despatches from the department; though I have received newspapers. I trust all papers directed to me, will hereafter be sent Via Mazatlan, as well as letters. Some of the packages addressed to me, were marked at the Department "via Mazatlan" but came by the Ship Lausanne from New York. Papers from N.

Orleans to the 17th of Feb[ruar]y were received here last month, by the way of Vera Cruz, While my latest are only to November 18th. I think one of the surest ways of forwarding letters &c to me will be, to send them to the Post Master at New Orleans, to be sent via *Vera Cruz*, Care of our Consul at Mazatlan, and by the Vera Cruz Packets via New York.

I shall leave in a day or two for the island of Kauai to spend a few days. It is said to be the most fertile of the Group, and contains the largest and most flourishing Sugar Plantations.

I do not know by what route this will reach you; but as there is a vessel leaves in a few days for Lima, shall probably send it to our Consul there to be forwarded via Panama.

If one or two of our small Vessels could be rigged with [John] Erics[s]ons propellers they might no doubt be advantageously employed in facilitating communications, between the different ports in the Pacific. I have the Honor to be with great respect Y[ou]r very Ob[edien]t S[ervan]t, Geo. Brown.

ALS (No. 13) with Ens in DNA, RG 59 (State Department), Diplomatic Despatches, Hawaii, vol. 1 (T-30:1, frames 83–87), received 11/13. NOTE: This despatch was addressed to Abel P. Upshur.

To CHARLES A. CLINTON, New York [City]

Department of State
Washington, May 4th 1844

My Dear Sir, I have just received your note of the 2nd inst[ant; *not found*] recommending Mr. [George E.] Baldwin for the situation of Despatch Agent at New York. Your recommendation is a sufficient warrant as to his character and qualifications—and your wishes a ready passport to my favorable consideration. But I have it not in my power to act in accordance with them in this case; as I promised, some weeks since, (being thereto requested by several friends in Congress acquainted with the Hon. Mr. [Fernando] Wood) that in the event of a removal of the present Agent [William Henry LeRoy], he should receive the appointment. You will therefore readily appreciate the reasons which restrain me from acting agreeably to your wishes. With high regard I am, Sir, Your friend and servant, J.C. Calhoun.

LS in NN, Ford Collection.

From JAMES DAVIS

Enon Grove[,] Heard County, Georgia, May the 4th 1844
Dear Sir, I see from a public speach made by the Hon. Mr. [Henry]
Clay, in A[u]gusta Georgia, that he appropriates the whole honor of
the *Compromise Bill* to himself. That Mr. Clay bore an honorable
part in that transaction I have never doubted but at the same time I
have always regarded you as entitled to an equil division of the honor.
The object then ["of" *canceled*] I have in view in writting to you at
present is to obtain from you a historey of this entire transaction *"The
Compromise Bill."* Will you be so kind as to answer me through the
Columns of the [Washington] Madisonian the following on that subject in connection with ["others" *changed to* "other"] things[?]
   Question 1st[.] Did I not address you a letter from Ellerton
Georgia on the subject of *"the Compromise Bill"* and did not said
letter contain all the principals of the Compromise Bill and did it not
suggest the person to propose it and the one to accept. Did you not
previou[s]ly to its proposial in the Senate confer with Mr. Clay and
was there any thing ever said publicly in the papers previous to your
reception of my letter, and nid [*sic*] you not immediat[e]ly answer
my letter saying in these words[:] "Rev. James Davis[.] Dear Sir[,]
I received your letter with much interest and will profit by your kind
suggestions[.] I cannot but have strong hope of the final success of
our great and good cause, when I see so many, good men, take shuch
deep interest in its triumph. As to myself if it shall please God to use
me as an instrument to establish the great truths for which we contend and which I sincer[e]ly believe are necessarey to secure our
freedom and to preserve our institutions my ambition as to the concerns of this life will be satisfied[.] With great respect I am & &,
J.C. Calhoun.["]
   question 2nd[.] Would ["you" *interlined*] if elected President
either in [18]44 or or [18]48 give your approbation to a measure of
Compromise on the currency question that would not be inc[ons]is-
tant with your sense of constitu[tio]nal obligations. In a plan of an
Exchuquer for receiving and disbursing the public Revinue; and
distinct from the gover[n]ment as its fiscal Agent, a Commercial
Bank—wholey seprearte and distinct from each other and would not
two shuch institutions act as a check on each other and could they
not be made so in detail both to be expediant and constitu[tio]nal[?]
   question 3rd[.] If his Excellency the Hon. John Tyler President
of the U.S. is run as a candidate for re election as the first Chief

Magristrate will you lend him your aid and support in prefference to Henry Clay and Martain Van Buren[?]

question 4th[.] Would you not approve of a bill for the agustement of the Tariff retaining all the principals of the Compromise Tariff though it might afford incidental protection[?]

Dear Sir, ["Though" *changed to* "Through"] the request of many Whigs and Democrats of [18]40 as an old friend I have been requested to submit these questions to your consideration to which it ["is" *interlined*] our wish you would respond as soon as convenient Through the Medium of the Madisonian or some other channel. Wishing you and all men well for time and eternity I subscribe myself your fellow Citizen In high consideration and in the hope of Immortality, James Davis.

May 9th

N.B. Mr. Calhoun can select any portion of this letter and answer that or let it alone as he may see p[r]oper but I shoulould be truly glad ["to" *interlined*] hear from him on the first question but I leave it all to his better Judgement. Yesterday we held a large meeting in this County in favour [of] the administration. I would be glad of a copey [of] Tyler[']s vindication[.]

Enon Grove is the Post Office[.] J. Davis.

ALS in ScCleA. NOTE: An AEU by Calhoun reads: "Re[veren]d Mr. Davis[.] Answered two first questions ["genl"(?) *canceled*] generally & declined answering the others for the present." No correspondence, such as Davis described above between himself and Calhoun at the time of the Compromise Tariff in 1833, has been found; nor has Calhoun's answer to the above letter.

From Lucius Q.C. Elmer, [Representative from N.J.], 5/4. "Have the goodness to inform me whether any information has been received at the State department from our Consul at Vera Cruz, respecting the Schooner Vigilant, seized there by the Mexican authorities, since the letter to me from Mr. [Abel P.] Upshur of the date of February 27th last." ALS in DNA, RG 59 (State Department), Miscellaneous Letters (M-179:104, frame 302).

From MIERS W. FISHER, "Private"

East-ville [Va.], May 4th 1844

My dear Sir, But for the anomalous condition of the political parties, and especially of the Republican party, at this time, I would not, upon my limited acquaintance, venture to address you in regard to the proper line of conduct to be pursued by the State rights party. And I hope in that will be found a sufficient apology.

The purpose of this letter is rather to ask than to express opinions; but, nevertheless, I cannot refrain from saying, that the States right portion of the Republican party, are in the condition to yield nothing to Van Burenism, but rather to require that their prejudices even shall be consulted. But without concert of action with every division of the party, defeat is inevitable. But temporary defeat might not be worse than temporary success. Mr. [Henry] Clay cannot possibly serve longer than one term, if elected, and the world has not yet designated his successor, but it has Mr. [Martin] Van Buren's, and he is as objectionable, if not more so, than Mr. Van Buren himself. Now, under present circumstances, shall the republicans of the land whose only aim is to preserve the rights of the States and the Federal compact inviolate, keep aloof alike from Clay and Van Buren, or ought they not rather to present a candidate of their own under whose banner all might honorably fight without any sacrifice of feeling or principle?

Is it not desirable that we should have a candidate in the field for the purpose of keeping our party together, so that in future contests we may rather prescribe terms to our friends than have them prescribed to us?

We cannot expect to keep the great mass of our party from voting for either Mr. Van Buren or Mr. Clay, unless we have a candidate of our own. Indeed unless we do have a candidate Mr. Clay, in this part of Virginia, will beat Mr. Van Buren very far. Last fall, when your friends expected confidently that you would be a candidate, they claimed a majority for you in this (Northampton) County. The result between Mr. Clay & Mr. Van Buren would be, that the latter would get about 75[?] out of 350 votes. There is a very strong & growing prejudice in eastern Va. against Mr. Van Buren.

Mr. Clay & Mr. Van Buren have both declared themselves opposed to the annexation of Texas to this confederacy. Their motives for this lie rather above than below the surface. The one had a competitor in his own party to silence, if not defeat, and both of them prefer to look to the North rather than to the South for support. But let their motives be whatever they may, it behooves the South to watch with vigilance her own especial interests, and to guard them in every possible honorable way.

I dislike the election of a President by the Ho[use] of Rep[resentatives] exceedingly, but had we not better risk that result than let the election go by default against us? We have suffered in the local elections in this State this spring, in many counties, because we had no presidential candidate and could not cordially unite upon Mr. Van Buren. Judge [Thomas H.] Bayly fought nobly in this District, but if they could not in any ["way" *interlined*] have connected his fortunes with Van Buren's I verily believe he would have been elected by a majority of from [*ms. torn; several words missing.*] Those who are opposed to Mr. Clay & not friendly to Mr. Van Buren, and even many of the latters friends on this [Eastern] shore, would unite on either you or Mr. [John] Tyler. And if Mr. V[an] Buren & Mr. Clay are alone candi[d]ates, the former will not get more than half the republican vote of this shore. Some of your friends here as well as myself, would like to have your views upon the course which our party ought to adopt, but I do not ask you to write a letter for publication, because that would be improper. And your views whatever they may be, will not be made public. Permit ["me" *interlined*] to ask that you will answer this at your earliest convenience & to request you to accept assurances of friendship from one who has been uniformly your friend, Miers W. Fisher.

ALS in ScCleA.

From J[OHN] G. FLUGEL

United States' Consulate
Leipsic, May 4, 1844

Sir, Most sensible of the losses our Government has sustained of late of the several most valuable statesmen—the more so from the cruel accident [aboard the *Princeton*] which occasioned them—I feel myself particularly called upon to offer my warmest and deepest regret, trusting that Providence may avert in future similar calamities.

Informed by the public papers—of you having become the head of the Department of State I beg leave to offer to you my most respectful congratulation.

It has been my lot that my various communications to the Department have reached Washington when the heads of it were no more. I would therefore beg leave to refer to my letters No. XVIII–XXI trusting that due note will be taken of their contents.

I hope also that the representations of our worthy Minister at Berlin [Henry Wheaton] and his Secretary Mr. [Theodore S.] Fay on me and my consular duties will enable you to form a proper judgment of my position; in regard to this and my performances I would beg also to refer to my Reports which I have composed for the Department and the special interest of *native* Americans since my appointment with indefatigable assiduity; and I hope that under your direction my claim for the necessary official outlays which I have had since my appointment will finally be settled as I have in justice every reason to expect.

I enclose to you a Leipsic Paper containing a Statement on the Receipts and Expenditures of the Customs' Union of Germany (Zollverein) from 1834 to 1843. Also a paper representing Leipsic during the Fair on which I have so largely spoken in my Reports. The present Fair seems to offer very good prospects of becoming a good one. Cloths and Leather have as usual found great sale; of the article of Cloth 7/8ths of the stock brought in from Saxony and Prussia amounting to about 100,000 pieces have been disposed of; several manufacturers have sold all their stock and received new orders of considerable amount. Two small manufacturing towns have sold of themselves 16,000 pieces; the prices have nearly remained at the low rate as of late years. Within a week about 2 millions of Thalers have changed hands in the article of cloth and purchases are still going on; a true statement however of the whole can only be made after the completion of the Fair. The manufacturers and merchants look with great anxiety forward upon the result expected from the Treaty and hope to see the trade with the United States acquire new life from a reduction of the duty on German manufactures.

Recommending myself to your Honour's kind protection I have the honour to be Sir Your Most Obedient Servant, Dr. J.G. Flugel, U.S. Consul.

LS (No. 22) with Ens in DNA, RG 59 (State Department), Consular Despatches, Leipzig, vol. 2 (T-215:2), received 7/11. NOTE: Besides two newspapers, Flugel enclosed a German-language publication of his own, the title of which translated is *Literary Sympathies; Or, Industrial Bookmaking. A Contribution to the History of More Recent English Lexicography*, published in Leipzig in 1843.

From JA[ME]S W. HALE[?]

New York [City,] May 4th 1844
Sir, Some two years since an application was made by some of my friends to the then Sec[retary] of State, (Hon. Mr. [Daniel] Webster) for my appointment as United States Despatch Agent for this city,

then vacant by the death of Mr. Bedicut[?], the former incumbent. I saw Mr. Webster in this city at the time, and he told me that he was so well satisfied with my capacity to do the duties of the situation, that he would think favorably of me, if he made *any* appointment— but that he had requested Mr. Dan[ie]l Le Roy (his wife's brother) to attend to the business, temporarily. Since that time the salary has been paid to Mr. D. Le Roy or his brother [William Henry LeRoy], altho' one or both have been absent from the city for months at a time. Mr. D. Le R[oy] was in New Orleans 7 or 8 months, while he was nominally despatch agent—and the duty which he should have performed was attended to by some of the Post Office or neglected altogether. The duty of the agent here is to recieve [*sic*] and forward all documents from the State Department to the various Consuls and Commercial Agents throughout the world. And if such documents and despatches are of value at all, it must be necessary that they should be forwarded with as little delay as possible.

My business during the last 8 years has been that of forwarding Foreign Letters to all countries—and I now ask to do that for the Government, which I have done for the public satisfactorily for several years. Should the appointment be made, I would state that the salary attached is but a minor consideration and may be reduced by the Secretary of State if he should deem it advisable.

I would further state, that it is quite a frequent circumstance that Consuls abroad send their despatches to my care, and that I forward them to Washington without the slightest remuneration—this I have frequently done for several years past. If you will refer to the documents rec[eive]d from the Am[erican] Consul at Genoa, you will find that they ["were" *canceled and* "have been" *interlined*] sent through me for a long time past.

Never having been a seeker for any other office under government than the one I now ask for, I do not trouble you with a pile of recommendatory letters—but, should you be disposed to think favorably of my application I can confidently refer to any of the Merchants of New York, for testimonials of character, industry and ["proptitude" *altered to* "promptitude"].

I would also refer you to Edmund S. Derry, Geo[rge] D. [*sic*; E.] Baldwin, John A. Morrill or Ja[me]s Bergen, for any ["other" *interlined*] information respecting me. Very respectfully Your Ob[e]-d[ien]t Serv[an]t, Jas. W. Hale[?], Foreign Letter Office, 58 Wall Street.

ALS in ViU, Crallé-Campbell Papers.

From ROB[ER]T MONROE HARRISON, "Private"

Consulate of the United States
Kingston Jam[aic]a, 4th May 1844

Sir, Being under the impression that it cannot be otherwise than agreeable to you, to receive authentic information concerning the working of the free labour system, as well as the conduct of the negroes generally in this Island; I with great deference and respect do myself the honor to send you herewith [my] answers to certain Interrogatories which have been put to me by a distinguished individual who was writing a work on Domestic Slavery: but as he has recently met with a premature death (which I shall ever lament) it will not now be published.

As a native citizen of the State of Virginia, I have devoted much of my time in my private as well as public character to enquiries concerning the effect which emancipation has already had on this colony, and what are likely to be the ruinous consequences hereafter. With profound respect I have the honor to be Sir Your ob[edien]t & most humble serv[an]t, Robt. Monroe Harrison.

[Enclosure]

What has been the effect of emancipation in the price of Real estate, exemplified by instances under your observation, and by some of the most striking you have heard of?

That of reducing the price of Freeholds generally to half or even a third of their real value. As an instance of which the late Mr. J. Maillet who possessed one of the finest Coffee properties in the Parish of St. George, called Mammee Hill, was in the latter days of Slavery offered Five thousand one hundred pounds St[erlin]g for the Freehold by a Gentleman of Kingston; but Mr. Maillet refused the offer being unwilling to take less than Seven thousand five hundred for it. Since the emancipation this fine Settlement has been appraised and Sold for no more than One thousand eight hundred pounds. Many other valuable properties have suffered, and are daily suffering a similar proportional deterioration in their intrinsic worth, without having the least prospect from ever recovering from their ruin. It is to be observed that sugar estates as well as those of other cultivation are included in the preceding remarks. In towns, fine large substantial buildings with every requisite out office, Coach Houses, stables, large yards and gardens, which could not have been erected for less than Two thousand pounds St[erlin]g are every day disposed of for five, four and even so little as three hundred pounds.

What has been the effect on the annual product of the Island? State particularly the relative products in Sugar and Coffee with such remarks as you may deem interesting.

Having no Custom House annual Returns of the exports of the Island before me to Consult, I cannot say to what extent its yearly product has decreased since the emancipation, but I know that the Crops upon the sugar and Coffee properties as well as others, have gradually diminished to half, one third and even one Fourth of what they used to average yearly. "Spring Garden" sugar estate in the Parish of St. George belonging to the Hon. John Rock Grosett in time of Slavery made annually Six hundred Hogsheads of Sugar and three hundred Puncheons of Rum and could grind weekly from 25 to 30 Hogsheads of Sugar, but at present it hardly makes Two hundred Hogsheads of Sugar and One hundred Puncheons of Rum and will at most grind but twelve Hhds. of sugar per week in full crop time; added to which the extravagant charges of the labourers for their in- adequate work, and the yearly contingencies, swamp all the profits, and leave little or nothing for the use of the proprietor. Gibraltar sugar estate, a property of the same magnitude, situated in the new Parish of Metcalfe, and once the princely Seat of Thomas Wentworth Bayley Esq., is in the same sad predicament. In the Coffee line the large plantation in St. Georges called Orange Vale has fallen off in its yearly crops from One Hundred thousand lbs. to ten thousand and even less; which is the case with many others throughout the Island of ["varies" *altered to* "various"] culture.

What is the moral condition of the negroes? what relation do they bear to the whites? what feelings exist between them? Are assassinations more frequent? and what is the Cause?

They are generally very fond of Chapels, which they attend in great numbers and very regularly; those places are to them, what Theatres and places of amusements are to the people in Europe— places of agre[e]able pastime where they meet to display their dress and fineries; to procure which they will go to any length save work- ing. They are religious only in outward appearance, and have so confused an idea of their christian duties that they have repeatedly been guilty of blending the rites of their religion with those of African paganism. With this absurd combination of novel worship here called Myalism, they have often committed serious mischief among their class in the Country; and lately to such an alarming and danger- ous extent, that the authorities have been compelled, for the Sake of public safety, to use all their influence and power to check that fast spreading evil. They have a natural mistrust and dislike of the whites, and will ever be jealous of them. When affranchisement began in Europe it took place gradually, and among people where no difference of Colour existed—as a brand to revive in the minds of the late bondmen or their offspring, imaginary or real grievances suffered at the hands of their former lords. After the affranchisement the ancient lord and serf could meet together without experiencing a feeling of antipathy towards each other; there remaining no brand mark or sign of recognizance to feed the late serf[']s hatred against his former lord. Al[l] the past fell into oblivion; and in a rigorous climate like that of Europe, the emancipation of the Serfs turned to the real advantage of the nations that adopted the change of system; but here the Color, that everlasting brand mark or sign exists between the whites and blacks, and hourly signalizes the former master to the late Slave and by that means continues to Nourish those deep rooted prejudices which exist between the two Classes; at the same time that it procludes the possibility of a future change; for instance, at the late dreadful conflagration of this town, the Streets where the fire was raging ["was" *altered to* "where" (*sic*)] thronged with thousands of the late emancipated blacks, men and women; none of whom would give any assistance to arrest the fury of the flames; one and all of them on the contrary, appearing to enjoy the destruction of "Buckra's" property and ["a" *interlined*] great ["many" *interlined*] of them were caught inhumanely and basely robbing the goods and furniture of the unfortunates who had their house[s] burnt down, and who were making a last and desperate effort to save some of their moveables from the general wreck. Without the timely and indefatigable exertions of the Military, and Crews of the Royal and merchants ships in the harbour, God only knows what would have been the final fate of Kingston and its pitiable inhabitants.

Though assassination is of rare occurrence here, still it has been much more frequent since the emancipation than in the days of Slavery; but as to all other crimes in general, they have increased and are, of late, yearly increasing to an ["allarming" *altered to* "alarming"] degree. The cause, I attribute to this—by the existing laws in the time of Slavery, to guard against rebellion, and insure public safety, the master or his representative was invested, and did act, with fully as much power as possesses the present special magistrate, to enforce and keep up that necessary discipline which is indispensable to maintain peace and good order on each property, among its semi barbarian African Slaves; the law protected them, but did keep them in due obedience, and clear of the bad results of idleness; while at present, instead of one magistrate to each property, as formerly, to enforce good order, we have but two or three paid Special magistrate[s] at most to each Parish, to keep the peace, and check the wicked in their vil[l]ainies. Moreover ["the circumstance of" *interlined*] these late emancipated blacks having been treated until now, as spoiled children and favourites; and the Authorities not strictly enforcing the law against them; encourages them to those acts of shameful misdeeds which we have so repeatedly cause to complain of, and bitterly to suffer by. Our emancipated as above observed, meeting with little or no restraint to their bad propensities, give full vent to their unruly passions, dreading no evil consequence as a natural result therefrom. Such, in my opinion is the most material cause of the general misbehaviour and culpability of our newly emancipated black population.

In the debates in the Chamber of Deputies the encreasing laziness of the negroes was proved by citing the diminishing products of Sugar and Coffee. The speakers however on the other side said that although Sugar and Coffee had diminished and real estate fallen in value yet that the whole amount of products must have encreased because the imports had regularly encreased ever since the emancipation. Can this be true?

The assertion that the imports of Colonial produce have regularly encreased since the emancipation might be very true; but it must be by the unfair and clandestine introduction of the East India and slave colonies sugars and coffee &c: but the supposition that our exports of the Same Commodities are also on the increase, is absurd; from the fallen state of our trade nearly annihilated: and when our exports are so well known to have decreased to such an incredible extent as to be the actual and irretri[e]vable ruin of the poor duped planters!

In by gone days, I have seen the harbour of this town covered with upwards of five hundred square sail at one and the same time, now it is commonly almost empty of any ships. Since the emancipation, I have known some vessels from Europe ["to" *interlined and* "being" *altered to* "be"] in the necessity of stopping Six and Eight months in our ports so as to enable them to make up a load which they could not procure in proper time for their return home. This speaks for itself and ought to show how ill founded is the supposition now treated upon; but still this supposition that our exports must have increased because our imports here, might have somewhat increased in the first years of the emancipation, is not a criterion to judge by, and is an enigma taken advantage of to puzzle *John Bull* and persuade him that the *grand experiment* is doing *wonderfully* well! but I would explain this false appearance thus: Upon the emancipation taking place all the money the labourers had by fair or foul means been treasuring up during the time of Slavery, leaving its lurking places was suddenly put into circulation to procure those good and fine things which their appetite and vanity so much coveted; but like a reservoir thoughtlessly and improvidently burst open, its content dashes out with impetuosity in the first instants and soon leaves it empty and dry; time will prove the truth of the comparison.

What is the condition of the negroes in St. Domingo? Are they advancing or retrograding in industry and Civilisation? How do they stand by comparison with our Slaves?

Who has been in this island and has visited our maroon towns before their dissolution may fancy having seen Haiti. Represent to yourself a fine ["sett" *canceled and* "race" *interlined*] of people, men and women good looking, well shaped, supple and agile in their persons; but lazy and indolent; having an unconquerable aversion to labour, however light; fond of all kinds of amusements attainable by them, such as hunting, fishing, gambling, feasting, dancing, drinking, love making &c &c, famous and persevering bushfighters in their recesses of the double mountains where they are always of difficult and dangerous approach; on the other hand, timid and weak opponents in a champaign country, remarkably shy in broad day light, but bold and most daring under the dark veil of night; and as all true Cowards most cruel in their vengeance. These people in this island had received from Government, hundreds of acres of most excellent and fertile lands in full property to them, and for their private use, and though enjoying the advantages of living under mild and protective laws, and being in the midst of civilisation, they never were stimulated by example to elevate themselves in the scale of Society through their industry and exertions and remained to the very last perfectly stationary in their ignorant and half civilised condition, without the least improvement whatever! Such is on a larger scale the nature and Character of the mass of our emancipated blacks; and such is also the disposition and present state of the generality of the black population of the interior of Haiti. The knowing one[s] are comparatively few, inhabit the low lands and Towns, and have taken good care to take the reins of government into their own hands, patriotically for the happiness of the Sovereign people, to govern the Sacred Republic at the point of the bayonnet!

Witness the accusations against, and the expulsion of the late President [Jean Pierre] Boyer! After nearly fifty years of full possession of so fine and fruitful an Island as Haiti, its people making little or no progress in civilisation, and remaining nearly stationary in their difficienties of all sorts, prove indisputably their want of energy and industry, and that something is faulty in their intellectual powers; and that indolence and idleness overpower and inslave the Haitian Citizens! Unfortunate effect of a fine climate, a beautiful sky, and too generous a Soil!

Does emancipation have the effect of immediately separating the blacks and whites? Or do they remain in about the same proportion to each other in any given district after as before emancipation.

The labourers are quitting the properties of their former masters as fast as their acquired means can permit them to purchase land and form little establishments of their own; they congregate together and form new villages most rapidly, towards the lowlands, and as near the market towns as possible; many plantations having now but few of their former slaves remaining on them, while others are already entirely deserted.

Notes. The grand experiment here, proves itself a complete failure, considered in a commercial point of view; the island under the free system being no longer profitable to the mother country; the cultivation of its main staples being daily forcibly abandoned by the planters in consequence of the want of labourers, too high wages and the scarcity of money. To compete with the Slaves colonies, the average price of the labourers work should not exceed six pence St[erlin]g a day of at least nine hours; ["and the negro" *interlined*] should be willing to undergo the fatigue he proves himself so positively an enemy to. Free emigrants from Africa, or blacks from any part of the world, without becoming a profitable acquisition to our agriculture, will only augment the present already too strong physical force of our black population, and endanger the safe possession of the island, already too precarious, with the example, communication and the near neighbourhood of Haiti. Should the question be put to me whether the Slaves are happier under the Change than before, I will unhesitatingly answer *most certainly;* but at the expense of the land holders whose interests have been most inhumanely and cruelly sacrificed; and ["whom" *altered to* "who"] by whole families have been thrown into distressing misery! It is not to be lost sight of, that since the emancipation there is hardly a black man to be found unprovided with fire arms &c. &c. furnished by the British merchants themselves, ["and" *canceled*] from whom they are daily purchased. The Contest seems to be between the West and the East India's interest; and the influence and preponderance of this last, has, under the mask of phylanthropy, achieved the irretri[e]vable ruin of the first.

The innocent and unfortunate possessor of Slaves, ["here" *canceled*] was forced to take only One third of the real value of his lawfully acquired property as a pretended compensation; his freehold despoiled of its former labourers like a dismasted and dismantled ship on the ocean after a tremendous and irresistible storm, remaining still afloat braving the billows a few moments longer, only inevitably to perish.

LS with En in ScCleA. NOTE: The author of the interrogatories to which Harrison replied has not been identified.

From Em[anue]l B. Hart, New York [City], 5/4. He informs Calhoun that Lovell Purdy, in attempting to procure an appointment to be the U.S. Consul at Leghorn, will submit proofs that [Joseph A.] Binda, the incumbent, is guilty of "gross neglect" of the duties of that office. These proofs will be presented through A.S. Dias, whom Hart knows to be respectable and of good standing. ALS in DNA, RG 59 (State Department), Applications and Recommendations, 1837–1845, Purdy (M-687:26, frame 702).

From J[ohn] Y. Mason, [Secretary of the Navy], 5/4. He encloses a copy of a letter written today to Lt. H[enry] H. Bell, "commanding the U.S. Steamer Union," [concerning the transportation of Wilson Shannon, appointed Minister to Mexico, to that country]. Mason suggests "that Governor Shannon be desired to apprise Lieut. Bell, at Pensacola, on what day he will be ready to embark from New Orleans." LS with En in DNA, RG 59 (State Department), Miscellaneous Letters (M-179:104, frames 303–304); FC in DNA, RG 45 (Naval Records), Letters Sent by the Secretary of the Navy to the President and Executive Agencies, 1821–1886, 4:501 (M-472:2, frame 632).

To THOMAS M. RODNEY, U.S. Consul, Matanzas, [Cuba]

Department of State
Washington, May 4, 1844

Sir: I have to acknowledge the receipt of your letter No. 13, with the correspondence in regard to an outrage committed upon Mr. Christopher Boone, a citizen of the United States, and the reference to the Department of one of the 13th ultimo to the President [John Tyler], transmitting the memorial of Mr. Boone.

The President fully approves the course you have taken in relation to this case, and he has directed that one of our ships of war should immediately proceed to Matanzas with special instructions respecting it, and in order that in the present disturbed state of the Island, the rights and liberties of our citizens residing there, may be more effectually guarded and protected. In the meantime you will in every instance which may come to your knowledge of injustice done to an American citizen, firmly and resolutely remonstrate with the Authorities, and use every exertion compatible with your official duties, which may tend to afford relief and resistance to the injured party. Every such case, as it occurs, you will promptly and specifically report to the Department, together with such authenticated evidence as you may be able to obtain, and upon the arrival of a ship of war you will confer fully with the Commanding officer and co-operate with him in rendering such aid and protection to our citizens as you can afford and their situation may require. I am, Sir, &c, J.C. Calhoun.

FC in DNA, RG 59 (State Department), Consular Instructions, 10:241–242; transcript in DLC, Carnegie Institution of Washington Transcript Collection.

From G[ILBERT] L. THOMPSON

Southwest Pass
Mouth of the Mississippi
Saturday Ev[enin]g May 4th/44

Respected Sir, I have the pleasure to inform you that we ar[r]ived here this eveni[n]g and are taking in wood, for Galveston, about 60 hours run, reserving our Coal for the run from there to Tampico.

The newspaper announcing the ar[r]ival of Mr. [Peyton A.]

Southall with important despatches from Mexico has just been sent on board by the Pilot. If on my ar[r]ival at Galveston the Potomac Com[mo]d[ore David] Conner is not there I shall proceed directly in the Steamer Poinsett. Respectfully your Ob[edien]t S[er]v[an]t, G.L. Thompson.

ALS in DNA, RG 59 (State Department), Diplomatic Despatches, Special Agents, vol. 13 (M-37:13, frame 77), received 5/21.

From J[ohn] Tyler, 5/4. Tyler wrote as follows on a resolution of the House of Representatives which he had received: "The Secretary of State will oblige me by communicating a copy of this resolution to the B[ritish] Minister with such remarks as may aid the object of the resolution." The resolution of 5/2 requested the President "to interpose his good Office with the British Government for the release" of Benjamin Mott of Vt., Samuel Newcome of N.Y., "and all other American prisoners at Van Diemans Land." AES on DS in DNA, RG 59 (State Department), Miscellaneous Letters (M-179:104, frames 278–279).

From G[EORGE] F. USHER

Commercial Agency of the U. States
Cape Haytien, May 4th, 1844

Sir, Since my communication to the Department of State of the 16th of March, (No. 15), I have the honor further to state, that the "Army of the North" was entirely unsuccessful in its attack on the Spanish city of St. Jago; and after a few hundred of them were killed, the whole army made a precipitate retreat to this place, and was suffered to disband itself.

Early in the night of Wednesday, the 23d Ultimo, information was received here that Gen[era]l [Jean Louis] Pierrot had collected a considerable force in the vicinity of Acul, about thirty miles off, and was marching for the Cape, without assigning to the Authorities here any reason for such a movement. Great consternation and alarm were produced, and particularly among the mulattos, who it had been conjectured, would be the object of the vengeance of this army.

As soon as information was given, that this supposed hostile force, had reached within a few miles of this City, I procured the boats of all the American vessels in Port, and advised the Americans, and also other Foreigners, to send their articles of value that were easily portable on board the vessels, which advice was readily adopted. Also many mulattos, principally women, repaired on board the shipping for personal safety.

A Deputation was sent out before morning to meet this army, and returned at noon, saying that Gen[era]l Pierrot intended no personal injury to either colour, but declared his intention to separate the north part of this Island from the Government at Port-au-Prince.

In the course of the succeeding night, he marched his army without resistance, into the Cape. And these people uniting with him, have declared the North part of this Island independent of the General Government.

They express a desire to be on friendly terms with the Spaniards; and also with the other parts of the Island, if practicable.

They have assumed a national Standard which is the Haytien flag, with the addition of a white star in the upper or blue half of it. The "Dominicans," as the Spaniards term themselves, have hoisted the Haytien flag with the addition of a white Cross in the center.

It appears that almost the whole of this Island is in a state of Revolution. The Eastern, or Spanish, part having first revolted. The center, including Port-au-Prince, disaffected, but still under the Government of President [Charles Aimé] Herard. The south, declaring against his rule, and in open rebellion. And this, the north, including all the territory formally [*sic*; formerly] claimed by Christophe, declaring itself independent of all.

Such a condition of discordant interests and feelings, must necessarily jeopardise, in a degree, the persons, and more particularly the property of Foreigners. And the large amount of American property in the different Ports of this Island; it would appear, needed some more efficient protection than can be given to it by its owners. Thus far however, no outrages, of any description, have as yet been committed here.

Yesterday evening proclamation was made, that an additional duty was imposed on all coffee not already embarked, of ten Dollars Haytien currency, p[e]r one thousand pounds, to go into effect, this the next morning; raising the export duty on Coffee, from twelve, to twenty two dollars, Haytien currency, p[e]r one thousand pounds, with the one dollar for weighage & wharfage as formally [*sic*].

By recent letters from home, I am informed that circumstances have arisen which makes it desirable that I should visit the U. States about the middle of July, to remain about a month, and have respectfully to ask for that indulgence. I have the honor Sir, to be, with the

438

highest consideration, Your very ob[edien]t S[er]v[an]t, G.F. Usher, U.S. Com[mercia]l Ag[en]t.

ALS (No. 16) in DNA, RG 59 (State Department), Consular Despatches, Cap Haitien, vol. 7 (M-9:7, frames 132–133), received 5/17.

From Alex[ander] Wells, "member of the Calhoun Central Committee of the State," New York [City], 5/4. Joseph [A.] Binda has lived in New York [City] throughout the past three years but receives payment for fulfilling the duties of the U.S. Consul at Leghorn— duties performed by a foreigner there. Lovell Purdy, an applicant for that Consulship, is an honest, capable gentleman who is well acquainted with Europe. ALS in DNA, RG 59 (State Department), Applications and Recommendations, 1837–1845, Purdy (M-687:26, frames 703–704).

From [Brevet Maj. Gen.] EDMUND P. GAINES

Pittsburgh Pa., May 5th 1844

Sir, [*Ms. torn; one or two words missing*] unaccountable accident or mistake in the conveyance of a letter having retarded the movement of a part of my family from Binghamton N.Y. to this place has detained me here nearly a week longer than I had anticipated. This detention however is the less to be regret[t]ed as it has afforded me an opportunity of a delightful inspection of the vast augmentation and improvement of the means which this city affords for the speedy supply of all the materials we need for the construction and armament of War Steamers and Floating Batteries of Iron, for the protection of our southern Sea Ports and western frontier.

My detention here has moreover afforded me an opportunity of examining the lately published papers purporting to be the Treaty of annexation, between the United States and Texas and the documents upon which the Treaty was based, together with the letters of Mr. [Henry] Clay, Mr. [Martin] Van Buren and Senator [Thomas H.] Benton, adverse to the Treaty.

These important public documents appear to me to indicate clearly the propriety of immediate preparation on our part for war; convinced as I am that if Mexico is sure of the open cooperation, or even the secret support of England (with her newfangled Holy horrour at that feature of our institutions for w[hich?] under the chastening hand of an all-wise Providence we are mainly indebted to the habitual avarice and inflexible cupidity of this same England,) our good neighbor Republic ["of" *interlined*] Mexico will readily commence the crusade so politely threatened by Lord Aberdeen.

With these impressions firmly fixed in my mind I should not be surprised to see at or near New Orleans before the end of next month a Fleet consisting of all the [British] *mail Boats* and other War Steamers to be found in the Gulf of Mexico ready and willing under a Mexican abolition Flag to commence the crusade under the influence of that demoniack spirit which at the River Raison [and] Fort Mims [in 1813], and more recently at the Alamo, consigned some hundreds of unoffending men[,] women and children with unresisting prisoners of war to the cold blooded cruelties of wholesale massacre.

Though England may be anxious to avoid being seen as the prime mover in such a crusade, yet who but England is to be benefitted? certainly not Mexico. On the contrary that deluded nation, like most other victims of British intrigue and British treachery cannot but receive sooner or later a full measure of that retributive justice which though due to her as the *accessory* before the fact, and *the ostensible actor*, will be doubly due to the artful *principal* offender.

And how I may be asked is England to be benefitted? I answer— let the crusade commence under the auspices of England—let its first operation result in crushing, or materially changing the institutions of Texas, and in substituting a British colony or other dependent nation of *white slaves* in place of *black*—a dependent nation secured to England by loans, or by *a secret Treaty of alliance offensive and defensive*, in place of the present high-minded Republic of Texas, then will England enjoy the proud triumph of having thrown around us an Iron chain, the last link of which, like the lost keystone of an arch, will be the most important link in that mighty chain—a chain extending from the Rocky mountains and northern Lakes to St. Regis on the Saint Lawrence and thence to East Port Maine consisting of *British colonies*, thence upon the Atlantic and Gulf of Mexico to Texas consisting ["of" *interlined*] *British naval supremacy* with the *British west India Islands*—the *keystone link of this mighty chain to embrace Texas*, and extend from the Gulf of Mexico to the Rocky mountains and North western Lakes. This new link is sustained by a vast invisible power of Indians, Traders, and Trappers.

The possession, or even the occasional occupancy of Texas by England would enable her to construct with *English Iron*, shaped in

England by English ship builders for uniting with *Texian live oak,* from one to two hundred war steamers adapted to our shoal-waters of the south—war steamers of British Iron and Texian oak, such as might be constructed in one year after their commencement, in Texian seaports, within a few hours run of the Balize and other parts of Louisiana, and but little more than one days run to Mobile and Pensacola—war steamers supplied with British Engines and manned by British Seamen; while her Hudsons Bay Traders and Trappers would organize and bring upon our unfortified western frontier from 60,000 to 80,000 hungry Indian warriors of the Tecumpseh stamp, ready and willing with *British scalping knives to renew the war upon our Western women and children and revive the old traffick of Yankee Scalps for British Gold!* The possession or even the occasional occupancy of Texas by England would I apprehend enable her to rivet her chain of circumvallation around us (if indeed we tamely submit to the British process of rivetting her chains of Empire,) which would render us more powerless and more dependent than if we were still burdened with the chains of British colonial vassalage.

We may thus ere long find ourselves engaged in another war for our Independence; a war however that no truehearted descendant or disciple of *Washington* will ever agree to terminate as long as a single link of the British chain by which our country is fettered shall remain unbroken!

If the united Mexican and British views disclosed by the documents recently published warrant the foregoing conclusions even so far as to render immediate active operations on the part of Mexico at all probable, of which I apprehend there is no reason to doubt, I cannot but think it my duty to solicit authority to call into service such volunteer corps with such Steam Boats as I may find convertible into *war Steamers* or *Floating Batteries*—with such other means of defence as may be needed to put New Orleans, Mobile and Pensacola, with the whole south western frontier in a state of readiness to repel any probable invasion.

Although I am convinced that it is our duty as long as they shall abstain from actual invasion, or the capture of our vessels, to treat Mexico and Texas, and all other American republics with the courtesy and kindness due to brethren of the same family, and of which we can only claim to be the *natural Guardian* or the eldest sister; yet if they or any of them should have the weakness to yield to the intrigues of a European rival, often our deadly foe, as England is, or was, and so far give way to that spirit of fanaticism (so recently and so extensively disclosed by various publications and public men in England, and in some parts of our own country, and in effect sustained by the documents above refer[r]ed to,) as to *appear in force* in our waters, or upon any part of our unmarked Boundary, or upon our thinly settled frontier, surely we can do nothing less than *to hold ourselves ready to admonish to admonish* [*sic*] *them to keep the peace.* And, if an attack is unavoidable, we should be ready forthwith to follow our friendly admonitions *with prompt action*—to repel any such attack. Otherwise they might be induced secretly to inspect, and thus ascertain our defenceless positions, and take by surprize our most vulnerable, if not our most vital sea Port towns here refer[r]ed to.

It is not to be apprehended that they would at first have the temerity to attempt to *hold possession* of any of our sea port towns. As they could not hope to hold any one of them for a day, or for more than a few hours. But they could in an hour or two by a vigorous cannonade and Bombardment destroy by fire and otherwise, millions of dollars worth of Houses[,] Merchandize and other property: For such is the great revolution in the attack and defence of sea Ports by the application of Steam power to ships of war and Rail Roads, and such the defenceless condition of most of our southern Sea Ports, that it is quite practicable for five or six armed Steamers such as can enter the Harbour of New Orleans and Mobile, to enter either without much risk to their own forces—and commence a cannonade and Bombardment—and thus by taking the place by surprize, set it on fire in 50 to 100 places, and then retreat in safety before the best of our Regulars, or the most vigilant volunteers in America (such as those of New Orleans and Mobile are known to be,) could possibly be ready to destroy or materially to cripple the invader without previously prepared means of *Floating defence* to cooperate with our stationary works and land forces.

The foregoing remarks are intended first, to present to you an outline of ["my" *interlined*] impressions regarding *the military aspect* of Texas, taken in connection with the defence of our western frontier, and more particularly New Orleans, which place is in a military point of view by far the most important sea Port in America; and secondly, to show the necessity of the officer commanding the Western Division being authorised to provide against those *sudden assaults* which steam power affords the means of making, and which cannot but be expected in a country like ours, whose most important and most assailable sea ports are in part so remote as New Orleans and Mobile are from the seat of the General Government.

Hoping to hear from you in New Orleans by the middle of this month, I have the honor to be very respectfully your obedient s[ervan]t, Edmund P. Gaines.

note. I'm glad to find our professed *northern man with southern principles,* as well as our western men with some northern predilections, have been recently laboring upon the annexation treaty *to define their positions.* I hope they will ere long *unite with us* in honest efforts to preserve the *Republic,* by maintaining the true principles of the union. E.P.G.

ALS in ScCleA.

Louis Mark, "Steamer Hibernia off Boston," to President [John] Tyler, 5/5. Mark informs Tyler that [Henry] Wheaton has sent Mark to Washington with the original copy of the commercial convention recently negotiated between the U.S. and the German states [of the Zollverein]. Mark hopes that he can answer any questions about the convention during his stay in Washington. He asks Tyler to recommend him to Calhoun's attention. An AEI by Tyler reads: "Mr. Mark is entitled to the confidence of the govt." ALS in DNA, RG 59 (State Department), Miscellaneous Letters (M-179:104, frames 305–306).

From W[illiam] Allen, Senator [from Ohio], 5/6. "This will be handed to you by Mr. J.G. Hoster of Ohio. He is a young gentleman of most excellent character. He has some little business about which he desires the favor of a moment's interview with you. You will greatly oblige me by affording ["him" *interlined*] that opportunity." ALS in DNA, RG 59 (State Department), Passport Applications, vol. 31, no. 2093 (M-1372:14).

To Lucius Q.C. Elmer, [Representative from N.J.], 5/6. In response to Elmer's letter of 5/4, Calhoun states that there has been no information "relative to the schooner Vigilant" since 2/27. FC in DNA, RG 59 (State Department), Domestic Letters, 34:174 (M-40:32).

From J[OSEPH] R. FLANDERS

Fort Covington [N.Y.], May 6, 1844

Dear Sir, I take the liberty of availing myself of the situation which you hold in the Federal Government, to solicit your attention to the case of the Post Master at this place, against whom charges are said to have been preferred at Washington. The incumbent of the place is Mr. John Parker, a capable and honest man. He is in such circumstances in life as render him dependent upon the income of his office for support. He has held the office about three years, and has discharged its duties to universal satisfaction. He has been faithful, attentive, and upright. If any charges have been made against him they must, I think, have originated in some quarter seeking his situation. If you will be so kind as to lay this statement before [Charles A. Wickliffe] the Post Master General, informing him what you know of me, I shall deem it a particular favor.

In making this application, I trust you will not deem me obtrusive. I believe I act from no improper motive. I am in no way connected with Mr. Parker, nor shall I be personally benefited by his continuing in his present situation. And if I were interested, be assured I should not trouble you in this way. With my present views, I could ["not" *interlined*] allow myself to ask any thing of personal benefit, on the ground of my being your political friend. I believe it is a cardinal doctrine of the school of politics of which you are the acknowledged leader, and of which I am a humble follower, that the offices and patronage of the government are not to be used to purchase or reward political partizanship. We have preached this doctrine when in opposition; I trust we shall show to the world our integrity and consistency by adhering to the same principle when in power. I ask nothing, therefore, ["for" *interlined and* "of" *canceled*] Mr. Parker, on political grounds. Indeed, it is right that you should know that he is a moderate whig. But he is an honest man, and this should far outweigh every political consideration. As an evidence of this, I need only state that between thirty and forty thousand dollars have been mailed by him since he was in office, and not a cent has been lost that I have heard.

I hope I shall not be considered impertinent if I allude to present political aspects. I think you must be ["be" *canceled*] convinced that the Van Buren party are acting in bad faith. Whatever advances they make in a right direction are evidently compelled by a stern political necessity. Their course on the tariff and abolition questions conclusively shows that they have no fixed principles, but are playing fast and loose between the two sections of the Union, to retain the favor of both. They temporize and shuffle in regard to abolition petitions, and are altogether incomprehensible upon the tariff. So, too, on the subject of internal improvements, they are running into the wildest latitudinarian doctrines to buy up the west.

What reliance is to be placed upon men who cannot be brought to take a stand any where, but are shifting and dodging with more than lunar variation? Such men evidently have no heartfelt attachment to the fundamental principles of the party, and can never be depended upon when they may deem it expedient for the moment to betray them. We saw this in 1832, when the [Force] Proclamation was issued to cast its baleful influence upon the country. We have seen it in the declaration of principles put forth by the Syracuse Convention. We have seen it in the proposed organization of the national Convention. We have seen it in the action of the present *Democratic?* House of Representatives. These things should be a warning against trusting in future men who are capable of such treachery.

You may possibly recollect a Communication written by me, and published in the Washington Chronicle, while in the hands of Mr. [Richard K.] Cralle, under the signature of "Ninety-Eight," in which I warned the State Rights party against an alliance with Van Burenism. Whether that warning was wise or not let events disclose. For myself, the course which I thought right to pursue on that occasion, though it has been detrimental to my personal interests, by keeping me separate from all ["personal" *canceled*] party organization, has left me at this time in a position which I think many State Rights men will feel constrained to take, that of neutrality in any contest to which Van Burenism is a party. I do not think it right to countenance political hypocrisy, fraud, and deception, and to countenance the tyranny of party, even to keep the whigs from power. In my view it is better for the country that the democratic party should suffer yet another defeat, than that it should be restored to power unreformed and unpurified. It will be worse to reinstate the corrupt dynasty of Van Burenism than to be ["bet" *canceled*] beaten by the whigs. For— of the whigs and their measures we can rid ourselves whenever our party shall have sustained sufficient adversity to teach it honesty and wisdom. But let party tyranny and ["corruption" *interlined*] triumph at this time, and it will so have broken the spirit of the people, as to be able to perpetuate itself. These considerations will induce me to stand aloof from the contest, if Mr. Van Buren shall be the candidate. Pardon the suggestion of these views, and believe me, With great respect, your fellow-citizen, J.R. Flanders.

ALS in ScCleA.

From Bladen Forrest, Washington, 5/6. Forrest states that because of illness he was obliged to leave his Consular post at Chagres, New Granada. Acting on a physician's advice he took the first opportunity to leave the place and embarked on 4/2. Forrest had written to the State Dept. for permission to leave, but was so ill with "the fever of the Country, which generally proves *fatal to* persons, *who are not acclimated*" that he did not wait for a reply. He advised the U.S. Consul at Panama [William Nelson] of his departure. ALS in DNA, RG 59 (State Department), Consular Despatches, Colón, vol. 5 (T-193:5).

From BLADEN FORREST

Washington, May 6th 1844

Sir, According to instructions received from the Department, I made every enquiry in regard to the transmission of Despatches across the Isthmus, to Panama—and was informed that all letters & newspapers brought to any port in the Republic of New Grenada from a foreign Country—must be immediately placed in the Post office for transportation. The Post masters are directed to forward all despatches, in the course of Eight hours after their arrival, but this law is seldom respected by them.

The mail Bags placed in my possession, on my arrival at Chagres, by Lieut. Com[man]d[in]g A[rthur] Sinclair of the U.S. Despatch Schooner Phenix[,] were taken by me, and delivered in person, to William Nelson Esq[ui]r[e] our Consul & Despatch Agent, at Panama.

The present rates of postage in New Grenada are very exorbitant, for a single letter, from Chagres to Panama twenty-five cents is charged. Newspapers, are admitted free, provided they are not put up in packages exceeding a half a pound in weight.

I beg leave to suggest to the Consideration of the Department, That the letter bags, to cross the Isthmus, with letters for *private individuals,* be closed at the post office at Washington, and the postage thereon be paid, previously to their leaving the United States. This arrangement would save the Government from an *enormous expense.*

The Bags, for Public Despatches & newspapers may be closed & sent from the Department. I have the honor to be Sir Very Respectfully Y[ou]r Ob[edien]t Serv[an]t, Bladen Forrest, U.S. Consul & Despatch Ag[en]t at Chagres.

ALS in DNA, RG 59 (State Department), Consular Despatches, Colón, vol. 5 (T-193:5). NOTE: Found among Calhoun's papers at ScCleA is [Abel P. Upshur's] draft of a letter of 11/7/1843 appointing Forrest to be Despatch Agent at Chagres, New Granada.

From D[ANIEL] JENIFER

Legation of the United States
Vienna, May 6th 1844

Sir, Although no official notice has reached the Legation here of your acceptance of the Office of Secretary of State, sufficient information has been received to justify me in addressing you as the head of that Department, in which capacity I shall be gratified to make my communications to you.

With my last I forwarded duplicates of the Tables which had been sent with my Despatch No. 16 (the Originals of which I was advised had been mislaid at the Department) as far as the few hours before the closing of the Mail would allow. I now transmit others showing the American trade with the Port of Trieste from the commencement of the year 1841 up to the 24th April last. Nos. 1 to 4, inclusive, exhibit the number of Vessels, amount of Tonnage, Cargo and Value, from whence and destination outwards—in American Bottoms. No. 5, shewing the American trade in Foreign Bottoms, both inward and outward, within the same period. The amount of merchandize thus conveyed, may in some measure indicate what degree of advantage is derived from Treaties of Reciprocity. It would seem, at least in some instances, they have not proved beneficial to the shipping interests of the United States. Those Countries, which have few resources, except their vessels which by constructing and sailing at a cheaper rate, are brought into injurious competition with American vessels.

A comparative Statement of the principal articles of Import into the Port of Trieste for the last 13 years, which I also enclose may not be uninteresting. I am preparing and with my next will transmit an estimate of the Imports and Exports, Manufactures and Agricultural products of the Austrian Dominions generally with some remarks upon the present state of the Austrian trade and internal resources. With high respect I am your Obedient Serv[an]t, D. Jenifer.

LS (No. 21) with Ens in DNA, RG 59 (State Department), Diplomatic Despatches, Austria, vol. 1 (T-157:1, frames 252–259), received 6/3.

From ROBERT DALE OWEN, [Representative from Ind.]

House of Representatives U.S., May 6, 1844
Sir: May I ask, that you will have the Goodness, if in accordance with the rules of the Department to cause to be communicated to me

1. Any official document from Mr. [Daniel] Webster, while at the head of the State Department, expressing his opinion of the justice or injustice of the protracted war carried on by Mexico against Texas.

2. Any official expression of opinion by England on the Same Subject; or ["offering" *altered to* "offer"] to mediate between Mexico & Texas.

3. Any official expression by France, or any other European nation on the Same Subject; or any offer to mediate between Mexico & Texas. I am, Sir, Your ob[edien]t Serv[an]t, Robert Dale Owen.

ALS in DNA, RG 59 (State Department), Miscellaneous Letters (M-179:104, frames 306–307).

To RICHARD PAKENHAM

Department of State
Washington, 6th May, 1844
Sir: I have the honor to acknowledge the receipt of your letter of the 16th ultimo, requesting information in respect to the terms upon which this Government is permitted to send its correspondence across the Isthmus of Panama.

I have, in pursuance of your suggestion, referred your communication to the Postmaster General [Charles A. Wickliffe], and now enclose to you a copy of his reply [of 5/3].

It is proper to add, that in March, 1843, Congress made a small appropriation, to be expended under the direction of the Secretary of State, "for defraying the expenses attending the conveyance and forwarding, by land, and of the receipt and delivery of mails, letters, and despatches at and between Chagres and Panama," and the Diplomatic representative of the United States at Bogota, under instructions from this Department, accordingly addressed a representation to the New Granadian Government with the view of obtaining its express consent to the establishment, under proper regulations for the prevention of frauds upon the revenue of the country by the persons engaged in the carriage of these mails, of an occasional post between those places, under the direction of agents of the United States. No definitive reply was made to this application; and, as it was presumed that no serious objection could be urged against the measure proposed, the Consuls of the United States at Chagres and Panama were subsequently directed to take upon themselves the duty of Despatch Agents at those ports, for the purpose of carrying into effect the object of Congress in making the appropriation of funds above referred to.

In the mean time, a conventional arrangement on the subject has been entered into with the Government of New Granada, which has just reached this Department. This postal convention will be forthwith submitted to the Senate of the United States for its consideration and advice, and so soon as it shall have been approved and ratified by the respective Governments, I will take pleasure in placing a copy of it in your possession, for the information of Her Majesty's Government. With high consideration, I have the honor to be your obedient servant, J.C. Calhoun.

FC in DNA, RG 59 (State Department), Notes to Foreign Legations, Great Britain, 7:16–17 (M-99:36); PC in Jameson, ed., *Correspondence*, pp. 581–582.

From G [ILBERT] L. THOMPSON

U.S. Steamer Poinsett
Galveston Bay, Texas
Tuesday May 6th 1844

Respected Sir, I have the honor to inform you of our safe arrival at this place. Our run has been very pleasant but slow. It is much to be regretted that there are no larger vessels on the Station. Steamers are indispensable. We will however persevere and by the kind attention of Lt. Com[man]d[ing Raphael] Semmes we shall reach Vera Cruz in about five days. We are compelled to put into every port for fuel.

I have been entirely incognito here—and have learnt from a very intelligent officer of the Navy who has been driven into the port in distress, that the news of the treaty is extremely popular among all the Americans but the foreigners here are much opposed to it. We shall go to sea to night or tomorrow morni[n]g bound to Tampico. Your Ob[edien]t S[er]v[an]t, G.L. Thompson.

ALS in DNA, RG 59 (State Department), Diplomatic Despatches, Special Agents, vol. 13 (M-37:13, frame 78), received 5/22.

From J[ohn] T[yler, President], 5/6. Tyler directs to Calhoun the following endorsement on a letter dated 12/30/1843 from Richard P. Waters, U.S. Consul at Zanzibar, to Secretary of State Daniel Webster: "Would it not be well for The Secretary of State ["will" *canceled and* "to" *interlined*] order the horses on to Washington—The original letter from the Sultan is in my possession and will be communicated to Congress." The letter on which this note was written announces that the Sultan of Muscat had made a gift of two Arabian horses to the President, which were being sent by the *Eliza* to the care of David Pingree in Salem, Mass. AEI on ALS in DNA, RG 59 (State Department), Consular Despatches, Zanzibar, vol. 1 (M-468:1, frames 199–201), received 5/4/1844.

From R[obert] J. Walker, [Senator from Miss.], 5/6. "Permit me to introduce to your acquaintance, Mr. Tho[ma]s DeSilver, a highly respectable citizen of Philadelphia, & the Father of the gentleman [Robert P. DeSilver], in regard to whose application for a Consulship [at Port Louis, Mauritius], I spoke to you a few days since. I should be much gratified if Mr. DeSilver could succeed in this application." ALS in DNA, RG 59 (State Department), Applications and Recommendations, 1845–1853, DeSilver (M-873:23, frames 45–46).

From Alb[ert] S. White, [Senator from Ind.], 5/6. White encloses for Calhoun's attention a letter from a very worthy gentleman who was formerly employed as Register of the Land Office in Crawfordsville, Ind. This gentleman is intelligent and industrious and "would with a grateful promptness perform any duty to which you might assign him." The enclosed ALS, dated 4/29, is from Charles Tyler to White asking that he recommend Tyler to Calhoun for employment so that he may place his daughter, "who is now ringing in my ears the evidence of her being a raving maniack," in an asylum. ALS with En in DNA, RG 59 (State Department), Applications and Recommendations, 1837–1845, Tyler (M-687:32, frames 593–596).

To Weston F. Birch, U.S. Marshal, Fayette, Mo., 5/7. "I enclose you the President's pardon of William Mason, [witness for the prosecution against the McDaniel brothers,] the receipt of which you will please acknowledge." FC in DNA, RG 59 (State Department), Domestic Letters, 34:177 (M-40:32).

To J[OHN] R. BRADY, New York [City]

Department of State
Washington, May 7th 1844

Sir: I have just received your favour of the 3rd Inst[ant] recommending Mr. [George E.] Baldwin as Despatch agent in place of Mr. [William Henry] Le Roy. Had I received it earlier, I would have given to it the favorable consideration you ask, but before its reception, and, indeed, before any other applicant was known to me I had promised, in case of a change, that the Hon. F[ernando] Wood should receive the appointment. This was in compliance with the request and recommendation of many of his friends in Congress who knew him well, and the appointment has already been made. With great respect I am, Sir, your ob[edien]t Ser[van]t, J.C. Calhoun.

LS in ViHi, John C. Calhoun Papers.

From ROBERT B. CAMPBELL

United States Consulate Havana
May 7th 1844

Sir, I have the honor to transmit herewith a copy of a declaration of a blockade established on the Port of San Juan de Nicaragua furnished me by her B[ritannic] Majesty's Consul General Resident in Havana. I am with Great respect Y[ou]r Mo[st] Ob[edien]t Serv[an]t, Robert B. Campbell.

Copy

Whereas certain British subjects who have for some years been residents in the State of Nicaragua in Central America, have received grievous injury in their property, and have in vain appealed for redress to the persons in authority in that State from whom they are entitled to protection, and whereas the representations of the Consul General of her Brittannic Majesty that justice might be rendered to the said subjects of her Britanic Majesty instead of being received with consideration and attention have been met by evasion and discourteous replies, and all redress has been refused, and whereas I have received instructions from her Majesty[']s Government to employ the force under my command for the purpose of obtaining redress

451

By virtue of the power and authority to me given by the said instructions, and in order to enforce the said claims of Her Majesty[']s subjects I hereby declare the Port of San Juan de Nicaragua to be blockaded, and that all commercial intercourse with the said Port shall be prevented and cease until the claims of Her Britannic Majesty[']s subjects are satisfied, and whereas a sufficient force shall be forthwith detached to the said Port of San Juan de Nicaragua to carry the said blockade into effect I hereby give public notice of the same to all whom it may concern, and that all ships and vessels under whatever flag they may be, will be turned away and prevented from entering the said Port of San Juan de Nicaragua, and if after any Ship or vessel has been warned not to enter the Port, then and in that case, any such ship or vessel that may attempt to break the Blockade will be siezed and dealt with according to the rules established of a de facto Blockade.

Given under my hand and seal, on board Her Majesty[']s Ship Illustrious at Port Royal, Jamaica this twenty fourth day of January 1844. Sig[ned:] Charles Adam.

[P.S.] Note by the American Consul. Although this declaration of Blockade bears date 24th Jan[uar]y 1844 it does not seem to have been promulg[at]ed even at Jamaica until the second of May 1844.

ALS in DNA, RG 59 (State Department), Consular Despatches, Havana, vol. 19 (T-20:19), received 5/18; PC in the Washington, D.C., *Madisonian*, May 20, 1844, p. 2.

From W[illiam] S. Fulton, [Senator from Ark.], 5/7. He encloses to Calhoun a letter from Andrew Hammond concerning the conviction [of John and David McDaniel] for the murder of [Antonio José] Chavis. Although Fulton is not personally acquainted with the McDaniels, he states that their family in Ark. is "amongst our best citizens." He asks that President [John Tyler] grant a reprieve in the case. ALS in DNA, RG 59 (State Department), Petitions for Pardon and Related Briefs, 1800–1849, no. 292A.

From W[illia]m B. Gooch, U.S. Comm[ercia]l Agency, Aux Cayes, 5/7. Gooch informs Calhoun that Capt. [Thomas W.] Freelon, commander of the U.S.S. *Preble*, has consented to remain in port to protect American lives and property "until the fate of the city is known." ALS (No. 15) in DNA, RG 59 (State Department), Consular Despatches, Aux Cayes, vol. 2 (T-330:2), received 5/30.

Alex[ander] W. Jones, Edwardsville, Ill., to Richard K. Crallé, 5/7. Jones expresses gratification in the appointment of John C. Calhoun to be Secretary of State and congratulates Crallé on his appointment to be Chief Clerk of the State Department. He suggests that a newspaper be established at Washington to advocate Texas annexation, free trade, and cession of the public lands to the States. This newspaper would expose the errors and falsehoods of "Federalism." ALS in ScCleA.

From J[ohn] Y. Mason, [Secretary of the Navy], 5/7. "In reply to your reference I have the honor to inform you, that I have directed the name of K.S. Derickson to be entered on the register of applicants; but under the present restrictions of the law no more Midshipmen can be appointed." FC in DNA, RG 45 (Naval Records), Miscellaneous Letters Sent by the Secretary of the Navy, 33:398 (M-209:12).

From J[ohn] Y. Mason, [Secretary of the Navy], 5/7. As requested by Calhoun, he transmits "for your information such papers as are to be found on the files" of the Navy Department in regard to two incidents enquired into by the British Minister [Richard Pakenham]: the conduct of Capt. [Samuel] Denison of the O.C. Raymond; and the "case of two American citizens [Samuel S. Thomas and Joseph R. Curtis of the Zebra], released from imprisonment in the island of Hayti, by Commander [Joseph] Mattison, of the U.S. Brig Bainbridge . . . ." LS with En in DNA, RG 59 (State Department), Miscellaneous Letters (M-179:104, frames 310–311); FC in DNA, RG 45 (Naval Records), Letters Sent by the Secretary of the Navy to the President and Executive Agencies, 1821–1886, 4:502–503 (M-472:2, frame 633).

To James Miller, Collector of Customs, Salem, Mass., 5/7. Calhoun encloses a letter [of today] to be delivered to David Pingree, in whose care are two horses sent by the Imaum of Muscat as presents for the President [John Tyler]. Miller should "take such steps as the occasion may require for preserving the horses and forwarding them to Washington in the safest and most economical manner." Miller should also report promptly on expenses and on provision made for the groom who accompanied the horses. FC in DNA, RG 59 (State Department), Domestic Letters, 34:180 (M-40:32); CC in DNA, RG

233 (U.S. House of Representatives), 28A-E1; PC in House Document No. 256, 28th Cong., 1st Sess.

To David Pingree, Salem, Mass., 5/7. "I am instructed by the President [John Tyler] to acknowledge the receipt of your letter to him of the 2nd . . . and to thank you for your polite and prompt attention to the matter." Directions will be given to James Miller, Collector of the Port of Salem, to relieve Pingree of care for the two horses sent by the Imaum of Muscat and to receive a statement of Pingree's expenses. FC in DNA, RG 59 (State Department), Domestic Letters, 34:179 (M-40:32); CC in DNA, RG 233 (U.S. House of Representatives), 28A-E1; PC in House Document No. 256, 28th Cong., 1st Sess.

To Richard S. Rogers, Salem, Mass., 5/7. Calhoun acknowledges Rogers's letter of 5/3 and states in reply that the State Department has at present no communications to make to the Consular agents at the South Pacific ports that Rogers plans to visit. FC in DNA, RG 59 (State Department), Domestic Letters, 34:174 (M-40:32).

To William H. Stiles, [Representative from Ga.], 5/7. Calhoun replies to a letter of 4/15 [*not found*] "in behalf of Mr. Benjamin." Because [Gregory A.] Perdicaris has "apprized the Department of his intention to return to Athens and resume his official duties, it is deemed inexpedient to make any change in the consulate at that place." FC in DNA, RG 59 (State Department), Domestic Letters, 34:176 (M-40:32).

From McC[lintock] Young, Acting Secretary of the Treasury, 5/7. In reply to Calhoun's letter of 4/26 requesting information for [Alphonse] Pageot, he encloses a letter [of 5/1 from James W. McCulloh, Comptroller of the Treasury, to John C. Spencer, former Secretary of the Treasury], and five Treasury Dept. circulars "in regard to the construction to be given to certain portions of the Tariff act of 30th August 1842." LS with Ens in DNA, RG 59 (State Department), Miscellaneous Letters (M-179:104, frames 313–323); FC in DNA, RG 56 (Treasury Department), Letters to Cabinet and Bureau Officers, 1842–1847, 4:362.

To A[lphonse] Pageot, 5/7. In reply to Pageot's letter of 4/23 asking for information from the Treasury Dept., Calhoun encloses copies of five circulars issued by that Dept. and a letter [of 5/1] of

James W. McCulloh, Comptroller, accompanying them. FC in DNA, RG 59 (State Department), Notes to Foreign Legations, France, 6:80 (M-99:21).

From P.J. Caduc, Baltimore, 5/8. As attorney for Henry H. Williams, principal owner of the brig *Morris*, unlawfully seized and sold at Puerto Cabello, he asks that an agent be appointed to demand reparations from Ecuador. New Granada and Venezuela have agreed to pay their share of the indemnity. Caduc recommends that John W. Holding be sent to Ecuador. ALS in DNA, RG 59 (State Department), Miscellaneous Letters (M-179:104, frames 326–327).

From Franklin Chase, U.S. Consul at Tampico, 5/8. Chase relates in detail how a Mexican judge has seized the proceeds from the sale of the effects of a deceased American citizen, Patrick Mc. McCarthy, and has refused to give them up even after Chase obtained an order from a superior court in Mexico City. "Under this state of things, you will doubtless perceive what a difficult task the performance of this branch of my duty has become, and I would therefore most respectfully suggest, the propriety of adopting such measures, as will prevent the local authorities in this Republic, from having any control over Intestate's Estates, of such citizens of the United States as m[a]y die here." ALS (No. 49) with Ens in DNA, RG 59 (State Department), Consular Despatches, Tampico, vol. 3 (M-304:2, frames 57–67), received 6/10.

From James Cochrane, "U.S. Steamer 'Col. Harney,' N[avy] Yard, Washington," 5/8. Cochrane presents a memorial "setting forth his grievances caused by an act of impressment into the military, and naval service of Mexico [in 1832], with the affidavits" of three U.S. citizens. He identifies himself as "at present" Assistant Engineer in the Navy. The 21-page memorial discusses the circumstances of the claim and requests $25,000 damages from the Mexican government. Also enclosed is a document signed by five U.S. citizens, former merchants in Tabasco, who attest to the correctness of the facts. ALS with Ens in DNA, RG 76 (Records of Boundary and Claims Commissions and Arbitrations), Records of United States and Mexican Claims Commissions.

From W[alter] T. Colquitt, Senator [from Ga.], 5/8. "Mr. Tho[ma]s G. Casey of Columbus Georgia, is now in the city of New-York, on his way to Europe, for the purpose of arresting a man by the name of G. Koster, for defrauding some of the Banks of the State. I ask that you provide him with a general letter, directed to our diplomatic & consular agents abroad, that he may have their friendly aid in the object of his trip. I desire to forward him such letter by to day[']s mail." ALS in DNA, RG 59 (State Department), Passport Applications, vol. 31, no. 2099 (M-1372:14).

To Bladen Forrest, Washington, 5/8. "The resignation of the United States Consulate and Despatch Agency at Chagres, tendered in one of your four letters dated 6th Inst[ant] is accepted." FC in DNA, RG 59 (State Department), Consular Instructions, 11:242.

To W[illia]m Henry LeRoy, New York [City], 5/8. "I have to inform you that Fernando Wood[,] Esquire[,] has been appointed to succeed you as Despatch agent of this Department, at New York." FC in DNA, RG 59 (State Department), Domestic Letters, 34:190 (M-40:32).

From Hen[ry] A. Muhlenberg, [former Representative from Pa.], Reading, [Pa.], 5/8. Muhlenberg asks that Isaac T. James, a youth of much promise, be appointed a distributor of the laws of the U.S. James has been advised by his physician to travel, but he is unable to do so unless he can obtain some business to add to his funds. ALS in DNA, RG 59 (State Department), Applications and Recommendations, 1837–1845, James (M-687:17, frames 183–184).

From W[ILLIAM] S. MURPHY

Legation of the United States
Galveston Texas, 8th May 1844

Sir, The United States War Steamer Poinsett, Capt. Symmes [*sic*; Raphael Semmes], for Vera Cruz, put into this Port yesterday for fuel. She was well supplied today with good coal, & sails to night, at 3 o'clock.

Mr. [Gilbert L.] Thompson, the Special agent of the Govt. is on board, in good health, and says he will reach the City of Mexico in 8 or 10 Days.

The anxiety of the People, for the fate of the Treaty of annexation, in the Senate, is becoming extremely painful. They have heard with deep mortification of Mr. [Henry] Clay[']s letter in opposition to the measure: Their disappointment, would give rise to a revulsion of feeling and opinion extremely prejudicial to any future effort, at annexation. This Government entered reluctantly into the present negociation, and would by no means, be backward, in ceizing [*sic*] the first occasion to change its policy.

I arrived here a few days ago, with Mr. [Stephen Z.] Hoyle the private Secretary of Gen[era]l [Samuel] Houston. I left the President at Houston, and shall join him there again, in a few days. I find it necessary to keep near him, in order that I may keep up his spirits, & cheer his hopes of the final success of the Treaty—for he is often despondent of its fate.

I heard last evening by private traders from Corpus Christie, that a small party of Mexican troops, sent to the Rio Grande, to suppress smuggling, had been attacked on the 2nd Inst[ant] by a body of Texan traders, and that 16 of the Mexican soldiers were slain, and the remainder dispersed. I informed Mr. Thompson of the fact, that he might use it to strengthen the views of my Government with that of Mexico, in relation to a fixed and well guarded boundary between the two Nations in all future time. I also informed him, that this affair was wholly unauthorised by this Government, and I mentioned to him, that he might assure Gen[era]l Santa Anna (if it became necessary) that if he would make no hostile movement, in retaliation, this Government would be aided by the Government of the United States, in an immediate, and full investigation of the whole affair and the leaders of the lawless band, ["should be" *interlined*] brought to punishment.

I will suggest the propriety of placing a small armed vessel, at Corpus Christie to keep the peace—otherwise these lawless bands, may increase to such an extent, as to cause movements of a Hostile & threatening character on the part of Mexico against Texas, and thereby make a correspondent movement on the part of the forces of the United States necessary. This would be a state of things, which must be prevented, if possible.

I shall inform Gen[era]l Houston, to day, of the affair at Corpus Christie, and shall treat it as an affair of no great consequence.

The following statistical information which I obtained from the Custom House here may be useful to the Dept. of State.

"Exports from the Port of Galveston for the quarter ending 1st May 1844.

6,192 Bales of Cotton, C.H. Price, 35$ p[e]r B.	. .	$216,720.00
3,234 Hides . . . . . d[itt]o	. . . . . .	5,643.21
14,990 Staves . . . . . d[itt]o	. . . . . .	534

114 Spars . . . . . d[itt]o	4,800
178 Packages of Skins (Deer)	$767

other articles of less note—in the aggregate, of
value $227,695.50
Imports for the same period 122,471.05
In favor of Exports $105,224.45
Vessels in Port receiving cargoes of cotton not enumerated above.
5 English Brigs, 3 Brigs & one Barque from Bremen, 1 U.S. Brig
& 1 U.S. Steamer, one French & one Texan Brig.

The revenue received at the Custom House here for the quarter
ending the 1st May . . . . . . is . . . . . . $37,564.19."
With Sentiments of the Highest respect and esteem I have the Honor
to be Your ob[edien]t Serv[an]t, W.S. Murphy.

ALS (No. 23) in DNA, RG 59 (State Department), Diplomatic Despatches, Texas,
vol. 2 (T-728:2, frames 307–309), received 5/22.

From Stewart Newell, [U.S. Consul at the] Sabine, 5/8. He acknowledges the circular of 4/1 announcing Calhoun's appointment as
Secretary of State and will have great confidence in any advice or
instructions coming from "such an able, energetic, and patriotic head"
of the State Department. ALS (No. 12) in DNA, RG 59 (State Department), Consular Despatches, Texas, vol. 1 (T-153:1), received
5/28.

From T[homas] H. Perkins, Boston, 5/8. Perkins asks that Calhoun interest himself in the claim by the owners of the brig *Mace-
donia* against the government of Chile. This claim is of long standing
and has been supported by several Secretaries of State. He asks a
reply at Calhoun's earliest convenience. ALS in DNA, RG 59 (State
Department), Miscellaneous Letters (M-179:104, frames 330–332).

To Alfred Schücking, Washington, 5/8. "I have received your
note of the 2d Inst[ant] and will give early attention to the subject
to which it relates." [Schücking's letter of 5/2 has not been found,
but it perhaps related to the alleged misbehavior of Louis Mark, U.S.
Consul for Bavaria and the Prussian Rhine Provinces, or to Schücking's wish to be appointed to an office.] ALS in MdBJ, Mackall Collection.

From HENRY WHEATON

Berlin, 8 May, 1844

Sir, I have the honor to subjoin copies of my correspondence with the Minister of the Grand Duchy of Oldenburg at this court, from which it will be perceived that the Government of Oldenburg declines to conclude a Treaty of Commerce & Navigation with the United States, upon the basis of our Convention of 1840 with Hanover, upon which alone I was authorized to treat by the President's Instructions, contained in Mr. Secretary [Abel P.] Upshur's Despatch, No. 49, under date of the 18 November, 1843. The reasons for declining to accept this basis of negotiation are not specified in the Minister's communication; but the determination of his Government may doubtless be attributed to the fact that it now enjoys, under the President's Proclamation, issued in conformity with the Act of Congress of the 24 May, 1828, much more extensive reciprocal privileges, in respect to Navigation, than are accorded to Hanover by the Convention of 1840. This state of things must continue so long as the Act of 1828 remains in force, unless the Government of Oldenburg thinks fit voluntarily to change it, by agreeing to treat on the basis of the Convention with Hanover, or revokes, by its own legislation, the reciprocal exemption of our vessels & their cargoes from discriminating duties of tonnage & import in the ports of Oldenburg. I have the honor to be, with the highest consideration, Sir, your obedient servant, Henry Wheaton.

LS (No. 250) with Ens (in French) in DNA, RG 59 (State Department), Diplomatic Despatches, Germany, vol. 3 (M-44:4), received 6/3; FC with Ens in DNA, RG 84 (Foreign Posts), Germany, Despatches, 4:127–133. NOTE: This despatch was addressed to John Nelson as Secretary of State ad interim.

To FERNANDO WOOD

Department of State
Washington, 8th May 1844

Sir, You are hereby appointed Despatch Agent for this Department at a compensation of $800 per annum for the services including all ordinary expenses, as stationary &c. To enable you to discharge which the following statement of the principal duties with which you are charged, as also instructions for their performance is given.

Viz. The receipt of Despatches arriving by the Packets from Liverpool and Havre, or by any other conveyance, and their immediate transmission by mail (unless otherwise directed) to this Department.

The transmission of Despatches from this Department to the Legations and Consulates abroad. For this purpose it will be necessary for you to make an arrangement with respectable American Citizens, passengers in the packets or steamers to Liverpool and Havre, to take charge of the Despatches and to deliver them *free of expense* to the Consuls there. They will for this purpose be invested with the character of bearers of Despatches, and you will be furnished with blank Passports to be filled for them as such. It will be also necessary for you to make an arrangement with the Post office at New York by which all Despatches directed to your care may be immediately delivered to you, in order that there may be no delay in their transmission, or loss of opportunity of the vessel for which they may be intended. It will be well to keep advised of all anticipated departures of vessels, so that advantage may be taken of the earliest opportunities that may occur. A tabular account is to be kept of that portion of Despatches from hence which may be numbered on their envelope, noting the numbers of those received, and the date and mode of their transmission; a copy of which is to be transmitted monthly to this Department.

In case of the detention of Packets at Quarantine, the Despatches are to be sent for at the expense of the Department, and an arrangement may be made with the owners or commanders of Newsboats who may board the Packets, for bringing in, and delivering to you, the Despatches (if by such mode you can expedite their transmission)[;] for this a reasonable compensation may be made, which will be allowed to you in your account.

The despatches from this Department will consist generally of communications to the Ministers and Consuls of the United States abroad, and of Books, printed documents and newspapers for those officers.

It is desirable to save expense in the transmission, as far as may be consistent with saf[e]ty and the requisite despatch. Those intended for Consuls are not usually of an urgent nature, and are therefore to be sent by vessels sailing direct to ports of the Consuls['] residence, or if no such opportunities offer, to the ports from which they may be most readily transmitted; in which latter case, they are to be sent to the care of the Consuls, with a request that they may be forwarded by the first vessel, or in some other suitable and economical manner, to those to whom they are addressed. When communications for Consuls are to be sent otherwise, particular instructions will be given.

Despatches for the Minister at Madrid and Paris are to be sent to the Consul at Havre, who will forward them. But when the package for the Minister at Madrid consist of Books or printed papers they are not to be sent to Havre, but for Madrid, to the Consul at Cadiz. Despatches for the Minister at Constantinople are to be sent by the way of Gibraltar. Despatches for the Ministers in England, Russia, Sweden, Denmark, Prussia, the Netherlands and Belgium are to be sent to the Consul at Liverpool, by whom they will be transmitted to the Minister at London, who will forward those intended for the Continent. Despatches for the Minister in Portugal are to be sent to the Consul at Liverpool when there is no opportunity of send them direct to the Consuls at Lisbon or St. Ubes. Books and printed papers are to be sent only by vessels for those ports.

Despatches for the Consuls at Tangiers and Tunis are to be sent to the Consul at Gibraltar. Those for the Consul at Tripoli to the Consul at Malta.

Those for the Minister at Mexico to the Consul at Vera Cruz, between which place and New York there are regular Packets.

Those for the Minister at Guatemala to the Consul at Kingston, Jamaica[,] or by vessels for Balize or Omoa.

Those for the Minister at Bogota, to the Consul at Carthagina [*sic*; Cartagena], and when no direct opportunity offers, to the Consul at Kingston who will forward them to the Consul at Carthagina.

Those for the other Legations on the American Continent to the most convenient Consul as occasions may offer, but where the Minister resides at the port to which the vessel is bound, they will be sent direct to them, and not to the Consul.

No letters or papers are to be transmitted in the Despatch Bag or packages, except those sent from the Department, unless specially directed. No endorsement, note or stamp is to be put on Despatches received by you to be sent abroad. A list of the Despatches is to be sent with them to the Consul. You will keep yourself early informed of vessels about to sail from the principal ports in the United States, to those to which you have despatches to forward, and where there is time, advise the Department of them. It is important that the Department shall receive its Despatches as early as practicable after their arrival, and you will adopt such measures as may enable you to obtain them as early as private letters are obtained, and you will transmit them immediat[e]ly by mail, or, if too late to be enclosed in the mail, they may be sent by the same conveyance, or by some passengers at the same time. All reasonable and necessary expenses incurred in obtaining or transmitting Despatches early will be allowed.

In sending Despatches to the Department, you will state the day of the sailing of the vessel by which they were brought, when you can ascertain it. You will keep a Register of the Passports which may be given by you to bearers of Despatches, and will make returns of them to this Department, so soon as delivered[,] stating the number and date of the Passport, and the name of the person to whom it is delivered. On each passport you will note the number and address of the packages delivered to the bearer. This is necessary in order to prevent any abuse on his part, by representing as public Despatches packages which are not so. It may perhaps be necessary to add that the duties imposed on you are of a confidential nature, and that it is necessary for you to transact the business confided to you in that light, and carefully to keep all Despatches in your possession. I enclose open letters for the Post Master and Collector at New York, asking such aid on the part of their respective offices as may be necessary to the prompt discharge of your duties. I am &C, John C. Calhoun.

FC in DNA, RG 59 (State Department), Domestic Letters, 34:182–186 (M-40:32); PC in Jameson, ed., *Correspondence*, pp. 582–585.

To James Cochran[e], [U.S. Navy], Washington, 5/9. Calhoun acknowledges Cochran[e]'s letter of 5/8, "accompanied by a memorial and other papers relating to your claim on the Mexican Government . . . . All proper attention shall be bestowed upon the subject." FC in DNA, RG 59 (State Department), Domestic Letters, 34:180–181 (M-40:32).

From GEORGE R. GLIDDON, "Private"

Philadelphia, 9th May 1844
Sir, In compliance with the wish you expressed, last Monday evening, to be placed in possession of the latest ethnographical facts, I have now the gratification of introducing my distinguished friend, Sam[ue]l Geo[rge] Morton Esq.[,] M.D. of this city, to your honored correspondence.

It would be supereregatory [*sic*], on my part, to add a single remark to the accompanying letter from Dr. Morton; inasmuch as I am but the pupil in questions so ably discussed by the Author of "Crania Americana," and "[Crania] Aegyptiaca."

Before the middle of next week, I trust I shall ["have" *interlined*] the advantage of transmitting to you, from New York, a series of my little Pamphlets on modern, and on ancient Egyptian subjects; and, in the interim, beg leave to thank you most respectfully for your courtesy to a stranger, no less than to subscribe myself, Sir, Y[ou]r mo[st] obliged & ob[e]d[ien]t Serv[an]t, George R. Gliddon.

ALS in ScCleA.

From SAMUEL GEORGE MORTON

[Philadelphia, *ca.* May 9, 1844]

Sir, Having been informed by my friend Mr. [George R.] Gliddon of the interest you take in certain Ethnographic questions, I beg your acceptance of a memoir in which, among other subjects, I have briefly inquired into the social position of the Negro race in the earliest periods of authentic history.

With profound respect for one whose name has long been associated with the active promotion of Science in our country, I remain, Sir, your obed[ient] Servant, Samuel George Morton.

ALS in ScCleA. NOTE: Morton (1799–1851) was a member of the Philadelphia Academy of Natural Sciences and had been Professor of Anatomy at Pennsylvania College. He propounded a theory of the separate creation of the races of man. His *Crania Aegyptiaca* . . . (Philadelphia: John Pennington; London: Madden & Co., 1844), probably the work mentioned here, concluded that, "Negroes were numerous in Egypt, but their social position in ancient times was the same that it is now, that of servants and slaves."

From W[ILLIA]M HOGAN

Washington, May 9[?] 1844

Sir, I have the honor to enclose my private account, against the United States, according to your instructions, deducting the item of $300, which, I paid in Mexico, for the purpose of procuring certain information, which, otherwise, could not probably have been obtained.

Previous to my departure, I stated to Mr. [Abel P.] Upshur, that it might be necessary to give a *gratuity*, to the Jesuits of Mexico, to facilitate the object of my mission. He remarked, that the "secret service money was very small, but he would leave it to my sound discretion to make such use as I thought proper, of a sum not exceeding $500."

If this fact were known to President [John] Tyler, I am satisfied, that his well known and strong sense of justice would induce him to allow this item. I have the honor to be Sir your most ob[edien]t Ser[van]t, Wm. Hogan.

[P.S.] The account is made out to May 9, as I have been detained here for no other purpose, than to obtain its settlement, and have been to the State Department, almost daily, to ascertain, when it would be convenient to do so.

ALS in ScCleA.

From C[harles] J. Ingersoll, "Chairman[, House] Committee [on] Foreign Affairs," 5/9. Ingersoll asks that the Committee be supplied with "extracts from any despatches" of 1842 or 1843 "indicating the official opinion of this Government then expressed as to the character of the war between Mexico and Texas; or urging on Mexico, that it should be terminated." Any information "indicating, either on the part of England or France, their opinion of the war; or any evidence of a protest or remonstrance by either Power against its continuance," is also requested. LS in DNA, RG 59 (State Department), Miscellaneous Letters (M-179:104, frames 333–334).

DIXON H. LEWIS to [Franklin H.] Elmore, [Charleston?]

Washington, May 9th 1844

My D[ea]r Elmore, With a respect for your understanding which would be flattering even to your self love, you know I have often spoken of the slowness with which you fix your opinions on any new question. I never saw it more illustrated than in your last letter, when you wake up as from a dream, & ask me the A.B.C. of questions, which I had supposed the whole country by this time comprehended & to which it appears you have been paying the usual attention. But there seems to be a fatality over the Southern Country at this time, which prevents them from comprehending the effect or feeling the ordinary interest in questions, by which all they hold dear is at stake. I believe in my soul it is the organization of Party by Conventions, which destroys all independent acting or thinking except under a lead given from some central point. What else can explain the fact there have been so few meetings in the South on the Texas question & so little apparent feeling as to induce both [Henry] Clay & [Martin] V[an] Buren to think there was but little interest felt in the question of annexation.

You ask if it is intended to run any one for the Presidency but Clay & V[an] Buren—I answer, that it is determined to run no one who is not in favour of immediate annexation & hence the necessity to meet & speak out.

Ever since the first of the session V[an] Buren has been getting weaker & weaker both in the affections of the Party & in their belief of his ability to be elected. Since the defeat of the Party in Connecticut[,] the City of N[ew] York & more recently in Virginia but about thirty Democratic members of Congress have of late thought V[an] Buren could be elected or even wished him to be the candidate. In this state of things Van's letter against immediate annexation came out & dashed the only hope of electing him. Men then came out & openly give utterance to the pent up feeling against him & every one was surprised to find that only about twenty or twenty five men were for running Van & two thirds of the Party in Congress began to declare that in no event, would they support Van or any one else not in favour of immediate annexation. This drove the Globe & Benton to madness & hence their attack on Calhoun not only on account of old grudges, but because they looked to him as the agent who had worked the change against Van, but the man most likely to supplant him as a Candidate. Since that time Benton & the Globe have been as odious as their wor[s]t enemies could desire, & so far as the Democracy of Congress are concerned, are blown sky high.

Now we want Texas meetings in every Town[,] village & Hamlet in the South—first to carry the question which is in doubt because its real favour with the people has not been made known. Secondly to kill off Clay & V[an] Buren who have come out against it & to elect some one in favour of it. Who that man shall be we know not & are willing to leave it to the People. Whoever he be, we believe will be elected by the unaided strength of the Texas Question & his election will put down the old Hunkers & corrupt Leaders of both Parties such as [Francis P.] Blair[,] [Thomas H.] Benton &c. On one thing the friends of Mr. Calhoun have long since determined to make no move for him which would connect his name with the question while he stands as the Negotiator of the Treaty—At least to make no move *here.* If the *People* should take him up without any prompting from us it would be a different thing. We would of course fall in. Some of us have hoped Virginia, & particularly [Thomas] Ritchie might in dropping Van take up him. In that event, the larger portion of the old V[an] Buren men except Benton[,] Blair &c would fall in, but if the move came from Mr. Calhoun's friends either here or in the South, the jealousy of V[an] Buren's friends would defeat him. Now I believe that the fear of provoking this jealousy will prevent ["any one(?)" *canceled*] Virginia from taking up Calhoun although he is now the preferred man. I think it likely the choice will lye between [Lewis] Cass[,] [Richard M.] Johnson[,] [James] Buchanan[,] [Commodore Charles] Stewart & [John] Tyler. Either of these men who may be rallied on can ["elect" *canceled*] beat Clay & if Van runs beat both of them, so strong do we find the Texas question. I think you had better in your meeting indicate no one for the Presidency except to say you will vote for no man opposed to *immediate annexation.* I confess of all the Cider nags[?] I should prefer Tyler but I think we should not quarrel in taking whoever the Party may designate if in favour of immediate annexation. The object is to keep the pledged V[an] Buren Convention in Baltimore from nominating him & if they do nominate him, to make this question ride over all party organization so as to beat him. In the mean we say for Calhoun—we go for no one but for *one* term, as we mean to run him in 1848 if alive, in spite of Conventions. In this *all* except Benton & Co. seem to acquiesce & I believe he is stronger now than ever he was & if Ritchie were to blunder on him as a Candidate, would be the most available man in the field in the coming contest next fall. But putting aside men & making the great question of Texas override all Presidential hopes—bring it forward not as a Mexican Question but a British & American Question & one which is to settle the fate of the South & her Institutions. Mr. Calhoun advises you say nothing about the [Adams-Onís] Treaty of 1819. He says they can[']t hurt him on that point, and he wishes not to change the issue from one which is to settle the fate of the South into a mere question as to the fairness of Mr. [John Quincy] Adams' ["former" *interlined*] negotiations. Quit the dead issue & come to the living whether Great Britain through Texas is to establish hostile Institutions on our Borders inconsistent with our own. He says, you may take it for granted from the nature of things—*what I suppose he dare not state on authority*—that if Texas fail in being annexed to us by Treaty in fifty days she will form a Treaty of annexation or of Commerce, for offensive & defensive purposes—["which th" *canceled*] with England which that Government will not fail to ratify. *You can[']t state too strongly the* issue to us, of *Now or Never*. Texas must be *ours immediately*, or she is in the *power of Great Britain forever*. I say you can[']t urge it too strongly—provided you do not urge it on the authority of being communicated by him. Having in this running sketch tried to give you the real aspect of the Texian Question & other matters I say, hold meetings & agitate, agitate, agitate from the Potomac to the Sabine & make the question paramount to Presidents & every thing else. Yours truly, Dixon H. Lewis.

[P.S.] Campbell writes me he will try & save enough of Dowling's money to pay my order, if Dowling's mother will consent. Can[']t you get him to look into it & accept the order I sent to you if no more. D.H.L.

ALS in NcU, Franklin Harper Elmore Papers.

Rich[ar]d K. Crallé to J[ohn] Y. Mason, Secretary of the Navy, 5/9. "I am requested by the Secretary of State, (who has received your note with the enclosed copy of an order addressed [to] Leiut. [*sic*; Henry H.] Bell of the Steamer Union,) to inform you that the President [John Tyler] deems it unadvisable, at present, to send out Governor [Wilson] Shannon to Mexico—and that you will be informed, as soon as circumstances will permit, at what time he will take his departure." ALS in DNA, RG 45 (Naval Records), Letters from Federal Executive Agents, 1837–1886, 6:132 (M-517:2, frame 312).

To J[OHN] R. MATHEW[E]S, Clark[e]sville, Ga.

Washington, 9th May 1844
My dear Sir, I am so much engrossed with my official duties, that my friends must excuse me, if my letters should be brief & long between.

The time is come, when England must be met on the abolition question. You will have seen, that I have placed the Texian question on that issue. I am resolved to keep it there, be the consequence what it may. I shall rise at every step in the correspondence, which may grow out of it. Mr. [Richard] Pakenham replied to my communication, and I have answered his reply. I took the broad ground, that our policy was to interfere with no other country, & to permit ["any" *canceled and* "none" *interlined*] to interfere with ours, in any respect whatever, as it related to our internal concerns. It closed the correspondence, with a note from Mr. Pakenham, that he would transmit the correspondence to England. It will I doubt not recommence on that side of the Atlantick, with a good deal of warmth. I shall meet it without flinching let what will come. The last letters, the one from Mr. P[akenham] & my reply, is [*sic*] before the Senate & is not yet published.

[Martin] V[an] B[uren']s letter has completely prostrated him. There is great confusion in the ranks of the Democracy. If they can be united under the flag of annexation, an easy victory will be achieved over Mr. [Henry] Clay & the Whigs. It is a vital question to us. The South through all her borders ought to speak out, promptly & boldly. The cause is spreading every where with rapidity. Now is our time to meet England & put down abolitionism. If the occasion is lost, we shall never again get such another opportunity. Our watchwords ought to be Texas, Annexation & non Interference. Under them we may march to victory. Truly, J.C. Calhoun.

ALS in DLC, John C. Calhoun Papers; PEx in St. George L. Sioussat, "John Caldwell Calhoun," in *The American Secretaries of State and their Diplomacy*, ed. by Samuel F. Bemis, 5:154–155.

To Erastus Root, [former Representative from N.Y.], Washington, 5/9. Calhoun acknowledges a letter of 5/6 from Root concerning Cyrus K. Gleason, a Texan prisoner in Mexico. [Wilson] Shannon, who is about to leave the U.S. as Minister to Mexico, will be given directions in the case. FC in DNA, RG 59 (State Department), Domestic Letters, 34:178 (M-40:32).

"Statement" by EDW[AR]D STUBBS

[State Department] May 9, 1844
An order was given by the President [John Tyler] to the Agent of the Department of State in Nov. 1842 to discontinue the National Intelligencer sent to the Legations abroad, and to substitute for it the Madisonian. The Madisonian was, accordingly sent, but the order for the discontinuation of the Intelligencer was, upon suggestion of the Secretary of State [Daniel Webster], suspended for the time. The President renewed the order yesterday in the most peremptory manner and expressed surprise that it had not been long ago carried into effect.

I accordingly addressed a note to [Gales & Seaton] the Publishers of that paper requesting ["its discontinuance" *altered to* "them to discontinue"] the papers sent for the Legations abroad. This was done, in compliance with the President's direction. The Secretary was not informed of it. Edwd. Stubbs, [Disbursing] Ag[en]t [of the State Department].

ALS in ScCleA. NOTE: An AEU by Calhoun reads "Mr. Stubbs' Statement."

To Mrs. A[NNA] M[ARIA CALHOUN] CLEMSON, [Edgefield District, S.C.?]

Washington, 10th May 1844

My dear Anna, I am indebted to you one letter & to Mr. [Thomas G.] Clemson two. As ["as" *canceled*] I have to write a dozen of letters to yours & his one, you & he must be content with my paying off scores, with you both, with one, and that not a long one. Between business and visiters, I have but little time left for correspondence.

A letter from Washington must almost of course begin with politicks. Every thing, then, is in confusion with the democracy at present. [Martin] V[an] B[uren]'s letter has completely prostrated him, and has brought forward a host of candidates in his place; [James] Buchanan, [Lewis] Cass, Stuart [*sic*; Charles Stewart?], [Richard M.] Johnson, who, with [John] Tyler & V[an] B[uren] himself, make six, whose claims are to be settled at Baltimore on the 27th Ins[tan]t. To add to the confusion, there will be two conventions, Tyler's & the old V[an] B[uren]'s; and two parties, as opposed & hostile to each other, as Whig & Democrat; the one in favour of, and the other opposed to the immediate annexation. So there is a fair prospect, that confusion will be worse confounded.

In the mean time, I stand aloof. I regard annexation to be a vital question. If lost now, it will be forever lost; and, if that, the South will be ["lost" *interlined*], if some prompt & decisive measure be not adopted to save us. I would prefer Tyler to any northern man at present, because, I think, the South will be safer in his hands; and because, as far as annexation is concerned, I regard his claim as the ["safest" *canceled*] strongest; but my aim will be to obtain union among the friends of annexation. If that can be done, the whigs will be beaten. It is the all absorbing question, ["and is" *canceled*] stronger ["even" *interlined*] than the presidential. It is, indeed, under circumstances, the most important question, both for the South & the Union, ["since" *canceled*] ever agitated since the adoption of the Constitution. So much for politicks.

Say to Mr. Clemson, that I have not had leisure to see the Postmaster General [Charles A. Wickliffe] in reference to the change he desires to make in the route of the post from Edgefield to Newberry. I will devote the first leisure hour to it, if he should deem it necessary, after the peice [*sic*] of intelligence I have to give him.

I saw the President day before yesterday, & asked him, if he had disposed of the mission to Belgium. He said he had not, and that it was at my disposal. I named Mr. Clemson to him ["to which" *canceled*]. He readily assented; so that, if he desires to fill it, it is at his service. The present Charge [Henry W. Hilliard] will leave in August. It is near to Paris, &, I suppose, will suit him better than the one to Naples, which will not be vacant till next year. He must let me know ["early" *canceled and* "soon" *interlined*]. Say also to him, that I would be glad to oblige Mr. [George W.] Barton, but I have find [*sic*] it necessary to establish it as a rule, not to interfere with the appointments in the other departments, in order to prevent them interfering with mine; and ["that" *canceled*] I am averse to giving countenance to that system of turning out & putting in, which has been introduced in the custom Houses. If, however, any fair opportunity ["of serving him" *canceled*] should offer, I will take pleasure in serving him.

I regret, that John's [John C. Calhoun, Jr.'s,] visit to Pendleton should delay his coming on here. I wrote both to Mr. Clemson & his mother [Floride Colhoun Calhoun] (addressed to Edgefield) some weeks since, requesting that he should come on immediately. I suppose he has not been informed of my wish, in consequence of his leaving for Pendleton. I requested Mr. Clemson to advance him for me $40 or 45 to bear his expenses. I hope he has returned and is now on his way here. It will soon be too late in the season for him.

My health is good, notwithstanding, ["with" *canceled*] a cold accompanied with a good deal of cough, as is usual with me, ["with" *canceled*] when I have a cold. Patrick [Calhoun] is well. I hope you all continue so.

My love to Mr. Clemson. Kiss the dear children [John Calhoun Clemson and Floride Elizabeth Clemson] for Grandfather. Your affectionate father, J.C. Calhoun.

ALS in ScCleA; PEx in Jameson, ed., *Correspondence*, pp. 585–586.

From J[AMES] HAMILTON [JR.]

                    Charleston, So[uth] C[arolina], May 10[t]h 1844
My Dear Sir, I wrote you some time since from the Bend [in Ala.]
but presume your intense engagements have prevented you answering my Letter.

I drop you a line to say that the members of the Southern Dele-
gations who are prepared to make issue on the [Texas] Annexation
["Question" *interlined*] should before the adjournment of Congress
have a meeting and determine on a clear & definite course of action to
be followed up simultaneously by all the slave holding States but
more especially by So[uth] C[arolina,] Geo[rgia,] Ala. & Mississippi
["&" *canceled*,] Louisiana[,] Missouri & Arkansaw. I shall write to
[Dixon H.] Lewis in a day or two from Savan[n]ah suggesting a
course of action in which we must place young Alabama in ["the"
interlined] *van* & So[uth] Carolina as the *Rear* ["*Guard*" *canceled
and* "as the Old Guard" *interlined*].

We never had such an issue in the world on which to make battle,
with the certainty of securing our Rights & interests.

The Treaty itself is very defective, in some of its parts ["drawn
out I presume before you arrived at Wash(ington)," *interlined*] &
manifestly unjust in the discrimination in favor of Fred[e]rick Dawson[']s claim whose debt is ["by" *canceled*] not ["more meritorious
than others & by no" *interlined*] means as obligatory as mine for the
Sale of the Zavala[?]—["But"(?) *canceled and* "to say nothing of my
advances for the Republic" *interlined*]. This discrimination is the
result of the villa[i]ny of [Samuel] Houston. But let this pass. I go
for *the measure, regardless* of my own interests. The meeting will be
a most powerful one *here* next week & without time to draw out the
Resolutions I am deliberating with our friends on their character.
The first "note of preparation" must I think come from Alabama. I
return to the Bend tomorrow to which be so good as to direct to the
Bend.

We are in the midst of a great crisis in which if the South is true
to herself we shall obtain security for the future if not indemnity for
the past.

I wish you to send me a Copy of the Documents connected with
the Treaty the moment the injunction of secrecy is taken off—[*marginal notation*: "with every paper or publication necessary to a perfect
developement of the annexation Question—as annonymously I shall
this summer through the Press act in Geo(rgia) & Ala. & may have to
prepare some papers for the public meetings in both States."] I have

written to Major [John H.] Howard to attend the Baltimore Convention by all means & to reserve two Days previous for consultation with you & our other friends at Washington. Howard is the man for the occasion who will either blow the convention up or make it subservient to the best interests of the South. I shall keep in the back ground until the moment for action arrives.

I sent you a Copy of my Letter to the Editor of the Georgian[;] in the concluding part of that communication you will see that I have put myself in my old position—to guard against any possible misinterpretation of my Letter on [Henry] Clay[']s reception at Columbus [Ga.]. I remain My Dear Sir with esteem very respectfully & faithfully yours, J. Hamilton.

ALS in ScCleA. NOTE: Hamilton's letter to the editor of the [Savannah] *Georgian,* a clipping of which is found in ScU-SC, John C. Calhoun Papers, was dated 3/4/1844, and was written to decline an invitation to attend Clay's reception at Columbus. The letter, accurately described by its writer as a "long, rambling" one, recounted his personal esteem for Clay, Calhoun, and Van Buren, and stated that he now took "no part in the politics of the country."

From J[AMES] H. HAMMOND, [Governor of S.C.]

Silver Bluff [Barnwell District, S.C.] 10 May 1844
My Dear Sir, I rec[eive]d from you a few days ago a note, & a letter addressed by the British Minister [Richard Pakenham] to you. From the tenor of your note, & the letter of the minister I apprehend you have ["not" *interlined*] sent me the paper you intended. In this Mr. Pakenham merely informs you that he will notify the authorities of Canada that the American minister in London [Edward Everett] will apply to her majesty for a pardon of Robert Marsh transported to Van Diemen's Land. As an evidence of his good feelings it is equivocal & not to be put in the balance against his protest—if he has made one against the Treaty with Texas. I should like to know what right Great Britain has ["a right" *canceled*] to interfere with the Treaties of Nations on this Continent other than her colonies. Is it intended to endeavour to introduce here the European System of the Balance of Power according to European ideas? I was delighted with your note to Mr. Pakenham in reference to Slavery. It is precisely the thing that was wanted & I do trust it will be published in every European paper. I have not seen the attack on you in the [Washington]

Globe & am at a loss to conjecture on what ground you can be charged with hostility to the annexation. I should say ["the ch"(?) *canceled*] it was flatly impossible to make even a plausible showing, if I did not know that with the baseness & malice of the devil [Thomas H.] Benton has his power of invention also. I think however it is clear that he & [Martin] Van Buren have both split on this Rock. The feeling in favour of annexation—the reason & imperative necessity of the thing cannot be met in the South & S[outh] west by humbug or chichanery: and these two masters in this art will for once find their magic powers fail them. Benton's hatred to you is at the bottom of this movement & I am rejoiced that it has at length led him to his ruin. As to Van Buren after this letter & the Virginia election I don't see the use of assembling a Convention in his behalf. Is the Democratic Party then to make no show of hands even? It is never to be too much lamented that after your letter the [Charleston] Mercury & [Washington] Spectator so hastily withdrew your name. It was a great error though doubtless done with the best feelings towards you. I can make no conjectures that would ["be" *interlined*] worth offering to you who are at head quarters—but is it impossible yet to rally your friends so as at least to get your name into the House? Might not the Democratic Party run its favourites in each section? I think you could at least carry all south of No[rth] Carolina—if not of Virginia. No anti-Texas candidate could rally the slave States against you or any of them. At all events this Texas question should be pushed. If the union is to break there could not be a better pretext. With Texas the slave States would form a territory large enough for a *first rate power* & one that under a free trade system would flourish beyond any on the Globe—immediately & forever. I confess I despair of the Union more & more daily. The combat on the floor of the House—the violation of the secrecy of the Senate almost prove us both incapable & unworthy of having a Government as at present organized. The resolute adherence to the Tariff—the sectional hostility to Texas—the increasing zeal & impertinence of the abolitionists show that the North & the South cannot exist united. I have not been for any length of time in close contact with my negroes until this year since 1839. I am astonished & shocked to find that some of them are aware of the opinions of the Presidential candidates on the subject of Slavery & doubtless of much of what the abolitionists are doing & I am sure they know as little of what is done off my place as almost any set of negroes in the State. I fancy—it may be fancy—there is a growing spirit of insubordination among the Slaves in this section. In the lower part of this district they have fired several houses recently. This is fearful—horrible. A *quick* & *potent* remedy must be applied. *Disunion* if *needs* be.

It is very dry, but crops, particularly corn promising. Very truly & since[re]ly Yours, J.H. Hammond.

ALS in ScCleA; PC in Jameson, ed., *Correspondence*, pp. 953–955.

From HOMER & SPRAGUE

Boston, 10th May 1844

Sir, Some time since we obtained the Signatures of a number of highly respectable merchants of this City, recommending to the department, Josiah Raymond Esq. of Beverly Mass. as a suitable person to fill the office of U.S. Consul at Manzanillo, (Cuba).

Our friend & correspondent, Mr. Raymond, has for the past 20 years transacted an extensive business, between that Port & the U. States, & during the major portion of that period, has resided there— & through his enterprise & perseverance, the trade with this Country, has increased to a large extent; so much so, that we beg leave to state, our Sales alone, the past 5 years, have amounted to upwards of half million dollars; besides, our neighbors, & likewise the trade to New York has been to a much larger am[oun]t. As a natural consequence we are compelled to have more or less property at risk at that port, and we have often felt the importance of having an authorized officer of our Govt. to look after the interest of those who trade from this Country.

We would beg to state also, that Mr. Raymond from his long residence, & friendly intercourse with the authorities of that port, has rendered himself highly popular, & we believe his appointment would be gratifying to to [*sic*] the government officers. His knowledge of the language & laws of the Island may be considered an additional recommendation. In this neighborhood where he is known by a large circle of merchants & others, we could easily obtain many additional names to testify to his character & capacity, but we believe the documents, already sent forward & now in the possession of the department, will be sufficient to confirm in full, the representations made to you in his behalf, through the medium of Robert Rantoul Jr. Esq., & others of his friends. We beg leave to call this subject to your kind attention & with the assurance of our high esteem, We Remain Sir Your Most Obed[ien]t & Humble S[er]v[an]ts, Homer & Sprague.

LS in DNA, RG 59 (State Department), Applications and Recommendations, 1837–1845, Raymond (M-687:27, frames 222–224).

From R[OBERT] M. T. HUNTER

[Lloyds, Va.] May 10th 1844
My dear Sir, I was much obliged to you for your letter this evening. I have not time to answer you fully as I have company. I shall endeavor to comply with your request and will probably be in Baltimore at the Convention not as a member but a spectator. I hope the South will declare itself strongly upon this question. But the mean course of the Southern [Henry] Clay men since his letter is dispiriting. I think many very many of them would give up Texas and every thing else to elect Clay.

The pens of the Southern men on the spot ought to be in motion. A well directed assault upon [Thomas H.] Benton at this critical period of his destiny could be very effective.

I will weigh well your suggestions; in the main I already concur with most of them but some of them require reflection. In the mean time may I be pardoned for begging you to beware how you express a preference for any of the candidates. There is great danger in touching [John] Tyler. I will not say you are wrong for I have not yet made up my opinion, but he is very unpopular with the people, although gaining ground of late. Still it will not do for you to lead the movement in that direction. What you wish must be done through your friends.

Your own position is one of repose so far as the selection of candidates is concerned. You should seem to ask nothing but security for vital principles in the ["opinions of" *interlined*] the candidate and for the rest to be willing to harmonise and sympathise with the party no matter what its personal preference. Herein lies the moral strength of your position, such is the color ["in" *interlined*] which your conduct should appear to the world. Of this I am sure, but how to produce this impression you know much better than I. In great haste and with the kindest wishes, most truly yours, R.M.T. Hunter.

P.S. Ought not the assaults of the Intelligencer and Globe upon you to be at once repelled. [Dixon H.] Lewis or [Richard K.] Cralle could do it with effect.

ALS in ScCleA.

From THEOBALD C. JUNG

New York [City,] May 10th 1844

Sir, The undersigned begs leave to ad[d]ress Your Excellency respecting his recent application to be appointed U.S. Consul for the Kingdom of Bohemia in the dominions of his Imperial Majesty of Austria and to comply with the suggestion to submit to the Department of State the views upon which the solicited appointment for the interests of the United States should be made.

The Kingdom of Bohemia of which the City of Prague is the capital is an independent country governed by the Emperor of Austria under the title of King of Bohemia. It has its own laws and constitutions and is under the care of a Vice Roy. It forms the principal northern part of the Austrian dominions bounding on Silesia (Prussia) and Saxony. The manufactures of Bohemia are of a great variety and their importation to the United States increases rapidly every year. The principal course of the trade at present is to ship via Havre de Grace incurring a duty of 25 per cent to the french Government besides the increased charges for freight & commission &c which in addition to the great delay also considerably enhances the price of the article here and is of benefit only to the French. This circuitous route can be avoided by a shipment via Hamburgh or Bremen and the cost proportionally diminished did not the trade require official documents to be authenticated by the Consul of the U.S. for Austria whose residence is at Vienna several hundred miles distant from the manufacturer and which officer governs himself by requirements which are set forth in an extract from a letter [from a Bohemian merchant] a sworn translation of which I have the honor to transmit for the information of the Department. By reference to this letter you will at once perceive that sectional as is the spirit of those Countries the manufacturer is exposed to a great many inconveniences which ["thro'" *interlined*] a nearer authority would not be quite as great a hardship. Again, there is a wide field open for the exportation to that Country of machinery for Factories, Engines &ca. manufactured here but which to be productive wants some person from whom with but little delay and expense the necessary authentic Information could be obtained. The Laws of Austria, excluding by a most rigid censorship the more important geographical and historical books ["from"(?) *canceled*] relating to this country have operated in a manner that the resources of the United States are not generally or properly estimated or their advantages correctly valued. Should a new treaty of Commerce admitting on more liberal terms the produce of the United States be successfully negotiated the wants of Bohemia will also require greater attention.

Allow me again to refer to that very important practical point, the difficulty in procuring the consular Certificates. Many merchants here are to my knowledge under heavy penal Bonds to the Collector of this Port for the production of legalized Currency Certificates to the invoices and which for want of a consul to Bohemia cannot be obtained at a near or convenient distance from the spot but if at all can only be had on compliance with great restrictions at a Distance of several Hundred miles and loss of time and increased expences. There cannot be any doubt of the disposition of the Government of the U.S. to facilitate the American mercantile interests by an additional appointment either of a consul or such other official capacity as may be deemed advisable.

I shall esteem myself happy in succeeding to have established satisfactory reasons for the appointment and shall be highly gratified by receiving from our Government the charge of that office.

Should this application be decided upon Favorably I will feel under a great personal obligation by receiving my papers as early before the 16th inst[ant] as can be; that being the day fixed for my departure. On the other hand should you decide against me I would ask the favor of receiving a Passport to Prague in Bohemia by return of mail.

Any despatches which you may feel disposed to entrust me with for our Legations at London[,] Paris[,] Berlin[,] Vienna or to any other part of the Germanic Confederation shall be faithfully attended to ["on such terms as the Department may impose or consider usual" *canceled*] free of expense. I have the honor to subscribe myself with expressions of most profound respect Your Excellency's most ob[edien]t & h[um]ble s[er]v[an]t, Theobald C. Jung.

ALS with En in DNA, RG 59 (State Department), Applications and Recommendations, 1837–1845, Jung (M-687:17, frames 736–742).

From WILLIAM R. KING, [U.S. Minister to France]

New York [City,] May 10, 1844
Dear Sir, At my request Mr. [Charles Augustus] Davis has furnished a plan [*not found*] for the certain and speedy transmission of government despatches to England and France. I have the honor to enclose it to you and request your attention to it, as I am impressed with the belief that the arrangement he proposes would prove advantageous to the government, and particularly so to Mr. [Edward] Everett & myself. I shall sail on the 16 direct to Havre—that being the first Packet in which I could procure comfortable accom[m]odations. With the highest respect, I am your Ob[edien]t Ser[van]t, William R. King.

ALS in DLC, Richard K. Crallé Papers.

From E.F. Kortum, New York [City], 5/10. He has heard that an application has been made [by Theobald C. Jung] for an appointment to be a U.S. Consul in Bohemia; he joins in recommending that application. The establishment of a Consulate at Prague would greatly facilitate Bohemian trade with the U.S. Enclosed is a document in German, with a partial translation, showing that Kortum is an exporter of American "machineries, instruments, and implements." LS with Ens in DNA, RG 59 (State Department), Applications and Recommendations, 1837–1845, Jung (M-687:17, frames 743–748).

From J[AMES] C. PICKETT

Legation of the U. States
Lima, May 10th, 1844
Sir: I have the honor to inclose herewith, copies of documents, numbered from 1, to 20 inclusive.

I endeavored some months ago, to prevail on the government here, (see Nos. 10 & 12 of the copies) to pay the first instalment due on the adjusted North American claims; but without any success. There is a willingness to pay, I believe, but no means. The government is at present, bankrupt and no improvement in its fiscal affairs can be expected, until the country shall become more tranquil than it now is. I flatter myself ["though" *interlined*] that at all events one instalment at least, will be paid on the 1st of January next, and as the claimants will receive 12 per centum interest per annum on it, from the commencement of this year, they will be I think, very fairly indemnified for the delay.

The civil contest still continues in Peru and has assumed a very ferocious character. Gen. [Ramon] Castilla has declared *war to death (guerra á muerte)* against Gen. [Manuel] Vivanco's adherents, which is intended I suppose, merely as a measure of intimidation, for it cannot be possible that he intends to execute what he threatens. The reason he gives for this proceeding is, that Vivanco has caused to be executed unwarrantably, five or six officers who belonged to his party, and it is true that one, a colonel, was put to death in cold blood, by Vivanco's partisans, after being made a prisoner, and without cause. This assassination it is said, has been disavowed by the Director; but he has not yet punished the assassins, and until he does punish them, the sincerity of his disavowal may be doubted.

The enemies of Castilla affect to be transfixed with horror, at what they call, his atrocious barbarity, forgetting apparently, that he has done no worse than Vivanco did soon after he got into power, which was, to denounce death against any person who should conceal himself, after being ordered to leave the country, for political reasons, and without any other preliminary proceeding than that of being identified by a drum-head court-martial; which being done, he was to be executed forthwith—within twenty four hours. And those whose humanity is now so shocked at Castilla's ferocity, had not a word to say against Vivanco's: They approved it perhaps, it being another's ox that was then gored. I do not suppose however, that had a case occurred, Vivanco would have carried out his butcherly decree. It too was intended for nothing more than a measure of intimidation, probably. But the condition of a country must be very deplorable, when men high in rank and station do not scruple to avow themselves before the public, to be much worse than they really are, and these violent proceedings of the two competitors for the mastery, supposing them to be intended only *in terrorem,* shew pretty clearly that there is no such thing in Peru, as public opinion, or that if there is, it has no force. I have the honor to be, with great respect, Your Ob[edien]t Servant, J.C. Pickett.

ALS (No. 93) with Ens in DNA, RG 59 (State Department), Diplomatic Despatches, Peru, vol. 6 (T-52:6, frames 483–500), received 9/20. NOTE: Pickett enclosed twenty-one documents, primarily correspondence between himself and the Peruvian Minister of Foreign Affairs about old claims and a new one arising out of the civil war. This letter was addressed to A[bel] P. Upshur.

From A[braham] Rencher

Legation of the U. States
at Lisbon, May 10th 1844

Sir, On the 28th ultimo Almeida was surrendered by Count Bumfin to the troops of the Queen [Maria II] under the command of Viscount Fonte Nova. The soldiers were surrendered at discretion, while Count Bumfin secured terms for himself and his Officers. They were allowed to withdraw into Spain with their personal baggage and effects, where they are at present. This may be considered decisive of the revolution. Count Bumfin has met with no ["great" canceled] sympathy from the people, altho many acts of the Government has been well calculated to arouse to resistance. The personal guaranties which were suspended by the Cortes until the 22nd of March last, have been suspended ever since by royal decre[e]; while the meeting of the Cortes has been postponed from the 22nd of April till the 22nd of this month, and will probably be continued still longer—perhaps ad infinitum. The prisons and prison ships, in the mien time, have been filled of persons taken up upon bare suspicion and committed without the forms of trial and some have even been transported under the same system of summary justice. These things have been quietly submitted to either from fear or from indifference. In fact the mass of the people are too ignorant properly to appreciate a constitutional form of Government, and it may well be questioned whether a majority of them are not, at this time, in favour of the absolutism of Don Miguel. They measure the value of a government by the amount of burthen imposed; and guided by this rule, they complain that their taxes were never so oppressive while their commerce and business was never so dull and unprofitable as under their present constitutional form of Government. Any form of Government badly administered is bad for the people.

The great staple of this country is wine, and those now charged with the Queen's Government manifest a deep interest in the success of the Bill reported to Congress to carry into effect the treaty made with this country relative to that article. I hope the bill may pass and the matter arranged in conformity with the views entertained by this Government for now that they have been recognized by one branch of the Government of the of the [sic] United States, it would be difficult for the Executive to resist them. I certainly think that, as understood by the American negotiator, it was a treaty unfavourable to the United States, because it surrendered much to the commerce of Portugal, *without obtaining any equivalent in return*. I am well satisfied from the situation of public affaires in Portugal that those now charged with the Queen's Government would, if the matter were now agitated for the first time, make any reasonable concessions in favour of American produce to obtain the advantages which it seems they will now enjoy under this treaty. It may not be improper to mention that Oporto is considered the strong hold of Costa Crabal, the first minister of the Government. But for his supposed strength in Oporto, he could not be sustained; and the wine trade is every thing to that portion of the kingdom. They have been, and are still fed with the hope of an improvement in that trade, and the United States is looked to as one of the means of affecting it. It is not here a subject of negotiation, but in my intercourse with ministers the subject has more than once been alluded to, and I do not fail to endeavour to impress them with the belief that the most effectual if not the only means of increasing the wine trade with the United States, to any great extent, is to remove, in part at least, the present excessive duties levied upon all our bread stuffs as well as our tobacco. I can hardly hope that these things will be done voluntarily during the existance of the treaty, but when it shall come to be renewed, if it ever should be, I am well satisfied important advantages might be secured to American produce. I have thought these suggestions might be of importance to you if the bill now before Congress should not become a law & the subject should again become one of negotiation. With high consideration I am, dear Sir, Y[ou]r Ob[edien]t Servant, A. Rencher.

ALS (No. 3) in DNA, RG 59 (State Department), Diplomatic Despatches, Portugal, vol. 14 (M-43:13), received 6/21; CC in DNA, RG 84 (Foreign Posts), Portugal, Despatches. NOTE: Rencher was Representative from N.C. during 1829–1839 and 1841–1843 and Governor of New Mexico Territory 1857–1861. He was appointed by Tyler to be Chargé d'Affaires in Portugal in 1843 and continued in that post until 1847.

To HENRY WHEATON

Department of State
Washington, 10th May, 1844

Sir: The object of this letter is to acknowledge the receipt of your despatches to No. 147 inclusive, and to inform you that prompt attention will be given to their important contents.

I have just learned that you have asked official permission to pub-

lish the correspondence between yourself and the Prussian Government about the breach of your Diplomatic privilege, as illustrative of
an important question of international law; and I hasten to say that
I leave it entirely to your discretion to publish the whole or any
portion of that correspondence. I am, Sir, respectfully, Your obedient Servant, J.C. Calhoun.

LS (No. 56) in DNA, RG 84 (Foreign Posts), Germany, Instructions, 1:287; FC
in DNA, RG 59 (State Department), Diplomatic Instructions, Germany, 14:75
(M-77:65).

From J[OHN] S. BARBOUR

Warrenton [Va.,] May 11th 1844
My Dear Sir, I send you by this mail the paper printed at this place
which contains the proceedings of this County [of Fauquier] on the
Texas question. The article in it addressed to [Francis P.] Blair (the
Editor) is the offspring of the pen of your excellent friend Mr. Ed-
w[ar]d Dixon, a young gentleman of good talents, fine Character;
and brave, chivalrous & manly.

It is obvious to every eye that Mr. [Martin] Van Buren can no
longer be upheld. [Richard M.] Johnson & [Henry A.P.] Muhlenberg [of Pa.] have occurred to me as strong enough to carry the West
& the North. With a strong man in the South also holding to Muhlenberg for the Vice-Presidency, success would be ours.

The selection might then devolve on the Ho[use] of Rep[resenta-
tive]s. Evil as this is, it is lesser[?] evil than a surrender to the
Whigs, whose success *now* is probable success for twenty years to
come—perhaps to the euthanasia of our system, or the violent dis-
ruption of the confederacy.

Muhlenberg can carry Penn[sylvani]a—who else can? As to
[Charles?] Stewart, it is idle to think of. [John] Tyler cannot be
elected.

I have not the slightest doubt, of your having strength enough in
Virginia to carry the State. The talent of the State is with you, its
disinterestedness is with you, its principles with you, its virtue &
patriotism with you. I will not close my eyes tonight until I have
written [Thomas] Ritchie. I think his character is not well understood by you. Gen[era]l [Thomas H.] Bayly of the Ho[use] of
Rep[resentative]s has a fairer & truer appreciation of him than any

one I know. Ritchie is not selfish—he is not base. His character combines in it some of the noblest virtues. Steadiness in friendship, elevation in morals, stability of patriotism with great simplicity of character & therefore sometimes led astray by those to whom he may unwittingly have given his heart & his confidence. To these moralities[?] he unites no common ability. I told him in 1825 that he was utterly ignorant of you, and last winter he admitted it to me. He is valuable as a friend, from the possession of those virtues, that grow in value (like the books of the Sybil,) because their possessors have so greatly diminished in number. I never had his friendship, and have nothing from him to warp my judgement. I have narrowly watched him for thirty years & the result of my experience, is the high estimate I have placed on his head & his heart. Talk with Bayly of him, and do not allow Ritchie to do you longer injustice, by injustice in your opinions of him.

I write freely to you, for that is the province of friendship.

I have refused in several instances to give letters to you, for persons desiring office. I hope it will not be regarded as a departure from [*one word canceled and "the" interlined*] propriety under which I acted in these refusals, to bring to your care the claims of Edward Dixon.

In all haste and with all Respect Y[ou]rs faithfully & cordially, J.S. Barbour.

ALS in ScCleA; variant PC in Jameson, ed., *Correspondence*, pp. 955–956.

From Shepard Cary, [Representative from Maine], 5/11. A company has been formed jointly by Americans and British subjects to operate a boom on the Aroostook river in New Brunswick about six miles east of the Maine-New Brunswick boundary. This has been found to be of great advantage to the lumbering interests of both countries. The State of Maine has incorporated the company, and the provincial parliament of New Brunswick has done likewise, pending approval of the British government. Cary asks Calhoun to instruct the U.S. Minister in London to seek approval of the incorporation. ALS in DNA, RG 59 (State Department), Miscellaneous Letters (M-179:104, frames 344–345); CC in DNA, RG 84 (Foreign Posts), Great Britain, Instructions, 8:164–167.

From L [EVORITT] H. COE

Somerville Te[nn.,] May 11th 1844

Sir, The letters of Messr. [Henry] Clay & [Martin] Van Buren upon Texas Annexation have just reached us. It is unnecessary to say they produce great dissatisfaction. Many of Clay[']s friends would drop him for any friend of Texas. The Democrats almost en-masse avow their determination to drop Mr. V[an] Buren. They feel more deeply because the party character this question had gradually assumed of late led them to expect a different course.

It is time Sir that the South should set up for herself. A large majority of our people are determined to have Texas cost what it may. We feel that the opposition to Texas is a concession to abolition & to the fears of Tariff monopolists. We have submitted to the open insults of the one & grinding oppressions of the other long enough. To yield the Texas question is to agree quietly to be tied hand & foot & oppressed in all time to come.

We must have a Southern Ticket for President & V[ice] Pres[iden]t. If we cannot elect by the people, we send them to the House [of Representatives] with as large or larger a vote than ["any" *canceled*] either of the others can get.

We look to you to hold the helm and pilot us through the difficulties which surround us. By the next mail I will withdraw my name as ["any" *altered to* "a"] candidate for Elector for the State at large—But ready to assume the same position upon a different ticket from the one contemplated when I was nominated. Very Resp[ect]f[ull]y, L.H. Coe.

ALS in ScCleA; PC (mistakenly attributed to "L.A. Hoe") in Boucher and Brooks, eds., *Correspondence*, pp. 226–227. NOTE: An AEU by Calhoun reads "Hoe [*sic*] Elector for Tennessee."

From ISAAC E. CRARY, [former Representative from Mich.]

Marshall [Mich.,] May 11th 1844

Dear Sir, After receiving all the papers in the matter of the mortgage of Mr. [Jasper] Adams vs. W[illia]m Kirkland, a bill for a foreclosure was filed in our 3d Chancery Circuit against Mr. Kirkland and Wife and a Mr. Wines[?] who became a subsequent purchaser of a portion of the property included in the mortgage. As all the defendants proved to be non residents an order of publication will have to be obtained at the June term of the Court. Having made the necessary publication to bring non-residents into Court we shall be able to obtain a decree of foreclosure and sale at the next January term of the Court.

I have had the title to the lands carefully examined at the Register's office of Wayne County and find it unincumbered at the time Mr. Adams took his mortgage Deed. I have also obtained ["obtained" *canceled*] an abstract from the Auditor General's Office showing that the taxes were regularly paid down to 1844. If there should be any publication of their being offered for sale for taxes of subsequent years I will transmit to you the paper in order that Mrs. [Placidia Mayrant] Adams may be apprised of the amount.

The absence of my partner during the winter kept me so closely confined to office duties that I have hardly had time to observe the various movements upon the political chessboard. I read and highly approved of your views in reference to the proper organization of a National Democratic Convention. Here all Democrats approve of them whether they be [Martin] Van Buren[,] Calhoun, [James] Buchanan[,] [Richard M.] Johnson or [Lewis] Cass men. By the by we have few who advocate the claims of either of the three latter. In the Eastern part of the State the Cass men are more numerous. Of late their numbers have been rather increasing from the Van Buren ranks by reason of an impression that is spreading abroad that Mr. Van Buren is not after all as strong a candidate with the masses as his leading political friends endeavored to make us believe. Your friends are numerous and although a minority yet capable of doing most efficient service.

Mr. [Edward] Bradley who is a delegate to the Baltimore Convention from this State and a warm Van Buren man withal, called on me a day or two ago for a letter to you. From the whole tenor of his conversation at the time I inferred that he entertained some doubts of Mr. Van Buren's future prospects. These doubts are thickening fast. The only cause of surprise to me is that the Van Buren leaders did not for[e]see what would be the probable result in time to save us from our present position. Never was a party in better condition than we were in 1842 up to the day of the passage of the Tariff. That bill was passed by the votes of men who in my opinion thought they were playing a great political game at the time—but it may prove to them a poisoned chalice. At any rate that law has thrown us upon a defensive campaign. In politics the defensive party are always half beaten. Without a protective Tariff we should now have been equally prosperous and perhaps more so. With it we prosper but our prosperity is attributed to it. The Tariff is called the cause and we are driven upon the defensive to show that it is not. I look upon that Tariff Act as having retarded the progress of the cause of free trade for at least five years and perhaps much longer. Before the country will come to their senses again we must perform our revolution under it. I speak from what I have observed of the public sentiment around me, from the doubts now and then expressed by my own political friends and from the questions often asked whether protection is not best so long as other nations pursue the same course. I may be wrong—but if so the time will soon be along when the popular vote will satisfy me of it.

I suppose there is not much prospect of the admission of Texas by the Senate as at present constituted. In the North the Democracy will be found by a large majority in favor of admission if the terms are such as are honorable and the occasion a proper one. Some go for immediate admission[,] others approve admission on the terms suggested by Mr. Van Buren. It seems to me that we ought to admit now if we can do so and preserve the national faith and honor. I have an abiding confidence that you will not by any acts of yours allow either to be dimmed.

Mr. [Abner?] Pratt sends his respects[.] I have the honor to be With high respect Your obedient Servant, Isaac E. Crary.

ALS in ScCleA.

To [CHARLES J. INGERSOLL?, Representative from Pa.]

[Washington, *ca.* May 11, 1844?]

My dear Sir, I learn from Col. [Nathan] Towson that the meeting at Baltimore was called by the peculiar friends of Mr. [Martin] V[an] B[uren] and is to be addressed with an opening speech by one of his friends. Its professed object is to discuss the political topicks of the day, Texas among the others; and that it will probably be large. Truly, J.C. Calhoun.

ALS in PHi, Ingersoll Papers.

To W[ILLIAM] S. MURPHY

Department of State
Washington, 11th May, 1844

Sir: I transmit a copy of certain papers which have been referred to this department by that of the Treasury, from which it appears that Mr. W.V.C. Dashiels [*sic*; William C.V. Dashiell], the Collector of the Customs at Sabine in Texas, has attempted to exact tonnage duties from the United States schooners Louisiana and William Bryan, which had taken on board a cargo of Texan productions in the Sabine lake or pass, at a distance from the Texan shore. It further appears that the attempt was accompanied by threats of violence on the part of the Collector and that the vessels were released only upon the condition of their masters giving an obligation to pay the duties in the event that the two governments should agree as to the legality of the exaction.

This government certainly cannot admit that the charge of tonnage duties in such a case is warrantable. By the Treaty of Limits, the boundary between the two countries begins at the mouth of the Sabine in the Gulph of Mexico and follows the western bank of that river until it reaches the 32nd parallell of latitude. The line, as thus defined, has been distinctly marked by duly appointed agents of both governments. Texas, therefore, cannot rightfully claim any jurisdiction beyond the western shore of the Sabine pass, lake and river. The demand of tonnage duties in a case like that under consideration may be deemed tantamount to such a claim on her part, and if acquiesced in by this government, would defeat the objects in view when the line mentioned in the treaty was agreed upon.

There is no reason to doubt that the Texan government will concur in this opinion and it is presumed that the course of the Collector at Sabine was occasioned by a mistaken sense of duty and not by any orders of his government. You will, however, address a representation upon the subject to the Texan Secretary of State [Anson Jones], in which you will say that it is expected the Collector of the Customs at Sabine will be directed to cancel the obligation required of the captains of the Louisiana and William Bryan and that such instructions will be given to him and other fiscal officers of that government as will prevent a recurrence of grievances like that complained of in this instance. I am, Sir, your obedient servant, J.C. Calhoun.

LS (No. 18) in DNA, RG 84 (Foreign Posts), Records of the Texas Legation; FC in DNA, RG 59 (State Department), Diplomatic Instructions, Texas, 1:92–94 (M-77:161).

From W[ILLIAM] S. MURPHY

Legation of the United States
Galveston Texas, 11 May 1844

Sir, The United States Frigate Potomac, Com[mo]d[or]e [David] Conner, arrived off this Island on the 8th and sent in her boat yesterday. The Commodore being too unwell to come on shore, I shall go out to day in the United States Schooner Flirt to see him.

A war steamer, is also reported off the Bar, this morning, supposed to be the Union.

I shall hear from Gen[era]l [Samuel] Houston tomorrow, but as the Steamer New York leaves this Port to day, for New Orleans, I shall have no op[p]ortunity ["of transmit(t)ing" *interlined*] another note to you, until the Steamer Neptune comes in, and returns; which will occur in 6 or 8 days.

I learn from the officers who came on shore from the Potomac, that none of the vessels of Commodore Conner[']s Squadron can enter any of the Harbours in this part of the Gulf—and that all their charts are verry erroneous in their Lat[itu]d[e] & Long[i]t[ude] of Places, Islands, bays, Shoals, &c &c along this coast. I will suggest that the U.S. Cutter, Vigilant, Capt. [William B.] Taylor, with 16 men and 5 mo[nths'] provision[s], is lying at the Balize below N. Orleans, with little or nothing to require his presence there; and that he [is] well acquainted with this coast, having for several years commanded the light vessels of the Texan Navy. He is a prompt & efficient officer, and his schooner is a verry light fine sailor—and might be profitably employed here, at this time on this service. He would also prove useful in a variety of ways, in obtaining useful, early & important information along the Gulf Shore, where the Flirt, could not enter, or approach with safety. I have the Honor to be Your ob[edien]t Serv[an]t, W.S. Murphy.

P.S. The steamer seen in the offing this [day] and supposed to be the Union, proves to be the Neptune. W.S. Murphy.

ALS (No. 24) in DNA, RG 59 (State Department), Diplomatic Despatches, Texas, vol. 2 (T-728:2, frames 309–310), received 5/22.

To Thomas H. Perkins, Boston, 5/11. Calhoun acknowledges Perkins's letter of 5/8 and states in reply that Mr. [William] Crump, recently appointed Chargé d'Affaires to Chile, will be informed of the "second claim in the case of the Macedonian" [against the government of Chile]. FC in DNA, RG 59 (State Department), Domestic Letters, 34:189 (M-40:32).

From EUSTIS PRESCOTT, "Private"

New Orleans, 11th May 1844

My Dear Sir, As you will have discovered from the *Herald,* and *Republican* of this morning that one of the largest public assemblages ever convened in this city—last night placed your name before the Union as the *People[']s* candidate for the Presidency, connected with the all absorbing question of the reannexation of Texas, it is due to you that one of your warmest and most steadfast friends should assure you that this movement does not emanate peculiarly from your attached friends, (altho of course they have given to it all their aid) but that it is a spontaneous movement of the people—the mass, and that the announcement of your name was received with a burst of such applause—continued & reiterated with an enthusiasm that I never remember ever to have previously witnessed in a political meeting.

Caucuses and Conventions were repudiated in toto. No Committee was appointed to announce this movement to you, as it was avowed that you had not been consulted, but that as a public man, and patriot, you could not refuse a call of your countrymen, when you were satisfied what their will was.

The meeting was presided over by Gen[era]l [J.B.] Plauché one of the oldest—most respectable & consistent Democrats of the city who was a candidate for Elector on the [Martin] Van Buren ticket, but who at the meeting declined being longer considered as such. Gen[era]l Felix Huston formerly a devoted Whig was one of the Vice Presidents and addressed the meeting in the most animated strains in support of the resolutions, and in condemnation of Mr. [Henry] Clay[']s letter and course. Cha[rle]s Watts is Judge of the Commercial and A.M. Buchanan of the District Court—the other Vice Presidents were Lawyers, Merchants, Mechanics &c—nearly all men of very considerable influence.

It has been industriously circulated here that you have addressed a letter to your friends advising them to support Mr. [John] Tyler. I am wary of all such reports, but when we see such a letter, it will be time enough for your friends to determine as to their course—in the mean time we shall issue an address to the people of the State & form our Electoral ticket[.]

We are confident that we can give *you* the Electoral vote of the State, but I very much doubt if under any circumstances it could be obtained for Mr. Tyler—whom *next to yourself I* certainly would support. If Mr. Van Buren should be the nominee of the Convention, his defeat is certain, under no circumstances do I believe it possible for him *now* to receive the electoral vote of this State.

You may perhaps ask what effect we anticipate that this movement will have north & east of us. I believe that it will rouse *the people*, and that the ball here set in motion will roll on with a rapidity, which has never been equalled except in the case of Gen[era]l [Andrew] Jackson, and that it will cause the Baltimore Convention to adjourn without making a nomination.

I have written this very hastily, and beg you to excuse the style. I hope to have the pleasure of seeing you in Washington ere another month, and remain My Dear Sir Very sincerely & truly y[*ms. torn,*] Eustis Prescott.

ALS in ScCleA; PEx in Boucher and Brooks, eds., *Correspondence*, pp. 225–226.

To CHARLES S. TODD, [St. Petersburg, Russia]

Department of State
Washington, 11th May, 1844

Sir: Your despatches to No. 42, inclusive, have been duly received at this Department, and laid before the President [John Tyler].

I take advantage of a private opportunity afforded me by the approaching departure of Mr. Samuel Harrison, of Philadelphia, for St. Petersburg, to transmit to you Executive Documents No. 5 and 8, printed by order of the Senate during its present session, containing a copy of the Treaty of Annexation recently concluded between the United States and the Republic of Texas, and of the President's message and other documents which accompanied it when submitted for the consideration of that body. Although the favorable decision of the Senate as to the expediency of ratifying this instrument has not yet been made known, and may perhaps be regarded as somewhat doubtful, these papers, besides being interesting in themselves, may enable you, if an occasion should call for it, to explain to the Russian Government, the reasons which have operated on that of the United States in the course it has taken in this matter. With that view your attention is specially called to the correspondence accompanying the Treaty. I have the honor to be, With great respect, Your obedient servant, J.C. Calhoun.

LS (No. 15) in DNA, RG 84 (Foreign Posts), Russia, Letters Received, vol. 4336; FC in DNA, RG 59 (State Department), Diplomatic Instructions, Russia, 14:64 (M-77:136). NOTE: Samuel Harrison was apparently the same "young Gentleman" from Philadelphia who had been introduced to Calhoun by Postmaster General Charles A. Wickliffe as about to go to Russia to pursue his profession as a civil engineer. Wickliffe to Calhoun, 4/2/1844, in DNA, RG 59 (State Department), Passport Applications, vol. 30, unnumbered (M-1372:14).

To H[ENRY] A. WISE, [Accomack County, Va.]

Washington, 11th May 1844

My dear Sir, I spoke to Gen[era]l Bayley [*sic*; Thomas H. Bayly, Representative from Va.] about attending at Baltimore to morrow evening, but he left me uncertain, whether he would or not. I shall endeavour to see him this evening, and hope he will consent to go. [Senator Robert J.] Walker [of Miss.] is invited and so is Harcourt? [*sic*; Representative William H. Hammett] from Mississippi, but it is uncertain whether either will attend.

Since you left, we have had despatches both from Mexico & Texas. The former is pressed and threaten[ed] by the French, and will be little disposed to give us trouble. The internal Provinces are in a very unsettled & unquiet condition.

The information from Texas confirms the previous impression, that her government will throw her into the arms of England, if we reject her hand. Of this, I hold, there is not the least doubt. I cannot but hope, that the Whigs will see the Gulf into which they are about to fall, and to save themselves will approve the treaty. If they are not destitute of sagacity, such will certainly be their course.

The riot [between Irish and nativists] in Philadelphia is the legitimate fruit of fanaticism & the spoils principle & that of the numerical majority. When will you be in the city again? With great respect Yours truly, J.C. Calhoun.

Transcript in DLC, Carnegie Institution of Washington Transcript Collection; PC in Lyon G. Tyler, *Letters and Times of the Tylers*, 3:135–136.

From ROB[ER]T MONROE HARRISON

Consulate of the United States
Kingston Jam[aic]a, May 12th 1844

Sir, Herewith I have the honor to enclose you the copy of a letter received yesterday from Captain [Thomas W.] Freelon of the "U.

States" Sloop of War "Preble"; and if I am to judge from it, and other sources of information which I have had access to, no time should be lost in sending two of our fast sailing Brig's of war to co-operate with the Preble in protecting the property and persons of our fellow citizens.

From the great extent and variety of Ports in Hayti, they ought to be of this class of vessels, to be constantly in movement, in order to afford protection at the different Ports where insurrection breaks out.

In great haste I have the honor to be Sir With profound respect Your very Ob[edien]t & most humble serv[an]t, Robt. Monroe Harrison.

[Enclosure]

Tho[ma]s W. Freelon to R[obert] M. Harrison

U.S. Ship Preble
Aux Cayes, May 5th 1844

My dear Sir, I arrived at the Isle á Vache at 2 A.M. on the morning of the 3rd inst. having as usual had a long passage. We were becalmed four days off Cape Tiburon and during that period did not make an inch headway. Yesterday afternoon I succeeded in making this place. This morning, in company with [William B. Gooch] the [Commercial] agent and the Capt. of the [H.M.S.] Griffon, I waited on the Governor, Gen. Accaau [that is, Acaau], and was received with much courtesy by him. He is a shrewd intelligent negro of about 35 or 40 years of age, and affects much simplicity of dress. He wore a check shirt dungaree jacket and trowsers and was barefooted. He appears however to be a man of a very resolute character and has his heterogeneous troops in a state of as perfect discipline as could be expected under the circumstances of the case. He has preserved from pillage the property of all foreigners, without distinction; and in doing so has been compelled to make some awful examples of his marauding troops. Whether this is owing to fear or to a sense of justice of course I am unable to determine. I find however that the sympathies of all the foreigners here are with him and against the mulattos. Doctor [Richmond] Loring found his house, and apothocarie's shop (and the latter is very extensive) untouched in every respect as far as he could judge from the hasty examination he made of it. The black army is now at Aquin about 25 miles from here. Where the army of the mulattos is, no one knows as nothing has been heard from them since they left here to quell the insurrection in the Spanish part of the Island. It is generally supposed however that the two armies will meet at Aquin and that the decisive battle will be fought tomorrow or next day. The defeated party which ever it may be, will endeavour to reach this place and a scene of pillage and slaughter will undoubtedly take place. I shall do all in my power to protect American Interests here, and I have recommended to Mr. Gooch, in the event of an irruption of the troops of either side, to hoist the American Ensign on the house of Doctor Loring, and I will send him a guard to protect him and it. I hope however that this will not be necessary.

There is here at present the French man of War Brig "Euryale" the English Brig Griffon, and several American vessels who in consequence of the existing state of things can neither dispose of their outward Cargoes nor procure a return freight. One of them has a large quantity of provisions on board, and the Gen[era]l has been in negotiation for them, for some time but the Captain would not part with them unless for cash, and as this article is very scarce with the General, I have no doubt but he would have seized them had he not been deterred by the presence of the Foreign men of War.

If nothing is heard of the contending parties in a few days I think I shall send a boat to Aquin to learn the news, and if any thing of importance occurs shall not fail to take the earliest opportunity of informing you.

I have written this in great haste as I have despatches to make out for the Government to send by a Brig that sails tomorrow morning. With my best respects to your lady & family, and my sincere wishes for your health and happiness, I remain Very truly Yours, Thos. W. Freelon.

LS (No. 282) with En in DNA, RG 59 (State Department), Consular Despatches, Kingston, vol. 9 (T-31:9), received 6/14.

From J[OHN] H. HOWARD, "Private"

Columbus [Ga.,] May 12th [1844]
I wrote to you some days ["since" *interlined*] but have not yet had the pleasure of a reply. Perhaps, sufficient time has not transpired to admit of your letter reaching me. I have only to say this morning, that your withdrawall from the Baltimore convention is *nothing*, provided the democrats should prefer to put you in nomination. It is my judgement that an effort on the part of your friends should be made, to nominate you in *convention*. If we find that impracticable then we should put you in nomination as a third candidate. I wish

Mr. [John] Tyler would agree to this, for with all good feeling towards him, I have no idea he can succeed. Although his motives are pure, the people give him no credit & his former relations with the Whig party (at least in 1840) are such that he is far from being acceptable. [Lewis] Cass is not known here, and Johnston[']s [*sic*; Richard M. Johnson's] private relations are so subject to objection, that he cannot be thought of. I do hope with your confidential friends, you will have no delicacy in discussing the prospects of your success, and allow them to take such a course as to secure your nomination by the convention, or if that cannot be effected, then as a third candidate as I have already indicated. [Martin] Van Buren ought to get out of the way. He is a dead weight upon us at the South & it is impossible for him to succeed. Yours, J.H. Howard.

ALS in ScCleA.

From D ANIEL P. K ING, [Representative from Mass.]

Washington, May 12, 1844

Sir, Enclosed I transmit to you two letters which I have just received relating to the appointment of Josiah Raymond as Consul for Manzanillo [Cuba]. I entirely concur with the very respectable writers of these letters, and the signers to the Memorial heretofore presented, in the importance and necessity of the appointment of a consul for this port, and in the high character and qualifications of Mr. Raymond, and in behalf of many merchants in the District which I represent, I do very respectfully solicit a compliance with their wishes. With high Consideration I have the honor to be Your obedient servant, Daniel P. King.

ALS in DNA, RG 59 (State Department), Applications and Recommendations, 1837–1845, Raymond (M-687:27, frames 225–226).

From [J OHN R. M ATHEWES]

[Charleston] 12 May 1844

My Dear Sir, I am about leaving Charleston and cannot do so without expressing to you my gratification on reading your letter in reply to Lord Aberdeen[']s assurances. To some it appeared that you had taken too much pains to do away [with] the pretended impressions of British Ultra Philanthropy; to me, as far as I could judge, it was hitting the right nail on the head—it is the only means ["by" *interlined*] which we can obtain a patient hearing from Europe whose eyes have ["been" *interlined*] blinded & ears deafened by England against us, & no means hitherto used by our gover[n]ment ["to" *interlined*] undeceive foreign Nations upon the subject of our operatives & the withering libels of England against our credit. I see it afforded Johny Q. [John Quincy Adams] another opportunity of displaying the facility with which he arranges for the British Minister[']s Capital, out of our Congressional discussions, whereby they can subsequently act in conjunction with him; it is a new mode of treasonable correspondence & would entitle the inventor ["with" *canceled and* "to" *interlined*] as much distinction as his prototype, were he as able to controul Truth & fact for the same shameful purposes—the betrayal to England of a portion of his Country & fellow Citizens. The Tariff & all other subjects should be put aside for Texas—do not let President makers divert the nation from this *one* point. The ground work commenced is beautiful and if Mexico becomes satisfied—the nation will nod assent & I think ["if" *canceled*] even now the Ashland treaty & the consequent Trio [of Thomas H. Benton, Martin Van Buren, and Henry Clay] begin to totter; but much reflection, time & caution is requisite to mature this glorious movement by Mr. Tyler & yourself. You certainly can use other means if a factious Senate will persist in destroying this people for President making & worshipping a Golden Calf. Do not faulter [*sic*], do not tire but let your progress be slow and onward, cautiously cutting down or putting aside the Briars & thorns that are placed in your way by Tom, Van, & Harry.

So far we run before the wind. When the thing is done, so will England be with us forever, & reaction with her will then commence in our favour. She will then try to obtain with us what ["we" *interlined*] are ourselves struggling for—Free Trade. Mexico if she goes right will become our warm friend & the South & West will have themselves released from New England Hand Cuffs. All here are in breathless suspense upon the Texas treaty. I regret that my business prevents attendance at the great meeting to be held here on Tuesday next, being compell'd to attend the Geo[rgia] R[ai]l R[oa]d meeting at Augusta on that day, & the next will take me I hope to the [Ga.] mountains, & as soon as I get home I will write you the observations of Public Opinion on the way.

The South never has nor never will again have ["an hour" *interlined*] for commanding her enemies & inviting her friend[']s assistance; if she again is disunited then it requires her to take a Bird[']s eye view of the field of self preservation. This is a "Caesar aut Nullus" Question and we must find "that peace of mind dearer than all" that our posterity more strongly demands from present action, than we did of our forefathers when they were ["in" *canceled*] invited from affluence & peace to join New England in Poverty & Turmoil against the Parent Gover[n]m[en]t. Josiah Quincy in 1765 says that at the table of Miles Brewton Esq[ui]r[e] in King Street Charleston— he threw out hints of his mission to stir up the South. He was scarcely noticed, except by an Englishman, who remark'd that when Virgi[ni]a and South Car[olin]a ceased to be colonies of England Massachusetts would furnish us with Governors. Is she not now trying to do more? To annihillate [*sic*] us as ["a" *interlined*] people because we will not be *govern'd* by her, nor submit to her construction of the constitution. Was this not Prophetic? & this mother ["now" *interlined*] joins with the Pedagogue now to denude the parts & apply the whip to us, her once spoil[e]d Child, diverted from her embrace by the wiles of Poverty & Dogmatism. I wrote you a long letter a few weeks ago six pages!!! Ever yours with great respect and esteem. [Unsigned.]

[P.S.] I believe that the hand of God is with us; such a combination of events pointing to the same favourable results for the rescue of our oppress'd section of the Union originates from a cause beyond accident or the power & Ken of man.

ALU in ScCleA.

From W[illia]m Nelson

United States Consulate
Panama, 12 May 1844
Sir, I did myself this honor on the 14th March, since then I have received no communication whatever from the Department.

The French Government have established monthly packets between Callao and this port at an expence of $1300 p[er] month, which will enable me to forward despatches for the Squadron with more regularity.

The sudden interest shewn concerning the isthmus by the French Government has induced the natives to suspect they have designs on the Country.

I have the honor to enclose four despatches for the Department.

I have the honor to be Very respectfully Sir Your most ob[edien]t serv[an]t, Wm. Nelson, U.S. C[onsul and Despatch Agent].

ALS (No. 20) in DNA, RG 59 (State Department), Consular Despatches, Panama, vol. 1 (M-139:1), received 6/22.

From ALBERT SMITH

Washington, 12th May 1844

Sir, The charges in my account, as Commissioner under the Treaty of Washington, for the pay of Civil Engineers and Commissary, have been rejected ["by the 5th Auditor, on" *canceled*] the ground that there is no authority in the law for the employment of a Commissary or of Civil Engineers.

I do not consider the decision ["of the auditor" *canceled*] to be based upon a sound, and common sense construction of the law.

The Statute gives *no authority* to the Commissioner to employ *any body* but a Clerk. It merely fixes his salary and that of his Clerk, and makes an appropriation for the general purposes of the Survey. The *Treaty*, upon which the law is based, points out the duties of the Commissioner to be, to mark[,] run & trace the line described in the Treaty—to erect monuments thereon, and to make a Survey ["of the same" *erased*] and maps of the same.

Now, these duties cannot be performed by the Commissioner alone. He must have necessary assistance, from competent men.

Can these duties be discharged without Commissaries? No one, at all acquainted with them, will answer in the affirmative. Such surveys were *never* made without them, in this or any other Country, & this is the first time that the pay of a Commissary was ever objected to. In every Survey which has been made in the United States, ["the 5th Auditor has examined and allowed" *canceled*] the accounts of Commissaries ["have been allowed" *interlined*]. Upon the exploration of the North Eastern Boundary line in 1841, I was, myself, a Commissary. My account was allowed ["by the 5th Auditor" *canceled*], and my compensation was *precisely* the *same* as is *charged* by the officer, to whose pay ["he now objects" *canceled and* "objection is now made" *interlined*]. I venture to say that the law of 1840, under which the exploration of the N.E. Boundary was made, gave no authority to the Commissioners to employ a Commissary, and yet *three Commissaries* were employed by them, and paid by the Government.

In short, in all cases where persons are required by law to perform any duty, the inference always is, that the necessary instruments and agents are to be employed by him for its performance.

["The Auditor objects" *canceled and* "Objection is made" *interlined*] to the charges for *Civil Engineers*, not only on account of the want of express authority in the law, but because the second section *makes it "lawful for the President* to employ *one or more* of the officers of the [U.S. Army] Topographical Engineers as the public service may require to assist the Commissioner" &c &c. Now, it seems to me, that a fair construction of that section, does not *deprive* the Commissioner of the power to employ other persons, if, in his opinion their services were *necessary*. If so, in case of sickness, or the death of an Engineer, the Commissioner would have to suspend operations, until he had time to notify the President and have the vacancy supplied by him. The law does not say that "all the Engineers employed upon this Survey, to assist the Commissioner, shall be detailed by the President from the Corps of Topographical Engineers." Language very different from this is employed in the second section, leaving to the Commissioner, as I contend, the power to employ such operatives, as the work should require. Such *I know* to have been the *intention* of the framer of the Law. Mr. [Caleb] Cushing [then Representative from Mass.] who penned it, (and it was not altered afterwards) advised with me in regard to the employment of *Civil Engineers* or *Surveyors*, (which be it remembered are synonymous terms in Maine). He *assured* me that I had full power, by the law, to employ what civilians were necessary in my sci[e]ntific corps.

The law was also so construed by Mr. [Daniel] Webster, and he, himself, recommended to me the appointment of a Commissary, and also of a Civil Engineer. But, it seems to me, that the question is settled by the positive instructions of the Secretary of State.

In his letter of the 17th March he says I am to expend the appropriation, among other objects, "for the pay and subsistence of *assistant Surveyors.*"

Again on the 22d of March, *after the detail by the President of the Topographical Officers*, the Secretary says, "Lt. [Thomas J.] Lee & [George] Thom will also be detailed to be employed under your general direction and the supervision of Maj. [James D.] Graham in carrying on actual operations in the field, *with such additional Surveyors* assistants &c as you *may find necessary.*" ["Here it seems to me is" *canceled and* "Is not this" *interlined*] direct authority, (if not positive instruction) to employ Civilians in my Sci[e]ntific Corps, if I thought their services important to the Survey?

In regard to the term "Surveyor" I would observe, that such surveyors, as are required for *this service*, must also be Civil Engineers, if there be indeed, any distinction in the terms.

The persons, for whose services I have paid, and for which I am refused allowance, were both Surveyors and Engineers, and were absolutely indispensable for the work. A *"Surveyor"* upon the Texan Boundary line, under Major Graham, received two thousand dollars per annum. Again the Secretary, in the last named letter says—"the *number of parties* which *it may be useful to keep employed* at the same time on various parts of the line, is a matter for *the decision of the Commissioner."* Each of these parties would require an Engineer at its head. If I had the authority, therefore, to decide on the *number of parties* to be employed, it follows that I must have had power to organize them, and to place a competent person at the head of each.

I might, I think, leave the case here with the single remark, that no Survey has, to my knowledge been carried on in the United States, without the employment of one or more Civil Engineers—The Coast Survey—the Texan Boundary—the N.E. Boundary exploration and survey, and all others have I beleive been carried on, partly by Civilians. But I adduce one more authority only—Major Graham, who was appointed the Head of the Sci[e]ntific Corps under my direction and who had examined the law, in a letter addressed to me under date of March 25th 1843, says—"Under the impression that the number of officers detailed from the Corps of Topographical Engineers will be *insufficient* to perform the field operations, I beg leave to suggest, that, in the selection of Civil Engineers, regard should be had to the practical experience, as well as sci[e]ntific attainments of the persons to be employed."

"I have therefore taken the liberty to *engage*, provisionally, the services of Messrs. Fairfax and Schroeder whose labours upon this line have been hitherto most arduous and efficient. There are others who may also be beneficially employed of whom I will speak when I meet you."

Major Graham had, therefore, no doubts as to the power of the Commissioner, to employ Civilians, if there [*sic*] services were found to be necessary, to co operate with the British Commissioner, in carrying out the provisions of the Treaty.

The services of these gentlemen have been rendered, under the express instructions of the Secretary of State. The Government ["have" *altered to* "has"] received the full benefit of them—they have been paid for, by me in full. I have no remedy against ["them" *canceled*] the individuals, to recover back the money from them, either in law or equity. Would it be right or equitable, that I should ["then" *canceled*] lose the amount thus paid to them in good faith, &, as I verily thought, in obedience to the law, & the instructions of the Secretary of State? I have the honor to be with high Consideration Your ob[edien]t & humb[l]e Serv[an]t, Albert Smith, U.S. Com[missione]r.

N.B. I am just informed that, on the 27th March 1843—Mr. Webster made a requisition on the War department for two additional engineers from the Topographical Corps for service on the Boundary.

Of that fact I was not notified until long after my employment of the civil Engineers in my corps. And these individuals were engaged, by the approval of the Secretary of State, prior to the detail of March 27th & with the topographical Engineers did not form a Corps equal in number to that of the British Commissioner.

The authority & direction contained in his letter to me of March 22d remained & still remains, *unannulled* & in full force. A.S.

[P.P.S.] The persons in the corps of the British Commissioner, termed *sappers* & miners are all educated men, well acquainted with the use of Engineering instruments, & capable of take [*sic*] charge of a survey. A. Smith, Com[missione]r.

ALS in DNA, RG 59 (State Department), Letters and Accounts from Despatch Agents at New York and Boston, vol. for August 1840–November 1847.

From W[illiam] B. Calhoun, [former Representative from Mass.], Springfield, 5/13. William B. Calhoun asks that the State Department investigate the imprisonment of Henry Joseph Cavalier in Cuba. ALS in DNA, RG 59 (State Department), Miscellaneous Letters (M-179:104, frames 351–352).

From ROB[ER]T MONROE HARRISON

Consulate of the United States
Kingston Jam[aic]a, 13th May 1844

Sir, Herewith I have the honor to enclose you a Paper by which you will perceive that the People of St. Domingo (that is to say, the Mulattoes) are disposed to put themselves under the protection of Great Britain. I have long been aware from information received through some of the principal Exiles, that this would sooner or later take

place. With great respect I have the honor to be Sir Your Ob[edien]t
& most humble Serv[an]t, Robt. Monroe Harrison.

LS (No. 284) with En in DNA, RG 59 (State Department), Consular Despatches,
Kingston, vol. 9 (T-31:9), received 6/22. NOTE: Harrison enclosed a copy of the
Kingston, Jamaica, *Royal Gazette* of 5/13, which contained an article stating that
the Haitian government was soliciting the assistance of Great Britain to combat
the most recent insurrection.

From Philip O. Hughes, Jackson, Miss., 5/13. He asks Calhoun
to consider him to be an applicant for the office of U.S. Marshal for
Southern Miss. if a vacancy should occur in that position. Hughes
is a son of an old friend of Calhoun and wishes to apply on that basis.
He adds, "My Mother is still alive and in pret[t]y good health." ALS
in DNA, RG 59 (State Department), Applications and Recommendations, 1837–1845, Hughes (M-687:16, frames 532–533).

From John McDaniel, St. Louis Prison, 5/13. He transmits to
Calhoun papers concerning his conviction [for the murder of Mexican
trader Antonio José Chavis] and asks that Calhoun examine those
papers. McDaniel professes his innocence and that of those convicted with him; he states that his sole culpability was in capturing
Chavis "who lost his life most unfortunately in this affair." Mc-
Daniel states that he alone was guilty of that offense and that his
brother David McDaniel and the others convicted in the crime should
be absolved of guilt. He asks for a pardon from the President [John
Tyler]. Two ALS's in DNA, RG 59 (State Department), Petitions
for Pardon and Related Briefs, 1800–1849, no. 292A.

To Henry A. Muhlenberg, [former Representative from Pa.],
Reading, Pa., 5/13. "I have the honor to state, in answer to your let-
ter of the 8th instant, that should agents be employed to distribut[e]
the laws, the application therein made in behalf of Mr. [Isaac T.]
James will receive the most respectful Consideration." FC in DNA,
RG 59 (State Department), Domestic Letters, 34:191 (M-40:32).

To HENRY L. PINCKNEY, Charleston

Department of State
Washington, May 13 [18]44
Sir: I have the honor to acknowledge the receipt of a memorial of a
number of citizens of Charleston, signed by yourself as Chairman,

together with the affidavits of Capt. Merriman and seaman John Scott, in relation to the murder at Havana of Michael Murphy, a seaman of the United States.

This case was reported to the Department on the 19th ultimo by the U.S. Consul at Havana, who stated that it was then undergoing judicial investigation. When the result of that investigation is made known, he will, of course promptly communicate it to the Department. Relying, in the meantime, upon his full attention being given to the matter, I take the occasion to say that whatever may be the final decision of the Authorities in regard to it, it is the determination of this Government to see that ample redress is made for the outrage committed upon Mr. Murphy. I am, Sir, &c, J.C. Calhoun.

FC in DNA, RG 59 (State Department), Consular Instructions, 10:243–244; PC in the Charleston, S.C., *Courier*, May 30, 1844, p. 2; PC in the Charleston, S.C., *Southern Patriot*, May 30, 1844, p. 2; PC in the Washington, D.C., *Spectator*, June 5, 1844, p. 3; PC in the Edgefield, S.C., *Advertiser*, June 5, 1844, p. 3.

From [President] John Tyler, 5/13. "As a bill is now before Congress having originated out of the case of [David] Babe condemned for piracy at New York, ["and" *canceled*] which makes it proper to extend his reprieve to such time as Congress may act upon the subject, the Secretary of State will cause a further reprieve to be made out ["in Babe's case" *interlined*] until ["the" *canceled*] Friday the 19th day of July next." ALS in DNA, RG 59 (State Department), Petitions for Pardon and Related Briefs, 1800–1849, no. 6B.

From Fernando Wood, New York [City], 5/13. He acknowledges Calhoun's letter of 5/8 appointing him Despatch Agent of the State Department at New York City and gratefully accepts the office. ALS in DNA, RG 59 (State Department), Passport Applications, vol. 31, unnumbered (M-1372:14).

From J[OHN] S. BARBOUR, "Private"

Warrenton [Va.,] May 14th 1844

My Dear Sir, Our friend Mr. Edw[ar]d Dixon is now in my room & expresses some uneasiness lest you may think that the brief mention of his name in one of my late letters was at his request. It was done solely on my own thoughts. At the breakfast table on the morning of my letter, the Master in Chancery of the Superior Court sitting nigh to me mentioned Mr. Dixon[']s name & his attachment to you, with other incidents that put his (Mr. D[ixon']s) interests upon my mind and in writing quickly after to you, I assumed the leave of mentioning his name in the brief terms I employed to remind you of him. It is justice to Mr. Dixon to say this and I do so with the greater pleasure because he has a commendable delicacy in this matter, which I justly appreciate.

There is nothing of interest in this quarter. It seems that public opinion is yielding up all its former predilections for Mr. [Martin] Van Buren. I learn that some half a dozen or more of these people have sent a note to the [Washington] Globe asserting that the voice of this Country is for Mr. V[an] B[uren]. This is not so. Some of those who are reported to have signed the Globe note have said to me that it was profitless & culpable to run him as our Candidate.

Such publications do hurt by the delusion they impose on the public mind. It is equally true that Mr. [John] Tyler cannot command a single County in Virginia & the effort to chafe[?] the popular sensibilities into his support has a decided effect in retracing the wandering & doubtful sentiments of the people to Mr. Van Buren. I assure you (with the kindest feelings to ["Mr." *interlined*] Tyler) that there is not the faintest reason to hope for him.

My former letters speak distinctly enough on this topick.

In great haste, Y[ou]r sincere friend, J.S. Barbour.

ALS in ScCleA.

From JAMES H. CAMPBELL

Office of the Morning Herald
New Orleans, May 14th 1844

D[ea]r Sir, I hope you will excuse the liberty I take in enclosing to you the resolutions passed at a mass meeting of the citizens of New Orleans at which you were nominated for the office of president of the United States subject to no convention but your own decision and the will of the sovereign people. This step sir has been taken without as you are aware the slightest consultation with yourself or indeed I may say with your special friends who are advised of your views and wishes. If such you have here we have not been advised by them. You will then I hope sir not consider this a party moovement but the spontaneous voice of the people of this great city—that voice

I am well assured will be responded to from every parrish in the State. In this meeting (which was one of the largest ever convened in our city) there were to be found as active members of that meeting ["Wh" *canceled*] whigs as well as democrats.

I assure you sir that the subject of annexation is the all absorbing question with us and that in refference to it all former party lines will be abolished—at least to a great extent. That Mr. [John] Tyler cannot carry the friends of annexation belonging to the Democratic party in this State is almost absolutely certain. I think also that the same would be the case in Georgia[,] Alabama & Mississippi to say nothing of other southern States. These statements are of course made to some extent conjecturally but not without pretty ample means of information.

Whilst it would be ["the last" *canceled*] foreign to the wish of your friends (one amongst the humblest of whome I claim to be) to place you in a false position—the demonstrations of public opinion are so strongly in your favour that the anxious enquiry is constantly made "Will Mr. Calhoun permit his name to be run as the *people*[']*s* candidate[?]" This question we are not able to answer. We can simply say to them that your known fearles[s]ness of charracter will not long keep us in doubt.

You may have perceived before this that the journal (The Morning Herald) at the head of which I am has already drop[p]ed the name of Mr. Van Buren and raised yours. It will ther[e]fore becom[e] material for me to know either in the strictest privacy or otherwise whether I have been justifiable in that course. It is true that in seeking this confidence I ask much but I beg leave to refer you to the Hon. Walter L. [*sic*; T.] Colquitt[,] Senator from Georgia and whome I know to be one of your friends to show you that such confidence will not be abused.

I have had the pleasur[e] of meeting you myself in the upper part of Georgia during my long residence in that State but am not vain enough to suppose that you remember me.

If however you would favour me with a reply designating whether it should be made public or strictly private you would confer a lasting obligation upon, Sir[,] Your Ob[edien]t S[er]v[an]t, James H. Campbell, Ed[itor,] Morning Herald.

ALS with En in ScCleA; PC in Boucher and Brooks, eds., *Correspondence*, pp. 227–228. Note: Campbell enclosed a clipping from the New Orleans *Morning Herald* of 5/15/1844, "Annexation and Calhoun Meeting," which printed the proceedings and resolutions of a meeting on 5/14. The meeting passed resolutions advocating Texas annexation and nominating Calhoun for the Presidency. One of the resolutions read: "Resolved, That the choice [of President] should fall upon some statesman of acknowledged ability and high worth, whose private life is without taint or blemish, and whose public career has been marked out by his own intellect; one who is the friend of peace, yet ever ready to uphold the honor of our country without counting the cost, and one whose administration we may be certain will be conducted on principles that will work no shame to the simplicity of our institutions, nor wound the integrity of the national character."

From EDWARD EVERETT

London, 14 May 1844

Sir, I have received a letter from Mr. James Shaw, consul of the United States at Belfast in Ireland, in which he informs me, that he has appointed Mr. William B. Glenny Vice-Consul at the port of Newry in the room of Mr. Alexander F. Little resigned.

I have also received a letter from Mr. Thomas W. Waldron, lately appointed consul of the United States at Hong Kong, dated 28th of January last. Mr. Waldron's letter is an acknowledgment of one, which I addressed him on the 5th of October last, to which allusion is made in the first paragraph of my number 58. At the date of Mr. Waldron's letter, no intelligence had been received from Mr. [Caleb] Cushing.

In a debate on the factory bill in the House of Commons last evening, Sir Robert Peel is reported to have expressed himself, in the following terms, in reference to the commerce of the United States with China:

"The accounts we have from China state, that there is at this time a great crisis in the competition now going on, that America is sending many goods into the China market, but that the Chinese prefer English goods, and the question is which shall be predominant." Without being acquainted with the data, on which Sir Robert Peel represents the Chinese as preferring English to American fabrics, I am inclined to think his statement erroneous, at least in the broad terms in which he is reported (perhaps incorrectly) to have made it. I have derived from various authentic sources of information the impression, that the preference is generally given to American fabrics over the English of the same nominal description, in the foreign markets in which they come in competition.

In fact the very debate, of which that of last evening was the adjournment, furnishes ground to doubt the accuracy of Sir Robert Peel's statement. Sir James Graham alluded to the rapid progress of the manufactures of the United States, as affording "evidence of a successful competition in a third market with the produce of British Industry"; and after making a statement in reference to the manufactures of Switzerland, he went on to say: "With regard to America, Mr. Horner also reports, what occurred to him in his last visit to Manchester under my direction, making special enquiry in reference to the intensity of competition. He gives me the name of a person whom he there met connected with a very extensive export house in Manchester. He said that America had in some instances quite superseded us in the foreign market: that his house used to export some descriptions of drills to a very large amount: after some time they found it necessary to meet the American competition, by the manufacture of a somewhat cheaper and inferior article, but without success."

Lord Howick the same evening, in alluding to this point in Sir James Graham's speech, said he had received the same information as to the formidable nature of the American competition, and he mentioned the Chinese market as that where it prevailed. "He had seen" (he observed) "a trade circular from China the other day, which stated the very great importation of North American manufactures into that market, and the reason assigned was this: that in North America a very low duty was levied on tea; that its consumption therefore was rapidly increasing, and that the American manufacturers produced their goods, as the cheapest mode of paying for that tea which their countrymen required." Lord Howick then deduced an argument from this supposed state of facts in favor of the repeal of the English Corn laws, which would enable the Americans to send their corn to this country and take British manufactures in return, which they might carry to China in payment for tea.

I was myself informed by a distinguished manufacturer in Manchester, on occasion of a visit to that place about two years ago, that they had found themselves obliged to imitate the external appearance and marks of the American fabrics, giving them at the same time a rather higher finish, but working in poorer and cheaper stock, to enable them to undersell the American article in a foreign market.

Such being the facts, I should be inclined to doubt whether there can be the preference which Sir Robert Peel supposes, on the part of the Chinese, for English fabrics. If there is such a preference at present, it will probably cease should experience make them acquainted with the fact just mentioned, that the coarse cotton fabrics of the United States are an article so superior to the English of the same nominal description, as to lead to an imitation like that described.

One thing, however, is no doubt true, as stated by Sir Robert Peel, that the present is a moment of crisis, in the markets of the Chinese empire, in reference to the competition between England and the United States; and he justly states, that if England prevails, it will be a great public benefit to her.

Under these circumstances the arrival of an American mission on the coast of China at this juncture, supported by an adequate display of force, will be a most opportune event. It will confirm the Chinese authorities in the favorable opinion they have already formed of the American character & of the strength and respectability of our government. Such an impression will, of course, have its influence in reference to our Commercial relations. If, independent of experience of the comparative qualities of the fabrics of the two countries, a preference is likely to be given by the Chinese to those either of England or America, under the operation of other circumstances such as affect, to a greater or less degree, the intercourse of nations, too much cannot be said of the importance of a creditable representation of the Government and People of the United States, at this moment in China.

It seems in other respects important, that we should hold our commercial privileges in the newly opened ports, not in virtue of the stipulations of the English treaty, but under a public compact of our own. Such has been the uniform policy of our government in reference to powers, with which it is for the first time forming a friendly international connection. It may also be quite essential, by way of precaution against the dangers of a peculiar character incident to trade with the Chinese, dangers likely to be increased by the multiplication of the free ports, that some better system should be introduced than has hitherto prevailed of settling controversies between our citizens and the local authorities. Such an improved system would require the agency of Congress; but could hardly be undertaken with confidence, except on the basis of enquiries & observations made upon the spot, by a minister of the United States.

I have fallen into these remarks, in consequence of insinuations which have appeared in the prints of this country, against the utility of a mission from the United States to China. It is quite natural that the British press should be inclined to magnify the importance of what has been effected by England, toward opening the trade of China to the world; nor am I at all disposed to under value it; nor to deny that the policy pursued by Sir Henry Pottinger, under the instructions of his government, in abstaining from all stipulations of exclusive advantage, was as liberal as it was wise. But it does not follow that nothing remains for the other governments to do for the protection of their own interests; and where an intense competition, as Sir Robert Peel states, is at its crisis, in reference to commercial relations to be formed with the largest population living under one government on the face of the earth, it would seem to be the dictate of common prudence, that the United States should be represented in the most efficient manner. I am, sir, very respectfully, your obedient servant, Edward Everett.

LS (No. 124) in DNA, RG 59 (State Department), Diplomatic Despatches, Great Britain, vol. 52 (M-30:48), received 6/3; FC in MHi, Edward Everett Papers, 49:60–68 (published microfilm, reel 23, frames 30–34).

From David McDaniel, St. Louis Prison, 5/14. He again writes Calhoun concerning his conviction [for the murder of Antonio José Chavis]. If supporting petitions from Clay and other Missouri counties should not reach Calhoun by 5/25, McDaniel asks that he be granted a respite to allow time for a thorough investigation of his conviction. ALS in DNA, RG 59 (State Department), Petitions for Pardon and Related Briefs, 1800–1849, no. 292A.

From John McKeon, [former Representative from N.Y.], New York [City], 5/14. McKeon asks that Gerard H. Coster of New York City, who plans to visit Europe with his wife, be granted the character of bearer of despatches to "facilitate his movements." ALS in DNA, RG 59 (State Department), Passport Applications, vol. 31, unnumbered (M-1372:14).

To G[regory] A. Perdicaris, "now at Cheraw," S.C., 5/14. Calhoun acknowledges Perdicaris's letter of 5/2 and in reply, considering the circumstances mentioned in that letter, Perdicaris is granted an extension of his leave of absence from his post as U.S. Consul for Athens for 12 months. FC in DNA, RG 59 (State Department), Consular Instructions, 10:244.

From LOVELL PURDY

Fullers Hotel
Washington, May 14th, 1844

Respected Sir, After several ineffectual attempts to gain an interview with you Sir at the Department, and as my business necessarily causes me to leave this afternoon for home; I have taken the liberty of thus inclosing to you the few remaining papers left me, in relation to ["the" *canceled*] Mr. Joseph Binda, Consul to Leghorn, and at your perfect convenience, respectfully solicit your attention to them.

I trust Sir, that you will excuse me, if I add in this communication, that this is the fourth time within the last four months, that I have visited Washington on the same business, and, that a Petition, signed by thirty of the first Merchantile Firms in the City of New York, another by eighty Masters of Vessels sailing out of that Port, together with evidences of Mr. Binda's having in many instances, sold Paintings as originals of Old Masters, which were proven to be Copies, were placed by me into the hands of the late Sec[retary of State] Judge [Abel P.] Upshur for the removal of said Binda. I also left with His Excellency [John Tyler] the President, a few recommendatory letters in favour of myself as an applicant for the appointment to Leghorn.

The above named papers, I am inclined to believe Sir, have never been laid before you.

On this my last visit I expected to meet Mr. Binda, as he had made an appointment to that effect through his intimate friend at New York Mr. Poligani for the purpose of—as he said—resigning in my favor. It proved to be another of the many acts of duplicity on the part of Mr. Binda, and prevented me from procuring other, and stronger evidences against him.

I will only add Sir, that it is the general opinion amongst your political as well as personal friends in the City of New York, that Mr. Binda has most grossly deceived you, in his representation as to the cause of his delay in this Country; and as a sincere and devoted friend to you Sir, as well as in justice to the Merchants and Masters of Vessels, interested in this matter, I thought it my duty to lay it before you in as correct and brief a manner as lay in my power.

With assurances Sir, that, although an applicant for the appointment, to me—it is of slight importance to the desire I have of ever seeing you represented in your true character. I have the honor to be Very Respectfully Your Ob[e]d[ien]t Serv[an]t, Lovell Purdy.

ALS in DNA, RG 59 (State Department), Applications and Recommendations, 1837–1845, Purdy (M-687:26, frames 705–707).

To Ramon Leon Sanchez, U.S. Consul at Cartagena, 5/14. Sanchez's despatches no. 34 and 35 have been received; the latter, "recommending that Cartagena, be included in the route to be taken by the Chagres packets, has been sent to the Secretary of the Navy [John Y. Mason] for his perusal." FC in DNA, RG 59 (State Department), Consular Instructions, 11:244.

To Isaac Van Zandt and J. Pinckney Henderson, [Texan Commissioners to the U.S.], 5/14. "Mr. Calhoun presents his complimen[ts] to Mr. Van Zandt and General Hende[rson], and will thank them to call at the department at any time before three o'clock this day." LU in Tx, Andrew Jackson Houston Papers; FC in DNA, RG 59 (State Department), Notes to Foreign Legations, Texas, 6:70 (M-99:95).

From HENDRICK B. WRIGHT

Wilkes-Barré [Pa.,] May 14, 1844

D[ea]r Sir, Allow me to congratulate you on the position you have taken on the subject of the *reannexation* of Texas to the Union. The measure has added new laurels to your brow—and the country will sustain the act. Your correspondence too, on the subject of Great Britain interfering with our domestic relations, is no less cheering to the democracy of the Union. We have pursued a temporizing policy too long, and the day has ar[r]ived when it becomes us to speak out & proclaim to the world where we stand, and what our principles are. You have taken the lead and you will be sustained. If war be the consequence—let it come. The sooner the better. The country is prepared for it, and in this event the old land marks will be reestablished and the democracy can then be discovered as distinct from the federalist without a patent from some examining Committee.

I will be in Baltimore on the 25th as one of the Senatorial delegates of this State to the democratic Convention and if time will ["permits" *altered to* "permit"] me I will visit Washington before the session of the Convention, in which event I shall avail myself of the opportunity of making you a call. I shall be detained in Phil[adelphi]a next week: but will be at Washington if I possibly can.

After the Convention my business will call me immediately home. But, Sir, I cannot close this letter without again congratulating you on the firm and independent stand you have assumed on the side of our common country. Believe me to be Sir, Yours very truly, Hendrick B. Wright.

ALS in ScCleA. NOTE: Wright had recently been Speaker of the Pa. House of Representatives and in a few weeks was to serve as chairman of the Democratic National Convention. He became Representative from Pa. during 1853–1855, 1861–1863, and 1877–1881.

HENRY Y. CRANSTON, [Representative from R.I.], to John Tyler

Washington, 15th May 1844

Sir, William Bisby, a native of New Jersey, but for some time past a Citizen of Rhode Island, has recently been seized by the authorities of Cuba, loaded with chains, and thrust into a loathsome dungeon with felons of the most abandoned cast. This most violent outrage has been committed upon an American Citizen, under the groundless pretence, that he had been concerned in some way or other in countenancing the recent insurrection in that Island. Mr. Bisby is a most deserving and meritorious young man, and I am perfectly confident, from my knowledge of his character, that the charge brought against him is in all respects wholly unfounded. This young man has been employed for several years past as an Engineer, upon the Plantation of Theodore Phinney Esq., who has entire and unqualified confidence in him as a sober, peaceable, and most excellent man.

I enclose herewith a letter, this day received by me, from the Hon: George Engs, one of the most respectable citizens of Rhode Island, containing the particulars respecting the unfortunate condition of Mr. Bisby. Allow me, Sir, to request, most earnestly, that the President will be pleased to take such measures as he may deem proper to cause this outrage to be inquired into by the Agent of the United States residing at Cuba, and to effect the speedy release, and restoration of Mr. Bisby to his distressed wife and family. I have the honor to be very Respectfully, Sir, your Ob[edien]t Ser[van]t, Henry Y. Cranston.

ALS with En in DNA, RG 59 (State Department), Miscellaneous Letters (M-179:104, frames 366–370). NOTE: An endorsement by John Brown Francis, James F. Simmons, and Elisha R. Potter, Senators and Representative from R.I., respectively, reads "We cordially & earnestly unite in the within application." An AES by Tyler, dated 5/18, reads "The Secretary of State will please cause this case to be made known to Mr. [Robert B.] Campbell Consul at ["Cuba" *canceled*] Havana."

From C[ALEB] CUSHING

Macao, May 15, 1844

Sir, I enclose here with copies of two letters of great importance from the Governor General and of my reply.

These letters announce the appointment of Key ing, who conducted the commercial negociations with Sir Henry Pottinger, as Commissioner, with powers to conclude a Treaty with the United States, and his speedy arrival at Canton, in the double capacity of Commissioner and of Governor General of the two Kuangs.

They also signify the continued unwillingness of the Court to receive the Legation at Peking.

Ching's letter of the ninth with its enclosure of copies of his instructions from the Court was delivered to me on the twelfth instant by a deputation of civil and military officers of rank, namely Kisheo, a general of the second class under the Mantchu banner, wearing a red button and a peacock's feather—Ching Ying, a Che-Fu, or Magistrate of a Fu, wearing a blue button, and Tung Leën, a Tung Che, that is Assistant Magistrate of a Hëen, wearing a crystal button.

They were accompanied, also, by Woo Ting Hëen, an aide de Camp of the Acting Governor General.

Doubtless one object of a delegation so respectable was to show some attention to the Legation, though I presume it was still more its object to endeavour to give an imposing authority to the "Imperial Pleasure" as documents from the Court are somewhat affectedly denominated.

In a separate despatch of this date I shall enter into some exposition of the State and prospects of my mission to be transmitted in the overland mail by the way of Bombay and London. I am, with the highest respect Your obedient servant, C. Cushing.

LS (No. 59) with Ens in DNA, RG 59 (State Department), Diplomatic Despatches, China, vol. 1 (M-92:2), received 10/23. NOTE: This despatch was addressed to A[bel] P. Upshur.

To C[harles] J. Ingersoll, [Representative from Pa.], Chairman of the House Committee on Foreign Affairs, 5/15. In response to a letter of 5/9 Calhoun transmits extracts from three State Department instructions, two from [Daniel] Webster to [Waddy] Thompson [Jr., U.S. Minister to Mexico], dated 6/22/1842 and 1/31/1843, and one from [Abel P.] Upshur to Thompson dated 7/27/1843, indicating the views of the President [John Tyler] in relation to the character of the war between Mexico and Texas. "This department is not in possession of any document which shows the opinion of either British or French Government upon that subject or of any evidence of a protest or remonstrance by either against the continuance of the war." FC in DNA, RG 59 (State Department), Domestic Letters, 34:195–196 (M-40:32).

From John McDaniel, St. Louis Prison, 5/15. His attorneys are preparing a report of his trial and conviction [for the murder of Antonio José Chavis] to be transmitted to Washington for consideration. Since the time of McDaniel's execution (6/14) is rapidly approaching, he asks for a respite to allow time for the preparation and study of the report. ALS in DNA, RG 59 (State Department), Petitions for Pardon and Related Briefs, 1800–1849, no. 292A.

From R[obert] G. McHugh, "Saint Lucia, West Indies," 5/15. McHugh, a British subject, seeks appointment as a U.S. Vice-Consul at St. Lucia. He states why he believes the appointment would be in the interest of the U.S. [William R.] Hayes, the U.S. Consul at Barbados, had written to [Abel P.] Upshur about the matter before Upshur's death. ALS in DNA, RG 59 (State Department), Applications and Recommendations, 1837–1845, McHugh (M-687:21, frames 356–357).

To ISAAC VAN ZANDT and J. PINCKNEY HENDERSON

Department of State
Washington, 15th May, 1844

The Undersigned, Secretary of State of the United States, will thank Mr. Van Zandt and General Henderson to furnish any information it may be in their power, in reference to any armistice or proposed armistice between Texas and Mexico and the circumstances connected with the same.

The Undersigned avails himself of the opportunity of renewing the assurance of his distinguished consideration. J.C. Calhoun.

FC in DNA, RG 59 (State Department), Notes to Foreign Legations, Texas, 6:70 (M-99:95); CC in DNA, RG 46 (U.S. Senate), 28A-B12; CC in Tx, Records of the Texas Republic Department of State, U.S. Diplomatic Correspondence; CC in Tx, Records of the Texas Republic Department of State, Copybooks of Letters Received from Texan and Foreign Representatives, vol. 2-1/98, p. [500]; PC in House Document No. 271, 28th Cong., 1st Sess., p. 85; PC in Senate Document No. 341, 28th Cong., 1st Sess., pp. 85–86; PC in *Congressional Globe*, 28th Cong., 1st Sess., Appendix, p. 554; PC in the Washington, D.C., *Daily National Intelligencer*, May 24, 1844, p. 1; PC in the Washington, D.C., *Globe*, May 24, 1844, p. 2; PC in the Washington, D.C., *Daily Madisonian*, May 24, 1844, p. 2; PC in the Charleston, S.C., *Courier*, May 29, 1844, p. 2; PC in *Niles' National Register*, vol. LXVI, no. 16 (June 15, 1844), p. 251.

MAY 16–31, 1844

◫

The Texas annexation treaty was officially still awaiting its final dis-position in the Senate, though its defeat was expected. But the focus of the issue had shifted from the legislative to the political arena. The Democratic National Convention gathered in Baltimore in late May. Calhoun, who had previously expressed his disdain for these proceedings, now urged his allies to attend on the quite reasonable grounds that the friends of Texas might best exert themselves in that way. The convention emerged with a "dark horse," James K. Polk, and a strong annexation platform, and Calhoun seemed to be satisfied.

Meanwhile there was plenty of official business to occupy the Secretary's attention. There were many consular posts to be filled. Some attention would soon have to be paid to the embarrassing side-show that was developing in Texas among the U.S. representatives there. The two most important Consuls, Archibald M. Green at Galveston and Stewart Newell at the port of the Sabine, were at cross purposes with the U.S. Chargé d'Affaires to the Republic, William S. Murphy, to a degree that had become a public scandal and threatened direct personal encounter. It was exceedingly difficult to sort out the merits of the controversy from Washington, though it appeared that Murphy was at fault and was perhaps a casualty of drink. The situation was in the process of solving itself, however, because on May 23 the Senate rejected Murphy's nomination as U.S. Chargé d'Affaires to Texas, a nomination which had been submitted to it six months before.

In instructions to new ministers to Brazil on May 25 and to Chile on May 28 Calhoun showed himself to be in favor of peace, good feelings, and progress among the nations of the New World and of the maintenance of legitimate U.S. interests in a firm but quiet and moderate manner.

In a letter to a young Philadelphian, Francis Wharton, written while the Democratic National Convention was meeting but before its outcome was known, Calhoun made a considered statement of his own position in national affairs at that moment. He had come to Washington reluctantly, with the purpose of managing the most

515

pressing negotiations and then retiring. He had had no desire to be involved in the Presidential election either on his own behalf or anyone else's (including John Tyler's). The defection of Van Buren and friends to the Whigs on the Texas issue, however, had made it necessary to take a hand in assisting the Democratic party to find its correct ground.

To Wharton he expressed his deepest reflections on the situation that had been revealed by the Texas imbroglio. The South had always showed a willingness to defend the interests of the North against foreign threats. Now that the South was threatened, the North had failed to reciprocate. "There is something wrong in all this, and not a little ominous for the duration of our system," Calhoun concluded.

〚〛

From WILLIAM G. AUSTIN

St. Francisville La., May 16th 1844

Dear Sir, You might ask with some degree of propriety why an humble individual like myself should attempt to solicit a correspondence with yourself Or rather I would say solicit you ["to suffer yourself" *canceled*] to become a candidate for the Presidency. Sir you will pardon me when I tell you that I have been a strong State rights man ever since I was entitled to a vote which was in 1832 & long before that when a boy I was taught to revere the name of Calhoun[,] the advocate of Republican principles and the rights of the States. Sir I saw with regret the course pursued by some of the would be leaders of the republican party in some of the eastern States in order that they might defeat your nomination & nominate a man that has done but little for his counntry [*sic*] & one that can not possibly succeed, I mean Mr. [Martin] Van buren. I heartily approved of your course at that time, in refusing to let your name go before that packed convention, but now sir matters & things are changed. The South will not support Martin Van Buren and still farther will she be from supporting Henry Clay. You sir are the onley man we can look to for success. The Texas Question has Killed Clay & Van buren in the South. Allready have large meetings taken place in New Orleans & various parts of our State for the purpose of ["nomination" *altered to* "nominating"] you for the presidency. Living on the Mississippi river as I do I have a great opportunity of learning from western men there [*sic*] views relative to Vanburen or Clay, & I am told that you are decidedly more popular than either of them, & besides you are there choice (["of" *altered to* "among"] all other men) for the presidency & I do hope you will pay no attention to that Vanburen Convention in Baltimore, But will come out for the good of your Country. By suffering your name to go before the people you have nothing to fear, your election is certain. I would be glad to see some one answer Vanburen ["& Clay" *interlined*] on the Texas Question. If you are not a candidate many of your fr[i]ends will not vote in the election & the consequence will be Clay will be elected & then we will have his odious measures palmed upon us, such as Tarriff &c. I would be glad if you would give me your views relative to this war with Mexico. Have we not a right to an[n]ex Texas[?] If you will ["pleas(e)" *interlined*] give me a few lines Directed to St. Francisville[,] West Feliciana [Parish,] Louisiana. I have lately mooved to this Parish from Mississippi. Respectfully your unworthy Servant, William G. Austin, M.D.

N.B. I saw one of your nephews Lawrance [*sic;* James Lawrence] Calhoun the other day in New Orleans. He has lost his wife [Nancy Hunter Calhoun] & his brother Capt. Thomas Calhoun, also his wife[']s Brother James Hunter died the other day. Wm. G.A.

ALS in ScCleA; PEx in Boucher and Brooks, eds., *Correspondence*, pp. 230–231. NOTE: An AEU by Calhoun reads "W.G. Austin[,] relates to my self."

From J[OHN] S. BARBOUR

Catalpa [Culpeper County, Va.] May 16th 1844
My Dear Sir, At my return last night yours of the 11th [*not found*] was put into my hands. I agree thoroughly with you in all that you say. In some respects promptness & energy will be our duty, in others the Augustan maxim *festina lente* [make haste slowly] will give a wise precept for action. Hitherto we have in some measure committed ourselves to the fortunes of Mr. [Martin] Van Buren. Publick opinion is rapidly evolving its discontent with him. Yet your friends who were committed to him will be vulnerable to harsher suspicions than those of any other party. We must show that we were willing in good faith *to redeem honourably,* our pledges. But

that the new developements present us the alternatives of life or death. And[?] the treachery of a man (who ought to have been grappled to us of the South ["by the ties & plies of gratitude" *interlined*] with hooks of triple Steel) [*one word canceled and* "releases" *interlined*] us from every purpose or promise of & to his support. We need the support of the whole party. Let us show that we deserve it, by ["our" *interlined*] fidelity to all reasonable expectations, until imperative duty compelled us to quit his support. This is the true ground on which to stand & it is the ground on which we may honourably stand & successfully combat. We agreed to go into State Convention. We did so & were out numbered. We yielded to the influence of the principle expressed & implied that carried us into Convention. *We* have done the best battle for *their* cause—our adversaries admit & applaud our fidelity. There is no treachery to stain us, no suspicion to impeach us in the secret thoughts or open acts & words of the friends of V[an] B[uren]. Our escutcheon has no blemish on it, in the eyes of friend or the distrust of foes. The new position of parties, the Treason of our leader, his abandonment of the *Sanctum Sanctorum,* & the conservatism that is in it; have all combined to withdraw from him his best friends—his original friends. In this withdrawal (& the manifestations of it), we prefer that his original friends shall take the lead. When they are the first to cry out that "we are betrayed," we can without crimination, maintain our first position, & support our known & primary choice. We go into the contest with all the moral power, that lofty & unsullied motives can give us. I regret that I was not a Delegate to Balt[im]o[re]. I did not think it proper after signing the address of your friends at Richmond. And it w[oul]d have been inconsistent with your publication. I now think that I will go there. I have other business both at Washington & Balt[im]o[re]. It is the season for Spring purchases for my family and I will probably go on with part of my family.

I should be glad to hear promptly from you & especially from Mr. [Richard K.] Cralle. Next Monday the people are to meet here.

The assemblage will be large. I shall doubtless be called to address. I am obliged to be cautious. Everything I say, (if I had not heard from you for months) is set down as your wishes. A legion of Oaths & witnesses could not disabuse the minds of many from this delusion. Everything looks well. I agree with you perfectly as to [John] Tyler. His ambition has warped a candid mind, that nature & early education, put in a true place & gave to it a true direction. These are my views, but I agree with you that he is greatly preferable *if we could get him.* That is impossible but we can do better. Y[ou]r friend, J.S. Barbour.

N.B. You see that I write with a flying pen.

ALS in ScCleA; PEx's in Boucher and Brooks, eds., *Correspondence*, pp. 229–230.

From Edw[ard] Bates, St. Louis, 5/16. Bates, the defense attorney for John McDaniel who was sentenced to be executed on 6/14, submits a statement of the trial proceedings, which he feels were very rigid and predisposed to convict his client. Bates believes that the case [which occurred on the Santa Fe trail] should not have been tried in the U.S. District Court in Missouri and cites at some length various statutes in support of his opinion. He asks that Calhoun review the case and recommend a respite for McDaniel on the basis of "the justice of the verdict, the jurisdiction of the Court, or the regularity of the proceeding." He finds it "hard that the errors of a federal Court sitting among us should be incapable of legal correction—final and fatal." Two ALS's in DNA, RG 59 (State Department), Petitions for Pardon and Related Briefs, 1800–1849, no. 292A.

From Edm[un]d S. Derry, New York [City], 5/16. He writes in support of Gerard H. Coster's wish to act as despatch bearer. Derry states that Coster is from a very prominent, well respected N.Y. family "and this mark of your respect towards them might not be ill advised." ALS in DNA, RG 59 (State Department), Passport Applications, vol. 31, unnumbered (M-1372:14).

To Edward Everett

Department of State
Washington, 16th May, 1844

Sir: It appears from the accompanying transcript of a letter from Mr. Shepard Cary [Representative from Maine] to this Department, of the 11th instant, that a company, composed of American citizens and British subjects, some time since erected a boom across the mouth of the Aroostook, and within the Province of New Brunswick, for the security of the owners of logs and other lumber manufactured upon that river and its tributaries. The assent of Maine was afterwards prospectively given, with certain limitations, by a resolve dated 3d

March, 1843, (copy enclosed,) to an act of incorporation by the authorities of New Brunswick, extending to the corporations the right to erect such boom; and at the last session of the Provincial Legislature, an act of incorporation was accordingly obtained embracing the restrictions and conditions contained in the resolve of Maine, subject to the approval of the home Government. Maine and New Brunswick having thus signified their assent to the measure, the Provincial Act has, it is understood, been sent to England for the purpose referred to, and the citizens of Maine, who have much the larger interest in the timber trade on the Aroostook, are desirous that your good offices should be employed in endeavoring to attract to this subject the prompt and favorable notice of Her Majesty's Government. I have, therefore, to request that you will, in informal conferences with Her Majesty's Principal Secretary of State for Foreign Affairs, and by such other means as you may deem best calculated to attain the end in view, use your best efforts to promote the object of Mr. Cary's application.

You will also receive herewith copies of certain papers, (of which a list is annexed,) relative to an act of the Parliament of New Brunswick, passed on the 25th day of March last, imposing an export duty of one shilling (twenty cents) per ton on all timber shipped from any port in that Province, and releasing all claims for the right to cut timber on the Crown lands. A communication on the subject has been addressed to this Department by certain citizens of the State of Maine, complaining of the proposed exaction as an infringement of the letter and spirit of the stipulations contained in the 3d article of the treaty of Washington, of the 9th of August, 1842; going into an argumentative examination of the construction to be given to that article, and of the nature of the rights secured by it to the citizens of the United States; and asking the intervention of this Department with the British Government to defeat this measure of the Provincial Parliament.

As a perseverance in this policy by the British Provincial Authorities must seriously and injuriously affect the interests of many American citizens, and as the proposed exaction appears to be in obvious violation of conventional stipulations existing between the United States and Great Britain, you will lose no time in calling the attention of Lord Aberdeen to the subject, with a view to procure the total abandonment of this policy on the part of the Province of New Brunswick, and the adoption by Her Majesty's Government of such measures as shall insure, hereafter, a strict observance of the obligations of the treaty. I am, Sir, very respectfully, Your obedient servant, J.C. Calhoun.

List of accompanying papers.

Boom across the Aroostook.

Mr. Shepard Cary to the Secretary of
State, dated 11th May, 1844.   Copy.

Resolve of Legislature of Maine, 3d March, 1843.

Duty on American timber in New Brunswick.

Edward Kent to the Secretary of State, 28th March, 1844.   "

Printed letter from citizens of Maine
to same   "   "   "

Edward Kent to Secretary of State (one
enclosure)   4th April,   "   "

John Fairfield to the President,   26th   "   "   "

Massachusetts ["Senators" *interlined*]
and Maine Delegation in Congress
to the President U.S.

"Royal Gazette" of 3d April, 1844, containing act of
Provincial Parliament (7 Vict. c. 18) relating to
collection of duty on Timber, &c, passed 25th
March, 1844.

("R.G." published at Fredericton, N.B.)

LS (No. 87) with Ens in DNA, RG 84 (Foreign Posts), Great Britain, Instructions, 8:159–242, received 6/15; FC in DNA, RG 59 (State Department), Diplomatic Instructions, Great Britain, 15:194–196 (M-77:74); PC with Ens in House Document No. 110, 29th Cong., 1st Sess., pp. 4–18; PC in Jameson, ed., *Correspondence*, pp. 587–588.

From EDWARD EVERETT

London, 16 May 1844

Sir, I yesterday received your despatch number 84 of the 27th of April, transmitting sundry additional applications in behalf of American citizens, now imprisoned in Van Diemen's Land for their participation in the revolutionary movements in Canada in the year 1838. I have lost no time in addressing a note to Lord Aberdeen in their favor, and have sent with it a selection of the memorials and applications. I doubt not I shall shortly be able to give information of their having been pardoned.

Some delay may be expected in the cases of Joseph Thompson and Robert Marsh, represented to have been resident in Canada at the time of taking up arms, and in reference to whom the favorable report of the Governor General will be waited for.

Three of the individuals whose pardon is solicited, in the papers transmitted with your despatch Nro. 84, having already been set at liberty, vizt. David Allen, whose case is referred to in my despatch Nro. 94, & Bemis Woodbury, and George T. Brown, who are in the list of those referred to in my number 120, by this steamer, I withdrew the memorials in their favor. I am, sir, very respectfully, your obedient servant, Edward Everett.

Transmitted with Despatch 127.

Mr. Everett to the Earl of Aberdeen, 16 May 1844.

LS (No. 127) with En in DNA, RG 59 (State Department), Diplomatic Despatches, Great Britain, vol. 52 (M-30:48), received 6/3; FC in DNA, RG 84 (Foreign Posts), Great Britain, Despatches, 8:229–230; FC in MHi, Edward Everett Papers, 49:83–85 (published microfilm, reel 23, frames 41–42).

From BEN E. GREEN

Legation of the U.S. of A.
Mexico, May 16th 1844

Sir, I have the honor to inform you that no money has yet been paid on account of the Instalment, due on the 30th ult[im]o. I send you (nos. 1 & 2) a note [of 5/4/1844], which I addressed to the Minister of F[oreign] R[elations], José M. de Bocanegra] upon the subject, and his reply [of 5/6/1844], in which he promises that it shall be paid on the 7th Inst[ant]. Notwithstanding this, they still hold back, with their usual excuse, "tomorrow"; expecting from day to day to hear of the annexation of Texas, which will offer an excuse for not paying at all.

I send you files of the Diario del Gobierno, the official paper, in which the subject of Texas is treated with much warmth. In the paper of the 14th inst[ant], you will see a proclamation, calling together the Congress, for the purpose (as therein expressed) of increasing the army & of taking steps to reconquer Texas, and to "preserve the security and independence of the Republic."

In that of the 13th is contained the resignation of Gen[era]l [J.M.] Tornel, which has caused much surprise. It is in fact a dismissal. Santa Anna, it is said, is displeased at the honors, with which Tornel caused himself to be received on the occasion of a recent visit to Puebla.

The president, Santa Anna, is expected to reach the city shortly. The convocation of the Congress is an unexpected movement. It will depend on their pliancy how long they will be permitted to sit.

The country is in a very unsettled condition, and discontent is brewing in the Departments. You have already been informed of the Revolution of the Gaudaras in Sonora. Gen[era]l [José] Urrea, the Governor of that Department, was recently superseded and Gen[era]l Ponce de Leon appointed in his place. It has been rumoured in this city for several days that Urrea has refused to yeild to the latter: that he has joined the Gaudaras and is marching upon Mazatlan, & that as soon as he has taken that port and secured what money may be there, it is his intention to declare Sonora & Sinaloa independent. Threatening rumors are also received from the northern provinces. (See the article upon Tamaulipas in the Diario of the 14th.) I have no certain information of the truth of these rumors; but have reason to believe that the northern provinces are much disaffected. I have the honor to be Very Respectfully Your ob[edien]t Serv[an]t, Ben E. Green.

ALS (No. 4) and 2 Ens (with a State Department translation) in DNA, RG 59 (State Department), Diplomatic Despatches, Mexico, vol. 12 (M-97:13), received 6/24; FC in DNA, RG 84 (Foreign Posts), Mexico, Despatches, pp. 493–494; PEx with Ens in Senate Document No. 81, 28th Cong., 2nd Sess., pp. 13–14; PEx with Ens in House Document No. 144, 28th Cong., 2nd Sess., p. 14.

From JOHN L. H. MCCRACKEN

New York [City,] 16 May 1844

Dear Sir, In reply to yours of 14th I will state to you briefly what Mr. [Fernando] Wood is charged with, & on what evidence I receive the charge. If further particulars should be wanted for any purpose, I shall readily give my attention to obtain them if desired.

Mr. Wood kept a bank account in this city (I think with the Lafayette Bank) where he discovered that a sum of money had been placed to his credit by mistake—about $1400—which money he drew out and used; and the error on the part of the bank was not discovered for some months, or even years; I cannot now say how long this time was; but it was more than ample to give *him* time to find his mistake if he had made one. When the Bank discovered the mistake they sued him for the amount; and the circumstances became public in the report of the trial. Mr. Wood attempted to clear himself of the charge of appropriating this money intentionally & fraudulently; but his exculpation did not appear to be sufficient; ["but" *canceled*] on the contrary the amount of money which he was used to have on hand at any one time, appeared to be so small as to render it morally certain he could not have received an accession of $1400 without perceiving it. Part of his defence consisted in showing that some of his books had been destroyed by a fire, and especially the bank book which contained the portion of his account in question.

Mr. Wood has been personally civil to me & has taken some pains to be so—though I do not know him by sight. I would much rather do him a kindness than an injury; and have interfered in this matter reluctantly, and solely under the influence of motives which my note to Mr. [Robert Barnwell] Rhett has no doubt explained to you. With the highest respect I remain, Sir, Your Ob[edien]t Serv[an]t, John L.H. McCracken.

ALS in ScCleA.

From David McDaniel, St. Louis Prison, 5/16. "Will you be so kind as to get the Editor of the [Washington] "Spectator" to publish the enclosed "Sketch"; the *truth* of which no person *can* or *will* deny. You will find your unfortunate fellow-being forever obliged to you for your kindness." ALS in DNA, RG 59 (State Department), Petitions for Pardon and Related Briefs, 1800–1849, no. 292A.

From Sam[ue]l McLean, U.S. Consul at Trinidad, Cuba, 5/16. He encloses copies of correspondence with the Captain General of Cuba [Leopoldo O'Donnell] which show his refusal to recognize the appointment of a U.S. Consul at Cienfuegos. ALS (No. 41) with Ens in DNA, RG 59 (State Department), Consular Despatches, Trinidad, Cuba, vol. 2 (T-699:2), received 6/14.

From F[RANCIS] W. PICKENS

Edgewood [Edgefield District, S.C.] 16 May '44
My dear Sir, On my return a few days since from my River place I found yours which I ought to have rec[eive]d a week ago. I will try & get a meeting 1[st] Monday in June. You know we can get no

meetings of importance except on sale days. However I think it well that we do not meet too soon. We ought to see the whole ground and give others in Va.[,] N. Ca[rolina,] Geor[gia] &c [the chance] to move if they will, for whenever So[uth] Ca[rolina] moves first there are thousands who fall back under the everlasting slang of "So[uth] Ca[rolina] ultraism[,] So[uth] Ca[rolina] Disunion &c." There is no dif[f]iculty in our taking the highest position. As I hear nothing from any one ["from" *canceled*] at Washington I am ignorant of all the under currents that are running there now.

I am rejoiced to see Va. moving as she is at this time. By a high & bold course at this juncture she can do much not only to save this Union but to give permanent protection & tranquility to the South, and if she vacillates and betrays her power & her honor into the hands of New York, this Union is gone & God only knows the blood & ruin that must follow.

If the Texas treaty is lost (& I take it for granted it will be & I never for a moment believed otherwise from the first) it will make a new division of parties, & even if [Henry] Clay comes in now (& I think he will) his Adm[inistration] will be broken up in the first three months—it cannot stand together. I am inclined then to think that your name will be placed at the head of the most powerful party that has ever risen in this country not excepting the party in 1828 that brought [Andrew] Jackson into power. It will give you the Government under the very best possible condition of things that could happen.

I was security for Gen[era]l [Alexander O.?] Anderson on a note in the *Metropolis* Bank (I think it was or perhaps it may be the Bank of Washington) for $5,000, and I have heard not a word of it since. Although I have written the Gen[era]l about it he has not answered at all. I directed to Washington but perhaps he may have left. When I signed he assured me that the Bank had agreed to take pay for the note out of a contract he had made with the War Department to remove some Cherokee Indians &c—& that I would not run any risk at all as this was the agreement & the contract was good for $30,000 &c. Now you know my dread of being in any pecuniary difficulty at all. [*Marginal interpolation*: "One reason of this dread is that I have no near relation at all who could take charge of my affairs, if I should die, & I have only helpless little girls whose interests are involved. My situation is peculiar & I therefore avoid all obligations."] Will you therefore be kind enough to cause information to be given me as to the true state *of the note* & my liabilities & the probability of its being paid &c. The note was given in March *1843.* I do not wish you to do any thing inconvenient or disagreeable to you, but if you could give ["the" *canceled*] me the information I desire on this point I would take it as a great personal favour. I think very strangely Gen[era]l Anderson has never written me a word about it, particularly as I advanced him at the same time all the money I had to purchase in his house & place for his family. This of course is confidential between us.

We have the most parching drought I ever knew at this season. I have 500 acres of oats that will be utterly ruined without rain in a very few days. It is dreadful hot too & has been for weeks—the Thermometer at 84° to 87° & 88° constantly—nearly all day too. I never had such a prospect of corn & cotton in my life. The cotton is nearly 4 weeks more forward than last year—it will bloom the 1st week in June, or by the 10th at furthest.

I have been so much engaged in planting &c that I have had no time to read the papers even. I had no idea that I could have so entirely lost all my relish for politics.

Anna [Maria Calhoun Clemson] & family were perfectly well when I heard & she is perfectly happy with her new situation, & I hear Mr. [Thomas G.] Clemson is much more interested now than he was. I am going out to see them in a week. Very truly & sincerely, F.W. Pickens.

ALS in ScCleA; PEx in Boucher and Brooks, eds., *Correspondence*, pp. 228–229.

To [JOHN TYLER]

Department of State
Washington, 16th May, 1844

To the President of the United States.

In compliance with the directions of the President, I have the honor to submit to him herewith, the enclosed copies and extracts of correspondence, calculated to show what will probably be the course of the government of Texas in the event that the treaty of annexation should at this time fail.

It will be perceived that among the papers are one from General Andrew Jackson, and one from President [Samuel] Houston to General Jackson. The writers of the other letters are believed from information which I have received from sources worthy of credit, to be gentlemen of high respectability, with ample means of obtaining information on the subject. Their statements are believed to be fully entitled to credit.

The parts of the correspondence omitted, are either irrelevant, or have a personal bearing. Respectfully submitted, J.C. Calhoun.

LS with Ens in DNA, RG 46 (U.S. Senate), 28B-B12; FC in DNA, RG 59 (State Department), Reports of the Secretary of State to the President and Congress, 6:102; PC with Ens in House Document No. 271, 28th Cong., 1st Sess., pp. 102–110; PC with Ens in the Washington, D.C., *Spectator*, July 16, 1844, pp. 1–2; PC with Ens in the Washington, D.C., *Daily Madisonian*, July 17, 1844, p. 2. NOTE: Calhoun's letter and enclosed documents were transmitted by Tyler to the Senate on 5/16. Their point was to sustain Tyler's contention that if the treaty of annexation then before the Senate was not approved, the opportunity of annexing Texas might be lost forever. Enclosed were copied extracts of six documents: the letter that appears above in this volume "from an unidentified Texan," 4/20/1844; the letter above to Calhoun from M[ilford] P. Norton, 4/29/1844, without the author identified; an unidentified Texan from Galveston to Abel P. Upshur, 11/20/1843; A.C. Allen, Houston, to Senator Robert J. Walker, 3/1/-1844; Andrew Jackson to an unidentified person, 3/11/1844; and Sam Houston to Jackson, 2/16/1844.

To [JOHN TYLER]

Department of State
Washington, 16th May, 1844

To the President of the United States.

The Secretary of State, to whom was referred the Resolution of the Senate of the 13th instant, requesting the President to communicate to that body the copy of the armistice agreed upon between Mexico and Texas, and a copy of President [Samuel] Houston's Proclamation declaring the same, provided the evidence of such armistice and proclamation be in the Department of State, has the honor to lay before the President a copy of and extracts from all the papers on file in this department which relate to the subject of the Resolution. Respectfully submitted, J.C. Calhoun.

LS with Ens in DNA, RG 46 (U.S. Senate), 28B-B12; FC in DNA, RG 59 (State Department), Reports from the Secretary of State to the President and Congress, 6:102; PC with Ens in House Document No. 271, 28th Cong., 1st Sess., pp. 82–86; PC with Ens in Senate Document No. 341, 28th Cong., 1st Sess., pp. 83–87; PC with Ens in the Washington, D.C., *Daily Madisonian*, May 24, 1844, p. 2; PC with Ens in the Washington, D.C., *Daily National Intelligencer*, May 24, 1844, p. 1; PC with Ens in the Charleston, S.C., *Mercury*, May 29, 1844, p. 2; PC with Ens in *Niles' National Register*, vol. LXVI, no. 16 (June 15, 1844), pp. 251–252.

NOTE: Tyler transmitted this letter and its accompanying documents to the Senate on 5/17. Enclosed were a letter from William S. Murphy to the Secretary of State, 6/16/1843, enclosing President Houston's armistice proclamation of 6/15/1843; J.M. Tornel, Mexican Minister of War, to General Adrian Woll, "commander-in-chief of the army of the north," 7/7/1843, ordering an armistice (translation); Waddy Thompson, Jr., Mexico, to Abel P. Upshur, 2/2/1844, reporting that peace negotiations have been broken off and the armistice suspended; Calhoun to Isaac Van Zandt and J. Pinckney Henderson, 5/15/1844, and their reply of 5/16/1844. The Senate resolution of 5/13, to which this letter was a response, can be found in RG 59 (State Department), Miscellaneous Letters (M-179:104, frame 353) and in *Senate Executive Journal,* 6:276.

From ISAAC VAN ZANDT and
J. PINCKNEY HENDERSON

Legation of Texas
Washington, May 16th 1844

The Undersigned &C., &C. in reply to the note of Mr. Calhoun ["Secretary of State of the United States" *interlined*] of yesterday['] s date, have the honor to submit for his information the following facts, in relation to the origin and history of the alledged armistice between Mexico and Texas, to which he refers.

By the terms of a convention, concluded between Texas and Great Britain on the 14th of November 1840, the British Government agreed to offer its mediation for the settlement of the difficulties between Mexico and Texas, upon the basis of the recognition of the Independence of Texas by Mexico. In pursuance of this convention, the mediation of Great Britain was tendered to, and declined by Mexico, information of which was communicated to the President of Texas [Samuel Houston]. Afterwards in the year 1842 representations were made, by Texas to Great Britain, France, and the United States, requesting their joint interposition for the settlement of the difficulties between Mexico and Texas. To this request the Governments of France and the United States indicated their ready willingness to accede. The British Government however for reasons deemed by it sufficient declined to be thus associated, suggesting at the same time that each might act separately. Subsequently the Texian Chargé d'Affaires in London [Ashbel Smith], was informed by the Minister of Foreign Affairs of the British Government [Lord Aberdeen] that the mediation, as before pursued, was utterly hopeless, and that Her

Majesty's Chargé d'Affaires in Mexico [Percy W. Doyle] had been directed to propose a *new feature* in the same to Mexico.

In the month of May 1843, in reply to the representations upon the subject, made by Her Britannic Majesty's Chargé de'Affaires in Mexico, to Gen[era]l Santa Anna, the latter indicated his willingness to agree to a suspension of hostilities, and to receive commissioners from Texas to treat on the terms of a peace. This fact was communicated by Her Britannic Majesty's Chargé d'Affaires in Texas [Charles Elliot] to the President of Texas, on the 10th of June 1843, who, on the 15th of the same month, issued his proclamation for an armistice, annexing certain stipulations, by which it should be terminated. When these were communicated to Gen[era]l Santa Anna, through the British Chargé d'Affaires, he declined to assent to them, suggesting that it would be better that the terms, duration &C should be arranged by Commissioners, appointed by the respective Governments, for that purpose. Information of this was communicated to the Texian Government, both, through the British Chargé d'Affaires in Texas and in a communication from Gen[era]l [Adrian] Woll to Gen[era]l [Samuel] Houston, in which it was stated, in substance, that he (Gen[era]l Woll) was authorized, by Gen[era]l Santa Anna, to appoint commissioners to meet any persons, similarly commissioned by Texas, to arrange the proposed armistice. In pursuance of this the Texian Commissioners were appointed and proceeded to Mexico. They were instructed that no arrangement made by them would be binding until approved by the President. When the agreement entered into by them was submitted ["by" *canceled*] to the President of Texas, he declined approving it. Refer[r]ing to Texas as a Department of Mexico was a sufficient reason for its prompt rejection, and precluded all possibility of official action under it.

The negotiations having thus terminated, and this agreement being held to be null and void, there is at present no subsisting arrangement of any character between Mexico and Texas.

The Undersigned avail themselves of this occasion to offer to Mr. Calhoun renewed assurances of their distinguished consideration. Isaac Van Zandt, J. Pinckney Henderson.

LS in DNA, RG 59 (State Department), Notes from Foreign Legations, Texas, vol. 1 (T-809:1); FC (dated 5/15) in Tx, Records of the Texas Republic Department of State, Letters and Dispatches Sent by the Texas Legation in Washington, 1:509–512; FC (dated 5/15) in Tx, Records of the Texas Republic Department of State, Copybooks of Letters Received from Texan and Foreign Representatives, vol. 2-1/98, pp. [500–501]; CC (dated 5/15) in Tx, Records of the Texas Republic Department of State, U.S. Diplomatic Correspondence; CC in DNA, RG 46 (U.S. Senate), 28B-B12; PC in *Congressional Globe*, 28th Cong., 1st Sess.,

Appendix, p. 554; PC in Senate Document No. 341, 28th Cong., 1st Sess., pp. 86–87; PC in House Document No. 271, 28th Cong., 1st Sess., pp. 85–86; PC in the Washington, D.C., *Daily National Intelligencer,* May 24, 1844, p. 1; PC in the Washington, D.C., *Globe,* May 24, 1844, p. 2; PC in the Washington, D.C., *Daily Madisonian,* May 24, 1844, p. 2; PC in the Charleston, S.C., *Courier,* May 29, 1844, p. 2; PC in *Niles' National Register,* vol. LXVI, no. 16 (June 15, 1844), pp. 251–252.

To W[illia]m S. Archer, [Chairman of the Senate Committee on Foreign Relations], 5/17. "I take leave to transmit to you a copy of a despatch recently received from Mr. [Henry] Wheaton, containing information which it is supposed may prove useful to you." [Enclosed was Wheaton's despatch No. 245 of 3/30 with statistical information "illustrating the great importance of the Tobacco trade between the United States and Germany." This En is identified not by Calhoun's letter but by endorsements on the despatch of 3/30 itself: LS in DNA, RG 59 (State Department), Diplomatic Despatches, Germany, vol. 3 (M-44:4).] FC in DNA, RG 59 (State Department), Domestic Letters, 34:203 (M-40:32).

To Francis M. Auboyneau, 5/17. Calhoun informs Auboyneau that he has been nominated and confirmed as U.S. Consul at La Rochelle and sends documents related to the office. FC in DNA, RG 59 (State Department), Consular Instructions, 12:82.

To William Bevan, Bridgeton, N.J., 5/17. In response to Bevan's letter of 5/14 concerning the seizure of the schooner *Vigilant* by Mexico, Calhoun states that the U.S. Consul at Vera Cruz has been directed to obtain information, upon the receipt of which the State Department will determine proper measures of redress. LS in DNA, RG 76 (Records of Boundary and Claims Commissions and Arbitrations), U.S. and Mexican Claims Commissions; FC in DNA, RG 59 (State Department), Domestic Letters, 34:198–199 (M-40:32).

To Henry J. Brent, "Care of Tho[ma]s Aspinwall, Esq., U.S. C[onsul at] London," 5/17. Calhoun informs Brent that he has been appointed and confirmed as U.S. Consul for Ravenna in Italy and encloses materials relevant to the duties of the office. FC in DNA, RG 59 (State Department), Consular Instructions, 10:246–247.

To Robert P. De Silver, 5/17. Calhoun notifies De Silver that he has been appointed and confirmed as U.S. Consul at Port Louis, Isle de France, [Mauritius]. Calhoun encloses materials related to the duties of the office. Application is to be made in London for De

Silver's exequatur, which will be sent to him when obtained. FC in DNA, RG 59 (State Department), Consular Instructions, 12:82.

To Joseph W. "Fabers" [*sic*; Fabens], 5/17. Calhoun notifies him of his appointment and confirmation as U.S. Consul at Cayenne, French Guiana, and encloses documents related to the duties of the office. FC in DNA, RG 59 (State Department), Consular Instructions, 12:82.

To Paul S. Forbes, U.S. Consul at Canton, 5/17. "Your nomination as Consul of the United States for Canton having been confirmed by the Senate, I herewith transmit to you your Commission." FC in DNA, RG 59 (State Department), Consular Instructions, 10:245.

From GEORGE R. GLIDDON, "Confidential"

Globe Hotel, New York [City,] 17th May 1844
Sir, A singular and unexpected affair, the heads of which are given in the annexed "New World," has prevented my having the honor of addressing you at earlier moments, but, during my passage through Philadelphia, I left a few lines of introduction to your correspondence, in favor of my distinguished friend, Sam[ue]l Geo[rge] Morton, M.D., who (probably ere this) has had the advantage of transmitting to you his two Works, "Crania Americana" and "[Crania] Aegyptiaca"; with a letter expressive of his desire to furnish you with all kinds of ethnographical materials.

I have now the gratification to subjoin three of my little Pamphlets; viz.

1–"Memoir on the Cotton of Egypt"; } London—1841.
1–"Appeal to the Antiquaries of Europe["]; }

2 Copies of my "Ancient Egypt";—New York—1843.
in favor of which I crave your indulgence.

These trifles have been *given* away to the public; nor have I any pecuniary object or interest in their wide circulation. Of the "Chapters" the publishers have sold 16,000 copies, in one year. Each one has been forced upon me by circumstances, which compelled me to oppose *facts* to opinions engendered by ignorance, and promulgated by hostile partisanship, in order that, in the race of life, I might not be altogether distanced by my fellows. Such are my only apologies for their humble form, and errors of style and typography.

531

In their rambling pages, your glance will perceive many *Oriental* facts, bearing on some of those vast Southern interests, which may be said to centre in your name and person—*facts*, which are certainly but little known in England, and which the cant of the day seems anxious to suppress. These, if interesting, can be extended at your command.

The subject of *Cotton* has suggested an addition, which is appended to the "Memoir."

Points relating to *Slavery* in *modern* Egypt are scattered throughout the two London "Brochures": while the "Chapters on Hierology" have cut *Negro*-questions away from all confusion with the earliest denizens of that most ancient Country—whose *monumental* history extends to at least 2750 years B.C. Dr. Morton's researches prove, that Negro-Races have ever been *servants* and *slaves*, always distinct from, and subject to, the *Caucasian*, in the remotest times.

I have long arrived at the conviction, that our current *illusions*, on these important questions, arise from the false translation of our *English* version; wherein we have misunderstood the meaning of the *original* Genesis of Moses. I have indicated one instance in relation to *Cotton*—nor will I adopt errors perpetuated by the shallowness of bigoted commentators, whose ignorance of *Science* leads them to twist Scripture to their theories, and vainly endeavor to stem the onward march of *Truth*. Yet, Genesis can outlive them all; and, our admiration for the *Science* of Moses, "learned in all the wisdom of the *Egyptians*"—who flourished *1000* years *after* the Great Pyramid!—will rise in exact ratio to the advance of knowledge. Moses will be vindicated in regard to *Ethnography*, more forcibly than even in Geology.

To collect the *evidences*, for this crude opinion of my own, serves to wile away my hours of monotony; but the materials, time, and means required, far exceeds the contracted limits of my trumpery sphere.

Deem me not presumptuous, Sir, in trespassing on your invaluable time with themes that, however interesting to me, are not of a nature for epistolary elucidation. You will generously forgive the impulse caused by your urbanity to one, who had no claim upon your patient hearing, and who has been excited by the depth of your Statesmanlike remarks.

Permit me to assure you, Sir, that (so far as my narrow observation extends) independently of all political associations, or your elevated official position, whenever *you* desire the solution of any *ethnographical* problem, in respect to *African*-subjects, the cooperation of the following Gentlemen is important and accessible; each in different branches, and in infinitely diversified measures—Dr. *Morton* of Philadelphia—Dr. [John E.] *Holbrook* of Charleston, S.C.—W[illiam] B. *Hodgson* Esq. of Savannah—and Richard K. *Haight* Esq. of New York. The resources of these Gentlemen, when viewed collectively, exceed all others in the world, in a new branch of Science of which Dr. *Morton* is the mastermind. In short, we have any amount of *facts* at our disposal to support and confirm all those doctrines, that, for so long and bright a period, have marked the illustrious career of *John C. Calhoun.*

At a very great distance my own studies lead me in the same direction; but, beyond my readiness to comply with your respected behests to the extent of my feeble ability, I am too conscious of the insignificance of my attainments, to do more than declare myself, with respect and admiration, Sir, Y[ou]r mo[st] obliged & ob[e]d[ien]t Serv[an]t, George R. Gliddon.

ALS in ScCleA. NOTE: George R. Gliddon was the son and brother-in-law of John Gliddon and Alexander Tod, successive U.S. Consuls at Alexandria, Egypt. A work by George R. Gliddon and Josiah C. Nott, *Types of Mankind: or Ethnological Researches* . . . (Philadelphia: Lippincott, Grambo & Co., c. 1854), pp. 50–52, describes Gliddon's conversations and visits with Calhoun during 5/1844 and later and reports remarks by Calhoun on the distinctness of the races and the relevance of that to the problems of the statesman.

From [the Rev.] Joseph Grisham, West Union, S.C., 5/17. He asks that Calhoun use his influence to obtain a pardon for [David and John] McDaniel, Grisham's relatives. Grisham has recently seen a newspaper article that suggests that the court that tried the McDaniels had no jurisdiction. (An AEU by Calhoun reads "The case of John McDaniel.") ALS in DNA, RG 59 (State Department), Petitions for Pardon and Related Briefs, 1800–1849, no. 292A.

To [JAMES H.] HAMMOND, Governor [of S.C.]

Washington, 17th May 1844

My dear Sir, I discovered shortly after I enclosed you the letter of Mr. [Richard] Pakenham, that the wrong one was by accident transmitted. I will thank you to return it. The one intended related to a man of the name of [John L.] Brown, who had been condemned [in S.C.] for enticing a way a negro, but who it was discovered had been pardoned. Mr. Pakenham wrote me a private note in reference to his case, originating in the request of some of his friends in Ireland.

The fate of the treaty is not yet decided. The prospect is that it will be rejected; but I am not without hope, that the Senate will approve. There is not a doubt in my mind, that if Texas should not now be annexed, she is lost to our Union. The Senate has been furnished with evidence to that effect, perfectly conclusive. I hope, that it may change the votes of the Whigs Senators from the South & west, especially if backed by a strong expression of publick opinion in favour of annexation in those sections. It is to us a question of life & death. Every city, town & County & District in the South & west ["must" *canceled*] should speak out promptly & loudly. Strange as it may seem, [Thomas H.] Benton & his wing object to the admission among other things, because in my letter to Mr. Pakenham, I should dare place the issue where it does! This, with many other things, clearly prove, that [Martin] V[an] B[uren] was courting the abolitionists. Thank God both of them lie prostrate, never to rise. They have done the party & country infinite mischief.

My letter was intended to lay the foundation, on which to stand in the future progress of the correspondence. I shall rise at every step untill England shall be placed on the defensive. I only ask the South to stand by me. Now is the time to vindicate ["& save" *interlined*] our institutions. If this tide is lost we shall never have another. Why do you all, I mean our men of influence & leisure, like yourself, not put in your pens at this great crisis? Our papers ought to be crow[d]ed with animated communications. Truly, J.C. Calhoun.

ALS in DLC, James Henry Hammond Papers, vol. 11; PC in Jameson, ed., *Correspondence*, pp. 588–589.

To Michael Kennedy, care of Sidney Breese, Senator [from Ill.], 5/17. Calhoun informs Kennedy that he has been nominated and confirmed as U.S. Consul at Galway, Ireland, and encloses documents related to the duties of the office. FC in DNA, RG 59 (State Department), Consular Instructions, 12:82.

From JOHN L. H. MCCRACKEN

New York [City,] 17 May 1844

Dear Sir, The New Era (N.Y.) of 3 Nov[embe]r 1840, and the New York American of same date contain the main facts on both sides of the case of Mr. [Fernando] Wood. From this point any one who pleases may trace out the whole matter through the papers of that period. I find my letter of yesterday contained some errors; but with this direction you can get the whole truth if it is now necessary to inquire into it. Very respectfully Your Obed[ien]t Serv[an]t, John L.H. McCracken.

ALS in ScCleA.

To John McKeon, [former Representative from N.Y.], New York [City], 5/17. "Your letter of the 15th instant, has been received, and in reply to the request it contains I have to inform you that if Mr. [Gerard H.] Coster intends going to Berlin, he will be furnished with a Courier[']s passport, and a small packet for the United States Legation there." FC in DNA, RG 59 (State Department), Domestic Letters, 34:200 (M-40:32).

From LOUIS MARK

European Hotel Washington, 17 May 1844

Sir, I had this Week frequent Interviews with Mr. [William S.] Archer [Senator from Va.] on the subject of the German Convention, and at his request gave him such explanations as he wished as to its merits and its bearing on the Commercial Interests of this Country and as its chief opponents in the Senate are those who fear its influence on our present Tarif[f], I drew up at Mr. Archer[']s request the inclosed Paper showing that it is for the Interest of those in favor of our present Tarif[f] to favor this Convention, and I have herewith the honor to submit this Paper to you, as you will be able to add many more powerful arguments and it is most important that the Tarif[f] interest should ["be" *interlined*] convinced on this Subject as soon as possible. With the greatest Respect, Your Ob[edien]t Ser[van]t, Louis Mark.

ALS with En in DNA, RG 59 (State Department), Miscellaneous Letters (M-179: 104, frames 373–374). NOTE: Mark enclosed a one-page memorandum entitled "Convention with the Zoll Verein."

From NAT[HANIEL] L. MITCHELL

Pearlington [Miss.,] May 17th 1844
My Dear Sir, So great a length of time has elapsed since you heard
from me, & so great have been the changes that I have recently
passed through, (& you have not been exempted from change) that I
am at a loss to know how to address you; perhaps I should not attempt ["it" *interlined*] now, or ever again at any subsequent time, so
unimportant do I feel myself to have grown—but that I feel sure that
change of *place can* never affect your principles, nor *will* it ever mine,
besides, since my removal to this place, about six weeks since, I have
become acquainted with a worthy family residing here for many
years, *on whose account* I have been induced to write to you.   Perhaps it was from something that our friend Volney E. Howard, (late
bond paying Calhoun candidate for Congress who was present) might
have said, or, perhaps it was from my defence of the course of Mr.
[John] Tyler in the house of a worthy Lady in this place, (Mrs.
Arnold,) that she became troubled with the belief that I might assist
her son John in procuring the situation of midshipman in our navy;
in being delivered of this belief, & in soliciting my support, she manifested so much intel[l]igence & address, that I should perhaps have
refused her nothing within my power.   I told her however that I was
entirely unknown to Mr. Tyler—[John Y. Mason,] the Secr[etary] of
the Navy—nor in fact had I ever the honour of seeing a single member
of the cabinet. "But (said she) you are not *unknown* to Mr. Calhoun,
& he when he returns to the Capitol, in the character of Secretary of
State, & he so distinguished, he must be the St. Peter of that place.
The Keys he will carry, rely upon it, & his friends are so attached to
each other, & to him, that doubtless such devotion can never be confined to one side; So that a request from one so ardently attached[,]
Sir, as you evidently are to him, will scarcely be regarded with indifference."

I acknowledged to her, that if I yet hailed from Columbus Mi[ss.]
that you would most probably recognize my signature—&, that attached friends were not new things to you—that you had verry many
such—& that there was *one* principle that pervaded the whole of us,
from yourself down to the humblest friend, all were *too proud to ask
for office*—from those we disagreed with, because of that disagree-
ment—& from those of our ["party" *altered to* "friends"] because we
feared we might embarrass them, & thus injure their usefulness.
"Well (she rejoined) I am verry glad to see that, that *principle* wilnot
[*sic*] prevent your *suggesting* the name of my son as a fit subject to

be shot by order of the Govt." I of course promised her to do my best, & I think in repeating what she said I have fully redeemed my promise. I will only add, that my young friend John Arnold is a youth of promise—well connected—has a brother who has been recently promoted in the army—his father is collector of customs at this place (a worthless office). I shall feel flattered *by your procuring* him a midshipman[']s birth [*sic*]—if you can do so without detriment to your influence in matters of more importance.

In the late struggle for a democratic candidate for the Presidency in the section of the State from which I then hailed (to wit) Columbus—no exertions were relaxed till the battle had been fought, & won in Monroe, an adjoining county—& lost in Noxubee (where at first you were strongest) by the over anxiety of *one* of our party (Doct[o]r [William D.] Lyles) to be himself distinguished—his unpopularity lost us that county. I was there at the organization of our party, was invited to participate, & put on the committee to draft resolutions—on which occasion I saw that Lyles would ruin us—& I was long engaged in silencing him, two or three months, before I succeeded. In Lowndes [County] we met the Vans & fairly whip[p]ed them appointing five delegates all *professedly* for you—though none nullifiers. Through the artful mano[e]uvering of S.F. Butterworth ["&" *canceled*] up to then your *professed* friend—who held a halter round the necks of a majority of the *five*—by the assistance of Mr. Ewing F. Calhoun[,] a hater of yours—the delegates a majority of them were corrupted—on ascertaining which we called an other convention of the whole ["people" *canceled and* "democracy" *interlined*] of the county. The meeting was full, & we succeeded in *instructing* the delegates to vote for Calhoun delegates to attend the Baltimore convention. It was the most exciting little struggle I ever witnessed. The Vans called out for counts *three* several times after drumming up all the *boys* they could find & *induce*, which ["was" *altered to* "were"] not many. We beat them a *little* at every count. Still did the traitor delegates refuse *obediance*—& Old [Isaac?] Worthington who was a participator, & became heated in the proceedings of the meeting, refused to publish the proceedings of the convention in his paper— where upon, having hitherto kept old Worthington strait, now that he would assert his liberty—I determined to set out immediately to [New] Orleans & buy a press, & printing materials on my own hook, relying upon the more talented of our friends for matter for my paper. I did so—purchased all the materials—& had them delivered into an office I had rented to receive them in the town of Columbus. The paper was to issue in one week—("The Mississippi Republican") So headed our prospectus, to which were appended a snug lot of names—among which was that of Gen[era]l Jesse Speight present Senator, in leiu [*sic*] of [John] Henderson[,] who subscribed $100—Col. Volney E. Howard[']s was 2 or $300, besides many other distinguished names with large donations were volunteered. At this particular juncture of time I became the subject of afflictions of heart, & body, that over threw all my calculations, & well nigh my verry being, & terminated in my forcing sales of my plantations, town property—& printing materials &c &c—at a sacrifice during the last year, & my removal last winter to Mobile, & from thence to this place. Thus *I paid all my debts*, & not by bankruptcy. I saved a remna[n]t of my negroes[,] about twenty five, half of which are children, & now I am about engaging in the Tar, & turpentine buisness. I am delighted with this coast country, having been raised on that of N.C. I have only to regret the want of schools for the benefit of my children—which in Columbus they had the advantage of—& which they would have continued to enjoy, *if you had at that time occupied the office I am so glad to see you fill under existing circumstances.* Many friends were exceedingly desirous of seeking the removal of the Blairs from the Columbus post office, (who are inveterate Van Buren men, & *whispering* revilers of Mr. Tyler, & unaccommodating in Office) & recommending me to succeed them. I do not doubt the whole would have been accomplished at once, had I not refused their interference, on the ground that *you must hold office, or be no more*, ere I would hold an office other than from the *people*, at whose hands I had also for many years refused place. It is too late now—however pleasant 2 or 3 thousand of extra dollars ["pr annum" *interlined*] would be to a half broke man, with a large & expensive family. Still I have insurmountable objections to *returning* to a place once occupied & left.

The corrupt policy of *parties*, & those who have recently led them, have so corrupted the *people*—that it has become impossible to get an expression of their will. For want of *patriotism & sense* in the democratic party, may Mr. Van Buren ascribe the success he anticipates before the Baltimore convention—& the defeat that awaits him before the people. Judging from my own feelings, I should think but fiew [*sic*] of your nullification friends who voted for him before, will ever do so again. In truth I would much prefer to see [Henry] Clay President, disagreeing with him as I do in every thing, to Van Buren—for the former is bold & honest—& against his measures the democracy would present an unbroken front—not so of the latter. Still I would wish in this *alternative* to see S.C. vote for Van [Buren]. I sincerely wish that my letter will reach you of a Saturday night to insure its reading—for I feel that it must prove as "tedious as a twice told tale." Still I will fill my sheet. The three months I remained in Mobile last winter I occupied a rented house next door to our friend Hallenquist late ["ed" *canceled*] Co editor of the "Ala[.] Tribune." We were verry much together, being capable of sympathising with each other. His attention to, & expenditures for the Tribune has nearly broke him—not withstanding it seemed well sustained. I got them in its start $100 worth of cash subscribers in Columbus. Hal[l]enquist's family is large & expensive. The young man Bal[l]entine[,] one of the other editors, on learning that I had been talking to Holland[,] an other part owner of the press, about buying him out, to prevent the fall of the paper—signified at once his readiness to work for his victuals & clothes, sooner than the paper should fall through—but I had forgot my own poverty in this last chat about *buying*. That paper has whip[p]ed Wilson[']s paper, the Van Buren organ there so much, & so severely that on being introduced to him as a most unmerciful democrat, he ceazed [*sic*] my hand with great cordiality—but drop[p]ed it as quickly, on being told by myself that I regarded Mr. Calhoun as not only the only available man—but as the only true representative of Jeffersonian Republicanism. We often met at the whist table, until I got so cordially to hate him—that to beat him was not full satisfaction to me—& I quit his company altogether. I saw your Son [Andrew Pickens Calhoun] there once only & regretted that I could not make his acquaintance. I also fell in with [Charles L. Woodbury] the son of Mr. [Levi] Woodbury whom I left not insensible to the advantages his father was acquiring in the South by his connexion with yourself. I could not write to *you* otherwise than as I have—still the oft recur[r]ing reflection of *whom you are*, boggles me, at the opening of every theme. You have the sincerest wishes for your success in Your friend, Nat. L. Mitchell.

ALS in ScCleA.

To Thomas G. Peachy, Williamsburg, Va., 5/17. Calhoun informs Peachy that he has been appointed and confirmed as U.S. Consul for Amoy, China, and sends documents relevant to the duties of the office. FC in DNA, RG 59 (State Department), Consular Instructions, 10:247.

F[rancis] W. Pickens, Edgewood, [Edgefield District, S.C.], to J[ames] Edward Colhoun, Calhoun's Mills, Abbeville District, S.C., "Care of Dr. [Henry H.] Townes," 5/17. "I have re[ceive]d two extraordinary letters from Mr. [John C.] Calhoun a few days ago urging me to go on immediately to Washington & to Baltimore. He writes under great excitement and says this State ought to be represented at Baltimore &c &c. This is strange as he urged as you know to have nothing to do with the Convention & the State has acted accordingly. However I have written to Charleston [to the Calhoun campaign committee?] and will await their answer, & if they wish it I will go on immediately. But it will be rather awkward. So I hold myself 'waiting orders' & will start at a moment[']s warning. I may therefore be absent until the 2d June. Mr. C[alhoun] says [Martin] V[an] B[uren] & [Henry] Clay can both be beaten & all is confusion at Washington. I have also rec[eive]d letters from members from Miss: & Tenn: to go on &c." Pickens comments on the "reports" concerning himself in Charleston and on the dry weather prevailing recently in his area. ALS in ScU-SC, Francis W. Pickens Papers.

To Josiah Raymond, 5/17. Calhoun notifies Raymond that he has been appointed and confirmed as U.S. Consul for Manzanillo, Cuba; he encloses various documents relative to consular duties and discusses steps taken to secure Raymond an exequatur from Madrid. FC in DNA, RG 59 (State Department), Consular Instructions, 10: 245–246.

From C[HARLES] S. TODD

Legation U. States of America at St. Petersburg
5/17th May 1844

Sir, I had the honor to receive on the 5/17th April Despatch No. 13 from the Department in which the Hon. Mr. [John] Nelson, Secretary ad interim, announced the disastrous affair on board the "Princeton." Having already expressed my deep sympathy for the great public and private loss sustained on that melancholy occasion I will merely add that in the death of Mr. [Thomas W.] Gilmer I have experienced a peculiar misfortune in losing his cordial and efficient friendship in the Cabinet and I beg to offer my sincere condolences to the President [John Tyler] upon an event which has deprived him, at a critical moment, of the faithful services of two such able and honest counsellors as Messrs. [Abel P.] Upshur and Gilmer.

At the same time allow me, in anticipation of the receipt of your official despatch, to congratulate my country upon the opportunity which your present position affords of adding, to your previous reputation, the high renown of adjusting some of the most difficult questions in our foreign policy. I recur with great delight to your Career in 1812 when your talents and patriotism constituted you one of the efficient arms of Mr. [James] Madison's administration then struggling in a just and necessary War for the defence of national rights; and your subsequent participation in the Cabinet Councils of Mr. [James] Monroe tending to confirm the public prosperity and develope the national resources in a period of peace, equally entitled you to the public confidence. It was my good fortune at that period to form your personal acquaintance and to receive, in the intercourse with which you honored me and for which I desire to express a grateful sensibility, impressions as to your ability which no time nor distance can efface. Will you allow me, then, to feel a personal gratification in the high destiny that awaits your enlightened labors?

I have the honor to enclose a copy of my note to each of our Consuls in conformity to the views expressed by Mr. [John] Nelson in Despatch No. 13 and to transmit you the substance of a recent Ukaze which adds further restrictions to the existing regulations permitting his Majesty's subjects to travel in foreign Countries. It has been published in Russian but not in the St. Petersburg Journal and I cannot therefore send it to you in French. It does not admit persons over 50 years of age to leave the Country upon any pretext whatever. None can leave it before they arrive at the age of 25 and if born whilst their parents were travelling abroad they must return in due time for their education, or they forfeit all right to inheritances &c. In all cases of permission to travel out of the Country a heavy tax is imposed upon each member of the family who may go. It will probably occur to you that the Ukaze is designed to be a Commentary upon the liberal opinions introduced by the Russians who have travelled into other Countries and is part of a system of measures intended to strengthen the reigning dynasty after the death of the Emperor [Nicholas I]. His commanding personal character renders any such precaution at present unnecessary, though it must be admitted that whilst he is idolized by the Clergy, the Army and the peasantry constituting the great Mass of the population, his supposed inroads occasionally upon the ancient priveleges of the Nobility have given rise to some jealousies from that quarter but not of a character to excite any immediate disturbance. The Hereditary Prince [Alexander], however, when he shall come to the Throne, will be powerfully aided by the genius and energy of his next brother the Grand Duke Constantine now in his 17th year who is preparing by regular study and actual service to become the High Admiral of

the Empire; and ["by" *interlined*] his Cousin, the very able Prince of
Oldenburg, who, although scarcely 30 years of age, is even now an
efficient and confidential Counsellor of the Emperor, being charged
with the superintendence of the important Departments of Civil and
Ecclesiastical affairs.

As tending to a consolidation of the power and interests of Russia
at home and abroad it may be well to look at the existing family connexions formed by the Imperial dynasty. Independent of the fact
that Catharine the 1st was of German descent, and that Catherine the
2nd and the Empress Mother were from Germany, we see that a
sister [Anna] of the Emperor is the Queen of Holland; that another
was the wife of the reigning Duke of Mecklenburg Schwerin and another was the wife of the reigning Duke of Oldenburg—that the Empress [Charlotte] is a sister of [Frederick William IV] the King of
Prussia and a cousin of [Victoria] the Queen of England and thus
connected with the Cobourgs, a sister of the Empress being, also,
the sister in law of [William II] the King of Holland; the Grand
Duchess Helene is a Cousin of [Lewis I] the King of Bavaria—the
Grand Duchess Marie, wife of the Hereditary Prince and who will be
the next Empress, is a daughter of the reigning Duke of Darmsdat—
a recent matrimonial alliance has taken place with the reigning Duke
of Nassau, the richest principality in Germany—the youngest daughter of the Emperor has just married the son of the reigning Prince of
Hesse Cassel and who will be *sooner or later* King of Denmark and
lastly, though not of less importance, the Duke of Leuchtenberg
Grandson of Josephine, and son in law of the Emperor is brother to
[Josephine] the present Queen of Sweden and Norway. Thus a
family cordon is formed around the shores of the Baltic which is
destined to become a "close sea" long before a similar claim once
avowed in relation to the North Western Ocean between the Russian
possessions in North America and Kamschatka in Asia shall be recognized as valid by other nations. If the negociations, recently held and
reported to have been broken off in consequence of the jealousy of
Prince Metternich, shall ever succeed in marrying the Grand Duchess
Olga to the Arch Duke Stephen of Austria, now Vice Roy of Bohemia,
a decided influence for the preservation of peace will be obtained in
the Councils of the neighbouring Empire of greatest extent and
power; and there are yet three young Grand Dukes who will soon be
ready to extend the chain of influence.

Count Reyneval has just been received as the Chargé of France
and it is reported that the late Chargé Baron D'Andre has been recalled and sent to the inferior position at Turin, because of his in-

discreet conduct in endeavouring *officially* to ascertain the views of the Imperial Government touching a supposed visit of the Duke of Bordeaux. The Emperor, it is said, did not choose to be questioned on the subject and the consequence is seen in the recal[l] of Baron D'Andre, a measure very creditable to the prudence and conciliatory spirit of the French Government.

In completion of the record of official notes I have the honor to enclose copies of notes from the Grand Master of Ceremonies inviting to a Court Circle on the $\frac{27\ March}{8\ April}$ and to a Ball in the Concert Hall $\frac{23\ April}{5\ May}$ the former having been Countermanded. I send, also, the Correspondence with Count [Charles Robert von] Nesselrode touching the legalization of some Russian proceedings in relation to the inheritance of the estate left by General Kosciouski who died without issue and I beg leave to transmit the further testimonials as to the application for the Consulate at Moscow which were inadvertently omitted in my last Despatch.

I have the honor to enclose a copy of a letter [of 4/17] from Mr. [John] Ralli our Consul at Odessa requesting leave of absence for 6 months upon indispensable private business in Turkey and Greece and appointing Mr. [J.W.] Edwards to attend to his duties—supposing no public interest will suffer in the mean time, I have granted the request in a letter under date 1/13 Inst. of which a Copy is herewith forwarded. I send, likewise, the Supplement to the very interesting Annual Report of the Minister of the Interior giving an extract of the Account rendered for the last year by the Russian American Company which may contain views and details of interest during the pending negociations as to the Territory of Oregon. To this report is added, also, a valuable essay upon the manufacture of Steel, in the Government of Nishnei Novogorod on the Wolga, from the Iron Mines in the Oural Mountains. I have the honor to be, with high Consideration, Your Ancient friend & ob[edien]t Ser[van]t, C.S. Todd.

ALS (No. 43) with Ens in DNA, RG 59 (State Department), Diplomatic Despatches, Russia, vol. 14 (M-35:14), received 6/21; FC in DNA, RG 84 (Foreign Posts), Russia, Despatches, 4406:213–217. NOTE: Charles Stewart Todd (1791–1871) was a Kentuckian and had been a military and political protegé of William Henry Harrison. He had been a U.S. representative in Colombia during 1820–1823. A Whig, he was appointed Minister to Russia by John Tyler in 8/1841.

To Thomas W. Waldron, Hong Kong, 5/17. Calhoun informs Waldron that his nomination as U.S. Consul at Hong Kong has been confirmed by the Senate and transmits his commission. LS in NhHi,

Miscellaneous Collections; FC in DNA, RG 59 (State Department), Consular Instructions, 12:81.

To F[rancis] M. Dimond, U.S. Consul at Vera Cruz, 5/18. "The parties interested in the Schooner Vigilant, captured by a Mexican Commander, and sent into Vera Cruz, for an alleged breach of the blockade of Yucatan, have applied for the interposition of this Government, for the purpose of obtaining redress from that of the Mexican Republic." Any information Dimond may have on that subject not already communicated to the State Dept. will be helpful, especially "whether there were any judicial proceedings, and what final disposition was made of the Vessel and cargo." FC in DNA, RG 59 (State Department), Consular Instructions, 11:245.

From EDWARD EVERETT

London, 18th May 1844

Sir, I duly received by the steamer of the 1st your despatch Nro. 85, transmitting the printed document containing the treaty relative to the annexation of Texas with the accompanying papers submitted to the Senate, together with your subsequent correspondence with Mr. [Richard] Pakenham.

I have delayed acknowledging the receipt of these most important papers to this the last day of writing by the Steamer, in the expectation that some communication might be made to me on the subject by Lord Aberdeen to be transmitted to you. This, however, is not the case.

You will perceive by the papers of this morning, that some conversation arose in the House of Lords last evening, in reference to the Treaty, on occasion of a question put by Lord Brougham to Lord Aberdeen. Lord Brougham assigned as a reason for his enquiry, that the conversation between Lord Aberdeen and himself on the 18th of August last had been (as he gathered from the documents which had appeared in the papers) deemed highly significant by the Government of the United States, and stated that it was far from his intention in what he then said to counsel any interference with Slavery as existing in the United States.

Lord Aberdeen was very reserved in his reply. He stated that the annexation of Texas raised a question as he believed new and unexampled in the history of public law, which demanded and would receive the earliest and most serious attention of Her Majesty's Government. There was no doubt that the Treaty was signed, but he shared with Lord Brougham the hope and belief that it would not be ratified; but it was impossible to speak with confidence on such a point.

The question to which Lord Aberdeen referred as "new and unexampled in the history of public law," was not stated by him, but from the remarks with which Lord Brougham commenced, as reported in this morning's papers, may be inferred to be, the effect of a union between two separate independent States on their previously existing relations with other powers.

In reply to a farther question from Lord Brougham, Lord Aberdeen said that the explanation which he had made of their conversation of the 18th August had been correctly reported by me, (a matter of necessity, I may observe, with the precaution which I took of submitting the memorandum to his inspection), and that he had confirmed it in a despatch to Mr. Pakenham, alluding apparently to that of 26th December 1843, of which a copy was furnished to Mr. [Abel P.] Upshur.

The intelligence of the Treaty has been less a subject of comment on the part of the press than might perhaps have been expected, at least, in the papers which I see. It seems to have taken the public generally by surprize, and the conductors of the press are probably waiting for further information, and for suggestions in parliament as to the ground to be taken by the Government and the leaders of the Opposition. There is an article on the subject in the "Times" this morning, which like most of the comments of that Journal on American affairs is of a hostile and acrimonious character. It is probable that the steamer which sails tomorrow will take out some instructions from this Government to Mr. Mr. [sic] Pakenham, under which he will communicate to you the views they are disposed to take of the Treaty. I infer this from not having received any such communication myself. I am, Sir, very respectfully, Your obedient Servant, Edward Everett.

LS (No. 129) in DNA, RG 59 (State Department), Diplomatic Despatches, Great Britain, vol. 52 (M-30:48), received 6/3; FC in DNA, RG 84 (Foreign Posts), Great Britain, Despatches, 8:236–240; FC in MHi, Edward Everett Papers, 49:103–106 (published microfilm, reel 23, frames 51–53); CC in DNA, RG 46 (U.S. Senate), 28B-B12; PC in Senate Document No. 367, 28th Cong., 1st Sess., pp. 1–2; PC in House Document No. 271, 28th Cong., 1st Sess., pp. 100–101; PC in the Washington, D.C., *Daily National Intelligencer*, June 8, 1844, p. 3; PC in the Charleston, S.C., *Courier*, June 11, 1844, p. 2; PC in *Niles' National Register*, vol. LXVI, no. 16 (June 15, 1844), p. 252.

From A[RCHIBALD] M. GREEN

Galvezton, 18th May 1844

Sir, It is very painful to me to be compelled by every mail to write you on disagreeable subjects, but disagreeable as they are it is what I owe to myself and it may benefit the country in the end. I have submitted to insult and indignity, impudence and impertinent messages from Gen[era]l [William S.] Murphy until my patience is worn out and if I permit such a state of things to exist much longer, I cannot expect to preserve even the respect for myself or that of others. And nothing has induced me to submit to the least outrage to my feelings but for the respect that is due to the station he occupies.

I have been patiently waiting to receive your answer to my communication of the 19th April No. 33 and Second May No. 34.

I must preserve my own dignity and my own character which I regard above all other considerations and should be very unwilling to do an act that would give offense or umbrage to the Department.

It was no longer than yesterday that Gen[era]l Murphy applied to Gen[era]l M[emucan] Hunt to be the bearer of an impertinent message to me without the least provocation. Gen[era]l Hunt knew that Gen[era]l Murphy was unjustified in sending such a message and told him to be the bearer of it himself.

Gen[era]l Murphy may be so unwise as to repeat in some short time his impudent messages. And if he does, I shall be compelled to notice them on the spot and at the time, in a manner that will reflect no credit on the Government be the consequences what they may. I am Sir most Respectfully y[ou]r ob[edient] S[ervan]t, A.M. Green.

ALS ("Private") in DNA, RG 59 (State Department), Consular Despatches, Galveston, vol. 2 (T-151:2), received 5/30.

From WILLIAM HALE

Detroit Mich., May 18, 1844

Dear Sir, I trust no apology will be required for obtruding myself briefly upon your attention. I desire to submit for your consideration, at this peculiar crisis in the democratic party, a few ideas gathered from observations that I have made upon the interesting questions, now agitating the party & the country. If productive of no other good, they may tend to furnish a clew to public sentiment here, or confirm & render certain, what, in the conflic[t] of parties, is involved in doubt.

The leading & primary questions that agitate the democratic party of Michigan, more than all others at the present moment, and which are deemed vitally important to our future success, are, 1st, The reannexation of Texas, 2d, Opposition to a protective tariff. The other leading questions of the democratic creed, are considered so far settled as to be of lesser interest. In whatever light then, we may be regarded at Washington, such is the position of the democracy of Michigan, and I believe I may safely add, of the entire Northwest.

With reference to the first question, the reannexation of Texas, I believe our views are not fully understood or fairly appreciated by many of our Southern friends. I make this inference from the tone & language of Southern papers. They discuss the question too much, as if its chief merits rested on local grounds. They seem to view it too exclusively in reference to its bearing on southern interests. They forget or overlook the relative position of the west to the south, their strong affinity in other interests, our national pride, our love of acquisition, & hatred of British power & control. These various influences, combined with the intrinsic merits of the question itself, are making the annexation of Texas the strongest issue we can tender to our opponents. It is true the project was not received at first, with any very decided tokens of favor. Many among us even looked upon it with distrust. We wanted time for inquiry & deliberation. But the result has been as might have been anticipated. A few weeks since, it had only here & there an advocate; now, the almost entire democratic party of the State, are virtually committed in its support. It is now looked upon as important, not only as tending to promote the welfare of the whole country, but as the question, that is to save the democratic party from defeat in the coming contest, if anything can. I hazzard nothing, therefore, in saying, that when the voice of the democratic party in the west can be fairly heard, it will be found to be in exact unison with that which we already hear from the South. We shall be found to a man united in favor of the great measure. Let not then our southern brethren look upon themselves any longer as its sole guardians, nor treat it so much in reference to its sectional bearings. If I might venture the suggestion, I would say, that a more enlarged & national turn to the discussion at the South, while it would not retard its progress there, would have the effect to hasten it more rapidly at the west & north.

With reference to the other question, opposition to a protective tariff, there is with us an entire unity of sentiment, as well as identity of interest, with the south. We are fellow sufferers, under a common system of oppression & extortion, imposed by a common task master. The machinery & ingenious contrivances of the present tariff, by which the west & the south, are made to pay tribute to the Manufacturers of the east, are as well understood here, as with the citizens of your own State. The term incidental protection, grates just as harshly in our ears. We regard it as a mere subterfuge, by which the ends of a protective tariff are sought to be secured, while the obnoxious principle is concealed or disguised. We are in favor of a tariff as a means of raising a revenue for the support of the Government, but in imposing duties, we discard the doctrine that it is proper or just to discriminate below a certain maximum, for purposes of protection, or with a view to protection. The recent votes of our northwestern delegation in congress, are stronger proof of our sentiments even, than appear on their face. Some of our representatives are tinctured from early association, with tariff views, but their keen sense of the views of their constituents has constrained them to vote as they have done. Such then is the aspect of our party in this section with regard to these measures, but with reference to men it has been less clear & distinct. My own preferences are not unknown to you, and I adhered to my favorite flag as long as it waved. But a majority of the party, following old leaders & what seemed to be the preferences of our friends elsewhere, had generally acquiesced in the nomination of Mr. Van Buren. Such was the case until the disastrous result of some recent elections was known, & especially until the appearance of his Texas letter. This feeling is now changed, and an impression that some other candidate should be selected prevails among reflecting democrats. If your own name had ["not" *interlined*] been withdrawn I think that a majority of our party in this State, would desire your nomination. But as it has been, most of us have turned our eyes towards General [Lewis] Cass. There may of course be some local feeling in the preference. But under all the circumstances, I am inclined to regard him as the most eligible man. He can doubtless bring to the aid of the party in this crisis, a greater degree of personal popularity, than any of the Gentlemen who have been named. His views on public questions are not less satisfactory. He is an open & decided friend of the immediate annexation of Texas, and his well known views respecting English Encroachments, will tend to place that question on the strongest & most popular grounds. On the subject of the tariff his official career in the Executive offices alone, has afforded him less occasion to express decided opinions on either side, but I have reason to believe that his administration ["but" *canceled*] would be generally favorable to the principles of Free Trade. His views I am aware have not been as clear & explicit as some of our friends and as I could wish, but his practical conduct I believe, would be found quite as acceptable as those of any democrat, whose nomination can now be secured. Certainly he is as little objectionable on this score even as Mr. Van Buren, with his tariff associations & sympathies; while in regard to the Texas question, & to ulterior considerations, he is surely far preferable.

Of course I know nothing of the intended course of our Southern friends in the Baltimore convention, but with their aid I believe that Gen. Cass might obtain the nomination. He will receive a large vote from western delegates, which, with the united vote of the South & with some aid from the middle ["States" *canceled*] & eastern States, would doubtless control the result. The decision, in my judgment, will rest with our southern friends, and their choice must be made between Cass & Van Buren. Neither [Charles] Stewart, [Richard M.] Johnson, [James] Buchanan or [John] Tyler can command sufficient strength to compete with the latter, and if the southern vote should generally be cast for either of these, it must result in Mr. Van Buren's nomination. Cass alone has friends enough in all sections of the Union to stand any chance of success. Stewart is unknown, Buchanan supposed to be withdrawn, & Johnson regarded as scarcely equal to the position. It is then for our Southern friends to choose between Cass & Van Buren. In all respects Cass, it seems to me must be equally or more acceptable, and so far as any reference to the future may be taken into the account, he is perhaps all that could be desired. He is committed to the single term principle. He lives in a western & non Slave-holding State. His successor would reasonably & justly come from an eastern & Slave holding State. It would be naturally his policy to promote harmony & good feeling ["during his administration," *interlined*] by favoring such a result. I know of no method by which the designs that have been formed, for transferring the succession from the banks of the Hudson to those of the Missouri, could be so readily and effectually counteracted. But it does not become me to enlarge on this point.

I have been tempted to trespass upon your time much farther than I intended. I beg you to pardon the freedom with which I have written, & to believe that I am actuated solely by a desire to promote the success of our principles, & of him who has done most to illustrate & defend them. Very Truly, Your Ob[edien]t Ser[van]t, William Hale.

ALS in ScCleA; PC in Boucher and Brooks, eds., *Correspondence*, pp. 231–234. NOTE: An AEU by Calhoun reads "Mr. Hale, Relates to the election of Gov[erno]r Cass."

From T. WOODHOUSE STEVENS

London[,] 21 Austin Friars, May 18th 1844
Sir, I have the honour to enclose a letter [dated 5/7] from the Respectable House of Brothers Nottebohn of Antwerp on the Subject of the Project now before the Belgian Chambers for increasing the duty on Tobacco. The only observation I have to make on the subject is, that it seems rather extraordinary that the only moment since the residence of Mr. [Henry W.] Hilliard [U.S. Chargé d'Affaires] at Brussells, when he could be useful in promoting the Interests of his Countrymen he should be absent on a Trip of Pleasure of [*sic*] *Paris*. I have the Honour To Be Sir your Ob[e]d[ien]t Servant, T. Woodhouse Stevens.

ALS with En in DNA, RG 59 (State Department), Miscellaneous Letters (M-179: 104, frames 379–382), received 6/4. NOTE: The letter from Nottebohn Brothers to Stevens described problems anticipated by Belgian merchants of American tobacco in the event new duties were imposed.

To [JOHN TYLER]

Department of State
Washington, 18th May, 1844
To the President of the United States.

The Secretary of State, to whom was referred the Resolution of the Senate of the 29th of last month, requesting the President to transmit to that Body copies of any communications to our Ministers in Mexico or Spain, concerning the purchase of or title to Texas and any replies relating to either subject which have not heretofore been made public nor sent to the Senate, has the honor to report to the President that there is not on the records of this Department any communication whatever to a diplomatic agent of the United States in Mexico, nor any communication to a diplomatic agent of the United

States in Spain, since 1820, upon the subject of the Resolution, which has not been made public or communicated to the Senate. The papers which are now laid before the President are an extract from a private letter of Mr. [Joel R.] Poinsett to Mr. [Henry] Clay and extracts from and a copy of other letters from Mr. [Anthony] Butler to the President and Secretary of State [during the Andrew Jackson administration], and are all the unpublished communications and parts of communications from diplomatic agents of the United States in Mexico relating to the purchase of or title to Texas; and, also, all the unpublished communications and parts of communications from Diplomatic agents of the United States in Spain, since 1820, upon the same subject, which, after a careful collation with previous reports from this Department, can be found upon its files. The report of the Secretary of State upon another Resolution of the Senate of the 29th ult[imo] will be accompanied by such unpublished correspondence between the Department and the mission to Spain, previously to and including the year 1820, as may be discovered.

All which is respectfully submitted. J.C. Calhoun.

LS in DNA, RG 46 (U.S. Senate), 28B-B12; FC in DNA, RG 59 (State Department), Reports of the Secretary of State to the President and Congress, 6:103–104; PC in Jameson, ed., *Correspondence*, pp. 589–590. NOTE: Tyler transmitted this letter and its Ens to the Senate on 5/18. The resolution to which the above is a reply can be found in RG 59 (State Department), Miscellaneous Letters (M-179:104, frames 266 and 309) and in *Senate Executive Journal*, 6:264.

To [ROBERT J. WALKER, Senator from Miss.]

[Washington, *ca.* May 18, 1844?]
Dear Sir, I hear [Thomas H.] Benton has made another abusive speech, & fierce assault on the Treaty. I do think that a reply &, that too a decisive one, ought to be made. It will not do to let the speaking ["to" *canceled*] be all on one side, & that at the very close of the session. It is indispensible to success, that our friends should leave here in high hopes & sperit, which cannot be, if he go without a reply.

No one can so effectually answer him as yourself. You are so familiar with the subject, that it will give you but little trouble to meet him at all points.

I do trust, you will view the subject in the same light, and that you will make an occasion, if no regular one should be afforded you, to expose the absurdity of his scheme & arguments. That is necessary to crown your great exertions in favour of the glorious cause. Truly, J.C. Calhoun.

ALS in ScU-SC, John C. Calhoun Papers. NOTE: An EU on this undated letter reads: "J.C. Calhoun. Texas[,] an[swere]d, 1844." Benton spoke on the annexation treaty on 5/16, 5/18 and 5/20 and was replied to by Walker on 5/20 and 5/21. The date given this document is approximate and conjectural and the recipient is identified only through a notation made on the ms. by an unknown person at an unknown time.

From A[RCHIBALD] M. GREEN

Consulate of the U.S. of America at Galvezton
Repub[lic] of Texas, 19th May 1844

Sir, This communication is addressed to you as it contained views of my own and believing that it is a subject which has long since sug[g]ested itself to you I had promised Mr. [Gilbert L.?] Thompson on his way to Vera Cruz to communicate the facts (& what is stated in this letter) to the Chairman of the Com[mit]tee of Foreign Relations of the Senate (Mr. [William S.] Archer) & on further reflection I have thought it my duty to make the communication direct to you, that you may do so, if thought advisable.

It would be well to bear in mind that Texas has passed through the ordeal of a Revolution, on which she staked every thing and which has left her no time to fix and determine those principles of policy by which her future course was or may be regulated.

Matters of such vast importance and which after all constitute the chief end and aim of a people, require time, repose and peace before they can be digested and arranged. She was poor and needy in the beginning of her struggle with a power: which, when compared with herself, was in appearance as to population and wealth and ability to conduct a war, as a giant is to a pigmy and if she has at the end of the struggle become still poorer and with nothing but the semblance of a Government ["she" *canceled*] she is not more unfortunate in these particulars, than other nations, who have been compelled to pass through the same difficulties and extraordinary trials.

When she is at peace and is given an opportunity to develope her resources, when the citizens and the farmers can ["return" *canceled*] return to their usual avocations and feel a proper degree of security in property and person, what reason can be assigned why all the necessaries of life for the comforts of every one, should not be as cheap here as in any portion of the South or West.

In a few years the many advantages of this country for farming and grazing purposes will more fully devellope themselves and there will be seen, the time when emigrants will experience as little inconvenience and may expect to encounter less privation and hardship than in most new countries.

The citizens of that part of Texas in which I have had an opportunity of Judging, may be said to be a Law abiding, intelligent and worthy people. Whatever may have been the habits and recklessness of many heretofore, their course of conduct seems to have been improved and past offences buried in oblivion and forgotten.

They are not only a Law abiding but a church going community whose habits and common sense have however superseded the necessity of legal enactments, and not only do the citizens of this part of the country usually unite in observing the Sab[b]ath by the discontinuance of the labours and business of the week themselves, but by allowing the same privilege to their *Servants.* The day is set apart and observed with the same religious ceremonies here as in the United States, and is marked with the same order, quiet, and decorum, as may be observed in any city embracing a like population in any portion of the United States.

The subject of the annexation of this country to the United States is one of great interest to the latter Country. If Texas be united to the States, the interest of every portion of that vast republic will be subserved.

To the north it will furnish an extensive market for her manufactories. The Sugar and Cotton growing portions of the United States will be equally benefitted. The growers of these products will then be on a footing with those of other nations but should the country be independent it will be impossible to compete with that class in this country. Here the farmer will have every thing free of duty and his produce will be admitted into Europe free of duty. It is in contemplation here, if the country be not annexed, to establish the free trade system, and it would be doubtless done at the next Congress. There has always been a large and respectable class of people in this country who have been in favour of this system. The opponents heretofore of this measure are now agitating the subject and will warmly advocate its adoption.

It is very easy to see what effect this system will have on the northern and southern portions of the United States. The importations from that country already dwindled to less than *one fourth* of what they formerly were, would cease altogether, Europe will be the recipient of all the products of this country and all the wants of the country will be *supplied* from the *same source.*

When we take a view of the geographical exposition of the southern line of the United States, extending from the mouth of the Sabine in Lat[itude] 29°30′ to 34° N[orth] L[atitude] following the course of said River and the imaginary line between the U. States and Texas, supposed to be a distance of more than twelve hundred miles, thence with the southwestern line of the United States bordering on Red River running parallel with the sea coast of Texas and at right angles with the dividing line between Louisiana and said Republic, until you reach the western limit at an immense distance—Enquiry may be made as to the practicability of reaching a point on Red River, so high up, with the imported goods from the European markets.

Let it be remembered that the principal rivers of Texas, have their sources in the mountains of that country and in a highly elevated country at the distance of many hundred miles from their mouths—for instance, the Trinity has been navigable for steam Boats during the present season and may be considered so generally during one half of the year to Fort Houston or a distance of five hundred and fifty miles, running parallel with the Sabine, only a much longer and better navigable stream. Then how easy would it be to freight goods that may be imported to Texas free of duty from Europe to some point on Red River on the southern coast of Arkansaw where they can be carried to a point so high up the Trinity and within comparatively so short a distance of the south western line of the United States.

The Brazos and Colorado are both navigable for steam boats a greater portion of the year to a great distance and thence in open boats to perhaps double the distance in steamers. These sources furnish the outlet and facilities for reaching the territory of the United States at a point the least expected, and though not of much moment at the present day, yet in the process of time may be regarded as of great interest and whilst the goods may be introduced into the United States through Texas from European markets free of duty a good supply will likewise be on hand at all times for the Mexican markets, and all northern Mexico will be supplied from that source.

I call your attention to the map of the country, and by a single glance of the eye, you will perceive how much the distance is shortened by the route from the upper Brazos or Colorado, to ["the" *canceled*] *Santa Fee*—by the above described rout[e] the distance in land carriage saved in going and coming ["is" *interlined*] upwards of 1200 miles, this saving of distance will necessarily be the means of breaking up that trade which has so long been carried on from St. Louis with so much advantage to our enterprising merchants and tradesmen. And whenever the day may come that the blessings of peace may prevail in Texas, is it not reasonable to anticipate a direct rout[e] through Texas to that region of country which has been the receptacle of so many manufactured goods of the United States.

The revenue of the U.S. would be very seriously diminished for the whole South would be supplied through Texas. Smuggling could not be prevented—it would require an army of men to prevent it. Texas would become emphatically a Republic of smugglers. The trade of the United States with Mexico would be almost entirely distroyed. The smugglers and importers of Texas would likewise supply that country. The whole coast from this country to Cape Florida would have to be guarded, and more ["effectually" *canceled and* "efficiently" *interlined*] and at greater cost than it has ever been heretofore in order to prohibit such trade being carried on directly in violation of our revenue Laws. And there is no telling to what extent this traf[f]ic is to ["be" *canceled*] assume, in some short time to come. Annexation, ["and" *canceled and* "or" *interlined*] a tariff corresponding with that of the United States are the only means to remedy an evil so much to be deprecated and destructive to our best interests— not only in a diminution of our revenue but destructive to the morral habits and character of our citizens.

If this Country be not annexed there is every probability that her institutions may be changed whenever the European population have the assendency. It is consequently the interest of the South to have this question put at rest forever by annexing the Country.

The northern people or those who are opposed to slavery would not increase the evil but if any, they, would lessen it. Virginia, Maryland & several other slave holding States would be entirely drained of slaves and what would be lost in one section would be gained in another. Should Annexation not take place, I then beg leave to suggest that no time be lost in preparing a Commercial Treaty with Texas at the earliest possible moment, which will save the 5 p[e]r c[en]t additional duty imposed over and above that fixed by other govts. which have a treaty with Texas on the same articles. I have the honor to be most Respectfully y[ou]r ob[edien]t S[ervan]t, A.M. Green, 19th May 1844.

ALS (No. 36) in DNA, RG 59 (State Department), Consular Despatches, Galveston, vol. 2 (T-151:2), received 5/30.

From J[AMES] HAMILTON [JR.]

Barn[e]sville[,] Pike County
Georgia, May 19[t]h 1844

My Dear Sir, I am just on my way to the Bend and have hauled up here to drop you a line.

You will perceive in So[uth] Carolina & this State, we have fairly set the annexation Ball in motion. I addressed enthusiastic meetings two nights since in Savan[n]ah and last night in Macon.

Both [Henry] Clay & [Martin] Van Buren stand before the America[n] public convicted of such flagrant inconsistency [*"th" canceled*] and from motives so eminently discreditable that they both must go to the [*one word canceled and "Wall" interlined*], if the discussion is driven home [*"&" interlined*] followed up by a proper series of measures.

Resolutions will be [*"followed" canceled and "adopted" interlined*] at Macon on Monday night & on Tuesday night [*"at Savan-(n)ah" interlined*] that the [*"members of Congress" interlined*] friends of Annexation should meet before [*"the" canceled*] its adjournment and organize for the call of a great National Annexation Convention at Philadelphia or some other convenient place at an early day to take measures to insure the success of *immediate* annexation & to nominate a Candidate for the Presidency confirmatory of the Baltimore Convention or *irrespective* of it. I believe if your friends are zealous & stand by you like men in the event of your nomination your chance to say the least of it would be [*"f" canceled*] a fair one.

If after the adjournment of Congress we do not resort to some decided action the measure dies by sheer inanition[?] & the South perishes with it.

With a good Candidate for the Presidency the Tables in Georgia will be turned on Clay compleatly.

I write [Dixon H.] Lewis by this Mail to arrange with him the means by which Alabama may be put in strong motion. As the Treaty *must* be defeated, Texas must [*"as"(?) canceled*] *de jure* as a Territory of the United States demand at the next session of Congress [*"admission into the Union" canceled and "that our Laws be" interlined*] extended over her Territory. She must *come* in or be *rejected* before[?] Clay either is elected or defeated.

I wish I was near you with all my heart. But at a distance I am doing all the good I can.

Direct to me [*"at the B" canceled*; at] Columbus[,] Geo[rgia] & believe me my Dear Sir with esteem Yours faithfully, J. Hamilton.

P.S. Major John H. Howard went on to day [to Baltimore]. He is a man on whom you can rely. I missed him but have written him fully by this day[']s mail.

ALS in ScCleA. NOTE: Puzzlingly, this letter was postmarked in Washington on 5/22.

To FRANCIS WHARTON, [Philadelphia]

Washington, 19th May 1844

My dear Sir, I placed your letter in favour of Judge [John B.] Gibson, as the successor of Judge [Henry] Baldwin [as Associate Justice of the Supreme Court], before the President [John Tyler] for his consideration. It is uncertain when the nomination will be made, and still more so, whether it will be acted on by the Senate this session. My impression is, that the Whig senators are resolved not to fill any of the important vacancies, which they can possibly avoid, and especially those of the supreme bench. The prospect is, that the majority of the places on it, will be vacant, including the two that now are, in a short time. Judges [Joseph] Story & McKindly [*sic*; John McKinley] are both said to be in infirm health.

I do hope, that the President, in making the selection to fill Judge Baldwin[']s vacancy, will be governed exclusively by a regard to character & qualifications, including sound principles moral & political. The working of our system depends in no small degree on the character of the Bench.

The Democratick party is in a state of complete decomposition here. It had been long coming to it. Mr. [Martin] V[an] B[uren]'s Texian letter has but hastened the process and made it more complete. The party now is resolving itself into two others, the cohesive points of which is annexation & antiannexation. The former will embrace nine tenth[s] of the whole. A considerable portion of the latter will be absorbed by the whigs.

It is now admitted on all sides, that Mr. V[an] B[uren] cannot be elected, should he [be] nominated at Baltimore. Many think, that he would not carry a single State; and yet it is thought by not a few, that he will receive the nomination. What a comment on the caucus system! I hold it certain, that there will be a candidate in the field on the side of annexation. Who it will be is still uncertain. An effort will be made at Baltimore to rally all the friends of annexation on some one candidate. If they can be, on any sound capable man, it can hardly be doubted he would defeat both [Henry] Clay & V[an] B[uren]. I fear, however, it will be found impossible to make such a rally.

I wrote you a few days before I left home for Washington. I fear you did not get my letter, as you make no allusion to it. I hope you may make it convenient to visit Washington. I would be glad to see you. Truly, J.C. Calhoun.

ALS in ScU-SC, John C. Calhoun Papers; transcript in DLC, Carnegie Institution of Washington Transcript Collection.

To ——

19th May 1844

My dear Sir, I write to acknowledge the receipt of your letter, & to say, that I have read it with great pleasure & much interest. It is in the proper tone & expresses the proper sentiments. Would to God all felt & thought as you do. How great & glorious would be the country & how great & triumphant the party.

I do hope you will make a point to visit Washington before the Convention. I would be very glad to see you. Truly, J.C. Calhoun.

Transcript in DLC, Carnegie Institution of Washington Transcript Collection.

From HENRY W. ANDREWS & CO.

Philadelphia, May 20, 1844

Sir, The undersigned merchants largely interrested in the St. Domingo trade respectfully call y[ou]r attention to the unprotected state of American commerce in the above island. In the course of many years but two or three of our national vessels have visited Hayti & at present not only property but the lives of our citizens are in jeopardy from the civil Commotions there Existing. The Brig Jos. Atkins at N. York from Aux Cayes brings information of the most alarming Character— & as we have a commercial house established at Cape Haytien in which not only ourselves but others in Boston are interrested we respectfully beg that you may give us that protection which citizens of other nations there enjoy, by a demonstration of force calculated to insure our rights. Very Respectfully Y[ou]rs, Henry W. Andrews & Co.

LS in DNA, RG 59 (State Department), Miscellaneous Letters (M-179:104, frame 383).

To Richard H. Belt, 5/20. Belt has been appointed as U.S. Consul at Matamoros, Mexico. His exequatur is to be applied for by the U.S. legation in Mexico City. FC in DNA, RG 59 (State Department), Consular Instructions, 11:246.

To W[illiam] B. Calhoun, [former Representative from Mass.], Springfield, Mass., 5/20. A copy of [William B.] Calhoun's letter of 5/13 has been sent to [Robert B. Campbell], U.S. Consul at Havana, "with instructions to enquire into the circumstances of the case of Mr. [Henry J.] Cavalier" and to take appropriate steps in regard thereto. FC in DNA, RG 59 (State Department), Consular Instructions, 10:247.

To R[obert] B. Campbell, U.S. Consul at Havana, 5/20. Calhoun transmits to Campbell a copy of a letter [of 5/13] from W[illiam] B. Calhoun concerning the imprisonment at Havana of Henry J. Cavalier, and also a copy of a letter [of 5/15 to John Tyler] from Henry Y. Cranston concerning the imprisonment of William Bisby, to both of which cases Campbell's attention is directed. FC in DNA, RG 59 (State Department), Consular Instructions, 10:248.

From SAMUEL CHURCH

Salisbury, Litchfield Co[unty,] C[onnecticu]t
May 20, 1844

My dear Sir, You may possibly recollect that on a former occasion and before your retirement from the U.S. Senate I addressed you in behalf of a young friend Mr. Henry F. Fish then residing in Bermuda and who had applied for an appointment as Consul at that Island.

Mr. Fish has since returned from Bermuda but the State of his health is such that he cannot safely reside under the influence of a northern climate and he will seek a warmer one.

I have known Mr. Fish from his boyhood. He is a young gentleman of much intellectual and moral worth, and his parents and relatives are among the most respectable and worthy of our Citizens; and if he should receive from the Government an Appointment of Consul or Agent at Bermuda, Madeira, or some other Southern port, I feel an assurance that he will not disappoint its just expectations.

Mr. Fish will hand you this note. With great & sincere regard Your Ob[edien]t Serv[an]t, Samuel Church.

ALS in DNA, RG 59 (State Department), Applications and Recommendations, 1837–1845, Fish (M-687:11, frames 270–272). Note: An AEI by Calhoun reads "Submitted for the consideration of the President. Judge Church the writer of the enclosed belongs to the Supreme bench of the State and is one of the first citizens of Connecticut." An AES by R[oyall] R. Hinman, Deputy Postmaster at Hartford, reads: "I fully concur in the request of Judge Sam[ue]l Church of Ct. who I know to be one of the friends of the President"; another AES by Joel W. White says, "I concur in the above." An AEI by Tyler reads: "Bermuda is a very important position and my impression is that the Consul should go from the South."

Circular from F[ranklin] H. Elmore, H[enry] Gourdin, James Gadsden, and P.D. de la Torre, Charleston, 5/20. As a committee appointed by a public meeting, they address citizens in various locations asking their opinion about public feeling in regard to the annexation of Texas and to the means for pursuing the same. Printed letter in ScU-SC.

To Henry Y. Cranston, Representative [from R.I.], 5/20. Calhoun acknowledges Cranston's letter of 5/15 [to the President], a copy of which has been sent to [Robert B. Campbell], U.S. Consul at Havana, with instructions to investigate into the case of [William] Bisby and take appropriate action. FC in DNA, RG 59 (State Department), Consular Instructions, 10:247–248.

From W[illia]m Crump

Powhatan C[ount]y, Virginia
May 20th 1844

I[n] my letter to the department of State bearing date the 20th of April, I informe you I should be prepar[e]d to enter on the dutys of ["my" *interlined*] appointment of Charge d Affairs of the United States to the Republic of Chile, on this day the 20th of May. I intended to have left home on Saturday the 18th for the City of Washington & should have done so, but for the arrival here of Mr. Geo[rge] W. Hopkins of the House of Representatives on Friday evening, by whom I was informed that the Revenue bill makeing the necessary appropriations for the expences of our representatives at foreign government, had not been acted on in the House of Representatives, and most probably would not be finally acted on for several days to come. That information determined me to decline my trip to Washington for a few days, and to await the final passage of the Bill makeing the necessary appropriation for my outfit. If, should any thing occur to retain me at home I should deam it great favour if the Department would inform ["me" *interlined*] at what time it is expected I shal[l] take my departure for the Republic of Chile. I am Sir Very Respectfully Y[ou]r Ob[edien]t S[er]v[an]t, Wm. Crump.

ALS in DNA, RG 59 (State Department), Diplomatic Despatches, Chile, vol. 6 (M-10:T6, frame 206).

To HENRY DOLLIVER, Somerville, N.J.

Department of State
Washington, 20th May 1844
Sir, I have to acknowledge the receipt of your letter of the 29th Ultimo upon the subject of your claim against the Mexican Government. A convention has been concluded between the two Governments which, if it goes into effect, will provide for all such claims and persons generally interested in them will when the Convention is published, learn the form of proceeding which it may then be necessary to adopt. Nothing can be done by this Department towards prosecuting any claim, until the fate of the Convention shall be known. I am, Sir Y[ou]r Ob[edien]t Servant, John C. Calhoun.

FC in DNA, RG 59 (State Department), Domestic Letters, 34:202 (M-40:32).

From W[ILLIA]M P. DUVAL, "Private"

St. Augustine, May 20th 1844
I consider the treaty with Texas as a dead letter, party feeling and selfish ambition has I fear triumphed over the dearest interests of the nation. [Henry] Clay & [Martin] Van Buren are fit companions,

either would sink[?] half the States to become President of the nation[.] I trust that the voice of the nation will soon be heard in tones, of deep condemnation, of the conduct of those who love England, better than their own country. We have many traitors among us—native as well as foreign[.] The Globe abuses you, it is the richest compliment it could pay to your talents & virtues. The Editor [Francis P. Blair], who betrayed his party to aid in the election of John Q[uincy] Adams as president, is capable of any other acts of treachery. The rascals who have sold themselves to to England, & her mermidons are the first to charge the loss of the Treaty in the senate to your intrigues as they term it—we the people are not such asses as to be duped by such slanderous slang. I do not know who will be governor [of Fla. Territory Richard K.] Call[']s successor. I would greatly prefer his reappointment, but my impression is that he is no favorite with the President [John Tyler]. I am opposed to the appointment of W[illia]m H. Brockenbrough, whos[e] name I hear has been before the President for that office. I write to you with truth & candor, do not favour his appointment[;] he is no friend to the administration and is certainly hostile to you[.] I have never had any difficulty or dispute with Mr. Bro[c]kenbrough. He was my partner in the practice of law for somewhat more than a year. I found him the most selfish and avaricious man I ever knew. He will hate a man who confers a signal favour on him and you could as soon, obtain the gratitude of a cat, as his. Cold[,] cautious & selfish[,] he is incap[a]ble of friendship—or noble feeling. I am somewhat of a judge of men, and depend on it I am not mistaken in this man[']s temper[,] feeling & character. If Gov[erno]r Call cannot be reappointed, I most earnestly insist that my early and noble friend Gen[era]l James Gadsden should be appointed Governor of Florida.

His appointment would give more satisfaction to the people of Florida than that of any man I know. His talents, & services, in and out of this Territory—the confidence we all have in his sterling integrity, and manliness of heart, present no ordinary claim, for the station. Gadsden is too proud a man to seek office, and unless his friends press his claims—his modesty will be found equal to his merit, and he will be overlooked. I would sooner trust Gadsden in any high & responsible office than any man in Florida—and if the administration will not continue Gen[era]l Call, who bye the bye is a noble man—then I beg that Gadsden may succeed him. I do not expect you to answer my letters, that is not in your power unless you neglect your duties but as one of your long tried and unwavering friends—I will speak to you every thought that I deem as a friend I should communicate[.] Your letter to the British minister [Richard Pakenham] is such as will sustain your high character and proves that a few patriots are yet to be found among our statesmen[.] Yours sincer[e]ly, Wm. P. Duval.

ALS in ScCleA. NOTE: During the War of 1812 Duval had been Calhoun's colleague in the House of Representatives (from Ky.), and he had been Governor of Fla. Territory when Calhoun was Secretary of War.

From H[enry] L. Ellsworth, Patent Office, 5/20. "Will it be convenient for the Hon. Sec[retar]y to attend to a case of extension of a patent at some hour tomorrow[;] if so please name the time. Very sincerely, H.L. Ellsworth." (Clerks' endorsements indicate that this letter was answered affirmatively.) ALS in DNA, RG 59 (State Department), Miscellaneous Letters (M-179:104, frames 388–389).

From JAMES GADSDEN

Charleston S.C., May 20 1844

My Dear Sir, This will be handed you by Mr. Francis Bulkley, who I beg leave to introduce to your particular notice. Mr. Bulkley has been residing for several years, in Richland District, and has been the principal of an academy in the neighbourhood of our mutual friends the [James H.] Adams'. His health having suffered in a climate, unfriendly to his constitution, he has been recommended to seek relief, or restoration in a latitude further south—and more congenial to him. Italy, the South of France, or Some favourable location in the West Indies, or South America, he is disposed to migrate to, but will be influenced in his determination, by the prospect of obtaining employment from our Government. The Adams', one and all, give the highest testimonials of his high moral character and qualifications, and express to me the deepest interest in his welfare. Are there any Consulates or other agencies vacant, which you could confer upon him, thus securing to the Government a faithful public servant, at the same time that you enable a worthy young man to enjoy the blessings of health in a climate more congenial to his constitution than the one in which his lot has been hitherto cast. Respectfully your ob[edient] S[ervan]t, James Gadsden.

ALS in DNA, RG 59 (State Department), Applications and Recommendations, 1837–1845, Bulkley (M-687:3, frames 587–589).

From C. W. HALL

Kingsport [Tenn.,] May 20th [18]44

Dear Sir, It is apprehended that the Texan treaty will be rejected by the Senate. In that event, what course will the friends of annexation take, to bring to the Question the Greatest amount of strength[?] Some sort of committal, on the part of the present opponents of the measure, to future annexation, would seem to be desirable[,] something more *definite* and *tangible,* than the *contingencies,* upon which the Question now rests in the minds of some of our prominent statesmen. It has been suggested, that the sum of two or three millions of dollars be placed at the disposal of the President, by an act or resolution of Congress, to be loaned ["by the President in his discretion" *interlined*] to the Texan Government to sustain its independence or to strengthen its power. This it is thought, will keep Texas in a Good humour, will enable it to organize such a fleet and army, as to deter Mexico, from the further prosecution of hostilities—if not Texas might commence offensive operations and carry the war into Mexico.

This measure would, it is thought, commit the U. States to a connexion with Texas, which connexion, would result in annexation.

Will not many Go for such a measure who are not prepared to meet the Question of annexation as presented by the Treaty—Will it not divide those who oppose the treaty from timidity, sense of honor, or principle, from the naked Anti Slavery men—and is it not most important that this should be attained[?] If this fund should be thus set apart and used, those who Granted the loan, could ["not" *interlined*] oppose the ulterior measures, to which the loan dire[c]tly points. Upon the rejection of the treaty, could not some of those who shall have voted against it, be induced to propose the loan, to save themselves from odium in the South and West. Of course the Northern Abolitionists, will oppose the measure, and may not the issue be made at once, in Congress, and the opposition to annexation be thus, *practically,* riven asunder.

The Question of Annexation is dire[c]tly involved in the nominations for the Presidency and Vice Presidency. The excitement growing out of it, as you have observed, is spre[a]ding over the entire south. It cannot be kept out of the present canvass. Under these circumstances what will the Baltimore Convention do—Can it be brought to unite on any one man for the first office[?] I regard it as very improbable. Should the convention divide, and make two tickets, for the Democratic party—Would it not be best, that the convention, should make no nomination, and upon its disbandment may not the Republican members of Congress make a caucus nomination ["a nomination, in the event, which is probable, that the" *and several other words canceled*] for the whole party. Many of the delegates to the Baltimore convention, have been instructed. It is now too late to call another convention of the people. May not the nomination be made at Washington, (merely recommendatory of course) which nominations may be ratified in county and State conventions.

In the event that the Baltimore convention shall nominate Mr. [Martin] Van Buren what will the friends of annexation do—Will they bring out a man of their own[?] I think they should. The South and West must unite in support of such a candidate. Fourteen of the southern and western States could, it is thought, be brought to his support—without doubt—leaving him the chance for Ohio, Michigan, Delaware and possibly Pennsylvania.

The South relies on You, far more than any other individual, to secure the success of this measure. You are, unquestionably, the man of their choice, for this undertaking. Nevertheless, if the success of the measure, should require the *postponement* of Your claims, (and I do not see how it should), the Glory of such success, will be Yours in a preeminent degree, and ["it" *interlined*] will still more endear You to the Southern people that You have made the sacrifice.

I have written this letter after consultation with a distinguished friend of the States right school of politics and an ardent friend of the annexation. The thoughts are hastily thrown together and You will value them according to their worth. I have the Honor to be most respectfully Y[ou]r ob[edien]t ser[van]t, C.W. Hall.

P.S. In the event that Mr. Van Buren is nominated by the Baltimore convention, I suppose that it would be impr[a]cticable, for the friends of annexation to Get up a regularly organized convention, for the purpose of bringing forward a candidate friendly to that measure. Should not members of Congress, friendly to the measure, make a Caucus nomination to be ratified in county or State conventions[?] C.W.H.

ALS in ScCleA.

From ROB[ER]T MONROE HARRISON

Consulate of the United States
Kingston Jam[aic]a, 20th May 1844

Sir, Herewith I have the honor to enclose you a letter from Capt. [Thomas W.] Freelon of the U. States Ship Preble, as also one from Mr. [William B.] "Gooch" the Commercial Agent at Aux Cayes: by which you will perceive that additional Naval force is required for the protection of our fellow citizens and their property at that place.

Owing to the immediate departure of the vessel which takes this, I have not time to make copies, and therefore send them as they are, which I trust you will excuse. With profound respect I have the honor to be Sir Your ob[edien]t & most humble Serv[an]t, Robt. Monroe Harrison.

P.S. As the vessel which takes this has made a stay of a few hours longer than was intended, I have been enabled to take copies of the letters of Mr. Gooch and Capt. Freelon; which I now have the honor to enclose.

[Enclosure]

Tho[ma]s W. Freelon to R[obert] M. Harrison, "Copy"

U.S. Ship Preble
Aux Cayes, May 15th 1844

My Dear Sir, Things here remain pretty much in the same state as when I last wrote you, only worse if any thing. Accao, who has proved himself to be little better than a Savage beast, has commenced confiscating and pillaging the houses and stores of the Haitien Merchants who have emigrated. The House of Blanchard & Co. went yesterday, and to day the House of Castell & Co., besides several minor houses. In these confiscations considerable American and English property has been seized, as Mr. Gooch our Commercial Agent has been acting for the firm of Lecour & Co. emigrés now in Jamaica, and Mr. Smith the Acting English Vice Consul has been acting under a Power of Attorney from Blanchard & Co. Gooch has acted very foolishly throughout the whole matter; and I fear will be a large sufferer, as he has mixed up his affairs with the Haytiens in such a manner, that it will be a difficult matter to unravel them. In the meantime I can do nothing but make a reclamation upon Acaou for the amount of American property in his hands, which will be of no more weight with him than a piece of blank paper, as he sets all laws, human and divine, at defiance; and to make reprisals would be the certain destruction not only of the property, but of the lives of

566

every white in the Town. Yesterday he ordered Mr. Smith the English Vice Consul and Mr. Gooch into prison; but before they were seized by the guard, they escaped on board this ship, where they remained during the day. Every person on shore is in a feverish state of excitement, and none know how long they will be safe. In the meantime the Army has elected Gen. [Philippe] Guerrier an old General of [Henri] Christophe, President. He has issued his proclamation calling upon the people to join him for the sake of their common country. Acaou has issued his counter proclamation framed with much cunning, in which, though he does not accept nor reject Guerrier, yet he objects to some of the promotions in the Army &c. The Deputation sent to him by Gen. Guerrier, he would not see for four days, and when he did see them, treated them with much contumely. They left this morning to rejoin Gen[era]l Guerrier, with a firm conviction that nothing can save the town, but his immediate march upon it. He has here but about Five hundred troops, if troops they may be called, consisting of ragged and naked negroes, armed principally with long poles sharpened at the end, but holding him in such awe that they do his bidding with the greatest promptitude. Last evening he surrounded Fort Boyer, where his prisoners are confined, with a detachment of these wretches, marched out the prisoners, more than a hundred in number, and caused them all to be unmercifully flogged with oxwhips. He then locked them up again. Besides shooting a great number of men by a file of *soldiers*, some of them, now admitted by all to have been guiltless of the crimes imputed to them; he has shot with a Blunderbuss which he always carrys with him, at least six persons with his own hands. In fact he is one of the most atrocious monsters that ever existed in ancient or modern times. His natural ferocity is stimulated by a free use of the rum of the country. I have seen him three times, and the two latter times he was literally drunk. I[n] my presence, both times, he knocked down one of his aides de Camp, tore their swords from their sides, and would have killed them had they not escaped by jumping downstairs. They were then sent to prison. When I first saw him, and read his proclamations, I had rather a favorable opinion of him, but I am now satisfied that he is a savage and ferocious beast rather than a man. This afternoon the Sch[ooner] Talma from Washington N.C. arrived here with a cargo of lumber consigned to Blanchard & Co. I have saved this cargo from his clutches by advising the Captain to leave the road instantly and make for some Port in Cuba, as the cargo would certainly have been confiscated as the property of Blanchard

& Co. the moment she entered the inner harbour, as was the proceeds of the sales of the cargo of the Joseph Atkins which was consigned to the same house. During this state of things, where are the West India Squadrons of our Navy, and of that of G[rea]t Britain[?] Five days ago, the Brig Griffon, the only British vessel of war in Port, left here for Jacmel. This morning the Sch[ooner] Pickle arrived to supply her place. There are millions of English property at stake, and a large amount of American; and yet the two nations most interested have not a force here, sufficient to command respect. The French have one Brig here, but there is no cooperation with them, as I have no doubt but they rejoice to see the Island in such a distracted state, as it will facilitate their once more getting a foot hold here; which I have no doubt they intend to do, at the earliest opportunity. Excuse this hasty scrawl, and Believe me My Dear Sir With sentiments of high respect Your friend and ob[edien]t serv[an]t, signed Thos. W. Freelon.

ALS (No. 286) with Ens in DNA, RG 59 (State Department), Consular Despatches, Kingston, vol. 9 (T-31:9), received 6/22. NOTE: Harrison also enclosed a copy of a letter to himself from W[illia]m B. Gooch, U.S. Commercial Agent at Aux Cayes, dated 5/15. Gooch described the situation at Aux Cayes and emphasized the need for a show of U.S. naval force. He characterized Acaau as "a complete land Pirate, two thirds of the time intoxicated and a perfect ferocious brute." A State Dept. Clerk's EU, dated 6/24, reads "Respectfully referred to the Sec[retar]y of the Navy [John Y. Mason] for perusal with a request that the letter & enclosures may be returned to the Dept. of State."

From L[ANSFORD] W. HASTINGS

New Madrid Mo., May the 20th 1844
Dear Sir, I have just received your favour of the 11th Inst., for which please accept my thanks.

You express a wish to receive from me, any information which I have in my possession, in relation [to] Oregon and California, not having time at this moment, to communicate to you as fully as I would wish to do, I have thought proper, at this time, merely to forward to you, a letter that I have in my possession, which I wrote immediately upon arriving in the United States from Oregon. This you will observe, gives you briefly, the present political condition of Oregon, also a brief description of California. I shall write to you more fully however, in reference to both those countries, at some future period.

There are some revolutionary arrangements, now being made, in California, of which I stand fully advised. If you are of the opinion, that information in relation to ["which" *canceled*] that matter would be of any importance to the U.S. government, I shall feel myself in duty bound, as a citizen of this government, to inform you more particularly in reference to ["every thing" *interlined*] appertaining thereunto.

From the seeming neglect of our government, of her citizens in Oregon, great dissatisfaction exists throughout the entire country, hence the question is constantly discussed (among our citizens there, and other[s] also,) whether it would not be more conducive to the interests and happiness ["of" *interlined*] all citizens and subject[s] there, of all governments to absolve all allegiance to their particular governments, and to form and organize a separate and independant government. If the U.S. do not give the people of Oregon, a government of some kind soon, an attempt will be made at an organization of an independant government.

That you may the better know who it is that addresses you, allow me to remark, that I am a native of Ohio, a lawyer by profession, I think I remarked to you in my last, that I have recently returned from Oregon via California, the City of Mexico and Vera Cruz, also that I intend returning to Oregon & California next spring.

Permit me further to remark, that it is absolutely necessary that the people of Oregon have the aid of the U.S. soon, in Establishing a government; without such aid, it is impossible for them to protect themselves against the ravages of the numerous tribes of savage and barbarous Indians, with whom they are everywhere surrounded.

I purpose publishing a small work, in pamphlet form, to be entitled the Emigrant[']s guide, to Oregon and California. This will contain a description of both Oregon and California, also of the intermediate country between the U.S. and those countries. The work above alluded to, will give a more full and accurate description of those countries, than I shall be able to do otherwise, however as you request, I shall write to you in reference to the subjects to which you allude previous to the publication of the above mentioned work. Allow me to subscribe myself, Dear Sir, Your ob[edien]t humble Serv[an]t, L.W. Hastings.

ALS in ScCleA; PC in Boucher and Brooks, eds., *Correspondence*, pp. 234–235.

From Whitemarsh B. Seabrook, Edisto Island, [S.C.], 5/20. He introduces Hugh Wilson, Jr., who plans to visit Europe "with a sick relation." Wilson is well educated, a planter, and "a zealous disciple of the Jeffersonian school, and fought bravely in the glorious cause of nullification." ALS in DNA, RG 59 (State Department), Passport Applications, vol. 31, nos. 2206 and 2207 (M-1372:14).

From W. W. T. SMITH

Consulate of the U.S., Port La Baca [*sic*] in
Matagorda Bay, Texas, May 20th 1844

Hon. Sir, Permit me to call your attention to a subject of great importance to the commerce of the U.S. as far as Texas is concerned. I allude to the non-existance of a commercial Treaty between the two countries. Goods and merchandize imported into this country in U.S. vessels pay 5 per cent duty more than those imported in Texas vessels or in vessels belonging to those countries between which and Texas commercial Treaties exist. U.S. vessels have also to pay a Tonnage duty of one dollar per Ton on entering into any of the ports of this republic. This matter is regulated by treaty with England & France. I would also call your attention to the injury sustained by the shipping interest of the U.S. in consequence in consequence [*sic*] of the duty imposed by the Tariff law of the U.S. on cotton imported into that country. I can not see that any interest in the U.S. is benefited by the imposition of this ["law" *canceled*] duty. It affords no protection to the cotton planter for an article cannot be protected when the supply of the article exceeds the demand in the country in which it is produced. It is only when the demand is greater than the supply that protection can be afforded. It is of no advantage as a revenue law for importation is only made with a view to exportation subject to the drawback law[,] the duty in other respects amounting to a prohibition. No interest then is benefited. Let us see the injury that results from this as I think impolitic law. If no such law existed in the U.S. almost all the cotton of Texas would be shipped there and in our vessels for Texas has no shipping and it will be many years before it will be her interest to have any. Then this cotton would be shipped from the U.S. to England, France and other European countries the U.S. having the advantage again in this re-shipment. This would be of immense advantage to the shipping interest besides furnishing employment to thousands of labourers, draymen, and commission and forwarding and receiving merchants &c &c. But the advantages would not rest here. The vessels that would carry the cotton of Texas to New York, Philadelphia, Boston and New Orleans would bring back the manufactures of the U.S. and the manufactures of other countries that would thus pass through the U.S. to Texas as well as many of the products of the U.S. not now raised in Texas. According to the relations now existing between the two countries most of the carrying trade is done by European vessels. Those nations that have commercial treaties with Texas have an immense advantage in conducting this trade. Their ships come here after Texas cotton and bring the manufactures and products of their own countries to Texas which ought naturally to be supplied by the U.S. I have thus hastily but as succinctly as possible called your attention to this subject. Should annexation be delayed I consider it a subject of great importance to the U.S. It will afford me great pleasure in accordance with my duty to furnish any information on this subject. Hon. Sir I am your obedient servant, W.W.T. Smith, U.S. Consul.

ALS (No. 12) in DNA, RG 59 (State Department), Consular Despatches, Texas, vol. 1 (T-153:1), received 6/15.

From MOSES STUART

Andover (Mass.), 20 May 1844

My dear Sir, I am happy to address you as *Secretary of State;* a place that I doubt not you will fill with honour & profit to the country, although the times are unpropitious to profitable action. But of one thing I feel assured, which is, that you will not tarnish your own reputation by either proposing, or acceding to, any measures which will bring dishonour on yourself or on your country. The high minded course which you have always pursued, commands, & will command, respect from all quarters, however the sentiments of any may differ from your own.

I feel embar[r]assed in stating to you the object of this note. Once or twice before I have felt obliged to trouble you with our concerns here in respect to our *post-office.* It is a contemptible business; & yet there is a constant scramble for it. I will tell the story in the fewest possible words.

Some half year since, Mr. [William] Pierce, our former postmaster, was displaced in order to appoint a *Mr.* [Samuel] *Phillips,* formerly Collector (under Mr. Van Buren's administration) at *Newbury Port,* Mass. Mr. P[hillips] is a N[ew] Eng[land] Democrat—not a rabid one, but a gentlemanly sort of a man, accurate in business, & agreeable *as a post-master* to this whole place—to both parties.

A young man of the village, for want of other employment, is trying to *oust* him, by professions of strong *Tylerism*, & all that sort of office-hunting apparatus. This young man (by name *Clark*) would be absolutely offensive to nine-tenths of the people here. They are content with *Phillips*, so far as the question concerns these two men; & indeed, in himself, he is a really good officer, & a change w[oul]d be preposterous, after his obtaining the place on the ground that he did—viz. as a friend of the present administration.

Mr. P[hillips], at all events, is a strong friend of yours; & there is no ground whatever to dismiss him from office. If you see it in your way to say a word on this subject, [*partial word canceled*] so as to prevent another *faux pas* of the government, & oblige the people of this place, it will be most gratefully remembered. It will prevent much mischief, & many broils. It would be preposterous to make another change, so quick, & without any reason whatever; & specially to appoint a young aspirant, who has nothing to recommend him, but assumed & temporary zeal for the present administration, i.e. for Pres[ident John] Tyler.

Please to excuse so dull & dry a letter, from one who would like to pour out his heart to you in respect to topics of deep interest to you & country, but who is in a *sick chamber* at present, & can write no more. Excuse the illegibility of this Note, which comes from a hand made trembling by a long protracted fever. With high respect & much affection, Truly your Friend & obed[ien]t Ser[van]t, Moses Stuart.

P.S. Please to consider this as *private*, & to destroy it when read. The parties here go to Washington, *hunt up all letters*, etc., & come back to make mischief about them. M.S.

ALS in ScCleA. NOTE: Stuart marked this letter "Care of Mr. Phillips," by whom it was likely hand-delivered to Calhoun. An AEU by Calhoun reads "Professor Stuart [of Andover Theological Seminary]. In reference to the P[ost] Master at Andover."

To [JOHN TYLER]

Department of State
Washington, 20th May, 1844

To the President of the United States:

The Secretary of State, to whom has been referred the Resolution of the House of Representatives of the 22nd ult[im]o requesting the President to inform the House, "what measures, if any, are now in progress to obtain from the Government of Denmark, indemnity for three ships and their cargoes, sent by Commodore John Paul Jones, in the year 1779, as prizes into Bergen, and there surrendered by order of the Danish King to the British Minister, in obedience to the demand of that Minister," has the honor to submit copies of the following letters, which appear to contain the information called for by the former portion of the Resolution.

The latter part of the Resolution inquires "whether the treaty concluded between our Government and Denmark, in 1830, in pursuance of which $650,000 were paid by Denmark to the Government of the United States, in satisfaction of all claims which had theretofore been preferred by citizens of the United States on the Government of Denmark, did, in its execution, embrace the claim to indemnity for the aforesaid prizes sent by Commodore John Paul Jones into Bergen; and, if not so included, are the claimants to those prizes excluded, by the terms of that treaty from further claim on the Government of Denmark?"

In regard to the inquiry embraced in the latter part of this Resolution, the Secretary of State is unable to perceive any thing in the Treaty which would bar the claim in question.   J.C. Calhoun.

LS in DNA, RG 233 (U.S. House of Representatives), 28A-E1; FC in DNA, RG 59 (State Department), Reports of the Secretary of State to the President and Congress, 6:106–107; PC in Jameson, ed., *Correspondence*, pp. 590–591. NOTE: Enclosed were extracts from four letters exchanged by the State Department and William W. Irwin, Chargé d'Affaires in Denmark, in 1843 and early 1844.   Tyler transmitted this letter and its Ens to the Senate on 5/20.   The House resolution of 4/22 to which it is a response can be found in DNA, RG 59 (State Department), Miscellaneous Letters (M-179:104, frame 217), and in *House Journal*, 28th Cong., 1st Sess., p. 843.

From Fernando Wood, New York [City], 5/20.   In undertaking his duties as Despatch Agent at New York, Wood has found numerous letters and boxes of material for various missions and consulates from the State Department that were not forwarded by his predecessor. He asks whether the State Department will pay the expenses involved in forwarding this material.   He also asks that he be sent blank passports for despatch bearers since there are numerous highly respectable citizens who would willingly carry despatches free of charge.   ALS in DNA, RG 59 (State Department), Passport Applications, vol. 31, unnumbered (M-1372:14).

To Henry W. Andrews & Co., Philadelphia, 5/21.   Calhoun acknowledges their letter of 5/20 and replies that steps have already been taken to protect the interests of U.S. citizens living in or trading with Santo Domingo. FC in DNA, RG 59 (State Department), Domestic Letters, 34:205 (M-40:32).

From J[OHN] S. BARBOUR, "Private"

Catalpa [Va.] May 21st 1844

My Dear Sir, The people of Culpeper had a meeting on the Texas question yesterday. It was contemplated to pass a resolution denouncing [Martin] Van Buren: & strange to say, Extra Smith [that is, William ("Extra Billy") Smith] urged it. I thought this unwise, as I do denunciation of any of the candidates, now before the public. My son [John S. Barbour, Jr.] drew upon his knee two brief resolutions, declaring for immediate annexation and that it was indispensable to us at this time and paramount to all other topicks for the publick deliberation. These were unanimously carried. And the resolution intended[?] (but not offered) ag[ains]t V[an] B[uren] w[oul]d have passed too, but it w[oul]d have kindled dissention & was therefore, (*I thought*) unwise. If we succeed at all, it will need *all our strength*; & if success be worth acquisition, it is worth the concord, that can alone secure it.

This is my view. Any other course is at once to surrender the citadel to the enemy. I hope to be with you in a day or two. Every thing in this particular will turn upon the tidings that may reach me tonight by the mail. If I can do good, I will go to Balt[im]o[re]—if not, it were an idle waste of my[?] time & money. If [Richard M.] Johnson & [Henry A.P.] Muhlenberg were run in one quarter & you & [Levi] Woodbury in another, [Henry] Clay might be defeated & the election devolved on the Ho[use] of Rep[resentative]s. But in that is the rub. The Whigs w[oul]d hold the bal[an]ce[?] & bargain & intrigue carry the point—and were it made with perfect purity distrust would still cloud it.

The temper of Virginia through all her border is Anti-V[an] Buren, and it is much stronger Anti-Tyler. It is singular in this quarter that his worst foes are those on whom he has lavished the trusts[?] & the money of the Country. He has given several offices & other "Keys"[?] in this quarter & the families he fostered by the use of the patronage in his hands, are the most bitter & denunciatory. The effort to run Tyler will do you mischief. I distrusted the policy of your going in to the Cabinet, unless with a distinct understanding that you were to discharge your office, & *no more*, and I was unwilling to see you accept it, after hearing from Mr. [William C.] Rives [Senator from Va.] the expressions of ["his" *interlined*] Tyler[']s letter which he ["(Rives)" *interlined*] said he had heard from Mr. [William] Wilkins Sec[re]t[ar]y [of] War; and the expressions were, that he w[oul]d not have tendered you the office, if your name had not been withdrawn from the list of candidates for the Presidency. In this he was begging the question. You had set up no pretensions & had therefore none to withdraw. But the language implied an expectation that you w[oul]d aid his own views. As a choice among others, united with a prospect of giving effect to [*one word canceled*] to [*sic*] the choice, he is to be preferred & greatly preferred to most others. It is a *felo de se* to think of him, & the thought should be a *deodand* at the shrine of credulity. We thought last winter of making him Governor of the State, at the expiration of his term; & the purpose would have been accomplished, in return for ["the" *interlined*] odium & opprobrium of the whigs. In great haste, y[ou]rs Sincerely, J.S. Barbour.

ALS in ScCleA.

From Weston F. Birch, U.S. Marshal, St. Louis, 5/21. Birch acknowledges receipt of Calhoun's letter of 5/7 enclosing a Presidential pardon for William Mason, who has been "forthwith discharged from imprisonment." ALS in DNA, RG 59 (State Department), Petitions for Pardon, 1789–1869, Tyler Administration.

To R[OBERT] M. T. HUNTER, [Lloyds, Va.]

State Department, 21st May 1844

My dear Sir, I would take pleasure in meeting your wishes in reference to Mr. Parker, should an opportunity occur. I have one or two engagements for the place of bearer of dispatches. After that, should there be a necessity for one, I would be glad to confer it on him.

I regret, that I had not an opportunity of seeing him when he was here. He left his letter of introduction at the office with his card; but before I had an opportunity to call on him, he had, I learned, left the city.

I am glad to learn, that you will be at the Convention. Its proceedings will be pregnant with much good or evil. You must make a point to take Washington in your way. It will be indispensible, I should see you, in order to explain what is the actual state of things here. Without that it will be impossible to act intelligently and with effect; and it would ["be" *interlined*] difficult to give you a full explanation within the ["ordinary" *interlined*] limits of a letter. I will expect you, and you must not disappoint me. Yours truly, J.C. Calhoun.

ALS in ScCleA; PEx in Jameson, ed., *Correspondence*, p. 591.

From LOMBARD & WHITMORE and JOSEPH W. GREEN

Boston, May 21st 1844

Sir, The undersigned Merchants of this City extensively engaged in commerce with the Island of St. Domingo respectfully & earnestly request that a sufficient Naval force may be kept on the Coasts and at the ports of that Island to protect the property of American Citizens.

The late revolutionary movements at Aux Cayes and the apprehension of immediate similar ["events" *interlined*] at Port au Prince and other ports have placed their property in great danger. With the highest Respect Your Very Ob[edien]t Ser[van]ts, Lombard & Whitmore, Joseph W. Green.

LS in DNA, RG 59 (State Department), Miscellaneous Letters (M-179:104, frames 395–396).

From John McKeon, New York [City], 5/21. "Mr. [Gerard H.] Coster will go to Berlin. I shall be extremely obliged to you if you will send the papers by return mail. Mr. Coster intends to leave immediately and will take good care of your despatches." ALS in DNA, RG 59 (State Department), Passport Applications, vol. 31, no. 113 (M-1372:14).

From JOHN T. REID

City of Washington, 21st May 1844

Sir, In consequence of the conversation which I had the honor of holding with you a few days ago, I wrote the Secretary of the New

York and South American Steamboat Association, and have received his reply.

As mentioned in my former letter [of 5/1], the claim of the Association amounted to $150,000, (One hundred & fifty Thousand Dollars). Upon the ground of delay of justice, the Brazilian Government are liable for Interest on this sum, and therefore the gentlemen interested, are desirous that the claim should in the first instance, be pressed for payment both of principal and interest. Annexed I send a statement of the Claim with Interest calculated at various rates. If Mr. [Henry A.] Wise however should ascertain that the insisting on interest presents an obstacle to a settlement, and that giving it up would end the matter, my constituents as a last resort, are willing that he should agree to accept, Two Hundred Thousand Dollars, or even One Hundred and fifty Thousand Dollars, *as a compromise* in full of the claim of the Association.

From a conversation I had with the gentleman in the [State] Department who has charge of the correspondence with Brazil [William Hunter, Jr.], I understand the other claims which Citizens of the United States have against the Brazilian Government are few, and that the claim of the Steamboat Company is the only one of any importance. As it stands on ground peculiarly its own, and in all probability will have to be compromised, the gentlemen interested, are desirous that it should be urged separate and distinct from the other claims, until some final arrangement shall be made with the Brazilian Government, fixing and ascertaining the precise sum to be paid by them to the Claimants. Of course they would desire that any amount for which their claim might be compromised should be paid at as early a day as possible, but if any delay is to take place interest can be stipulated for.

It is perhaps necessary to mention to Mr. Wise, that all former Powers of Attorney by the Association relating to this subject have been revoked, and that a Letter of Attorney has been executed in my favour to take charge of it hereafter. In all probability I shall shortly proceed to Rio to afford him any aid I can in the prosecution of the claim. With great respect I have the honor to be Sir Your Obedient Servant, John T. Reid.

CC with En in DNA, RG 76 (Records of Boundary and Claims Commissions and Arbitrations), Miscellaneous Claims Records, Brazil Convention, January 27, 1849.

From H. GOLD ROGERS

Pittsburgh United States of America
May 21, 1844

Sir, The Undersigned [former] Chargé d'Affaires of the United [States] of America to Sardinia by virtue of a Commission from the President of the United States [Martin Van Buren] and late Envoy Extraordinary after treaty formed to Italy respectfully solicits from the Secretary of State of the United States of America the appointment of Envoy Extr[a]ordinary and Minister Plenipotentiary to Austria with *plein Pouvoirs* to make treaties with Tuscany, Modena[,] Parma and Plaisance [*sic*; Piacenza or Placentia]. I am Sir with great respect your obedient Servant, H. Gold Rogers.

ALS in DNA, RG 59 (State Department), Applications and Recommendations, 1837–1845, Rogers (M-687:28, frames 476–477).

To I[srael] K. Tefft, Savannah, 5/21. Calhoun acknowledges receipt "by the hand of Mr. [William B.] Hodgson [of] my Diploma of Honorary membership of the Georgia Historical Society, and the two volumes of its collections. . . . The delay in transmitting this receipt is to be attributed to the great pressure of my official duties, which has in a great measure suspended my private correspondence since my arrival here." ALS in CtY, Sterling Library, Miscellaneous Manuscripts.

From J[oseph] A. Woodward, [Representative from S.C.], 5/21. He encloses a letter [to himself, dated 4/21] from Francis Bulkley and endorses Bulkley's wish for a Consular appointment in a southern locale. ALS with En in DNA, RG 59 (State Department), Applications and Recommendations, 1837–1845, Bulkley (M-687:3, frames 590–593).

From ARCH[IBAL]D H. ARRINGTON, [Representative from N.C.]

House of Representatives
May 22d 1844

Sir, I am at a loss to know whether under the Treaty with Denmark the Claim to which the letter which I have the honor herewith to enclose alludes, is embraced or not. Will you do me the favor to cause the same to ["be" *interlined*] examined and furnish me with the desired information. With great Respect Your ob[edien]t Serv[an]t, Archd. H. Arrington.

[Enclosure]
Wallace D. Styron to A[rchibald] H. Arrington
Straits near Beaufort N. Carolina Carteret County
March 18th 1844

Sir, You must pardon me for Troubling you with a line as I know of no other channel through which I can obtain the information wanted. I must therefore solicit of you the favour to inform me in the first place if the Government of the United States has not received from the Kingdom of Denmark Indemnity for certain prizes taken by [John] Paul Jones in the time of the Revolutionary war & sent in to Denmark and there retaken by the British and if so if those concerned in the Capture and carr[y]ing in of those prizes are not Justly intitled to a part of that indemnity as prize money and if they were entitled if their Heirs are not also entitled and if so what proof would be necessary to inable the Heir to obtain his parent['s] part. My reason for the above inquiries is this. My Father George Styron with another young man from this place by the name of Henry Salter were ingaged in the taking of said prizes and my Father acting as prize master & Salter as prize master[']s mate Carried one of Said Ships into Denmark where he was taken with his prize by the Brittish and my Father and Salter confined in Mill Prison England untill the close of the war. Both of these men beign now dead nothing more can be proven now only what they both told when they returned and during their lives. Please make all the necessary inquiry as to the amount due if any and the propper course to persue to obtain it and inform me by letter as soon as convenient and much oblige your cincere friend, Wallace D. Styron.

ALS with En in DNA, RG 59 (State Department), Miscellaneous Letters (M-179:104, frames 396–398).

From FLORIDE [COLHOUN] CALHOUN

Forthill, May 22d 1844
My Dear Husband, I hope ere this letter reaches you, John [C. Calhoun, Jr.] has arrived at Washington. I was very uneasy fearing he would not be in time, but he lost nothing by coming home, as there was no way for him to go to Edgefield, from his Uncle[']s [James

Edward Colhoun's]. And he was so anxious to see all at home once more. I had all he required made here, he ondly [*sic*] needed some pockethandkerchieves. I was sorry he would not take on some of his wo[o]llen clothes, at any rate he ought to have taken his frockcoat, and one pair of pantaloons. I tryed my best to persuade him to do it.

I saw Mr. Fred[e]ricks last night, he says all is going on well on the plantation. His wheat is nearly ready to cut, and looks finely. His corn, and cotton, is remarkably good considering the drouth. It is now raining, and looks as though the season would be fine. The crops at Abbeville, have suffered much more than ours.

James [Edward Calhoun] has gone down to his Uncle['] s in the Dearborn, he went down prepared to stay at school, provided it was safe to do so. The rumour here is that Lowndesville is very sickly in summer. If so he is to return in the Dearborn, with Andrew, James [Edward Colhoun's] Stone mason, and bricklayer. He has loaned him to me for one month. As soon as he comes I shall set him to cut stone, like Mr. Kirkseys, under his pillars at the [Pendleton] Village. And after that put him to the well place to arch[?], and fix it compleatly. I told James to ask his Uncle, to let me have him longer than a month. He is as good a workman, and better, than Hall.

I have written Martha [Calhoun Burt in Washington], to get the articles for me, I wrote you, and Patrick for. She wrote me to say she would attend to any thing I wished. You can read her letter. I requested her to consult with both yourself, and Patrick, as to what things had he got, so that there can be no mistake. I wrote her to get [Martha] Cornelia [Calhoun], a mourning breastpin, as she has none. I also requested her to get the articles as reasonably as possible. As soon as the things are ready, do send them on. I mean by the first person that comes on here or near us. If Martha does not come sooner than than [*sic*] the Adjournment of Congress. Perhaps Mr. [Richard F.] Sim[p]son [Representative from S.C.] will bring them directly here, it will be the best anyhow.

Do let me know if there is any prospect of your coming home this summer. If the two questions should not be settled when Congress rises, I think you might leave the business of the Department to some one while you come on. All are well but myself. I have occasionally a stricture in my chest, and great weakness in my back, so much so that I cannot bear my corsets, but sit almost doubled at times, to get relief. The fatigue, and anxiety has been too much for me. I have Mrs. G[a]illard[?] staying with me, she makes me take long walks. The first evening we went by the mill, and returned by the Millpond. I have not walked as much in a long time. The crop looks very clean, and the fence is far further than I thought. I have Mrs. Ga[i]llard[']s coachman helping us, which I am glad of. He is a steady boy. Mr. Mann is at work at last on the Piasa[?]. He seems to work very steady. He has a hand working with him. I did not send William Lowndes [Calhoun] down with James until I heard about the place. All join me in much love. Your affectionate Wife, Floride Calhoun.

P.S. I have received the check, and sent 50 to Edgefield by My Brother. I let John have 11 to take him to Edgefield.

ALS in ScCleA.

From R [ICHARD] K. CALL, [Governor of Fla. Territory]

Tallahassee, 22nd May 1844

Sir, I beg leave to place before you charges of a grave and serious character against Charles S. Sibley Dist[rict] Att[orne]y of the United States for the Middle District of Florida.

First I charge the said District Attorney with aiding and promoting malicious prosecutions to gratify personal and political animosity. The Specifications for this charge will be found in two indictments for "nuisance" prepared and signed by said District Att[orne]y against myself at the May term 1844 of the Superior Court for the County of Wakulla.

The first of these indictments charges in the usual form that Richard K. Call did on the 1st day of January 1844 "*unlawfully wilfully* and *maliciously*" erect a pier or piller composed of wood and stone, in the St. Marks River, a navigable stream, by which the navigation of said River is obstructed. An examination of the facts of this case, facts universally known in this community, and to no one better than to the said Attorney, will prove to the satisfaction of any unprejudiced mind, the wanton malice, or gross ignorance, in which this prosecution originated.

Here where the facts are known this proceeding excites only the contempt and ridicule of all honest and intelligent men. But at Washington where it was intended to operate, and where the facts are unknown, to have it said that the Governor of Florida has been indicted, leaves the impression that he has been guilty of some violation of law or good morals, which renders him amenable to criminal justice. A brief narrative of the facts will shew the injustice of such a conclusion. In the year 1834 the Legislative Council of Florida, granted a charter to the Tallahassee Rail Road Company. I soon after became one of the principal Stock holders, and the President of that Company which situation I still hold. The charter authorized in express terms the company to construct a draw bridge over the St. Marks River at the intersection with the Rail Road. This was accordingly done, and the pier, for the erection of which I am now indicted was built by the direction of the Company, and under the express authority of Law as early as the year 1839. The draw of this Bridge was sufficient for the accom[m]odation of all vessels navigating the St. Marks River, and from the time of its construction until the 13th of Sept. 1843, a period of near five years, no difficulty or delay attended any vessel bound up or down the river in passing the bridge. At the date above mentioned the bridge was swept of[f] by a storm which desolated that part of our Sea Board, leaving the pier standing in the River with a clear and unobstructed passage on each side of it, sufficient to admit with convenience the passage of the largest vessel which can ever ascend the St. Marks River.

The charge then of obstructing the navigation of the St. Marks River by the erection of the pier is false and unfounded, and the charge of erecting the pier unlawfully, and maliciously is also false and known to be so, by the District Attorney before and at the time of drawing the Indictment. I make this unqualified charge against the District Attorney, because I know he has been frequently on the Bridge, was well acquainted with its localities, and that he had every opportunity of reading the charter in our Statute Book, under which the Bridge was constructed.

The disastrous storm of the 13th of September 1843, by which I sustained a loss of not less than $50,000 carried the Bridge erected on the pier, and deposited it, partly on the Bank, and partly in the River, a short distance above its former position, and this combined action of the elements, directed by the hand of Providence, constitutes the ground of the second indictment which charges that Richard K. Call did "*unlawfully*" and "*maliciously*" fix place put and set a certain [w]reck of a bridge in the St. Marks River, a navigable stream, by which the navigation is obstructed, when it was well known to the said District Attorney, that the Bridge was removed and placed where it now is, by the will of God.

I therefore charge, and from facts and circumstances, shall I think be able to prove that the said District Attorney well knew every material statement contained in both indictments to be false at the time of drawing them, and that he has prostituted the authority of his office for the most unwarranted, and malicious purposes.

I further charge the said District Attorney with high misdemeanor, in compromising various criminal prosecutions in the courts of this District for private ends, and I charge him with official impropriety in receiving pay in the name of fees from defendants in criminal cases, as an inducement to dismiss proceedings against them, after indictments found, and in cases where the facts and the law made it his imperitive duty to prosecute to conviction.

I will sir in a few days forward evidence to support these charges. But if a more public investigation of them should be deemed proper I respectfully recommend that Ex Gov. W[illia]m P. Duval, James E. Broome[,] Judge of the County Court of Leon County ["residing at Tallahassee" *interlined*] & David L. White, Judge of the County Court of Gadsden County, Quincy, be appointed commissioners to take testimony, and report the result to the proper Department of the Government. I have the honour to be Very Respectfully Your Ob[e-dien]t S[ervan]t, R.K. Call.

LS in DNA, RG 59 (State Department), Applications and Recommendations, 1837–1845, Sibley (M-687:30, frames 80–83); PC in Carter, ed., *Territorial Papers*, 26:905–907. NOTE: Call's term as governor expired on 8/11. On 6/14 John Branch of N.C. was appointed to succeed him.

From CH[ARLES] AUG[USTU]S DAVIS, "Unofficial"

New York [City,] 22 May 1844

My D[ea]r Sir, I am in rec[eip]t of your kind notes [*not found*] on the subject of special "dispatch bag" which I had the honor at the instance of Mr. [William R.] King to suggest to you—and fully appreciate the reasons and motives that govern you in declining to make any alteration. I beg only to repeat that I knew of no existing agency here or I should not have troubled you.

I think I can see here among those I mingle with a very material change of opinion in regard to *"Lord Aberdeen[']s despatch"*—since your last published letter to Mr. [Richard] Pakenham has appeared. It has induced them to read that despatch again and they find matter there which tho' it escaped their notice did not escape yours. I said from the first and on all occasions have spoken and written since— that it contained the most imprudent and dangerous sentiments that for many years had ever been presented by that Gov't to this—but these Sentiments were so *kindly* decorated with *rose leaves* and spread over with so much *honey*—no wonder many were misled. Your last publish'd Letter to Mr. Pakenham has so effectually scraped off these rose leaves & honey—that people begin to see it in its right light and decide accordingly. And that *general rule* you suggest as best calculated to keep the world in harmony and peace—is capital— and will fail to find favor only among those who are most busy in meddling with other people[']s affairs—and even they can't except to it. I predict that *that one remark* alone will open more eyes in England to the impolicy and the inequity of the "meddling principle" than all that Diplomacy has said for years.

I have sent as many copies of it as I could obtain to every body I knew there for it struck my fancy exactly. I am with great respect Y[ou]r Ob[edien]t Ser[vant], Ch: Augs. Davis.

ALS in ScCleA.

BEN E. GREEN to [Gilbert L. Thompson]

Legation of the U.S. of A.
Mexico, May 22d 1844

Sir, The Secretary of State, in his letter to me of the 19th April, states that you are acquainted with the views of the Government of the U.S. in relation to Mexico; and that he wishes me to converse and consult freely with you.

In order to [reach] a more clear understanding you will oblige me by giving me in writing an abstract of those views, and a succinct outline of the propositions, which are to be made to the Mexican Govt. I am, Sir, very respectfully Your ob[edien]t Ser[van]t, Ben E. Green.

ALS (retained copy) in NcU, Duff Green Papers (published microfilm, roll 5, frames 508–509).

From ABBOTT LAWRENCE

Boston, May 22d 1844

My Dear Sir, I have great pleasure in stating that Mr. Henry G. Wolcott has been personally known to me since he attained the age of fourteen years—and that he is in *all respects* qualified to discharge the duties of the office which is sought for him by his brother [J. Huntington Wolcott]. Mr. Wolcott was born in Litchfield Connecticut, and is the son of the late Judge Wolcott of that place—and nephew of the late Governor Oliver Wolcott. He has received an excellent early education, and served an apprenticeship of six years in a large Mercantile House in this City—possessing great energy of character, excellent principles with perfect integrity—["energy" *canceled*] and ability. I have no hesitation in recommending Mr. Wolcott to your favorable consideration, and hope he may be appointed Consul at Ningpo. I have the honor to remain Your Ob[edien]t S[er]v[an]t, Abbott Lawrence.

ALS in DNA, RG 59 (State Department), Applications and Recommendations, 1837–1845, Wolcott (M-687:35, frame 3).

From LOUIS MARK

Washington, 22 May 1844
Sir, Agre[e]ably to your wish I have the honor to inclose a Copy of Mr. [Henry] Wheaton's last Letter to me.

As Great Britain places her claim on the single word of *like* Articles as mentioned in our Convention of 1815, I would suggest that the Goods we import from the Zoll-Verein, Silks, Laces, Toys[,] Embroideries, Glass, Wines and most other Articles included in this Convention with the Zoll Verein, are mostly manufactured by hand, *and* are quite *unlike* any of the Articles now made in England, but if there should be any *like* article, which can only be one of small Amount, might we not at once grant Great Britain the right to enter it at the reduced Duty, if our Custom house find it *like* the Article imported from Germany? I remain with the greatest Respect Your Ob[edient] Ser[van]t, Louis Mark.

ALS with En in DNA, RG 59 (State Department), Miscellaneous Letters (M-179:104, frames 400–402). NOTE: Mark enclosed a letter from Henry Wheaton, dated 4/23, in which Wheaton discussed the question of reduction of duties upon British goods as a result of the proposed German commercial convention.

From J[ohn] Y. Mason, [Secretary of the Navy], 5/22. "In answer to the enquiry contained in the letter of Mr. William J. Kennedy, referred by you to this Department, I have the honor to inform you that, under the restrictions of the law of 1842, it is not probable any appointments of Midshipmen can be made for several years.

Mr. K[ennedy] has already passed the age fixed by the [Navy] Department for an entrance into the Navy as Midshipman." FC in DNA, RG 45 (Naval Records), Miscellaneous Letters Sent by the Secretary of the Navy, 33:427 (M-209:12).

From STEWART NEWELL, [Galveston, Texas Republic]

Consulate of the United States
Port of Sabine, May 22d 1844

Sir, Having closed all official buissiness, requiring my immediate attention, at Sabine, I arrived at this place, on a visit to my family (resident here) several days since, and on the 16th inst[ant], after paying a visit to a Foreign vessel, in this harbour, in Company with President [Samuel] Houston, and our Chargé de Affaires, Gen[era]l [William S.] Murphy, I was in the Afternoon of same day, invited by the latter, to Dine with him. A few minutes before the Dinner was announced, Gen[era]l Murphy called my attention, to a gentleman just passing the Hotel, at which he Gen[era]l Murphy resides, and the questions were asked me, by him, Did I know the person, then passing. I replied in the affirmative.

I was then asked his name, occupation, and qualification, as a Consul of the United States, he being an applicant to Gen[era]l Murphy, for such an Appointment, to Corpus Christi, an inland Port, between the Nueces, and Rio Grand[e] Rivers, within the disputed limits of Mexico, and Texas. I answered the enquiries of Gen[era]l Murphy, as follows. His name is [Alexander] Stevenson, his occupation a Carpenter, that I did not think his associations, and profession, could have qualified him, for such an appointment, as the one named, particularly, as the Trade of the place, is entirely with a view to smuggle, the Merchandize imported through Texas, into that place, thence, over the Rio Grand[e], into Mexico. On the Morning of the day following, I called at the Office of A[rchibald] M. Green Esq[ui]r[e], U.S. Consul, for the Port of Galveston, and was immediately accosted by him, with the same enquiries as above, and stating that he, Mr. Green, ["was" *canceled*] was then addressing a Letter, to Mr. [W.W.T.] Smith, U.S. Consul at Matagorda, reccommending said Stevenson, for an appointment as Vice Consul, to Corpus Christi. To these enquiries, the same answers were given, by me, adding a doubt, that the Govt. of the United States, would confirm, such an appointment, under the state of things, now existing, between Mexico and Texas. While in Mr. Green[']s office, said Stevenson, came to the Door, and requested me, to step outside. I, immediately done so, and there, found another person, with Stevenson, one having a large Cane, the other a heavy Whip, which I learned subsequently, were intended, to be used upon my person, if such enquiries as Stevenson, should make, were answered in the Affirmative, and Stevenson then stated, he had been informed, by a gentleman in Galveston, that I, had spoken lightly of him, Stevenson, and desired to know if such, was the fact. I replied to him, that I had the day before, answered certain enquiries of Gen[era]l Murphy, relative to him Stevenson, but as the Enquiries, and answers thereto, were official, I was not at liberty to divulge them, but assured him, that nothing derogatory to him was said by me. Upon this Stevenson, was requested by me, to step into Mr. Green[']s office, and ask Mr. Green, if any improper reference, had been made by me, relative to him, Stevenson. Upon Mr. Green[']s assurance, Stevenson expressed himself satisfied, of the misrepresentations, made to him.

Upon reflection of the matter, and of escape from a Public Insult, I deemed it due to myself, to ask of Gen[era]l Murphy, if my answers to him, had been made known, by him, to any person (as p[e]r my ["Copy" *interlined*] Note *No. 1*) to Gen[era]l Murphy, and herewith enclosed) dated on the morning of the 17th. Receiveing no answer up to the evening of the 18th, I addressed Note No. 2, to Gen[era]l Murphy, to which his reply No. 3, dated 19th was received, on the Morning of the 20th, the latter after having been placed in a Public Bar Room, without Seal, or Envelope, and as I am informed, opened and read, by several persons, before it was sent to Mr. Green[']s Office, and where I received it, on the 20th. The manner in which said Note (it being Official) was forwarded to me, without Envelope, or Seal, and addressed as p[e]r Original, herewith enclosed, was deemed, by me, as well as all, who saw it, as an intention to insult. I remained in Mr. Green[']s Office, until about Two O[']clock P.M. When Mr. Green and myself, left, he proceeded to his Hotel, opposite his office, and I to my House. Upon my arriving opposite the Hotel, at which Gen[era]l Murphy, and Mr. Green lodged, and while passing, on the opposite side of the Street, I saw Gen[era]l Murphy, shaking his Finger on clenched hand, at me, and with a violent gesture, and loud tone of voice, he, demanded of me, if I, had received his Note. This was repeated a second time, from the side walk. Then, Gen[era]l Murphy having advanced into the Street, again demanded, in a more violent manner, if I had received his Note. I then approached him, with a view to avoid, an exposure of his violence, and feelings, in public, as was evident, must now be the case, unless I did so approach him (although his Note, *and then*, manner, had determined me, otherwise, until I had reflected upon the matter). Upon arriving at the Spot where he Gen[era]l Murphy stood, the question was repeated, in the same rude, and violent manner, to which, I replied, I had received his Note, at Mr. Green[']s office. Upon this, in an increased violent tone, he required, that I should not name, that *Damned rascall, Green*, to him, and demanded of me twice, in rapid succession, to know, if his Note was satisfactory, to which enquiry, I replied, it was not, so far as its being open, and chargeing me, with intention to menace him. To this reply, Gen[era]l Murphy, then apparently, excited to the highest pitch of Rage, (exclaimed) then *God Damn*, you, why don[']t you, answer it. Damn you, answer it, and I will show you two, rascally Consuls, up to the Government, for leagueing together against me (Gen[era]l Murphy) to bring the Govt. into disrepute. I then requested him, as mildly as possible, to have some respect for his Official character, and not bring it, and the Government, and its Officers, into disgrace, by such improper conduct, at the same time, assureing him, that such language and manner, was not only improper, but would not be permitted, towards me, from any person, but that if he, Gen[era]l Murphy, would retire to his Room, with me, I would afford him, every opportunity, to discuss these matters. His reply was still, abusive, and upon my being about to leave him, he again repeated, that he would expose "you two Consuls" to the Government as disreputable (meaning Mr. Green and myself). Upon thus hearing his name used, Mr. Green advanced to Gen[era]l Murphy, and forbid his useing such language, relative to him Green.

I then interfered, and separated Gen[era]l Murphy, and Green. We each then retired, and the Assembly of persons present, dispersed. On the same Evening, as demanded, I addressed my Note *No. 4*, to Gen[era]l Murphy, and to which I have received no reply, nor indeed, did I expect one.

From this plain statement of facts, the Hon. Secretary, will see the unfortunate state, of our Diplomatic relations, in this Country, with all official and friendly relations, broken off, by the acts of the Minister, in consequence of a free indulgence, as I believe, in stimulating drinks, and associations with, Men of a low and vulgar standing, in this community. His foibles ministered to, by such sycophants, as he attracts around him, his manner, and language, has become of the most overbearing, vulgar, and indecent, character, and not to find a congenial spirit, in a person, is sufficient, to change *his* feelings, towards such person, and I assure the Hon. Secretary, this is not the first time Gen[era]l Murphy, has treated me, with unbecomeing conduct, on his part, even when applying to him, for information, and advice, as to official duties, and which I had determined to bear patiently, during the important negotiations, for annexation, and not to intrude private differences, upon the Department, at so all important a time, for both Governments, but the last Outrage, being committed upon me, in the Public Street, and in open daylight, in presence of an assembly of more than Twenty respectable Citizens, and Strangers, leaves me, no other alternative, than to communicate the same to the Department, for a settlement, of this unpleasant difference, and trust that such consideration, will be given to it, as the case may require, and I beg leave here to remark, that Gen[era]l Murphy, has even descended to request, of a highly respectable gentleman, to find out something, that would operate against me, and enable *him*, to Act against me, for what reason I know not, unless from my intimacy with Mr. Green, and with whom Gen[era]l Murphy, has had some difference.

I have allways, met the most Courteous, and friendly offices from Mr. Green, towards me, Officially, and Privately, and his Official and private conduct, here, has secured ["to" *interlined*] him, many warm friends, but this has apparently, been sufficient to arouse the envious feelings, of the Minister, towards me, and thank God, he has not been able, to detect in my Official, or private Character, or Acts, any thing, that would afford him, the opportunity he, seems so desireous of, to *Stab* me, in the Back, whilst professing, so much friendship to my Face, and I trust the Department, will do me, the justice, to acknowledge my forbearance, in this matter, and trust the report herein made, will be duly appreciated.

As Mr. Green, will furnish the Department, with sufficient proof, of the nature of the transaction of the 20th, refer[r]ed to above, I have deemed it, unnecessary, to add thereto, but as I had never been in dispute, with Gen[era]l Murphy, nor entitled to such treatment from him, but on the contrary, quite the reverse, from the many friendly offices, rendered by me to him, I beg leave to refer, the Hon. Secretary, to Hon. Alcee Labranch [*sic*; Alcee L. La Branche] M[ember of] C[ongress from La.], as to my character & disposition &C. I have the Honor to be Most Respectfully Your Ob[edien]t Servant, Stewart Newell, U.S. Consul, Port of Sabine.

ALS (No. 14) with Ens in DNA, RG 59 (State Department), Consular Despatches, Texas, vol. 1 (T-153:1), received 6/11. NOTE: In addition to the four enclosures mentioned by Newell in his despatch, a letter of 5/17/1844 from Newell to Green and Green's reply of the same date indicate that nothing "improper" was said of Stevenson in their discussions.

From R[ICHARD] PAKENHAM

Washington, 22 May 1844

The Undersigned Her Britannick Majesty's Envoy Extraordinary and Minister Plenipotentiary, has been instructed to enter into communication with the Government of the United States, with the view to ascertain whether it would be agreeable to the said Government that an arrangement should be concluded for the transmission through the United States of the Mails to and from Canada and England, which are now landed at Halifax and thence forwarded through British Dominion to their destination.

There seems to be reason to think that these Mails if landed at Boston instead of Halifax, and thence forwarded by the most direct route to Canada, would reach their destination sooner than by the route now followed, and that while advantage would thus be gained on the side of England in the more rapid transmission of the publick correspondence, the arrangement in contemplation might likewise be advantageous to the Post Office of the United States, by reason of the compensation to be paid, according to agreement, for the transport of the Mails in question.

If it should suit the views of the Government of the United States to accede to the principle of the arrangement which the Undersigned has thus the honor to propose, the Undersigned will be prepared to concert with the Post Master General [Charles A. Wickliffe] or with such authority as the President [John Tyler] may be pleased to designate, the detailed measures which it may be expedient to adopt for the complete execution of the plan.

The Undersigned takes advantage of this occasion to renew to the Hon[ora]ble Mr. Calhoun the assurance of His high consideration. R. Pakenham.

LS in DNA, RG 59 (State Department), Notes from Foreign Legations, Great Britain, vol. 22 (M-50:22).

From John Shackelford, Culpeper Court House, Va., 5/22. He recommends his friend, William Augustine Broadus, for employment "in a Clerk[']s office of one of the departments of the Government" and states Broadus's qualifications. ALS in DNA, RG 59 (State Department), Applications and Recommendations, 1837–1845, Broadus (M-687:3, frames 365–366).

From FRANCIS WHARTON

Philadelphia, May 22d 1844

My dear Sir, I am much indebted to you for your goodness in noticing my letter of a few weeks since. In common with most of the members of the bar here, of which though a young, I am somewhat an ambitious member, I feel a deep interest in the nomination to the vacant judgeship [on the U.S. Supreme Court]. I wish the matter were in your hands—I still trust that such matters may some day be—but as it is, both the bar & the country will hope for the best in the filling of that, and the remaining important vacancies.

I cannot refrain expressing my anxiety at the troubles brooding over the northern wing of the Republican party. The south may be safe enough, but I see here no prospect of a safe reorganization. You ["may" *canceled and* "will" *interlined*] allow me to speak frankly on the subject of Mr. [John] Tyler; ["but" *canceled and* "and" *interlined*] I believe I can truly say that so great is the distrust felt here towards him, that nominated or not nominated, anti-Texas or pro-Texas, he will not collect a thousand voters in the State. Were not your own great name connected with his, the Texas question would be dragged by him into the dust. I am in the habit of occasional conversation with the old recognised leaders in this city, and I believe that it is the fear of his nomination alone that prevents them from coming out manfully. As it is, the argument for immediate annexation has not come to us fairly. Mr. Tyler's advocacy is suspicious, Mr. [Robert J.] Walker's Quixotic. Mr. [Thomas H.] Benton's speech, as I glanced at it in this evening's [Washington?] Globe, will produce a strong and abiding effect, unless its reasoning be controverted from a source entitled to the respect of the community. What Mr. [James] Buchanan [Senator from Pa.] may do, I know not, and perhaps he may succeed in working a change. If such should be the case, and *you* should be brought forward as the annexation candidate, or Mr. Buchanan himself, or perhaps General [Lewis] Cass, Pennsylvania, New York, and New Hampshire might be snatched from Mr. [Henry] Clay. But with Mr. Tyler as a candidate, the game is up. The Texas scheme will become as ridiculous as the Exchequer, and will be almost as easily crushed, at least in its present shape. Whatever office-seekers or office-keepers may say, I have no doubt that if the issue is to [be] made upon Mr. Tyler[']s reëlection, we will not only be miserably, but ludicrously defeated.

If you could find time and opportunity to exhibit the bearing of the present treaty in such a manner as to recommend it to the republicans of the North, a great point would be gained. The published documents, to a Northern eye, have a baldness which made me for one almost believe that the hand which purloined, had garbled them. Our instinct is in favour of the scheme, but our reason has not been sufficiently courted. The frankness, and I must add, the unexpected *logicalness* of Mr. [Martin] Van Buren's letter, has shaken some of our best friends, and I believe that to turn things round suddenly enough for the November election would require exertions superhuman.

What then can be done? I answer, we must bide our time. So great & unexpected a change of popular sentiment as that called for by the treaty cannot take place in a flash. I see no reason for doubting the opinion we held but a short time since, that the next election must go by default. Put Mr. Clay in the Whitehouse, and, with a moderate degree of prudence & conciliation on our part, we will have the reversion to ourselves. If the states-right's party acts wisely, in one year, under a Whig president, it will dry up the Albany regency, & draw over its subjects. Mr. Clay will be elected easily enough, and though good faith & policy both require we should oppose him, there is no probability that by doing so he will be defeated. Would not his election be safer for republican principles, with the necessary reaction in our favour which would follow, than would the election of any pro-Texas, pro-Tariff caucus democrat, such as Mr. Buchanan or General Cass? If we could succeed in November with a good and true man, we will ["be" *interlined*] doing well, but of that I fear there is no hope. Under such circumstances I cannot but believe that our true policy is to prepare for the organization of such an opposition as prudence and energy will enable us to collect, for the purpose of hampering Mr. Clay for his first term, and defeating him for his second.

[*Several words canceled.*] I hope to go to Washington in the course of the spring, and I believe I would long since have made the visit, in spite of the business claims, which, small as they are, I am trying to nurse into respectability, had I not been frightened by the accounts of the host of office hunters by which both you and the president are beset. I am still so young, and have still so very little political experience and political weight, that I feel almost backward, ["also," *interlined*] to attract a moment of your attention. Not being, therefore, either an office seeker, or a politician, I am almost unwilling to intrude upon the occupations of the capitol. But if in any manner or way I can be useful either to you, or our own great cause, even a suggestion from you, will give me will to do, and energy in doing. Your faithful friend & servant, Francis Wharton.

ALS in ScCleA; PC in Jameson, ed., *Correspondence*, pp. 956–959.

From J. Huntington Wolcott

Boston, May 22d 1844

Sir, My Brother Henry Griswold Wolcott is now in China and informs me that he has about completed his arrangements to engage in Mercantile pursuits at Ningpo, one of the northern ports now opened to trade by the recent treaty. He is in every respect qualified to perform the duties of Consul, and I respectfully request his appointment as Consul at Ningpo. Very respectfully Your Ob[edien]t Serv[an]t, J. Huntington Wolcott, of the firm of A. & A. Lawrence.

ALS in DNA, RG 59 (State Department), Applications and Recommendations, 1837–1845, Wolcott (M-687:35, frames 1–2).

To A[rchibald] H. Arrington, Representative [from N.C.]

Department of State
Washington, 23d May 1844

Sir, In reply to your note of the 22nd instant, enclosing a letter from Mr. [Wallace D.] Styron of Beaufort N.C. concerning the claim of John Paul Jones against the Danish Government, in which he holds a certain interest, I have the honor to inform you that the present Diplomatic representative of the United States at Copenhagen [William W. Irwin] has been instructed to call the attention of the Danish Government to these claims and to demand indemnity therefor, but that no decision has yet been made known to this Department.

For fuller information on the subject I beg to refer you to the correspondence recently communicated to the House of Representatives in answer to a Resolution dated on the 22d Ultimo respecting these claims. I am, Sir, respectfully Your Obedient Servant, John C. Calhoun.

FC in DNA, RG 59 (State Department), Domestic Letters, 34:206–207 (M-40: 32); PC (addressed to "H. Archibald Arrington") in Jameson, ed., *Correspondence*, pp. 591–592.

From FRANKLIN CHASE

Consulate of the United States of America
Tampico, May 23d 1844

Sir, I have the honor to enclose to you herewith, a memorial signed by the principal American and such Foreign merchants, as are concerned in commercial pursuits between this Port and the United States—the purport of which is, to point out to your Excellency the extreme inconvenience which this commercial community has been laboring under for some time past, for want of means of direct communication between this Port and the United States, and also suggesting a plan by which this serious obstacle could be effectually removed, in the event of that plan appearing feasible to you.

And I would most respectfully beg leave to add, that I have also experienced numerous delays and inconveniencies in the absence of direct means, to enable me to forward Despatches to my Government, which are frequently sent to this Consulate from the United States squadron in the Pacific, and other Official sources from the western coast of this [Mexican] Republic.

I have also one more reason for bringing this subject to your notice, which is to provide means to relieve distressed citizens of the United States, whose misfortunes have in various ways thrown vast numbers of them in this country, and many of whom have recently presented themselves in this City, so extremely destitute, as to become a burthen to the more fortunate class of their countrymen. During the last twelve months, large contributions of money has been raised by me, in common with my countrymen to relieve the distressed condition, and defray passages of Americans to the United States. I will not however pretend to assert, that in every instance the person applying for such assistance was really deserving so much charity from his countrymen, but I believe that nothing can excite the sympathies of an American ["to such an extent," *interlined*], and more particularly so in such a country as this, as when he sees his fellow countryman reduced to penury and abject want.

Craving your indulgence for thus intruding these remarks upon your notice, I am, with the greatest respect, Sir, Your most Obedient Servant, Franklin Chase.

ALS (No. 51) with En in DNA, RG 59 (State Department), Consular Despatches, Tampico, vol. 3 (M-304:2, frames 69–72), received 6/17. NOTE: The enclosed "memorial" appears immediately below.

From JOHN G. MCCALL and Others

Tampico [Mexico,] May 23, 1844

Sir, We the undersigned, American Citizens and others merchants intimately connected with American interests, and consequently deeply interested in the trade between the United States of America and this port—Do respectfully represent

That owing to the daily decrease of the means of direct communication between Tampico and New Orleans naturally consequent upon the severe prohibitions and heavy duties enacted by the Government of Mexico, we have suffered and shall probably continue to suffer in our respective commercial interests.

That for the above reason our direct communication with the United States is limited to long intervals, and for want of other means our correspondence is most frequently forwarded and received through Havana or Vera Cruz by H[er] B[ritannic] M[ajesty's] Steamers or by casual conveyances, occasioning great delay and expense.

Wherefore we would respectfully intimate to your Excellency, that if the plan be practicable; two Government Schooners or as many as the Government may think proper, be fitted out to run from New Orleans to this port as United States packets. The correspondence brought and carried by them might be subject to fixed rates of postage, and at times when the Exchange in New Orleans on other countries is favorable, large quantities of specie would be thrown into that city.

Your Excellency is better able to judge than ourselves, of the practicability of the plan. We can only say that in our humble opinion it would give increased activity and stability to our commercial connections with the United States of America. We have the honor to subscribe ourselves, Sir, Your most humble Servants, Jno. G. McCall,

J. Labruere, Man[ue]l Blandin, J.M. Layendain, Salvador Dargen[?], Franklin Chase, U.S. C[onsul], Sam[ue]l Walley, S.W. Aldrich, Tho[ma]s Walley, Geo[rge] W. Van Stavoren, Watson Labruere & Co., Droegea Co., Stewart L. Tolly[?] & Co., Claussen & Treibs, Baker[?] Bissens & Co., Lelong Comacho & Co., J.F. Alberdi, Z. Lacroix[?], Eug[eni]o Maliano, W[illia]m L. Ameyer & Co.

LS (in McCall's hand) in DNA, RG 59 (State Department), Consular Despatches, Tampico, vol. 3 (M-304:2, frames 71–72), received 6/17.

From Rufus Choate, [Senator from Mass.], 5/23. "I have the honor to enclose the within from a house of great respectability in Boston, whom I know to be largely engaged in trade to the ports of which they speak." [Probably enclosed was the letter of 5/21 to Calhoun from Lombard & Whitmore and Joseph W. Green, concerning "St. Domingo."] ALS in DNA, RG 59 (State Department), Miscellaneous Letters (M-179:104, frame 404).

From W[ILLIAM] W. IRWIN

Legation of the United States
Copenhagen, 23 May 1844

Sir; I have the honor to acknowledge the receipt of your Circular No. 11, dated the first ultimo, informing me of your appointment as Secretary of State, which fact I, this morning, announced, in the course of an interview with his Danish Majesty's Minister of Foreign Affairs [Adam Wilhelm von Moltke].

The Minister expressed the most lively satisfaction, and congratulated me on the very fortunate selection made by the President for that responsible station, at this deeply interesting juncture.

I pray you, Sir, to be assured that no one will take more pleasure than myself in receiving and following the instructions of one whose experience, virtues and eminent public services, throughout a long and distinguished career, give the strongest assurance to the world that the honor and interests of our beloved country have been confided to safe hands. I have the honor to be, Sir, very respectfully, Your obedient servant, W.W. Irwin.

LS (No. 24) in DNA, RG 59 (State Department), Diplomatic Despatches, Denmark, vol. 3 (M-41:5), received 7/19; FC in DNA, RG 84 (Foreign Posts), Denmark, vol. 1843–1847:[132].

To J[ames] Miller, Collector of Customs, Salem, Mass., 5/23. In response to Miller's letter of 5/18 [*not found*] Calhoun authorizes him to "present to the Groom of the Imaum of Muscat, who had charge of the horses, if he has not sailed, a watch of the value of one hundred dollars; or, money to that amount, at his option." FC in DNA, RG 59 (State Department), Accounting Records: Miscellaneous Letters Sent, 1832–1916, vol. for 2/1–9/30/1844, p. 185.

From W[illiam] H. Newman, New York [City], 5/23. Newman states that [Daniel] Webster promised in 2/1843 to appoint him to be the U.S. Consul at St. Johns, Newfoundland. He asks Calhoun to examine his recommendations and to grant the promised appointment. He wants it not so much for its salary as for its opportunity to advance the interests of the business firm with which he is associated in New York City, R.W. Newman & Co. (An EU refers to an earlier letter to Newman "objecting to appoint a Consul for St. Johns.") ALS in DNA, RG 59 (State Department), Applications and Recommendations, 1837–1845, Newman (M-687:24, frames 152–154).

G[ILBERT] L. THOMPSON to Ben E. Green, Chargé d'Affaires, Mexico

Mexico [City], May 23d 1844

Sir, In answer to your note of this date [*sic*; 5/22], I have the honor to inform you, that in addition to the despatches, which I presented to you on my arrival yesterday, I was confidentially instructed by the Hon. John C. Calhoun, Secretary of State, to authorize you to propose to the Mexican Govt., that its Minister at Washington shall be authorized to receive propositions and open negotiations for a boundary line between the two countries.

2dly. You are authorized also to state to the Mexican Govt. that whatever Mexican Territory may fall on the American side of the proposed boundary will be liberally paid for in proportion to its value and extent.

3dly. You are authorized to say that for the purpose of avoiding all misunderstandings and ill feelings for the future, the United States are willing to guaranty the line of Boundary, which may be agreed upon. I have the honor to be Very Respectfully &c &c, G.L. Thompson.

ALS in NcU, Duff Green Papers (published microfilm, roll 5, frame 519).

From CALEB ATWATER

Washington, May 24, 1844

Dear Sir, Yesterday I called for the purpose of showing you my "Mysteries" but Gen. [Alexander O.] Anderson came and so I was compelled to retire. However, I hope in a few days to present the whole volume to you, without reading the work, it is impossible to get an idea of it. Compelled to write for my bread, I cannot do more than present a medley of matter, so as to catch as many readers as I can. I am grateful for any patronage that I can obtain. The administration being unfriendly to me, as a whole, I must support such portions of it, as are friendly to me, and let the rest alone. I have no interest in supporting any party, at present, & must walk along in my narrow path turning neither to the right or left from it. It is pos[s]ible that I have said more for the Secretary of State than I have for any other man and so have offended others. Men are but large children always suspecting partiality. I had hoped that my work would be read with interest by our foreign ministers, consuls &c. and that some how there might be some 100 copies purchased for them by the state Department.

I have not even one subscriber and I depend on the members of congress and the officers of government for my patronage. In the war Department so far as [William] Wilkins, [Daniel] Parker & [T. Hartley] Crawford are concerned, I expect opposition, not encouragement. I have not named them nor said aught of them, after having my *private letters made public by them.* I am aware of their malice and so I leave them to be dealt with, in another volume, provided their hostility continues towards me. This is the first of a series of volumes. "Mysteries of Washington" is the present volume—"Humbugs of Washington" is the 2nd volume; and, if that does not reform them, I intend to publish "The crimes of Washington city." Should the government give me ["some" *interlined*] suitable employment, the other volumes will not be published, otherwise they will be forth coming, as soon as my health and means will permit.

Your suggestion yesterday, as to breaking down the present corrupt parties, pleased me, and [I] would be glad to converse further on that matter. My "Humbugs" might be levelled at their strong holds, firing pistols, rifles and finally Paixhan guns at them. If I only knew some time when *Gen. Anderson* would not come in upon me, and I could see ["you" *interlined*] alone, except your son [Patrick Calhoun], and Mr. [Richard F.] Simpson or [James A.] Black, I should be glad to call at your house, in an evening, and then we could talk about matters & things in general. I must feel quite differently from my present feelings or I shall take no part in the next election. Your Old friend [William] Creighton knows what you did for Mrs. [William S.] Murphy, but he wishes her to come home and take care of her young babe and children now neglected by her, a charge on her relatives. Can she not be sent home? Her cousins refused to call on her here, but thanked me & requested me to thank you for what you did. They wish her to be sent home to Ohio. Yours ever, Caleb Atwater.

ALS in ScCleA.

From W[illia]m P. Duval

St. Augustine, May 24th 1844
My dear Sir, I beg leave to introduce the Hon[o]r[ab]le W[illia]m Marvin judge of the Southern judicial district [of Fla. Territory] to you, as one of those friends, whom I have long known & highly esteemed. Few men have fallen in my path through life who have more frankness—candor and sterling virtue than Judge Marvin. I trust you will make his acquaintance. I see the Globe hangs on you with the ferocity of a bloodhound, but he [Francis P. Blair] is only shewing his cloven foot which he had cunning[ly] put ["into" *changed to* "in"] a *boot*—since he became a *Jackson man*. The nation will do you justice[,] such a corrupt creature of Blair, cannot tarnish your fame. He is like a child, crying to pull down a star. A combination of the leaders of both great parties is now formed to distroy the administration—and the *prosperity of our country*. I yet believe that the Texas treaty and the action of the Senate on it, will result in as signal a revolution in public opinion as occur[r]ed in 1800. The voice of the people, is now rising, and those who have given up their country[']s banner for the British flag, will have little, honor by the exchange. The light of wisdom is shining on your path and it will lead you[,] Mr. [John] Tyler and the nation to Glory. I well know the steady firmness of the President, his purity, and love of country. I know too the energetic power of your mind &, principles—the iron nerve that braces your determination, never to yield under the most trying circumstances, those principles ["to" *canceled and* "which" *interlined*] secure the union & prosperity of your country[.] Your [sic] are engaged in a mighty struggle which must soon result either in ["the" *canceled*] triumph over British influence, and the honor of

the union—or in treacherous & mortifying disgrace to the nation[.]
The people are comming to the resque & like a might[y] wave, will
wash the decks of our national ship clear, of the virmin that now
defiles her. Your friend, Wm. P. Duval.

ALS in ScCleA. NOTE: An AEU by Duval on the address page of this letter
reads: "Fare by Judge Marvin." William Marvin (1808–1902), a native of
N.Y., became a U.S. District Judge and was Governor of Fla. during Presidential
Reconstruction.

From W[ILLIA]M B. GOOCH

U.S. Commercial Agency
Aux Cayes, May 24th 1844

Sir, Since the date of my last letter this City has been in the greatest
state of excitement. The General commanding here, with his troops,
can be called only a company of freebooters.

They forcibly entered my room, took possession of my trunk containing all my Official papers, as well as private letters & funds—Also
the press & seal by which all public documents are authenticated,
property of the U.S. They also confiscated twenty five Bbls. of provisions belonging to me, which were in stores of Commercial houses,
who had left the country & their property confiscated. I made a demand of my property but was refused. The Brittish V[ice] Consul
[C. Smith] accompanied me, but the General [Acaau] issued an order
for our arrest. We were fortunate in making our escape on board the
U.S. Ship Preble. I then directed a letter to Captain [Thomas W.]
Freelon, commander of the U.S. Ship Preble, making a statement of
the amount of property taken, & requested his assistance.

He made a demand of Gen. Acaau for the amount of property
taken. In a few days my trunk, papers & private funds with the Press
were returned, but not the provisions. A division of the army of Gen.
Acaau, who has been in command of this City, were ordered for Port
au Prince. Having intelligence that General [Philippe] Guerrier had
been appointed President, returned to this place on the 20th inst.
and announced their adherance to the new president, thoug[h] opposed by the commander of the city. A battle was feared between
the the [sic] parties, & the commanders of the vessels of war were
requested to interfere for the protection of the city; but an arrange-

ment was made without their interposition, & yesterday tranquility, it is to be hoped, was again restored to the city. It is of great importance for the protection of of [*sic*] our Commerce at this Island, that our vessels of war (as the civil commotions are so frequent among this people,) should be ordered to call at the different ports on the island. The Preble is the only Ship of war belonging to the U.S. which has been in this port for more than twenty years, although three revolutions have commenced in this place within the past year, and a large amount of American property in the city requiring protection.

Captain Freelon has endeared himself to every foreigner. His gentlemanly deportment, his conciliatory manner & his activity & perseverance to protect the lives & property, not only of his country-men but others, has produced a fear & respect of our Navy from the blacks, and the warm gratitude of the English as well as American residents.

Vessels from the U.S. with cargoes consigned to houses whose property have been confiscated, we have advised to sail to other Islands for a market. They were taken under the protection of the U.S. Ship of war, & when they sailed the Captain ordered a strong guard to protect them until out of danger: thus he has preserved several cargoes from confiscation.

I would inform the Department that recent intelligence from my friends of domestick afflictions, renders it important that I should return to the U.S. as soon as I can mak[e] necessary arrangements. I shall visit Washington, if in my power, on my return, & give you a statement of the affairs of this Island which may be of importance to our commercial interests. With high regards I am dear Sir your obedient & devoted Servant, Wm. B. Gooch.

ALS (No. 16) in DNA, RG 59 (State Department), Consular Despatches, Aux Cayes, vol. 2 (T-330:2), received 6/17.

From Lorton & Kirksey, Pendleton, 5/24. "Yours of the 18th instant came to hand by to day[']s mail, enclosing check on Planters & Mechanics Bank of Charleston, for Five Hundred Dollars, which we have placed to your credit." LS in ScU-SC, John C. Calhoun Papers.

From W[ILLIAM] S. MURPHY

Legation of the United States
Galveston Texas, 24 May 1844

Sir, I transmit this correspondence merely to shew to the Dept. of State, the frivolous and degrading means resorted to, for the purpose of harrassing this Legation.

The constant association of the Consuls [Archibald M.] Green and [Stewart] Newell—the correspondence in the dates of their several attacks upon me—their similarity in form and substance all shew a joint purpose.

I hear that Mr. Newell intends to make this correspondence the subject of a charge against me, to the Dept. of State. How he will work it I know not—But his general character here is such, that I should not be surprised at any thing from him. I am satisfied that this Legation cannot be at peace whilst these men are retained in office here. I have the Honor to be, Your ob[edien]t Serv[an]t, W.S. Murphy.

ALS (No. 25) with Ens in DNA, RG 59 (State Department), Diplomatic Despatches, Texas, vol. 2 (T-728:2, frames 317–320), received 6/11. NOTE: Enclosed are ALS's of 5/17/1844 and 5/18/1844 from Newell to Murphy asking whether Murphy had repeated to Alexander Stevenson, an applicant for a consular appointment, Newell's assessment of Stevenson made at Murphy's request. An enclosed copy of Murphy's reply of 5/19/1844 to Newell indicates that his opinion on Stevenson's unsuitability for a Consular position was repeated to Stevenson since it was an official matter and "therefore had nothing of secrecy or of a private character in it."

From W[ILLIAM] S. MURPHY

Legation of the United States
Galveston, 24th May 1844

Sir, You will not be surprised, that the communication which it is my duty to make to you at this time, is extremely painful to me. It afflicts me the more, because I know how painful it will be to my Government.

The enclosed hand bill, addressed "To the Public" and signed by "A[rchibald] M. Green U. States Consul" at this port, was handed to me on the 21st Inst[ant] at my office, and I was circulating in Town.

The reason of its publication, is explained in the "Hand bill" itself by its author, to be, that I did not reply to his note of the day previous: which note is set forth at length in the "Hand bill."

The facts, in relation to this note, and its delivery to me, are these. On the evening of the 20th May, I was in my office, preparing, or about to prepare for supper. I heard a loud knocking at the office door, and I requested the person to come in, at the same time advancing, or placing myself near the Door, so as to know what was wanting, without opening the door too wide, as I was partly undressed. A stranger to me, presented himself, with a stick in one hand, and a note in the other, handing me the note, and saying, in a threatening tone, and menacing attitude, that the note was from his friend "Green" and that he demanded an answer in 20 or 30 minutes.

I will not pretend, that I remember the exact words, but such was their import. I replied, that the Gentleman need not trouble himself, I would look at the note, and reply when I had time. The note bearer replied, that he would call in ½ an hour and demand a reply. This remark was accompanied with greater menace, and a shaking of the stick—which drew from me an angry demand that he go away, or be off—or words to that effect.

Surprised at this strange mode, which the Consul had pursued, in sending me a note accompanied with menace and insult, partly undressed, as I was, I read it, and after dressing and taking tea, I read it again, and soon after retired for the night, thinking that in the morning I would make such enquiries as to enable me, to give him a proper answer: For the note itself gave me no information of the gentlemen with whom it accused me of having held the conversation complained of: or the name of his informant, who had certainly in this instance slandered me the most. Then the note enlarged its demand on me, for a reply touching any other conversation, connecting his name, or the names of his relations &c &c &c &c.

I could not fail to see in all this, a studied effort to insult me, or to provoke me to do, or say something derogatory to my character and station. Nevertheless I had decided upon giving him a calm reply, such as I had a day or two before given to Mr. Consul [Stewart] Newell, in a case nearly similar, and which is also presented to the Department in another despatch (No. 25). But, as if in anticipation of such an answer, as would effectually defeat his purposes, on the next day, the 21st May, the Consul Green, caused these handbills to be put in circulation.

So they must have been printed between the evening of one day, & the time of their circulation the next: making the slander against me, the foundation of a Libel of the most monstrous character.

If he really wished for a reply, ought he not, to have given me, at least a few hours of day light, to write it in? and much more time, than that, to make necessary enquiries, as to who heard, and who told to him, the conversations imputed to me—what they really did hear, & what they really did report to him?

But I will not argue the question, thus. There is his official signature to a paper, which no officer of the United States, should sign either officially, or unofficially.

This effort on his part to degrade, or provoke me, has fallen harmless to the ground—and the citizens of the Town are indignant at his conduct.

The idea held out in this "hand bill," of my talking in Bar rooms &c &c is wicked, and malicious. I do keep my office in the Hotel, called "Shaw[']s Hotel." The office of the French Legation is at the "Tremont Hotel." These are the best Hotels in the place. I have an office room, and a sitting Parlour. I found it necessary to keep the Legation office in this Hotel, because I could get good rooms, and having to leave my Legation verry often, under the orders of my Government, my archives were more safe, under the care of the Landlord, than if they had been in an office, seperate & apart to itself. I was more than a month at Washington[-on-the-Brazos] last winter & spring—and have had to meet Gen[era]l [Samuel] Houston, at Houston frequently since, and ere long, shall have to meet him there again, by agreement. This is necessary from the peculiar state of the negociations between the two Countries. I am never in the "Bar room" except to pass through, or on necessary business with the Landlord, or Keeper of the House. The imputation implied in this "hand Bill" is ridiculous & untrue. Such is not, and never has been, my manner of life.

Sir, There is a British party in Galveston, though contemptable in numbers, yet Proud, overbearing, impudent and ferocious. They are goaded to madness, by the appearance of an American fleet in the Gulf, and American officers about the streets of Galveston—as well as by the successful negociations of my government, and the certainty of the final consummation of the great measure of annexation: and I am satisfied (though I have no direct & positive evidence of the fact) that they have entrap[p]ed, or seduced the consul of my country into into [sic] a line of conduct which led him to the commission of the degrading act complained of. I have been warned of their machinations against me, from time to time, by the American party here. But no prudence, no circumspection on my part, could avoid an act, not my own, or prevent the malicious and secret actions of others. If

the consul had given me a reasonable time, or if I could have anticipated his real object, I would have answered his note in the most
conclusive, and satisfactory manner. I repeat it, as my settled ["conviction" *interlined*] from all I have heard & seen, within the last 4
months, that the language imputed to me by the consul, was art-
fully put into his head, by some of the British party here—and by that
Party, he has been duped, and led to do an act, as brutal towards
me, as it is derogatory to my country, and degrading to his station.

But I will trespass no further on your feelings, or patience. I have
served my country faithfully, I have gained the approbation of the
People, and the confidence of the Government of Texas. And I wish
(it is natural I should wish) to remain here, until the great question of
annexation, which has cost me so much toil, pain & anxiety is settled.

I enclose herewith, the Galveston "Evening News" the Paper of
the American party here—and refer you to an editorial which I have
marked, to shew the existance of the two parties, and that the "Galveston Civilian," refer[r]ed to in that editorial, is the organ of the
British party here—informing you at the same time, that Consul
Green, is the near relation by marriage of the Editor of Civilian—
and his constant associate.

I sent you not long ago, one number of the "Evening News," in
which were resolutions of the citizens of this Town, passed in Public
meeting, complimentary to me, for my arduous & faithful services &c
&c. I hope you, received, that paper, but lest it may have miscarried,
I will send you another number, if I can get one. With sentiments
of the highest respect, and esteem, I have the Honor to be, Your
ob[edien]t Serv[an]t, W.S. Murphy.

ALS (No. 26) with Ens in DNA, RG 59 (State Department), Diplomatic Despatches, Texas, vol. 2 (T-728:2, frames 321–327), received 6/11. NOTE: The
enclosed handbill of 5/21/1844 by Green contains a letter of 5/20/1844 from
Green to Murphy asking whether Murphy had accused Green of "dishonorable"
banking transactions in Virginia. Upon receiving no reply to that letter by the
next day, Green states "I am left no other alternative than to proclaim him the
Charge aforesaid, a most gross and infamous Slanderer, Liar, and Cowardly
Scoundrel." The enclosed issue of the Galveston *Evening News* of 5/25 contains
a quotation from the *Civilian* that accuses the U.S. of negotiating a treaty "not
such as was expected" in Texas, especially concerning the Texan national debt;
takes issue with that statement and accuses the *Civilian* of being "the organ of
the British party in Texas"; and commends Murphy for his role in obtaining the
proposed treaty despite [Samuel] Houston's reluctance. On 5/25 Murphy
wrote a long letter to John Tyler in which he reiterated what he had told Calhoun in regard to Green, portrayed Green and his connections as political opponents of Tyler, asked for Green's removal, dwelled upon his own feeble health,
and stated that he had informed President Sam Houston that, to his great regret,

his nomination as Chargé d'Affaires to Texas would probably be rejected by the Senate, forcing him to leave "before the final issue, of the important measure of annexation, should be completed." ALS in DNA, RG 59 (State Department), Diplomatic Despatches, Texas, vol. 2 (T-728:2, frames 311–314).

From William H. Powell, New York [City], 5/24. He plans to visit Europe for "pleasure and to cultivate my talents for the fine arts" and asks for introductory letters to U.S. Ministers abroad "in order to gain access to those Collections which are confined almost exclusively to the Sovereigns and nobility of Europe." Powell is related by marriage to David J. McCord, Langdon Cheves, and other friends of Calhoun. As further references, he mentions Albert Gallatin, Charles A[ugustus] Davis, and others. ALS in DNA, RG 59 (State Department), Passport Applications, vol. 31, unnumbered (M-1372: 14).

From Edw[ar]d Richardson & Co., New York [City], 5/24. They ask if U.S. vessels would be molested if they attempted to obtain from the west coast of Africa "Guano" to import into the U.S. Great Britain is about to "take possession in the name of her Majesty" of the district from which this guano must be obtained, and Richardson is anxious to obtain information on U.S. commercial relations in that case. LS in DNA, RG 59 (State Department), Miscellaneous Letters (M-179:104, frames 408–409).

From T[homas] M. Rodney

Consulate of the United States of America
Matanzas [Cuba], May 24th 1844
Sir, It affords me great gratification to acknowledge the receipt of the Department[']s letter of the 4th Inst., informing me of the President's approbation of of [sic] the course pursued, in relation to Christopher Boone, and of the action the government has been pleased to adopt.

And I now deem it my duty to inform the Department that on the evening of the 18th Inst. I received such intelligence as warranted me in believing, and which has since been strengthened, that the American schooner Cavallero, of Baltimore, Morgan Gordon, master, had landed at Camarioca, a few miles to Eastward of this, a cargo of slaves direct from the coast and afterwards sailed for Baltimore.

As there was a vessel to sail immediately for Charleston S.C. I wrote to the Collector of Baltimore, in ["the" interlined] hope my letter might reach him before the Cavallero arrived and he might, by a little management bring the violators of the law to condign punishment.

The Department may not be aware that in this country it would be neither safe nor profitable for any one to testify against persons engaged in this business; nor do I think it would be possible to obtain legal proof if fifty cargoes were landed in this Harbour.

The enclosed is believed to be a true copy of my letter [of 5/18] to the Collector of Baltimore. I have the honor to be Sir, with high respect Your obedient Servant, T.M. Rodney.

ALS (No. 18) with En in DNA, RG 59 (State Department), Consular Despatches, Matanzas, vol. 4 (T-339:4), received 6/8.

From J[ohann] W. Schmidt, Prussian Consul at New York [City], 5/24. Schmidt encloses a newspaper article containing a letter written by L[ouis] Mark, U.S. Consul to Bavaria, accusing Schmidt of opposing the recently negotiated U.S.-Zollverein trade treaty. Schmidt asserts that this accusation is false and refers Calhoun to the correspondence on file in the State Department for proof of that. He protests this publication by a person acting as U.S. Consul, thereby giving the accusation an official character, and demands that the accusation either be proved or publicly retracted. ALS with Ens in DNA, RG 59 (State Department), Consular Despatches, Munich, vol. 1 (T-261:1).

From ALFRED SCHÜCKING

Washington, May 24th 1844

Sir: In pursuance of what I deem *my most imperious duty*—which I shall discharge maugre the unrequitted loss of time, the expense of labor and perhaps the Contraction of personal malignity—I have the honour herewith to submit further illustrations of the character of *one* busy meddler [Louis Mark], who has thrust himself as a self-constituted agent (paid, avowedly, by the manufacturers of Germany) between this government and those of Germany. I have now on hand documents, which, as soon as the translation Can be prepared, I shall submit as still more Conclusive evidence, Sufficient to demand an instantaneous investigation at your hands, to redress the injury done to the interests & good fame of this Country by the appointment of this man.

I have to regret again on this occasion, that I am not placed in such official Connection with the Department, as would no doubt enable me, to be of some service in this matter. I think that in the present negotiations, and generally, the absence of persons in the American Department of State, Sufficiently or at all Conversant, with the language in question, is as much to be regretted as such an acquaintance would afford great advantages and facilities.

I hold myself responsible for all I have asserted. I am Sir With great respect Your most obed[ien]t Serv[an]t, Alfred Schücking.

ALS in DNA, RG 59 (State Department), Consular Despatches, Munich, vol. 1 (T-261:1). NOTE: An AEU by Calhoun reads "Mr. S[c]hücking. Charges against Mr. Marke [*sic*]."

From THO[MA]S WATTSON & SONS

Philad[elphi]a, May 24th 1844
Sir, The Undersigned, In behalf of themselves and others engaged in the trade between this City and Port au Prince in the Island of St. Domingo, beg leave to request your attention to the unprotected state of our vessels engaged in Trading with that Island and more particularly in the Bay of Port au Prince, where vessels are liable to be becalmed near the shore for several days, in which case we feel apprehensive that our vessels laden with provisions may be molested by the Natives, a number of whom are reported to be in a starving condition. Under existing circumstances, therefore, We would feel much more secure in prosecuting our business if one or more of our vessels of War was near the Island to protect our Interest, and deter the Natives from plundering our property. We are with great respect Your Ob[edien]t Serv[an]ts, Thos. Wattson & Sons.

LS in DNA, RG 59 (State Department), Consular Despatches, Port au Prince, vol. 2 (T-346:2). NOTE: A State Dept. Clerk's EU reads "Refer for perusal to N[avy] Dept."

To Fernando Wood, Despatch Agent, New York [City], 5/24. In reply to Wood's letter of 5/20, Calhoun states that courier's passports will be furnished to Wood only when despatch bags are sent to him.

"The Department will from time to time when it may be thought expedient for them to be used, transmit them to you." FC in DNA, RG 59 (State Department), Domestic Letters, 34:208 (M-40:32).

From JOHN J. CHAPPELL

Columbia, 25th May 1844

My Dear Sir, Permit me to introduce to your acquaintance my Friend Mr. Francis Bulkley who has for several years been engaged as a Teacher in the Families of our Friends the Adam's[,] Weston &C. in this neighbourhood & who by his Talents, assiduity & devotion to his charge has earned the entire approbation of these Gentlemen. They wish to retain him but his declining health renders it advisable that he shall change his employment, & these Gentlemen with a worthy philanthropy have interested themselves to afford him the means of doing so, & have joined in the request that I shall bespeak your favourable consideration in his behalf.

Mr. Bulkley wishes an appointment under the United States as Consul or in any other Capacity, & desires to go to the South of Europe, or either Shore of the Mediterranean; or if no situation can be obtained there, he would be pleased to accept an appointment to any of the West India Islands, to Mexico, or to any part of South America.

The Education & acquirements of Mr. B[ulkley] are spoken of so favourably, that he may be considered qualified to fill creditably the grade of appointment which he desires, & his Character ["is" *canceled*] is so unexceptionable, that the Government need not apprehend any but the most honourable & faithful discharge of its duties. If you can subserve his wishes compatibly with your official duties, you will gratify his recent employers, & oblige your old Friend, Jno. J. Chappell.

ALS in DNA, RG 59 (State Department), Applications and Recommendations, 1837–1845, Bulkley (M-687:3, frames 594–596).

From [Matthew St. Clair] Clarke and [Peter] Force, Washington, 5/25. Clarke and Force report the publication of vols. 4 and 5 of the *Documentary History of the American Revolution.* Publication costs of the two books were $48,297. Volume 6 of the series is nearly complete and its estimated cost will be $24,174. They request Calhoun to make "the usual estimate to the [Senate] Committee of Finance,

and of [House] Ways & Means in Congress, as soon as practicable."
Two CC's in DNA, RG 233 (U.S. House of Representatives), 28A-
D30.6.

From T. Hartley Crawford, [Commissioner of Indian Affairs],
5/25. Crawford asks that Calhoun take steps to obtain the release
from prison in Mexico of John Hoffer. Any efforts in Hoffer's behalf
will be greatly appreciated. ALS with En in DNA, RG 59 (State
Department), Miscellaneous Letters (M-179:104, frames 419–420).

To George Evans, [Senator from Maine and] Chairman of the
Committee on Finance, 5/25. "I have the honor to transmit to you
the enclosed copy of a letter [of today] addressed to me by Messrs.
Clarke and Force, in which they desire that the usual estimate may
be made to your Committee, and that of Ways and Means in the
House of Representatives, for the cost of the fourth, fifth, and sixth
volumes of 'The Documentary History,' as therein stated." LS with
En in DNA, RG 233 (U.S. House of Representatives), 28A-D30.6;
FC in DNA, RG 59 (State Department), Accounting Records: Miscellaneous Letters Sent, 1832–1916, vol. for 2/1–9/30/1844, p. 192.

From F[e]r[dinand] Gardner, U.S. Consul, Villa da Praia, St.
Jago, Cape Verde Islands, 5/25. Gardner reports that the [Portu-
guese] governor general of the Cape Verde Islands has informed him
that the concession permitting the storage of supplies for the U.S.
African Squadron will expire on 3/24/1845 unless extended. He nar-
rates his role in establishing the fleet storehouse and comments upon
the present arrangement concerning payment of duties on the public
stores of the squadron. Gardner feels that, contrary to the present
practice, the cargoes of merchant vessels chartered by the U.S. to
ship goods for the squadron should be admitted duty free. ALS
(No. 68) in DNA, RG 59 (State Department), Consular Despatches,
Santiago, Cape Verde Islands (T-434:3).

From Jos[eph] Grinnell, [Representative from Mass.], 5/25.
Grinnell encloses a letter complaining of port regulations in Paita
and other ports of Peru and Bolivia. These regulations are changed
at the will of the government and shipmasters are not informed of
changes until they have somehow incurred a charge. Grinnell suggests that the U.S. representatives in Peru and Bolivia transmit to
the State Department for publication a copy of the commercial regulations in those countries. (Enclosed was a letter of 1/20/1844 from

Paita [Peru] to the owner of a New Bedford, Mass., whaling ship, describing the ship's narrow avoidance of a $1,000 fine because of a recent and unexpected decree.) ALS with En in DNA, RG 59 (State Department), Miscellaneous Letters (M-179:104, frames 416–419).

From ALLEN A. HALL

Legation of the United States
Caracas, May 25th 1844

Sir, Herewith I transmit to you the copy and translation of a confidential communication I have received from the Venezuelan Government on a subject of no little delicacy. It embodies the observations which [Gen. Carlos Soublette] the President of the Republic had previously made to me, in person, at an interview requested by him for that purpose. I think he has just grounds for the apprehensions he entertains as to the possible consequences to Venezuela of a war of races in Hayti. The great danger of internal commotions of any description, or from what cause soever arising, in this country, is that they will eventuate in, or lead to the breaking out of, a war of color. What is commonly called the Reform Revolution of 1835 was merely an attempt—for the moment successful—of a few discontented officers of the army to acquire possession of the Government by force; but it was followed by Farfan's Rebellion, the notorious object of which was to array the colored population against the white. One of the most intrepid acts of General [José Antonio] Paez's life was his his [sic] charge, at the head of greatly inferior forces, upon Farfan's troops—lancing two or three hundred on the spot, and dispersing the rest. It is not a question between master and slave, but one of color only, which it is feared may one day or other arise in Venezuela. All slaves born since 1822, are unconditionally free on attaining the age of eighteen. There are not, at present, more than twenty six, or twenty seven, thousand slaves in the whole country, and it is computed that, in fifteen years from this time slavery will be extinct in the Republic.

The population of Venezuela in 1839 was estimated as follows:

Indians	221,415
White Spanish Americans & Foreigners	260,000
Mixed races	414,151
Slaves	49,782
Total	945,348

Since my residence in Caracas, I have frequently asked intelligent Gentlemen, Creoles, as well as Foreigners who have long resided here, what prevented the colored part of the population from taking the reins of Government into their own exclusive keeping—by means of the ballot box, if they had any scruples as to the use of force—and the invariable answer has been, "The ill will and jealousies existing between the blacks and mulattoes." Such a state of things cannot continue much longer. The scepter will, at no distant day pass from the hands of the white, into those of the colored, people, and then comes a revolution of the social system. At present, whites of respectability will not intermarry with persons of color, nor will they admit them into their houses upon terms of social equality and intimacy. Into the best circles of Caracas society, mulattoes can no more gain admission, than they can into those of the United States. Superior in numbers, and once in possession of the Government of the country, is it likely that the colored population will quietly submit to any further assumption of social superiority on the part of the whites?

I have thrown out the foregoing suggestions, that you may the better understand and appreciate the grounds which the Venezuelan Government have for the apprehensions they feel with regard to the future tranquillity of the country. They appear to be entirely and helplessly unprepared for the horrible condition of affairs which they fear *might* be produced here by the evil and contagious example of Hayti; nor is it at all probable that, should the dreaded contingency hereafter arise, it will find them better prepared to meet it than they are now. To give you some notion of their want of energy and moral power, I need only describe a scene exhibited in this City in February last. An Editor of a newspaper being on trial for libel, a band of disorderly persons (the most of them colored) entered the Court House—showed their knives, dirks and pistols—interrupted by their clamors the proceedings of justice—forcibly ejected the policemen (soldiers) who were called in to preserve order—intimidated the Judge, and, breaking into the room where the jury were deliberating, extorted a verdict of acquittal. This accomplished, they procured a band of music and marched up and down the principal streets until a late hour of the night, knocking at the doors of such of the citizens as were particularly obnoxious to them, and crying out with a loud voice, as they did so, "Death to the Oligarchists!" For the protection of the Court and Jury, in the first instance, or for the preservation of the public peace afterwards, neither the National or State authorities made the slightest effort. The omission was generally ascribed to *fear*. It is believed by some very respectable, intelligent persons, that had the Government interfered, they would have been overcome by the mob. A feeling of insecurity prevails to a considerable extent at this moment. It is very common to hear fears expressed that disturbances will arise during the present year, particularly at, or about the time of, the elections, which take place in August. I have no confidence in the continuance of domestic tranquillity, and shall not be at all surprised if intestine commotions do arise in the course of the year. The public mind is unsettled. There are thousands of restless men in the country, without character or property, ready to lend themselves to any movement that promises anarc[h]y and confusion.

Under these circumstances, I would submit to your consideration the propriety of orders being issued to such of our men-of-war attached to the West India squadron as can conveniently do so, to touch at La Guayra as often as practicable and communicate with me. In the event of a revolution, I should consider the property of foreigners by no means safe.

The President desires that the accompanying communication may be regarded as strictly confidential. As I do not like to trust it to the ordinary channels of conveyance, I shall detain this despatch until a suitable opportunity occurs for its careful transmission. I have the honor to be, Sir, with great respect, Your ob[e]d[ien]t serv[an]t, Allen A. Hall.

ALS (No. 36) with Ens in DNA, RG 59 (State Department), Diplomatic Despatches, Venezuela, vol. 2 (M-79:3), received 7/22. NOTE: Hall appended a Spanish-language copy with his English translation of a note, dated 5/17, from Juan Manuel Manrique, Foreign Minister of the Republic of Venezuela. Manrique commented upon the recent rebellion of the Spanish portion of Haiti. He expressed fears that the African government of Haiti will crush the rebellion and institute a race war against the rebels. The President of Venezuela and Manrique fear that the proximity of such a race war might lead to a similar occurrence in Venezuela. Acting upon the orders of the President, Manrique requests Hall to inform U.S. authorities of these fears.

From J[AMES] HAMILTON [JR.], "Private"

Oswichee Bend [Chattahoochee River, Ala.] May 25[t]h 1844
My Dear Sir, I received yours of the 15th inst[ant] on my return to this place from Savannah.

The intense interest felt in the annexation Question is augmenting in the South.

My own impression however is and I have written to this effect to Mr. [Dixon H.] Lewis, that if the Treaty fails in the Senate that without there exists an entire & *absolute certainty* of the passage of the Joint Resolution which you suggest by both Houses adopting it—This move ought not to be hazarded. ["You" *canceled.*] We should have the members in the House who vote against the Treaty committed against us & this would only strengthen the party opposed to annexation.

In case the Treaty is rejected in the Senate, (about which there can be no doubt) we then go before the people with a tremendous excitement to act on the presidential Question & all others in which the South is interested.

At the meeting of the next ["U.S." *interlined*] Congress, the Congress of Texas can memorialize ours & demand admission under the provisions of the Treaty of 1803. Or annexation can be ["made" *canceled and* "consummated" *interlined*] by the action of her Congress in some other mode by a Joint legislative act of both Governments.

Depend on it we hazard an important card by going before the House of Representatives after a defeat in the Senate.

In my view nothing could be better than the nomination of [Martin] Van Buren by the Baltimore Convention ["if it takes place" *interlined*]. We should then have an annexation Convention and in all probability nominate you, and if we did not elect you carry you into the House of Representatives with a fair prospect of success. Your friends I have all along seen have committed a sad mistake in relation to yourself as I have just remarked to Lewis ["that" *canceled and* "They" *interlined*] have always ["looked to" *canceled and* "calculated" *interlined*] the opp[os]ition to you without ever estimating your strength. They never seem to have recollected that the largest streams have the most powerful eddies.

I perceive the embarrassment of your position in Mr. [John] Tyler[']s Cabinet in permitting your name ["to be used" *interlined*] as a Candidate. But a powerful annexation Convention by its decision, would soon obviate this Dilemma.

But what is all this fire to end in? I see no plan of a Campaign and on this point I have ventured to write Mr. Lewis somewhat at length, to whom I must refer you.

In the mean time My Dear Sir be assured of the esteem with which I am faithfully yours, J. Hamilton.

ALS in ScCleA.

From JOHN W. HOLDING

Washington, 25th May 1844

Sir, It Having been communicated to me, the Inexped[i]ency of a Public Agent, being sent to the Republic of the Ecu[a]dor—for the Purpose of Promoting the Interests of the citizens, of the United States, claim[an]ts against the late Govern[men]t of Colombia—I most respectfully ask Permission to State, That the constituti[o]nal Provision for the Government aforesaid, Provides for a Congress, but once in two years, and will convene in Jan[uar]y next, as I am credibly Informed by a Gentleman now in this city, direct from Bogata—New Gran[a]da.

There being claims already Liduidated [sic], and Provided for by the Govern[men]ts of New Granada, and Ven[e]zuela, and others in Progress, and all the remainder, may or should find a Settl[e]ment, in the course of the Present year, and If no agent should be in Quito to comm[and?] the Several Interests of the citizens of the U.S., they will Stand Suspended as a matter of course untill the year 1847.

In case of civil discord, what may be regarded as a Point of the common Law in such Republics, The Ex[e]cutive can Invest himself with Extraordinary Power and Suspend the ordinary Provisions of Legislation, and under Such a course of Provably[?] contingencies, I most respectfully solicit the consideration of the Sec[retar]y of State—and sincerely hope that It will not be found Predijucial to the public good, If such a Measure could be deemed to accelerate or Promote Individual Interests. I Have the Honor to be Most Respe[c]tfully Your Obed[ien]t Serv[an]t, John W. Holding.

ALS in DNA, RG 59 (State Department), Miscellaneous Letters (M-179:104, frames 421–422).

From S[AMUEL] D. INGHAM

N[ew] Hope [Pa.,] 25 May [18]44

My dear Sir, The papers have recently announced the appointment of Warder Cresson [as] Consul to Jerusalem. This man is the brother of Elliot Cresson who is much distinguished for his activity in the cause of colonization, but the consul has been laboring under an aberration of mind for many years; his mania is of the religious species. He was born a Quaker wanted to be a preacher but they would not; since, he has gone round the compass from one spot to another, sometimes preaching about the church doors & in the streets. His passion is for religious controversy & no doubt he expects to convert Jews & Mohammedans in the East—but in truth he is withal a very weak minded man and his mind what there is of it, quite out of order—he is extensively known and the appointment is made a theme of ridicule by all who know him & cannot make allowance for the gross imposition practised on the appointing power. Very Sincerely Yours, S.D. Ingham.

ALS in DNA, RG 59 (State Department), Applications and Recommendations, 1837–1845, Cresson (M-687:7, frames 156–157).

From John McDaniel, St. Louis Prison, 5/25. He asks that Calhoun examine a report of the trial proceedings that resulted in his conviction [for the murder of Antonio José Chavis, a Mexican trader]. Since McDaniel is scheduled to be executed on 6/14, he is sending a friend, J[ames] B. Martin, to Washington to return to St. Louis with any respite or pardon that may have been granted. McDaniel adds in a postscript that in the hurry of departure, Martin left this letter behind. (An AEU reads *"Post Master,* send this to Mr. Calhoun *immediately."*) ALS in DNA, RG 59 (State Department), Petitions for Pardon and Related Briefs, 1800–1849, no. 292A.

To J[ames] I. McKay, [Representative from N.C. and] Chairman of the House Committee on Ways and Means, 5/25. Calhoun encloses a copy of a letter to himself [dated 5/25] from Clarke & Force in which they request that "the usual estimate may be made to your Committee, and that of Finance in the Senate, for the cost of the Fourth, Fifth, and Sixth volumes of 'The Documentary History,' as therein stated." LS with En in DNA, RG 233 (U.S. House of Representatives), 28A-D30.6; FC in DNA, RG 59 (State Department), Accounting Records, Miscellaneous Letters Sent, 1832–1916, vol. for 2/1–9/30/1844, p. [193].

From E [ZEKIEL] PICKENS

Cahawba [Ala.,] 25 May 1844

Dear Sir, Some days since I promised Mr. W[illiam] H. Bonneau, of this County, to write in a request that you would use your influence to obtain for his son "a Cadet[']s commission at West Point." Constant engagement has heretofore delayed the fulfilment, & I wish I could decently have withheld a promise, for I presume one in your situation is likely to be molested in this way; but I could not well do so, seeing that he is a Kinsman, apparently deserving, with a large family, & in moderate circumstances.

The young man[']s name is Richard Vanderhorst Bonneau, well grown, & indeed likely. If then you can gratify the father[']s feelings, without encountering any thing disagreeable to your own, I doubt not it would afford you as much satisfaction as myself.

From the violent assaults recently made I began to wish you had not assumed your present station; but from the sensation now indicated here I have no doubt it will recoil & be the severest blow to [Thomas H.] Benton he has before felt in this region.

But strange to say very few of the Whigs here can be brought to pledge themselves not to vote for one opposed to annexation—such a resolution was presented to a meeting of both parties & carried by but a few votes[,] almost every Whig voting against it, as I was informed.

I have not heard directly from your son Andrew [Pickens Calhoun] recently, but all your friends, in this vicinity, are well, & we never had a better prospect for crops—have just had a fine season, apparently general, & that after a good deal of dry weather. Accept my best wishes. Yours truly, E. Pickens.

ALS in ScCleA. NOTE: Ezekiel Pickens (1794–1860) was a native of S.C. and a grandson of Gen. Andrew Pickens, and therefore a remote kinsman of Calhoun. Since his mother was a Bonneau he was also related to Mrs. Floride Colhoun Calhoun. He was a judge on the Ala. bench during 1839–1848 and 1850–1852.

From WILSON SHANNON

St. Clairsville Ohio, May 25th 1844
D[ea]r Sir—I perceive by the public papers that the Senate have had under consideration the Treaty of annexation for some ten days or more. I presume the discussion is drawing to a close and that a final vote will be taken in a few days. I have all my business arranged so as to be able to leave for Mexico as soon as I receive my instructions. The season is rapidly advancing and I am exceedingly anxious to leave in time to pass over the unhealthy portion of my journey before the sickly season sets in. I hope therefore the president [John Tyler] will find it consistent with his sense of public duty to direct me to

leave for Mexico immediately after the final action of the Senate on the Treaty.

The question of annexation is much stronger in Ohio than I had supposed it would be when in the city [of Washington]. The great body of the democratic party with a respectable portion of the whigs, are sound on this question. They go for the Treaty and the public servant from this State who goes against it will have a fearful responsability to encounter. The manifestations among the people are so strong in favour of the measure that I hazard nothing in saying that a large majority of the voters of Ohio are in favour of it. It is a question that enters deep into the feelings of the great mass and will control more votes in the approaching presidential election than any other great question of public policy before the country. No democratic candidate for the Presidency will be sustained in this State who is opposed to the Treaty. It is folly to think of running such a candidate. Nay it is worse—it is treason against the democracy. Let the friends of immediate annexation be of good cheer. On this great question they have the people, if not the aspiring politicians, with them.

Hoping to hear from you immediately after the final action of the Senate on the Treaty I have the honor to be yours with great respect and esteem, Wilson Shannon.

ALS in ScCleA; PEx in Boucher and Brooks, eds., *Correspondence,* p. 235.

From DAVID A. STREET

Purdy, Tenn., May 25th 1844

Dear Sir, Having been for many years a devoted admirer of your political course, I have ventured—not I confess with much sanguineness of hope, amid the onerous and multiplied duties of your office, that you can find time, or inclination to attend to one who moves in so obscure a sphere as myself—to approach you, by letter; and ["to" *interlined*] express to you, my fervent congratulations for your services, rendered under auspices so forbidding, to that portion of our country ["with" *canceled and* "which" *interlined*] I feel myself identified with. I would not have you believe, my object in addressing ["you" *interlined*] to be, to flatter you; far otherwise; but there are circumstances in a nation[']s history, which justify, the voluntary gratulations by the humblest citizen, without the possible imputation of obsequiousness, of those who have applied themselves devotedly, to the advancement of the public good. Let me then tell ["you" *interlined*] that since your election to the Vice Presidency—then I had no vote—until the present time, I have watched you narrowly—scanned every speech or observation that ["has" *interlined*] fallen from you, when you were in favor, as well as when the dark cloud of proscription hung over you—as well when the smiles and approbation of an overwhelming majority of your countrymen marked you out—*not by a packed convention* but by your own distinguished services, as worthy of confidence, and raised you to the second office in the Government, as when you dared, in defiance of the frowns of power—perhaps your personal interest—to plant the standard of *Justice*, and *Right*, upon the ramparts of the Constitution, and bid defiance to its myrmidons. Remember Sir that it ["is" *canceled and* "will not be" *interlined*] for the number of the offices you have held, that posterity will render you their grateful homage, but for the sacrifices you shall make, to transmit to them untarnished the liberty you enjoy. Need I call your attention to one near you [John Quincy Adams?], who has filled offices, from almost the dawn of manhood, but who has lived to witness the period when impartial men ["only" *interlined*] through charity for the imbecilities and infirmities [*ms. torn; two or three words missing*] to pu[e]rility[?] are willing to ["forgive" *canceled and* "connive" *interlined*] at a fanaticism, inspired by the hatred of disappointment—the most direful of all hatred—they would otherwise blast with indignation? Virtue, and patriotism are at last, the safest reliance. The devotion of Tully to the principles of a republican form of government, cost him his life, but he left behind him, for the benefit of posterity to the latest generations, a name associated with virtue and a love of freedom.

It was with much ["pleasure" *canceled and* "gratification" *interlined*], that I beheld the pleasure of all parties, expressed in your behalf, when you accepted the office you now hold. Before the letters of Messrs. [Henry] Clay & [Martin] Van Buren giving their views upon the propriety of the annexation of Texas, were published, there were few—indeed I may say no Administration men in this part of the Country: but since they have declared ["themselves" *interlined*] against the Treaty, Administration men begin to spring up on all sides. You will perhaps have seen, that many primary meetings have been held by the people of Tennessee, and amongst the rest one was held by the people of this County (McNairy). Judge [William C.] Dunlap—whom you perhaps know, as he was in Congress with you—presided. Mr. [Adam] Huntsman—of Crockett notoriety—a democrat, and Mr. [Christopher H.] Williams—of the last Congress from this District and a Whig made speeches. After they were done, the people of the county well-knowing my political opinions—that I was opposed to all encroachments upon the *grants* of the Constitution for every trifling *expediency,* and that I had often and openly avowed by approbation of the reason suggested for your going into the Cabinet—loudly called for me to address them. I did so; but am doubtful of its propriety even now: for while I had much influence to check the zeal of the Van Buren men, many of whom now declare they will not sustain him, with the views of his letter before them, as opposed in *any way* to the Annexation of Texas, I feel well assured that such is the devotion of the Clay men to their idol, that nothing short of a miracle, or providential interference can change them. However mortifying and disgusting such a spectacle may be, the fact is so, that half the people of our country have thrown away their freedom and independe[nce; *ms. torn; one or two words missing*] and ["are" *interlined*] willing to be dragged like beasts behind the car of a political demagogue. What hope have freemen, from the author [of] such a speech as Mr. Clay[']s at Raleigh, elevated to the highest office in their gift? Is such a man capable of vindicating their constitution from the incroachments of wild and misguided fanaticism? May God defend us, we are fallen on inauspicious times!

In order to free you from any embarrassment in regard to my *identity,* I refer ["you" *interlined*] to Mr. [Milton] Brown, and Mr. [John B.] Ashe, members of Congress from this section of Country, Messrs. [George C.] Dromgoole & [John W.] Jones of Va.[,] President [Thomas R.] Dew and Prof[essor]s [Nathaniel Beverley] Tucker & [Robert] Saunders of William & Mary College, & Judge [John B.] Christian of Williamsburg.

I am young and need much the advice of those whose age and experience have disciplined them against the arts of designing men; and therefore if you can find time, from your the [*sic*] duties of your office, and ["shall" *interlined*] feel inclined to give your opinions to one whose zeal in your behalf though humble, is yet fervent, but which from indiscretion, may over [*ms. torn; one word missing*] itself, he will be obliged to you. And Sir with [*ms. torn; one word missing*] of the highest regard for your public & private worth I am yours most respectfully, David A. Street.

P.S. Colo[nel Ephraim H.] Foster of the Senate, knows me ["personally," *interlined*] and from him you may learn, that you may safely communicate to me, any views that you entertain. D.A.S.

ALS in ScCleA.

620

To HENRY A. WISE

Department of State
Washington, 25th May, 1844

Sir: You will receive herewith a copious synopsis of the correspondence between this Department and the mission to Brazil. It is very desirable that all points in dispute between the two governments should be promptly and satisfactorily settled. You will accordingly apply yourself to the adjustment of the claims of our citizens upon that government as soon after your arrival at Rio de Janeiro as you may deem expedient. The claim in the case of the schooner J.S. Bryan seems to be one which will deserve your earliest attention. Nothing is wanting to complete a discharge of the obligations of Brazil in this case, but the payment of the money acknowledged to be due. If, as is understood to be the fact, an appropriation for that purpose by the Brazilian Legislature will be necessary, you will omit nothing which it may be proper to do towards bringing about that measure. The other claims are not numerous or great in amount. It is not unlikely that your predecessor may have settled those in the cases of the Shamrock and the cargo of the Smack Felicidad. In transacting business of this kind, it is usual for our diplomatic agents when the claims are few and the pecuniary indemnity expected is not large, to take up the cases singly and discuss them with the foreign government. This has been the course which your predecessors have pursued. The changes in the Brazilian Ministry have however been so frequent and their reluctance to bestow the necessary attention upon business of this character is so apparent, that the President [John Tyler] is willing that you should conclude a Convention providing for the settlement of all unadjusted claims of citizens of the United States upon that government, if, upon proper examination, the aggregate amount of the claims should be found to warrant such a proceeding. Owing to a practice which formerly prevailed of sending to the missions abroad all the original papers relating to claims without keeping copies of them, the department has not the means of stating with precision the sum total of the unadjusted claims upon Brazil. It is believed, however, that the amount is at least three hundred thousand dollars, which would be sufficient under the circumstances, to justify the conclusion of a Convention upon the subject. You will accordingly herewith receive a power for that purpose. You may adopt as a general model for the Convention any of those upon the same subject between the United States and other powers, bearing in mind that its most essential features must be a

621

payment by Brazil of a sum of money in full discharge of all the claims, and securing to this government the distribution of the money among the claimants. The President is aware that the finances of Brazil are not as flourishing as might have been expected from the resources of that country and the skill which has generally been shown in the administration of its government. Consequently, he will not insist that the amount of our claims should be paid at ["at" *canceled*] once, but is willing that you should stipulate for a payment by instalments with interest, the last instalment being payable within five years from the signature or from the exchange of the ratifications of the Convention. In estimating the amount of the claims, you will by no means leave out that of the South American Steam Boat Association of New York. A copy of two communications upon this subject which have been addressed to me by Mr. [John T.] Reid, the agent of the claimants here, is now presented to you. The department concurs generally in the views of Mr. Reid and is decidedly of the opinion that the Brazilian government ought to make amends for the actual losses sustained by the Company in consequence of prohibiting the Steam Boat to ascend the Amazon after the invitation given in the instructions to Mr. [José Silvestre] Rebello. This part of the case should be kept distinct from any claim for speculative damages, which this government never patronizes in any way, and, also, from any claim for a breach of contract for an exclusive privilege to navigate the Amazon or for disappointment in not obtaining such contract, as it is not customary for this government to interfere officially in cases of this character.

In forming your judgement upon the subject generally, the decree of the Brazilian government of 1822, referred to by the Consul at Para in his protest, will be of material assistance. The department is not in possession of that decree. You will however endeavor to obtain it for your own use and a copy of it would be acceptable to the Department.

The instructions of Mr. [Abel P.] Upshur to Mr. [George H.] Proffit upon the occasion of the departure of the latter on his mission are so full upon the political and commercial relations between the two countries, and are of such recent date, as to require but little to be added to them at this time. You are accordingly referred to them and will be guided by them.

The mission to which you are appointed is regarded as the most important of any in this hemisphere. Next to the United States, Brazil is the most wealthy, the greatest and most firmly established of all the American powers.

Between her and us there is a strict identity of interests on almost all subjects, without conflict, or even competition, on scarcely one. Thus fortunately situated in reference to each other, there should ever be peace and the kindest feelings and relations between them. To preserve the existing peace and to cherish and strengthen their present kind feelings and relations, will be the first of your duties.

You will find, accompanying this, a copy of the Treaty negotiated with Texas and the President[']s Message transmitting it to the Senate for its approval, with the accompanying documents. You will embrace some early and suitable occasion to explain to the Brazilian government the motives which led to the adoption of the measure at this time. It is important it should be made to understand, that it originated in no feelings of disrespect or hostility to Mexico. For that purpose it will be necessary to explain fully the views and policy of Great Britain in reference to Texas, especially as they relate to the subject of abolishing slavery there, and to point out the danger to which they would expose us and the necessity it imposed on us to adopt the measure we have, as the only one which could effectually guard against it.

You will avail yourself of the occasion to impress on the Brazilian government the conviction, that it is our policy to cultivate the most friendly relations with all the countries on this continent, and with none more than with Brazil. You will assure it that it is our most anxious desire to see them all settled down in peace under well established governments and employed in developing their great resources and advancing in wealth, population, power and civilization, free from all interference from any quarter in the regulation and management of their domestic concerns. It is our established policy not to interfere with the internal relations of any other country, and not to permit any other to interfere with ours. Brazil has the deepest interest in establishing the same policy, especially in reference to the important relation between the European and African races as it exists with her and in the Southern portion of our Union. Under no other can the two races live together in peace and prosperity in either country. The avowed policy of Great Britain is to destroy that relation in both countries and throughout the world. If it should be consummated, it would destroy the peace and prosperity of both and transfer the production of tobacco, rice, cotton[,] sugar and coffee from the United States and Brazil to her possessions beyond the Cape of Good Hope. To destroy it in either, would facilitate its destruction in the other. Hence our mutual interest in resisting her interference with the relation in either country, and hence also the importance of each country firmly opposing any attempt on the part of Great Britain to disturb the existing relation between the two races within their respective limits, and of each discountenancing any such attempts in that of the other.

You will endeavor to impress the importance of this on the Brazilian Government and avail yourself of the occasion to express the satisfaction felt by this Government at the firm resistance it made against the attempt of Great Britain in the late negotiation, to make the abolition of slavery in Brazil a condition on which her sugar should be admitted on an equality into the British market with that produced in the Colonies of Great Britain. You will see the importance, in this connexion, of keeping yourself well informed and the Department promptly advised of all movements on the part of those acting under the authority of Great Britain in Brazil, and on that of the agents or emissaries of her abolition society to interfere with or disturb the relation between the two races in Brazil, and the measures which may be adopted on the part of her Government to counteract and defeat such attempts. I am, Sir, your obedient servant, J.C. Calhoun.

FC (No. 4) in DNA, RG 59 (State Department), Diplomatic Instructions, Brazil, 15:100–105 (M-77:23); CC in DNA, RG 84 (Foreign Posts), Brazil, Despatches, 11:20–24; CC in DNA, RG 84 (Foreign Posts), Brazil, Instructions, vol. 2.

From W[illiam] S. Fulton, [Senator from Ark.], 5/26. He asks that Calhoun attend to an enclosed petition [asking for the release of Fitzaymer W.T. Harrison, a prisoner in the castle of Perote, Mexico]. Fulton will appreciate Calhoun's action in this matter and asks that he receive such information as will enable him to "return such answer to Mr. [Jared C.] Martin, as the information now in your Department affords." ALS with Ens in DNA, RG 59 (State Department), Miscellaneous Letters (M-179:104, frames 423–426).

From W[illia]m C. Sully, Charleston, 5/26. He asks Calhoun's aid [in securing a place in the Revenue Cutter service]. Several individuals have recommended Sully for his good conduct; any assistance rendered by Calhoun will be deeply appreciated. ALS in DNA, RG 26 (Records of the U.S. Coast Guard), Revenue-Cutter Service: Miscellaneous Letters Received, 1844, p. 78.

To [Matthew St. Clair] Clarke and [Peter] Force, 5/27. In response to their request of 5/25, Calhoun has transmitted their letter of that date to the chairmen of the Senate Committee on Finance and the House Committee on Ways and Means. FC in DNA, RG 59 (State Department), Accounting Records: Miscellaneous Letters Sent, 1832–1916, vol. for 2/1–9/30/1844, p. 194.

To T. Hartley Crawford, [Commissioner of Indian Affairs], 5/27. Calhoun acknowledges the receipt of Crawford's letter of 5/25 concerning John Hoffer, "one of the Texan prisoners in Mexico taken at the battle of Mier. According to the information in possession of this Department, the prisoners taken at San Antonio have been set free, but the survivers of those taken at Mier are still detained. I will commend the case of Mr. Hoffer to the good offices of Governor [Wilson] Shannon." FC in DNA, RG 59 (State Department), Domestic Letters, 34:212 (M-40:32).

From C[ALEB] CUSHING

United States Legation
Macao, May 27, 1844

Sir, I have just been informed that the English Steamer, Vixen, is to sail from Hong Kong to-morrow, for Singapore and Trincomalee, by means of which a letter may possibly reach Bombay in season for the mail of July.

There is no time to complete, for transmission by this conveyance, several despatches which I have in hand, but I will not lose the opportunity of giving to you, in brief, intelligence which is of importance.

On the thirteenth instant I received from the Governor General copies of three several despatches addressed to him from the Court, which in substance made known to him—first the unwillingness of the Imperial Government to receive the Legation at Peking and, second, the appointment of Keying, who negotiated, in behalf of China, the late Commercial Convention with Great Britain, and who has now received full powers to negotiate with the United States.

I have replied to this letter expressing my satisfaction in the prospect of meeting a Commissioner so competent and so well disposed as Keying, but signifying, also, that I do not relinquish the purpose of ultimately repairing to Peking.

On the twenty fourth instant I received a letter from Keying himself, notifying me of the same facts and communicating his anxious wish to meet me at Canton.

So far as regards the object of adjusting in a proper manner the commercial relations of the United States and China, nothing could be more advantageous than to negotiate with Keying at Canton, instead of running the risk of compromising this great object by having it mixed up, at Tiensin, or elsewhere at the North, with questions of reception at Court.

Add to which the fact, that with the Brandywine alone, without any Steamer, and without even the St. Louis and the Perry, it would be idle to repair to the neighborhood of the Pih ho, in any expectation of acting upon the Chinese by intimidation and obtaining from their fears, concessions contrary to the feeling and settled wishes of the Imperial Government.

To remain here, therefore, and meet Keying, if not the most desirable thing, is at present the only possible thing.

It is understood that Keying will reach Canton from the fifth to the tenth of June.

Meanwhile I have the pleasure to inform you that the Antelope of Boston, which arrived at Macao, this afternoon, reports having this morning spoken [to] the St. Louis, outside the Lamma, on her way into Hong Kong. This intelligence is truely grateful on all accounts. Indeed so long a period had elapsed without hearing from her and she had come to be so far behind all reasonable time, that the belief was becoming general here that she had either foundered at Sea or returned to the United States.

And I am still utterly at a loss to conceive what are the causes which have protracted her voyage to such an extraordinary length.

I have the honour to acknowledge the receipt of your despatch of the fourteenth of December, numbered "5" which came to hand a fortnight since, enclosing a copy of Mr. [Henry] Wheaton's letter respecting the new commercial and political relations of the Chinese Empire. I am, with high respect Your obedient servant, C. Cushing.

LS (No. 63) in DNA, RG 59 (State Department), Diplomatic Despatches, China, vol. 2 (M-92:3), received 10/22. Note: This despatch was addressed to A[bel] P. Upshur.

To W[illiam] S. Fulton, [Senator from Ark.], 5/27. Calhoun acknowledges the receipt of Fulton's letter of 5/26 concerning F[itzaymer] W.T. Harrison, a Texan prisoner "confined in the Castle of Perote." While the State Department cannot "with propriety officially demand" Harrison's release, [Wilson] Shannon will be requested to do all within his power towards effecting that object. FC in DNA, RG 59 (State Department), Domestic Letters, 34:213 (M-40:32).

To Joseph Grinnell, [Representative from Mass.], 5/27. Calhoun acknowledges receipt of Grinnell's letter of 5/25. "This government has no diplomatic agent in the Republic of Bolivia, but it will give me pleasure to direct the Chargé d Affaires [*sic*] of the United States at Lima to send hither from time to time the fiscal regulations of Peru. When received, they shall be published as you request." FC in DNA, RG 59 (State Department), Domestic Letters, 34:214 (M-40:32).

From James Harper, Philadelphia, 5/27. He seeks Calhoun's influence "to obtain for me a clerkship under Government." He has a large family, was employed for more than seven years by one man, and has now been unemployed for two years, since that man's death. "I was educated under the care of my uncle the late Condy Raguet Esq. with whose character and opinions you are well acquainted." ALS in DNA, RG 59 (State Department), Applications and Recommendations, 1837–1845, Harper (M-687:14, frames 549–550).

From P[ERLEY] B. JOHNSON, [Representative from Ohio]

Washington, May 27th 1844

Sir, I have received a letter from Charles E. Baldwin one of my constituents who states that his nephew named Henry J. Cavalier a citizen of the United States is imprisoned in Cuba under a charge of having been engaged in the late servile insurrection in that island and desiring that all the aid and protection which the government can properly give may be extended to him. He states "that said Cavalier was induced to leave the mint in New Orleans in the spring of 1839 in consequence of offers made to him by the proper authorities of Cuba to be employed on the Havana & Cardenas rail road as engineer."

I respectfully call your attention to the matter. Yours Respectfully, P.B. Johnson.

ALS in DNA, RG 59 (State Department), Miscellaneous Letters (M-179:104, frame 449).

From J[OHN] Y. MASON, [Secretary of the Navy]

Navy Department
May 27, 1844

Sir, I have the honor to transmit herewith a copy of a report made to the President of the United States on the 17th inst. in relation to a line of Steamers between New York and Havre; and tender to you an apology for not having notified you thereof at the time. I have the honor to be Very resp[ectfull]y Y[ou]r Obed[ien]t Serv[an]t, J.Y. Mason.

LS with Ens in DNA, RG 59 (State Department), Miscellaneous Letters (M-179:104, frames 434–442); FC in DNA, RG 45 (Naval Records), Letters Sent by the Secretary of the Navy to the President and Executive Agencies, 4:517 (M-472:2, frame 640).

From WILLIAM MILES

Baltimore, 27th May 1844

Sir, I went from this City to Haiti in April 1831 & remained until 1836 without leaving the island. From 1833 or thereabouts I was Com-[mercial] Agent at Aux Cayes. I resided previously at Port au Prince. I have travelled a good deal in the island. When I first went to St. Domingo or Haiti, The prejudices of the people were not strongly shewn towards the whites, because the French had not settled the claims under their Ordonannces, but as soon as the treaty indemnity was settled with France by reducing its amount & tranquility was restored with France, the French & English increased their trade, & when it was ascertained by the Pres[iden]t [Jean Pierre Boyer] that altho' thus tolerated, by others the U. States would not give up the 10% discriminating duty on Haitian vessels coming to our ports, nor appoint Consuls or answer a letter, there very soon arose considerable prejudice against us, & in favor of the English & this feeling increased until after the British emancipation act it became annoying. The prejudices against all whites now commenced, were increased by the Mulattoes, & lighter colored people, who were jealous of the whites & tho[ugh]t *they* ought to become the merchants & traders, & by the year 1836 & 1837 foreigners generally began to leave the island.

I resided with my family, in Haiti, natives of this City, & one of my children about 5 years old said to me one day "Father I wish I was like Amelié Ligondé." This was a colored child. My little girl must have been told something to make her wish herself colored. I state this to you to shew you that beyond all question, the same repugnance exists in colored people towards us, we have for them. All my observation confirms this. As to negroes I am of opinion that when let alone, they feel their relative position, & there exists no real innate hatred. The negroes of Haiti have as a common proverb, The white man is a horse. The Black man is a (Borich [*sic*; bourique]) Jackass but the Colored man is a mule & add, The White man has a country, the Black man has a country (Africa) The Colored man has no country.

Except in the cities & towns & in contact with the foreign residents, I could not discover any advances towards a a [*sic*] higher Civilization than exists in what we know of Africa. It is true the people are catholics, but are not instructed & do not conform to their duties. There are but few priests on the island & these many of them not worthy persons. The negroes in the mountains & interiour live in concubinage, & so they do very much in the towns. They have some of them their African idols. They beleive in the evil eye, in charms, in curses & bad & good influences. They are fond of music of course & sing & dance, but they will pursue pleasure to excess all night & lie listless all day unless compelled.

The greatest industry I saw was always among the old men & women who had been slaves, & become habitually industrious &c— but in general they seemed disposed to reduce their wants rather than to labour.

The Scotch Abolitionists sent an agent to Haiti in 1831 or thereabouts to report its condition. Mr. Hill the above agent was a colored person & he told me, his information was most discouraging.

I wrote a letter to Mr. [Daniel] Webster about a year ago on this subject. I suppose it is on file in the Department.

I have been in Chile, Peru, New Granada, in the islands of Porto Rico, St. Thomas[,] Trinidad & Barbados, & all over our West & South West—but I never saw such a country as St. Domingo. I have heard the Phillipines described as a perfect Paradise. But it appears to me the Haitiens have the most beautiful spot on this earth. The mountains of Azua are snow clad in winter, tis said. I have myself eaten the Cabbage & irish potatoe of the mountains as good as our own, & also apples & peaches—of course they have all the Tropical products— pure streams, & navigable rivers, & timber for ship building. Cotton grows every where, & the woods & plains produce spontaneously almost the means of living.

The government of Boyer was bad & selfish, but still that will not account for what must I fear be called a retrograde march in society. What I saw in Trinidad last year was also discouraging—while there, a ship was lying in port from St. Helena of 300 tons with 380 or 400 negroes on board, & the Small pox raging. These were volunteers of captured slavers for the plantations of Trinidad. With them came their priests Mahommedans—persons taking these *Volunteers* pay all their expenses, which they contract to refund by labour.

The most industrious negroes I saw under the new English system were at Turk's island where nothing grows & they must work or starve, & there they will drink.

I was appointed Commercial agent at Aux Cayes by General [Andrew] Jackson in 1833 (myself in Haiti) by the influence of Judge [Roger B.] Taney, Mr. [James A.] Pearce of the Senate [from Md.] & others.

If the Government should wish to send an agent to St. Domingo, I should be glad to go.

The Haitiens have *no title whatever* to the Spanish part of the island but occupancy.

If I can give you or procure you any information relative to negroes that you may need I will cheerfully do so.

Mr. [John Pendleton] Kennedy & Mr. Pearce [Representative and Senator from Md., respectively] know me, also, Clement Cox Esq. of Georgetown.

I do not wish any answer to this, & ought perhaps to apoligize for writing it—but I know the negroes pretty well, & could not help, giving my testimony, tho' at times, I have hoped & tho[ugh]t more favourably. An elder brother of mine knew you on Rhode Island near Bristol in 1810 or thereabouts. I remain—with the highest respect, Your obe[dien]t S[er]v[an]t, William Miles, formerly Com[mercial] Agent at Aux Cayes.

ALS in DNA, RG 59 (State Department), Miscellaneous Letters (M-179:104, frames 431–434).

From JOHN [S.] PENDLETON

Santiago de Chile
May 27th 1844

Sir, My dispatch No. 20 by the ship "Lennox" informed you of the state of the negotiation in regard to the affair of Sitana, as it stood on the 14 of February last. Since that time I have made every exertion, that I felt myself authorised to make, to force the Chilien Minister to a decision in regard to that claim. Precisely one hundred days after the date of my note of the 14th of February his answer came in—viz two days ago. It is now in the hands of a translator, and I expect to reply to it in the next seven or eight days—after which I shall take my leave of the Court—so soon as I can make some effort to induce the Congress of Chile to modify the law providing for the payment of the money in the first case of the Macedonian according to your instructions and the wishes of Mr. [Thomas H.] Perkins.

I shall sail from Valparaiso about the last of June in the Ship Eric.

The Minister in his note of the 25th inst. takes no new ground whatever, nor has he yet offered any evidence in opposition to the proofs submitted on my part. The whole object is to gain time and thus save to Chile the difference of interest on the original principal and the whole sum as now compounded of interest and principal.

I shall be gratified, if you deem that my energy in the premises has been equal to the tone of my instructions.

The money can never be made—or at any rate for a long time can not be made unless the agent here is instructed to say distinctly, that if this Govt. does not instantaneously shew other reasons for refusing payment than have as yet been given, that force will be forthwith applied. I shall however write in as positive a tone as I think will meet your approbation and that of the President [John Tyler], in my next, and I presume last communication.

The note of the Minister covers forty five pages. Of course I am not able to send a copy as this must leave today in order to be in time for the Steamer to Lima.

I should not avail myself of the President's permission to return, until late in the year or the arrival of my relief, if there were a possibility of my rendering service by remaining a few months longer—But the Congress meets five days hence and for four months thereafter it is absolutely certain, that the Minister will not take one step in this or any other business of the sort. All the heads of Departments here, are members of congress and during its sessions, they suspend all correspondence—at any rate when they are likely to have to pay money. In such a case as this it is certain they will profit by such an excuse as their Congressional duties afford.

The books, records and property of the Legation, will be put in a safe place, subject to the order of the American Consul at Valparaiso [Eben R. Dorr] or my successor [William Crump]. I have the honor to be Your Excellency's Most Ob[edien]t S[ervan]t, Jno. Pendleton.

ALS (No. 21) in DNA, RG 59 (State Department), Diplomatic Despatches, Chile, vol. 6 (M-10:T6, frames 166–168), received 12/30. NOTE: John Strother Pendleton (1802–1868), a Virginian and lawyer, had been appointed Chargé d'Affaires to Chile by Tyler in 1841. During 1851–1854 he was Chargé d'Affaires to the Argentine Confederation.

To Edward Richardson & Co., New York [City], 5/27. "I have received your letter of the 24th instant, and have to state in reply that this Department is not possessed of any Official information on the subject of your communication, and is consequently not prepared to answer your inquiries." FC in DNA, RG 59 (State Department), Domestic Letters, 34:213 (M-40:32).

From McClintock Young, Secretary of the Treasury ad interim, 5/27. Young reports the decision of the Treasury Dept. upon questions raised by [Jean Corneille,] Chevalier Gevers, Dutch Chargé d'Affaires to the U.S., in his letter of 4/21 to Calhoun. Young reviews the Tariff of 1842 and existing treaties between Holland and the U.S. and sees no conflict between the twenty per cent duty on Java coffee and the treaties. He suggests that legislation would be necessary to remove the duty on coffee and thus "to meet the views of Mr. Gevers." Young has received an inquiry from Gevers relating to duties upon coffee imported directly from Java into the U.S. and encloses a copy of the Treasury Dept. decision in that case. LS and CC with En in DNA, RG 59 (State Department), Miscellaneous Letters (M-179:104, frames 443–448); FC in DNA, RG 56 (Treasury Department), Letters to Cabinet and Bureau Officers, Series B, 4:371–373.

To Weston F. Birch, U.S. Marshal, Fayette, Mo., 5/28. "I enclose you the President's [John Tyler's] respite of John McDaniel, David McDaniel and Joseph Brown, untill the 12th day of July next, the receipt of which you will please acknowledge." (An EU indicates that an identical letter was sent to the Marshal on 6/3.) FC in DNA, RG 59 (State Department), Domestic Letters, 34:216 (M-40:32).

From P[IERCE] M. BUTLER

[Washington,] 28 May 1844

My compliments to Mr. Calhoun. Many of his old friends—The Cherokees—Mr. [John] Ross & others—wish to call & see him. Will he indicate at what hour tomorrow—it will be agreeable to see them. Truly, P.M. Butler [of] So. Carolina.

ALS in DNA, RG 59 (State Department), Miscellaneous Letters (M-179:104, frames 450–451). NOTE: This note was addressed to Calhoun "at Mrs. King's." A State Dept. Clerk's EU reads "Answ[ere]d tomorrow 30th May at 2 p.m." Butler was Indian Agent to the Cherokees and a former Governor of S.C.

From ROBERT B. CAMPBELL

Consulate of the United States of America
Havana, May 28th 1844
Sir, I have this day received your Official communication of Ap[ril] 26th accompanying the duplicate of Mr. [Franklin] Gage[']s letter & a copy of the reply of the Dept. to him. I assure you, and the President through you, that under ["your" *canceled*] your present instructions, no effort shall be wanting on my part to protect both the persons & property of our countrymen residing on *any part* of this Island. Being Consul for Havana, I have not at all times felt myself authorised to enquire into & attempt the redress of wrongs, (if any have been committed) in the jurisdiction of other Consulates, unless personally applied to by the parties, or their friends. Justice to myself requires a history of the Cardenas affair so far as known to me. I heard about the end of April that three American citizens had been arrested as parties to a contemplated insurrection. One was bailed, and [William] Bisby and [Samuel] Moffat placed in stocks. I immediately wrote Mr. Gage enquiring into the truth of the report. His reply confirmed my previous intelligence. On the receipt of his letter I called in person to see the Capt[ai]n Gen[era]l [Leopoldo O'Donnell], who I did not see, but learned from one of his Officers that the men had already been relieved and were only kept in custody to await their trial on charges against them. This affair occurring beyond the limits of my Consulate, I did not feel authorised in doing more or presuming that my influence was greater than the Consul having it in his immediate charge and at his own residence. Had I demanded their immediate discharge without trial there was no probability of its being conceded, and I might have been requested to limit my action to the limits of my Consulate. Observation has satisfied me, that to be officially influential and efficient, it is generally necessary to act with promptness and energy in all things over which you may rightfully claim jurisdiction, not too often attempt

to trespass on the jurisdiction of others. Your last communication changes my situation, and I shall hereafter feel fully authorised to interfere on any part of the Island and justify the act, under your authorising it in your official favor of the 26 April. Immediately on the receipt of yours of the 26 Ap[ril] (to wit this day) I addressed a letter to the Capt[ai]n Gen[era]l in relation to Bisby and Moffat but have not the time to furnish a copy as the Vessel which bears this sails in a few hours.

It is due from me to the past & present Cap[tain] Gen[era]l to say That in the limits of this Consulate I have no cause of complaint. They have treated all communications and applications made by me with attention, respect & favor, and altho occasionally compelled to ask favors for others in direct violation of existing laws, they have been invariably granted. I have at all times found them disposed to treat our citizens kindly & leniently, & when their stations in life was known to justify attention they have never failed to shew them marked respect. I will adduce a few instances in evidence. The laws expressly prohibit the landing of slaves or free persons of color on the Islands. Notwithstanding this legal prohibition, they have always granted permission on my application to visiters from the States with slaves or free servants to have them in attendance on themselves while here for months, on one occasion during the races of last year it was granted to great numbers. Two American Women imprisoned in Matanzas for three years on charge of crime have been released on my application. An American Ship Master who had committed several serious assaults & batteries was arrested & confined, on my application he was discharged without trial. A young man (an American) suspected of being a party to a riot for which several Spaniards of respectability were banished the country was on application delivered up to me without trial. A Mr. Goodwyn from the North recently attempted the commission of suicide, was arrested, and under the law would have been subject to several years of labor in chains upon the public Works, was upon my representation of the act itself as evidence of insanity given up to me. Recently an order has been issued expelling all free persons of color not natives from the Island. Those born in the United States (few in number) called upon me, and I offered to interest myself to enable them to remain altho the law made no exceptions, there was only one who would consent to stay. I drew a memorial for him, backed by a letter from myself and the permission was granted him to stay. On a recent visit of Gen-[era]l [William J.] Worth and Staff I introduced them to the Cap-

[tain] Gen[era]l. They were treated with marked respect and among other evidences of attention the crack Reg[imen]t was ordered out to be reviewed by him. These are among the many evidences of good will, and the disposition to respect my Official applications given by this Gov[erno]r. Tis true I have not yet obtained satisfaction for the death of [Michael] Murphy of which I informed you, but a court Martial was ordered and held, the sentence however being more mild than the Capt. Gen[era]l thought the offence required has ordered a review of it and from the multiplicity of cases growing out of the insurrections, it is not yet concluded. In this Consulate there has been only one arrest as a party to the insurrection, who claims to be an American, he is a colored dentist, has suffered no cruel infliction, has a room to himself in the prison, is allowed to receive that [which] may add to his comfort which his friends please to send him and his confinement is only strict enough to secure him. Letters from the notorious abolitionist [David?] Turnbull have been found upon his person (it is said) and the chances of acquittal are against him. I shall endeavor to secure him a fair trial and it is but just that he should abide the result. I have the honor to be with great Respect Y[ou]r Mo[st] Ob[edien]t Serv[an]t, Robert B. Campbell.

ALS ("Duplicate") in DNA, RG 59 (State Department), Consular Despatches, Havana, vol. 19 (T-20:19), received 6/17.

From R[obert] S. Chew, "Department of State, Consular Bureau," 5/28. Chew asks that he be granted leave of absence from the State Department for "a week or ten days. Mr. [James S.] Ringgold will, should the permission be granted, attend to the business of my Room, during my absence." (An AEI by W[illiam] S. D[errick], Clerk in the State Department, reads: "Granted.") ALS in DNA, RG 59 (State Department), Miscellaneous Letters (M-179:104, frame 454).

To T[HOMAS] G. CLEMSON, [Edgefield District, S.C.]

Washington, 28th May 1844
My dear Sir, I had a conversation, with Dr. [James H.] Relfe [Representative from Mo.] in reference to the subject of your letter. He says that he knows nothing about the case, or the condition of the

estate of Dr. [Lewis F.] Linn [former Senator from Mo.], as he had no time to look into his affairs before he sat out for Washington; but that he will attend to the subject of your letter, as soon as he returns home, & will write to you in reference to it. He evinced a proper sperit, & spoke of you kindly. You had better inform Mr. Mr. [*sic*; J.B.] Crockett of the conversation. I told him, that I knew you did not desire to give any unnecessary trouble, & that you would prefer a compromise, if one could be had on fair terms. I return Mr. Crockett[']s letter.

I informed you some time since, that the the [*sic*] mission to Belgium (a Charge) would be vacant this summer, and that the President [John Tyler] would tender it to you, if you should desire it.

John [C. Calhoun, Jr.] is still here. He will leave in a few days. Patrick [Calhoun] will accompany him. They will make fort Bent their head quarters. It is situated near the head of the Arkansaw, about 700 miles from St. Louis. It is said to be one of the best spots for persons, whose lungs are effected, as well as for hunting. I have highly favourable accounts of the beneficial effects of the tour to it, on persons whose lungs were effected. Dr. Relfe says he has no doubt of John's restoration to health.

The Convention is now sitting in Baltimore. There is, I understand, great excitement. [Martin] V[an] B[uren]'s defeat is thought to be certain; but it is doubtful, who will be nominated, or in fact whether any one will be. Tyler[']s convention has nominated him.

I hope your crop is doing well, and that you ["are" *canceled*] all continue to enjoy health. You must not remain too long. I would by all means advise you to leave by the middle of next month, for Fort Hill.

John gives a fine account of the children; how they grow & how they improve. I was surprised to hear him say, that little Floride [Elizabeth Clemson] was running all about. Kiss them for Grandfather; & tell [John] Calhoun [Clemson] that Grandfather wishes to see him very much.

Patrick & John ["join" *interlined*] their love to you & Anna. My health is good, though I am not free from a cough. Your affectionate father, J.C. Calhoun.

ALS in ScCleA.

To WILLIAM CRUMP, [Powhatan County, Va.]

Department of State
Washington, 28th May, 1844

Sir: The commercial relations between the United States and the Republic of Chile, are governed by the Treaty between the two countries concluded on the 1st of September, 1833, which is still in force. Of that instrument you will herewith receive a copy and will make yourself familiar with its provisions.

The United States have a high interest in the preservation of concord and good understanding with that country. Its government is more stable and more wisely administered than any of those of the other Spanish American Republics whose shores are washed by the Pacific. Chile has been comparatively exempt from the desolating and sanguinary civil wars which are almost incessantly waged in many of the others of those States, and has derived the full benefits from this exemption, as is shown by the flourishing condition of the arts of peace within her confines, and the more rapid increase of her population.

The direct trade of the United States with Chile is of considerable extent and is understood to be lucrative to those concerned in it. Valparaiso, the principal port of that country, is, besides, a place of deposite for many commodities carried thither in vessels of the United States, which are consumed in the neighbouring Republics of Bolivia and Peru. To the ports of Chile the vessels of the United States engaged in the whale fishery in the Pacific also resort, for the purpose of making repairs and obtaining refreshments. The expenses consequent upon these are in a great measure defrayed, not by specie carried from this country nor by bills drawn on it, but by a barter or sale of the products of the fishery or of the productions of the United States carried into the Pacific by the whalers themselves.

In a country, therefore, with which we have so much commercial intercourse susceptible of enlargement, it is desirable that we should have a representative whose position will give him access to political information in advance of the ordinary channels or not to be obtained through them.

You will consequently cultivate the acquaintance of persons of influence and in authority at Santiago. You will, however, be careful not to identify yourself with either of the political parties into which the country may be divided, and you will be particularly careful not to give just cause of offence to the religious opinions or prejudices of the authorities or of the people.

The power with which you are furnished authorizes you to negotiate with that government upon the subject of unsettled claims of citizens of the United States, to sign a Convention upon that subject and to receive money in payment of claims already adjusted. It is not, however, believed that the number or amount of the just claims would warrant the conclusion of a Convention. Your predecessors have settled them one by one, and it would perhaps be best for you to pursue the same course. If, however, any such material change of existing circumstances should take place as to render a Convention preferable, the power will enable you to avail yourself of that change.

The claims upon the Chilean government which have recently been adjusted are those in the cases of the brig Warrior and the first claim in the case of the brig Macedonian. Three instalments in the case of the Warrior have been paid and four remain to be paid, the first of which will be due in November, next. When you receive the amount, you will remit the same to this department, being careful to choose such means of remittance as will be best for the interest of the claimants.

In the case of the Macedonian which has been adjusted, several instalments are due. These, as you may receive them, you will either remit directly to Mr. T[homas] H. Perkins of Boston, who is the recognized agent of the claimants, or place the funds, for that purpose in the hands of any person at Valparaiso whom he may designate.

The unadjusted claims upon Chile are;

1. The second in the case of the Macedonian.
2. The whale ships Franklin and Good Return.
3. The brig Garafilia and the Argyle.
4. The ship Franklin and brig Clifton.

The second claim in the case of the Macedonian is for the seizure, in 1822, and conversion to the use of the authorities of Chile, of a large amount of treasure, the proceeds of the cargo of that vessel. There can be no doubt of the accountability of that government in this case. So far as the department is informed, that accountability has not been seriously denied, the principal objection offered by that government to the claim being the length of time which elapsed between the act complained of and the presentation by this government of a demand for reparation. The causes of that delay, however, are fully explained in the memorial of the claimants to this department and the documentary proof seems to be as complete as the nature of the case would allow. It is not unlikely that Mr. [John S.] Pendleton will have settled this claim previously to your arrival. If, however, you should find it to be still pending, you will prosecute it with all proper diligence.

The claim in the cases of the whale ships Franklin and Good Return is for an unjust detention of those vessels at the port of Talcahuano in Chile for an alleged breach of the revenue laws of that government. The correspondence on file in the Legation will acquaint you with the particulars of the subject. According to the last information from Santiago respecting it, the Chilean government had referred the matter to a Commissioner for a report.

The claim in the cases of the Garafilia and the Argyle is for the detention of those vessels by embargo in Chilean ports during the late war between Chile and Peru. Our right to a reparation arises from the clear and positive stipulation in the fifth article of the Treaty. The claim has been resisted upon the ground that the Spanish version of the Treaty admits of a different construction from that contended for by this government for the English version. If, however, the obvious intent of the article be considered, the obligation of the Chilean government to make amends in this and all other similar cases would remain, even if the construction of the treaty contended for by that government were to be admitted. Upon this subject you are particularly referred to the instruction from this department to Mr. [Richard] Pollard, No. 15, of the 3d of August, 1837.

The claims in the cases of the ships Franklin and brig Clifton are founded on contracts entered into with the owners of those vessels at an early period of the Chilean war of independence, by alleged authorities of Chile. It is not usual for this government to interfere except by its good offices, for the prosecution of claims of this description. Your course in regard to them will consequently be regulated by that principle.

These are believed to be all the claims of citizens of the United States on that government which the correspondence between the department and the Legation at Santiago shows to be in any way pending. It is not improbable that during your residence there, other cases may occur in which your countrymen who may visit Chile or whose abode may be in that country, will expect you to interpose between them and the Chilean authorities. In deciding upon the propriety of your interference, you will in the first place consider whether the case involves any breach of the treaty, and if so, whether the aggrieved party might not obtain redress through the judicial tribunals, for if proper reparation were to be obtainable through that channel, it would be the duty of the complainant so to seek it, at least in the first instance. Cases not contemplated by the treaty may occur, and yet involving a breach of the law of nations for which the Courts of the country can provide no remedy. In such cases there will be a strict propriety in asking reparation through the diplomatic channel.

In cases arising under the municipal laws of the country only, it will very seldom be proper for you to interfere at all, and you will admonish our citizens there that the treaty itself requires them to submit to those laws.

Although the intestine broils in the greater number of the Spanish American States have been almost incessant since their emancipation from the mother country, and wars between the States themselves have been frequent, it is probable that in a controversy between any one of those States and a foreign power, the former will always, more or less enjoy the sympathies of the others. The Chileans may be deemed particularly sensitive on this point. This is shown by many circumstances, but by none more strongly, than by their requiring, at the time of the negotiation of our treaty with them, an exception to the principle of the most favored nation, to the advantage of the other Spanish American States. As this feeling is a natural one, springing from the identity of origin, language and religion of the people of those States, we have no reason to complain of it, unless it should be indulged to an extent sufficient to give an undue bias to a judgement upon proceedings of this government.

There is reason to believe that Mexico has heretofore attempted to inculcate an opinion in the governments of those States that the United States entertained ambitious designs upon her acknowledged territory and sought unfounded pretexts for the accomplishment of those designs. It is not known that any insinuations to this effect which may have been made in Chile have been favorably listened to, but as that may possibly be the case, it is proper that you should be prepared to counteract them by a representation of the facts. Those necessary for that purpose you will find in the documents which accompanied the President's Message to the House of Representatives of the 10th of June, last, a printed copy of which you will receive herewith. I am, Sir, your obedient servant, J.C. Calhoun.

LS (No. 2) in NjMoN, Lloyd W. Smith Collection (Morristown National Historical Park published microfilm, reel 8); FC in DNA, RG 59 (State Department), Diplomatic Instructions, Chile, 15:49–55 (M-77:35).

From LATHROP J. EDDY

Baltimore, May 28th 1844

Respected Sir, Before returning to my constituents of New-York I pen to you a hasty account of our proceedings in [the Tyler] Convention. The respectable portion of the New-York Delegation as you will perceive by the proceedings were not heard, but were put down by the dishonest & contemptible parasites who seem to have got the ear of the President. "The Calhoun Ex[ecutive] Com[mittee] of New-York" have heretofore occupied a high & most honourable position before the People—and they intend at all hazards to maintain that position. We came to this Convention with the most friendly feelings for John Tyler—but loving our principles & your standing more—We intended to act for the Democracy only & were so instructed by our Constituents. When we came here we found your enemies, the secret friends of Henry Clay—and men without such standing in society or influence as to enable us to even be presumed as acting with them, acting in conjunction with Mr. Rob[er]t Tyler & Doct[o]r [John G.] Miller & others and without any consultation with us controlling everything. Every attempt which we made to act with discretion & honesty was put down by a tumult[u]ous assemblage which had no business there; but brought there for the sole purpose of gagging us & ["humbugging" *altered to* "humbuging"] Pres[iden]t Tyler.

The result I doubt not will be that no Tyler Elector Ticket will be made in a majority of the northern States—and in the remainder no State will give him 5000 votes. We are not by such influences to be placed in any such ridiculous position. We regard you & those principles of which you are the exponent too highly.

If Mr. Tyler has made selection of such advisers as have here controlled, no good can come to the country from his administration.

We stand as we did; opponents of Mr. [Martin] Van Buren—Your friends & [*one word canceled and* "in" *interlined*] the course of the coming fortnight we shall publish an address to the People setting forth our position, and advising our friends as to the course to be taken in the coming contest. In so doing we shall have a single eye to your eventual success and the adoption entire of your principles by the People. In much haste I remain with the highest respect Your friend, Lathrop J. Eddy.

ALS in ScCleA. NOTE: An AEU by Calhoun reads "Mr. Eddy[,] relates to the proceedings of the Tyler Convention."

From A[RCHIBALD] M. GREEN

Consulate of the U. States of America at Galvezton
Republic of Texas, May 28th 1844

Sir, I have the honor to acknowledge the receipt of yours of the 2nd Inst[ant].

I have in former communications reported the conduct of the Ch[arg]e de Affaires & intimated to the Department that his conduct might be of such an ["offensive" *interlined*] nature as to require prompt action on my part.

His conduct at all times insulting and offensive, has recently been of such a nature as to require and compel me to redress my own wrongs. A few days since he publickly proclaimed in a public Bar Room of a public Hotel of this City that I was engaged in fraudulently abstracting money from the Bank of Virginia—in consequence of which I had run off to Canada. That I was in bad repute with my government and that in consequence of swindling the Bank of Virginia I dare not return home. It became necessary for me to notice promptly this vile and ["slanderous" *canceled*] & false charge.

It was due to myself, due to my Government. The Govt. may say that as one of its officers I had my redress & that by referring the matter to the proper tribunal ample justice would have been done me—but I appeal to you and to every high minded honorable man whether longer forbearance would not have ceased to have been a virtue.

My character stamped as a swindler and rogue in a foreign Land amongst strangers and by the Charge d'Affaires of my own Government.

I have persued the only course that my feelings as an honourable man would allow. Upon hearing his charge, I immediately addressed him a note calling upon him to know whether he had made any such charge—to which note he made no ["reply" *canceled*] response, and as unpleasant & as mortifying as it was to me, I was compelled to post him. Although it is true that under the very excited state of my feelings, produced by these calumnies, I used language at the close of the last paragraph of my handbill which upon reflection I ought not to have applied to the *Charge d'Affaires*, however justly it may have been merited—

I was left no other alternative. His age protected him from proper chastisement and the ["impulse of the" *interlined*] moment governed me. In answer to my card he endeavours to create the impression that he could not so far forget his station as to condescend to repeat the language used by myself—yet he could basely and falsely slander an officer of his Government in a public Bar Room, get drunk, use the most vulgar, indecent and loathsome language that ever escaped the tongue of man.

This matter will doubtless be investigated by the Department— and I am satisfied that my conduct will be perfectly justifiable as a man—if not as an officer. And I am also satisfied that my official conduct & my deportment as a gentleman has met the entire approbation of those with whom I have had any intercourse.

If it be the pleasure of the Department to enter into a full investigation of my conduct, I should ["like" *canceled*] be gratified and it will afford me pleasure to make in person suitable explanations and with permission of the Department, I will without delay make any that a justification of my conduct might seem to require.

I herewith enclose you evidences, that will go far to establish the truth of what I say and a justification of my course. A memorandum of which is as follows.

No. 1. Conversation with Gen[era]l Murphy (the charge d'Affaires) at three different times.

" 2. Colo[nel Alden A.M.] Jackson['s; "letter" *interlined*; of 5/- 25/1844] former Collector of the Port of Galvezton as to conversation and words used by the Ch[arg]e d'Affaires.

" 3. Letter [of 5/21/1844] from W.J. Gourlay as to the language used by Ch[arg]e d'Affaires.

" 4. Letter from Maj[o]r Ja[me]s A. Hamilton as to words used in bar Room by the Ch[arg]e de Affaires.

" 5. Letter of [5/22/1844 from Stewart Newell] the Consul of the United States at ["the" *interlined*] port of Sabine, as to Gen[era]l Murphy[']s indecorous language.

" 6. Letter [of 5/28/1844] from Capt. J[ohn] A. Davis U.S. sch[oone]r Flirt.

" 7. Letter [of 5/24/1844] from Judge [R.C.] Campbell as to the conduct of the Ch[arg]e d'Affaires.

" 8. Letter [of 5/23/1844] from Judge [Robert D.] Johnson.

" 9. d[itt]o [of 5/25/1844] from the Mayor of Galvezton [John M. Allen].

" 10. A Certificate [of 5/22/1844] voluntarily given by the shipping merchants of the city of Galvezton.

" 11. Gen[era]l [Memucan] Hunt[']s Letter [of 5/23/1844].

" 12. Printed cards [of 5/21/1844] of Mr. Green & [of 5/22/1844 of] W[illia]m S. Murphy to the public.

I have the honor to be Sir Most Respectfully your Ob[edien]t Servant, A.M. Green.

ALS (No. 37) with Ens in DNA, RG 59 (State Department), Consular Despatches, Galveston, vol. 2 (T-151:2), received 6/11. Note: Murphy's response to Green's handbill was a statement in the Galveston *Evening News* of 5/23/1844 in which he refused to engage in a public controversy with Green and left the decision of the affair to "my government."

Bill from [Mrs.] E. King, [Washington], 5/28. This document bills Calhoun $166 for four weeks' board with six extra dinners [for guests?], and $153.50 for two dinner parties of ten persons each with waiters. Payment was receipted on 5/31. ADS in ScU-SC, John C. Calhoun Papers.

To J[AMES] I. McKAY, Chairman, Committee of Ways and Means, House of Representatives

Department of State
Washington, 28 May 1844

Sir, I have the honor to state, for the information of the Committee of Ways and Means, that appropriations will be necessary, in addition to those stated in my communication of the 24th Ultimo, for Outfits of a Minister to Austria, and of a Chargé d'Affaires to Belgium, $13,500.

I have the honor to invite the attention of the Committee to items included in the estimate from this Department, which are omitted in the appropriation bill, (No. 32,) now before the House of Representatives, Viz:

For Outfits of a Minister to China, and of a Chargé d'Affaires to Texas,	$13,500
For the salary of a Minister to China,	9,000
For Salary of a Commissioner to the Sandwich Islands	3,000
For Salary of the Consul at Beyrout	500

and to the following reductions from the estimates; Viz:

The item for the Contingent expenses of all the Missions abroad from $20,000, to $15,000. The appropriations for this object have usually been $30,000. The estimate for the ensuing year was for $20,000 only, as it was expected that a saving would result from the operation of the act fixing the value of the pound sterling in all payments to be made from the Treasury. The demands upon this appropriation will, however, during the ensuing year, be heavier than ordinary, in consequence of the return of several Diplomatic Agents of the United States. The salaries of those agents will cease at the date of their audience of leave. The customary allowance for the expenses of their return to the United States will be chargeable to this appropriation.

The item for the relief and protection of American Seamen in foreign countries, estimated at $75,000, has been reduced to $30,000. The appropriation for the year ending on the 30th June, proximo, was $50,000, which proving insufficient, a further appropriation of $40,500 was made at an early period of the present session of Congress to meet the deficiency. A reduction of the appropriation for the ensuing fiscal year to $30,000, would, probably, before the commencement of the next session of Congress, leave the Department destitute of means to pay the draughts of the Consuls of the United States for their reimbursement for money actually advanced by them, in obedience to law. Such an event could not but be productive of serious injury to the credit of the country and of its agents abroad, not only present, but prospective; It would also be attended with pecuniary loss in the way of costs and damages upon protested bills.

The amount for Contingent expenses of this Department, including publication and distribution of the laws, estimated at $20,000, has been reduced to $18,600. The reduction appears in the item of "Extra-Clerk hire and copying,["] from $3,400, to $2,000. The estimate under this head was greater for the ensuing year than for the past one, that for the latter having proved insufficient and requiring a resort to the transfer of surpluses from other heads, provided for by law. The aggregate amount of the estimate was not however increased; the amount, added to the item for extra clerk-hire, having been deducted from other heads of expenditure, as heretofore appropriated.

The item for preparing indices to the Manuscript papers of the Confederation, and of [George] Washington; including an arrearage for the year ending on the 30th of June 1844, of $1108, was $2360. It has been reduced to $1252, thus taking off the precise amount of the arrearage.

I have the honor to State, that, from information received from Mr. Albert Smith Commissioner to mark the Boundary between the United States and Great Britain, it appears that the estimate for the salary of the Commissioner and Clerk, and for other expenses of the Commission, including the purchase and repair of instruments, wages of persons employed and other contingencies, was too low. He states that for the operations of the past season there was a deficiency of $8,000, and that for those of the present season the sum of

$35,000 will be required; making together $43,000, instead of $15,000 as estimated by this Department. I have the honor to be, Sir, Your obedient servant, J.C. Calhoun.

LS in DNA, RG 233 (U.S. House of Representatives), 28A-D30.6; FC in DNA, RG 59 (State Department), Accounting Records: Miscellaneous Letters Sent, 1832–1916, vol. for 2/1–9/30/1844, pp. 196–199.

From F[RANCIS] W. PICKENS

Baltimore, Tuesday 10 O'Clock [May 28, 1844]
My dear Sir, I would have written before but for constant engagements. There are some things I cannot understand. I saw it the moment I mingled with members at Washington. Your own friends talked of your name as out of the question at present &c—whereas I had been thinking that circumstances had taken place which made it eminently fit & proper that you should be pushed, & had so talked all the way on. Well I find hundreds here who all say you ought to be the man, but they cannot get at you &c. There has been something wrong *somewhere* but where I cannot tell.

Every thing is uncertain here. [Robert J.] Walker [Senator from Miss.] I have been with much—he fights nobly, but does not see the end of his own moves. If they dispute all points, as they will do I think, it will end in confusion and blowing up of the convention. All the members begin to see the nomination is in fact the election, & therefore they will contend for every inch. The whole amount is that there will be no other conventions, & we have made the platform upon which they will break them down.

It seems probable that, if any one is nominated it will be [Lewis] Cass & [Richard M.] Johnson, but still a slight circumstance may change the whole. I never saw such excitement in my life—immense crowds every night & addresses in the streets &c—of the most vulgar demagoguism.

As I return I will see you and hope to recieve [*sic*] a letter from home which will be enclosed to you. I shall have no time to stay in Washington, and as I cannot get an interview with Gen[era]l [Alexander O.] Anderson at all, I enclose the within note so that I can recieve the answer when I call to see you. Will you be so kind as to make a servant drop it at the Bank for me. Very truly, F.W. Pickens.

P.S. My own impression is that the best result *for us* is the nomination of [Martin] V[an] B[uren] by a [*manuscript torn*; large] majority, & if it does [*one word canceled*] not force rebellion it will bring defeat and odium upon his N[ew York] clique & *future prostration* to [Thomas H.] Benton[,] [Silas] Wright &c [*manuscript torn*; and] the whole Dynasty. Perhaps it is better this than for us to be forced to acquiesce in a weak & uncertain ticket.

8 O'Clock night. Convention adjourned—last bal[l]ot Cass 123[,] V[an] B[uren] 99—Johnson 21—[James] Bucchanan [*sic*] 26[,] Calhoun 1. I begin to doubt any nomination being made. The V[an] B[uren] men desperate—great excitement. They will not agree to Cass. It is best for us to break up without agreeing. V[an] B[uren] dead forever. They begin to see the consequences of things. It does seem to me that the South ought to agree to push you. I do not see why they don't—but all are lifeless. F.W.P.

ALS in ScCleA; variant PC in Jameson, ed., *Correspondence*, pp. 959–960. NOTE: This letter was postmarked in Baltimore on 5/30.

From S[tephen] Pleasonton, Fifth Auditor of the Treasury, 5/28. He advises how certain items in the accounts of Albert Smith, Commissioner for running the northeastern boundary line of the U.S. in accordance with the Treaty of Washington, should be handled under a statute of 1843. The cost of provisions and of transporting them should be allowed, as being necessary to accomplish the stipulated object. The law mentioned only the use of Topographical Engineers loaned by the Army, but instructions to Smith have also ambiguously authorized the use of civilian engineers; so those items in his accounts might also be approved. LS with En in DNA, RG 59 (State Department), Letters Received from the Fifth Auditor and Comptroller, 1829–1862; FC in DNA, RG 217 (General Accounting Office), Fifth Auditor: Letters Sent, 5:126–127.

From EDWARD UHRLAUB

Hannoverian Consulate
Baltimore, May 28th 1844

Sir! Having been informed thro' the medium of the newspaper of this country, that a commercial treaty has been agreed upon by the President of the United States and the German League, called the "Zollverein" and which is now before the Senate for ratification, I beg you to allow me to make the following remarks in regard to it. One of the features in this treaty is as I understand a reduction of duties on the part of the United States on Linnen, Cotton and other manufactures, but whether it discriminates between manufactures of the states of the German League and those of other states, or not, I do not know. Should the former be the case, it would in a still greater degree affect the manufacture of Linnen in the Kingdom of Hannover than the present high duty of 25% has done already.

The Kingdom of Hannover together with the Grand Dukedom of Oldenburg do not belong to the German League, but have formed an alliance for leviing duties between themselves. The duties levied by these two states on American tobacco are very moderate indeed, say only one fifth part of that raised at present by the Prussian Government on this article. The United States would insure themselves a continuance of this low duty in Hannover and Oldenburg should the former reduce the present duty on Linnen, an article, the importation of which does little or not at all interfere with American Industry.

In closing these remarks I leave them trustfully for your consideration and beg you, if your Excellency thinks proper to communicate the same to the President of the United States. I have the honor to remain Sir your most ob[e]d[ien]t Serv[an]t, Edward Uhrlaub, Royal Hanoverian Consul.

ALS in DNA, RG 59 (State Department), Notes from Foreign Consuls, vol. 2 (M-664:2, frames 387–390).

To FRANCIS WHARTON, [Philadelphia]

Washington, 28th May 1844

My dear Sir, I am always gratified with the free expression of the opinions of my friends. I infer from your remarks, that you are of the impression that I am some how or other connected with Mr. [John] Tyler in reference to the Presidential election. Nothing is farther from the fact. I have no understanding, or connection with him whatever in reference to it. I accepted the office I hold with the utmost reluctance, and with an express declaration on my part, that I accepted it wholly in reference to the pending negotiations and that I should be at liberty to retire as soon as they were closed. I came here resolved to take no part in the presidential election, or the party politicks of the day unless forced by circumstances over which I could have no control to do so. The unexpected opposition of Mr. [Henry] Clay and Mr. [Martin] V[an] B[uren] to the Treaty, and the wholly unjustifiable assaults on me by the friends of the latter, have compelled me to oppose him and them, which I have done decidedly; and to that extent, and no farther, have I interfered. Their course has made a thorough reorganization of the party necessary, and when I say their course, I do not refer simply to it in reference to Texas, but on the subjects of the Tariff and abolition, on both of which they have identified themselves with the Whigs, and that in violation of the most open and solemn pledges often given.

If the Texas question to a northern eye does not appear sufficiently sustained by the documents, I must think, it is owing to the fact, that that portion of the Union has not duly weighed the danger to which the movements and avowed policy of Great Britain in reference to Texas would, if consummated, expose the southern and western States, and the obligation which this Government is under to defend them. I must say, that I fear from what I see and hear, even from the enlightened and well disposed at the North, that the zeal, which the South has ever evinced to defend the North, when her interest is involved, will never be reciprocated on her part. On three memorable occasions, the war of the Revolution, that of 1812, and the threatened war of the Maine boundary, when the interest of the north was mainly involved, we evinced a zeal not less than her own, for her defence. In none of these cases, had we any particular or local interest, yet we did not on that account hold back. Even in the local question of the Maine boundary, which involved a few hundred thousands of acres of barren land, we came up unanimously to the rescue; but now, when for the first time we ask for defence; when our very safety is at stake, the great body of the enlightened portion of the North either hold back, or oppose. There is something wrong in all this, and not a little ominous to the duration of our system. If our safety and the great interest we have in maintaining the existing relation between the two races in the south, are of no estimation in the eyes of our northern friends—if they see neither insult nor danger, in the Declaration of the Earl of Aberdeen, in reference to that relation, in connection with Texas, it is time we should know it. If they are insensible or blind to our danger on that vital point, they may rest assured we are not.

I think you will find, when you come to look in to the facts, that you have permitted Col. [Thomas H.] Benton's unfounded assertions to make an erroneous impression on your mind. His whole speech is a mass of contradictions, resting on baseless assumptions, as I think you will see, should [you] read the replies, which have been made to him. He, and, I must say, Mr. Clay and Mr. V[an] B[uren], have

649

involved themselves by their course in a web of contradiction, from which they can never extricate themselves.

As to myself, I am of the impression, if we shall have the folly or wickedness to permit Great Britain to plant the lever of her power between the U. States and Mexico, on the Northern shore of the Gulph of Mexico, we give her a place to stand on, from which she can [*illegible word*; "brave"?] at pleasure the American Continent and control its destiny. There is not a vacant spot left on the Globe, not excepting Cuba, to be seized by her, so well calculated to further the boundless schemes of her ambition and cupidity. If we should permit her to seize on it, we shall deserve the execration of posterity. Reject the treaty, and refuse to annex Texas, and she will certainly seize on it. A treaty of alliance commercial and political will be forthwith proposed by Texas to her, and I doubt not accepted. This for yourself.

PC in Jameson, ed., *Correspondence*, pp. 592–594.

To [Jean Corneille,] Chevalier Gevers, [Dutch Chargé d'Affaires to the U.S.], 5/29. Calhoun acknowledges receipt of Gevers's letter of 4/21 relating to the "injurious operation" of the U.S. tariff of 1842 upon Java coffee imported from the Netherlands to the U.S. According to Gevers, the twenty per cent duty upon coffee discriminates against that product and contravenes the U.S.-Dutch treaty of reciprocity of 1839. Calhoun has referred Gevers's letter to the Acting Secretary of the Treasury [McClintock Young] and now transmits to Gevers a copy of his reply. Calhoun agrees with Young on the tariff issue but will "lose no time" in sending to [Charles J. Ingersoll] the Chairman of the House Committee on Foreign Affairs their correspondence on the subject with a view to alter the tariff by legislation. FC in DNA, RG 59 (State Department), Notes to Foreign Legations, Netherlands, 6:33–34 (M-99:75).

From HENRY W. HILLIARD

Legation of the United States
Brussels, 29th May 1844

Sir: I have the honor to acknowledge the receipt of your letter of notification of the 1st April, informing me of your appointment to the office of Secretary of State. Before receiving your communication, I had ventured in an unofficial letter to express my gratification that you had consented to enter upon the duties of that office, at this important juncture, and I congratulate the country upon the choice the President has made.

In my despatch of the 26th February, last, I presented to the late Secretary of State, Mr. [Abel P.] Upshur, a full statement respecting the project of a law submitted to the Chambers by the Minister of Finance, proposing to tax the consumption of tobacco, and I forwarded a copy of my correspondence with Count [Albert Joseph] Goblet, Minister of Foreign Affairs, upon that subject. I take the liberty of inviting your attention to that correspondence, and of referring you to my communications to the Department of State in relation to the subject. I have endeavored to put the Department in possession of the question, but I have reason to believe that it was not clearly apprehended. I have endeavored to exhibit this idea; that the proposition of the Minister of Finance to subject the tobacco belonging to citizens of the United States imported into Belgium upon the faith of existing laws, to the provisions of a new law was in a high degree unjust and that the measure was *retro-active* in its character. I have insisted that the tobacco brought into this country, upon which the duty of importation is paid has acquired certain rights, and that its consumption ought not to be taxed; that to subject it to the payment of duties of any description, not imposed by laws in existence, at the time of its introduction would be unfair and unjust.

The reply of Count Goblet to my representations is before you, and the view taken of the question by the late Secretary of State will be seen by reference to his despatch addressed to me under date of 24th February last. It is urged by the Minister of Finance that the proposed law will not affect American tobacco unless it should be put into consumption, that it may lie in warehouses or be circulated through the country, without paying an additional duty or that it may even be re-exported; to which I have replied that the tobacco was sent to this country for consumption, that to leave it in store would be unprofitable and to re-export it would be ruinous. The report of the central section appointed by the Chambers to examine the project of the law submitted by the Minister of Finance has been made and I shall forward it by some early opportunity, it is too bulky for the ordinary post. I have expressed myself so clearly and strongly upon this subject to the Minister of Finance in conversation, and in my correspondence with the Minister of Foreign Affairs, that I do not see how I can effect anything more until I receive instructions from the Department of State, which will enable me to speak with the authority of my Government.

It will be seen by my correspondence with Mr. Nothomb, Minister of the Interior, already forwarded, that the applications of claimants for indemnity for losses caused by the destruction of the entrepôt at Antwerp, are under consideration and will be disposed of as early as possible. The claimants are naturally impatient, but I do not see that the business can be at all expedited.

On the 1st March last, in a letter to the President, I stated that it was my wish to return home in the course of the summer and I had hoped by this time to have had a favorable reply from him. The considerations which induced me to make the request are chiefly of a family and private nature, and they are so imperative that I cannot consent any longer to defer forwarding a formal resignation. I must, respectfully, request the President to permit me to leave the Legation by the 12th August, and to consider this a resignation of my office to take effect on that day. I select the 12th of August, not merely for personal reasons, but because it closes regularly a quarter of a year, regarding the date of my appointment and it will make it rather more convenient for the settlement of accounts. I have the honor to be, Sir, Very respectfully Your obedient servant, Henry W. Hilliard.

LS (No. 18) in DNA, RG 59 (State Department), Diplomatic Despatches, Belgium, vol. 2 (M-193:3), received 6/21. NOTE: Found among the papers of Calhoun's Chief Clerk, Richard K. Crallé, at ViU (Crallé-Campbell Papers) is a letter of 2/24/[1844] from John Winge, Petersburg [Va.], to President Tyler, enclosing a petition of 26 tobacco merchants making complaint of a proposed Belgian duty of $50 per hogshead on tobacco to be imported and already on the market. An undated AEI by Tyler on these papers directs them to the attention of the State Department: "State[;] an immediate explanation of this should be asked of the Belgian minister." Henry Washington Hilliard (1808–1892) had been Professor at the University of Alabama and was appointed Chargé d'Affaires to Belgium by John Tyler in 5/1842. He was subsequently Representative from Ala. 1845–1851, a Colonel in the Confederate army, and U.S. Minister to Brazil 1877–1881.

To P[erley] B. Johnson, Representative [from Ohio], 5/29. In reply to Johnson's letter of 5/27, Calhoun informs him that the U.S. Consul at Havana [Robert B. Campbell] has already been instructed to inquire into the case of [Henry J.] Cavalier. FC in DNA, RG 59 (State Department), Consular Instructions, 10:248–249.

From GEO[RGE] H. JONES

Petersburg [Va.,] 29th May 1844

Dear Sir, I received a few days scince [*sic*], a letter from our mutual friend Judge [John Y.] Mason in which he mentioned your having united in recommending me for office. For this evidence of your Kind feelings I beg you to accept my warmest gratitude and also to assure You, I would not again ask your assistance, but for the suffering condition of my family, not made so from any imprudence on my part, if I am free from fault, it is from *dissipation* of every discription [*sic*]. I had the misfortune to lose my Father at the age of 12 years old with but 4 years schooling & *not a dollar*, a mother and 7 Sisters to assist. I managed by strict economy & close attention to business to aid them & save some little of my earnings. A few years since I commenced the dry good business & finding it prosperous I thought it most prudent to marry, but a few years afterwards I was blest with four little children, and in the midst of my happiness, rev[e]rse of fortune came upon me and I was deprived of every thing, even the cradle, that wrocked my children taken from me. In addition to this, I had the misfortune a few weeks scince to lose my Dear good Mother. All my troubles seem to thicken & I have borne them with that fortitude, which becomes an honest man, and used every exertion to obtain employment, but I deeply regret to say, I have been thwarted in every way.

Unlike others I have no relatives whose situation will admit of their lending me a helping hand, nor have I friends, upon whom I have any claim to their friendly aid. Deprived then of every comfort, with my wife & children, actually in want, and I unable to assist them, You may well imagine my feelings. Aside then My Dear Sir from every political friendship I appeal to you as a parent, I implore you, once more to see the President [John Tyler] in person & endeavour if possible to get me some appointment. I am satisfied if he could appreciate my situation & knew my kind feelings personally and politically, he would not lend a deaf ear to your entreaties in my behalf. Do grant this request and I promise you the gratitude and prayers of a pious wife[,] the thanks of my little suffering children & the continued gratitude of an unfortunate man.

I presume ere this, the convention have settled on some one as the candidate of the Democratic Party and should any one north of the Potomac be the nominee, I am at a loss what course to pursue. I am satisfied all the north (without distinction of party) are in fav[o]r of a high tarif[f], a measure I think destructive of the most vital interests of the South & as such I am unwilling to aid in elevating any candidate who is the least *tinctured* with a Tarif[f]. I have always been one of your warmest admirers and regarded You, as giving tone to all my political views and I trust you will not hesitate to advise me, what course to adopt in the coming election. I had fully made up my mind, that in the event of your not being a candidate to support Mr. [John] Tyler should he be run by any Party. I do so upon principle. I really think he has been greatly misrepresented and certainly has administered this government, with a degree of independence rarely to [be] met with.

I shall *certainly expect* your reply. I am Dear Sir Y[ou]r friend mo[st] Truly, Geo. H. Jones.

P.S. Should you have occasion to send abroad any despatches I should like to be the bearer.

ALS in ScCleA. Note: An AEU by Calhoun reads "Mr. Jones of Petersburg."

From W[illiam] S. Murphy

Legation of the United States
Galveston, 29th May 1844

Sir, The enclosed copies, of notes, between Mr. [Archibald M.] Green[,] Mr. [Stewart] Newell and myself, coupled with much verbal and contradictory matter, which has reached me from other sources (upon ["which" *interlined*] but little reliance can be placed,) is all the information in the possession of this Legation, in relation ["to" *interlined*] the Steamer "Scioto Belle."

My last note, of yesterday, to Mr. Newell, (you will remark,) calls upon him for the paper evidence in his possession, to enable me, to present the case to you, in a manner intelligible to the department of State.

Until this is done, I do not deem it respectful to the Department of State, or agreeable to that accuracy of information, which this Legation should strictly observe, in all its correspondence, to present the uncertain and equivocal circumstances, as they now appear before me.

I may remark, however, that this ["is" *interlined*] the second Steamear, owned by American citizens which has been brought from the Sabine to this port, under the official supervision of the Consuls

Green and Newell; The first was made (in some way or other) to become a total loss to the owners—and a suit has ["been," *interlined*] and perhaps is yet, pending, in New Orleans, against Mr. Green, on account of the loss of that Boat, under his official supervision. And I fear, that the present case, under the supervision of Mr. Newell and Mr. Green, both, will result in the same way. You will observe, from the enclosed correspondence, that both have addressed me on the subject; but I have called on Mr. Newell for the authentic papers and evidences in relation to the case, because I supposed him, to be most certainly in possession of them.

The steamer New York, sails tomorrow for N[ew] Orleans, and by her, I forward this despatch, and also Nos. 25 and 26. With Sentiments of the highest respect and Esteem, I have the Honor to be Your ob[edien]t Serv[an]t, W.S. Murphy.

ALS (No. 27) with Ens in DNA, RG 59 (State Department), Diplomatic Despatches, Texas, vol. 2 (T-728:2, frames 328–336), received 6/11; FC in DNA, RG 84 (Foreign Posts), Records of the Texas Legation. NOTE: An enclosed letter of 4/13 from Murphy to Newell introduces the bearer, Carter Beaman, an owner of the *Scioto Belle*, and asks that Newell settle the difficulties concerning that steamer. In letters of 5/24 from Green and 5/25 from Newell to Murphy, they protest the action of the Texan government in assuming jurisdiction over the *Scioto Belle* case after that U.S. owned and operated vessel was sold, following Murphy's directions, and the crew paid accordingly. Murphy replied to Green on 5/24 and to Newell on 5/25 that he would investigate the matter as soon as his other duties allowed. In a final letter of 5/28 to Newell, Murphy stated that he would submit the case for the decision of the State Department and asked for "authentic" copies of all relevant documents in Newell's possession.

From W[ILLIAM] S. MURPHY

Legation of the United States
Galveston Texas, 29th May 1844

Sir, The enclosed Letters from citizens of this Town addressed to the President of the United States, have just been handed (unsolicited) to me and I deem it proper, that they should reach His Excellency, through the Department of State. They have reference to the subject matter of my Despatches to you, Nos. 26 & 27.

The enclosed affidavits, have also just been handed to me, by the Captain of the Steamer "Scioto Belle"—and refer also, (in part) to the subject matter of the same previous despatches. They confirm all my previous information, on the painful subjects to which they relate; and I forbear any commentary upon them.

Permit ["me" *interlined*] however to say, that I do not think, ["that" *interlined*] a Consulate at the Sabine, is, or has been, of any advantage to the Citizens of the United States. Rather the reverse, as it[s; "duties" *interlined*] have been hitherto executed. I have the Honor to be, Your ob[edien]t Serv[an]t, W.S. Murphy.

ALS (No. 28) with Ens in DNA, RG 59 (State Department), Diplomatic Despatches, Texas, vol. 2 (T-728:2, frames 336–348), received 6/11; variant FC in DNA, RG 84 (Foreign Posts), Records of the Texas Legation. NOTE: Enclosed are affidavits of 5/29 and 5/30 by J[ames] J. Wright and George A. Hudson, former master and crew member of the *Scioto Belle*, respectively, claiming that irregularities by Stewart Newell, U.S. Consul at Sabine, in selling that vessel tended to favor Carter Beaman and discriminate against the crew and other owners of the vessel. A letter of 5/29 from J.C. Shaw and Dan[ie]l Marston, Jr., to [John Tyler] attests to Murphy's good character and industriousness and states that he has gained enemies in his attempts to bring about Texan annexation to the U.S. An enclosed copy of the Galveston *Evening News* of 5/11 contains proceedings of a public meeting at which resolutions complimentary to Murphy were adopted. A final enclosure of 5/23 from P. Edmonds to John Tyler regrets the public dissension between Murphy and [Archibald M.] Green because of its bad effect on annexation efforts. Edmonds feels that Murphy has been effective in his attempts to further those efforts.

From W[ILLIAM] S. MURPHY

Legation of the United States
Galveston Texas, 29th May 1844

Sir, I received, late last evening, a verbal account, from a merchant, just arrived from Corpus Christie, of a revolution which had just broken out on the Mexican border, and that Gen[era]l [Antonio] Canales, was at the Head of 2000 men, and leading the revolutionary party—but it was generally believed, that Gen[era]l [Mariano] Ariste, was really the prime mover, and would shortly make a decisive demonstration, at the head of a larger force. Gen[era]l Canales has his head Quarters at a point opposite Comargo, on the North side of the Rio Grande. Gen[era]l [Adrian] Woll's head Quarters, are at Sabinas, an inland vil[l]age, where he has about 1200 men.

Gen[era]l Woll, being ignorant of the amount of the forces of Gen[era]l Canales, sent 200 men to, arrest him. But Canales, without attacking these men, sent them back, with a request to Gen[era]l Woll, that if he wished to arrest him, he must come himself, with 20,000 men.

There are the reports (of course) of traders from the border & interior, of that part of Mexico. But we may safely conclude, that a real and considerable force, in open rebellion against the Mexican Government is actually in the field, under Gen[era]l Canales. And, that consequently, there is no danger of any invasion of Texas, by Mexico, at present.

All agree in this, that the Texan border is in peace—and likely to continue so for a long time to come.

The Vincennes, Capt. [Franklin] Buchanan is, at anchor off this port—officers & crew, all well. The Somers, is daily expected here. I have the Honor to be, with great respect & esteem Your ob[edien]t Serv[an]t, W.S. Murphy.

ALS (No. 29) in DNA, RG 59 (State Department), Diplomatic Despatches, Texas, vol. 2 (T-728:2, frames 348–349), received 6/11; variant FC in DNA, RG 84 (Foreign Posts), Records of the Texas Legation.

From STEWART NEWELL, [Galveston]

Consulate of the United States, Port of Sabine
R[epublic] of Texas, May 29th 1844

Sir, In my No. 14, addressed to the Department, I trust the unpleasant duty, of reporting therein, the impropriety of conduct, on the part of our Chargé, Gen[era]l [William S.] Murphy, towards an Officer of his Government, you find in it nothing, that appears to go beyond, the duty, as I believed imposed upon me, to report any thing, that may tend to affect, our Commerce, with this country, and that a dispute between the Officers of the Government, resident in this country, would have that tendency, and of a most serious kind, the Department can have no doubt.

I have done that duty, and leave the result, to the fair and impartial views, and decissions, of the Department, which its character merits, and which I feel well assured, it will receive, and which a sense of duty to myself, and desire to render my feeble aid, in sustaining the Dignity of our Government, has alone prompted me, in the communication of.

I have now to report to the Department, an attempt at violence, and improper interference, on the part of the Courts and Officers of this Government, which calls loudly, for some prompt and decisive action, on the part of our Government, to give protection to our Officers, which perhaps is more necessary, in this Country, than in any Foreign Country, with which we have Commercial relations. The whole matter has been communicated by me, Officially, to Gen[era]l Murphy, Charge de Affaires, and as requested by him, I shall as speedily as possible, furnish him, with the Copies of all the Papers necessary, and Documents, to enable him, to make a proper report thereof, to the Department.

After stating to the Department, some of the important points, in the case, I beg leave to enclose a Copy of my Protest, made against the interference of the Courts of Texas, and hope when the matter is fairly before the Department, that the Protest, and all my action, in the matter, may meet the entire approbation of my Government.

On or about the 14th day of Febr[uar]y ult[imo], the American Steamer Scioto Belle, arrived at Sabine from New Orleans, under command of J[ames] J. Wright, he placed in command, by and with consent of Carter Beaman Esq[ui]r[e], and Thomas Barrett Es-q[ui]r[e] of New Orleans. Said vessel was chartered by said Bea-man, and who joined Wright, in the Charter, and Thomas Barrett, intervened, and became a third party, by becomeing security for the fulfilment of the terms of the Charter. Said Beaman, deposited with Barrett, securities satisfactory for Five thousand Dollars, to meet terms of said Charter, which was as follows, The Charterers to pay Three hundred dollars, p[e]r month, for Six Months, with privilege of purchasing for Three thousand dollars, within a certain time, and the Monthly payments, upon the Charter, to be considered as payments of the purchase. The notice to purchase was given in due time. The vessel proceeded on her voyage, to Sabine, and up Sabine River. Upon arriving there, Beaman found, that the rep-resentations made by Wright, ["were" *changed to* "to"; "false" *canceled and* "induce" *interlined*] him, Beaman, to join in this adven-ture, *was false*, he Wright, being of notorious bad character, in this country, and that no employment for the vessel, could be had, if he, Wright, remained in command. Upon this, after arrival of the vessel at the Port of Sabine, from a voyage up River Sabine & back, with-out Freight &C, Beaman, applied to me, as Consul for the U. States, (the vessel having been Entered, previously, at the Texian Custom House, and received a Coasting Liscence) to take the matter in hand,

and to dispossess Wright of the command. After a very patient investigation, of the whole circumstances, fully satisfied of the Character of Wright, and beleiveing his intention to be dishonest, and after the Crew had demanded their Wages, and which the Master had no Money, or credit, with which to pay, said Wages or necessary repairs, to the vessel, or to provide provissions, or supplies, of any kind, for the Crew I made demand upon said Master, and Beaman, as Owner, to pay or cause to be paid, the Wages, and claims due, by them, and said vessel, both of whom declared, thier inability, and unwillingness, to pay. Therefore I as Consul, upon the written libel filed by the Crew, before me, and the written application of Beaman, and authority of Barrett to Beaman, and by him, recorded and filed in this Office, I advertised said vessel for Sale, to pay Seamen and other claims, against her. After the expiration of Ten days notice, said vessel was sold, at Public Outcry, and Beaman, became the purchaser, to the amount of Two thousand dollars. He, having just claims, admitted by the Master, against said vessel, for Monies expended by Beaman for use of said vessel, they were admitted by me, as part of the payment of the purchase, after which Beaman paid the ballance in Cash, required, to satisfy the other claims as Wages &c, against the vessel. Wright gave notice at time of Sale, of his, not wishing the vessel sold, but became a bidder, to an amount less than Beaman, although Wright, had up to that time, declared his inability to pay, any of the Claims, and for proof of his inability, all contracts for Provissions, neccessary for the Crew, until paid off, were made, and settled by me, at the expence of the vessel. I stopped the pay of the Crew, from the day of libel, until paid from the Sale of the vessel, when all of them, reshipped, on board, excepting Wright and four others. The latter, with Wright, pursued the vessel to Galveston, there, have instituted a Suit in the Admiralty court, for Wages, alledged to be due them, and have caused the vessel to be arrested, and detained here, from being employed, and in danger of being entirely destroyed, in the Salt Water, by the destructive Worms thereof, Wright having declared, his intention, to effect such a purpose, before the Court can act upon the matter. All this is done by Men, who have joined in the libel before me, lived on board the vessel, at the expence of the Purchaser, until the day they were paid off, received thier Money, receipted for it, and now institute another suit, against the vessel, for alledged Wages, the whole being done at the instigation of the late Master.

Under these circumstances, both Mr. [Archibald M.] Green and myself as Consuls, and the Owner and Master, have Protested against said Proceedings, and determination thus, and openly expressed, on the Part of the Courts of this Country, the Officers thereof, and the Class of Attorneys, employed, to destroy if possible, and interfere with, the authority of our Consuls, and Officers, and by bringing the Office of Consul, into disrespect, with the Citizens and Seamen, thereby destroy confidence in thier Acts, and thereby, create litigation, for thier especial benefit, which if the Official Character, of the Consul, was properly supported ["here" *interlined*] and protected, would not be the case, and yesterday, on a part of this matter, being under investigation, in a Magistrate[']s Court, much abusive and unbecomeing censure, and remarks, were made by the Lawyers, relative to the rights and authority of Consuls, and a demand was made upon Mr. Green, for some Original Documents, belonging to said vessel, which if delivered, would have remained in Court, as part of the Records. He refused them, but tendered Certified Copies of them, upon being paid the proper fees therefor. The parties demanding the Papers, did not wish to incur the expence, and refused to accede, to the proposal of Mr. Green, and applied to the Court, for an Attachment against Mr. Green, and myself, and requireing us, to be Imprisoned, upon this as a contempt of Court, and perhaps only for the suggestions of a gentleman standing present, the order would have been carried into effect. But however mortifying, such a course towards us, would have been, yet I should have submitted, with a view of bringing the matter fully before my Government, that ["the"(?) *canceled and* "her" *interlined*] Action, would have been prompt, and deciseive, in the matter, and have more fully defined, to this Government, the Position her Consuls, and Officers, are to be considered, as occupying in thier Official capacities. I have the Honor to be Most Respectfully Your Ob[edien]t Serv[an]t, Stewart Newell.

ALS (No. 15) with En in DNA, RG 59 (State Department), Consular Despatches, vol. 1, Texas (T-153:1), received 6/11. NOTE: The enclosure is a protest of 5/25 by Newell against the action of the Texan authorities in assuming jurisdiction in the case of the *Scioto Belle*, a U.S. vessel whose claims had recently been settled by Newell as Consul. He feels that the seamen bringing the case to court are guilty of "Molesting and disturbing" the new owner in his legal possession of the vessel. Newell also feels that the suit evinces a disrespect for the U.S. Consul's office and will foster distrust and a lack of confidence in the authority of that office.

From S[ETH] T. OTIS

United States Consulate
Basel (Switzerland), May 29/44

Sir, I have the Honor to herewith Enclose to you a translated copy of a Letter Rec[eive]d at, And another one sent from this consulate, within the last few days. You will perceive by reference to them that they appertain to matters of some considerable importance to the commerce of the United States, and I doubt not they will receive that prompt attention from your Department that they may require.

Having so recently entered upon the duties of this Consulate, I am reluctant to speak with much Certainty upon the subject to which these communications relate, but I deem it proper to remark, That this Confederacy is one of undoubted wealth, and the amount of Silks (their principal manufactures) sent an[n]ually to the United States is very Considerable, and much Jealousy & ill feeling pervades the minds of the people relative to the Entrance of their Fabrics into the United States upon terms less Advantageous to their interests, than what is to be granted to their neighbors in Germany. And I have no doubt but what this Government will do *all in its power,* to bring about Equal facilities and advantages to the commerce of the United States, that shall have been secured to them by the Treaty alluded to.

Should you be of the opinion that Any good would result from an attempt at negotiating with them upon the subject, I should feel greatly Honored by being empowered to act in the matter under the instructions of my Government, *And would Endeavor to do something creditable for the Interests and character of the United States.* Awaiting anxiously Your reply to this communication, I have the Honor to be Sir with unfeigned Respect Your Ob[edien]t Servant, S.T. Otis, Consul.

ALS (No. 6) with Ens in DNA, RG 59 (State Department), Consular Despatches, Basle, vol. 1 (T-364:1), received 6/21. NOTE: Otis enclosed a translated copy of a letter of 5/26 to himself from the President and Federal Directory of Switzerland asking whether Swiss silks imported into the U.S. on German vessels will be admitted on equal terms with German silks under the treaty pending between the U.S. and the Zollverein. Otis replied on 5/29 that he had not been informed of the terms of the pending treaty but felt that if Switzerland "in *all respects* afford equal facilities and advantages" to U.S. trade as those granted by the German states under the treaty, then the U.S. would reciprocate.

From ALFRED SCHÜCKING, "(Confidential)"

Washington, May 29th 1844

Sir: Enclosed I beg permission to present to the notice of the State Department further allegations as to the Character of a Certain Lewis Mark. Having had in view only the duty of any man, Connvirsant with the facts in the Case, I shall here terminate my Communications on the Subject, resting satisfied with having brought the Circumstances generally to your notice, and with a most humble and abiding Confidence in the wisdom of the application to be made of them by you. I have the honour, Sir, to be With great respect Your most obed[ien]t Serv[an]t, Alfred Schücking.

ALS with En in DNA, RG 59 (State Department), Consular Despatches, Munich, vol. 1 (T-261:1). NOTE: Schücking enclosed his own translation of an article, datelined Leipzig, published in the German-language *New-Yorker Staats-Zeitung*, relating to alleged bribery and other activities of "Lewis Mark" in behalf of German manufacturers. Among the records of the State Dept. is another translation by Schücking of an article that appeared in the *Staats-Zeitung* of 4/27. In this article, also datelined Leipzig, "A Good Democrat" opposed at length Mark's appointment as U.S. Consul for Bavaria and the Prussian Rhine. The writer stated that, despite his claims, Mark was not an American citizen and was a disreputable businessman. Copy in DNA, RG 59 (State Department), Miscellaneous Letters (M-179:104, frames 246–250).

From WADDY THOMPSON [JR.]

Washington, May 29, 1844

Sir, I beg leave to submit the following remarks in relation to the charge in my accounts [as Minister to Mexico] of $3600 for which I gave a draft to L.T. Hargoos & Co. [*sic*; Louis T. Hargous & Co.] for money advanced by him to the Texan prisoners liberated by President Santa Anna in 1842. I had been instructed by the Secretary of State to use all the influence which I possessed to obtain the liberation of those men. On the 15 of June 1842 they were set at liberty in a condition of absolute want and destitution and must have suffered the utmost extreme of hunger & misery if I had not assisted them. Those who had been confined in the City of Puebla did actually suffer for food for three days and until a messenger could be sent to me in Mexico [City]. A still greater difficulty then presented itself as to the mode of sending these men home. The British minister Mr. Packenham [*sic*; Richard Pakenham] and the Prussian Chargé des affaires Mr. Gerrolt [*sic*; Baron F. von Gerolt] proposed to defray all the cost of transporting such of said prisoners as were natives of their respective countries. I also found a precedent of the action of our own government in a case precisely similar. In the year 1820 certain natives of the U. States were in confinement in Spain who had been captured in Mexico fighting in the armies of that country in its civil war with Spain. They were released on the application of Mr. [John] Forsyth the American minister in Spain—who issued an order to all American Consuls in Spain to furnish to those men thus liberated the means of transportation to the U. States and to charge the same to their government. See Niles' Register Vol. —— Page [*blank space*]. Out of extreme caution I forbore to do this but advanced them $2500 of my own funds and at my own risk which has since been paid me by the government. As this sum was wholly insufficient Mr. Hargoos of Vera Cruz an American merchant and our acting consul at that port advanced ten or eleven thousand dollars more. Before he did so however he wrote to me to enquire whether our government would repay him. I referred him to the precedent to which I have above alluded and expressed the opinion that our government would indemnify him. I drew a draft on the government for the $2500 advanced by me which was at first refused payment but an appropriation was made at the close of the session of Congress in 1842 of $6000 to cover the disbursements of the Legation in this matter—whereupon Mr. [Daniel] Webster wrote to me that if the drafts were again presented they would be paid out of this appropriation. The draft of $2500 drawn by me was so paid, but when the draft of $3600 in favor of Mr. Hargoos was presented he was told that it could not be paid, Because the balance of the appropriation had been exhausted in paying for the transportation of certain of the Santa Fé prisoners sent home by my predecessor Mr. [Powhatan] Ellis. I remonstrated against this—on the ground that Mr. Ellis had been expressly instructed to draw on the contingent fund of the State department for all such expenses incurred by him and no appropriation had been asked by the department for that purpose and it was perfectly well known that the only object of this appropriation was to indemnify me for the charges subsequently incurred for those liberated afterwards to wit on the 15 of June. The draft for $3600 was subsequently paid as I had supposed out of the ["appropriated" *altered to* "appropriation"] above referred to and that the charges incurred by Mr. Ellis were transferred where they properly belonged, to the contingent fund. But to my surprize I found that it had been charged to my individual account. I wrote to the Secretary of State remonstrating against this Because the Draft which I gave did not authorize any such thing, as in that draft I expressly stated that it was to be paid out of this appropriation of $6000 and was drawn on the authority of a letter from the Secretary of State. If it was not considered proper to pay it out of that fund the draft should have been refused payment which would not have involved me, as I was not personally liable for its payment, and had never authorized its payment out of my own funds, and there was no more authority so to pay it than there was to pay it out of the money of any other individual, whose funds might have been in the power or controul of the government. Mr. [Abel P.] Upshur in a letter to me bearing date July 11, 1843, says "you are not warranted in supposing that it is intended to deduct the amount from your Salary &c["]—see his letter. I rested satisfied with this and sent the vouchers required. But on my arrival at home to my infinite astonishment I find a letter from the department informing me that it is so charged and will remain so unless I can show that the persons sent home by me were those for whom I had officially interfered and demanded their release—some fifteen or twenty of them were so—but it is now impossible for me to obtain the requisite evidence on that subject. But if this ground was intended to be assumed why was it not done when my own draft was presented and paid. That draft was not for persons thus situated but for Texans taken in arms against Mexico—and having no claims upon our protection—or why was not the draft for $3600 refused payment instead of being paid out of my funds. I was in no way responsible for its payment, had not authorized any such payment, but had expressly stated *in the draft* the fund out of which it should be paid—and besides such was not the class of Englishmen and Germans, paid for by their respective ministers for not one of whom had those ministers interfered. I trust that you will upon this statement of the facts see the injustice which has been done me and order my account to be credited for the amount. Very Respectfully Your ob[e]d[ien]t Serv[an]t, Waddy Thompson.

P.S. I beg leave to add that the appropriation of $6000 was moved by Mr. [William C.] Preston of the Senate expressly for the purpose of indemnifying the expenses incurred and authorized by me for prisoners released who were not American citizens—no appropriation being necessary for such as both my predecessor Mr. Ellis & myself had been expressly authorized to draw upon the contingent fund of foreign missions for all such disbursements—and no appropriation for that purpose was ever asked of Congress—and the appropriation is in general terms for prisoners. Very Respectf[ul]ly &c, Waddy Thompson.

LS in DNA, RG 59 (State Department), Accounting Records: Miscellaneous Letters Received. NOTE: The postscript only is in Thompson's handwriting.

From H[ENRY] BAILEY, [Attorney General of S.C.]

Charleston, 30th May, 1844

Dear Sir, The inclosed letter for Baron [Friedrich] Von Raumer was handed to me at Columbia, & was forwarded by me to Charleston, but unfortunately did not reach this place until an hour or two after the departure of the Baron & his Son for the North. I take the liberty now of forwarding it to you, as it is probable you may be able to give its proper direction. It is from Dr. [Ernest L.] Hazelius, who is filled with inexpressible chagrin at learning that Baron Von Raumer had been in Columbia for three days, and had departed without his seeing him.

Your favor of 29th ult[imo], conferring upon me the pleasure of an introduction to the Baron was forwarded by him to me at Columbia, where I was in attendance on the Court of Appeals, & as he subsequently visited that place I had the pleasure of there making his acquaintance, & that of his intelligent & accomplished son, who combines with excellent gifts & extensive attainments a modesty which adds much to their lustre. It gave me great pleasure to offer any attention to them; & I believe that the utmost hospitality & attention were extended to them both in Charleston & Columbia. They arrived at the latter place in season to witness a highly creditable exhibition by some half dozen orators of the senior class, of the [South Carolina] College, which impressed them very favorably. They also were hospitably entertained at the plantations of [Wade] Hampton [II] & Tailors [sic; Thomas Taylor, Jr.?], which they examined very minutely, & thus had a very full & fair opportunity of seeing something of the economy of a cotton plantation, & the treatment of our slaves. It was too late in the season to venture into the rice culture region. They made good use of their time in Columbia, & examined every thing worth seeing there; they even attended our Courts, and had our system explained to them, in which the young man, who is a jurisprudent[,] took great interest. In a word we have shewn them every thing there was to see, & I trust that when

665

they come to report these matters, if they extenuate nothing, they at least will not set down aught in malice.

We are awaiting here in trembling anxiety the intelligence of the doings at Washington & Baltimore at this most eventful crisis of our political history—I cannot, in the midst of much doubt & darkness, avoid indulging strong hopes; & perhaps for no better reason ["than" *interlined*] that it seems to have been *providential,* that you should so unexpectedly [be] placed at the centre of movement at this juncture.

The rumor is, that Mr. [James] Buchanan will be nominated by the Convention, which is I think the best nomination, but one, that could be made; but I doubt much whether it will avail for much more than to enable us to keep our friends together during the coming contest. There is but one name that can kindle enthusiasm of feeling any where, or rally even the South, upon the Texas question with sufficient energy to rescue us effectually from the trammels ["of" *changed to* "and"] delusions of whiggery. Mr. Buchanan is our next best, but Mr. [John] Tyler won[']t do at all.

But I am trespassing upon your time & will only add the assurance of the high regard & esteem with which I am Your Obe[dien]t Serv[an]t, H. Bailey.

ALS in ScCleA; PEx in Boucher and Brooks, eds., *Correspondence,* pp. 236–237.

From EDWARD EVERETT

London, 30 May 1844

Sir, I received on the 21st instant your despatch of the 10th of April number 82, transmitting additional papers in relation to a claim of Messrs. N[athaniel] L. Rogers and brothers on the British Government, growing out of the imposition of duties upon a large quantity of spirits imported into the Bay of Islands and landed there, before the assertion of the English sov[e]reignty over New-Zealand.

I have caused these papers to be transcribed and shall send them to Lord Aberdeen together with a note of which a copy is herewith enclosed on the subject of the claim. In bringing the case again to Lord Aberdeen's consideration, I have endeavored to comply with the instructions of the late Secretary of State [Abel P. Upshur], directing me, in treating this subject, not to commit the United States to a recognition or a denial of the British right of Sov[e]reignty over New-Zealand. The interests of the United States, however, in that quarter are so important, that I cannot but think it highly desirable, that our relations with the colonial government of New-Zealand should be more definitely ascertained. On this subject I beg leave to refer to my despatch Nro. 72, dated 26th December last.

I observe that the Messrs. Rogers, in the statement of their claim subjoined to their memorial, charge the spirits at seventy eight cents per gallon, which would appear to be even less than the price for which this article had been sold in New-Zealand a short time before. This is, however, I suppose, nearly three times the original cost of the article in the United States; and I cannot consider it prudent, in advancing a claim against a foreign government, to make a demand for so high a rate of consequential damages. However manifest the equity of such a demand may be, it would not, I think, be allowed by a committee of claims of the House of Representatives. For this reason, in order not unnecessarily to prejudice the claim of the Messrs. Rogers in advance, I have thought it best, in sending the additional papers to Lord Aberdeen, to omit this statement of their claim. No harm can result from with[h]olding it, till the principle of indemnification is settled. I am, sir, very respectfully, your obedient servant, Edward Everett.

Transmitted with Despatch 133.
Mr. Everett to the Earl of Aberdeen, 30 May 1844.

LS (No. 133) with En in DNA, RG 59 (State Department), Diplomatic Despatches, Great Britain, vol. 52 (M-30:48), received 6/21; FC in DNA, RG 84 (Foreign Posts), Great Britain, Despatches, 8:251–254; FC in MHi, Edward Everett Papers, 49:146–149 (published microfilm, reel 23, frames 73–74).

From BEN E. GREEN

Legation of the U.S. of A.
Mexico, 30th May 1844

Sir, I send you (nos. 1, 2, 3 & 4) two notes [of 5/4/1844 and 5/18/-1844], which I addressed to the Minister of Foreign Relations [José M. de Bocanegra] upon the subject of the Instalment, which fell due on the 30th ult[im]o; and his replies [*sic*; of 5/23/1844] thereto. In addition I need only state that daily application has been made for the payment, but as yet none of the money has been paid. The

Minister of Foreign Relations, in his note of the 6th, states that the payment would be made on the following day, and in that of the 23d, he says that the Minister of Hacienda had two days previous issued an order for the payment. Notwithstanding this, the money has not been paid, and the *order has not been issued.* This needs no comment.

In the present posture of affairs, they do not wish to acknowledge their unwillingness or inability to pay; but the fact is that at present they have not the money.

In relation to the Convention for the liquidation of claims, I have already explained the difficulties in the way of its settlement. The same posture of affairs continuing, their excuse for not entering upon and concluding that convention now is, that they are waiting for some documents of the late commission. This is nothing more than an excuse.

Col. [Gilbert L.] Thompson arrived in this city on the 22d inst[ant]. After consulting with him as directed in your letter of introduction, I requested an interview with the Minister of Foreign Relations for the following day. In that interview I presented the note [of 5/23/1844], of which I send you a copy (No. 5); and requested, that the Mexican Minister at Washington should be authorized to receive propositions and open negotiations for a boundary line between the two countries. I also requested that, if the Mexican Govt. should think proper to authorize its Minister to do so, I might be informed thereof on tuesday, the 28th. This was promised; but on tuesday the Mexican Minister informed me, that the President requested that Mr. Thompson's departure might be postponed, in order that he might previously have a conference with me on the subject of the proposed negociations. No. 6 is a protocol of the conference with the President. No. 7 is a copy of Mr. Bocanegra's reply [of 5/30/1844] to my communication. This reply was promised to me this morning; but was not received until 9 o'clock tonight; and owing to the lateness of the hour, & want of time, I must refer you to Col. Thompson, who accompanied me to the conference with the President, & who will be able to give you a full account of all that has transpired.

He will also inform you that the course of the Mexican Govt. is entirely owing to the fact that they are under the impression that the Treaty for the annexation of Texas will be rejected by the Senate, and that they calculate upon our internal dissensions, growing out of the question of slavery.

I send you files of the official [news]paper, and refer you particularly to the article of the no. of the 21st May, which I have marked. I have the honor to be Very Respectfully Your ob[edien]t Serv[an]t, Ben E. Green.

[Enclosure]

Ben E. Green to J[osé] M. de Bocanegra

Legation of the U.S. of A.

Mexico, May 23d 1844

The undersigned, Chargé d'affaires ad interim of the U.S. of A., has the honor to inform H[is] E[xcellency] J.M. de Bocanegra, Minister &c &c, that he has just received by a special messenger, despatches from his Govt., by which he is instructed to inform the Mexican Govt. that a Treaty for the annexation of Texas to the U.S. has been signed by the Plenipotentiaries of the two Govts., and that the said Treaty would be immediately submitted to the Senate of the U.S. for its approval.

The President of the U.S. has enjoined the undersigned to accompany this communication to the Mexican Govt. with the strongest assurance, that in adopting this measure, the Govt. of the U.S. is actuated by no feelings of disrespect or indifference to the honor and dignity of Mexico, and that it would be a subject of great regret, if it should be otherwise regarded by the Mexican Govt.

The undersigned is also instructed to state to the Mexican Govt., that this step was forced upon the Govt. of the U.S. in self defence in consequence of the policy adopted by Great Britain in reference to the abolition of slavery in Texas. It was impossible for the United States to witness with indifference the efforts of Great Britain to abolish slavery in that territory. They could not but see, that she had the means in her power, in the actual condition of Texas, to accomplish the objects of her policy, unless prevented by the most efficient measures; and that, if accomplished it would lead to a state of things dangerous in the extreme to the adjacent States, and to the union itself. Seeing this, the Govt. of the U.S. has been compelled, by the necessity of the case and a regard to its constitutional obligations, to take the step, it has taken as the only certain and effectual means of preventing it. It has taken it in full view of all possible consequences; but not without a desire and hope that a full and fair disclosure of the causes, which induced it to do so, would prevent the disturbance of the harmony subsisting between the two countries, and which the Govt. of the U.S. is anxious to preserve.

The undersigned is also directed by the President of the U.S. to assure the Mexican Govt., that it is his desire to settle all questions between the two countries, which may grow out of this Treaty, or any other cause, on the most liberal and satisfactory terms, including that of Boundary. And that the Govt. of the U.S. would have been happy if circumstances had permitted it to act in concurrence with that of Mexico in taking this step; but with all its respect for Mexico, and anxious desire that the two countries should continue on friendly terms, it could not make, what it believed might involve the safety of the union itself, depend on the contingency of obtaining the previous consent of Mexico. But while it could not, with a due regard to the safety of the union, do that, it has taken every precaution to make the terms of the Treaty as little objectionable to Mexico as possible; and amongst others, has left the boundary of Texas without specification; so that, what the line of Boundary should be, might be an open question, to be fairly & fully discussed and settled according to the rights of each, and the mutual interests and security of the two countries.

The undersigned avails himself of this occasion to renew to H[is] E[xcellency] Mr. Bocanegra, the assurance of his high consideration. (Signed) Ben E. Green.

[Enclosure (Translation)]
[Protocol of a conference with Valentín Canalizo]
[Mexico City, May *ca.* 29, 1844]
It is proposed that the Mexican Minister at Washington shall be authorized to receive propositions and open negotiations for a boundary line between the two countries.

There is a treaty which determines the boundary line between the United States and Mexico. It is asked whether the former proposition takes it for granted that that that [*sic*] Treaty is to stand, or is it proposed that new limits are to be assigned, apart from that Treaty? The proposition is to enter into a new Treaty of Limits. So far as that Treaty differs from the old one, it will be a substitute for the old Treaty; which of course may be varied by one of later date.

Mexico having been promised an indemnity for so much of her territory as the United States may acquire by the new Treaty which is proposed, it is desired to know "What rule or what data will serve to distinguish Mexican territory from that of the United States?["]
To answer this question rather pertains to the Plenipotentiaries who will be appointed to make the Treaty, or to the Commissioners who may be appointed to run the line under that Treaty.

Without allowing that Mexico doubts the value of the existing treaty, it is desired to know whether the United States acknowledge the line marked out in that Treaty?

Upon this point I have no advices from my government.

[Enclosure (Translation)]

J.M. de Bocanegra to Benjamin E. Green

National Palace

Mexico [City,] 30th May 1844

The undersigned Minister of foreign affairs and Government has had the honor to receive the note which the Chargé d'affaires ad interim of the United States of America has been pleased to address to him, under date of the 23d instant, in which he communicates the arrival of a special messenger sent with despatches from his Government for the Legation of the United States of America, with the object of informing the government of this Republic that the Executive of those States had signed and transmitted to the Senate a Treaty for the annexation of the Department of Texas to the union of the United States.

The simple reading of the note to which the undersigned is replying is sufficient to recognise the magnitude and gravity of the subject which it contains, and it is certainly wonderful that a Government ennobled and governed by institutions so liberal and so well founded in the known admitted principle of committing no aggression, and especially to guard and respect in every sentiment and in every manner the imprescribible [sic] rights of man in society, has proceeded to the negotiation, approval, and even transmission to the Senate of a treaty which indubitably and notoriously despoils Mexico of a Department, which by ownership and by possession belongs to her, and has always belonged to her, according to the contents of the clear, conclusive, repeated and very early protests which the Government of this Republic has made, laid not only before the government and Republic of the United States, but before nations and the world.

An event such as the note of Mr. Green announces, leads without doubt to consequences the most serious and of the highest importance, since no one is ignorant that in treating with Nations the principles and law should be observed and considered, which are observed and considered even with respect to individuals. Thus it is that the obligations of contracts are the same and the respect to individual and social g[u]aranties are the same and they are arranged among themselves. And has the step taken by the Government of the United States of America been adjusted to these rules and principles of reason, of political truth and of justice, which as Mr. Benjamin Green knows are laid down among nations in the respect and consideration which are due to themselves, and reciprocally among each other. The act speaks for itself, and makes manifest that in its exercise were forgotten the principles which always protect Governments and men in their relations, in their compacts and generally in their actions.

Mr. Green with reference to advice from his Government gives to the government of Mexico the most conclusive assurances that in adopting the measure of adjusting a treaty for the annexation of Texas, no other principle has actuated it, and it fulfils no other end than that of its own security and defence from the policy which Great Britain has adopted for the abolition of Slavery.

The undersigned does not, nor ought he to enter upon the question of what may be and what should be the course which the United States should pursue in their relations with Great Britain nor what the policy which it becomes it to adopt with respect to said nation, neither should he for a moment consider what may be the benefits or disadvantages which may be produced in the United States by the variety or division which is observed, and which the press exhibits to us in a public and undeniable manner relative to the abolition of slavery, it being sustained in some that this should be protected, and in others that it should be extinguished, seeing with horror this relic of barbarous ages, proscribed by philosophy, and by the intelligence of the epoch. These questions should not in truth occupy the undersigned, nevertheless in alluding to them the Chargé d'Affaires of the United States [*blank space.*] The resolution of these depends on emergent circumstances, and on the progress which no one can arrest.

But when in order to sustain that slavery, and avoid its disappearing from Texas, and from other points, recourse is had to the arbitrary act of depriving Mexico of an integrant part of her possessions as the only certain and efficacious remedy to prevent what Mr. Green calls a dangerous event; if Mexico will be silent and lend her deference to the present policy of the Executive of the United States, the reproach and the censure of nations ought to be her reward.

If a succession of events which are known to the American Legation, the publicity whereof it is sufficient to insinuate, have gone on to put the colonists of Texas, and the adventurers who have come in more lately, without more character, nor mission than their own will and the inspirations and impulses which have been given them, putting them in an attitude to usurp a territory, over which those had not a full and absolute dominion, and which in the part not colonized, cannot nor ought not to be considered *primi occupantes.* If that same series of events has retarded the reconquering of that territory altho it has not been abandoned, this does not give a legal title, either to the rebellious colonists, or less to the new comers to consider themselves masters of it, whatever may be the reasons which might be brought forward, since the repeated acts and protests of Mexico to preserve the plenitude of her rights would be sufficient against them.

The best titles of dominion are those which are based on good faith, and this is not found in the conduct of those who directly or indirectly have constituted themselves true usurpers.

Mexico being persuaded of this truth generally recognized and considered in the law which has never denied to nations what it grants to individuals, has sustained the Territory of Texas as its own even though a series of causes foreign to its will may have impeded its constant action to resubdue them.

With this Motive Mexico has been always seen to operate to repossess herself of Texas by the means proper to nations, without being able to point out a single act, which may indicate that she may have had even the intention of separating herself, and renouncing her imprescribible rights, rights so much the more sacred, inasmuch as they are founded in the same nature with which she acquired them and in her legal possession.

Mexico, repeats the undersigned, consistent always in the conduct, which she has preserved to sustain the justice of her cause, protested before the whole world, and in the most solemn manner against the acknowledgement by the United States of the independence of Texas, as an act aggressive to her sovereignty, since that acknowledgement being well considered, effected so hurriedly, abandoning or disdaining diplomatic facilities and without regard to right, it will be unable to qualify the national morality as sound, nor good feeling, but as the political apotheosis of usurpation. Mr. Green knows what has been the conduct of the supreme Government of Mexico with respect to the United States, notwithstanding that circumstances were leading to a rupture.

The Government of the undersigned is instructed and it appears by unanswerable documents that in the proclamation and act of independence of Texas there did not assist but few Mexicans so small in number, that they scarcely amounted to ten, and that those who figured as principals are almost in totality natives of the United

States, who would never have taken so disloyal a step, if they had not counted upon assistance which should be rendered them elements to sustain a struggle in which they were going to enter, and with a Nation with whom they had the slightest cause of quarrel, nor without any other precedent than the kindness and frankness with which she admitted the first colonists.

Experience has just manifested that what at that period might have been reputed as conjectural or suspicious, is a lamentable reality.

The meetings publicly drawn together in New Orleans and other parts of the United States, for the purpose of exciting sympathy in favor of the so called Republic; the emigration of armed adventurers, warlike stores, armament, munitions and other acts of hostility, it is proved that they have proceeded from the same Republic, whose executive has signed the treaty of annexation.

The acts of aggression towards Mexico, and the chiefs, who have commanded them, have also proceeded from the same Republic of Washington, and many times has it been manifested with regret and formality by the Supreme Government of Mexico, through the undersigned, and through their Minister in those States by means of conferences and notes, without being able to succeed in having a stop put to similar acts, nor to act according to the treaties which bind both Republics as a strong conventional law.

At this very day the note of the 23d instant, May, ["to" *interlined*] which the undersigned is now replying, gives the most conclusive, full and clear proof that the Mexican Republic, under every aspect, is wounded in her rights and outraged in her honor and dignity. It is said by Mr. Green, by order of his Government, that the treaty of annexation of Texas to the United States was adjusted and signed, and that in order not to be wanting in the consideration due to Mexico from that Republic, it communicates to her that it has been rendered necessary for its safety and interest to take such a step. Let Mr. Green permit me to call his attention, as also that of his Government and the Nation whom he represents to (this) that this act which is said to be ["out" *interlined*] of respect to Mexico, is in reality but the manifestation of an event consummated, if not with the constitutional perfection, through want of the approval of the Senate, yet certainly on the part of the executive [John Tyler], who has done as much as he had to do in the exercise of his functions, without Mexico and her rights, her honor and dignity having the smallest part in a consideration, which he now manifests towards her in making her only a notification; and by this opportunity (ocaso) the Chargé d'affaires assures that his Government has taken that resolution, and has taken that step in full view of all possible consequences; and is it nevertheless affirmed that Mexico is respected and that her rights are considered? The undersigned and his government cannot reconcile the facts with the words; altho' it is perceived that the rights of the Mexican nation are as clear, as conclusive and obligatory as the same Government of the United States has expressly confessed in the note which is being replied to; it being very remarkable that a document, which carries on its face (consigo) so express a confession, is the same which tramples upon them, assuring that what belongs to Mexico has been indefutibly [sic] usurped by the United States.

With regard finally to the assurance of the Chargé d'affaires to Mexico that the settlement of all the questions which may result, including those of limits, considering the treaty as concluded, is desired; and the undersigned has express orders from the President of the Republic to say and affirm in the most conclusive and express manner, that Mexico has not renounced, nor should not renounce, nor in any manner cedes the totality or part of her rights, that the firm and constant resolution has been and is to preserve the integrity and dignity of the nation; that at this time as very opportune for the re-production of his protests, he gives them here as express, as if they were in full (como si lo fuesen una á una) especially recalling to mind as special that of the 23d of August 1843, in the words "that Mexico will consider as a declaration of war against the Mexican Republic, the ratification of that agreement for the incorporation of Texas into the territory of the United States.["]

The undersigned also states by order of his Government that a formal Treaty existing, as it does between Mexico and the United States, which fixes the line of limits between both Republics, the Mexican is disposed to its fulfilment, and to give it the perfection of scientific operation, as the only pending requisite: that all that may not be conducted by these principles of international law in the case, would be to remove a legitimate obligation in order to open a negotiation: which wanting legality in its origin, would not have any base upon which to raise any new operation which might be attempted.

And in concluding the undersigned cannot do less than call the attention of Mr. Green and his Government, to the satisfaction which, not only the fact of the adjusted annexation demands, but the outrage and atrocious injury which is done to Mexico, in her dignity and rights, in signing the cited treaty; and Mexico flatters herself with the hope that the Senate of a nation enlightened; free and founded by the immortal Washington [blank space] constitutionally an act which reason, right and justice condemn; but if unfortunately and contrary to this hope the said Treaty should be approved, Mexico in so painful an event will consider herself placed in such a position as that she ought to act conformably to the law of nations and to her protests.

The undersigned avails himself of this opportunity to repeat to the Chargé d'Affaires of the United States of America, the assurances of his distinguished consideration. Signed, J.M. de Bocanegra.

ALS in ScCleA, received 6/17; ALS (No. 5) with Ens and State Department translations in DNA, RG 59 (State Department), Diplomatic Despatches, Mexico, vol. 12 (M-97:13), received 12/13; FC in DNA, RG 84 (Foreign Posts), Mexico, Despatches, pp. 495–496; draft in NcU, Duff Green Papers (published microfilm, roll 5, frames 534–537); PC in Jameson, ed., *Correspondence*, pp. 960–961. NOTE: The enclosed Protocol and Bocanegra's letter of 5/30 are transcribed from State Department translations attached to the second-cited ALS.

To Ch[arles] J. Ingersoll, Chairman of the House Committee on Foreign Affairs, 5/30. "I transmit to you herewith for the information of the Committee, and with a view to such legislative proceedings, as may be deemed proper with referrence to the Subject, the copy of a recent Correspondence between the Department and [Jean Corneille, Chevalier Gevers] the Chargé d'Affaires of the Netherlands at Washington, respecting a discriminating duty levied in the ports of the United States on Java Coffee when not imported directly from that Island." FC in DNA, RG 59 (State Department), Reports of the Secretary of State to the President and Congress, 6:104.

From LOUIS MARK

Washington City, 30 May 1844

Sir, I have the honor to inclose a Table made at the request of Mr. [William S.] Archer [Senator from Va.] showing the great increase of consumption in the Zoll Verein for Tobacco, Cotton and Cotton Twist. Of the latter small shipments are now making from Mas[s]achusetts to Germany and as it ["is" *interlined*] entirely made by Machinery no doubt of our soon rivalling Manchester in the German Market.

An anonymous letter in a N. York Paper [the *Commercial Advertiser*] stated that I was employed by the Manufacturers of Germany to bribe this Government, and altho such accusations are farcical,

I replied to it as you will see by the inclosed which I take the liberty of sending to you, as I am most anxious for your good opinion and trust that you will place more confidence in Mr. [Henry] Wheaton's representations who has known me intimately from my Youth than in any statements made by Persons who are interested to defeat the German Treaty or who are jealous of its success. With the greatest Respect Your Ob[edien]t Ser[van]t, Louis Mark.

ALS with Ens in DNA, RG 59 (State Department), Miscellaneous Letters (M-179:104, frames 457–459). NOTE: Mark enclosed a clipping from the New York *Commercial Advertiser* of his reply to an anonymous letter published in that newspaper. He also enclosed a table showing the increased consumption of tobacco, cotton, and cotton twist among the Zollverein nations.

"Synopsis of charges against Mr. [LOUIS] MARK, U.S. Consul for Bavaria &c."

[State Department] May 30, [18]44

1. Swindling. In a letter to the Department, dated December 23rd 1833, Mr. [Charles] McVean, then a member of the House [of] R[epresentative]s [from N.Y.], states that Mr. Mark had received money from a gentleman in N. York on the strength of his appointment as Consul for Bamberg and that the money was never accounted for.

Mr. Rudisill states, in a letter of March 11th 1840, that $130 had been paid to Mr. Mark in Germany to be forwarded to the U.S. and that nothing has since been heard of the money.

Mr. R.M. Blatchford, of N. York, in a letter of 18th Septem[ber] 1839, charges Mr. Mark with having received, while Consul at Ostend, £500 St[erlin]g, from a Mr. Andudon to be invested for him in land in the U.S., and that neither land nor money could be heard of afterwards.

Mr. Mark has also been charged with being an Agent of the German manufacturers, and with having endeavoured to obtain money from them under pretence of its being necessary to secure the ratification of the Treaty with Germany (See letters of A[lfred] Schücking [of 5/29] & J[ohann] W. Schmidt [of 5/24].)

2. Forgery. Mr. Mark transmitted to the Department in January last his bond as Consul for Bavaria, &c. On account of an informality in its execution it was sent for correction to the house in N. York (P. Harmony's Nephews & Co.) whose names appeared as Sureties. It

was returned to the Dept. by those gentlemen who utterly disclaimed all knowledge of its existence. A letter was immediately written to Mr. Mark (who had then left the Country) demanding instant explanation. That letter was never answered. Upon his return to the U.S. some weeks since, a copy of it, together with a copy of that of Messrs. Harmony, was handed to him, but no explanation has yet been made.

ADU in DNA, RG 59 (State Department), Consular Despatches, Munich, vol. 1 (T-261:1). NOTE: This memorandum is in the handwriting of an unidentified State Dept. Clerk.

To [Alphonse] Pageot, [French Minister to the U.S.], 5/30. "The Secretary of State presents his compliments to Mr. Pageot, and will be happy to see him at this office, if convenient to him, at any time before three o'clock to-day." FC in DNA, RG 59 (State Department), Notes to Foreign Legations, France, 6:80 (M-99:21).

From JOHN REYNOLDS

Belleville, Ill., 30th May 1844

Dear Sir, In the crisis I find you and the Administration in relation to the annexation of Texas I think it my duty to write you: that I think our State Illinois will sustain you in the *immediate* annexation. We had a meeting last fall in October in which I was a member, which descided for the *immediate* annexation. We all over the State go it strong for Texas, and I would not be surprised; that the people would sustain some Democrat for the Presidency, who is in head and shoulders for the ["*immediate*" *interlined*] annexation. Messrs. Van Buren's[,] [Thomas H.] Benton's and other's letters are corks on the waves [having] no weight. Please write your *friend*, John Reynolds.

ALS in ScCleA. NOTE: An AEU by Calhoun reads: "Gov[erno]r Reynolds[,] States that Illinois is for immediate annexation of Texas." Reynolds, a native of Pa., was a former Governor of and Representative from Ill.

To [JOHN TYLER]

Department of State
Washington, 30th May, 1844

To the President of the United States.

The Secretary of State, to whom was referred the Resolution of the Senate of the 22d instant, in Executive session, requesting the President to inform the Senate whether any engagement or agreement has taken place between the President of the United States and the President of Texas [Samuel Houston], in relation to naval or military aid or any other aid, to Texas in the event of an agreement on the part of Texas to annex herself to the United States; and if so, all the particulars of such agreement or promise, with the copies of the same, if in writing, and also a copy of all communications, if any have been made, to the President of Texas, informing him of the march and sailing of portions of our army and navy and the orders given them to communicate with and report to, the said President of Texas, has the honor to lay before the President a copy of the following papers.

1. A note, dated the 17th of January, last, from Mr. [Isaac] Van Zandt, Chargé d'Affaires of Texas, to Mr. [Abel P.] Upshur, inquiring whether after a treaty for the annexation of Texas to the United States should be signed but before it should go into operation, the President of the United States would, if Texas should desire or consent to it, order such a disposition of the naval and military force of the United States as would be sufficient to protect Texas against foreign aggression?

To this note no answer was returned by the person to whom it was addressed.

2. A despatch from Mr. [William S.] Murphy to Mr. Upshur, dated the 15th of February, last, announcing the appointment of General [J. Pinckney] Henderson as a Plenipotentiary on the part of Texas and stating the assurances given by Mr. Murphy which led to that appointment.

3. A despatch from Mr. Murphy to Mr. Upshur, dated the 22nd of February, offering suggestions in regard to the protection of Texas from invasion, pending a treaty of annexation.

No despatch from Mr. Murphy of the 19th of February is on file in this Department. It is presumed, therefore, that in referring to a despatch of that date in his letter of the 22nd of February, he intended to refer to the despatch of the 15th of that month.

4. A note dated the 14th of February, last, from Mr. [Anson] Jones, Secretary of State of Texas, to Mr. Murphy, requiring as a condition of the appointment of General Henderson, assurances that this government would station troops and a naval force for the purpose of protecting Texas from invasion; and would guarantee the independence of Texas.

5. A note from Mr. Murphy to Mr. Jones, of the same date giving ["the" *canceled and* "certain" *interlined*] assurances ["required" *canceled*] in reply thereto.

6. A note from Mr. Jones to Mr. Murphy, of the 15th of February, announcing the appointment of General Henderson in consequence of the assurances given in Mr. Murphy's note of the 14th.

7. A secret order, dated the 19th of February, from Mr. Murphy to Lieutenant [John A.] Davis, in command of the United States schooner Flirt, directing him to proceed with that vessel to Vera Cruz.

8. An instruction from Mr. [John] Nelson, Secretary of State *ad interim* to Mr. Murphy, of the 11th of March, last, disavowing the arrangement entered into between Mr. Murphy and Mr. Jones.

9. A despatch from Mr. Murphy, dated the 14th ult[imo], acknowledging the receipt of the instruction of Mr. Nelson.

10. A note, dated the 12th ult[imo], addressed by Mr. Murphy to the Secretary of State of Texas, in compliance with the instruction of Mr. Nelson.

11. A note dated the 11th of last month, from the Undersigned to Messrs. Van Zandt and Henderson, referring to the note of Mr. Van Zandt to Mr. Upshur of the 17th of January, and informing them that during the pendency of a treaty of annexation, the President would deem it his duty to use all the means placed within his power by the Constitution, to protect Texas from all foreign invasion.

All which is respectfully submitted. J.C. Calhoun.

LS in DNA, RG 46 (U.S. Senate), 28B-B12; variant FC in DNA, RG 59 (State Department), Reports of the Secretary of State to the President and Congress, 6:104–106; PC with Ens in Senate Document No. 349, 28th Cong., 1st Sess., pp. 1–12; PC with Ens in House Document No. 271, 28th Cong., 1st Sess., pp. 87–98; PC with Ens in the Washington, D.C., *Daily National Intelligencer,* June 3, 1844, pp. 1–2; PC with Ens in the Washington, D.C., *Daily Madisonian,* June 3, 1844, p. 2; PC with Ens in *Niles' National Register,* vol. LXVI, no. 15 (June 8, 1844), pp. 230–232. NOTE: Tyler transmitted this letter to the Senate on 5/31. The Senate resolution to which the above letter is a reply can be found in DNA, RG 59 (State Department), Miscellaneous Letters (M-179:104, frames 399–400) and *Senate Executive Journal,* 6:291.

From Francis Bulkley, [Washington, *ca.* 5/31]. He respectfully requests Calhoun's attention to his wish for a [Consular] appointment and the reasons for it and points to his recommendations from prominent South Carolinians [James Gadsden, Joseph A. Woodward, and John J. Chappell]. ALS in DNA, RG 59 (State Department), Applications and Recommendations, 1837–1845, Bulkley (M-687:3, frames 597–599).

From F[RANCIS] M. DIMOND

United States Consulate
Vera Cruz, 31 May 1844

Sir, Herewith I have the honour to transmit a letter and papers from our Legation at Mexico [City], which have been waiting an opportunity some days. In fact there has been no opportunity before this to acquaint you with the arrival at this port of the U.S. Steamer Poinsett on the 13 inst[ant].

Colonel [Gilbert L.] Thompson immediately went out to Manga de Clavo, and after an interview with the President [Santa Anna], continued on to Mexico [City], on the 24 after his arrival there, the ministers were called together, to consider the nature of the mission, and the President[']s views on the subject.

I am informed, Colonel Thompson was kindly received by Gen[era]l Santa Anna, and by a Letter from the Commander of the Poinsett [Capt. Raphael Semmes] (who accompanied the Colonel) I am led to believe, the object of the mission will be accomplished.

The President is to be in Mexico on the 2d June, and Congress is to be convoked on the 3d—and altho our Secretary of Legation informs me that Colonel Thompson will be here on the 3, or 4th prox[im]o, I am inclined to believe he will wait the arrival of the President.

About a week since Gen[era]l Santa Anna was here, and visited the Castle de Ullua, and expressed his opinion, that the French, would not get it again. The Papers seem to talk about war with us, but as the President is the Government, I am inclined to believe that negociation will suit him better than war. In fact I believe he would be glad to get clear of Texas on any Honourable terms.

There has been a report here, that Gen[era]l Semana [*sic*; Francisco Sentmanat] (former Governor of Tobasco and who was by

the supreme Government expelled [from] the republic) was collect-
ing a force at New Orleans and was to sail for Tobasco in two
Sch[oone]r[s] and the Government have sent forces down there to
prevent his landing.

I have stated to the Governor of this place that they would not
be allowed to leave New Or leans or the waters of the U. States
publicly known to be coming to attack any port of Mexico.

The Brig Kirkwood has this moment arrived from N. Orleans
and the Barque Eugenia last evening from N. York and Dispatches
for our Legation at Mexico sent up by the mail last evening. I have
the honour to be Sir most Respectfully your Ob[edient] Servant, F.M.
Dimond.

ALS (No. 221) in DNA, RG 59 (State Department), Consular Despatches,
Veracruz, vol. 5 (M-183:5), received 6/24.

From EDWARD EVERETT

London, 31 May 1844

Sir, With my despatch Nro. 127 of the 16th May, I transmitted to you
the copy of a note which I had addressed to the Earl of Aberdeen,
making application for the pardon of seventeen American citizens
therein named, for having taken up arms in Canada in 1838. I have
now the pleasure of forwarding to you the answer of Lord Aberdeen
acquainting me that their pardon has been ordered. I also transmit
a copy of my note of acknowledgment.

You will observe that of two of the persons spoken of in your
despatch 84, as having probably been resident in Canada at the time
the disturbances broke out, one, Joseph Thompson by name, has
already received a pardon, (subject to the usual condition of good
behaviour in Van Diemen's land) on the recommendation of the Governor General of Canada. The other, Robert Marsh, appears to have
been included without qualification, among those whose pardon is
announced in Lord Aberdeen's note of the 29th.

In the closing paragraph of my despatch Nro. 79 of 20th January
last, I mentioned the case of Dresser and Wright two of the American
prisoners in Van Diemen's Land, who had been pardoned for good
behaviour, in assisting to apprehend some outlaws, and who had received from the colonial authorities a free passage to this city. As
they were here without funds to take them to the United States and
applied to the consul and myself for assistance, I advised Colonel

682

[Thomas] Aspinwall to give them such aid as a liberal construction of the law would permit. As it is not impossible that a considerable number of those recently pardoned may arrive at London nearly at the same time, and require assistance to get home, I beg leave to request, that you would give such directions as you may think proper on that subject. To make the matter, however, as little burdensome to the public as possible, I propose by the next Australasian mail, to address a letter to Mr. [Elisha] Hathaway [Jr.], our consul at Hobartstown, Van Diemen's Land, requesting him to find passages as far as practicable, for those whose pardon has been lately ordered, on board the American vessels which resort to that port. I am, sir, very respectfully, your obedient servant, Edward Everett.

Documents transmitted with Despatch 134.

1. The Earl of Aberdeen to Mr. Everett, 29 May 1844.
2. Mr. Everett to the Earl of Aberdeen, 30 May 1844.
3. Mr. Everett to Mr. Hathaway, U.S. Consul for Hobartstown, 31 May 1844.

LS (No. 134) with Ens in DNA, RG 59 (State Department), Diplomatic Despatches, Great Britain, vol. 52 (M-30:48), received 6/21; FC in DNA, RG 84 (Foreign Posts), Great Britain, Despatches, 8:254–257; FC in MHi, Edward Everett Papers, 49:151–153 (published microfilm, reel 23, frames 75–76).

From CHRISTOPHER HUGHES, "Private"

The Hague; 31 May 1844

My dear Sir, There is absolutely nothing—of direct interest to us—to write! I act regularly & *dutifully* in sending a formal acknowledgement of the receipt of your "circular," notifying me of your appointment; and having executed this official act & obligation, I have really not one other word to say.

All our concerns, in Holland, go on well & amicably; & promise to continue to do so! I do all I can, to maintain this comfortable state of things. I live harmoniously & kindly with all the classes—and I receive constant and welcome evidence of good feeling & confidence from all. Having said this I have nothing more to add.

Our quiet residence was thrown into great excitation—yesterday, by the unexpected arrival of the Emperor of Russia [Nicholas I], on his way to England. H[is] I[mperial] M[ajesty] arrived at Eleven, A.M.! & he left the Hague—at Nine, this morning—to embark, at Rotterdam, for London. After his visit to Queen Victoria, he will return, and pass (it is said & hoped;) some days at the Hague: this is the Emperor's first visit to Holland! You know, how very ["close, &" *altered to* "closely" *and two words canceled*], H.I.M. is allied with the House of Nassau. The Queen of the Netherlands is his Sister; and the Princess Frederick of the Netherlands (the wife of the King's only Brother; and daughter of the late, & sister of the Reigning King of Prussia:) is a sister of the Empress of Russia! Thus, it is as near and as manifold a family alliance as well can be.

The Emperor made a most rapid journey—day & night—as is his custom—& is said to have been but 8 days on the road—from Petersburg to the Hague. His object was to give a surprise to his sister—the Queen. He declined receiving the respects of the Corps diplomatic—assigning as a reason—his short stay & fatigue. I saw him, yesterday, for a few moments, walking from the Palace—in which he lodged—to the Palace (the Residence) of the King! He appeared to me heavier & looking *much older*—than when I last saw him (in 1840) at Czarsko Zelo [that is, Tsarskoe Selo]—his favourite Country Palace near Petersburg. He is, always, however, the noblest, most commanding & magnificent man, the eye can light on. I have never seen, and I doubt, if the world has ever seen—a more noble, imposing & magnificent human being. The Emperor's suite is small & composed of only five or 6 persons & his Physician. It is thought not *impossible*, that he may be exposed to some danger, in England if he move about in his usual free & careless manner. Some desperate & revengeful Pole (& there are a great many such in England:) may attempt his Life.

It was amusing—here—to see the agitation—and almost terrour—excited in the Russian Legation—by the news of the Emperor's approach—which preceeded, by a few hours—his actual arrival. The first thing the Secretaries of Legation attended to—was to have their fashionable *mops* of hair & long locks—cut *close* to their heads! The Emperor cannot tolerate any thing that is French—or that smacks of Young France.

If you follow up the European, & especially the English Press—you will see that you & the Prince de Joinville have given the journalists full occupation. Your Note to Mr. [Richard] Pakenham & the Prince's Naval Note—are most zealously & inveterately handled & discussed. I enclose, herein, lest it may have escaped you—a very sharp article from "The [London] Times"—on the P[rince] de Joinville's Pamphlet; and this article may be taken as the measure of the public feeling excited in England by this very remarkable production.

Our last dates—from U. States—to 1st May—were brought by the Acadia Steamer; we are expecting now the Steamer of 15th May.

I wrote you a *private* letter [dated 4/30]—before I had received official news of your acceptance of the office, which makes you my Chief! You may depend upon one thing & that is—that no one of your subordinates will communicate with you, my dear Sir, with more satisfaction, pleasure and unqualified esteem & confidence— than I shall do; for I have—I may say—*all my life*—entertained, & in the highest possible degree—these sentiments for you—as a Gentleman, a Statesman & a Patriot. No circumstance ever has occurred— or ever can occur—to make ["me" *interlined*] feel & think otherwise of you. But my *"despatches"* are, & must be—from this post—few & of little interest; for I really see no motive for writing long *official* papers—when there is nothing of any interest, *to us*—to say.

I beg to be most respectfully recalled to the kind recollection of the President [John Tyler], & that you will believe me to be respectfully & faithfully Y[ou]r obed[ien]t Serv[an]t, Christopher Hughes.

ALS with En in ScCleA. NOTE: Enclosed is a clipping from the English language *Galignani's Messenger* of Paris, 5/27, reprinting an article from the London *Times* concerning the Prince de Joinville and the French navy.

From S[tephen] Pleasonton, Fifth Auditor, 5/31. Waddy Thompson's accounts as U.S. Minister in Mexico are now being given a final settlement. [Abel P.] Upshur expressed doubt last February whether any expense in relation to Texas prisoners engaged in the Santa Fe expedition could be allowed. Pleasonton asks whether relief given to Texas prisoners by Thompson can be refunded, as his outlays for U.S. prisoners in Mexico are to be. Pleasonton asks also when Thompson's salary terminated and whether or not he is to receive the usual additional salary for one quarter for his return to the U.S. LS in DNA, RG 59 (State Department), Letters Received from the Fifth Auditor and Comptroller, 1829–1862; FC in DNA, RG 217 (General Accounting Office), Fifth Auditor: Letters Sent, 5:128–129.

To S[tephen] Pleasonton, Fifth Auditor, 5/31. "The amount charged in Mr. Waddy Thompson's account for expenses incurred for the prisoners in Mexico, Texan, as well as American, may, for reasons expressed in his letter of the 29th instant, be allowed. The Salary of Mr. Thompson as Minister to Mexico terminated on the 25th of March, and he is to have the usual allowance for the expenses of his return to the United States." FC in DNA, RG 59 (State Department), Accounting Records: Miscellaneous Letters Sent, 1832–1916, vol. for 2/1–9/30/1844, p. 206.

From THO[MA]S P. SPIERIN

Abbeville Courthouse [S.C.], 31st May 1844
Sir, By the 4th [*sic*; sixth] Article of the Treaty for the Annexation of Texas to the United States it is agreed that four Commissioners shall be appointed by the President of the United States [John Tyler] by and with the advice and consent of the Senate, who shall be authorized under certain prescribed regulations ["]to hear[,] examine and decide on all questions touching the legality and validity of the claims &c."

In the event of the Confirmation of the Treaty, and in advance of it, I have taken the liberty of requesting you to place my name before the Pres[iden]t as an applicant for an appointment on this Commission. As I am a Stranger to the Pres[iden]t and comparatively a Stranger to the Senate; The responsibility of vouching for my Capability and integrity for such a Confidential trust and appointment will chiefly devolve upon yourself, our two Senators[,] and my immediate representative Mr. [Armistead] Burt, whom I have addressed on this subject.

I am aware that in all Commissions of this kind the Government is well informed as to the nature of the Claims and will shape their instructions accordingly, leaving but little to the discretion of the Commission. The indebtedness of Texas being chiefly Bonds and Exchequer Bills, will principally swell the Amount of claims, and I have taken it for granted, that business talents, methodical arrangement, and correct calculation will be the requisites, and qualification[s] necessary on this Commission, involving few legal or constitutional, or international questions, (and if any) to be decided under special rules and instructions, subject to the appellate power and approval of the Govt. These being my views of the nature of the Trust to be conferred, I offer them, as some evidence, together with my Acts on file in the War Department, and your own personal knowledge of my fitness, to prove or establish my worth and qualification for the Trust I ask to be conferred upon me. Your Agency in my behalf, whether successful or not, will be a favor I'll duly apprec[i]ate. Yours very Respectfully, Thos. P. Spierin.

ALS in DNA, RG 59 (State Department), Applications and Recommendations, 1837–1845, Spierin (M-687:31, frames 155–156).

To R.H. Weyman, Charleston, 5/31. Calhoun has received Weyman's letter of 4/8 and its enclosure concerning Weyman's claim against the "late Republic of Colombia." No other information is on file in the State Department about the subject, and no "definitive opinion" can be reached. Calhoun asks Weyman to submit an account of all material facts in the case "and an account against the Government from which you expect reparation." When these are received, Calhoun will determine what course to follow. FC in DNA, RG 59 (State Department), Domestic Letters, 34:219 (M-40:32).

From FRANCIS WHARTON

Philadelphia, May 31st, 1844

My dear Sir, I thank you most warmly for touching what with me, has turned out to be the true key on the Texas question. My "northern" eyes have at last opened, and the eyes of the one or two to whom I read your letter, who were previously strong opposers of the measure, have opened also. It is a duty owed by the North to the South. If I can be in any way useful, as a writer, on the subject, let me know. If in the course of the campaign, a pamphlet ["should" *canceled and* "is to" *interlined*] be written, to embrace the Northern view, and if my services would be of any value, they are at your command. I wish my practice was sufficiently extensive to enable me not only to *write*, but to *publish*.

I trust you consider [James K.] Polk's nomination safe—it certainly has very much dashed ["my" *canceled and* "the" *interlined*] politicians in this neighbourhood. The first feeling was that of delight, not at Polk's nomination, but that any nomination was made at all. The second feeling is one of wonder & curiosity. The Pennsylvania editors[,] I mean, the editors of the Pennsylvania Newspaper[s], have started on the hunt after Mr. Polk[']s opinions, and have discovered, to their horror, that he is not only pro-Texas, but anti-Tariff. So far, so good. I ["am" *canceled and* "will be" *interlined*] very much gratified if Mr. [Francis W.] Pickens & Mr. [Franklin H.] Elmor[e], turn out to represent your opinions. As to Mr. [George M.] Dallas [Democratic nominee for Vice-President], whom I know very well personally, there is no one who professes for you a

687

greater admiration. I met him a short time ago, when he told me he had just read my late review [of *Speeches of John C. Calhoun*] in the Democratic Review, & agreed with it thoroughly. He went on to say that there was one man who was the great man of this country, and that was Mr. Calhoun.

I am going to say one or two words on a subject which if it should not meet your convenience, I hope you will at once dismiss. I am struggling somewhat against wind and tide in my profession, as you know must necessarily be the case with a young man in a large city, and I am making every effort which my ["limited influence" *canceled and* "imperfect purchase" *interlined*] will enable me to make, to obtain professional independence. In the large cities, there are things called *commissionerships,* offices the holders of which are appointed by the governors of the various States, for the purpose of acknowledging deeds and taking depositions, &c. Such offices are valuable to a young man, much more from the business connection they ["induce" *canceled and* "establish" *interlined*], than the actual emoluments they produce. I mentioned that the nominating power rests in the hands of the governors; ["who" (?) *canceled and* "and" *interlined*] in the case of the ["governors" *canceled and* "States" *interlined*] of Virginia, New York, and Ohio, the two last especially, the office is productive of some business advantage. Should it be in your power by mentioning my name, either to the governors in [*partial word canceled*] question, should you be in the habit of correspondence with them, or to any of their congressional friends, you would be doing me a great benefit. I should not presume to intrude upon your attention were the offices themselves of any political value, or of any importance to the functionaries by whom they are to be made. Such is not the case, and yet to me, in lack of many of the claims on the attention of the community which better known practitioners must have, they may be of much value. If, however, the subject may be in any way embarrassing to you, do let me assure you that nothing would hurt me more than that personal considerations should induce you to give it a moment[']s attention. With great respect, I am yours[?], Francis Wharton.

ALS in ScCleA; PEx in Jameson, ed., *Correspondence,* p. 962.

From W[ILLIA]M P. DUVAL, "Private"

[St. Augustine, May 1844?]
. . . ultimately occupied, they will be the best safety-valves, to prevent the explosion of the union. Oregon will make three free States—and Texas as many, the latter having much the most fertile soil—thus keeping up the proper ballance [*sic*] between the States. If we are so madly wicked, as to exclude Texas, and thus throw her into the arms of England, she will soon bring us to witness our consum[m]ate folly. Her emissarys will combine, ["the" *altered to* "in"] vast ar[r]ay the Indian tribes, on our western borders, against us—and Missouri, Arkansas, and Louisiana, will be covered with the blood of our people. What man of common mind can doubt this? In this event, will not the slaves of those States unite with the savages in spreading death and conflagration to [the] banks of the father of waters? But admit England[']s forbearance for a time, may avert the calamity. Yet controling Texas she will flood the great vall[e]y of the Mississippi with or[?] goods—through red river, & other channels. What then becomes of our revenue? What then will be the fate of our petted manufactories? As a nation we are older in folly than any other in existence, and younger in wisdom, than the least enlightened of the sister republics. Your friend with sincere regard, Wm. P. Duval.

ALS (incomplete) in ScCleA. NOTE: This fragmentary letter can only be dated approximately.

UNIDENTIFIED VIRGINIAN to Littleton W. Tazewell

[Washington, *ca.* May, 1844]
I promised to give you a faithful and impartial account of the state of affairs in this City, as soon as I could ascertain how the currents and counter currents were running. I redeem the pledge with the more pleasure as I write to one who is no partizan—I myself being none.

The crisis of our fate is at hand. Party-organization has, for many years past, been gradually breaking down the once proud spirit of the South, and preparing the Leaders and the People for unconditional submission. We have at length reached the last stage in this sad retrogradation; and in a few days more you will see Southern Senators affixing the seal of degradation and disgrace on us and our children forever! Start not at what I say, Sir; the deed will soon avouch the declaration.

It is now well ascertained that the Treaty of Annexation is to be voted down by *Southern Senators.* The hands which we armed for our defense are the hands that are to stab us. Yet, Sir, we shall not be offered up on the Altar without some patriotic pretexts. The victim, as is usual, will be crowned and adorned with appropriate ornaments—the common trumpery of the sacrifice.

I have said our fate is near at hand. A majority of Northern Senators has determined that there shall be no more slave States in this Union; and that those now composing a part of this Union shall have no securities whatever, no, not even against the machinations of a *Foreign Power.* This is their edict; and *Southern Senators* will shortly record[?] it. I express, Sir, no surprise at this—for I feel none. For ten years past I have looked to this event as inevitable. We have been utterly degraded by Presidential Elections, and now, no man pretends to think any other object worthy of his notice. The friends of Mr. [Henry] Clay are perfectly willing to give up, not only our territory, but every Constitutional safeguard, in order to secure his election; while the followers of Mr. [Martin] Van Buren and Mr. [Thomas H.] Benton are equally disposed to offer the same price with compound interest. Mr. Clay's letter, as you will have seen, proposes the surrender of Texas as the price to be paid, on his part, for Northern votes; and his followers at Baltimore have endorsed the Contract. With remarkable promptitude Mr. Van Buren steps forth, and, before the bid is cried, puts in his own to the same effect; and Mr. Benton and his *clique* have since offered to go *his* security. Both these letters or *bids,* were submitted, as is confidently believed, to a *joint commission,* composed of the leading friends of both in this City, before they were published to the world.

You will readily perceive the object of both these aspirants. Each desired the other to be his competitor; and concurred in the purpose of preventing any competition by the introduction of new issues. Mr. Clay trusted to the zeal, intrepidity and fealty of his friends; and Mr. Van Buren to the iron despotism of his organization. Thus arrayed each was anxious to join battle at once; and their respective L[i]eutenants, Messrs. Benton and [John J.] Crittenden, consulted ["with each other" *canceled and* "together" *interlined*] with all the politeness and condescension of seconds in the *duello.* This, I believe, is known and admitted.

Now, Sir, in all these arrangements there was not the slightest regards [*sic*] had to the public interest. The momentous considerations involved in the question of annexation were entirely overlooked. Nay, Sir, they actually took ground with Great Britain *against* their own Country, in the reckless effort to advance the objects of their ambition: and, humiliating as is the truth, I must tell you they have consulted more with the British Minister, Mr. [Richard] Pakenham, on the subject of the Treaty, than with any of the officers of our own Government. I say this advisedly; and I believe it is the first instance in our history when a Foreign Minister has been invited freely to converse with the *agents* of the People and the States, on questions deeply involving the harmony, happiness and safety of both; and when the Government of such Foreign Minister and our own was [*sic*] directly at issue. Such conduct appears to me to involve all the guilt of actual *treason*. And yet to this "complexion have we come at last"!

As to the positions assumed by Messrs. Clay & Van Buren ["and their adherents" *canceled*] and the arguments urged to cover their gross delinquency, I need say nothing to you. They are too trifling and absurd to require comment. Indeed, they are sufficiently exposed and refuted *by themselves,* in their correspondence on this very subject while they were respectively Secretaries of State. This they well know—and the world knows. They are condemned *by* themselves, and need no severer sentence than that they have pronounced *on* themselves.

But while I refrain from commenting on their quibbles, it may not be improper to say a word or two in regard to the course of their British associates and coadjutors. [*Here the manuscript ends.*]

Ms. in ScCleA. NOTE: This ms. copy of a letter or part of a letter, undated and identified only by a heading: "To Littleton Waller Tazewell Esq.," is found among Calhoun's papers and was probably given to him by the unidentified writer. Tazewell was a lawyer of great repute and former Senator from Va.

JUNE 1–8, 1844

〖〗

The first act of the Texas annexation drama closed on June 8. By a vote of 16 to 35 the Senate of the United States refused its consent to Calhoun's treaty of annexation. The friends of annexation immediately moved resolutions looking toward a direct admission of Texas to the Union as a State. These were tabled. The Southern Democrats and several Northeastern and Northwestern Democrats not closely tied to Martin Van Buren voted for Texas. Calhoun could rightfully criticize the defection of the Van Buren Democrats, but in fact this was not decisive. The solid opposition of both the Northern Whigs and the Southern Whigs doomed the treaty. The Southern and border State followers of Henry Clay cast a solid block of negatives, which, if it had been reversed, would have put the treaty within a few votes of the necessary two-thirds. If, as Calhoun contended, fixing Texas to the Union was essential to the South, then the South, once more, had defeated itself.

However, the play was not over, but was about to enter its second act. This act would be carried out in the volatile arena of a Presidential campaign, which might enflame public opinion even further. Rejection of the treaty had settled nothing except a few political scores. The position of Texas still loomed large and problematic on the continent of North America. The relationship between the United States and Mexico remained in festering condition.

The long first session of the 28th Congress, which had begun last December, was winding towards its end. The last weeks of a session were always hectic for a department head. The Senate still had not acted on the next most important diplomatic matter on its agenda, the Zollverein treaty. When Congress adjourned, on June 17, the Secretary might relax a bit, and then turn his attention to the British Minister and another great issue. But if the Presidential election promised to bring Texas to a settlement, its effect was likely to be the opposite when it came to Oregon, which was, by virtue of having become a live political issue, probably further from settlement than it had been a few months before. On June 3 the Senate asked for the documents on the Oregon negotiation, but the President "in the present state of the subject matter," refused to send them.

◫

From ANNA [MARIA CALHOUN CLEMSON]

Canebrake [Edgefield District, S.C.,] June 1st 1844

Dear father, I received your letter [of 5/10] last Sunday [5/26] but as the part *relating to Belgium* touched Mr. [Thomas G.] Clemson more nearly than myself he replied to it immediately. That letter you may or may not have got such is the glorious uncertainty of our mail[,] but as this goes to Edgefield [and] therefore will be more certain & [perha]ps earlier in its arrival I will give you at his request the outlines of what he said. In the first place as you may suppose he is much pleased with the idea & very much obliged to you for interesting yourself *personally* in the matter which was even more than he expected & the next he would be glad to hear from you as soon as possible as to when it would be necessary to start[,] what is the pay? whether there is an outfit? &c &c that he may know what he has to depend on. He would be glad also for your advice as to what arrangements had better be made here & this is I believe all he told me but if you think of anything else necessary for him to know as a perfect ignoramus in such matters he begs you will mention it. And now I suppose you want to know what I think & feel about this weighty matter. In the first place were I a few years younger or my children [Floride Elizabeth Clemson and John Calhoun Clemson] a few years older I should enjoy the idea of visiting Europe much but as it is I expect to have more of the fatigues & disagreeables of travel than the pleasures. Moving about has not for me the pleasures it had & my children are at the most troublesome age. If *they* were old enough to be amused or profitted by the trip I might enjoy their pleasure. Then I am so completely out of [the] habit of society that the idea of returning to [its] ceremonies & ettiquettes especially in a position that in however small a degree renders them incumbent on me is rather irksome than otherwise so you see on the whole ["you see" *canceled*] I am so dull as to prefer all things considered to remain at the Canebrake for the present at least more especially as I cannot for the life of me see what arrangement we can make here that will not subject us to the greatest evils of absentees. We have an old neighbour[,] a Mr. [John] Mobley[,] a most excellent & worthy old man whose wife [Lucretia Simkins Mobley] is a niece of Col. [Eldred] Simkins & who as his children are all married off & he is very fond of riding about especially on this place which he regards with a great deal of interest who might be of great service in receiving monies[,] keeping a supervising eye & writing you if he detected any abuses[,] but Mr. Clemson sounded him & he seemed unwilling (only on account of the responsibility) but the real reason I expect is that being & [sic] uneducated man he dreads the writing to you from time to time at least so I judged from an observation he mentioned. If he does not give an eye to the place I think it is a thin chance unless you can suggest some plan of inspection for altho' we like our overseer much as far as we know him the position is liable to too much abuse to intrust to one we have know[n] so short a time with unlimited authority. Notwithstanding all these objections & misgivings I am on the whole pleased that Mr. C[lemson] has received the appointment. He is so anxious to revisit Europe & thinks of it so much that I don[']t think he will be contented till he does & I hope the visit will have one of two good effects—either to reconcile him to this country or give him an opportunity of seeing what he can do for himself there & either way put an end to his constant desire to go there. I think the first the most probable for he is becoming daily more interested in planting & will look back to it with regret I hope when he leaves. My greatest trouble now I have made up my mind to go is about a nurse & that is a great difficulty with two such little children as I have. As soon as we hear definitely from you about the time of starting &c &c I shall write to cousin Anna Bonneau to try & procure me a decent person at least to go as far as Washington & I would be really glad if Pat[rick Calhoun] & yourself would without giving yourselves much trouble make inquiries among your lady friends if they know of a white woman[,] a good nurse & kind to children who would suit me. I should prefer a middle aged woman. Should you hear of such a one she might be spoken to but no positive arrangement made as I might suit myself in Charleston which would be more convenient to me. I have left myself no space to reply to your letter or to discuss politics. As to the latter I have ceased to take much interest in such a dirty business as it has become except so far as it concerns you & even if I did I am so far behind the news in this out of the way corner of creation that I should only prove my ignorance by attempting to say anything about the matter.

I hope John [C. Calhoun, Jr.] arrived safely at Washington & that you have made satisfactory arrangements about his trip west. I am very anxious about him & do hope he may experience benefit from the excursion. We miss him much especially [John] Calhoun [Clemson] who is perfectly devoted to him. Did Pat go with him? If he did not do give my love to him & tell him I hope he has received my letter written before John started & beg him to write me. I have not heard from home for some time but I suppose it is the mails. I write regularly.

The children are quite well. Calhoun send[s] love to "faddy[?] & Uncle Paddy" & is very anxious to know if you got the letter he wrote you in mine to Pat. He is *very smart*. Your devoted daughter, Anna.

[P.S.] Mr. C[lemson] desires me to say that he forgot in his to mention about Mr. [George W.] Barton's letter that it was the second application & he merely sent it to you to get rid of the matter.

ALS in ScCleA.

From F[rancis] M. Dimond

United States Consulate
Vera Cruz, 1 June 1844

Sir, In the absence of any mail from Mexico [City] allow me to add to my respects of yesterday and to observe, that there appears to be no expedition either by sea or land preparing against Texas[.] All is quiet, nevertheless the Proclamation of the President in calling Congress together seems to have for its main object the furnishing of means to support the Honour and dignity of the country and for the reconquest of Texas.

Notwithstanding which, allow me again to repeat, that I firmly believe the President would much rather treat with the United States for a boundary line including Texas, than again to invade that little but gallant State.

There are at Sacrificios but two French vessels of war[,] one English and our little steamer Poinsett.

The British Steam Packet leav[e]s here Tomorrow with a million and [a] half Dollars—our last instalment due on the 30 of April remains unpaid as yet. I have the Honour to be Sir most Respectfully Your Ob[edient] Servant, F.M. Dimond.

ALS (No. 222) in DNA, RG 59 (State Department), Consular Despatches, Veracruz, vol. 5 (M-183:5).

From F[RANCIS] M. DIMOND

Consulate of the U. States
Vera Cruz, 1 June 1844

Sir, Since I had the honour a few hours since to address you I have by mail rec[eive]d a Letter from Capt. [Raphael] Semmes of the Poinsett dated Mexico [City] 30[t]h ult[im]o wherein he observes, that Mr. [Ben E.] Green and Colonel [Gilbert L.] Thompson, had an interview with [Valentín] Canalizo, President adinterim, and ministers yesterday, and are to have their ultimatum today; and there is no doubt but it will be entirely favourable notwithstanding the gasconades of the public prints.

I take the liberty to say thus much trusting it will turn out so—and as there will be no opportunity again for some days.

The Poinsett will no doubt depart hence on the 4th ins[tant]. I have the honour to be Sir most Respectfully Your Ob[edient] Serv[an]t, F.M. Dimond.

ALS (No. 223) in DNA, RG 59 (State Department), Consular Despatches, Veracruz, vol. 5 (M-183:5), received 6/24.

From EDWARD EVERETT

London, 1 June 1844

Sir, I transmit the last monthly circular of the Messrs. [G. and H.] Davis, of whom I have formerly spoken as the most considerable dealers in Tobacco in the Kingdom. You will perceive that they make a reference to the Executive document on the subject of Tobacco published the present session, by our House of Representatives No. 173. They have stated to me that on page 100, of this document, the number of pounds of Tobacco retained for home consumption should be 16,222,111 and not 22,095,588 as printed.

I learn from one of the partners of this house who has been examined before Mr. [Joseph] Hume's committee, that the committee are pursuing their investigations as to the quantity of smuggling and adulteration in the article of Tobacco in a very thorough manner, and that he thinks a strong impression has been made upon their minds, by the testimony given and the evidence produced before them. Mr. Davis exhibited to me the proof sheets of a portion of his own testimony, disclosing a state of facts well calculated to arouse the attention of Parliament to the alarming extent of the evil, and the expediency of applying the only effectual remedy, vizt. a great reduction of the duty.

I thought it might be useful in this state of the enquiry, to confer with Lord Aberdeen on the subject; and I had an interview with him for that purpose on the 28th of May. He said that at the time the government granted Mr. Hume's committee, there was (he thought) rather a decided opinion on their part that the duty could not be safely reduced. It might, however, be, that a state of facts would be disclosed by the Report as to the extent of smuggling and adulteration, and the prospect that a lower duty might be collected on the entire consumption, that would warrant a change. He did not feel sanguine that such would be the case; but as it was a matter not pertaining to his particular department he was not prepared to speak confidently about it. He might, however, he believed, say that no determination existed on the part of the government to oppose reduction at all events. They regarded the question as one exclusively of revenue; they were in favor of any thing, which would extend their trade with the United States; and if they could lower the duty on Tobacco without injury to the Treasury they would gladly do it.

I shall lose no time, when the report of the committee appears, in sending you a copy. I am, sir, with great respect, your obedient servant, Edward Everett.

LS (No. 137) in DNA, RG 59 (State Department), Diplomatic Despatches, Great Britain, vol. 52 (M-30:48), received 6/21; FC in DNA, RG 84 (Foreign Posts), Great Britain, Despatches, 8:261–264; FC in MHi, Edward Everett Papers, 49:161–163 (published microfilm, reel 23, frames 81–82).

From ALEX[ANDER] W. JONES

Edwardsville, Ill[inoi]s, June 1, 1844

Sir, I am encouraged to request your Kind Offices, with the President, in my behalf, by the reflection, that you never forget or desert a friend, however obscure, so long as he remains worthy—and that my character for honor and integrity, is as unsullied, as when I removed, from Virginia. Senators [Sidney] Breese and [James] Semple, from this State, who Know me well, will cheerfully bear testimony.

Almost from the date of my Appointment as Register of the Land Office, at this place, I have been from time to time, earnestly importuned to advance money, and lend my aid, to sustain the [Washington] Madisonian, and other Journals of a similar character. On these communications, as well as that of a Mr. [Alexander G.] Abell, who modestly requested me to assist in extending the circulation of his life of Mr. [John] Tyler, contrary to the letter and spirit of my instructions, I have never bestowed the slightest notice. I am now, from this cause, classed among the "disaffected," and from the tenor of a letter I received, from Mr. Abell yesterday, I suspect that an effort will be made, perhaps has already has [*sic*] been made, to remove me, from Office.

To you, I will frankly say, what I would scorn to say, to the Sycophants and parasites of the Court, who beset Mr. Tyler, and have rendered even his name odious to many, who would otherwise have been his friends, that in truth, on all questions of constitutional Law, and national Policy, with the exception of the Exchequer Scheme, I fully concur with the Executive. On the Subject of the re-annexation of Texas, to its former and rightful Proprietor, and the resumption of sole and supreme sovereignty over the Territory of Oregon, with or without a war with Mexico and England, or either, or any other, and all other foreign Powers, I am with four-fifths of the people, occupying the great Valley of the Mississippi. But I am no Tyler-man Altho' I prefer him to Mr. [Martin] Van Buren. There is One whose elevation to the presidency, I have long desired, and I rest with unshaken confidence in the belief, that Providence, that so often and so signally has manifested itself, in our behalf, will yet, in its good time, select him as the instrument for the deliverance of its chosen People. I have therefore refused to pledge or commit my self to the fortunes of any aspirant, and I owe it to my self to state candidly, that there ["are" *interlined*] others, in the Democratic ranks, for whom, I shall vote in preference to Mr. Tyler.

In the Legislature of Virginia, at a critical juncture in his political life, I warmly and zealously sustained him against one of the most distinguished men of Virginia, who was supported alike, by his own formidable family influence, and every Prominent Leader of the Democratic Party.

I am in straitened and very reduced circumstances, and altho the salary and perquisites of my Office average scarcely $600, Per annum, yet that amount is sufficient, for the few wants of my family, and should I be removed, I should not only be greatly embarrassed, even distressed; but I should have to encounter the suspicion of failure or neglect of official duty, which would throw an obstacle, in the way to honorable employment, in some other pursuit.

Upon reference to the Hon. Tho[mas] H. Blake, he will unhesitatingly say, that I have performed my official duties, in a manner entirely satisfactory to the General Land Office. With great respect, Alex. W. Jones.

ALS in ScCleA.

To Aaron Leggett, New York [City], 6/1. "Your letter of the 30th Ins[tan]t [sic; 4/15?] relative to the claim of Mrs. Mary Hughes against the Mexican Gover[n]ment has been received and, with the documents which accompanied it[,] has been placed on file." FC in DNA, RG 59 (State Department), Domestic Letters, 34:220 (M-40:32).

From J[oseph] C. Luther

Port au Prince, June 1st 1844

Sir, I have the honor to inform you that I arrived at this Port to day in the Brig Republic of and from New York, which port she left, on the 17th of May last past, and have again resumed the duties of my office, as Commercial Agent of the United States. The late disturbances in this Island have resulted in another complete overturn of the Government, and a new President has been procla[i]med in the person of *Guercere* [sic; Philippe Guerrier], who is now in full command of this portion of the Island, The South Eastern or Spanish part of the Island having declared themselves independent and established a distinct Government, which they will doubtless maintain. I have the honor to be very respectfully your ob[edien]t Servant, J.C. Luther.

ALS (No. 8) in DNA, RG 59 (State Department), Consular Despatches, Port-au-Prince, vol. 2 (T-346:2), received 6/20.

From R[ichard] K. Call, [Governor of Fla. Territory], Tallahassee, 6/2. Call encloses two statements from citizens in support of his charges against Charles S. Sibley, U.S. District Attorney for the Middle District of Fla. If the evidence is insufficient, he recommends the appointment of a commission to investigate the matter. If this is done "other and stronger cases, of official impropriety, will be found to support the charges against this officer." ALS with Ens in DNA, RG 59 (State Department), Applications and Recommendations, 1837–1845, Sibley (M-687:30, frames 95–102).

3 June 1844

From W[ILLIAM] S. ARCHER, [Senator from Va.]

Senate Chamber, June 3d [18]44

Sir, A motion will be made as I have reason to believe, for the rejection of the appropriation for the Salary of the Chargé d'Affaires to Sardinia, on the ground of the want of any occasion for, or utility to be expected from the Mission.

I have to request to be furnished with any information you may deem pertinent, as regards the grounds, on which the Mission has been instituted, or may be thought deserving of retention, at as early a moment as may be suited to your convenience. I am Respectf[ul]ly Y[ou]r Ob[edien]t S[ervan]t &c, W.S. Archer, Ch[air]m[a]n F[oreign] Relat[ion]s of the Senate.

ALS in DNA, RG 59 (State Department), Miscellaneous Letters (M-179:104, frames 482–483). NOTE: Tyler had appointed Robert Wickliffe, Jr., of Kentucky to be Chargé d'Affaires to Sardinia (to succeed Ambrose Baber) during the recess of Congress in 1843, and Wickliffe was already at his post.

From R[ichard] K. Call, [Governor of Fla. Territory], Tallahassee, 6/3. "I herewith enclose a paper accidental[l]y omit[t]ed in my communication of yesterday, to which I beg leave to invite your attention." (Appended is a Clerk's EU that reads, "To be filed with the Papers in this case & laid before the Secretary.") ALS in DNA, RG 59 (State Department), Applications and Recommendations, 1837–1845, Sibley (M-687:30, frames 103–104).

From ROBERT B. CAMPBELL

Consulate of the United States of America
Havana, June 3d 1844

Sir, I have the honor herewith to enclose to you a copy of a letter addressed by me to the Capt. Gen[era]l [Leopoldo O'Donnell] and a copy of his reply in relation to the arrest and imprisonment of [William] Bisby and [Samuel] Moffat at Cardenas, referred to in your communication of the 26th of April last. I have the honor to be with considerations of very great respect y[ou]r mo[st] ob[edien]t Ser[van]t, Robert B. Campbell.

700

[Enclosure]
Robert B. Campbell to Captain General Leopoldo O'Donnell
Consulate of the United States of America
Havana, June [*sic*; May] 28th 1844

Sir, I have the honor herewith to enclose to your Ex[c]ellency a copy of a letter just received from an unhappy (and if the statement be correct) a cruelly treated American citizen of the name of Bisby. My knowledge of the firmness, impartiality and mercy evidenced on more than one occasion with which your Ex[c]ellency has administered the duties of your exalted office does not permit me to doubt that all unnecessary and cruel treatment inflicted upon the unfortunate who may fall under the suspicion of the Government is without the sanction of your order and may not have been brought to your notice. Your Ex[c]ellency I am convinced coincides with me in the opinion that in all civilized nations conviction does and should precede punishment. That all the requirements of law and Government are fulfilled by the securing the persons of the suspected in such a manner as to ensure their being brought to trial. This being conceded it follows that the treatment of Bisby has been wanton, cruel & unnecessary. Mr. Phinney of all others the most interested as the owner of the slave upon whose evidence Bisby appears to have been arrested has just seen me and represents Bisby as an amiable, worthy and law abiding individual. That he is only now recovering from a serious indisposition induced by the severity of his treatment. His family are in the United States. Are of respectable standing and he is most anxious to return to them. Should there be no sufficient evidence to justify the beleif of his guilt y[ou]r Ex[c]ellency would be performing but an act of justice to place him at my disposition. Of Mr. Moffat another American citizen whose name is mentioned in Bisby's letter it is said his character not only places him above suspicion but in the insurrection which occurred at Bemba last year he bravely fought the negroes while the others fled. That he was near losing his life in consequence of wounds received in the engagement with them. If this statement is correct y[ou]r Ex[c]ellency I am satisfied will feel the disposition to protect and reward him. Should there be no sufficient evidence against Moffat to require his continued imprisonment Y[ou]r Ex[c]ellency will doubtless give him up to me. If the representations made to me of the innocence of these men do not correspond with the evidence before the tribunal which set upon them & the policy of the Government or the safety of the institutions of the Country require their longer duress, I must urge

701

upon y[ou]r Ex[c]ellency the importance of ordering the Governor of Cardenas to treat them with all the lenity compatible with their safe custody. I embrace this occasion to say to y[ou]r Ex[c]ellency that I have no sickly sensibility on the subject of slavery. I beleive it to be a salutary institution in the present condition of the black race and no punishment can be too severe for the intermeddling fanatic who attempts to arm the slave against the master. I admit that in the excitement produced by servile insurrections the innocent may often suffer with the guilty but a benificent Government will and ought to make those sufferings as short & light as possible and take the earliest opportunities voluntarily to repair any wrongs that may have been inflicted. Y[ou]r Ex[c]ellency may perhaps think me subject to the charge of officiously interfering beyond the limits of this Consulate to releive myself from this imputation I must plead the instructions of his Ex[c]ellency the President of the United States just received through the Secretary of State. I have the honor to be with considerations of very great respect y[ou]r Ex[c]ellency's most ob[edien]t Ser[van]t, Robert B. Campbell.

ALS with Ens in DNA, RG 59 (State Department), Consular Despatches, Havana, vol. 19 (T-20:19), received 6/17. NOTE: Campbell also enclosed O'Donnell's reply in Spanish of 6/1. In his note O'Donnell disclaimed knowledge of the Bisby incident but said that he had written the Lieutenant Governor of the Cardenas District for information. If Bisby's statements have merit, the conditions of his incarceration will be changed.

From F[RANCIS] M. DIMOND

United States Consulate
Vera Cruz, June 3th 1844

Sir, I had the honour to address you on the 1st inst[ant] via N[ew] Orle[a]ns, and now [have] the honour to transmit documents rec[eive]d by this day[']s mail from the other side.

Colonel [Gilbert L.] Thompson arrived this morning from Mexico [City], and sailed in the U.S. Steamer Poinsett at noon to day for Galvaston, and I regret to *add,* that the object of his mission has *not* been accomplished, and that this Government *only* repeated that the annexation of Texas to the U. States would be a declaration of war and that in no courteous terms.

The Steamer I forward this by is chartered by the Government and departs in great hast[e]. I have the honour to be Sir most Respectfully Your Ob[edient] Serv[an]t, F.M. Dimond.

ALS (No. 224) in DNA, RG 59 (State Department), Consular Despatches, Veracruz, vol. 5 (M-183:5), received 6/19.

From Lathrop J. Eddy, New York [City], 6/3. He asks that George E. Baldwin, a long-time friend and supporter of Calhoun, be appointed despatch bearer. Baldwin is in poor health, and his appointment would gratify numerous N.Y. friends. (Clerks' EU's read "Rec[eive]d June 8/44" and "Answ[ere]d by Mr. Craulle.") ALS in DNA, RG 59 (State Department), Passport Applications, vol. 31, unnumbered (M-1372:14).

From H[enry] L. Ellsworth, Patent Office, 6/3. He discusses 12 applicants for the position of Chief Clerk in his office and indicates a preference for E.G. Smith. ALS in DNA, RG 59 (State Department), Applications and Recommendations, 1845–1853, Ellsworth (M-873:26, frames 350–355).

To B[en] E. Green

Department of State
Washington, 3d June, 1844

Sir: I have to inform you that your draught, dated the 18th of April, last, for one thousand and twenty-seven dollars, part on account of your salary as Secretary of the Legation of the United States at Mexico and part on account of your salary as Chargé des Affaires, has been presented to this Department. You were mistaken in supposing that you were authorized to draw for the salary of a Chargé des Affaires. There may be an equitable claim on your part to the difference between the salary of a Secretary of Legation and that of a Chargé d'Affaires, for the interval between the departure of General [Waddy] Thompson [Jr.] and the arrival of his successor [Wilson Shannon], but you cannot with propriety draw for that difference and this department cannot by any means honor such draughts until Congress shall have made an appropriation therefor.

An arrangement has however been effected by which seven hundred dollars, the amount due you as Secretary of Legation on the 24th ult[imo] has been paid on account of the draught above mentioned, and the residue will be paid as your salary in that character may become due. I am, Sir, your obedient servant, J.C. Calhoun.

LS (No. 4) in DNA, RG 84 (Foreign Posts), Mexico, Instructions, vol. 5.I; FC in DNA, RG 59 (State Department), Diplomatic Instructions, Mexico, 15:296–297 (M-77:111).

From W[ILLIA]M HOGAN

New York [City,] June 3d 1844

Sir, The proceedings of the Baltimore Convention place it beyond my power to render yourself or President [John] Tyler, any further service; your friends have given up the game, which they held in their own hands to your opponents, & I am now forbidden to move an inch except in a track, pointed out to me by gentlemen, a portion of whom, have been faithless to you & all of whom have most unworthily—in my opinion—["have" *canceled*] sacrificed the interests of the South. Under these circumstances, allow me, Sir, to ask you for the Consulate of Trieste, now filled by an English gentleman [George Moore]; or if you & the President have any objection to giving me that, I will thank you for that of Bremen, in case Mr. [Francis J.] Grund is rejected—but if he should be ["rejected" *canceled*] confirmed, give me any other in the British West Indies, where you think I may be of some service in giving you such information as our peculiar relations with Great Britain demand at the *present moment.*

I have accepted my present Consulate in Nuevitas from Mr. Upsher [*sic*; Abel P. Upshur], with the sole object of giving him more effectually such information as he desired in relation to affairs in Cuba. The fees of the Office are not worth one hundred Dollars per annum, & I am already out of pocket over $1200 in consequence of the president not understanding Mr. Upsher[']s views in sending me out to Cuba & Mexico. Under these circumstances ["I these circumstances" *canceled*] I think that justice allows me to ask for a better situation.

Will you do me the honor of dropping me a line & as evidence that I am not unworthy of your kindness, I beg to refer you to any of the following gentlemen. The Hon. Messrs. [Isaac E.] Holmes [Representative from S.C.], [Levi] Woodbury [Senator from N.H.], [Charles G.] Atherton [Senator from N.H.], [Duncan L.] Clinch [Representative from Ga.] or [John M.] Berrien [Senator from Ga.]. I have the honour to remain Sir Respectfully, Wm. Hogan.

ALS in ScCleA.

From STEWART NEWELL, [Galveston]

Consulate of the United States
Port of Sabine, June 3d 1844

The following short statement, of affairs connected with the Steamer Scioto Belle reported to the Dep[art]m[en]t, being deemed neccessary, to a correct understanding of the matter, is most Respectfully presented to the Department, by Most Respectfully Your Ob[edien]t Serv[an]t, Stewart Newell.

The Steamer Scioto Belle was chartered by Carter Beaman, who took, [James J.] Wright into the interest, from a kindness of feeling, on part of Beaman, and Wright[']s representations of ability, to advance the interests of Beaman, in the contemplated trade. For the vessel, Beaman & Wright, gave joint notes for payment of Charter. Beaman has paid all the notes due, and Deposited such security as required for the ballance, and has paid all the expences. Wright had, nor has neither credit or Money. Tho[ma]s Barrett of New Orleans became interested by his endorsement of the Notes and holds Beaman[']s securities to indemnify him Barrett. The latter has paid the Money and cannot be reimbursed until next Fall or Spring. In consequence of Wright[']s inability to command buissiness for the vessel on credit or money to defray expences, and his determination to carry the vessel to some other Port or Ports not expressed in the Shipping Articles and the vessel not adapted to go to Sea the Crew demanded to be paid off at Sabine although the time stipulated for in the agreement between the Master & Seamen, of three months had not yet expired but within a short time would do so, and as the vessel could not be employed under the command of Wright from his notorious bad character, and destitute of any means, and the Crew dissatisfied, and determined not to go to Sea in the Steam Boat, and which to all acquainted with that Class of vessels would say was prudent in them. In the mean time demand was made by me upon the Master and Beaman to satisfy said claims. Both declined as stated in letters enclosed (in *No. 3*, accompanying this) upon which I went to Galveston to consult the Charge of the U. States [William S. Murphy] and was directed by him to sit in Admiralty upon all such matters, useing many arguments in presence of Witnesses to prove that the duties of Consuls were entirely such as the Admiralty Courts of the U. States were invested with, that I must so consider it, and by his verbal order then given, I must proceed to sell the vessel, or suffer censure from him and the Department. I proposed various modes of avoiding this course. He objected to all. I then travelled

85 Miles to consult the District Judge of that District of Sabine. He replied that no Court could be held for Six weeks thereafter and that I should proceed to dispose of the vessel. Advertisement was then made through the Tri-Weekly Newspaper, and upon the Crew, Beaman and Barrett[']s joint application the vessel was sold, the Crew paid off up to the time of thier libel, Wright removed from the command, and Beaman placed in possession and the vessel proceeded to buissiness by going to Galveston during a Calm time at Sea. Upon her arrival at Galveston Wright instigated three of the former Crew to libel the vessel for alledged Wages with a view to get her into the hands of the Law, and cause a loss of her to Beaman, between whom and Wright no friendly feelings existed. The whole Crew were paid off and gave receipts corresponding to the Copy of one enclosed signed ["by" *canceled*] G[eorge] W. Phillips, each for thier respective Am[oun]ts. Beleiveing it to be the intention of Wright to ruin the Boat and Beaman by such a course, Mr. [Archibald M.] Green and myself protested against the Jurisdiction of the Courts in such cases where the whole parties were American. Gen[era]l Murphy sanctioned, the whole, commanded it to be done, and now, seeks to cast censure upon me for doing, and Counsels and advises, Wright to commence a Suit for damages against me for displaceing him of a command of the vessel, in which he had been placed, by Beaman & Barrett, these Gentlemen being to pay all the Debts and purchase of the Boat, requireing Wright[']s dismissal, Wright in Law or Equity not an Owner, Beaman & Barrett being both in Law and Equity Owners, and Men of Respectable Character and responsible. Wright possessing wherever known just the reverse character and well known to me for his general bad character for Six years.

I did not under these circumstances hesitate and feel quite satisfied the Department will justify the Act, and at least give me credit for disposition to obtain instructions how to act as my numerous and lengthy Letters to Dep[art]m[en]t, will show.

ALS in DNA, RG 59 (State Department), Consular Despatches, Texas, vol. 1 (T-153:1), received 6/24.

From W[ADDY] THOMPSON [JR.]

Washington, June 3 1844

Shortly before I left Mexico I received a commission for a gentleman whose name I do not remember [Richard H. Belt] as American Commercial agent at Matamoros. When asked what was meant by Commercial agent I really could not explain it and the Exequatur was refused. I presume therefore that the consulship at Matamoros which Mr. [Isaac D.] Marks has recently resigned is still vacant. I therefore take leave to recommend Mr. J[ohn] P. Schatzel[l] for the office. The emoluments of the office are very trifling not more than three or four hundred dollars a year and Mr. Schatzel[l] who is a man of large fortune only desires it for the protection which it will give him. It is of the utmost importance and particularly so at that port that the consul be a man of intelligence well acquainted with the country & its customs and withall a man of wealth, as the necessities of our countrymen frequently force him to expend to them pecuniary aid not authorized by Law. No man is more able & very few so willing to expend such aid as Mr. Schatzel[l]. The Hon. Mr. [John J.] Crittenden [Senator from Ky.] requests me to use his name in this matter. Indeed it is at his request that I write this, as he feels a deep debt of gratitude to Mr. Schatzel[l] for kindness to his son [George B. Crittenden] when a prisoner in Mexico. Very Respe[ct]f[u]lly, W. Thompson.

ALS in DNA, RG 59 (State Department), Applications and Recommendations, 1837–1845, Schatzell (M-687:29, frames 412–414).

To [JOHN TYLER]

Department of State
Washington, 3d June, 1844

To the President of the United States.

The Secretary of State has the honor to acknowledge the receipt of the Resolution of the Senate of the 28th ult[imo] requesting the President to communicate to that body "the whole of the 'private letter' from London with its date quoted by the American Secretary of State in his letter of the 9th (8th?) of August, 1843, to the United States Chargé in Texas, so far as the same applies to Texas; and all other letters from the same person relative to the annexation of Texas to the United States; also that the President be requested to inform the Senate of the name of the writer of said '*private letter*,' and whether the said writer was employed by the government of the United States, in Europe, and if so, a copy of the instructions under which he acted, or of the letters or papers which accredited him, the character in which he acted, by whom appointed, the amount of money which he received, and out of what fund it was paid."

In reply, the Undersigned has the honor to report to the President that, after diligent inquiry, no letter of the character referred to can be found on the files of this Department; nor any evidence that such has ever been placed on them. He is unable to ascertain the name of the writer in question from any documents in possession of the Department, and presumes that the letter referred to in the Resolution of the Senate being *"private,"* is amongst the private papers of the late Mr. [Abel P.] Upshur. Respectfully submitted. J.C. Calhoun.

LS in DNA, RG 46 (U.S. Senate), 28B-B12; FC in DNA, RG 59 (State Department), Reports of the Secretary of State to the President and Congress, 6:107–108; PC in Senate Document No. 351, 28th Cong., 1st Sess., p. 1; PC in House Document No. 271, 28th Cong., 1st Sess., pp. 98–99; PC in *Congressional Globe,* 28th Cong., 1st Sess., Appendix, p. 569; PC in the Washington, D.C., *Daily National Intelligencer,* June 4, 1844, p. 2; PC in *Niles' National Register,* vol. LXVI, no. 15 (June 8, 1844), pp. 232–233. NOTE: Tyler transmitted this letter to the Senate on 6/3. The resolution to which the above letter was a reply is found in RG 59 (State Department), Miscellaneous Letters (M-179:104, frame 453), and in *Senate Executive Journal,* 6:294.

To the Rev. [WILLIAM] CAPERS, [New York City]

Washington, 4th June, 1844

My dear Sir: I have felt a deep interest in the proceedings of your [Methodist Episcopal] conference [in New York City] in reference to the case of Bishop [James O.] Andrew. Their bearings, both as it relates to Church and State, demand the gravest attention on the part of the whole Union, and the South especially.

I would be glad if you and Judge [A.B.] Longstreet, and other prominent members of the conference, would take Washington in your route on your return home, and spend a day or two with us, in order to afford an opportunity of exchanging ideas on a subject of such vital importance. Yours truly, J.C. Calhoun.

PC in John Nelson Norwood, *The Schism in the Methodist Episcopal Church, 1844: a Study of Slavery and Ecclesiastical Politics,* in Alfred University Studies, vol. I (Alfred, N.Y.: Alfred University, c. 1923), p. 190, reprinted from the *Richmond Christian Advocate,* August 7, 1851; Ms. copy in NcD, Whitefoord Smith Papers. NOTE: Capers was a S.C. Methodist minister, subsequently a bishop. The copy of this letter in the papers of Whitefoord Smith, another S.C. Methodist minister, carries no addressee and is probably a transcript of the letter to Capers.

To [THOMAS G. CLEMSON, Edgefield
District, S.C.]

Washington, 4th June 1844

My dear Sir, The pay of a Charge is $4500 with an outfit of the same amount. The present Charge [Henry W. Hilliard] will resign, say in August, and an appointment will be made as soon as his resignation takes place. You ought to leave here shortly after. It is usual to allow pay for about a month, before the departure on the mission, to make arrangements & preperation. It is hardly probable, that there will be a vessel of war going cross the Atlantick at the time.

If you should ["conclude to" *interlined*] dispose of your cook, I would be glad to take him; and, if not, to keep him for you, in your absence. If we can dispose of our carriage & Horses, I would be glad to take yours. I would be glad, if you, or Anna [Maria Calhoun Clemson], would write to Mrs. [Floride Colhoun] Calhoun on the subject.

Patrick [Calhoun] & John [C. Calhoun, Jr.,] leave this evening for St. Louis.

John looks better than when he arrived, but coughs a great deal. I am much encouraged by the information I have received from several sources of the highly beneficial effects of the excursion he is about to take. Dr. [James H.] Relfe thinks, there is little doubt of his restoration. Patrick has orders to join a detachment of dragoons, which will visit the western frontier, & ["will" *interlined*] be out the greater part of the summer. John will go along with him, which will exactly suit.

I am much engaged at present, and must pass over politicks ["to" *canceled and* "till" *interlined*] my next.

If the season has been as fine with you of late, as it has been here, your crop must look well. Our rains have been both abundant & gentle.

I must entreat you, not to remain too long at your place. It will, in my opinion, be full time to leave by the time you receive this. You had better go without delay to Fort Hill, & remain there till you think it time to set out for Washington. I hope you all continue well. My love to Anna & kiss the dear children [John Calhoun Clemson and Floride Elizabeth Clemson; *here the extant manuscript ends.*]

ALU (fragment) in ScCleA.

To F[rancis] M. Dimond, U.S. Consul at Vera Cruz, 6/4. Henry A. Holmes [*sic*], "bearer of this letter, has a claim against the Mexican government, for provisions furnished the division of the Mexican Army under General [Pedro de] Ampudia, which was recently employed in subduing Yucatan." Calhoun asks Dimond's assistance in obtaining payment of the claim. FC in DNA, RG 59 (State Department), Consular Instructions, 11:246.

From W[ILLIA]M B. GOOCH

U.S. Commercial Agency
Aux Cayes, May [*sic*; June] 4th 1844

Sir, In my last letter to the Department, I stated the importance of my returning to the United States, on account of domestick affliction.

Deeming it of the greatest importance to have our Commercial interests representeded [*sic*] at this port, I have advised with Captain [Thomas W.] Freelon, Commander of the U.S. Ship Preble, who concurs with me in opinion.

I have advised him to authorise some person among the American residents, who he thinks best qualified to perform the duties of U.S. Comm[ercia]l Agent, until an appointment is made by Government.

He has selected Richmond Loring M.D. and I fully acquiesce in his opinion that Dr. Loring is the most suitable person that could be appointed under the existing difficulties of the Island.

Inclosed are copies of letters, one to Capt. Freelon & his answer— also a letter [from Gen. Diugua Zamor] to the Nations represented by their Agents & our answer.

Captain Freelon has prolonged his departure on account of the danger to which American property is exposed. Captain Freelon made a demand of this Government for my property which had been confiscated & it has been returned.

I must again urge the necessity of having some vessels of war call at the different ports, of importance, on this Island during their revolutions. Our property, I fear, will soon need protection along the coast, as well as the harbours & cities.

I expect to embark for the United States on the 6th inst. and on my arrival shall probably visit Washington, (if you are not absent;) when I will fully explain to you the great importance of U.S. Vessels of War being on this station. With high regards I am Sir your most devoted & obedient Servant, Wm. B. Gooch.

[Enclosure]
Tho[ma]s W. Freelon, U.S.N., to W[illia]m B. Gooch

U.S. Ship Preble
Aux Cayes, 30th May 1844

Sir, I have the honour to acknowledge the receipt of your letter of the 25th inst. in which you inform me that it is the opinion of the American residents, that my prolonged stay here is necessary to their protection. In one sense this is doubtless correct, as in this country of revolutions & anarchy, protection is necessary; but that there exists any powerful cause for remaining longer, I take the liberty of controverting for the following reasons.

In the first place, the power of President [Philippe] Guerrier appears to be recognized, & established over all the Island excepting that portion which formally belonged to Spain.

In the second place, I have received the most solemn promises, both from General Zamar [*sic*; Diugua Zamor] the Military Chief of this Arrondis[se]ment, and Mr. Solomon, who has recently been appointed by President Guerrier, the civil Cheif of the South, that the persons & property of resident foreigners, should be guarded & protected with the utmost care and vigilance. Such being the case, and there being but one American vessel that will be left in port when I shall leave, & sufficient time having elapsed since my arrival to give notice of the existing state of things here to the Merchants in the United States, and to the Government, to send out a Vessel of War if so disposed, I deem it my duty to proceed to complete the orders received from the Department on my leaving the United States. I shall therefore leave here as soon after the first of June as the wind & weather will permit. I am Sir Very Respectfully your most Obedient Servant, Thos. W. Freelon, U.S.N.

ALS (No. 17) with Ens in DNA, RG 59 (State Department), Consular Despatches, Aux Cayes, vol. 2 (T-330:2), received 7/3. NOTE: Another En was a copy of a letter from Gooch to Freelon, dated 5/25, requesting Freelon and the *Preble* to remain at Aux Cayes until Gen. Guerrier's arrival to prevent "rapacity" and "plunder." Two others were a notice from Gen. Diugua Zamor of 5/25 requesting French, English, and American consuls to accompany Zamor to inventory and seal the houses and stores of refugees and a reply from C. Smith, Acting British Vice Consul, A. Elesse, Acting French Vice Consul, and Gooch, also dated 5/25, refusing Zamor's request on the grounds that many houses and stores had already been pillaged. To accede to their being inventoried and sealed would be to countenance the prior thefts.

C[HARLES] J. INGERSOLL to [Richard K. Crallé], "Private"

[Washington,] June 4, '44

Dear Sir, In the peculiar state of things now it will be difficult to get salaries and outfits passed by the house of R[epresentatives] without strong reasons for whatever charges may be necessary, even tho' indispensable or accidental.

I explained this to Mr. Calhoun yesterday, and beg you after conferring with Mr. [William S.] Derrick, Mr. [Francis] Markoe or whoever else may be familiar with the subject, to favor me *to day* with an informal memorandum of the following particulars.

1. Mr. [George H.] Proffit [U.S. Minister to Brazil] having had one outfit and now receiving salary, another outfit & salary are asked for, for Mr. [Henry A.] Wise, for the same time and place. Any precedents, analogies or reasons for this will be important to me.

2. How long, precisely, have Mr. [Charles S.] Todd and Mr. [Daniel] Jenifer been appointed to Russia and Austria? Why are their places to be filled by other appointments? I suppose that the important questions arising from the Zollverein Treaty and its results may have some connexion with Mr. Jenifer's succession. Has he not signified thro' Mr. Joseph [R.] Ingersoll [Representative from Pa.] & Mr. Markoe his intention of coming home?

3. Why are outfits asked for, for Belgium[,] Chile and Sardinia? The particulars are necessary to enable me to explain why. I understand that there is an official letter from Mr. [Henry W.] Hilliard [U.S. Chargé d'Affaires in Belgium] stating his wish to return.

4. If there are any other missions for which any appropriations are asked please to let me know as soon as you can, by a memorandum sent to me at the house [of Representatives] to day. I am, very Respectfully Y[ou]rs, C.J. Ingersoll.

ALS in ScCleA.

From LOUIS MARK

Washington, 4 June 1844

Sir, Mr. [George] Evans of the Senate requested me to state in writing the present Exports of England of Cotton Twist and I have the honor to inclose a Copy of my Letter [of 6/1] to him showing how it bears on our trade and that of the Zoll Verein. England finds this a most profitable trade by which she profits annually over 6 Millions of dollars and it of right belongs and can in the present humour of the Zoll Verein be easily secured for this Country. With great Respect Your Ob[edien]t S[ervant], Louis Mark.

ALS with En in DNA, RG 59 (State Department), Miscellaneous Letters (M-179:104, frames 487–489).

From ALLEN PIERSE

Milliken[']s Bend, Parish of Madison La.
4th June 1844

Dear Sir, Having recently seen it stated in the newspapers that the present *Chargé de affair[e]s* to Texas [William S. Murphy] would probably be rejected by the Senate, it occur[r]ed to me, (if he should be) to apply for the office, if I could make such an interest as would warrant me in making the application with any hopes of success. I have consulted my friends on the subject, & some of them entertain strong doubts of my being able to get the office. They know more about office seeking than I do; & they think that if the place becomes vacant, there will be such a swarm of applicants for it, that one who has not a strong political influence to recommend him will stand a poor chance to succeed. These doubts have greatly damped my hopes, & determined me not to go to Washington, unless there be a possibility that I may succeed in my object.

I have taken the liberty to write to you as the head of the department with which the office is connected, to make inquiry; I hope there is no impropriety in my doing so; if there is, you will destroy this letter, & think no more about it. I can bring to Washington the petition of a few friends, who will recommend me as a suitable person to fill the office. Through them I can get a few members of Congress from this State & Mississippi, & one or two from North Carolina to join in the petition: none however, making a strong personal solicitation in my behalf. I could be *confirmed by the Senate*, & could *retain the office under Mr. Clay* should he be elected president.

I detest office seeking, & never expected till recently to apply for one: But I have been unfortunate here; become involved in the days of a redundant currency, & have had to sell every thing I owned, even to my library, to extricate myself. A broken man, no matter under what circumstances he fails, looses [*sic*] cast[e]. At least he does not feel right. According to the *reasoning* of my friends I ought to remain where I am, but according to my own *feelings* I should not. I have no family (tho I probably shall have soon) & the Scenes of my misfortunes being any thing but pleasant, I am strongly inclined to leave them, & profit elsewhere by my experience here. This is the only reason that could have induced me to think of applying for an office.

I shall make no application to the president [John Tyler], unless supported by you. With you principally, I shall try to make interest. All the interest I ever felt in politics has been connected with the hope of seeing you President of the United States. That hope has been above any thing like party feeling & entirely unconnected with it. It has had reference to the good of my country alone. The office could add nothing to your fame or your glory; but so exclusive has been my partiality in your favor, that I should not feel at liberty to apply to any other for an office, nor should I be willing to be indebted to any other for one.

I intend to vote for Mr. Clay at the ensuing election, taking it for granted, though the proceedings of the Baltimore convention have not reached here, that you will not be a candidate; and what few friends I have being mostly whigs, I am satisfied they would induce him to retain me in any office I might hold on his coming into power.

Thus, sir, I have told you frankly, what I want, & what I can do to obtain it. And now do you think there is any necessity for my coming on to Washington? I do not wish to spare the time, nor incur the expense of the trip if there is no hope of success. If I could receive any thing to aid my present low estate, no favor ever was granted that was more thankfully received, than I shall receive it; nor did the recipient of one, ever try harder to deserve it, than I shall try to deserve any that may be confer[r]ed on me.

I trust you will excuse me for the trouble of ["re" *canceled*] reading this letter, & if you should have a leisure moment ["&" *canceled*] to devote to one so humble, that you will write me an answer. With the greatest respect I am your ob[edien]t Servant, Allen Pierse.

[P.S.] I shall send this letter to Vicksburg to be mailed, but if you write me, please address me at this place.

ALS in ScCleA.

From T[HOMAS] M. RODNEY

Consulate of the United States of America
Matanzas [Cuba], June 4th 1844

Sir, I avail myself of an opportunity for Charleston to enclose to the Department copies of letters passed between this Consulate and the government of Matanzas in relation to Maurice Hogan a citizen of the U.S. and a coffee planter, residing near Cardenas, and now confined in prison at this place, and also a communication made to the government this morning in relation to Samuel Moffort [*sic*; Moffat] and William Bisby both American citizens, young enterprising men who have been treated in perfect wanton[n]ess of cruelty. The first of them is from one of the slave holding States and distinguished himself on his arrival in the Island, in March 1843, at the time of the negro insurrection at Bemba, (a few miles from Cardenas) by attacking on horse back, single handed and alone, and holding in check two or three hundred negroes. In this he was desperately wounded and will bear the marks to his grave, and it is not easy to discover why he has been so persecuted unless in spite to the gentleman (Mr. Phin[n]y also a citizen of the U.S.) on whose plantation he works at his trade of carpenter.

Mr. Phin[n]y is perhaps too free in his speech in this country and has brought upon himself the ire of the public functionary at Cardenas. His estate was made a scene of havock and confusion more than forty of his hands were desperately whipped Eight of whom died under the operation and in the end the old man was obliged to buy off, by paying thirty or forty onz's[?] to the Fiscal, or officer having his district in charge.

I hear of other American Engineers arrested and in prison in the country, on negro testimony, obtained by leading questions under the lash, but as yet have not been able to obtain the whole statement of facts.

In relation to the American sch[oone]r Cavallero alluded to in my last, as having arrived with a cargo of slaves, I learn that instead of sailing for Baltimore, she ran down to a small port to the westward of Havana where she now lies.

This vessel was purchased in Baltimore and sailed from New York on the 26th day of October last under the command of Morgan S. Gordon a citizen of the town of Portland, Maine. She obtained Portuguese papers on the coast, and either used her own register or one obtained in Havana, which was procured about two years since to suit a vessel of her class. Seven of the American crew died on the coast, and she landed at Camarioca 337 slaves. This information is derived from an unquestionable source, but, with the solemn assurance that the name must in no case be given.

I wait most anxiously the arrival of the ship of War, and live in the hope that when she does come we may be able to relieve our Countrymen from their present suffering condition. I have the honor to be your obedient servant, T.M. Rodney.

ALS (No. 19) with Ens in DNA, RG 59 (State Department), Consular Despatches, Matanzas, vol. 4 (T-339:4), received 6/17. Note: The Ens included letters from Rodney to Antonio Garcia Oña, dated 5/27, 6/3, and 6/4, relating to the arrest and imprisonment of Hogan, Moffat, and Bisby. The letter of 5/27 states that Hogan was arrested on 3/24 and charged with holding communication with his brother in New York. The letter of 6/4 reveals that Moffat and Bisby had been named as conspirators in the slave insurrection by a slave named Nicholas after he had received 1,200 lashes. The fourth En, from Oña to Rodney and dated 6/3, was a notice that the trial of Maurice Hogan would soon end.

To [JOHN TYLER]

Department of State
Washington, 4th June, 1844

To the President of the United States.

The Secretary of State, to whom was referred the Resolution of the Senate of yesterday, in Executive Session, requesting the President to communicate to that body "a copy of the letter from Messrs. Van Zandt and Henderson to Mr. Calhoun, calling his attention to the letter of Mr. Van Zandt of the 17th of February [*sic*], 1844, to Mr. Upshur, and to which Mr. Calhoun replies in his letter of the 11th of April, 1844"—has the honor to report to the President, that no such letter as that of which the Resolution requests a copy was addressed by Messrs. Van Zandt and Henderson to the Secretary of State, but, in the course of the negotiation of the Treaty for the annexation of Texas, those gentlemen orally invited the attention of the Secretary of State to the note of Mr. Van Zandt to Mr. Upshur, of the 17th of January last. Respectfully submitted. J.C. Calhoun.

LS in DNA, RG 46 (U.S. Senate), 28B-B12; FC in DNA, RG 59 (State Department), Reports of the Secretary of State to the President and Congress, 6: 108; PC in Senate Document No. 361, 28th Cong., 1st Sess., p. 1; PC in House Document No. 271, 28th Cong., 1st Sess., p. 99; PC in the Washington, D.C.,

Daily National Intelligencer, June 6, 1844, p. 3; PC in *Niles' National Register*, vol. LXVI, no. 15 (June 8, 1844), p. 233. NOTE: Tyler transmitted the above to the Senate on 6/4. The Senate resolution of 6/3 being responded to can be found in DNA, RG 59 (State Department), Miscellaneous Letters (M-179:104, frame 479), and in *Senate Executive Journal*, 6:305.

From [Capt.] Tho[ma]s W. Freelon, U.S.N., "U.S. Ship Preble, Aux Cayes," 6/5. Freelon explains that he has issued to Richmond Loring a provisional appointment as U.S. Commercial Agent at Aux Cayes and asks that the appointment be made regular. He encloses five letters between himself and William B. Gooch, the departing Commercial Agent, explaining the situation. ALS with Ens in DNA, RG 59 (State Department), Applications and Recommendations, 1837–1845, Loring (M-687:20, frames 78–84).

From Henry A. Holms, Baltimore, 6/5. He recommends Eneas McFaul, Jr., for an appointment to be the U.S. Consul either at Vera Cruz or at Laguna, Mexico. Holms considers McFaul to be a worthy gentleman whose extensive mercantile experience makes him well qualified for the position solicited. McFaul has been for many years a merchant in Baltimore but was born in Ireland. ALS in DNA, RG 59 (State Department), Applications and Recommendations, 1837–1845, McFaul (M-687:21, frames 301–303).

From Richmond Loring, Aux Cayes, 6/5. Loring requests the State Dept. to confirm his provisional appointment by Capt. Thomas W. Freelon to be U.S. Commercial Agent at Aux Cayes. He has served as Acting Commercial Agent during William B. Gooch's absences during the last year. ALS in DNA, RG 59 (State Department), Applications and Recommendations, 1837–1845, Loring (M-687:20, frames 76–77), received 7/3.

From J[AMES] I. McKAY, [Representative from N.C.]

Committee of Ways and Means, June 5, 1844
Sir, The Committee have received your Communication asking an appropriation for three volumes of the Documentary History of the Revolution. In the act of the 3rd of March 1843 there is a proviso

"that the materials which shall compose each successive volume shall before any appropriation is hereafter made for the Cost of the same be submitted to and approved by the Secretary of State for the time being." Will you be so good as to state whether the materials which compose the three volumes have been submitted to and approved by you, and also whether the parties [Matthew St. Clair Clarke and Peter Force] who stipulated to publish the Documentary History complied with the requisitions of said act in delivering to the Secretary of State a written agreement adopting as part of the said original articles the restrictions and limitations and making the same legally binding and operative as portions of the said Original articles, in all respects, as if they had been in terms incorporated into the same. Also whether the same was accepted and approved by the Secretary of State. With respect Y[ou]r Ob[edien]t Servant, J.I. McKay.

ALS in DNA, RG 59 (State Department), Miscellaneous Letters (M-179:104, frames 492–493).

To J[AMES] I. McKAY, "Chairman, Comm[ittee on] Ways and Means, H[ouse of] R[epresentatives]"

Department of State
Washington, 5 June, 1844

Sir: I have the honor to state in reply to your note of this morning, that [Clarke & Force] the parties stipulating to publish the Documentary History of the American Revolution, have executed an agreement, adopting, as part of the original articles, the restrictions and limitations required by the act of 3[r]d March, 1843, and that the same has been accepted and approved by the Secretary of State. It also appears that the materials for the 5th and 6th volumes were duly submitted to, and approved by, the Secretary of State for the time being—the previous four volumes having been printed prior to the date of the act referred to. I am, Sir, with great respect, Your obedient servant, J.C. Calhoun.

LS in DNA, RG 233 (U.S. House of Representatives), 28A-D30.6; FC in DNA, RG 59 (State Department), Accounting Records: Miscellaneous Letters Sent, 1832–1916, vol. for 2/1–9/30/1844, p. 212.

From STEWART NEWELL, [Galveston]

Consulate of the United States
Port of Sabine, Texas, June 5th 1844

Sir, I beg leave most respectfully, to enclose to the Department, Copies, of communications to the Legation, to this Country, and my answers thereto, and submit them for examination, by the Department, that the Hon. Secretary, may judge, if any thing is expressed, or implied, that savors of studied, or implied insult, to the Legation, as Gen[era]l [William S.] Murphy, has on more than one occasion, charged me with, and I will take occasion here, to remark, that the course pursued by him, towards me, may be, for the purpose of provoking something of that, from me but I have endeavoured to avoid it, and shall continue to do so, with a firm reliance, upon the liberality of the Department, in giving a proper consideration, to all or any of my communications, and that at least, my acts, may receive that charitable interpretation which they appear not destined, to receive, from this Legation at Texas.

On the 25th May Gen[era]l Murphy, returned me, as p[e]r Note No. 1 annexed, a Protest, prepared by me, against the interference ["in" interlined] of what was deemed by me, ["with" canceled] my Official duties. On the 28th May, Gen[era]l Murphy addressed me a Note, No. 2, and demanding Copies of all Papers & Documents, in my office, relative to the Case of the Steamer Scioto Belle, and which vessel, I gave a short notice of ["to" interlined] the Department, in my No. 15 [of 5/29], my answer to which demand, marked No. 3 [dated 5/28/1844], also enclosed, with a Copy of my Letter [of 6/2/- 1844] to Gen[era]l Murphy, accompanying the the [sic] Documents furnished him ["No. 4" interlined] and his reply [of 6/3/1844; "No. 5" interlined], also the original receipt, to which Gen[era]l Murphy takes offence, and the answer [of 6/5/1844] last addressed him, and which I hoped, would have proved sufficient to satisfy any reasonable person, as to my feelings, but this day, I have been informed, of a most uncalled for, and unjustifiable abuse, and attack upon me, and my official acts, contained in a Letter to Mr. [Archibald M.] Green, U.S. Consul at this Port.

The Department will readily perceive, how much injury could arise, to the Public or private duties of the Consulates, in Texas, under such feelings, as are evidently entertained, and openly expressed, by the Charge, while it is equally apparent, that good feeling, cannot, exist under such a state of affairs. I, much prefer laying such matters, before the Department, than to take any such measures, on my part, as the disposition, and acts towards me, from Gen[era]l Murphy, would seem to justify, and which if the Hon. Secretary, could see *for himself*, would better understand, than any Pen, can describe, and I shall continue my present course, under the circumstances, and communicate every new act, to the Department, which seem on the part of the Charge, as intended to interfere with, my Public duties, or private rights, and shall deem it sufficiently in time, for me, to resent them personally, when such aggressions, should be overlooked in a Charge, and which I, am too well convinced, will not be, for one moment by the Department.

The Hon. Secretary will find reference in Gen[era]l Murphy[']s Letter ["to Mr. Green" *interlined*] to certain difficulties, on the part of the Legation, to give Mr. Green, answers to his enquiries, for want of the proper Documents or Papers, relative to the case refer[r]ed to. These Papers were furnished, as required, and as named in the receipt now enclosed, and after returned to me, by Gen[era]l Murphy. This Gentleman, cannot at this late date, answer Mr. Green, yet some 2 or 3 weeks previous to my decission, in the matter, and ["at" *interlined*] an interview with the Owner of the vessel, who was seeking protection from me, as U.S. Consul, against a Man, then, as Master of said vessel, who was seeking an opportunity, to defraud the Owner, out of his vessel, at that time, Gen[era]l Murphy declined seeing any papers, stating he was well aware of all the facts, and that, *if I did not sell the vessel, immediately*, and pay the Crew, and claims, *he* Gen-[era]l Murphy, would have the vessel brought to Galveston, and sell her himself. His positive order to me, subsequently, was the same, and the Sale was made, with consent of the only real owners, or persons, who were likely to suffer in the matter.

Hoping the Department may entertain such proper views of this matter, as will do only justice to all concerned, I have the honor to be Most Respectfully Your Ob[edien]t Servant, Stewart Newell.

[P.S.] The Documents ordered by Legation, and returned to Consulate, are herewith Enclosed, to Department of State by, Very Resp[ectfull]y Your Ob[edien]t Serv[an]t, Stewart Newell.

ALS (No. 17) with Ens in DNA, RG 59 (State Department), Consular Despatches, vol. 1, Texas (T-153:1), received 6/24. NOTE: An enclosed receipt dated 6/1844 by Newell lists the documents requested by and sent to Murphy as "No. 1, Copy of Charter [of 4/1/1844] of Scioto Belle. [No.] 2, [Copies of] Letter[s] from Master & Owner to U.S. Consul & Petition of Crew relative to Wages [dated 3/16/1844, 4/17/1844, and 4/18/1844, respectively]. [No.] 3, Copies of Letters [of 4/18/1844] addressed to Master & owner by Consul, replies [of 4/18/1844] to same and Consular Entry of Notice of Sale &C. [No.] 4,

Copies of Depositions of James Taylor and Edmund Jones [dated 3/22/1844 and 3/23/1844, respectively], also receipt [of 5/3/1844] of George W. Phillips [for payment of wages]." The final enclosure, a "statement of affairs" of 6/3/1844 by Newell to the State Department, appears above under its own date.

F[rancis] W. Pickens, Edgewood, [Edgefield District, S.C.], to J[ames] Edward Colhoun, Pendleton, 6/5. Pickens has recently arrived home from [the Democratic National Convention at] Baltimore. "You saw what we have done at Baltimore. There was great excitement, and we overthrew [Martin] V[an] Buren forever. [James K.] Polk is sound & with us. Rallying on him will give a sound basis to move together on Mr. [John C.] Calhoun immediately after the election." Pickens discusses local politics and family affairs. "Judge [Daniel E.] Huger will certainly resign his seat [as Senator from S.C.] immediately after the adjournment of Congress or soon enough to notify the Legislature. I hardly think [George] McDuffie will resign at all. I think he is fond of his place. The Charleston Delegation have requested me, or at least the largest portion of them, to run for Huger's place. I shall leave it pretty much to Charleston." His crops are doing well. "I left Mr. Calhoun very well and he says we must go for Polk cordially &c. I think his situation in the Cabinet of a weak man very unpleasant." He sends regards to Floride [Colhoun Calhoun]. "Patrick [Calhoun] & John [C. Calhoun, Jr.] were[?] to start to the Rocky Mts. in a few days." ALS in ScU-SC, Francis W. Pickens Papers.

From C[HARLES] A. WICKLIFFE

Post Office Department
June 5th 1844

Sir, I have received and read to-day the communication of Mr. [Richard] Pakenham, Envoy Extraordinary and Minister Plenipotentiary of Her Britannic Majesty's Government to you of the 22d May, by you referred to me for information to enable you to reply to the same.

Mr. Pakenham desires to ascertain if it would be agreeable to the Government of the United States to enter into an arrangement for the transmission, through the United States to some point on the Canadian Frontier, of the British mails to and from Canada, which are now landed at Halifax, and thence forwarded through the British Provinces to their destination.

I am not aware of any objection to such an arrangement. By it the transmission of the British mail would be greatly expedited, without any possible disadvantage to the United States.

As the laws of Congress now are, this Department has not the power to make an arrangement such as seems to be contemplated by the British Government, viz. a transit of the British mail through the United States between Boston and Canada, under the British mail-lock. I would recommend that power be asked of Congress to authorize the Department to make such arrangement. This could be obtained by the passage of a joint Resolution in the following form:

"Resolved; by the Senate and House of Representatives of the United States in Congress assembled, That the Postmaster General be and he is hereby authorized to make such arrangements, as may be deemed expedient, with the Post Office Department of the British Government for the transportation of the British mail, in its unbroken state or condition between Boston and Canada."

The United States have now a daily line of mail transportation between Boston and St. Johns [New Brunswick], via Burlington [Vt.], in summer, and Highgate [Vt.] in the winter by which this mail could be transported with advantage to the British public and to the United States. Without some such general power as this, the only mode by which the British mail could pass between Boston and Canada, under existing laws, would be by mailing its contents at Boston at great expense and at an increased charge of postage, to be paid at Boston. This ["mode" *interlined*] would be wholly inconsistent with the object which the British Government is understood to have—that of expedition. The mode which could be adopted under the authority contemplated by the Resolution proposed, would greatly expedite the mail, and at much less trouble, cost and expense to the United States and to the British public.

If you concur with me in the views expressed, I would respectfully suggest that the President, by message, ask the consideration of Congress upon the propriety of passing a resolution or some other provision similar to that suggested. I am with high respect your Ob[e]d[ien]t serv[an]t, C.A. Wickliffe.

LS in DNA, RG 59 (State Department), Miscellaneous Letters (M-179:104, frames 493–495); variant FC in DNA, RG 28 (Records of the Post Office Department), Letters Sent by the Postmaster General, N.2:29–30.

To Col. [John J.] Abert, [Bureau of Topographical Engineers, War Department], 6/6. "Mr. Calhoun's respects to Col. J.B. [*sic*]

Abert, and desires the favour of an interview with him at the Department of State at the earliest hour that may suit his Convenience."
LU in ScU-SC, John C. Calhoun Papers.

To W[ILLIAM] S. ARCHER, Chairman of the Senate Committee on Foreign Relations

Department of State
Washington, 6th June 1844

Sir, In reply to your letter of the 3rd instant, asking for information in regard to the Sardinian mission, I have the honor to state that the motives for the establishment of that mission, and the advantages to be anticipated from diplomatic relations with Sardinia will be found clearly set forth in the papers accompanying the Treaty of commerce with Sardinia communicated by the President [Martin Van Buren] to the Senate, on the 24th January 1839, to which I beg leave to refer you. It may be proper to observe for the information of the Senate that Genoa, the Commercial capital of the Kingdom of Sardinia[,] is the largest commercial Emporium in the Mediterranean. It is the principal point from which the smaller ports of Italy, the Levant, and Africa are supplied with the Colonial products of this hemisphere.

Before the Treaty of 1838, the United States had comparatively, very little commerce with Sardinia, but that Treaty having encouraged our commerce by giving to it all the advantages which were previously enjoyed by national vessels, our trade there has been rapidly on the increase, as will be seen by the accompanying abstract from the consular returns of Genoa, from 1830 to 1843 inclusively. By this Treaty unusual facilities for the transit of the products of the United States, without liability to any duty, were secured, and the correspondence of this Department goes to show that many Cargoes of tobacco imported into Genoa have been carried in transitu through Sardinia into Lombardy and other places. American vessels arriving in Sardinia usually take in a part of a cargo consisting of medicinal articles, marble, in block or manufactured, olive oil &C. and then proceed to the ports of Sicily and the Levant, of Spain or of France to complete their Cargoes, so that return cargoes are rarely entered as coming from Genoa or Nice[,] which are the two principal ports [of Sardinia] on the continent. Our importations from the Kingdom of Sardinia consist, principally, in manufactured silks estimated at about 8,000,000 francs per annum and are received in transitu through France by Havre. The population of the Kingdom of Sardinia [is] 5,000,000. The greater portion of the supply of tobacco for that country is of American growth, the culture of the article being entirely suppressed. Formerly the article of Cotton consumed in that Country, the growth of the U. States reached its destination by the way of England, but the removal of the very onerous quarantine regulations which served to repress all direct commerce with America having been removed since the year 1838, the importation of that article has been constantly on the increase.

It is believed that the commerce between this Country and the Kingdom of Sardinia, considerable as it has already become, is susceptible of steady and important increase, not only in raw products, but also in the cotton manufactures of the United States. Hitherto the Coarser manufactures of Cotton for the poorer classes in Italy have been chiefly furnished from England, but as we already compete successfully with her in other parts of the world, in the supply of coarse cottons, it is believed that an extensive market will be found in the Mediterranean for similar goods of our manufacture. In view of the foregoing facts and considerations, as well as of others which will be obvious to all, it is the opinion of this Department that the public interests require that the Mission to Sardinia should be maintained. I have the honor to be, very respectfully Your Obedient Servant, John C. Calhoun.

FC in DNA, RG 59 (State Department), Domestic Letters, 34:224–226 (M-40: 32); PC in Jameson, ed., *Correspondence*, pp. 594–596.

From D[ABNEY] S. CARR

U.S. Legation
Pera [in Constantinople], June 6th 1844
Sir, In my No. 2 of the 3d of Febr[uar]y last, I informed the Department of the application which had been made to me, by the American Missionaries here, on behalf of their brethren in P[e]rsia. A short time ago I received the letter of which the inclosed paper marked A. is a Copy. At an early day after its receipt I addressed a note, of which paper marked B. is a Copy, to Mr. Titow, the Russian Minister near this Court, to which I received a reply of which the enclosed paper C. is a Copy. Mr. [A.L.] Holladay, who writes

me the letter for himself and brother Missionaries in Persia, I have known, personally, from his boyhood. He is a gentleman of distinguished intelligence and a member of one of the best famalies in Virginia. Indeed, the American Missionaries in the East, without one exception that I have heard of, are a credit to our Country.

Events of the deepest interest and greatest importance were happening and expected in the United States when the Arcadia Steamer left N. York on the 1st of May, as I glean from the meagre extracts of American news Copied into Galignani [a Paris monthly periodical], but I received not a single Washington or other American newspaper, although none had been forwarded me previously of a later date than the 20th of March. If it were not for Galignani (the subscription to which I dare say will not be allowed in my Accounts,) I should never hear any thing from the United States until weeks after it ceased to be *news* here. What the Diplomatic Corps here think of my ignorance of what is passing in my own Country I know not. It is not my fault, yet it is very mortifying to me, both on my own account and that of my Government. By the Arcadia I *might* have received papers &c. in *thirty five* days, whereas it is *seventy five* days since the date of the last paper received by me from Washington. I have the honor to be With great respect Your very ob[edien]t Serv[an]t, D.S. Carr.

ALS (No. 10) with Ens in DNA, RG 59 (State Department), Diplomatic Despatches, Turkey, vol. 10 (M-46:12), received 7/19; FC in DNA, RG 84 (Foreign Posts), Turkey, Despatches, G:133–134. NOTE: In En A, dated 3/28/-1844, A.L. Holladay described to Carr tensions between Roman Catholics and Nestorian Christians in Constantinople over ownership and use of a church.

From A[RCHIBALD] M. GREEN

Consulate of the U. States at Galvezton
Rep[ublic] of Texas, 6th June 1844

Sir, My previous communications in relation to the exportation of Cotton from Texas to the U.S. free of duty, anticipated the event which has actually occurred.

One of the Steamers trading between this & New Orleans brought five hundred bales of Cotton from N[ew] O[rleans] for shipment from this port to Europe.

This fact shows that better prices can be afforded; for the Cotton bought at the latter place, will bear the expense of being shipped to this. It is also worthy of remark as showing the advantage, which this port possesses over N[ew] O[rleans] on account of the saving in Towage up and down the river—worfage [*sic*], Tonnage & various other charges in the shipment of commodities for Europe and the receipt of goods in Exchange. I have the honor to be Sir most Respectfully Y[ou]r ob[edien]t S[ervan]t, A.M. Green.

[P.S.] My communication of the 28th May through error was not numbered. It should have been marked No. 37, which you will please have endorsed thereon. A.M. Green.

The U.S. Sloop of war Vincennes Capt. [Franklin] Buchanan and the Brig Summers Capt. [*blank space*; James T. Gerry] are off Galvezton Bar. Officers and Crews all well.

ALS (No. 38) in DNA, RG 59 (State Department), Consular Despatches, Galveston, vol. 2 (T-151:2), received 6/25.

From JAMES OMBROSI

Consulate of the United States
Florence, 6th June 1844

Sir, The present will serve to inform you that I have received several letters for Mr. Edward Gamage who has not yet arrived at this his Consular residence, nor have I received any accounts of him, though I have written to him & looking for his appearance from day to day. I have continued to verify the legality of the trade of the U.S. with Florence up to the present time.

It is now reported notwithstanding the appointment of Mr. Gamage that the Consul of Leghorn Mr. [Joseph A.] Binda intends to unite the Consulate of that port with Florence. The Manufacturers & Merchants of this latter place having been accustomed to have their Invoices certified by me here the last 25 years, the above intertention, if true, will be to them a most serious inconvenience, all of which is communicated for your information, and if the Department in reply should think fit to give their orders to the Writer (an old public Servant) on the Subject for his guidance, they will be gratefully received. I am, Sir, respectfully Y[ou]r Ob[edien]t S[er]v[an]t, James Ombrosi.

ALS in DNA, RG 59 (State Department), Consular Despatches, Leghorn, vol. 3 (T-214:3), received 7/29.

To S[TEPHEN] PLEASONTON, Fifth Auditor

Department of State
Washington, 6 June 1844

Sir, I have received your letter of the 28th Ultimo, and having taken into consideration the facts stated by you, in relation to the charges in the account of Mr. A[lbert] Smith, Commissioner to run and mark the Boundary line between the United States and Great Britain, for the compensation of Commissaries, I am of opinion that those charges ought to be allowed. I am, also, of opinion, that, in consideration of the reasons stated in Mr. Smith's letter of the 12th instant, the charges for compensation of civil Engineers may be admitted. I am, Sir, Your obedient Servant, J.C. Calhoun.

FC in DNA, RG 59 (State Department), Accounting Records: Miscellaneous Letters Sent, 1832–1916, vol. for 2/1–9/30/1844, p. 213.

From L[EMUEL] SAWYER

Newyork [City,] June 6, 1844

Dear Sir, As we are led to expect another move on the executive checker board soon after the adjournment of Congress, as the temporary president [John Tyler] uses men mer[e]ly as counters in keeping his game, by placing them to the right or to the left of the board, and as an unexpected nomination of a new candidate [James K. Polk] for the presidency on the part of the loco-Focos has taken place since my last letter, it may be thought respectful & perhaps obligatory on me to add my views on this new posture of the presidential question.

Excuse my asking you a pertinent question or two, without wishing the answer to escape your own bosom—in words ["but where" *canceled and* "as" *interlined*] I may be permitted to judge, by your conduct, that such answer will be exhibited as I have good grounds to anticipate, from some knowledge of your independent spirit & high sense of your official rights & dignity.

Do you ["meant" *altered to* "mean"] to allow John Tyler to remove from & appoint to, an office, within your rightful jurisdiction, without consulting you, or contrary to your advice? I ask this question, because it is understood that he intends to remove Silas M. Stilwell the marshall of this district, & appoint Gen[era]l [Philip?] Arcularius in his place. Now it does not become me to raise any objections to that course, for although Mr. Stilwell is a personal friend of mine, & a man of *very* superior talents, particularly as regards the science of finance, yet as he, with Edward Curtis & many other officers of the customs, of the higher grades, are friendly to the election of Mr. [Henry] Clay, it may comport with the policy of the executive to remove them, to make way for ["their" *canceled and* "his" *interlined*] friends. In case of the removal of Mr. Stilwell, & you think the appointment of his successor worthy your interposition, I beg leave to crave your special attention to one favour, that I ask at your hands, *but yours only*, that I may be provided for, as his deputy, & that it shall be insisted on as a condition to the new nomine[e]. At the time of making this request, I am aware that both Mr. Tyler & yourself know that I am no friend of his—& he knows the cause of my hostility, which you do not, but which I will summarily assign to you presently. But as regards him, I will promise this much, that if I am appointed the deputy, & United States Commissioner, in the place of Mr. Rapelje, I will do him as much good in his election to the presidency as any one of his most active partisans, which is just none at all, for he stands not the least earthly chance of getting a single vote. You know sufficiently, without any letters of recommendation, ["of" *canceled*] my suitableness for that station, perhaps above all others in your gift, from my long career in the halls of national legislation [as Representative from N.C.], of a tolerable acquaintance with the laws of the United States, their just interpretation, & their construction & application to the revenue system—by which I trust I might act the part of Judge, in many important questions which are of frequent recurrence before the tribunal of Mr. Rapelje.

You would have a friend *ever ready*, to defend you from all attacks with his utmost ability, & that such an adjutant is highly important here is but too evident on witnessing the lame & impotent defenses, when any are offered, in favour of the president, particularly ["on" *canceled and* "against" *interlined*] the late powerful & annih[il]ating ones in the columns of the [New York] Courier & Enquirer. All that pretend to draw the pen in his favour, are a few foreigners, of little standing or consequence, the conductors of the Auraro [*sic*; the New York *Aurora*]. He is now so low, that no one is found to do him reverence.

Now let me add a few words on my treatment at the hands of John Tyler—merely intermixing with it a simple declaration, that on the score of morality[,] respectability & private standing, I will compare with him or any of his cabinet, except yourself, whatever I might have been formerly when a member of congress. Of this declaration, the

truth of it may be verified by refer[r]ing to the rev[eren]d Mr. Van-
horsighe[?], of Capitol Hill, & Col. Sam[ue]l Starkweather now in
your city—who is also cognisant of the circumstance of my ill treatment at the hands of Mr. Tyler.

About the close of Mr. V[an] Beurens [*sic*] administration in
Dec[embe]r 1839—A friend of mine, Col. A[mbrose] C. Kingsland,
one of the wealthiest merchants here, who owns a sperm oil & candle
manufactory at Jersey City, informed me that Do[cto]r [John M.]
Cornelison, the deputy assistant collector of Jersey City had resigned,
& taken passage ["of" *canceled and* "in" *interlined*] his ship, the
Autumn on a south seas whaling voyage. I was mostly a resident,
during the summer season, ["of Orange," *canceled and* "at" *interlined*]
Orange Spring in N.J. ten miles distant. He advised me to apply for
it, as it was worth $1000 per an[num] & but little or nothing to do.
I did so, & he & his brother & a few friends from Jersey City joined
me in it, & wrote strong recommendatory letters. Mr. [Levi] *Woodbury* of the senate, whom I had obliged by vindicating his ["tittle"
canceled] title to a seat in the senate by several numbers in the
Journal of Commerce & the Express—which were sent him, (& which
were never answered, but which answered our purpose) went himself to the treasury department & urged my nomination. He informed me by letter, that the answer was, it was a sinecure, & would
be abolished. Some time afterwards Sam[ue]l [L.] Southard went
there & insisted upon the appointment of a friend of his, H. Southmayd. It was complied with. August 12 months ago Cols. James L.
Curtis & Sam[ue]l Starkweather had an audience with the president,
& stating the fact as to this appointment, & the president recognising
me as an old acquaintance, immediately promised to correct it, &
bade[?] his son John [Tyler, Jr.] to make a memorandum of the circumstance, with a view to refresh his memory when the case came
regularly before him. The loss of his wife came soon after & this
matter was postponed, out of delicacy to his feelings—at length word
was brought me that another candidate had taken the field & urged
the removal of Southmayd & the appointment of himself. I then
recalled the president[']s notice to his promise, & forwarded the letters of Mr. Woodbury to prove the injustice that was shewn me. He
refer[re]d the matter to John C. Spencer. Spencer wrote me about a
year since, that he had refer[re]d the question to Mr. Curtis the Collector, to report whether the office was a sinecure & ought to be
abolish[e]d. Curtis reported that *it was*, & gave his opinion that it
ought to be abolish[e]d. I have his correspondence on the subject.
I acquiesced, as a matter of course, under a sense of my duty to sub-

mit to what was supposed the necessity of the case demanded. What was my astonishment, & that of my friends to learn shortly afterwards, that this sinecure, was fill[e]d by a professed Tyler man from New Brunswick [N.J.]. It has created no little sensation where it is known, both in Jersey City & here, & is not calculated to enlist many recruits in the Tyler ranks. John C. Spencer has kept Woodbury[']s letters that I sent him, & has been treated as he deserves &—Curtis holds his office by the frail tenure of John Tyler[']s will, which is alone governed by his private interests. You see therefore that I have ample cause for my enmity to John Tyler, for *preventing* my obtaining that which had been promised me, *mer[e]ly* because he calculated that he could make more capital out of the new appointment—But which he will find by no means the case.

I find my letter extended to too great length to add any remarks under the head of the presidental question, merely reiterating my former opinion that Mr. Clay[']s election's assurance is "now doubly sure." Most Resp[ectfull]y, Your Ob[edient] se[rvan]t, L. Sawyer.

ALS in ScCleA.

From JAMES SOMERVALE

Clarksville, Va., June 6, 1844

Dear Sir, When in Washington, the other day, I would have called upon you; but I had an object in view, which I held of more importance than idle ceremony. That object is accomplished in the final termination of the fox-hunt, which I hope has ended, now & forever.

I was rather too much fatigued with that chace to begin a coon-hunt immediately, & therefore did not return thro' Washington.

Tho' clothed with powers to go into the [John] Tyler convention I did not unite in recommending that honest & sincere patriot for re-election; because I am not satisfied in my own mind that he does not come under the exclusion of The great one Term principle. As against an *ex president* he of course was my choice; but for the sake of *re-union* of the great Jackson & Calhoun party of 1828 I thought it best to wait the course of events & if possible to play into the hands of The *Vanburen* National convention.

Whether I shall unite with the Irish in rearing young Mocking Birds on Polke Berries, will depend greatly upon whom shall the management of The Republican Garden be devolved.

When you are informed that Tho[ma]s J. Green & Memucan Hunt, & the "Wretch" Bullock are my near relations, & that Gen. [J. Pinck-ney] Henderson the Texian minister is a lineal descendant of that great & good woman Granny Henderson of Nutbush N.C. who aided my mother in bringing me into this world—That one of my surviving sons is a Tyler man, the other a Calhoun man, & my excellent son in law a nephew of Col. John & Lewis Williams [former Representative from N.C.] & an own[?] uncle of young [Richard] *Dodge* lately ap-pointed to the military academy—you can have no doubt as to my wishes for the success & continuance of this administration. I often say to my neighbours; if we can[']t trust Calhoun & [Abel P.] Upshur; [William R.] King & Jno. Y. Mason; to say nothing of Tyler, [Richard M.] Johnson, [Lewis] Cass, [Andrew] Jackson, [James K.] Polk & [George M.] Dallas—in whom can we place confidence? The mother of all my children was an Irish woman from Limerick—& The Roman Catholics are many of them my near relations.

Make me a subscriber to the Spectator or the leading paper at Washington which goes for *Texas & The Navy*—Capt. *Tyler & Capt.* [Robert F.] *Stoc[k]ton*—or a reunion of the old Republican party upon the issues made by [Thomas] Jefferson in his Message of Nov. 8, 1808 & by the Republicans in Nov. 1828: if there be such a paper. I take the Madisonian & National Intelligencer.

And now with the most entire conviction in my own mind that our cause must triumph at the ensuing election, if the great leaders of the Republican party will bear & forbear; forget & forgive; & unite in a long pull & a strong pull & a pull altogether; for our great cause; Liberty of Speech, liberty of the Press; The liberty of conscience; the security of life & the stability of our glorious Federal Republic, I pray God to have you & yours in His Holy Keeping at all times! With great respect your old acquaintance, James Somervale, "The Nullifi-cationist."

[P.S.] (not for publication) But of course any man whose name is called is at liberty to read it.

P.S. "Moses & Aaron"[,] A Jewish Dynasty in America & above all places in Maryland, Virginia, New Jersey, Pennsyslvania & "The Good Old North State[.]" What can [North Carolinians George E.] Badger & [Kenneth] Rayner, & [Willie P.] Mangum & [James] Iredell [Jr.] & Shell & Shelton say to such a coalition[?] J.S.

ALS in ScCleA.

From Col. J[OHN] J. ABERT

Bureau of Topographical Eng[inee]rs
Washington, June 7th 1844

Sir, In answer to your enquiries of yesterday, I have the honor to state, that in compliance with an application from the State Department, and with the orders of the War Department, a party was detailed for the survey of the north eastern boundary line under the treaty, consisting of

Major J[ames] D. Graham
Capt. J[oseph] E. Johnston
1st Lieut. Tho[ma]s J. Lee
2d   "   Geo[rge] Thom
2   "   Geo[rge] W. [*sic*; G.] Meade

This party was organized early last spring, and duly reported to the State Department. Two plans of action had been suggested; one, that the party should report to the State Department and receive its directions from that Department. The other, that the State Department should apply to the War Department for the execution of the work, the results to be reported to the State Department when executed.

The second plan was in my judgment the best, but inasmuch as the surveys previous to the Treaty, had been made according to the first, it was decided that it was better to continue the same system.

The party was therefore, as before stated reported to the State Department, from which it receives all orders in reference to the work. The Honorable Secretary will therefore perceive, in answer to one of his enquiries, that directions for the party to take the field will have to be given by the State Department.

Since the first organization of the party, Lieut. (Brevet Capt.) Johnston has been relieved from it, also Lieuts. Lee and Meade. In their places Lieutenants [William H.] Emory and [William F.] Raynolds have been assigned, and Lieut. [Amiel W.] Whipple, now in New Hampshire will join the party whenever it takes the field, which will make the party equal to its original detail.

These Officers execute the drawings of their own work, but a draftsman might probably be required for the map of the whole, so as to keep the general map as forward as the detail protractings. Upon this point however Major Graham could speak more advisedly.

In reference to the "rank and file" ordered upon the duty, it is not in my power to give any information, as the applications for this portion of the detachment are unknown to me. Very respectfully

Sir Your Ob[edien]t Serv[an]t, J.J. Abert, Col. Corps T[opographical] Eng[inee]rs.

LS in DNA, RG 92 (Quartermaster General), Consolidated Correspondence, Boundary, Northeast Survey; FC in DNA, RG 77 (Office of the Chief of Engineers), Letters Sent by the Topographical Bureau, 1829–1870, 7:262 (M-66:7, frames 138–139).

To Asbury Dickins, Secretary of the U.S. Senate, [*ca.* 6/7?]. Calhoun asks Dickins to report, for the information of the President [John Tyler], "the vote of the Senate on the nomination of Mr. [Weston F.] Birch" to be U.S. Marshal in Mo. Abs in *The Collector: a Magazine for Autograph and Historical Collectors,* vol. LIII, no. 1 (November, 1938), p. 5.

From A[RCHIBALD] M. GREEN

Consulate of the U.S. of America at Galvezton
Repub[lic] of Texas, 7th June 1844

Sir, I beg leave to refer the enclosed documents to the Department for their consideration—without further comment from myself except to state that I learn from a reliable source that Gen[era]l [William S.] Murphy addressed his letter to me intending as he said, to publish it in the public Journals of the country and that it was shown to many before it reached my hands. My answer to Gen[era]l Murphy forwarded to him and returned to me is also enclosed. I have the honor to be most Respectfully y[ou]r ob[edien]t S[ervan]t, A.M. Green.

ALS (No. 39) with Ens in DNA, RG 59 (State Department), Consular Despatches, Galveston, vol. 2 (T-151:2), received 6/25. NOTE: An enclosed letter of 6/4/1844 from Murphy to Green, labelled "*Instructions* From the Legation of the U.S. to the Consulate at *Galveston Texas,*" is in response to a letter of 5/29/1844 from Green concerning the *Scioto Belle,* a trading vessel whose nationality is in question between the U.S. and Texas and which is the subject of a pending case in the Texas admiralty courts. Murphy strongly advises Green to take no action that would impair relations between the U.S. and Texas; he adds "Your suggestion or request that I would order the Commander of the United States Schooner Flirt, now in this port, to seize by force the Steamer 'Scioto Belle', Take her out of the hands of the proper officer of the Court in which she is libelled, and place her under the guns of the Flirt, cannot be entertained by me for a moment." He adds that Green has "no right under any circumstances that can possibly occur to command or direct any part of the naval or military arm of the United States, however small or wherever stationed." Murphy feels that the Texas admiralty court before which the *Scioto Belle* case is pending will render a fair judgment and directs Green to abide by the decision of the court. Murphy complains of Stewart Newell's discourtesy to him in this and other matters. Green's letter of 6/6/1844 to Murphy states in reply that he has every respect for the admiralty court and its presiding judge. Green studied the opinions of [Thomas] Jefferson when Secretary of State, and the writings of [James] Madison, [John] Adams, and Patrick Henry before determining on his course; he has followed the precedent established by Jefferson in 1793 in a case similar to that of the *Scioto Belle*. He adds that Murphy's views are "somewhat the same." Green continues, "If *occasion require* it and I should give an *order* to the commander of any portion of the naval forces that may be in the Gulf & off Galveston, however great or *small* and that *order* not obeyed by said commander—The responsibility will rest where it belongs without just reference to Your Excellency." Because of Murphy's declaration that he would remove the *Scioto Belle* from the care of [Stewart] Newell, U.S. Consul to Sabine, unless the vessel was sold and the claims against her paid, Green assumed that Murphy was familiar with the details of the case. He disclaims any interest in or responsibility for the discourtesy and bad feelings between Murphy and Newell and advises Murphy to address Newell directly on the subject.

From BEN E. GREEN

Legation of the U.S. of A.
Mexico, June 7th 1844

Sir, Col. [Gilbert L.] Thompson will inform you that Mr. [José M. de] Bocanegra's note of the 30th inst[ant], in reply to mine of the 23d, (copies of which I sent you by him) was received so late on the night before his departure, that I had barely time to make out a copy and to refer you, in my despatch [of 5/30], to him for particulars. It was my intention to leave it entirely to you to answer that note; but on further consideration I have thought it proper to rebut at once the admissions, which Mr. Bocanegra has so adroitly endeavoured to deduct from the conciliatory tone of my note of the 23d. This I have thought the more necessary, as the Mexican Govt. has sent copies of the correspondence to each of the Foreign Ministers here, & intend to publish it immediately. I presume that it is not intended to recede from the ground taken by Mr. [Abel P.] Upshur, in his despatch (no. 51) of 20th Oct. '43. No. 1, accompanying this, is a copy of my reply [of 5/31/1844], in which I have taken that despatch for my guide. I shall not follow the example of this Govt., by sending copies to the Diplomatic Corps; for I can not suppose that the U.S. recognize that, or any other tribunal, than their own sense of right and justice.

Judging from the newspapers received from the U.S., this Govt. is confident that the Treaty will be rejected by the Senate. Otherwise it would immediately agree to any reasonable proposition on the subject of Boundary. As it is, confident in the supposed hostility of the Senate to the President, it assumes a lofty & warlike tone, expecting to strengthen its popularity by making the Mexican people believe that the failure of the Treaty was owing to its firmness and threats.

The Congress has met for the purpose of increasing the army, and of providing means to invade and reconquer Texas. I do not yet, (nor do many here) believe that Santa Anna will be able to send another army thither. He will not trust his valuable person there again, and he will be very lo[a]th to send another general to do that, in which he failed. If he had all the disposition, he has not the money to raise the necessary army. On Saturday last, the Minister of the Treasury applied to a foreign merchant to loan the Govt. $9,000. The person applied to refused to loan the Govt. one dollar, but consented to loan the Minister $3,000 on his personal responsibility. The Mexican Minister of War, in a conversation with Gen[era]l [Waddy] Thompson [Jr.] before his departure, said: "Texas is gone from Mexico; it is impossible for us to reconquer her, and all we wish is to save the national decorum." Now, however, it is urged that the present is the time for effectual action against Texas. It is contended by those in favor of another effort, that this occasion must not be lost. Partisan spirit, they think, will prevent the annexation during Mr. Tyler's term of office. But the great importance of Texas to the security & commerce of the U.S. is appreciated here better, perhaps, than in the U.S.; and few, or none, doubt that the measure will soon be carried into effect, unless Mexico by immediate action shall recover possession, or at least those rights (if she ever had any), which she has lost by eight years of inaction.

In the mean time Santa Anna calls for $4,000,000 and 30,000 men. Commerce is so drained that it can stand no more exactions, and it is proposed to disencumber the clergy of this sum of $4,000,000. But Santa Anna wishes the Congress to propose the measure, and they insist on his doing so; and the matter now rests "in statu quo"; both Congress & Santa Anna standing in awe of the potent arm of the Church. The Clergy begin to feel very insecure, and are much opposed to any further attempt upon Texas. The rich and well informed of the laity are mostly of the same opinion, for they know that they will have to pay the costs, & that the contest is a hopeless one.

Some of Santa Anna's movements, however, bear the appearance of a determination to make one effort more for Texas. I learn from a priest, in the confidence of the ArchBishop, that 1,000 men have been secretly despatched from this city, via S[an] Luis Potosi; and that a larger body has been sent from Jalapa.

A messenger was sent in the last Havana Steamer to France and England; to arrange the difficulties with the former, and to ask aid of the latter. Upon the answer, which this messenger brings, will probably depend the course to be pursued in relation to Texas. If it is favourable, Santa Anna may carry his hostile threats into execution; if otherwise, he will probably consent to some amicable arrangement, reserving to himself the credit of having striven to the last for the "national rights and honor." I have the honor to be Very Respectfully Your ob[edien]t Serv[an]t, Ben E. Green.

[Enclosure]

Ben E. Green to J.M. de Bocanegra

Legation of the U.S. of A.

Mexico, May 31st 1844

The undersigned, Chargé d'affaires ad interim of the U.S. of A., has the honor to acknowledge the receipt of the note of His E[xcellency] J.M. de Bocanegra of yesterday's date; a copy of which has been forwarded by the undersigned to his Govt.

The undersigned might then, with propriety, content himself with simply acknowledging its receipt, leaving it to his Govt. to make what reply it may deem proper to so extraordinary a paper. He considers it alike unbecoming the importance of the subject, & his official character, as the representative of a powerful people, whose generosity Mexico has more than once experienced, to retort injurious epithets with H[is] E[xcellency] the Minister of Foreign Relations. But there is one passage in the note of H[is] E[xcellency] Mr. Bocanegra, which he feels called upon to notice. It is that, in which H[is] E[xcellency] says, "It is said by Mr. Green, by order of his Govt., that a treaty for the annexation of Texas to the U.S. has been agreed upon and signed;" & that, not to be wanting in the respect due to Mexico, he communicates to her Govt. that the U.S. have been forced, by their own safety & interests, to take this step &c &c. It being very remarkable that a document, which contains so express an acknowledgement—(of the rights of Mexico)—should be the same, that tramples upon those rights &c &c."

If H[is] E[xcellency] will refer to the note of the undersigned, he will see that he has entirely mistaken its import. The undersigned would be sorry to believe that H[is] E[xcellency] Mr. Bocanegra, has wilfully perverted his meaning.

The Govt. of the U.S. in making that communication to the Mexican Govt., neither directly nor indirectly, admits that Mexico is the legal proprietor of Texas, or that any apology or explanation is due to her, as such. The independence of Texas having been recognized, not only by the U.S., but by all the other principal powers of the world, most of whom have established diplomatic relations with her, she is to be regarded as an independent and sovereign power, competent to treat for herself; and as she has shaken off the authority of Mexico, and successfully resisted her power for eight years, the U.S. are under no obligation to respect her former relations with this country.

The Govt. of the U.S. however, has thought proper, in a friendly and candid manner, to explain to Mexico the motives of its conduct; & this it has thought due to Mexico, not as the proprietor of Texas, either de jure or defacto, but as a mutual neighbour of Texas & the U.S., and one of the family of American Republics.

The undersigned must be allowed here to express his surprise, that Mexico should renew her unfounded protests against the course, which the Govt. of the U.S. has thought proper to adopt, in relation to the Republic of Texas; and more especially, that she should address those protests to that community of nations, which by recognizing the independence of Texas, have long since denied to Mexico any right to complain. The ground assumed by H[is] E[xcellency] that Mexico by futile protests upon paper, could retain her rights over the territory of Texas, notwithstanding the facts, which are notorious, that Texas has declared and maintained her independence for a long space of years, that during that length of time Mexico has been unable to reconquer her, and has of late ceased all efforts to do so, is truly novel and extraordinary. As well might Mexico, by similar protests, declare that the world is her empire, and the various nations, who people it, her subjects; and expect her claim to be recognized.

The undersigned also begs leave to express his regret, that Mexico should have rejected in a manner so little to have been expected, the friendly proposal of the Govt. of the U.S. to settle the questions, which may grow out of the present relations, by amicable negotiations; and he takes this occasion to say, that if war does ensue, as threatened by Mexico, Mexico herself will be the aggressor, and will alone be responsible for all the evils, which may attend it. In the mean time the U.S. will pursue the policy, which their honor & their interests require, taking counsel only of their own sense of what is due to themselves and to other nations.

The undersigned has reason to congratulate his country upon this correspondence. For the world will now see that the U.S., throughout the whole course of this matter, have conducted themselves with honor, justice and forbearance towards Mexico; and that in so long deferring to do that, which the society of nations, by recognizing the independence of Texas, has declared it to be their right to do, and in forbearing to exercise that right, until it became necessary for their own security, they have done all, & more than Mexico could reasonably ask of them. The world will also know the manner, in which the friendly overtures of the U.S. have been met by Mexico, and if war, with its long train of evils, does result, will lay its censure where it will be justly due.

The undersigned avails himself of this occasion to assure H[is] E[xcellency] Mr. Bocanegra, of his distinguished consideration. Ben E. Green.

ALS with En in DNA, RG 59 (State Department), Diplomatic Despatches, Mexico, vol. 12 (M-97:13), received 7/12; FC (dated 6/2) in DNA, RG 84 (Foreign Posts), Mexico, Despatches, pp. 497–499; draft (dated 6/2) in NcU, Duff Green Papers (published microfilm, roll 5, frames 553–557); PEx with En in Senate Document No. 1, 28th Cong., 2nd Sess., pp. 57–59; PEx with En in House Document No. 2, 28th Cong., 2nd Sess., pp. 57–59.

From J[AMES] H. HAMMOND, [Governor of S.C.]

Silver Bluff, 7 June 1844

My Dear Sir, I inclose you as you request the letter of Mr. [Richard] Pakenham forwarded to me by mistake. I should have been glad to have seen his note in the case of [John L.] Brown. Having seen it you have no doubt formed a proper estimate of its character. But it strikes me as most extraordinary that a British Minister should in any capacity either officially or otherwise attempt to interfere in any terms whatever with the execution of ["the" *interlined*] Criminal Laws of the U.S. & [*one word canceled*] more especially of ["the" *canceled*] one of the States. The Federal Government would seriously endanger itself by such an interference with the mere municipal & domestic regulations of a State & is it to be tolerated from a Foreign Power for a moment or in the smallest degree? Henceforth we may expect all our laws about slavery to be discussed in the British Parliament, & perhaps made subjects of official correspondence. Unless Mr. Pakenham's ["int"(?) *canceled*] note was of such an inoffensive character as I can hardly conceive a note from such a source on such a subject to be, it constitutes an era in the slave question & ought perhaps to be known to the Slave holders to put them on their guard by pointing out fresh dangers. These dangers are accumulating so rapidly that a crisis seems to me inevitable & political events appear to march in concert to the same point. The Texas Question is an immense stride in that direction. You need not have the slightest apprehension that you will not be fully[,] promptly & enthusiastically sustained by the whole South in all you have done or propose to do in reference to it. There never was such unanimity on any question before, or such determination *to act*. I have no doubt that four fifths of the South prefer Texas to the Union & are prepared to stand by that issue if made. For one I think it the true issue & that it ought to be made speedily. We must set the North seriously to calculating the value of the Union or we shall be embroiled in a civil war & possibly to some extent a servile one, tho' of the latter I have not much apprehension. You have seen that almost every section of this State has spoken out very plainly. We had two meetings in this [Barnwell] district neither of which I could attend being confined to my bed as I still am to a great degree. You may depend on my warm & decisive co-operation in the matter in every way I can & to the utmost extent that it may be deemed proper for me to do so officially ["&" *canceled and* "or" *interlined*] privately.

The mail yesterday brought the results of the Baltimore convention. They are to my mind pregnant with the most important consequences. No union or enthusiasm can be excited among the masses for [James K.] Polk & [George M.] Dallas. They will lose New York, Pennsylvania, Virginia & Ohio & be worse beaten than [Martin] Van Buren was [in 1840]. But this will be the least important consequence I apprehend. The Northern Democratic Party will dissolve entirely I fear. Those who constitute it ["must" *interlined*] with a few exceptions ["must" *canceled*] become whigs or abolitionists or both, & never will again act with the Southern portion of the party as they never have done cordially or for any disinterested purposes. The Southern Democrats will I trust unite thouroughly & rally on the true principles & give us a sound party if a small one. Larger however than the Nullification Party & on substantially the same grounds. These consequences I apprehend from the Baltimore break up, for in that light I regard this nomination notwithstanding the momentary enthusiasm exhibited on the occasion. But others will follow. The pressure of the combined Democratic Party ["united" *canceled and* "removed" *interlined,*] what is to keep the Whigs to-gether[?] The spoils cannot do it long. Southern men cannot support the Bank, Tariff, Distribution & *Abolition*, which lies at the bottom of Whiggism & cannot be very long concealed. The Whig party will divide into northern & Southern, & then the fragments of both parties united, will present great Northern & Southern or essentially slaveholding & non-slaveholding parties seperated by ["gre" *canceled*] other great political principles resting both on constitutional & sectional differences. The break up of the Democratic Party into northern & southern divisions which I think inevitable from this nomination will end in arraying the two sections against each other permanently in our national contests, & this event will be precipitated & brought about almost at once by the Texas Question. What then becomes of the Union? It is gone. Unless there is some Providential interposition or I am wholly wrong in the signs of the times it cannot drag on ten years & may not two. I fear you will think my views visionary. God knows they are sincere & the promptings of my reason solely. I have as little personal & selfish interest in public affairs as any man alive, for I never expect to be promoted by any turn of events & do not desire ["it" *interlined*]. But from your ["present" *canceled*] position, whether you will or no you must occupy a prominent part in every thing & ["cannot" *canceled*] will ["not" *interlined*] do amiss to consider the remotest & most improbable consequences of passing events. Do let me know when & how I can serve you or the country. Very truly & sincerely Yours, J.H. Hammond.

P.S. I pardoned Brown simply because I was satisfied of his *innocence* & for no other reason whatever.

ALS (partly mutilated) in ScCleA; autograph draft in DLC, James Henry Hammond Papers, vol. 11; PEx in Boucher and Brooks, eds., *Correspondence*, pp. 237–238. NOTE: Words lost in the mutilations of the recipient's copy have been supplied from the draft retained by Hammond. John L. Brown had been convicted of slave stealing and sentenced to hang, under a law dating from early colonial times, after he had absconded with a slave woman, apparently his mistress, from a plantation near Winnsboro where he had been employed. Hammond pardoned Brown, seemingly in deference to South Carolina public opinion, which considered the punishment too severe for the case.

To HENRY W. HILLIARD, [Brussels]

Department of State
Washington, 7th June, 1844

Sir: I am directed by the President [John Tyler] to inform you that, upon the different considerations presented in your letters to him, he feels inclined to yield to your repeated solicitations to be permitted to resign the post of Chargé d'Affaires to Belgium, and to return to the United States in the course of the summer. In accepting your resignation, however, the President desires me to say, that he wishes you to remain at Brussels, until the arrival of your successor, inasmuch as the now pending question of the new duties upon American tobacco is one of deep concern to the citizens of this country, and, as he conceives, your presence at Brussels at such a juncture, may become indispensably necessary, not only to watch and protect this great interest, but also to enable you to afford the advantages of your experience to the person who may be selected to succeed you, on entering upon the duties of his mission. Final instructions and a letter of recall will probably be sent to you before or during the month of August.

Your despatch No. 16 was received at the Department on the 25th of March, and on the 20th of May following, there arrived, unaccompanied by any despatch, copies of a correspondence between your Legation and the Belgian Government, respecting the Belgian indemnity, which appear to be in continuation of that portion of the correspondence communicated in your No. 16, relating to the same subject. The new delays which it seems must still retard the payment of this indemnity, are profoundly regretted by this Government, and you will take an occasion, before your departure, to say so to the Minister of Foreign Relations [Alfred Joseph Goblet], and to urge upon him the importance of inciting the commission of liquidation to prompt action, so as to afford to the Government of the United States some assurance that these long deferred claims of our citizens will be settled within a reasonable period.

In this connexion, and in view of the correspondence which passed between you and the Belgian Government on the subject, by which it now appears that the late bill, before the Belgian Legislature, fixes new duties on the manufacture and on the retail of all tobacco, whether foreign or native, in Belgium, your attention is called to the instructions written to you under date of the 24th February last. As no acknowledgement of those instructions has been received, and as indeed your last despatch is dated two days after those instructions were written, it is apprehended either that they, or your acknowledgement of them may have miscarried—a duplicate of the despatch of this Department, containing them, is accordingly herewith transmitted. The Department is unable to give you any further instructions on the subject at present, but you will take care, from time to time, to apprise your Government of the exact state of this business, and of the steps you may take in regard to it, that any measures which occasion may require may be resorted to by the Executive, or Congress, to check injurious legislation on the part of Belgium, or to remedy the evils that may accrue to American commerce from the apprehended action of the Belgian Chambers.

The volumes described in your No. 16, were duly forwarded by the Consul at Antwerp [Samuel Haight] to Washington; and it is presumed you did not fail, on the occasion, to make due acknowledgements to the distinguished President of the "Commission Centrale" for them; and to inform him, that no authority is vested in the Executive to make any returns in the way of exchange for such favors from foreign Governments. The Department regrets the absence of any provision for such an object, and entertains the hope that in considering the subject at some future day, Congress may be convinced of the expediency and advantage of placing at the disposal of the President such publications of this Government as are desired by Mr. [Lambert A.J.] Quetelet. I am, Sir, respectfully, Your obedient Servant, J.C. Calhoun.

LS (No. 14) in DNA, RG 84 (Foreign Posts), Belgium, Instructions, 1:251–255; FC in DNA, RG 59 (State Department), Notes to Foreign Legations, Belgium, 1:48–50 (M-77:19). NOTE: An FC of Upshur's letter of 2/24 to Hilliard can be found in DNA, RG 59 (State Department), Notes to Foreign Legations, Belgium, 1:45–47 (M-77:19).

From JOHN HOGAN

Utica N.Y., June 7th/[18]44
Dear Sir, The office of Post Master of Utica (this city) expires in July. The President [John Tyler] will have to appoint some person to this office. The present incumbent A[ugustine] G. Danby is an applicant and is sustained by men from this State [former Representative Samuel] Beardsley[,] Gov. [William C.] Bouck & I believe *John* Cramer—that class of men are the same who got us ["into" *interlined*] the Syracuse Convention and are bitterly opposed to the Annexation of Texas. My own opinion is that they will support Mr. [Henry] Clay *such* is their opposition to the annexation of Texas. *I understand* that they are encouraging through *some creatures* from this State Mr. Tyler to get up a seperate Electoral Ticket in every State in the Union. In that way or by that course Mr. Clay would carry every State & they would defeat indirectly the Texas question. *The mere* suggestion is sufficient *for you to penetrate them all*[.] With few *exceptions* that class of Gent[lemen] called Old Hunkers are bitterly

hostile to the annexation of Texas and unless Mr. Tyler is careful of those men he will give Mr. Clay 20,000 in this State[.] They are desperate in their efforts[.] You see that they have courted & got the Abolitionists & they are all Tarriff men all pretty much ["are"? *interlined*] engaged in manafacturing [*sic.*] It is their interest that Mr. Clay should be elected to affect[?] Texas & the Tariff & sustain the Abolitionists[.] It is your duty allow me to say to look to those men[.] The best part of your life and all your energies have been devoted to your country & a little more & we will be successful. We have done one great thing by the Convention. Let us now not loose by entriage [intrigue?] what we have achieved. *Depend* upon what I say to you that the ultra V[an] B[ure]n men will defeat [James K.] Polk & Tyler and all of us if they can[.] Their c[r]eatures *are now around you.* I wish I could by [*sic*] in Washington for three months to direct the contest[.] *In this State* I am fearful that our victory will be *turned to* ["our" *interlined*] *overthrow.* I look with the greatest apprehension to the result[.] It is idle for you to say my dear Sir that you will take no part with matters of office with the President[.] The time may not be far distant when things will occur that will *gaul* you to the quick & your country[.] Then and not until then will you see the fatal error you are committing now. You know that we have to contend with Mr. Clay[']s friends & Mr. V[an] B[u]r[e]n[']s friends on the Texas & Tarriff questions *therefore* let me beg of you to *reflect deeply*[.] If we loose Texas the South is reduced[;] if we gain Texas our country is *Free* & its institutions[.] *Texas now or never* with that question so vital in itself to the perpituity of our institutions every other thing should be lost sight of[.] If Texas is annexed the Abolitionists are prostrate[;] Texas defeated the Abolitionists *triumphant.* As small as those appointment[s] may be considered they may change the institutions of our country[.] If those men cannot be dislodged from the President[,] Mr. Clay[']s Election is sure. Your ob[edien]t Ser[van]t, John Hogan.

ALS in ScCleA. NOTE: This letter is marked *"private matters"* on the cover. An AEU by Calhoun reads: "Mr. Hogan relates to the Post office at Utica."

From Ja[me]s M. Hughes, [Representative from Mo.], 6/7. He recommends Robert C. Ewing for appointment as U.S. Marshal for Mo. in place of W[eston F.] Birch who has been rejected by the Senate. "The Appointment would give Entire satisfaction to our friends in Mo." ALS in DNA, RG 59 (State Department), Applications and Recommendations, 1837–1845, Ewing (M-687:10, frames 362–363).

From RICHMOND LORING

Aux Cayes, 7th June 1844

Sir, In view of the extensive commercial interests at stake in this Island, I would respectfully request that a small squadron of a few light vessels be stationed here to protect American interest in this Island, and as Tho[ma]s W. Freelon Esq. commanding the U.S. Ship Preble, has interested himself so much in the preservation of the property of the Americans and other foreigners residing ["here" *interlined*], I would respectfully request the Squadron may be placed under his command. I have the honor to be, Very respectfully, Y[ou]r most ob[edien]t Serv[an]t, Richmond Loring, Acting Commertial Agent Aux Cayes.

LS (No. 1) in DNA, RG 59 (State Department), Consular Despatches, Aux Cayes, vol. 2 (T-330:2), received 7/3.

To J[AMES] I. MCKAY, Chairman Committee of Ways and Means, House of Representatives

Department of State
Washington, 7 June 1844

Sir, I have the honor to invite your attention to the appropriation for the Relief and protection of American Seamen in foreign Countries. It has been reduced in the bill as now before the House to $30,000.

There was appropriated for the year ending 30th instant $90,500. When the first appropriation was made there were draughts of the Consuls lyeing unpaid to the amount of $15,358.59, leaving available for the year ending 30th instant $75,141.41. Of that appropriation there now remains in the Treasury $12,000 which will not, probably, be more than sufficient to meet the draughts that will appear before the end of the month.

It must, therefore, be evident, that the sum of $75,000, as estimated, will not be too great for the demands of the fiscal year ending on the 30 June 1845.

It can scarcely be expected that the bill, No. 374, now before the House, should it become a law, will curtail very materially the amount required for the relief of Seamen. It cannot, however, have any effect at distant Consulates, where the heaviest expenditures occur, for several months.

The act dispensing with the exaction of three months wages in certain cases upon the discharge of Seamen was passed in July 1840. It could not have had a general operation until the year 1841; Yet the appropriations for the relief of Seamen had been steadily on the increase from the year 1830, when the amount was $15,000[,] to 1840, when it was $40,000. When the latter amount was appropriated, draughts were lyeing unpaid on this Department to the amount of $9827.81 besides those in the hands of individuals. The amounts of draughts lyeing over each ["subsequent" *interlined*] year awaiting the passage of an appropriation has been greater, and should the appropriation be now reduced to $30,000, the amount of draughts that may be unprovided for before another would be made, would ["be" *canceled*] probably be much greater than it has yet been.

The duty of Consuls in providing relief to destitute American seamen is prescribed by laws. In its performance they necessarily advance their own funds, and, draw upon this Department for reimbursement. It cannot be necessary for me to urge the necessity of making provision for those draughts. To do so seems to be the dictate of policy as well as justice. A contrary course may be productive of incalculable evils. I have the honor to be, Your Ob[edien]t Servant, J.C. Calhoun.

LS in DNA, RG 233 (U.S. House of Representatives), 28A-D30.6; FC in DNA, RG 59 (State Department), Accounting Records: Miscellaneous Letters Sent, vol. for 2/1–9/30/1844, pp. 215–[217].

From J[AMES] I. MCKAY

[Washington,] June 7th 1844
Sir, In your letter of April 3rd 1844 transmitting to the Committee of Ways & Means copies of letters from the Senators & Representatives of the State of Maine & of Mr. S[amuel L.] Harris agent of that agent [*sic*], in relation to the necessity of a further appropriation to satisfy the claims of that State &c, you neither recommend that such appropriations should be made or express any opinion as to the character of the claims yet to be satisfied. Will you be pleased to inform me, whether any preliminary examination, has been made of the claims, by the proper officers of the Treasury & whether they are satisfied that the whole or what part of them are embraced within the stipulations of the Treaty of Washington. An early answer is requested. Y[ou]rs Respectfully, J.I. McKay.

ALS in DLC, United States Finance Collection. NOTE: A State Dept. Clerk's EU reads "Referred to the Fifth Auditor who is requested to report to this Department without delay." Another Clerk's EU reads "Mr. Calhoun replied to same date."

To W[illie] P. Mangum, [Senator from N.C. and] President [Pro Tempore] of the Senate, 6/7. "I herewith transmit the Corrected Map of Texas—together with the accompanying Papers, marked 1 and 2, which may serve to explain the corrections." LS in DNA, RG 46 (U.S. Senate), 28B-B12.

From S[TEPHEN] P[LEASONTON]

Tr[easury] Dept., 5th A[uditor's] O[ffice]
June 7, 1844

Sir, I have the honor to State in reply to the letter of the Hon. [James I.] McKay [Representative from N.C.] of this date which you referred to me that in September last accounts ["against" *canceled and* "of" *interlined*] the State of Maine against the United States under the Treaty of Washington were adjusted and allowed at this office to the Amount of $206,934 73/100 being equal to the Sum appropriated by the Act of March 3d 1843 in Satisfaction of said accounts.

In the accounts presented was an additional Sum of $6110 26/100 which was not allowed for want of an appropriation & the authority of Law.

Subsequent to the above Settlement the Agent of Maine filed in this Office a Statement of further claims on the part of Maine under the Treaty but without attaching the Amount which it was stated ["it" *canceled*] was not then ascertainable. It is not known therefore at this office what amount is still claimed by Maine or what sum may be admissable & for which provision ought to be made by Law. S[tephen] P[leasonton].

FC in DNA, RG 217 (U.S. General Accounting Office), Fifth Auditor: Letters Sent, 5:130–131.

A[ndrew] Stevenson, [former Speaker of the U.S. House of Representatives and Minister to Great Britain], Richmond, to F[rancis] J. Grund, Washington, 6/7. Stevenson states that he is "surprised" to learn that Grund has been accused of being "friendly to *Abolition*." He "cannot but suppose, that there must be some strange misapprehension on the subject" and hopes that Grund will experience no difficulty in being confirmed by the Senate as U.S. Consul at Antwerp. [This document, found among Calhoun's papers, was perhaps given to him by Grund.] ALS in ScCleA.

From W[illia]m Wilkins, Secretary of War

War Department
June 7th 1844

Sir, Believing it possible the measures of the officer commanding the 1st Military Department of the Army at Fort Jesup in Louisiana may become a subject of inquiry, through the Department of State, by the Texian authorities, I respectfully enclose herewith copies of the report and papers transmitted by Colonel D[avid] E. Twiggs to the Adjutant General of the Army [Roger Jones] on the 14th of May last, together with a copy of the orders given [to Twiggs on 6/6] in the case, through the Adjutant General by this Department. Very respectfully Your Ob[edien]t Serv[ant], Wm. Wilkins, Sec[retar]y of War.

LS with Ens in DNA, RG 59 (State Department), Miscellaneous Letters (M-179:104, frames 506–514); FC in DNA, RG 107 (War Department), Letters Sent by the Secretary of War, 25:340 (M-6:25). Note: The Ens concern a detachment of U.S. troops crossing the Sabine from La. into Texas territory in pursuit of marauders who were at work on both sides of the border, an operation undertaken partly at the request of a Texan justice of the peace. Jones approved Twiggs's orders for the pursuit with a caution about respect for the international boundary.

From Tho[ma]s J. Green, "(Private)"

Velasco Texas, June 8th 1844

Dear Sir: You have doubtless often been informed of the abideing interest which a large majority of this community have felt in the question of "annexation." Since the manifestation of op[p]osition to it in the U.S. and particularly from Messrs. [Henry] Clay and [Martin] Van Buren, the question is fast looseing ground here; and I am satisfied that the disgust created throughout the Texas public by those gentlemen, will in the event of either of their elections to the

Presidency, make a decided majority of our people opposed to the measure. I believe that your election to the Presidency can *only* effect it.

If then it is a matter of such vital concernment to both nations, is it not right that all lawful and constitutional means should be imployed in its accomplishment? If I am answered in the affirmative I believe that it may be thus effected.

John C. Calhoun, has sufficient popularity with the people of Texas and sufficient weight of character with the people of the U.S. united with his determined energy upon the question to ["accomplishment" *altered to* "accomplish it"]. His friends in So[uth] Ca[rolina,] Georgia, Alabama, Miss. & Louis[i]ana, and perhaps elsewhere, will give him the third highest electoral vote. Clay, *will* run, Van Buren, *should* run; and if neither the latter or Calhoun can get Penn. [James] Buccanhan, or some *fourth* man should do so. Clay, Van Buren, and and [*sic*] Calhoun, over in the house of representatives, there would be a constitutional election determined between them upon the paramount political question of the nation. Is it not better that such should be the result, than that the nation should be humbug[g]ed with the mockery of an uneaquelly represented and fraudulently contrived convention. I am settled in the opinion that the greater patriotism is to settle the election by the house of representatives, and break up such a mammoth fraud, such a wicked offspring of the old *Congressional Caucus*; and that John C. Calhoun, should not withhold his name from his friends.

These condenced thoughts are the unsolicited and candid opinions of his warmly devoted political and personal friend, Thos. J. Green.

ALS in ScCleA.

From A. N. MONTGOMERY

Jacksboro, Campbell County Ten[n.]
June 8[t]h 1844

D[ea]r Sir, I have Commenced a suit In the Federal Court at Wythe In the State of Virginia for a Tract of Land on Ready Creek Containing 640 Acres Against the Crockets[.] My Grand Father Hugh Montgomery I am told purchased this Land from your father who holds among his papers the original Grant[.] I am advised that you have the Care of your father[']s papers[;] if so I would be glad to obtain the possession of It through you[.] My Grand father gave my father a Life Estate in it ["at" *interlined*] his death he Devised it to me[.] Under the laws of Virginia I am Compel[l]ed to have the original Grant If I can precure [*sic*] It[;] If not I can precure a coppy at Richmond as I am compel[l]ed to shew a Clear Chain of Title down to this date you will therefore see my object in wanting the Grant[.] I hope you will have the goodness to give me Every information [on] this subject & Oblige yours with the Highest respect & Esteem, A.N. Montgomery.

ALS in ScCleA. NOTE: An AEU by Calhoun reads "Mr. Montgomery[,] relates to the grant of a tract of land sold by my father in Virginia to his Grandfather."

To [JOHN TYLER]

Department of State
Washington, 8th June, 1844

To the President of the United States.

The Secretary of State, to whom was referred the Resolution of the House of Representatives of the 29th of April last, requesting the President to communicate to the House, "copies of such portions of the correspondence, public or private, in the years 1816, 1817, 1818, 1819 and 1820, between our Ministers at the Court of Madrid and the Department of State, between those Ministers and the Spanish Secretaries of State, and between the Department of State and the Spanish Ministers accredited to this Government, and which correspondence may not have been hitherto communicated to either House of Congress and published under the authority of either["]—has the honor to submit to the President the accompanying copies of documents, of which a list is annexed, which appear to embrace all the papers called for by the Resolution. J.C. Calhoun.

LS in DNA, RG 233 (U.S. House of Representatives), 28A-E1; FC in DNA, RG 59 (State Department), Reports of the Secretary of State to the President and Congress, 6:112–113; PC with Ens in House Document No. 277, 28th Cong., 1st Sess., pp. 1–51. NOTE: Tyler transmitted this letter to the House on 6/8 with copies of 42 documents enclosed. The House Resolution to which the above was a response can be found in DNA, RG 59 (State Department), Miscellaneous Letters (M-179:104, frame 264) and in *House Journal*, 28th Cong., 1st Sess., p. 858.

To [JOHN TYLER]

Department of State
Washington, June 8th 1844

To the President of the United States—

The Secretary of State to whom was referred the Resolution of the Senate of the 7th Inst[ant] requesting the President "to inform the Senate whether Mr. Duff Green was employed by the Executive Government in Europe during the year 1843, and if so, to communicate to the Senate a copy of all the correspondence of said Mr. Green in relation to the annexation of Texas which may have been received from him, if any"—

Has the honor to report that there is no communication whatever, either to, or from Mr. Green in relation to the annexation of Texas to be found on the files of this Department.

Respectfully submitted. J.C. Calhoun.

LS in DNA, RG 46 (U.S. Senate), 28B-B12; FC in DNA, RG 59 (State Department), Reports of the Secretary of State to the President and Congress, 6:110; PC in House Document No. 271, 28th Cong., 1st Sess., p. 101. NOTE: This letter was transmitted by Tyler to the Senate on 6/10. The Senate resolution of 6/7 can be found in DNA, RG 59 (State Department), Miscellaneous Letters (M-179:104, frames 505–506) and in *Senate Executive Journal*, 6:310.

SYMBOLS

The following symbols have been used in this volume as abbreviations for the forms in which papers of John C. Calhoun have been found and for the depositories in which they are preserved. (Full citations to printed sources of documents, some of which are cited by short titles in the text, can be found in the Bibliography.)

Abs   —abstract (a summary)
ADS   —autograph document, signed
ADU   —autograph document, unsigned
AEI   —autograph endorsement, initialed
AES   —autograph endorsement, signed
AEU   —autograph endorsement, unsigned
ALS   —autograph letter, signed
ALU   —autograph letter, unsigned
CC   —clerk's copy (a secondary ms. copy)
CCEx   —clerk's copy of an extract
CtY   —Yale University, New Haven, Conn.
CU   —University of California-Berkeley
DLC   —Library of Congress, Washington, D.C.
DNA   —National Archives, Washington, D.C.
DS   —document, signed
En   —enclosure
Ens   —enclosures
EU   —endorsement, unsigned
FC   —file copy (usually a letterbook copy retained by the sender)
LS   —letter, signed
LU   —letter, unsigned
M-   —(followed by a number) published microcopy of the National Archives
MdBJ   —The Johns Hopkins University, Baltimore, Md.
Me-Ar   —Maine State Archives, Augusta
MHi   —Massachusetts Historical Society, Boston
NcD   —Duke University, Durham, N.C.
NcU   —Southern Historical Collection, University of North Carolina at Chapel Hill
NhHi   —New Hampshire Historical Society, Concord
NjMoN   —Morristown National Historical Park, Morristown, N.J.
NN   —New York Public Library, New York City
PC   —printed copy
PDS   —printed document, signed
PEx   —printed extract
PHi   —Historical Society of Pennsylvania, Philadelphia

751

Symbols

RG — Record Group in the National Archives

ScCleA — Clemson University, Clemson, S.C. (John C. Calhoun Papers in this repository unless otherwise stated)

ScU-SC — South Caroliniana Library, University of South Carolina, Columbia

T- — (followed by a number) published microfilm of National Archives

Tx — Texas State Library, Austin

TxU — Barker Texas History Center, University of Texas at Austin

ViHi — Virginia Historical Society, Richmond

ViU — University of Virginia, Charlottesville

BIBLIOGRAPHY

◫

This Bibliography is limited to sources of and previous printings of John C. Calhoun documents in this volume.

Aderman, Ralph M., and others, eds., *Letters [of Washington Irving]*. 3 vols. Boston: Twayne, 1978–1982. (Vols. 23–26 of *The Complete Works of Washington Irving*.)

Boucher, Chauncey S., and Robert P. Brooks, eds., *Correspondence Addressed to John C. Calhoun, 1837–1849*, in the *American Historical Association Annual Report* for 1929 (Washington: U.S. Government Printing Office, 1930).

Bourne, Kenneth, ed., *British Documents on Foreign Affairs. Reports and Papers from the Foreign Office Confidential Print*. Part One, Series C: *North America, 1838–1914* (4 vols. Frederick, Md.: University Publications of America, 1986).

British and Foreign State Papers (170 vols. London: HMSO, 1812–1968), vols. 33 and 34.

Carter, Clarence E., and John Porter Bloom, eds., *The Territorial Papers of the United States*. 28 vols. to date. Washington: U.S. Government Printing Office, 1934–.

Charleston, S.C., *Courier*, 1803–1852.

Charleston, S.C., *Mercury*, 1822–1868.

Charleston, S.C., *Southern Patriot*, 1814–1848.

The Collector: A Monthly Magazine for Autograph and Historical Collectors. New York, 1887–.

Congressional Globe . . . 1833–1873 . . . . 46 vols. Washington: Blair & Rives and others, 1834–1873.

Crallé, Richard K., ed., *The Works of John C. Calhoun*. 6 vols. Columbia, S.C.: printed by A.S. Johnston, 1851, and New York: D. Appleton & Co., 1853–1857.

Davids, Jules, editorial director, *American Diplomatic and Public Papers: The United States and China*, Series I [1842–1860], 2 vols. Wilmington, Del.: Scholarly Resources Inc., 1973.

Edgefield, S.C., *Advertiser*, 1836–.

Garrison, George P., ed., *Diplomatic Correspondence of the Republic of Texas*, in the *American Historical Association Annual Report* for 1907, vol. II, and for 1908, vol. II. Washington: U.S. Government Printing Office, 1908–1911.

Hammond, George P., ed., *The Larkin Papers. Personal, Business, and Official Correspondence of Thomas Oliver Larkin, Merchant and United States Consul in California*. 11 vols. Berkeley: University of California Press, 1951–1968.

Jameson, J. Franklin, ed., *Correspondence of John C. Calhoun*, in the *American Historical Association Annual Report* for 1899 (2 vols. Washington: U.S. Government Printing Office, 1900), vol. II.

London, England, *Times*, 1785–.

Manning, William R., ed., *Diplomatic Correspondence of the United States: Canadian Relations, 1784–1860.* 4 vols. Washington: Carnegie Endowment for International Peace, 1940–1945.

Manning, William R., ed., *Diplomatic Correspondence of the United States: Inter-American Affairs, 1831–1860.* 12 vols. Washington: Carnegie Endowment for International Peace, 1932–1939.

Meyer, Isidore S., ed., *Early History of Zionism in America.* New York: Arno Press, 1977.

Moltmann, Gunter, "Eine Deutschland-Korrespondenz John C. Calhouns aus dem Jahre 1844," in *Jahrbuch fur Amerikastudien,* vol. 14 (1969), pp. 155–166.

New Orleans, La., *Louisiana Courier,* 1807–1860.

New York, N.Y., *Evening Post,* 1832–1920.

Niles' Register. Baltimore, 1811–1849.

Norwood, John Nelson, *The Schism in the Methodist Episcopal Church, 1844: A Study of Slavery and Ecclesiastical Politics,* in the *Alfred University Studies,* vol. I (Alfred, N.Y.: Alfred University, c. 1923).

Richmond, Va., *Enquirer,* 1804–1877.

Sioussat, St. George L., "John Caldwell Calhoun," in *The American Secretaries of State and Their Diplomacy,* ed. by Samuel F. Bemis, vol. 5 (New York: Alfred A. Knopf, 1928), pp. 125–233.

Tyler, Lyon G., *The Letters and Times of the Tylers.* 3 vols. Richmond: Whittet & Shepperson, 1884–1896.

U.S. House of Representatives, *House Documents,* 28th and 29th Congresses.

U.S. House of Representatives, *House Journal,* 28th Congress.

U.S. House of Representatives, *House Reports,* 28th and 29th Congresses.

U.S. Senate, *Journal of the Executive Proceedings of the Senate of the United States, 1789–1852.* 8 vols. Washington: U.S. Government Printing Office, 1887.

U.S. Senate, *Senate Documents,* 28th and 29th Congresses.

U.S. Senate, *Senate Journal,* 28th Congress.

Washington, D.C., *Daily National Intelligencer,* 1800–1870.

Washington, D.C., *Madisonian,* 1837–1845.

Washington, D.C., *Spectator,* 1842–1844.

Washington, D.C., *The Globe,* 1830–1845.

INDEX

⑪

Abbeville District, S.C.: 580, 686.
Abbott, Amos: to, 198.
Abell, Alexander G.: mentioned, 698.
Aberdeen, Lord: from, 53; mentioned, 12, 55–56, 61, 125–128, 141–142, 154–157, 186, 243–244, 263, 273–274, 278, 284, 286, 288, 326–327, 346, 349, 351, 370, 377, 392–393, 410–411, 440, 494, 520–522, 528, 544–545, 583, 649, 666–667, 682–683, 697; to, xii note, xxv note, 331.
Abert, John J.: from, 198, 732; to, 722.
Abolition: xxv–xxvii, 22, 53–56, 76, 78, 144, 152, 154–158, 160, 191, 224–229, 243–244, 253–254, 263–264, 268, 273–278, 283–284, 286–288, 301, 304, 341, 346, 348–352, 358, 365, 370, 373–383, 393, 404–405, 408–409, 411–412, 429–435, 439–440, 444, 463–464, 466–468, 472–473, 484, 494–496, 510, 532–534, 544–545, 555, 562–564, 583–584, 599, 623–624, 628–630, 635, 649–650, 668–670, 672, 690–691, 704, 707–708, 738–740, 743, 746–747.
Acaau: mentioned, 492–493, 566–568, 600.
Academy of Natural Sciences: 463.
Acapulco, Mexico: 294.
Acosta, Joaquin: mentioned, 15–16, 18, 69, 71–72, 386–388.
Adam, Charles: from, 451; mentioned, 68, 360.
Adams, James A.: mentioned, 609.
Adams, James H.: mentioned, 563.
Adams, Jasper: mentioned, 484–485.
Adams, John: mentioned, 149, 374, 734.
Adams, John Quincy: mentioned, 127, 374–376, 379, 466, 495, 562, 619.

Adams-Onís Treaty: 64, 220, 375, 466, 749.
Adams, Placidia Mayrant: mentioned, 485.
Addington, Henry U.: mentioned, 154.
"Address of Mr. Calhoun to His Political Friends and Supporters": mentioned, 146, 153, 268, 473, 485.
Admiralty law: 734.
Africa: xix, xxxiii, 25–26, 34, 55–58, 78, 90, 136, 141, 227–228, 243–244, 260, 276–277, 311, 349, 360, 375–376, 378, 381, 405–406, 430–432, 434, 453–454, 461–463, 531–533, 560, 606, 610, 629–630, 632, 715–716, 723.
Agriculture: in Calhoun family, 580, 636, 694, 709; mentioned, 100, 301, 421, 434, 474, 526, 553, 617, 689, 721; Southern, 157, 179, 194–195, 204, 254, 359, 373, 665.
Aguirre, Maximo de: mentioned, 134–135.
Aiken, S.C.: 201.
Alabama: 35, 83, 168, 189, 211, 264, 291, 441–442, 471, 504, 538–539, 556, 614, 616–617, 652, 748.
Alamo: 440.
Alaska: 125, 127, 231, 542–543.
Albany, N.Y.: 177.
Albany Regency: 357, 592.
Alberdi, J.F.: from, 595.
Alcala, ——: mentioned, 134.
Aldama, Miguel: mentioned, 226.
Aldrich, S.W.: from, 595.
Alexander, Robert I.: from, 268.
Alfonso, Joseph E.: mentioned, 228.
Alfonso, Julian: mentioned, 227.
Allen, A.C.: mentioned, 68, 527.
Allen, David: mentioned, 522.
Allen, John M.: mentioned, 403, 643.

Ellsworth, Henry L.: from, 124, 409, 563, 703.
Elmer, Lucius Q.C.: from, 424; mentioned, 237; to, 443.
Elmore, Franklin H.: from, 148, 560; mentioned, 687; to, 359, 464.
El Paso: 330.
Emancipation: results of, 76, 276–278, 349, 429–435, 611–613, 628–630. *See also* Haiti; Negroes, free.
Emory, William H.: mentioned, 198, 399, 732.
Engs, George: mentioned, 511.
Ericsson, John: mentioned, 422.
Erskine, ——: mentioned, 375.
Escandon, Manuel: mentioned, 329.
Espartero, Baldomero: mentioned, 134–135, 226.
Ethnography: 462–463, 531–533.
Evans, George: from, 124; mentioned, 365, 712–713; to, 148, 610.
Everett, Alexander H.: from, 224; mentioned, 267.
Everett, Edward: from, 55, 59, 62, 114, 125, 141, 243, 244, 262, 264, 324, 326, 392, 409, 505, 521, 544, 666, 682, 696; mentioned, xv–xvi, xxii, 90, 116, 155, 157, 186, 225–226, 229, 320, 326, 378, 472, 478; to, 60, 188, 244, 255, 345, 519.
Everitt, Stephen H.: mentioned, 175.
Ewing, Robert C.: mentioned, 743.
Exchequer proposal: 423, 591, 698.
Executive patronage: 151, 161, 172–173, 268–269, 315, 318, 444–445, 470, 491, 574, 598, 727–730. *See also* Appointments and removals.
Expenditures. *See* State Department, U.S.: expenditures and accounts of.
Extradition: xix–xxi, 158, 171, 186–187, 210, 376, 411, 455–456.

Fabens, Joseph W.: mentioned, 338, 399; to, 531.
Fairfax, ——: mentioned, 499–500.
Fairfield, John: from, 124, 308; mentioned, 365, 521; to, 148, 400.
Fair, German: 427.
Fannin County, Texas: 190.

Farfan: mentioned, 611.
Farnham, P.J. & Co.: mentioned, 329.
Faulkner, ——: mentioned, 151–152.
Fauquier County, Va.: 482–483, 502–503.
Fay, Theodore S.: mentioned, 141, 196, 426.
Federalist party: 143–144, 358, 453, 510.
Ferdinand (of Austria): mentioned, 476.
Ferdinand II (of Sicily): mentioned, 395.
Ferris, Charles G.: mentioned, 316.
Figaniere e Morão, J.C. de: from, 142; mentioned, 174; to, 123, 173.
Fiji Islands: 117.
Finney, Walter: document signed by, 414.
Fisheries: 63, 203, 637. *See also* Whaling.
Fisher, Miers W.: from, 424.
Fish, Henry F.: mentioned, 559–560.
Fisk, Theophilus: from, 244; to, 255.
Fitnam, Thomas: mentioned, 413.
Fitzhugh, George: from, 138; to, 207.
Flanders, Joseph R.: from, 443.
Flirt, U.S.S.: 42, 47–48, 66, 81, 185, 237, 282, 488, 643, 680, 733–734.
Florence, Italy: 726.
Florida Territory: xx, 222, 226, 264, 277, 406, 435, 441, 555, 561–563, 581–583, 599–600, 689, 699–700.
Flour: 285, 296.
Flugel, John G.: from, 426; mentioned, 254–255.
Fonte Nova, Viscount ——: mentioned, 480.
Foote, John: mentioned, 78.
Forbes, Paul S.: mentioned, 64–65; to, 65, 531.
Force Act: 445.
Force, Peter: from, 609; mentioned, 610, 616, 718; to, 272, 624.
Forrest, Bladen: from, 445, 446; mentioned, 73; to, 446, 456.
Forsyth, John: mentioned, 37, 255, 551, 663.
Fort Bent: 635.
Fort Covington, N.Y.: 443–445.

Hooper, ——: mentioned, 117.
Hooper, William: mentioned, 10, 420.
Hope (brig): slave trading case of, 25–26, 57, 130–131, 258, 308.
Hopkins, George W.: mentioned, 561.
Horner, ——: mentioned, 506.
Horses: 32, 212, 405–406, 450, 453–454, 597, 709.
Hoskins, John: mentioned, 231.
Hoster, J.G.: mentioned, 443.
House, David: mentioned, 345.
House of Representatives, U.S.: Calhoun's career in, 540, 563; mentioned, 245, 445, 614, 696, 748; possible role of in Presidential election, 425–426, 473, 482, 484, 574, 614, 748; State Department relations with, xi note, 119, 142, 144–145, 148, 159, 162, 173–174, 186, 205–206, 213–214, 229–231, 256, 266–267, 272, 294, 296, 316, 321, 364, 395–396, 437, 448, 464, 512–513, 561, 572–573, 578–579, 593–594, 609–610, 616, 624–625, 644–646, 650, 676, 712, 717–718, 744–746, 749.
Houston, Samuel: mentioned, 14–15, 26–29, 32–33, 42–44, 47–49, 66, 83–84, 131, 146, 157–158, 164, 179, 185, 215, 221–223, 232–233, 250–251, 295–296, 305, 361–365, 403, 457, 471, 488, 526–529, 586, 604–605, 679.
Houston, Texas: 43, 66–68, 84–85, 109–110, 185, 295, 361, 363, 365, 457, 527, 604.
Houston, Texas, *Democrat*: mentioned, 365.
Hoveys, ——: mentioned, 150.
Howard, John H.: from, 300, 404, 493; mentioned, 472, 557.
Howard, Volney E.: mentioned, 536, 538.
Howick, Lord: mentioned, 506.
Hoyle, Stephen Z.: mentioned, 457.
Hubbard, Simeon: from, 149, 152.
Hubbell, James Gale: from, 240.
Hubbs, Paul K.: from, 129.
Hudson, George A.: mentioned, 656.
Hudson's Bay Co.: 110, 440–441.

Huger, Daniel E.: mentioned, 686, 721.
Hugg, John: mentioned, 386, 388.
Hughes, Mrs. ——: mentioned, 501.
Hughes, Ann-Sarah Maxcy: mentioned, 266.
Hughes, Christopher: from, 367, 683.
Hughes, George: mentioned, 246.
Hughes, James M.: from, 743.
Hughes, Margaret Smith: mentioned, 369.
Hughes, Mary: mentioned, 246–247, 699.
Hughes, Philip O.: from, 501.
Hülsemann, Johann Georg, von: from: 191; to, 123.
Hume, Joseph: mentioned, 114–115, 696–697.
Hungary: 88.
"Hunkers": 465, 742.
Hunter, James: mentioned, 517.
Hunter, Robert M.T.: from, 475; mentioned, xi, xii note, 138, 207; to, 384, 575.
Hunter, William, Jr.: from, 246; mentioned, 577.
Hunting: 730.
Huntington, Jabez W.: from, 191.
Hunt, Memucan: mentioned, 403, 546, 643, 731.
Huntsman, Adam: mentioned, 619–620.
Huntsville, Ala.: 168.
Huske, John: mentioned, 416.
Huston, Felix: mentioned, 489.

Illinois: 145, 147, 326, 453, 678, 697–699.
Immigration: 197. *See also* German-Americans; Irish-Americans.
Independence, Mo.: 36.
Independent Presidential nomination. *See* Tyler National Convention.
India: 512, 625.
Indiana: 58, 370, 374, 448, 450.
Indian Affairs, U.S. Office of: 176–178, 632–633.
Indians: 73, 175, 211, 354, 375, 440–441, 525, 569, 632–633, 689.

cations and recommendations:
for Post Office Department; Ap-
pointments and removals: in Post
Office Department); business with,
258, 417–418, 448–449, 460,
462, 470, 590, 721–722; men-
tioned, 347, 373, 378, 428. *See also*
Mails, international.
Potomac, U.S.S.: 437, 488.
Potter, Elisha R.: from, 511.
Pottinger, Sir Henry: mentioned, 51,
65, 270–271, 508, 512.
Powell, William H.: from, 606.
Powers, Stephen: mentioned, 169–170.
Powhatan County, Va.: 290, 560.
Prague, Bohemia: 476–478.
Pratt, Abner: mentioned, 486.
Pratt, Zadock: from, 213.
Preble, U.S.S.: 189, 331, 452, 491–
493, 566–568, 600–601, 710–711,
717, 744.
Prentiss, Francis: mentioned, 68.
Prescott, Eustis: from, 489.
Presidency, U.S.: appointing power
of, 205; Calhoun's candidacy for,
147, 153, 160–161, 163–164, 166–
167, 268–269, 292, 300, 306, 308,
314–316, 318, 334, 341–342,
347, 367, 377, 383–385, 396, 398,
404–405, 411–412, 423, 444, 465–
466, 469, 473, 475–476, 482, 484,
489–490, 493–494, 503–505, 516–
518, 536–539, 548, 556, 565,
575, 591, 614, 619, 641, 646–648,
654, 666, 704, 714, 748; treaty-
making power of, 79–80, 327;
war powers of, 81, 238, 284, 680.
See also Tyler, John.
Presidential election of 1824: 562.
Presidential election of 1828: 525,
730–731.
Presidential election of 1840: 166,
176–177, 314–315, 424, 494, 538,
739.
Presidential election of 1844: x, xxvii,
143–144, 146, 149–153, 160–161,
163–164, 166–167, 222, 253, 268–
269, 291–292, 300, 302, 306,
308, 314–316, 318, 334, 341–342,
347, 353, 355–356, 377, 383–

385, 396–398, 404–405, 411–412,
423–426, 439, 443–445, 456–457,
464–470, 472–473, 475–476, 482–
486, 489–491, 493–495, 503–505,
510–511, 515–519, 524–526,
536–540, 546–550, 556–558, 561–
562, 564–565, 574–576, 591–593,
599, 614, 618–620, 635, 641, 646–
650, 653–654, 666, 678, 687,
690–692, 698, 704, 713–714, 721,
727–731, 739–740, 743, 747–748.
Presidential election of 1848: anticipated, 268–269, 423, 466, 592.
Presidio del Norte: 330.
Preston, William C.: mentioned, 664.
Prevost, Stanhope: mentioned, 109.
Prime, Ward, & King: mentioned,
19, 72.
Princeton, U.S.S.: 3, 116, 139, 266, 426,
540.
Prisoners: American in Cuba, 233–
235, 254, 261, 328, 336, 436, 500,
511–512, 559–560, 627, 633–635,
652, 700–702, 715–716; American
in Van Diemen's Land, 345, 437,
472, 521–522, 682–683; Californian
in Mexico, 292–293; Texan in
Mexico, 87, 93, 95, 187, 189, 213,
290–291, 295, 299, 326, 342–344,
468, 610, 624–626, 662–665,
685–686, 707. *See also* McDaniel
brothers; Pardons.
Pritchard, ——: mentioned, 14.
Proffit, George H.: from, 56; mentioned, 210, 321, 622, 712.
Providence: 101, 426, 440, 582, 698,
740. *See also* God.
Prussia: ix, xxii, xxviii, 63–64, 79–80,
100–106, 123, 136–137, 174, 193–
197, 247–248, 252, 254–255, 318–
319, 324, 326–327, 359, 361,
369, 426–427, 458, 461, 476, 481–
482, 530, 535, 542, 607–608, 648,
662–666, 684. *See also* Zollverein
Treaty.
Publication of the laws. *See* Laws, U.S.
Public Lands, U.S.: 37, 216–218,
264–265, 444, 453, 677.
Puebla, Mexico: 662.

792

41–42, 69, 111, 131, 190, 203,
207, 245, 296, 400–401, 457–458,
487, 555, 570–571, 654–660,
705–706, 719–721, 725–726,
733–734.

Thom, Adam: mentioned, 127.

Thomas, Richard: mentioned, 9–10,
12, 14.

Thomas, Samuel S.: mentioned, 308,
348, 400, 453.

Thom, George: mentioned, 498, 732.

Thompson, Gilbert L.: from, 406,
436, 449, 597; mentioned, 253,
283, 456–457, 552, 668, 681,
696, 702, 734; to, 584.

Thompson, Joseph: mentioned, 345,
522, 682.

Thompson, Waddy, Jr.: from, 20,
94, 662, 706; mentioned, 47–48,
77, 87, 93, 107, 181–184, 187,
236, 256, 283, 321, 402, 513, 528,
685–686, 703, 735.

Thorndike, Andrew: mentioned, 352.

Thorndike, Timothy: mentioned, 352.

Thornton, James B.: from, 138; to,
207.

Tientsin, China: 626.

Titow, ——: mentioned, 724.

Toast: to Calhoun, 208.

Tobacco: 80, 88, 100–101, 103–106,
114–115, 194–195, 254, 285, 372,
392–394, 481, 530, 550, 623,
648, 651–652, 676–677, 696–697,
724, 741–742.

Tod, Alexander: mentioned, 533.

Todd, Charles S.: from, 540; mentioned, 712; to, 490.

Tod, John G.: mentioned, 32, 42,
48–49, 81, 185.

Tolly, Stewart L., & Co.: from, 595.

Tom (slave): mentioned, 200.

Topographical Engineers, U.S. Army:
198, 333, 398–399, 498–500, 647,
722–723, 732–733.

Tornel, J.M.: mentioned, 329, 522–
523, 528.

Torre, P.D. de la: from, 560.

Townes, Henry H.: mentioned, 539.

Towson, Nathan: mentioned, 486.

Treasury Department, U.S.: appointments and removals in (*see* Applications and recommendations:
for Treasury Department; Appointments and removals: in Treasury Department); business
with, xiv–xv, xviii, xxi, 23, 35,
113, 119, 138, 142, 145–146, 162–
163, 178, 190, 198, 203, 207, 260–
261, 267, 317, 333, 340, 366,
391, 401, 453–455, 462, 487–488,
597, 607, 632, 644, 647, 650, 662–
665, 676, 685–686, 727, 744–746;
mentioned, 320, 335, 371–372,
395, 537. *See also* Revenue
Cutter Service, U.S.

Treaties. *See* Adams-Onís Treaty;
France: extradition treaty with;
Mexican-U.S. Claims Convention;
Postal conventions; Texas Treaty;
Treaties, commercial; Treaty of
Washington; Zollverein Treaty.

Treaties, commercial: 11, 20, 31–32,
58, 73, 88, 141–142, 195–196,
262–263, 327, 363, 365, 392–395,
410, 447, 459, 477, 480–481, 570–
571, 585, 632, 637, 650, 723–724.
See also China; Zollverein Treaty.

Treaty of Annexation between the
United States and the Republic of
Texas: text of, 215–219. *See also*
Texas Treaty.

Treaty of Ghent: 379.

Treaty of Washington: and extradition, xix–xx; and Northeastern
boundary settlement (*see* Maine-
New Brunswick border issues); and
Northeastern boundary survey
(*see* Northeastern Boundary Commission); and slave trade, xix, 55–
56, 58, 78, 243–244; mentioned,
3, 301, 375–376.

Trebizond, Turkey: 30–31.

Trieste: 447, 704.

Trigueros, ——: mentioned, 329.

Trinidad (island): 629–630.

Trinidad, Cuba: 227, 524.

Trinity River: 554.

Tripoli: xxiii, 461.

Trueheart, G.W.: from, 295.

Trueheart, James L.: mentioned, 295.